THE OTHER COUNTRY
Patterns in the Writing of Alice Munro

JAMES CARSCALLEN

THE OTHER COUNTRY:
PATTERNS IN THE WRITING OF ALICE MUNRO

THE OTHER COUNTRY:

Patterns in the Writing of Alice Munro

JAMES CARSCALLEN

ECW PRESS

CANADIAN CATALOGUING IN PUBLICATION DATA

Carscallen, James
    The other country: patterns in the writing of Alice Munro

Includes bibliographical references and index.
ISBN 1-55022-163-9

1. Munro, Alice, 1931-   – Criticism and interpretation. I. Title.

PS8576.U57Z64 1993   C813'.54   C92-095258-5
PR9199.3.M85Z64 1993

This book has been published with the assistance of a grant from the Canadian Federation for the Humanities, using funds provided by the Social Sciences and Humanities Research Council of Canada. Additional grants have been provided by the Ontario Arts Council and The Canada Council.

Design & imaging by ECW Type & Art, Oakville, Ontario.
Printed and bound by Imprimerie Gagné Ltée, Louiseville, Quebec.
The cover photograph was taken by the author in southern Ontario.

Distributed by General Distribution Services,
30 Lesmill Road, Don Mills, Ontario M3B 2T6.

Published by ECW PRESS, 1980 Queen Street East, Toronto, Ontario M4L 1J2.

TABLE OF CONTENTS

Foreword

The following book is offered, not just to Munro specialists, but to anyone who has found her work enjoyable and moving. For this reason among others I have tried to write in plain English, even if in places I have had to stipulate a special meaning for a word or phrase. Similarly, I have not counted on knowledge that a general reader would not possess or have readily available. Munro's uncollected stories are no doubt hard to get at, not to mention her unpublished ones. Where I have felt the need to refer to these, I have tried to supply necessary information; in any case they play no great part in my argument. Draft materials play even less: the different versions of Munro's work merit a thorough study, but trying to incorporate one into this book would have produced chaos, as would unwillingness to posit that a Munro story is whatever it finally became. I have also stuck pretty closely to the stories themselves as my evidence, believing that a study of the present kind cannot depend on an author's conscious intentions. Thus I have used Munro's comments on her work only sparingly and never to settle a matter; I have consulted her personally only on a couple of factual points. Except simply as the author of her writing, she is not responsible for any of my interpretations, and has given none of them her certification. Anyone with Munro's books on hand is hence in much the same position as I have chosen for myself.

Part I of my study sets out my interpretative model as it applies to individual stories. To some extent this has meant going over familiar ground, much of it covered more thoroughly by others; to some extent my model differs from ones commonly used for Munro. What I would like to emphasize here is that it is Munro I am using it for.

Like any model it can be applied to more than one thing (though its particular form here is meant for the writing of a particular author); but where I have noted analogues in other writing, perhaps alluded to by Munro herself, it is always the form of her own work that I am trying to clarify. And just as I am not offering a general interpretative model, so I am not offering a general treatise on literary theory — or Canadian literature, or the short story. For the most part the only criticism I mention explicitly is that dealing with Munro herself. (I should add that some of this, such as Magdalene Redekop's study, appeared too late for me to use.) If I had gone farther — if I had, for instance, canvassed general theories of story form from Aristotle and Donatus to Propp, Greimas, Frye, Todorov, and beyond — an already long book would have turned out far longer and more elaborate, while losing such focus as it can claim. I do make clear, I think, what my interpretative principles are and why they seem to me to apply to their stated object.

In the second and longer part of my study, I both shift my emphasis from theory to practice and extend my scope from individual stories to the groupings they make. Munro's single stories seem to me to fit implicitly into a larger one of the same kind as themselves; they can be grouped by being associated with its individual phases, which they follow as well in their ordering — most plainly in the two novels but also, to a remarkable extent, in the five collections of independent stories. Here as elsewhere I try to make plain what I do not mean: the phases are not pigeon-holes, and no story is simply "in" one of them, since they not only mirror each other, but in principle can all be found in every story. Thus pieces from anywhere in a book may help to illustrate a phase with which those in a particular location are linked in a more special way.

If the relation of Munro's stories to groups, and these groups to each other, is a tricky matter to describe, so is her way of presenting such grouping and more generally her way of presenting meaning. Her work offers us the great human myths, but as half-concealed — both from the characters themselves and from the reader — behind a surface ordinariness that seems anything but mythical. To argue for something beneath this surface, and something with a structure, takes a fair amount of exemplifying and explaining — especially as structure in Munro can be fairly complex. To argue that a given story is linked to some one part of such a structure takes more explaining again: my exposition, consequently, has had to be a long one (and even as things are I leave a good deal to the reader). The concealing

I have mentioned also requires some compromise in sequence. The structure inherent in Munro's work is orderly like any structure, but in actual reading we come to it through what in a way is its opposite: associative connections like that of similar characters with names sounding like "Mary." When my argument moves like an exploring reader along paths of association, structure may not seem its concern at all. But not only will groupings like the "Mary" names reveal little structures of their own; they will turn out to be parts of the larger structure that, I hope, is building itself throughout.

When speaking of the structure of Munro's work, I of course mean that of her work up to the recent past: not owning a crystal ball, I have no way of knowing what she will do in the future. And much as I would have liked to use a story like "Carried Away," I have chosen to stop with the collection *Friend of My Youth*, after which there was a notable gap in her publishing. Even *Friend of My Youth*, for that matter, is not treated as fully as the earlier books: the stories it includes came out when my work was substantially complete, and while they do appear both in my main text and more especially in my notes, I generally use others to develop my argument. But then I have made no effort to give Munro's stories equal coverage: the earlier ones, for instance, get what may seem a disproportionate emphasis, since they often show clearly what appears in subtler and more complex forms later.

Since this study is not a survey — it does not follow Munro's dates of publication or, for the most part, deal with one story or collection after another — the editors and I have tried to help the reader both with a liberal amount of cross-referencing and with an index of stories and characters. At the same time, the ordering of the stories in their collections is important for my argument, and tables of contents for Munro's books will accordingly be found on pp. 548–50 — an aid that any reader without a freak memory is likely to welcome. American and British readers will want to know that what was published in their countries as *The Beggar Maid* appeared in Canada as *Who Do You Think You Are?* It may also be worth pointing out that, in this book as in most others, a title like *Dance of the Happy Shades* refers to an entire collection where one like "Dance of the Happy Shades" refers to an individual story. "Tener" in the notes, followed by catalogue numbers beginning with "37," refers to Jean M. Moore and Jean F. Tener, *The Alice Munro Papers, First Accession* (see bibliography); when followed by numbers beginning with "38," it refers to Jean M. Moore, *The Alice Munro Papers, Second Accession*.

ACKNOWLEDGMENTS

The writing of this book has proved a much longer and more taxing job than I at first expected; it would never have been finished without the advice, encouragement, and above all the plain friendship of a number of people. Walter Martin and I have been discussing Munro for many years now, carrying somewhat different critical baggage but almost always arriving at the same favourite stories; and my debt to both Walter and Trish is far more than literary. I owe the same debt to David and Masha Perlman, apart from David's free and copious provision of editorial skills. Michael Laing and Douglas Spettigue both read the whole manuscript when it was even longer than now, commenting most usefully; Brock Pennington produced a glossary of Munro's proper names that helped not only in my own work but in the preparation of the book's index. Friends who helped in less specialized ways will have to come as a mere list, but there is something special in the gratitude I feel toward each. They include Bruce Barnes, David Blostein, Eleanor Cook, Dennis Duffy, James Good, Jeff Heath, Chaviva Hosek, Jay Macpherson, Ward McBurney, Willard McCarty, and Doug Scott. Lastly I wish to mention the steady support and forebearance of ECW PRESS, particularly its general editor Jack David. Throughout our dealings, ECW has stood squarely behind an ungainly and perhaps eccentric book; and while the author with the same qualities takes full responsibility for the result, he wants others to know how much they have given him.

The Other Country

P A R T   I

Munro's Presentation

I: TRUTH AND REALITY

In the title story of Alice Munro's earliest collection we find ourselves at a social gathering: the narrator's old music-teacher, Miss Marsalles, is having one of her annual student recitals. The situation is the saddest imaginable — a run-down street on a hot afternoon, a poor and failing Miss Marsalles, new pupils who are mentally defective, a few older ones hanging on glumly from a more genteel past. Yet something happens here that is not sad: a girl plays the Dance of the Happy Shades from Gluck's *Orfeo ed Euridice*, and as she does so a strange grace comes into the room. Afterwards the narrator reflects that Miss Marsalles is not so pathetic after all. She is the serene dweller in an "other country" (224) — the Elysium of Gluck's opera, in effect — and the Dance of the Happy Shades was her "communiqué" to the land of bondage where the rest of us have to live.

"Other countries" in Munro's writings are not always Elysian, but they seem always to be there: again and again we have the sense of a place or time or order of things standing apart from our own.[1] One of Munro's uncollected early stories is in fact called "At the Other Place," and concerns itself with a remote property to which a family periodically goes from its very different home farm. In a much more recent story, "Miles City, Montana," another family on a holiday chooses the American route from Vancouver to Toronto, perhaps because "we just wanted the feeling of driving through a foreign, a

I

very slightly foreign, country — that extra bit of interest and adventure" (88). In "Walker Brothers Cowboy" Ben Jordan goes off his salesman's itinerary for somewhat the same reason; he introduces his daughter, moreover, to a world remote in time rather than space — the ancient landscape preceding the ice-age and the formation of Lake Huron. Journeying in both space and time, the Rosicrucian of "The Spanish Lady" takes the heroine back to the world of the Conquistadors.

In "Dance of the Happy Shades" Miss Marsalles's otherworld keeps its air of remoteness, even when favouring the immediate one with a communiqué; in "Marrakesh," however, the situation is more complex. No doubt the story's otherworld seems remote enough at first, being the exotic locale of an exotic travel story. Marrakesh, according to older versions of the *Encyclopaedia Britannica*, is a crumbling desert city full of thieves; more recent travel literature paints a tidier picture, but the city still has its great bazaar and famous minaret, flanked by gardens and commanding a splendid view. By contrast, nothing could be less romantic than the place where the Marrakesh story is told, an Ontario small town in hot summer weather. Yet with the elms all cut down to reveal the shabby houses, this town is as sun-baked as any desert city; it can also boast an impending bazaar and mosque, since a new shopping centre would have "flat-roofed stores and the immense, curved, dominating shape of the supermarket" (162). In its own way the Kinsmen's park is a match for the famed Marrakesh gardens, and if you went to the cemetery (or, as one character calls it, "Last Lookout" [156]) you would find both a view and signs of vandalism — it was the Vandals, we may remember, who invaded Africa.[2] We should notice events here as well: just as the tourist in the story was lured and accosted by a chance acquaintance in Marrakesh, so she is now introduced to a neighbour and ends making love with him — in fact they take to "relishing and plundering" (173) like any tourists or vandals. The other country, while remote, is also present in this country; and somehow it *is* this country.

If we look elsewhere in Munro, we can find the identifying of contrasted worlds in still more elaborate forms. At the end of "Something I've Been Meaning to Tell You" Char Desmond is found dead, perhaps by her own hand, while her ageless beauty remains untarnished. When Blaikie Noble, the lover she has supposed unfaithful, arrives a few hours too late, Char's sister Et is reminded of a story: *Romeo and Juliet*, which she perhaps read in high school. Et is less likely to have read *Antony and Cleopatra*, but anyone who has done so may think of still another Shakespearean heroine found dead and beautiful. Char's name (which I will come back to) is oddly reminiscent in this context of Cleopatra's maid Charmian, as well as, perhaps, the Greek *cháris* or "grace," not to say a charwoman: certainly Char works a toil of grace, while also doing the meanest chares in the form of her endless washings.[3] And so we have both Juliet here and a greater lady: a tragic and abased queen, complete with a splendidly unreliable lover.

If we keep listening to its suggestions, Munro's story will take us farther again. Char's husband is named Arthur Comber, and with his innocence and "galloping optimism" (16) makes a knight in shining armour if ever there was one — he even chooses to be Sir Galahad in a game of "Who am I?" Et, quickly guessing who he is, turns the conversation to King Arthur himself, the adulterous Guinevere, and the dark sequel: for there is an Arthurian as well as a classical form to the tragedy of the beautiful queen with her dashing lover, and now we can add a wronged husband as well. We find, moreover, that Arthur enjoys a book about the Duke of Wellington — Arthur Wellesley, as it happens — and that the world of this later Arthur crops up in other details of Munro's story. Et as a schoolgirl mimicked a teacher reading "The Burial of Sir John Moore": if not a poem about Wellington, at any rate one about a soldier killed in the Peninsular War. In another of Arthur Comber's parlour-games words are made out of "Beethoven" — a name that, with all the heroism and downfall in the air, recalls the *Eroica* Symphony and its funeral march for a hero. And we can note this symphony's intended dedication: to Napoleon, Wellington's great enemy.

A number of tragedies thus resonate in the background of Munro's story; nor do these belong to other times and places alone, any more than Marrakesh does. While neither Arthur Comber nor Blaikie Noble is actually a soldier, there are references here to both World Wars, and in fact the original affair of Char and Blaikie takes place in the summer of 1918 — if Blaikie were any older, we are told, he would be in France. No doubt the love-affair in a quiet resort town contrasts sharply with the fighting overseas, but then there is a war going on at home as well: "lovers," as Et observes, is not a gentle but a "cruel and tearing" (14) word. All in all, the story gives us a sense of powerful convergence. The Roman civil wars, the internal war into which the Arthurian kingdom degenerated, the Napoleonic wars, the wars of the twentieth century — all these convulsions of worlds divided against themselves become a single world of conflict, which is equally one of love. And this world "surfaces," as Et is uncomfortably aware, in the seeming peace of Mock Hill.

In the various stories I have mentioned, we have found on the one hand an exotic other place — or time or cast of characters — and on the other a home that is more homely. For our purposes we will need to go on from these places to general principles with fixed names, and Del Jordan of *Lives of Girls and Women* can be of help to us here. During her teens, as she confesses in "The Photographer," Del brooded on a secret novel, set in her own town of Jubilee but turning that town into a baleful gothic otherworld. However fantastic, the result had its own validity for her — "the main thing was that it seemed true to me, not real but true, . . . as if that town was lying close behind the one I walked through every day" (248). "Truth" and "reality" have interested a number of Munro's critics,[4] and in the senses Del intends (senses to which I shall generally be restricting them) these terms will do well enough for the principles we need here: for whatever we make of their ontological status, these seem to be the two poles between which human experience as seen by Munro endlessly shuttles. Reality — "unsatisfactory, apologetic and persistent," as another character puts it[5] — is like matter, the part of experience that cannot be spirited away. If Del thinks her novel has disposed of it, it will suddenly return to make its claims, in the light of which truth can only seem vain and spectral. Truth, on the other hand, is what Munro is asserting when she speaks of a literary world having its own distinctness and autonomy[6] — the world here of things made up, including real things made over as Del makes over Jubilee. Elsewhere in Munro truth may be a world of beliefs rather than inventions, but in any case it is a paradigm world, one of patterns distinguished from reality as such. And in this way it makes its own kind of claim, for as Roberta remarks in "Labor Day Dinner," "Isn't it funny how you're attracted — I am — to the idea of a pattern?" (149).[7] This ethereal pattern even has the power noticed by Et Desmond to invest the grosser world of reality; in certain paradoxical states we may feel, like Mr. Lougheed in "Walking on Water," that it has greater reality than reality itself. At other times, conversely, we will feel reality to be the truest form of truth, for each of the contraries has an authority of its own. More strangely, each seems to need the other: and they may turn out to be the same thing in the end.

*

From what we have seen so far, two distinct pairs of opposites have already appeared: on the one hand there are Home and the Other Place, as I will generally be calling them; on the other there are reality and truth. These would seem to be the same pair in different contexts, and yet we should not simply merge them. In some stories the Other Place is as rarefied as Miss Marsalles's Elysium; in some, as we will find, it can have the solid character of reality, even while remaining truth by virtue of its otherness. Two pairs is what we will need, then; and in fact we will have to equip ourselves with still others — potentially an infinite number — arising from the same matrix. What is of more immediate concern is the kinds of relation within any such pair of opposites.

The model that I find most useful for Munro distinguishes between two sorts of relation (to which I will eventually add a third). For convenience I am going to call these by an Eighteenth-Century pair of terms, sense and sensibility, keeping the adjective "sensible" for the first. Sense is a relation in which two elements, while remaining distinct and different, join neatly together at the same time: sense is like a contract, with the parties not really abandoning their basic differences but agreeing to get along with each other. To use another Eighteenth-Century analogy, sense is a Peace of Utrecht, whether between countries or between the sisters in Munro's story of the same name; or it is other concords that Munro's characters discover in school when they learn the Missouri Compromise or the Congress of Vienna.[8] Sensible people are the ones who enter into such concords — people who get over their own troubles and patch up their quarrels with others. We can think here of Valerie in "Labor Day Dinner," whose house is a place of "delicate checks and balances" (139) and who "will throw herself headlong into any conversation to turn it off its contentious course, to make people laugh and calm down" (156). Or, in a somewhat different vein, there is the equanimity of the Jordans as experienced by Del in "The Flats Road." Outside the family house disturbance may rage like a winter storm; inside, Mr. and Mrs. Jordan quietly play their card-game, and a world war comes only as radio news from far away. When they are being sensible, all other contraries behave like Del's parents in this story: they make the marriage work, they play the game by the rules. Thus cause fits effect; semantically, a sign fits a thing or class of things. Truth, in the same way, fits reality: the two live amicably together, and neither trespasses on the other's property.

But Munro, as critics have often noted, may take us into a different world.[9] The Del Jordan of "Walker Brothers Cowboy" sees her father as being like a "kindly, ordinary and familiar" landscape — except that at times this becomes "something you will never know, with all kinds of weathers, and distances you cannot imagine" (18). Similarly, the Del of "The Flats Road" may trust her parents' domesticity, but upstairs in bed she remembers something more threatening — "that we were in a house as small and shut-up as any boat is on the sea, in the middle of a tide of howling weather" (26). The same Del decides in the end that "people's lives . . . [are] dull, simple, amazing and unfathomable — deep caves paved with kitchen linoleum" (253). Whether we align it with truth or reality, this is the world, or anti-world, of sensibility, in which there are no truces or constitutions, no games with rules, and, as Et Desmond would say, "no fit" (18).

A suggestive image for this other world is the common one of a mirror, at least if we think of a mirror as something mysterious. No doubt mirrors can be explained in a sensible way: they send back the light rays that strike them, the reflection matches the original, and there is no problem. But they have always had something haunting about them as well: when one looks into a mirror one is seeing another person; and while this other is the same as the perceiving subject, the subject has been projected as well as reversed between left and right so as to be no longer subject but object, and an opposite sort of object. When Del, in her grief at the loss of Garnet French, looks into the hall mirror, it is reflection as mystery that she experiences:

Without diminishment of pain I observed myself; I was amazed to think that the person suffering was me, for it was not me at all; I was watching. I was watching, I was suffering. (241)

While each of Del's two selves here is authentic, the two cannot be reconciled; and yet, paradoxically, they are also the same self. Related elements are at once farther apart and closer together than sense would allow, alien and yet sharing what Frances in "Accident" calls "a bizarre and dreamlike intimacy" (99).

II. EPIPHANY

One context I have mentioned for sense and sensibility is that of signs and their meanings: here as elsewhere, sense makes us feel that two things fit easily together while remaining different things. Literary genres such as stories with morals, simple personification allegory, and *romans à clef* all belong with sense to the extent that we can comfortably exchange the images they give us for the conceptions these represent. With sensibility the relation of image to meaning is a more problematical one; it is this second relation, in a particular form, that various writers have seen as best characterizing Munro's kind of story.

In the first place, we can note that reality and truth are both present in all stories, though this may not be obvious in the world of sensibility, where either reality or truth — which I am aligning here with meaning — can withdraw to the point of invisibility. When we are being aggressive about the term "realism," we usually have in mind the documentary kind that "gets the facts" and "tells it like it is" — in other words, tries to purvey reality without truth. Yet the truth that is invisible here is not simply absent but conspicuous by its absence: perhaps it is secretly present all the time. Munro's "Working for a Living" is factual not only in effect but in substance — a story about her real family — yet it has the same informing shape as any of her fictional stories. And this should not be surprising: it is impossible to present facts without selecting, arranging, and otherwise articulating them, and selection is always assimilation to an idea — that is, to truth.[10] "Getting the facts," then, always means collecting in accordance with some criterion. Similarly, "what it is *like*," "the *way* it is," is not a thing but a mode; and in practice, writing that vividly expresses "the way it is" does so by being highly metaphorical — connecting an object with something more ideal, or two objects with an ideal third. The contrary of realism, which we can call symbolism in one sense of that word, seeks to have pure truth without the contamination of reality. For this an author must try to bring out the idea of things to the point where there are no things left at all, only their forms. And in the end he too will fail, since these forms can only be known as embodied in matter, or the words we use to refer to matter.

The narrators in Munro, as we will see, are often sticklers for reality: they want the factuality of fact, unadulterated by truth. Munro herself is speaking to the same effect in "The Colonel's Hash Resettled" when she insists that a house, for instance, has no idea behind it — that it is a house and not a "bloodless symbol."[11] She can be thought of here as guarding against allegory — sense allegory, that is, in which a thing can simply be traded in on a concept. Or, in a more sensibility way, her metaphor suggests a ghost or vampire secretly preying on the substance of the house: but at any rate she is saying that a house must not be connected to anything other than itself. This makes her sound like a realist, and so she is, much more obviously than a symbolist; yet the house as sheer reality is quite impossible. To say that it is a house at all we must connect a particular thing to the general idea of "house" (and we have done some connecting to think of a unitary "thing" in the first place). If we confine ourselves to saying that a thing is "itself," even this implies an essential self to which the material thing must be linked by a copula.[12]

Even as a pure realist, then, Munro would not be a writer without truth; and in any case her special genre is a somewhat different one, as we can see by looking again at the article I have just quoted. Munro goes on here to tell how her stories originate. They may draw on fact, or alternatively on anecdotes she has come across (as apparently with "Dance of the Happy Shades"); but the story as such, she says, generally arises from a highly charged image that simply appears to her.[13] Thus "Images" grew from the image of Joe Phippen advancing with his hatchet towards Ben Jordan; and if a story called "Images" seems a special case, "Visitors" grew from the image of Grace and Vera at their sewing, "Bardon Bus" from that of people shopping on Queen Street in Toronto.[14] Such an image, flashing from another country of the mind, is truth in relation to the story that will embody it. At the same time this image has all the givenness of a real world about it — it does not, Munro says, feel made up. Perhaps, then, truth and reality have traded characteristics, as I have suggested they might: what we have in any case is a very strange kind of interrelation.

The same thing can be said about the story that arises from the image. While we will later need to explore Munro's stories as narrative structures, these structures crystallize around epiphanies like the one from which "Images" arose: for that epiphany includes Ben's little daughter watching in amazement, and is thus an event within the story as well as in its author's mind. In the other epiphanies I have mentioned, the figures are no doubt more intent on their ongoing concerns, yet the resulting stories gather around special manifestations no less than does "Images." Such stories offer us, not simply realism or symbolism, but a general effect of intense — or perhaps merely dull — factuality crossed in a mysterious way by "communiqués" like the one sent by Miss Marsalles. According to the narrator of "The Shining Houses," the tales told by old Mrs.

Fullerton have the "pure reality" of things that are "at least part legend" (19). "Pure reality," thus imagined, is an odd combination: it makes a good formula for the kind of painting Munro has allied herself with, the "magic realism" of artists like Colville and Chambers;[15] and it makes a good formula for her own stories.[16]

*

What is the effect of this pure reality as we experience it? If we notice that Arthur Comber is like King Arthur, or an Ontario small town like Marrakesh, the likeness as such is acceptable enough to our sensible minds. What is less so is its "far-fetched" character, the way the remote meets the ordinary: perhaps the chapter "Lives of Girls and Women" can show us our resistance even more clearly. We can start by noting that this chapter contains two explicit references to the biblical David. Eager to display the glories of Florence, Mrs. Jordan on one occasion produces Michelangelo's version of David from the Encyclopaedia, with sensational effect. An effect that should be even more sensational but proves less so comes when Art Chamberlain exposes himself to Del: his penis, she finds, is "not at all like marble David's" (169). The very contrast here makes the comparison: oddly enough, Art Chamberlain is being paralleled with the greatest of kings, Del's fancy having been at work on the job ever since the evening with the Encyclopaedia.

In the second place, we can note a connection of David's within the Bible itself: he is the ancestor and type of Christ, as Munro reminds us by making Naomi's father quote the parable of the Wise and Foolish Virgins. And Munro's stories show us Christ in many other ways, especially the Christ of the Crucifixion. In "The Spanish Lady," for instance, a dying man utters a loud cry, and "as the cry fades out he half turns, staggers, tries to hang onto the air with fully raised arms and open fingers, falls, and lies on the floor, twitching" (190). A sufferer in a somewhat different plight is Allen Durrand, the hired man in "The Ottawa Valley." One hot afternoon Allen gets the job of piling hay in the stifling mow of the barn. The narrator's mother and aunt, girls at the time, conspire first to sew up the fly of his overalls and then to provide him with a pailful of lemonade, topped up with vinegar. When this has the desired result, Allen has to rip off his overalls completely; and for the girls, who secretly are watching like Del in "Lives of Girls and Women," the revelation is complete — " 'When he shot away there wasn't a thing we couldn't see. He

9

turned himself sideways'" (236). Once more, then, we have the Crucifixion here: the unbearable high place, the vinegar, the seamless garment or veil, exposure, the turning of the side, above all the emission of the fluid that is at once profane and, to the girls, sacred. And if we go back to the masturbating Art Chamberlain, with his "spasmodic agony" (170) and final moan of desperation, we will realize that he is the same martyr.[17]

No doubt there is something silly about all this: Art Chamberlain makes a very unlikely David, not to say Christ, and even where such a connection is explicit in Munro our minds cannot help struggling against it. But we can think here of the way we respond to dreams — what Munro has said her stories resemble. As long as we are asleep and inside a dream, we more or less take it for granted; when we are waking up, or going through the greater waking that brings us to the dream's meaning, it takes on a double character. On the one hand it is "just a dream," pleasant or frightening or neither, but not making much sense and hence not very important. On the other hand people have always felt that dreams must mean something — that in spite of or because of their absurdity they contain an important message. To the extent that we can interpret it, the dream and its meaning come together in the end; and yet there is something very unsettling about the process. And so we feel like Del at the English exam in "Baptizing," understanding what the words mean but unable to accept that they really mean it.[18] Or we are like Helena in "Executioners," who compares her state after the great fire to a light sleep — a state half-way between sleeping and waking, in other words — in which she cannot accept something that would be plain to a more fully wakened self.

*

To describe responses to Munro's stories is to raise certain further questions that will need to be considered at least briefly here: for the purpose we can notice two more hints of the Israelite Kingdom in "Lives of Girls and Women." At one point in the story Del and Naomi go wandering about town after supper. Presently they drift into the park and climb some cedar trees, where they hang pretending to be baboons; then they go off to the garbage-man's house and look at the peacocks in the yard. Cedars, apes, and peacocks: is the echo of the Kingdom real or imaginary? Elsewhere in the story we are told that Mrs. McQuade's whorehouse is located next to the B.A. service station. As I myself mused on this unremarkable but included fact, it first occurred to me that, in the world of the chapter, a whorehouse and a service station have somewhat the same function — one of the whores, in fact, was required to "serve a line-up" (153) on a legendary night. And since I was thinking of transportation and a whorehouse at the same time, I remembered that Solomon kept stables both of horses and of women. It then occurred to me that a B.A. is a university degree,[19] that Solomon cultivated wisdom as well as arms and pleasure, and that in Munro's story both Mrs. Jordan and her daughter are relentless pursuers of enlightenment. By this time I was feeling embarrassed: was I reading things into Munro's text that were not there at all? And if they were there, was a reader expected to notice them? But then the allusions in question are not just "there"; nor are we required to pick up a definite number of them. Munro has imagined a Jubilee of a certain kind: the biblical David appears at two key points in the story, so that our minds are set running on his world as well, and any correspondence it may have with the local one. Once she has established a pattern by putting two worlds in parallel, the pattern assimilates whatever will fit into it.

If we are wondering how much we need to get out of a Munro story, we will also be wondering how much she meant to put into it: and here we will have to pause over an old issue that has never vanished from literary criticism and that, in my experience, comes up strongly for readers of Munro when they notice correspondences of the kind we have just been dealing with. I will have to say firmly that I do not know Munro's intentions for her stories, and for my present purposes do not care. When it comes to works of literature — by which I mean any text read for its imaginative structure — an author's conscious intention is not what matters. Since Munro says "David" in "Lives of Girls and Women," no doubt she knew she was putting David there, at two junctures anyway; but did she realize how thoroughly David, and the Jewish Kingdom more generally, pervades her story? If we all create our dreams unconsciously, perhaps resisting their meaning afterwards, Munro may have done the same thing — her papers do not include anything like deliberate biblical plans for this story or any other, and she has repeatedly said that she does not consciously put meanings into her stories. During the rest of this book I am going to say a good deal about allusion; but while it is impossible to discuss it without suggesting intention on Munro's part, intention is not what I am concerned with — unless we mean that of the creator largely hidden from a writer's conscious mind, or of the creation itself as absorbing whatever is consonant with it.

III: NARRATIVE AND MEDITATION

In the last few pages we have begun to consider signs and meanings in Munro; and since a sign or a meaning is that only for someone experiencing it, we have been led along a path we will take repeatedly — the path from something there to something offered and received, from the "given" in one sense to the "given" in another. In the present context this path has brought us to Munro's stories as presentations — what they were first, perhaps, as sudden images in her mind, what they are also for their experiencers and, finally, for their readers. Now we can ask a further question: how does the relation that we have found between sign and meaning appear, not only in individual epiphanies, or a whole story taken as a single epiphany, but in the story as having an extended form? What I mean by "story" at this point is not strictly a narrative shape but, once again, a presentation. Presentation, after all, has its own narrative aspect: an epiphany may be timeless in itself, but it belongs to a process of experience which is also a process of understanding. And before we can proceed to matters more central for the present book, we will need to give this process some consideration, even if this again means covering a certain amount of familiar ground. More precisely, we will need to consider the process's own relation to epiphany, since in Munro this takes a sensibility form amounting to a crisis.

Discussing sense and sensibility, I suggested that we imagine the former as a compromise, a "Peace of Utrecht" in which contracting parties agree to act in the common interest. For something comparable in the world of narrative forms — the forms of action itself to start with — we can think of a well-made "plot": not just a series of events but an integrated structure of them in which, as Aristotle says, nothing can be added or omitted.[20] No party, in our diplomatic metaphor, fails to appear, and none works against the peace that is contracted for. There will be a similar peace between a presented story as a narrative progression and the same set of words as expressing what this progression is all about. No pure example of such a decent alliance exists, perhaps, but a novel of Jane Austen will do well enough. The events of an Austen novel all "advance the plot," and this plot is neither without a moral nor bound to any moral felt as disjunct from the events expressing it. The action of *Pride and Prejudice* and its theme — that of pride and prejudice — are co-ordinate and co-operative.

If on the other hand we turn to Joyce's *Portrait of the Artist as a*

Young Man, a novel with a clear influence on *Lives of Girls and Women*,[21] we find something we have already found in Munro: strange epiphanies — Joyce's own word, of course — standing out against the rest of the story; and while these sum up the story's meaning, we experience that meaning as a message from another order of things, discontinuous with the narrative texture of the novel. What may also strike us about Joyce as contrasted with Austen is his inclination to run on. Even in the revised *Portrait* there is a remarkable tolerance for passages that go their unhurried way; and Joyce is equally the author of *Ulysses*, not to mention *Finnegans Wake* with its endless river of blarneying sound. If epiphanic concentrations can take on a life of their own, so, it seems, can the story-line itself or anything else that wants simply to flow.[22] Joyce is thus writing what we can call a sensibility novel, one in which narrative and cognitive elements refuse any easy alliance. The same refusal is very pronounced in romance more generally. Homer's Ulysses, like Joyce's, has his separate confrontations with cyclops and sirens and suitors; he also voyages on and on, and the god Poseidon for one is in no hurry to let him reach home. The result is a story of continual diversion: the hero is forced to take an indirect route, and his adventures, while related to his homecoming, have a disruptive effect of their own, functioning both as epiphanic crystallizations and as further lines of action thwarting the main one. It is much harder than with Jane Austen to make sense of the story, because something is making sensibility of it; and this is what we will now have to consider as a matter of presentation.

*

Alice Munro is a writer of "short stories" — in fact even her novels are sequences of "linked short stories," as she herself has said. The term "short story" can, of course, mean different things: Munro's examples of the genre are distinguished not just by brevity (some of them, for that matter, are fairly long), but by the same sensibility character that we have just noted in forms of romance.[23] They might, then, be called little romances; more particularly they are like romances that emphasize epiphany more than line, and so it is their epiphanic side that we can best begin with. We have seen how a particular situation in a story comes to Munro as an emblem of the whole; and while the situation in question may not be experienced as intensely by her characters themselves, her stories show a strong tendency to focus on certain special incidents. Often, indeed, they seem to focus on just one: a girl plays the Dance of the Happy Shades at Miss Marsalles's recital; the heroine of "Marrakesh" is seen making love with the neighbour.

Later we will have to deal with such events as events, occurring at different points in narrative structures: one thing to be noted at present is that, like the stories that form around them, they are somewhat peripheral in relation to a larger action. Joe Phippen's sudden attack — certainly the most striking incident in "Images" — is quietly parried by Ben Jordan, and does not seriously disrupt his trap-round; the round itself is only a vestige of an earlier kind of life; nor are the sensational incidents in "Marrakesh" and "Dance of the Happy Shades" any more likely to have long-term practical conse-quences. On the other hand, such incidents are always central for someone's understanding: even when they take the form of actions, these are presented as revelations. In "The Flats Road," for instance, the effect of Uncle Benny's descent into Toronto is that "we could see it, we could see how it was to be lost there, how it was just not possible to find anything, or go on looking" (25). If the search for Madeleine and Diane has not come to much as an action, it has achieved what Benny secretly meant it to do, for it has produced a picture. This is not to say that he himself quite sees the picture — he has uncon-sciously executed it for the Jordans, and if they were less responsive the reader would be left to see it alone; but at any rate seeing, literal or metaphorical, is what is in question. In fact a title like "The Flats Road" implies that the whole of the story amounts to a picture — of a significant locality in this case.

When the little girl in "Images" sees Joe Phippen with his hatchet, she is struck silent and motionless — "I saw him and just waited" (38), she tells us. This makes her like a picture herself, "a child in an old negative" (38):[24] for as several of Munro's critics have noted, all pictures have something static about them, heightened when epi-phany and the onward movement of a story are as opposed as they are here. The other focal events we considered above are "stills" in much the same way. The Dance of the Happy Shades turns a whole fidgeting audience silent and motionless:

> The children are all quiet, the ones from Greenhill School and the rest. The mothers sit, caught with a look of protest on their faces. . . . (222)

Dorothy, the watcher in "Marrakesh," is "halted" (173) by the sight of the lovers; like the child in "Images" she is unable to call out, and when the spectacle is over "she sat on the steps for a few moments to get control of herself" (174). In the same way Benny, home from Toronto, "sat there for a moment, not looking at us" (22) — his wild ride itself, for that matter, is a kind of paralysis, a compulsion like that of Dorothy watching the lovers. Only when such spells have dissolved and receded can we get back to the shifting actions and feelings of ordinary life.

The more a story is arrested in this way, the more it turns into a set of isolated parts, the little units of incident or reflection into which Munro's stories tend to be divided, even typographically. In an extreme case like "The Ottawa Valley" we may feel, as the narrator herself feels, that we are looking at a series of distinct "snapshots" (246).[25] For the same reason Munro the novelist inclines toward the genre of the *Bildungsroman*, in which a life is often presented in discrete stages, with sizeable gaps in time between them and little in the way of transition. Del Jordan the student is a certain kind of person at the end of primary school, starting to like boys by dreaming of one as a vague presence; she is a very different person as a teenage sex researcher in high school, and a different one again as a young woman in her graduating year attempting real emotional bonds. These three Dels inhabit quite separate chapters: there are various girls and women here, each with a life of her own.

*

While one side of Munro's presentation is thus its tendency to focus and isolate, this tendency would be much less marked without its contrary, even if the latter is somewhat less prominent. "Wood," like other stories I have mentioned, centres on a single event, a sudden dangerous accident in the bush. At the time of the crisis there is a strong sense of focus: only by keeping his mind fixed on immediate necessity can Roy Fowler crawl to safety, and this is why not only the accident itself but the whole episode has a feel of timelessness about it. And yet the story as a whole is more than Roy's crisis or even the indispensable amount of preparation for it; and the rest is oddly discursive. We hear a good deal about Roy's wife Lila and her family — more than, from the standpoint of "plot," seems necessary to explain his liking for solitude. We are introduced to his step-daughter Karen, whose situation tells us something about Roy's mood on the fatal day, but who might have been dealt with much more briefly. The same could be said of old Percy Marshall, who does nothing but pass dangerous rumour; and most unnecessary of all, seemingly, is a long disquisition on different kinds of trees — what they look like, what they are good for, how they should be handled. Along with timeless epiphany, then, we feel a continuity wanting to continue — something in the story becoming an end in itself, once again, but an opposite kind of something.

Expansions like this catalogue of trees occur constantly in Munro. In *Lives of Girls and Women* there is so much miscellaneous information that the chapters have a hard time reaching their main incidents at all: "The Flats Road" carries on for several pages before Munro gets to what would seem her proper subject, Uncle Benny's disastrous marriage; in "Princess Ida" we are almost two-thirds of the way through before Bill Morrison arrives for his visit. The main story itself, for that matter, can have a very continuous aspect to it. A novel like *Lives of Girls and Women* may show us isolated phases of Del's development, but development is what it is showing us — Del's slow change from a girl to a woman; and our sense of ongoing line is very strong in a story like "Forgiveness in Families." Val, the narrator here, is an Ancient Mariner: tribulation follows tribulation (it must take several mugs of coffee) before she is ready to pull her monologue together and be done with it.

Mrs. Jordan is not formally the narrator of the stories in which she appears, but she too has a tale to tell: given the slightest opening, as we learn from her mortified daughter, she is off on her life and hard times. And if always an exception in some ways, Mrs. Jordan belongs to a whole world of rural and small-town storytellers — the world into which Munro herself was born and for which she has found counterparts in other worlds. In a small town, as the narrator of "Winter Wind" remarks, everyone is a tale: and while some of these tales are no doubt pointed anecdotes, a resourceful teller can easily combine or stretch anecdotes into endless yarns. More generally, this is a world of talk: the "jaw[ing]" (22) in "Something I've Been Meaning to Tell You," the kitchen-table chatter (complete with several stories) in "Half a Grapefruit," the schoolchildren's gossip in "Changes and Ceremonies."[26] It is in such a world that Benny, with his "monotonous, meticulously remembering voice" (25) compels us to share his journey to Toronto; "Flo" flows on, and the talk of Mrs. Jordan and Fern Dogherty is "a river that never drie[s] up" (71).

But what is more striking here than either epiphanic crystallization or hypnotic flow is, once again, the strange way in which these impinge on one another. It is true that some stories are fairly straight-ahead, whether ongoing confessions like "Forgiveness in Families" or single anecdotes like "How I Met My Husband" or "Mrs. Cross and Mrs. Kidd." Often, however, we find narrative movement suspended in its course as if by a charm.[27] A conversation in "The Ottawa Valley" is frozen half-way through a statement (which Munro has to repeat) while we are given a detailed account of the mother's church-going outfit and its preparation; a description of Aunt Lena, on the other hand, has to pause while Aunt Dodie tells a story about the narrator's dying grandmother. And even when having their own way, our two tendencies turn into their opposites by their very compulsion to be themselves. The insistence on filling out a picture leads to discursiveness; a line that insists on itself not only tends to have a static emblem at the end of it (the dying old man, for instance, at the end of the railroad in "The Spanish Lady") but itself becomes static, since a line seen to be a line turns into a defined figure as opposed to a sheer extension. Uncle Benny may not be quite as ruminative as Conrad's Marlow or one of Henry James's narrators, but he too runs on until he "makes you see" — accumulates until he produces a single vision of accumulation:

> As he talked a different landscape — cars, billboards, industrial buildings, roads and locked gates and high wire fences, railway tracks, steep cindery embankments, tin sheds, ditches with a little brown water in them, also tin cans, mashed cardboard cartons, all kinds of clogged or barely floating waste — all this seemed to grow up around us. (25)

And so the same element in a story can be experienced in both ways: the catalogue of trees in "Wood" has, as I have noted, something wilfully discursive about it, and yet from another point of view it is iconic and self-contained — a set piece.

*

The interchange we have just been seeing shows the sensibility crossing of emblematic and discursive clearly enough; but it is only the most obvious among a number of related symptoms in Munro. Another is a convention that might seem very strange to a time or culture different from our own. On opening *Lives of Girls and Women* a reader finds the following: "We spent days along the Wawanash River, helping Uncle Benny fish." Who are "we"? Who is Uncle Benny? Where is the Wawanash River? None of these things is introduced — it is as if we were suddenly tuning in to a programme that had begun some time before. We often find a similar phenomenon at the end of a story: in the last part of "Age of Faith" Major the dog is about to be shot, but the story breaks off before that happens (if it does). What we are given is thus like a deliberate fragment: a mere snatch of a larger story, with a resulting emphasis on some specially significant incident. Such a fragment may prove remarkably elastic — "The Flats Road," as we have seen, finds room for a huge amount of information — and it may also hold a complete story in little; but its effect is not simply one of completeness, and I wonder how many readers have come to the end of a Munro story and thought "Is that really the end?"

A narrative fragment of this kind is likely to need references to events preceding and following: these will have to be tucked inside the story as we are given it. (It is interesting to see from her drafts that Munro has often put material in simple consecutive order at first and then recast it in this encapsulating way.[28]) Many stories double back to show their antecedents — "Winter Wind," "Visitors," "Princess Ida"; less frequently, we find stories like "Miles City, Montana" interrupting themselves to point forward. The story proper and its larger circumstances thus make a temporal foreground and background, so to speak: and the relation between these varies considerably.[29] The background may of course be just background; yet often, as we have noted, the foreground story is or seems unimportant in itself — the foolish travellers' conversation in "The Spanish Lady," the tedious reunion in "Visitors," the uneventful island stay in "Dulse." An immediate situation may in fact be disposed of fairly briefly; and where it is slight enough, and the events behind it important enough, we will have a piece like "Material" in which the foreground events — the narrator's chancing on one of Hugo's stories and belated appreciation of it — can easily (if not quite properly) be seen as a mere frame. The foreground material of "Executioners" is hard to see any other way: while we are aware throughout that Helena as a narrator is much older than in the recollected story, only briefly and at the end do we learn about her present situation — a very drab one — and how she came to it. Often, however, both foreground and background have considerable weight, while behaving in a mutually disruptive fashion that prevents the story as a whole from having an ordinary kind of unity.

One form of this disruption is the doubling back and leaping ahead that I have noted. Another is what we often find in the course of this, a good deal of rearrangement: while the immediate events tend to appear in more or less their temporal sequence, those recalled may not do so at all. This is the case, for example, in a number of mature stories like "Dulse" or "Labor Day Dinner"; we also find it in certain complex and important early ones, beginning most noticeably with "The Peace of Utrecht." And even where background and foreground events both keep their sequence, the former may intrude on the latter in a confusing and seemingly random way, as in "Something I've Been Meaning to Tell You." There are two conspicuous stories in this case, associated with the First and Second World Wars respectively, and both these stories are given in about their chronological order: but Munro's presentation switches from one to the other in ways this order does nothing to explain. Some time after the Second War Blaikie Noble returns to Mock Hill, and Et reports to Char on his two marriages. The story suddenly shifts to the involvement of Char and Blaikie in 1918. When Char attempts to poison herself after Blaikie's desertion, we find ourselves back with the later story again, and Et's discovery of rat poison in Char's cupboard. Then, as the four principals are spending an evening on the porch together, the story once again veers to the earlier days, and we learn for the first time about Arthur's arrival and accident-prone career.

*

There is at least one evident reason why past and present behave so unpredictably here. If we look again at the back-and-forth movements of "Something I've Been Meaning to Tell You," we will see that to a remarkable degree it is a meditation, with Et as the meditator.[30] It is Et who, watching the others through the long evening on the porch, recalls things that in turn recall Blaikie's reappearance, the old love affair, and Char's attempted suicide. It is Et's connecting of this last with the rat poison that brings us back to the narrative present and the fatally matched group sitting together in apparent concord. It is Et's reflections on the disastrous Arthur that take us back to his first days in town. The comparison of the two situations, the shifting between them, the minor rearrangements of temporal order, are all part of her thoughts. In the same way a conversation in "The Ferguson Girls Must Never Marry" is twice interrupted by lengthy episodes from the past that are clearly memories touched off in Bonnie's mind. In "Dulse" two pieces of information from different times and places lie side by side because one suggests the other to

Lydia Cooper: Mr. Stanley likes to sit alone outside the empty house of Willa Cather; Lydia herself, jilted by Duncan, once sat for an hour outside the bathroom of her apartment.

In other stories we find the same meditative ordering of materials, but it may not be so clear who is doing the meditating. Almost all the reflections in "Something" can readily be attributed to Et: the narrator's mind seems continuous with hers. (It is significant that Munro often changes between first- and third-person narration in successive versions of a story without changing our sense of the story's experiencer.) Elsewhere, however, we may feel experiencer and narrator to be more distinct. This is most obvious where a first-person narrator comments critically on the earlier self whose story she is remembering — as Jessie does at the end of "Jesse and Meribeth," for instance.[31] And it may be no less obvious in the case of third-person narrative:

> She meant to be gone a couple of days, until she came to her senses and could face the sheets and the patch of readied earth and the place behind the bed where she had put her hand to feel the draft. (Why did she bring her boots and her winter coat, if this was the case?) (168)

Here we have what are evidently Rose's own thoughts to begin with, then the intrusion of someone else sceptical of Rose's sincerity. Perhaps this someone else can be merged with Rose herself in a more self-questioning vein; in any case, it seems that Munro's stories can have a plurality of experiencers, with a varying degree of continuity among these. That is what we find even in "Something I've Been Meaning to Tell You": along with Et's associations we occasionally feel those of another mind that may or may not be continuous with Et's own, or with its conscious workings. Coming on some rat poison, Et wonders what it means:

> She put it back where she had found it. She made Arthur his eggnog and took it in and watched him drink it. A slow poison. She remembered that from Blaikie's foolish story. (13)

Somebody is associating the rat poison not only with the poisoning wife in Blaikie's tour routine but with the eggnog: to what extent is this somebody Et?[32]

*

While there are implications here that will have to wait, we can go on to consider meditation in another story where it is neither as obvious nor as closely concentrated within a single experiencer as in "Something I've Been Meaning to Tell You." The main action of "White Dump" — consisting of events around Laurence's fortieth birthday — is introduced by a scene set a number of years later, when Laurence and his second wife Magda are being visited by Laurence's grown-up daughter Denise. The plane ride that had been Denise's birthday gift to Laurence on the earlier occasion happens to come up in conversation; Magda is curious, and the account of the birthday that occupies the rest of the story is given for her benefit. Or at least this account is what Munro gives us after the conversation: on the other hand, items like Laurence's love-making with Denise's mother or his own mother's unspoken memory from her childhood can hardly be part of what is told to Magda; and from the start of the main narrative the birthday has more the air of a direct experience than of a report. As we go on, in fact, we find ourselves inside a whole series of experiencers. The action in general may centre on Laurence, but the three divisions into which Munro formally divides it show us the parts played successively by the three women in his life: his daughter Denise, his mother Sophie, his first wife Isabel. And in each case the narration is presented in close relation to the woman's own thoughts.

To see the effect of this succession of minds, we can briefly follow the course of the birthday story. In the conversation from which it arises there is a casual mention of a "bad experience" (279) — something that happened to Sophie on the day in question. What was that? asks Magda. At first she does not get an answer, and by the time one arrives the impetus of the story is such as to carry us well past it — on to a number of bad experiences that somehow are all the same. We begin with Denise, whose idea it was to give Laurence the plane-ride in the first place: it is Denise who recalls (or has recalled for her) her mother's picking up of the birthday cake, baked by a picturesque catering-woman who also happened to be married to the pilot of the aeroplane. Then the story jumps to Denise's recollection of the same woman as she appeared a year later, distraught and accusing — Denise, being only a child, did not know why.

In the second part Sophie takes over as experiencer: her bad experience on her son's birthday, we now learn, was to have her bathrobe torn by three young hippies while she was swimming in the lake. Later, during Laurence's plane-ride, Sophie finds herself feeling intense discomfort: dismay at something that has happened (for which the bathrobe incident can stand at least metaphorically) as well as foreboding for the future. But it is only in the third part of the story that we approach the heart of the matter: the revelation and rending of which we have been getting omens and emblems and aftereffects. Isabel's day begins with a bad experience of her own — her dismay when Sophie, having lost her bathrobe, appears naked at breakfast. Isabel in fact is disgusted: the hippies, she is sure, are "brats" (301), and Sophie is coldly and hypocritically striking at her son by embarrassing him. Yet when the others have gone up in the plane and Isabel is thinking matters over, she wonders bleakly whether she is not as cold as Sophie: after all, she sees the birthday only as something to be got through without mishap. Now she also begins, in a vague way, to ask herself what she really wants — and soon we learn about the most divisive experience of all, her affair with the pilot of the plane and the marital collapse that results.

In the last pages of the story we go beyond even the three women as we have had them until now. The account of the tragic affair turns into a reflection on all such affairs, shared by Isabel and a grown-up Denise; and at the very end there comes, in effect, a still more comprehensive reflection — the gnomic assertion of fate that Sophie, followed by Isabel, reads in the Poetic Edda. What began as the answer to a casual question about a casually mentioned "bad experience" has gradually expanded into a general vision of human destiny — of all the evil done by and to the larger Sophie who contains the particular women of the story. It is, if we like, this looming "Old Norse" (280) who muses the whole tragedy: the memories of three Norns dissolve into the dream of a single ancient earth-mother,[33] to whom all experience must look the way love looks to Denise, "weird" (281).

IV. INVASION

In the presentation of "White Dump," then, a meditating woman who is also a trio moves toward the heart of her experience. Yet something is inhibiting her meditation, for in spite of Magda's direct question it needs the whole story to get where it has to go. Moreover, the saying from the Edda with which the story concludes (coupled, we can add, with the vision of a falling spaceman) comes as a kind of afterthought: it belongs to the end of the birthday, whereas the narration has already gone on to the affair that came later. Afterthoughts of this kind are a common feature of Munro's presentations. In "The Moons of Jupiter," for instance, Janet's last visit to her dying father's hospital room would make an acceptable ending to the story, but for some reason her account goes a bit further. She mentions a curious experience in the old Chinese garden at the Royal Ontario Museum — a vision that left her feeling briefly at peace. Since this vision occurred before her return to the hospital, we sense that she did not mean to bring it in, then found herself doing so just before stopping altogether.

A vision is an intimate thing: perhaps Janet felt embarrassed. That, certainly, is how Rose feels in "The Beggar Maid" after her own vision of "a radiantly kind and innocent Rose and Patrick" (95): for in all her modern candour about the breakdown of their marriage, this is something she never tells. In "A Queer Streak" Violet does tell about Wyck Tebbutt and the thornbushes, but only after a great crisis and just before her death; in her Marrakesh story Jeanette finally mentions being in love, but "apologetically" (171) and — it would seem — compelled by Dorothy's silent suspicion. Then there is the strange ending of "The Ottawa Valley," where the narrator gives us a scene of inexplicable happiness after the rest of her mother's tragedy, only to push it away with a paragraph of fumbling explanation and confession. The story, she says, ought to have ended before this scene; she was forced on by an urge to "bring back all I could" (246) — including something quite out of keeping with the rest of her memories.

*

When we find such narrators wanting and not wanting to tread on perilous ground, we can often detect what we have so far considered only in other contexts and in the most formal terms: an element of antagonism, indeed personal antagonism, in the interplay of opposites. Something is exerting its force, against great resistance; and the same something is somebody — in "The Ottawa Valley," as we learn at the end, the narrator's craving to remember is equally a sense of obligation to the dead mother pressing against her. In "A Queer Streak" we find a similar constraining figure, even if her identity and demands are less precise: as Violet begins to show her own queerness near the end of the story, she has the alarming sense of being possessed by "a helpless and distracted, dull and stubborn old woman, with a memory or imagination out of control, bulging at random through the present scene" (244) — virtually her mother Aunt Ivie. There are other kinds of figure that bulge in this way — Violet is plagued by an imagined horse with her father's name, the mother in "The Ottawa Valley" by a sweaty old man and, indirectly, by the wronged Allen Durrand — but in one specially illuminating story the intruder is again an old woman: the same, essentially, to whom the various meditators in "White Dump" must surrender their thoughts, willingly or not.

"Home," published in 1974, has never been put into a collection, perhaps because of its similarity to other stories, perhaps because Munro was dissatisfied with it as a formal experiment. In content it is much like "The Moons of Jupiter," being a story about a woman who visits her dying father; the situation also reminds us of "Half a Grapefruit," since the father has a boisterously practical second wife, Irlma, to whom he has transferred his allegiance. Since the narrator's own allegiance remains with her mother, one of Munro's cultivated, stricken women, we are also close here to stories like "Winter Wind" and "The Ottawa Valley." "Home" further suggests the latter story in having a bedeviled narrator, and in this case the narrator does not wait until the end to confide in us: in asides scattered throughout, she reveals what she thinks of her situation and in particular of her own story-telling.

She is a self-critical woman, remarkably so when we consider all the bitterness she has to fight back; and she is particularly uncertain — while also stubborn — when it comes to Irlma. No doubt she ought to say good things about Irlma; she wants to say good things about Irlma's sterling, and genuinely likeable, daughter Marge, who appears near the end as if to show what a daughter might be. But something alien is subverting all these good intentions: the story has been "invaded" (137), as we are told, by the narrator's dead mother, a very different person from Irlma and no friend to her. At the point where the father says "I know you love this place" (136), the narrator begins to think of the place as she did once love it — and of the books she read, and of the mother who bought the books and had Parkinson's disease and demanded attention her daughter would not give at the time.

Here we begin to see how the narrator's state of mind affects the form of what she writes. She is hard on herself in the first place for not coming up with a proper narrative: she has taken too long working into her story, she says, and has brought in too much description (as if postponing something, we may reflect). Suddenly, and against her better judgment, she reveals the mother; having done so, she is uneasy at saying so much so fast to "get her finished with" (137) — for the mother has her own claims, in death as in life. But should the narrator tell a dream she had about the mother? She holds back — until a point a few pages later when she is acknowledging Irlma's undeniable virtues as a wife. Then, with only a paragraph break, she does slip into the dream, one in which the dead mother came at night as the living Irlma does by day.

As if to restrain the dream, the narrator now forces it into a frame: it is only an illustration, we must understand, of her inability to deal with Irlma impartially. As if for good measure, she adds a little anecdote about her own snobbishness, omitted earlier out of shame. At the end of the larger story, however, she adds something quite different and strictly extraneous — something that seems to have forced its way in to offset the good things said about Irlma and Marge. Many years earlier the narrator had known a moment of closeness both to her father and, implicitly, her mother — a moment in which they had stood together against the whole encroaching world of Irlmas. Now she stubbornly remembers this moment, in spite of the fact that Irlma, as represented by a symbolic cow, survived where the mother, similarly represented, did not. And even here the narrator is unsure of herself. This memory would make an effective ending, she feels — one could "see" it (153): then she is caught between the need for such an ending and a desire to get rid of effects altogether.

*

In addition to much that we have found elsewhere, a story like "Home" shows what happens when a narrator is caught between two allegiances — or between an allegiance and a temptation if she feels the matter that way. We can put the same divided allegiance into a larger context as well, that of Munro's concern as to whether, and how, one should speak at all: for we often feel this to be at base a question of personal loyalty. Munro's elders provide conflicting models here — the Mrs. Jordans in her stories have no qualms about their monologues, the Mr. Jordans seem to have none about their reserve. As for the versatile Flo, she is a divided couple all by herself. It is Flo who says "You have to let them know" (57), and who bequeaths to Rose an irresistible urge to mimic and tell. It is also Flo who has some sense of her own mischievousness, and in moments of caution will remark "I shouldn't even be telling you this stuff" (7) — with the result that Rose, heeding her wisdom, manages in the end to keep back at least one story. If, in this general context, we sample views on speech held by Munro's other characters, what we find is a strange assortment.[34] To touch here on something that I will return to later in this book, Eileen in "Memorial" is convinced that "silence [is] the only possible thing" (221); Et Desmond, on the other hand, is uneasy about the something that she means to tell Arthur but never does. Del Jordan feels that her novel about a romanticized Jubilee (a secret and never-written novel, to make things more complicated) is a shirking of her duty to present the real Jubilee: she ends penitentially trying to collect all the facts, while seeing in this undertaking itself the vanity of an Uncle Craig, with his all-inclusive (and never completed) county history.

In the case of "Home" the narrator's problem is not simply that of speaking, but of different things that might be said: a fundamental issue that Munro presents in various forms. In "Miles City, Montana," for instance, we find it as a question of fact or fiction. Recalling the death of Steve Gauley, the narrator does her best to separate what really happened from what she remembers; in effect Del is doing the same thing when she tries to preserve the real Jubilee by getting it all down. The narrator of "Winter Wind," equally hungry for what really happened and equally scrupulous about tinkering with it, is nevertheless willing to trust intuitions as a source of information. She is sure her grandmother was a certain kind of person, even without factual evidence; in "The Progress of Love" the narrator goes so far as to defend a memory she knows to be contrary to fact. And apart from the facts — or non-facts — in themselves, what is one's duty as regards explaining? Janet at the end of "The Stone in the Field," torn between curiosity and a compulsion to dispose of her family, opts for the latter. She is not going to involve herself in the past, nor is she going to go beyond the facts — there must be no explanatory linking of these by some "horrible, plausible connection" (35). Yet it is equally typical of Munro's narrators to dwell on causes, as we shall see presently. They may well feel, as the narrator of "Home" does, that seemingly malicious or silly behaviour should be explained, and explained sympathetically: the alternative would be "vengeful reporting, in spite of accuracy" (149).

In one way and another, what all these self-conscious people want is to "do this with honour" (153), as the narrator of "Home" puts it:

to satisfy the demands of the conflicting principles that are also conflicting people. "Winter Wind," with its own tormented narrator, can sum the situation up for us. In spite of her bad record, this narrator has reformed — from now on she is sticking to ascertainable fact:

> I have used these people . . . before. I have tricked them out and altered them and shaped them any way at all, to suit my purposes. I am not doing that now, I am being as careful as I can, but I stop and wonder, I feel compunction. (201)

And the very stating of her compunction takes her to a different sort of thought, even a different compunction. The people about whom she is being careful are, after all, members of the rural world we have noted: they are forever telling surreptitious tales about one another. Perhaps even intimations — themselves secret tales of a sort — deserve respect. Perhaps such intimations will help the narrator to make her peace with the grandmother she once dismissed so impatiently. Perhaps similar intimations, as well as scrupulously remembered facts, will enable the "Ottawa Valley" narrator to do justice to her mother. Then she will be free of her: for what is going on in both these cases is a rite of exorcism.[35]

*

If conflicting obligations, and loyalties, are much on the mind of narrators like these, they appear more subtly in the very texture of Munro's writing — her narrators' general way of presenting the world. To see one side of the matter, we should first look more closely at a passage in "White Dump" that we touched on earlier. What sets off the main story, we found, is a question asked by Magda; and in fact there are a number of questions here, explicit and implicit. It seems that Denise gave Laurence a plane-ride for his birthday. Which year was that? 1969, because that was the year of the first moon shot, which happened a couple of days later. Why a plane-ride? Because Laurence had often said he wanted to see the neighbourhood from the air. How was it they went up together? Denise could only afford to pay for Laurence, but the pilot let everyone go for a single fare. (Isabel, however, stayed behind, there being one seat too few).

And so on: even in a situation of mere social pleasantry, a determined attempt is being made both to get facts straight and to account for them in a reasonable way. We find the same attempt again and again in Munro's narration; here is a fairly ordinary passage from "Fits":

> To avoid them, he went down a short dead-end street that branched off theirs. No houses had ever been built on this street, so it was not plowed. But the snow was hard, and easy to walk on. He didn't notice how easy it was to walk on until he realized that he had gone beyond the end of the street and up a slope, which was not a slope of the land at all, but a drift of snow. The drift neatly covered the fence that usually separated the street from the field. He had walked over the fence without knowing what he was doing. The snow was that hard. (127)

The tone here is very different from that of the chatter in "White Dump," yet we can discern the same need — that of a narrator more or less continuous with Robert himself — to give a satisfactory explanation of a carefully reported event. What this implies about the event itself is precisely that it takes explaining: walking over a fence in the snow without realizing it may not be all that remarkable, but it is at least a "happening." Elsewhere in Munro there are of course more remarkable happenings — the shocking incident on which "Fits" itself is concentrated, the scandalous goings-on connected with the birthday in "White Dump," numerous "accidents" like the one from which the story "Accident" takes its name. And yet events like these, however special, typify the world in which Munro's experiencers live at all times. They have to be dealt with very carefully if these experiencers are to be at peace with their compunctions:[36] for the compunctions are those of sense, and sense is just what such events challenge.

*

The accident that happens to Roy Fowler in "Wood" is "the most ordinary and yet the most unbelievable thing" (52): "it was what might happen to the most stupid daydreamer walking in the bush . . . . It has never happened to Roy in thousands of times of walking in the bush, or come near happening." Roy is preoccupied and in a hurry; walking on early light snow (as Munro is careful to explain) he for once steps without thinking, slips, and "falls disbelievingly." What happens to Bobby Makkavala in "Accident" — he gets killed when he ties his sled to a truck going down an icy hill — is perhaps even more ordinary and more unbelievable: ordinary because boys like Bobby do such things, unbelievable because the result is nothing less than death, a fatal accident. It will alert us to something important here to consider the term I have just used: when we speak of a fatal accident, we mean or can mean something quite self-contradictory, since logically fate and accident exclude each other — as do the ordinary and the extraordinary themselves.[37]

One person who notices this self-contradiction, if in a somewhat bleary way, is the whisky-drinking babysitter in "An Ounce of Cure." Her employers appear at the door just as her evening's adventure has reached an orgiastic climax, and she is forced to consider "the way things happen": "the shameless, marvellous, shattering absurdity with which the plots of life, though not of fiction, are improvised" (87–88).[38] The most obvious paradox here does not amount to much in itself — a narrator in fiction is free to say that what has happened to her does not happen in fiction — but it points to a more substantial paradox in the world this narrator is experiencing. (This latter paradox, whatever she may think, is one constantly represented in fiction, especially the comedy of errors of which this story is a typical example.) In the narrator's world the nature of chance and the art of fate coincide — she herself describes the Berrymans' entrance not only as improvisation but as a moment in "a well-organized farce" (84). When, at the end of "Accident," Frances thinks of the events that have brought her where she is, everything seems sheer happenstance, and so from one point of view it is. But in the very process of thinking this Frances is implying the opposite as well: for she is marvelling at a "long chain of things" (106), a chain linked just as it was, and bound to her rather than anyone else. A chain is not a random succession; and the story leaves us feeling that Frances's victory is not simply an accident.

If fatal accident is the way things ordinarily happen, that is something we have to get along with; and we do, most of the time — the world usually seems to make sense. But fatal accident becomes a tempter or an invader, like those in "Home" or "The Ottawa Valley," when we feel it as sensibility: when, that is, its elements of fate and chance seem both mutually exclusive and mysteriously congruent. Among Munro's papers there is a short fragment dealing with "Ella," a forerunner of Flo.[39] Ella is obviously a sensible woman, and can on the whole account for her life — she knows, for the most part, why she felt and acted as she did; but there have been three occasions that she cannot account for. The neutralizing of such occasions calls for immense effort on the part of Munro's various Ellas: it greatly concerns Et Desmond, for instance, "who didn't like contradictions, didn't like things out of place, didn't like mysteries or extremes" (7); and it concerns all the narrators who give their allegiance to an Irlma rather than a ghost-mother.

*

Their job does not seem hopeless: the unaccountable can almost always, even perhaps always, be accounted for. This is so, for instance, when someone like Callie in "The Moon in the Orange Street Skating Rink" evinces powers that to the Grazier cousins seem nearly "miraculous" (155) — for Callie penetrates first the Orange Street Rink and later the train on which the boys are escaping to Toronto. We will need to distinguish the two boys here: it is the romantic Edgar who especially senses a miracle, the practical Sam who tries to find reasons. The questions that fill a paragraph on Callie's latter appearance must, then, be Sam's; what are the answers that Sam elicits or infers?

> None of it was impossible. She had come back with the groceries and gone up to the attic. (Why? She didn't say.) She had found the note and guessed at once they hadn't gone home to the farm and weren't hitchhiking on the highway. She knew when the train left. She knew two places it went to — Stratford and Toronto. She stole the money for her ticket from the metal box under the hymn books in the piano bench. (Miss Kernaghan, of course, did not trust banks.) By the time she got to the station and was buying her ticket, the train was coming in and the station agent had a lot of things to think about, no time to ask questions. There was a great deal of luck involved — lucky timing and lucky guessing every step of the way — but that was all. It was not magic, not quite. (155)

Callie's feat, it seems, came about by an acceptable combination of calculation and luck; even the one fact that is left dangling — her going up to the attic — may for all we know have a simple explanation.

Yet the dangling fact stays dangling, as it so often does in Munro. The tidy-minded Et Desmond is never able to explain the missing rat poison at the time of Char's death — it has to remain as the something she never tells. In *Lives of Girls and Women*, similarly, the curious deaths of Miss Farris and Marion Sherriff remain as missing pieces of a puzzle; so of course does the shooting in "Fits," as well as something less gruesome but no less troubling, the discrepancy noticed by Robert in Peg's story. Faced with such embarrassments sense can only cover them, in either sense of the word: it can put them away or it can bring them out — acknowledge them, that is, as a means of neutralizing them. Robert, to keep his marriage running smoothly, chooses the former course; the latter is taken by the "Ottawa Valley" narrator as a means of placating her mother. It is taken again, if in a different way, by Janet in "The Stone in the Field" when she comes on the newspaper account of Mr. Black. Janet adheres respectfully to the facts, as well as to inferences that are themselves virtual facts (the Fleming sisters, she supposes, would have provided water and a quilt for the dying man, but then she already knows from the paper that they provided "nursing care" [33]); after that she considers herself done with the whole business. It may, for that matter, be the opposite of facts that one acknowledges. Peg in "Fits" is like Janet in limiting herself to facts or near-facts; Robert, on the other hand, keeps confessing to what we can loosely call sentiments — feelings and principles and reasonings, "old bad habits, old deceptions and self-deceptions, mistaken notions about life, and about himself" (128). Yet both Peg and Robert have the same underlying motive: as the latter remarks, "There are things I just absolutely and eternally want to forget about" (128).

Nor is it only fact and reason in isolation that these people want to forget: they want to dispose of connection itself when it starts to defy sense. When Janet resolves to stay with the facts, she may not be rejecting sense connection — ordinary thoughts as to the what and why of the Flemings' actions — but there is a more seductive and dangerous possibility here: the occult causation, and occult knowledge of it on Janet's part, that would have Mr. Black dying from cancer of the tongue because (as she would partly like to imagine) he was in love with one of the Flemings and never declared himself. It may occur to Sam that Callie was obeying a mysterious hunch in going to the attic; if so, his motive is all the stronger for sticking doggedly to reasons. The "Winter Wind" narrator may not be very different in clinging to hunches themselves, knowing her grand-mother's hopeless passion is not an attested fact but believing "that we get messages another way, that we have connections that cannot be investigated, but have to be relied on" (201). This narrator is honouring such connections just as the narrator of "The Ottawa Valley" honours the facts about her mother. And perhaps she is doing it for the same reason — perhaps she is yet another who wants to make peace and be rid of somebody. In other words, sense may again be leaning over backwards, acting in its own interest by recognizing its opposite.

The methods of such people can achieve a remarkable degree of success: what remains, though, is always some hint of precariousness. No doubt the account of Callie's appearance on the train makes sense, but we feel the effort that goes into the making — not only must reasons be looked for, and luck acknowledged, but the most one can say in the end is that what happened was not, after all, quite magic. If no doubts are apparent on the surface, that itself may raise doubts. Was the grandmother in "Winter Wind" secretly romantic? The narrator is duly cautious: "Nothing she ever said to me, or in my hearing, would bear this out" (201). Yet the very strictness of the grandmother's self-possession does something to bear it out. When sense becomes as rigid as this woman — not to say her rapidly stiffening grand-daughter — it is developing into a kind of sensibility, or one of a pair of sensibility opposites. Et Desmond is no less extreme: knowing that "something [goes] on" (13) and determined to protect Arthur from it, she turns into the sharp-eyed, sharp-tongued vigilante we find her to be. In one view it is the same anxiety that turns Del Jordan into a compulsive annalist, or Val into a compulsive explainer. And in the end the composure of such characters is never perfect: the grandmother in "Winter Wind" does break down once, though ostensibly over a matter unrelated to her hidden frustration; Et, always on guard for sense, can for that very reason be a prey to the most irrational of fears and fancies.

*

To see as we have just been seeing is to turn Et and the others into a squad of dedicated if not quite perfect police. But to appreciate a greater ambiguity in these figures, and in the stories where they so often serve as experiencers, we should note something else about them — or another way of understanding what we have already noted. The Et who acquires an interest in rat poison is being characteristically astute, and no doubt she is also an old maid "going a little strange" (14), as she herself supposes; but we feel something more when her sister is found dead. Many years before, Et had happened to step outside one night — and to look at just the place where Char and Blaikie Noble were lying. Dorothy in "Marrakesh" similarly walks out in the night — to just the place where she can see Blair King making love with her grand-daughter Jeanette. In fact, Dorothy had earlier called out an invitation to the same Blair King, wondering at herself for doing so; Et, equally amazed at herself, blurts out her fib about Blaikie's new woman. It is not merely that Et and Dorothy are helpless to repel the danger they perceive: they are strangely intuitive in perceiving it. More than that, they obscurely want to perceive it, even to bring it on.

Munro has a whole set of characters who, like these two, live by sense and yet flirt in some degree with sensibility. The Spanish Lady, with her scepticism, her willingness to listen, and her final sense of an unsettling "message" (191) is very typical here; in a less special way, all the major protagonist narrators — Del, Rose, Janet — share her susceptibility. On the male side we have encountered someone like Sam Grazier, who ends as a level-headed businessman drawn irresistibly back to the problem of Callie and Edgar. Even more remarkable are what we can call the lock-headed fathers, older men who resist the supernatural yet are curiously open to it, perhaps because they would secretly like to regain faith both in it and in themselves. In "Home" the narrator's father prepares rationally for death while refusing another man's Bible religion, and the narrator notices his face: "locked into itself in an unyielding weariness, so that it . . . looks shut for good and blind" (141). Yet the same father muses in his fever that "something may be going on we don't know the first thing about"(148). The very similar father in "The Moons of Jupiter," while sure you must not "start playing tricks on yourself" (226), reads articles about the experiences of the clinically dead. Rose's father keeps notes of strange occurrences, veering between robust dismissal of their strangeness and wistful conjecture that they may be the "will of God" (3). Deeper than any of these is Mr. "Lougheed" in "Walking on Water," from whom I have made up the term "lock-headed father." Mr. Lougheed is a rational man and an unbending one, very easy to shock; yet he continues to look about him, feeling "an odd apprehension of a message that could flash out almost too quick for the eye to catch it" (80).[40]

Messages do come, as if from another world: most notably, Mr. Lougheed finds himself recalling the end of a dream that has long escaped him. In the same way, the father in "The Moons of Jupiter" is searching for a word in an old school poem — Joaquin Miller's "Columbus" — when his daughter enters the room and the word suddenly comes out. At this point, as it happens, he is feeling buoyant enough to reject any nonsense on the subject:

> "It's not all that surprising. I ask my mind a question. The answer's there, but I can't see all the connections my mind's making to get it. Like a computer. Nothing out of the way. You know, in my situation the thing is, if there's anything you can't explain right away, there's a great temptation to — well, to make a mystery out of it." (225–26)

Yet there is something at work here stranger, and less subject to his conscious will, than any retrieving mechanism.[41] The poem in this dying man's head speaks of a voyage into unknown and shoreless seas ("shoreless" is in fact the missing word). He has secretly invoked this poem, though at the same time rejected — until his daughter's comforting or disturbing arrival — one element of it standing for what is unbearable about the whole. He has equally invoked the shoreless seas themselves: the mystery outside his finite under-standing and his finite existence. Rose's father invokes the same mystery in a brighter form: he mouths lines about cloud-capped towers and gorgeous palaces — lines that suggest to his daughter a splendour beyond any fading — while performing his humbler magic as a furniture repairman. Not only the depths but the heights, and with them the power to create, seem to wait outside the little life of the ordinary self; people like these fathers can glimpse them on condition that they shrug off their vision as "nothing out of the way."

*

To reach the full implication of what these people are experiencing, we can first go back to "White Dump," where certain things may now be more evident. In the first place, we will see that the answers covering the birthday in one sense cover it in the other sense as well. By being so cheerily informative, Laurence and Denise are trying to hide the most distressing aspect of the day behind a screen of sociability. And there are tiny holes in the screen: Laurence glancingly mentions Isabel's decision not to go on the plane ride, the pilot's wife who made the birthday cake. There is even a touch of bravado that comes into his manner, answered by a "cautionary" (279) tone in

Denise's. Detecting these things, we may detect something further about the whole scene. It is Laurence himself who brings up the dangerous subject — perhaps escaping the previous one but also unable to resist, just as he could not resist saying "Goat milk!" (278) a moment before. In fact Laurence is rather openly what Janet's father is much more guardedly: someone who, in spite of qualms, wants to challenge and show off — even to risk the greatest of gambles. Laurence wants to take to the air and see things; if space is his world as it is his son's, we can even say that he wants to voyage into a shoreless unknown. And without realizing it he is courting the unknown in its less ethereal form — what is summed up by the naked ancient confronting him in his triumph.

We will find something similar in the story's presentation. Throughout "White Dump" we find a narrating presence that, like the experiencers it contains and goes beyond,[42] has set itself the job of reporting and accounting. The job is carried out quite efficiently: questions arising ("What did he sometimes wonder?" "Why into the dining room?" "Why did she think so?" [276, 286, 291]) are all promptly and firmly answered. In other words, we have an "omniscient third-person narrator" here, seemingly in full command of the story's facts and reasons. If, on the other hand, we ask why this narrator should feel such a need to raise and answer questions, we sense the same uneasiness we have found elsewhere — the fear of the inexplicable. And yet the same narrator voices the meditation that moves toward the heart of the story, seeking an event no explanation can cover: once again sense is courting sensibility.[43] Indeed sensibility and sense — which as we have seen can become oddly like each other — are here courting something beyond either.

We have been seeing Munro's covering figures as representatives of sense, even when they respect the mystery beyond it; and we have seen that mystery taking the form, often, of a strange old woman. But now we should think further about the old woman herself: Sophie in "White Dump" will make a suggestive figure here. In the first place, we must acknowledge that Sophie has ample sense of her own: not Magda's more airy kind, to be sure, but certainly a body of solidly grounded opinions and practices. Yet when she quite rationally appears naked at breakfast, her daughter-in-law feels her to be covering something; and what this is is the brooding Old Norse — the woman who, while being a model teacher to the children on the plane-ride, is secretly possessed by a sybil's foreboding. The wise Sophie has a more terrible omniscience than any sensible provider of reasons: the knowledge of a fatality beyond comprehension. The question that remains is whether this too might not be a covering.

When, at the heart of things, Isabel first turns to meet the pilot's look, "they exchanged a promise that was no less real though they might never meet again. And the promise hit her like lightning . . ." (305). The all-knowing narrator — continuous or not with an Isabel reflecting on her own story — is plainly embarrassed here. This is only "high-school fantasy," she assures us in advance;[44] nor is such an experience really lightning at all, just something we put ourselves up to. The other aspect of the matter appears in the passage from the Edda to which, like Sophie and Isabel, the narrator is drawn at the end. What we choose, it says, becomes our fate: and there is surely something fatal about a world in which that would be so. Yet something has also happened to challenge this world of fatal choice as of fatal accident. Dorothy in "Marrakesh" is another Old Norse, as she discovers on looking in a mirror; and like Sophie, or the narrator who merges with Sophie, she is drawn to a vision of sexual meeting. She too is dismayed: for her, indeed, dismay comes as its own bolt of lightning — she feels she might be having a stroke. Afterwards she of course assures herself that nothing has really happened, that she will be all right once she has had a little time to collect herself. Yet something inappropriate has got into the classroom of the old schoolteacher's eye — something not only fatal but "festive"; and it has appeared there because she herself has had both "strength" and "gratitude" (174). Others in Munro feel the same intimation of festivity: "happiness undeserved, unqualified, nearly unbelieved-in" (113), to quote "Tell Me Yes or No." And they too feel grateful.

Gratitude is not fated but free, responding to a grace freely offered; there is the same grace in what Dorothy sees in the night, the mutual self-giving of the two lovers. No matter what may contaminate this grace in a world of passion, or come as its consequence in a world of chance and necessity, a dance of happy shades is taking place here. And such a dance is more disturbing than any wretchedness or folly: Miss Marsalles's guests sit "with a look of protest on their faces, a more profound anxiety than before, as if reminded of something that they had forgotten they had forgotten" (222). In terms of accounting, a story represents this dance when, beyond explaining the world or even acknowledging its mystery, it witnesses to the same forgotten thing in human experience. Indeed it itself becomes the dance — a dance of words — and so breaks free of simple dependence on "the way things happen," the world of sense or sensibility, comedy or tragedy.[45]

*

A story that can serve us as a parable here, as well as a last and extreme example of Munro's presentation, is "Characters," a Rose-and-Flo story published in 1978 though never collected. This is a bizarre affair, going further towards sensibility in a way than even "White Dump": for the latter deals on the whole with one set of events, redistributed as these may be, whereas "Characters," like some other of Munro's stories, not only combines originally separate materials, but even as published does not constitute anything like a single action. To begin with, we are told Flo's preferred method of killing chickens — after which chickens are never mentioned again. Then we find ourselves with Rose's science teacher Mr. Cleaver, and presently hear of his odd wooing of Flo, brought to a sudden end when she puts a Sen-sen packet in his bag of cookies (Mr. Cleaver has bad breath). On this occasion he is off to look at drumlins, whereas Flo is getting ready to give one of her bridal showers: thus loosely attached, the shower has its own little story, in which Flo is scandalized by some dolls equipped with genitals. At the end we have Rose's later thinking on the subject of Mr. Cleaver and Flo as a pair; and lastly Munro adds a bit of Rose's fancy — what, ever since Mr. Cleaver, she has imagined when she thinks of the word "drumlin" (82).

If we look about in Munro's papers, we find that the motifs of the chicken-killing and the drumlin occur apart from the rest and from each other: they were once items in an "Album" of vignettes meant for publication with attached photographs.[46] The story of Mr. Cleaver, moreover, might well have originated in her mind separately from that of the shower, since we often find such disjunctness in the elements of other stories. Thus Robina appears in Munro's drafts with her arm and her cooking long before Munro decides to put her in the story we know as "Executioners"; Rose's high-school adventures and the death of her father appear severally before Munro brings them together for "Half a Grapefruit." And in "Characters" she has exerted herself even less than in "Half a Grapefruit" to ensure narrative links: all we find, if anything, are bits of Scotch Tape like the timing of the Sen-sen incident to occur when Flo is preparing for the shower. At the same time, we can sense an implicit meditator groping for a different kind of link.

You should kill a chicken, according to Flo, by slitting its brain — that way it gives itself up, or at any rate does so in a sense acceptable to Flo. Mr. "Cleaver" takes much the same view in his own work: when confronted by his students' indifference to the remote past he attacks head-on, as it were, attempting to "rip this moment open" (72) and force a hidden world to reveal its treasures. Mr. Cleaver and Flo — the pedantic schoolmaster, the philistine storekeeper — could never have got along together, nor can they be called two of a kind in any ordinary fashion; for that matter, Flo is something of an ironist rather than a cleaver in the way she humours customers. But in general, as Rose notices, they defend themselves from the world in the same aggressive style, Mr. Cleaver inflicting his science on the drumlins, Flo inflicting her wrath on the ladies at the shower when the latter open the dolls' costumes to reveal the hidden genitals. As a result the two remain impenetrable and unpenetrating; and yet "Characters" has more to show us than that. At the end, with the hesitation we have seen in other stories, Rose remembers the word "drumlin":

> A celtic word, he said. *Little hill*. It made a hill sound smooth and hollow, and continued to remind her of what she used to hope for when she was little, though she never really expected to find it, at the base of hills: the little, grassy, perfectly fitted door, that can only be opened from the inside. (82)

Rose's imagined drumlin does not simply remain shut, but neither can it be cloven against its will: rather, it is to open itself freely. Mr. Cleaver's real gift to her — one for which she might have said thank you — was just this odd little word.

In a story like this, Munro's special genre stands out very clearly. A rag-bag of elements — a set of directions, a description of Mr. Cleaver at work, a couple of anecdotes, some reflection on Rose's part — come strangely together in the mind of an implicit meditator whom in this case we can readily identify with Rose herself. And what this meditator sees — more comically than in "White Dump," of course — is the way things happen: the fatal collision of Flo and Mr. Cleaver. But with the word "drumlin," and the sense of gratitude that it brings, Rose momentarily sees something more. In a quiet way she is experiencing her own bolt of lightning, and not just the lightning that merely gives way to another stretch of darkness, but the greater illumination that is always there within any lesser. By the same token, "drumlin" is not just the meditation that withdraws from action, or the epiphany that withdraws from narrative continuity. It fulfils meaning and happening alike; to the extent, moreover, that Rose can feel gratitude for it, it is a wedding of object and subject — a consummating and transcending, then, of the world of presenter, presented, and receiver that has been the main subject of this introduction. Rose will, of course, have to go on as a limited human being like all of us, yet in "drumlin" she is sensing a word of life — one in which she might find the free communion there could never be between Flo and Mr. Cleaver.

It seems, then, that what can be called a word, or the larger dance of words that is a story, unites what nothing else can unite: I will be returning to this idea at the end of the present book. In the meantime, however, there are matters of more immediate concern. So far we have considered the genre of the epiphanic story, embodying the way of seeing and communicating that I have called sensibility. Without by any means putting the problem of sensibility behind us (we will encounter it repeatedly, in fact), we can now turn to a different aspect of Munro's world: its character not as presentation but as thing presented — to make again a distinction that, for a moment, we passed beyond. The world as presented is what we also call the given one, not thinking of a gift uniting giver and receiver but merely of something objectively "there." Such a world's connections divide most readily, in their verbal form, into counterparts of the meditation and action we have already been dealing with: there is the static or quasi-spatial linking that is metaphor — in the limited sense I am now implying[47] — and there is the moving or temporal one that is narrative in the sense of events in sequence. Comparing the two, we may feel that we have not left presentation behind at all, since metaphor, associated with the showing and seeing that belong to space, has a noticeably presentational quality, whereas narrative is what we simply engage ourselves with until we are ready to "see" the whole of it. Yet for present purposes we can confine our distinction to the world of the presented by itself; and it is by investigating this world that, in the end, we can return with fuller understanding to that of "drumlin." Since in Munro we have to do with a story-teller, the metaphorical side of our new world can be dealt with here more briefly than the narrative. It is metaphor, then, that I will begin with; and in particular I am going to dwell on a remarkably prominent and suggestive feature of Munro's writing: her names.

NOTES

¹ For a sensitive essay from a point of view close to my own, see Catherine Sheldrick Ross, "'At Least Part Legend': The Fiction of Alice Munro," in MacKendrick, 112–25.

² Marrakesh is also a red city: for the associations of such a place, see below, 81, 426.

³ See below, 64–66, 79. Blodgett suggests "char" in a fiery sense, very aptly, as well as the French "chair" or flesh (79).

⁴ See for instance Eldredge 113.

⁵ "The Peace of Utrecht" 197.

⁶ See "The Colonel's Hash Resettled."

⁷ Del feels her imaginary Jubilee to have its own kind of authenticity, "as if I had discovered, not made up, such people and such a story" (248). She is not alone in Munro in hesitating to give up her truth; yet the "Bardon Bus" narrator is also speaking for many when she describes her "uncalled-for pleasure in seeing how the design wouldn't fit and the structure wouldn't stand, a pleasure in taking into account, all over again, everything that is contradictory and persistent and unaccommodating about life" (127–28).

⁸ See "Something I've Been Meaning to Tell You" 15; "Characters" 79.

⁹ A few of the studies that have emphasized paradox as such in Munro are Martin, *Paradox and Parallel*; Hoy, "'Dull, Simple, Amazing, and Unfathomable': Paradox and Double Vision in Alice Munro's Fiction"; McMullen, "'Shameless, Marvellous, Shattering Absurdity': The Humour of Paradox in Alice Munro"; and Noonan, "The Structure of Style in Alice Munro's Fiction." My own attempt is to relate paradox to other kinds of relation. Macdonald's "Structure and Detail in *Lives of Girls and Women*" makes a distinction similar to my own.

¹⁰ Either truth or reality can be imagined as signifying the other. The other then is its meaning; or meaning can be located in the union of the two principles.

¹¹ "The Colonel's Hash Resettled" 181.

¹² In her interview with Hancock, Munro has spoken of her love of "surfaces" — meaning the reality of commonplace things. Yet what excites her is that "they seem to mean something way beyond themselves" (101).

¹³ This was Munro's statement at a reading during a conference at the University of Waterloo, March 1982.

¹⁴ Munro mentioned the origin of "Visitors" at the Waterloo reading; those of "Bardon Bus" and "Hard-Luck Stories" (Julie transformed by her affair with Douglas) in the interview with Hancock (82). She uses "Images" and "Dance of the Happy Shades" as examples in "The Colonel's Hash Resettled" 183.

¹⁵ See among others Conron 110. Djwa, who uses the same term (183), sees Munro as combining the southern gothic tradition from the United States with the Canadian tradition of documentary realism (181). See also Martin, "The

Strange and the Familiar in Alice Munro."

16 Unlike Rasporich (*Dance* 159ff.) I cannot see sensibility (to use my word for it) as belonging specially to an *écriture féminine*. The basic proposition of the theorists followed by Rasporich is that, since the norms of our culture have been imposed by men, anything that can be construed as abnormal (or subversive, which apparently follows) is female — in the circumstances though also, as Rasporich often argues, inherently. But the short story form, to take only one of her examples, has not been used by women writers more than the traditional novel, nor is there anything "fractured" (162) about the tale-telling Rasporich associates with women elsewhere (93). It is the same with characters: Munro's do not divide neatly into men with sense and women with sensibility (see Ch. 1 below).

17 Cf. below, 429, 430, 472–73, 507, 509 (with n106), 516.

18 See "Baptizing" 228. In a way Del here is the reverse of a sensible self unable to take a dream seriously: as bemused by Garnet French, she feels sense and reality themselves to be "nonsensical, oblique, baleful as some sentence in a dream."

19 At a party in "Mischief" Rose produces a Tom Swiftie, to the chagrin of a writer who cares about language (107). Munro evidently cares about language in a different way.

20 See *Poetics* 1451a.

21 See Struthers, "Reality and Ordering"; Martin, "Alice Munro and James Joyce."

22 What I am concerned with here is not a story as *a* line, bounded because a story as such is bounded (see below, 119), but simply as "line," something that might go on forever.

23 Writing in a different context, Howells sees Munro's stories as shifting between realism and gothic fantasy (reality and truth, in the senses I have been using), with neither mode prevailing; she also sees these as making a traditional well-made plot impossible (73ff.).

24 For a discussion of Munro's work generally in terms of photography see Lorraine York's " 'The Delicate Moment of Exposure': Alice Munro and Photography" in *Other Side* 21–50.

25 York goes so far as to argue that there is no further structural principle in Munro (*Other Side* 48): I will attempt a different argument in Part I, Ch. 2 below.

26 The early story "The Edge of Town" presents this narrating world more directly, perhaps, than any of Munro's collected ones. A local talker is telling an outsider about life "up here" (368) and soon gets onto the story of Harry Brooke. In other early material, preserved only in draft form, we can see how Munro might have become more of a Faulknerian raconteur than she in fact did.

27 See Conron 111.

28 For Munro's development in this respect see John Orange, "Alice Munro and a Maze of Time"; Martin, *Paradox* (especially 77ff.).

29 By "background" here I mean the events preceding and following the story, not primarily the world in which it is set or its own less salient elements.

30 The sense in which I am using the idea of meditation here is rather different from that of Margaret Gail Osachoff in " 'Treacheries of the Heart': Memoir, Confession, and Meditation in the Stories of Alice Munro." Osachoff is thinking of a first-person narrator speaking only to herself (or an imaginary listener) and moved by "the desire for truth, for self-knowledge, and for order through art" (64). I am thinking of any imitation of the succession of thoughts in an experiencer's mind.

31 See Robert Thacker, " 'Clear Jelly': Alice Munro's Narrative Dialectics," for the development of this technique in Munro.

32 To take a further step, the story contains allusions hardly possible for Et herself — I have suggested, for instance, that she would not have read *Antony and Cleopatra*.

33 The sibyl in the *Völuspa* is the mother of the giants; Wagner turns her into Erda when he adapts *Baldrs Draumar* for the purposes of *Siegfried*.

34 See Carrington 14ff., connecting the embarrassment of Munro's narrators primarily to Munro's personal background in rural Ontario. While agreeing with Carrington's findings, I will ultimately be more concerned with difficulty of communication as a condition of a fallen world. For a more general study of narrators, knowledge, and their problems, see Blodgett's *Alice Munro*, with which my own study concurs at certain points.

35 See Carrington 185ff.

36 This can be so whether a narrator tries to stick to facts or not. Narrators like Janet in "The Stone in the Field" (e.g., those of "Winter Wind," "Friend of My Youth," or "Meneseteung") dearly love to imagine stories for people they find interesting; in "Fits" Robert imagines, at least in part, Peg's entry into the house of the shooting (111). But such people usually want their imaginings to have likely forms. The narrator in "Tell Me Yes or No" recommends "detail, solidity" (109); the one in "Royal Beatings" thinks of reasons why Flo and Rose would be where they are, in the mood for a scrap; Del, even in the throes of her gothic novel, is bothered that her heroine could hardly drown in the local river during summer low water (247).

37 We can say simply that the ordinary is challenged by the extraordinary; more complexly, it is challenged by an extraordinary — as sensibility sees it — coincidence of the ordinary and extraordinary themselves. In any case, sense does its best to see "the way things happen" as merely normal. See also Blodgett 115.

38 Lorraine McMullen, in " 'Shameless, Marvellous, Shattering Absurdity': The Humour of Paradox in Alice Munro," discusses this passage in relation to a general paradoxicality in Munro.

39 See Tener 37.13.10–13.

40 Cf. I Cor. 15:51–52.

41 In the same way, the narrator in "Bardon Bus" finds certain lines of poetry

coming into her head, often running counter to her conscious mood; if she thinks about the matter, she finds a subversive connection with herself — "I can usually see that the poem, or the bit of it I've got hold of, has some relation to what is going on in my life. And that may not be what seems to be going on" (122).

42 See Carrington 159, 171. Carrington feels that a point of view beyond those of the three experiencers is first introduced at the moment of Isabel's exchanging of looks with the pilot. See also Slopen 76.

43 Often we can feel this in a narrator's questions themselves. In "A Queer Streak," for instance, a narrator close (at this point) to Violet wonders "Why did Violet do this? Why did she send those ugly letters to Trevor, and put such a note in with them?" (228). Neither Violet nor the narrator seems to have a clear answer.

44 Cf. Del Jordan's first awareness that Garnet French is looking at her: "I thought what nonsense; like a recognition in an opera, or some bad, sentimental, deeply stirring song" (211). (The narrator in "White Dump" says "operatic story" [305].) In the *New Yorker* version of "White Dump" the narrator puts the sentences on the exchange of looks in italics (39); in the collected version they are in normal print.

45 I am generally aligning sense with comedy and sensibility with tragedy in my argument, but it seems to me that either can go with either. When the narrator of "An Ounce of Cure" sees "the way things happen" as "shameless, marvellous, shattering absurdity" (87), she is seeing the world as a sensibility comedy.

46 Tener 37.13.10–13.

47 While I often use the word "metaphor" in a general sense in this study, I will also use it in the following two chapters especially to mean the *identity* — in varying degrees — of two things, and this as something both static and objective. In particular I will use the word for the most paradoxical identity that can still be called objective; and in the final chapter I will suggest a kind of metaphor that goes beyond the objective.

Names

I: SIGN-POSTS

When, in "The Photographer," Del goes for winter walks with Jerry
Storey and looks down at Jubilee from the railroad bridge, what
appears to her is the town as a "pattern of streets named after battles
and ladies and monarchs and pioneers" (248). In "Princess Ida" a
younger Del, moving into town from the Flats Road, is similarly
aware of "the order, the wholeness, the intricate arrangement of town
life, that only an outsider could see" (70). As on her later walks with
Jerry it is streets that she notices — "River Street, Mason Street, John
Street, Victoria Street, Huron Street, and strangely, Khartoum Street"
— and what matters about these streets is once again their names.
For names are what the whole town seems to come to: all its varied
things and doings not only tend to have names of their own, but are
gathered into in a single name that expresses them all:

> . . . the evening dresses gauzy and pale as crocuses in Krall's
> Ladies' Wear window; the Baptist Mission Band in the basement
> of their church, singing *There's a New Name Written Down in*
> *Glory, And It's Mine, Mine, Mine!* Canaries in their cages in the
> Selrite store and books in the Library and mail in the Post Office
> and pictures of Olivia de Havilland and Errol Flynn in pirate and
> lady costumes outside the Lyceum Theatre — all these things,
> rituals and diversions, frail and bright, woven together — Town!
> (70)

There can be few authors who take such delight as Munro in this sheer giving and listing of names. If we are to have a story of three boys — the Three Jokers in "Half a Grapefruit" — they will of course need names, but that will not be enough: Munro must add the names of the three female jokers as well, even if she tells us nothing about their jokes. She must name the girls Del Jordan worships at school, and the boys they are matched with. She must name Garnet's girl-friends and Janet's aunts and the Baptist Young People; the villages Ben Jordan visits in "Walker Brothers Cowboy," the towns the family travels through in "Miles City, Montana," the places in the Encyclopaedia, streets, ships, operettas, books, drinks, foxes, trees. Munro's characters, moreover, seem often to crave names as much as she does. Del at various times can rhyme off the articles in Uncle Benny's house, the presidents of the United States, even the "hotels, streets, restaurants, in London, Paris, Singapore" (175). When last seen she is trying to recall the name of everything in Jubilee, even to name the things that have no names — "every layer of speech and thought, stroke of light on bark or walls, every smell, pothole, pain, crack, delusion" (253).[1]

In the present chapter we will see some of the patterns that emerge from this endless naming; before starting, however, we can note a peculiarity of names — or signs more generally — that needs to be kept in mind here, even if its full significance will appear only later. A street in Jubilee would no doubt have sign-posts to identify it: in any case its name would be set inside the mental frame or quotation-marks that we put around objects of cognition to separate them from reality. Names, that is, are most simply truth — to use "truth" and "reality" again in the senses I have taken from Del Jordan. When at one point Del herself speaks of Garnet French living in a "world without names" (221), it is evidently a world of reality she means. (Jerry Storey, on the other hand, could be said to live in a world of truth: one with names — or perhaps mathematical symbols — but without things.) In a different view we could put names with reality, leaving only pure idea as truth; but as long as we are dealing with a simple duality of truth and reality, names must be assimilated to one or the other in this way — they have no place of their own.

They acquire one when we allow the scheme another term. Del, we have seen, is far more intrigued by names than either Garnet or Jerry; "Caroline" (242), the name she hits upon for the heroine of her novel, seems magically right to her — so much so, in fact, that we feel it taking on its own identity. The same thing happens with any name when we dwell on it. The "Khartoum" in "Khartoum Street" is not Khartoum itself, much less the heroic ideality that the namers of the street must have associated with that city. On the other hand, the "Street" in the name is not a stretch of pavement in Jubilee: while connecting "Khartoum" to a street — truth to reality — "Khartoum Street" remains something in its own right. In this ternary model a name takes on a medial or mediating role: we can say that it "means" an idea, or means a thing, in the sense that it represents either to the other. Both models, of course, must be understood as models: ideas, names, and things here are not entities but ways of experiencing. But our world is experience, and we do usually see it as consisting of things with names, or things connected by names to ideas, whatever philosophical problems may be lurking. In the same way, as we have already found, we experience Home, an Other Place, and a communiqué that somehow passes between them.

To see mediation at work more generally in Munro's naming, we can choose a form of it that stands out clearly when Del moves into town. Some of the things she finds there — religion, the mail, the soldiers on leave from the war — can be associated with the serious "rituals" we have heard her mentioning. Others, like songs and movies, are only "diversions"; yet elsewhere Munro has a good deal to say about serious joking,[2] and as this passage shows, solemn rituals and recreational games have much in common. Both are set apart from ordinary life; both require set forms such as costumes, which tell what roles the participants are taking. Both, in other words, are forms of art. And the town produces its own official form of this in *The Pied Piper*, the operetta put on by the local school-children in "Changes and Ceremonies." The story here is the familiar one, more or less — children are led away to a strange world by a magician who then disappears; and when we turn to the youngsters who perform the operetta, we recognize the same story in a less idealized form, for they themselves are being drawn away to the colourful, perilous world of their sexuality. When we note which child takes which role, the correspondence grows even clearer. As her dancing partner Del gets Jerry Storey, her inevitable consort for the next few years; Del's friend Naomi plays the bossy mother she is destined to become in later life; and the Pied Piper himself is Frank Wales, the first boy to call forth the girl in Del. *The Pied Piper*, in other words, brings the age-old myth of the psychopomp to the real life of the children, while bringing the children to the myth.

Another example of art as mediation will be more cryptic — so much so, in fact, that I must ask the reader to take it partly on faith for the present. In "Something I've Been Meaning to Tell You" Blaikie Noble knows things about the hotel entertainers that he gleefully passes on to Char and Et Desmond:

> He told them the Scottish ballad singer was a drunk and wore corsets, that the female impersonator even in his hotel room donned a blue nightgown with feathers, that the lady ventrilo-quist talked to her dolls — they were named Alphonse and Alicia — as if they were real people, and had them sitting up in bed one on each side of her. (9)

Clearly the entertainers, while having much more squalid lives offstage than on, play their stage-selves in real life as well — and real selves on the stage; but there is a further meeting of art and life here that we may not immediately notice. We should think of Blaikie Noble with his Scottish name and romantic wooing — the Blaikie who, in spite of these things, can only pretend to be a boy like others. We should think of Char, who poses gracefully in blue but conceals a most unladylike wrath and wilfulness underneath; and of Et, who subtly creates the roles in which others are cast. Blaikie, Et, and Char are themselves the three entertainers — "You'd have a fit if you could see" (10), Blaikie remarks. And in this correspondence there is mediation: the roles played by the hotel entertainers — or by the young people themselves — link mundane humanity to the archetypal world of the lover, the trickster and the blue-robed queen of heaven. In "Lives of Girls and Women," again, that noted performer Art Chamberlain stands between David the fabled lover-king and a world of small-town adultery that includes his own less glamorous self.

*

Now we can turn to the main business of this chapter, the exploration of Munro's world as a whole seen as one of names.[3] For a preview of what we are going to discover, we can consider an individual example that is also a central and a very rich one: "Del Jordan." "Jordan," of course, will immediately suggest the Jordan River, where the Israelites cross into the Promised Land and John the Baptist later does his baptizing. Del Jordan, correspondingly, reaches the crisis of her girlhood in a chapter called "Baptizing," in the course of which she gets immersed in the Wawanash River; later and in a more metaphorical way she gets baptized into the vocation of writing, like the George Herbert of the "Jordan" poems. The name "Del" takes rather more introducing. Evidently it is a pet-form of some such name as "Adela": since Del is called "Della" (82) by her uncle, that may in fact be the official form of her name (her mother's name "Ada" being another version of it). Names of this family go back to a Germanic root meaning high or noble (as in the German "edel"): an Albert or Adelaide or Edith or Edgar, to mention related names in other Munro stories, is always in some sense — perhaps paradoxical — a privileged being. So is Del if she receives baptism in the Jordan.

This is to see "Del Jordan" as a simple unity, its members reinforcing each other's suggestions. What, though, if we were to see "Del" and "Jordan" as contrasted? There are two opposite perspectives we can take here. We have just seen the Jordan as a sacred river: a passage to the Promised Land. If we set "Del" in opposition to such a river, we will be reminded of "delta" — for of course there is another river, that of Egypt, to be associated with the Exodus. "Del," then, will suggest a land of bondage, an underworld to be escaped from; it can also suggest the fertility associated with a delta, or more vaguely that of the genital triangle, which we can see as base if we like. "Jordan," by contrast, is the water of purification — the putting off of every-thing that belongs with Egypt or wilderness. Yet when we remember that "Del" means something like "high" or "noble," we get opposite results: it is "Jordan" that now sounds low — in fact we will be meeting the Jordan again as a river of death. We may even recall that "jordan" is an old slang term for a chamber-pot.

No two people will agree as to the particular content of "Del Jordan" — what exactly is "there" in the name: and yet the principles I have isolated seem plain enough. For our imagining selves the relation of elements in a name, like the relation between a name and its bearer, is the metaphoric one of similarity in difference; difference, moreover, produces a mirroring in which either element can play either of the opposed roles — in the case of "Del Jordan," those of the high and low. The same principles seem to govern many other of Munro's names: so many, in fact, that we have good reason to look for these principles in her naming generally. "Arthur Comber," "Art Chamberlain," "Clare MacQuarrie," "Jerry Storey": while these names will have more to tell us as we go on, we can readily see that each contains an oxymoron.[4] Art Chamberlain is a kingly Arthur and a menial chamberlain; Jerry Storey is, among other things, a low jerry — another sort of chamber-pot — combined with a high storey. Even single names can be oxymoronic in the same way. Eugene in "Walking on Water" is "well-born" — what his name means — in the sense that he is something of a natural aristocrat. But we are made aware of a different Eugene, one who suffered some kind of breakdown and whose higher Eugene-ness strikes Mr. Lougheed as artificial; and when another character mockingly calls "Yew-gene" (89) we can hear Eugene's doubleness in the very syllables of his name. It is the same when Uncle Benny calls Madeleine's baby "Di-ane" (15), making her combine a principle of light and superiority ("day," "dea") with "anus."[5] We hear some such duality again, perhaps, when in "Heirs of the Living Body" Del taunts a cousin by repeating "dead cow" as "day-ud cow," "expanding the word lusciously" (44). In fact word-play of this kind seems to be going on whenever one of Munro's characters produces a singsong version of a word — as with Art Chamberlain's "pea-cocks" (160), in which we can hear opposition not only between stately peacocks and urinary "pee cocks" but between "pee" and "cocks" by themselves.

If we are exploring, however, we cannot often be so microscopic, or even limit ourselves to full names taken in isolation: our chief job will be to map the larger complexes into which these group themselves. Arthur Comber and Art Chamberlain may be very different persons, but they are both Arthurs; nor is "Comber" the only name in Munro to suggest a wave. With such groupings the metaphoric likeness and difference we have been seeing will reappear as relations within, or between, whole families of names. For reasons that will become apparent, a good family to start with is that associated with the simple colours black and white — colours that, as it happens, figure prominently in Munro's naming. If we want a talisman on setting out, the mysterious "Blanche Black" in "Visitors" is an obvious choice; and for good measure we can add "Blaikie" (as in "Blaikie Noble"), which by a fluke of etymology means both black and white.

II: MARY

Apart from Blanche Black, Munro has only one character of the same surname, Mr. Black in "The Stone in the Field"; but she has various other names that mean the same thing. Sir John "Moore," recalled in "Something I've Been Meaning to Tell You," is a Mr. Black; Morris in "Oh, What Avails" is another, echoed by an Archibald Moore in the background of the same story; and Morris can lead us to a more important figure — the Mrs. Jordan who began life as Miss Morrison. We can add that one of the townships of Wawanash County is Morris; that in "Miles City, Montana" the family travel in a Morris car;[6] and that in the same story Andrew's family live near "Muir Park" in Toronto (suggested, it would seem, by the actual Moore Park). These are common names, of course; nor is it surprising that in 1918 (when the earlier part of "Something I've Been Meaning to Tell You" takes place) a schoolteacher would read "The Burial of Sir John Moore" to a class.[7] But the Blacks and Moors in Munro seem more than casual: we find, for instance, that Sir John Moore, like Blaikie Noble, belongs to a story with a significant amount of darkness, notably in the form of holes.

Walking by the lake, Char hears invitations from the "dark holes" of the workmen's cottages (8).[8] She herself, lying with Blaikie Noble in the darkness, produces a similar effect: for as seen by her sister, "their mouths were big and swollen, their cheeks flattened, coarsened, their eyes holes" (10) — dark holes in the faintly lit faces. Other holes, while not so named and not always so dark, are no less distressing. Arthur Comber cannot visit the Grand Canyon because of dizzy spells, but he creates a dark lake by spilling ink on the floor; Et in effect discovers another lake when she comes on the bottle of rat-poison. Behind all of these there is Lake Huron itself, or the face that Et thinks of when she sees the lovers in the night — that of her younger brother Sandy, drowned in the lake before the beginning of the story.

Things dark or cavernous, then, can be linked with names meaning "black" — not too surprisingly. There are other names as well to link them with, and combining some of these with "Moor" we arrive at a group, connected more by sound than etymology, that is going to be specially significant for this study. In "Heirs of the Living Body," along with molasses, a dark cow's eye, Boston Blackie, a Black Watch dress, and a black dot in a maze, we find the lugubrious Aunt Moira Oliphant: a woman swathed in dark fabric (down to her "earth-coloured" [40] stockings) and possessed of a voice that, recounting tribulations, spreads over the yard "like black oil" (41). Similar-sounding names occur with noticeable frequency in Munro: Aunt Moira's own daughter, for instance, is a Mary Agnes, and elsewhere we find Marie, Maria, Maureen, Myra, Maya, and Molly — to go no further for the moment. We also find various surnames: there is a

Mr. Malley in "The Office" and a Mr. Morey in "Walking on Water," not to say June Morey in "Characters" and the rough Morey boys in "Privilege." Another form of "Morey" is "Murray," as in Murray Street, Murray Heal, Pierce Murray, Heather Sue Murray, and Murray the protagonist of "Oranges and Apples."[9]

Once again, it is not especially remarkable that Munro would pick a certain number of names starting with the letter "m," or even "m" with a following liquid; it is also true that these names point in various semantic directions.[10] But where we are told about their bearers, we find that these have something in common. To ignore complications for the present, we find not only an outraged Aunt Moira but a molested Mary Agnes, a luckless Mr. Malley, a dispirited Mack,[11] a withdrawn Mattie, a frail and outcast Alva-Marie, a guilt-ridden Maddy, Morgan the irate turkey-killer, Morgy his blubbering son, Maria the hapless victim of her sexual urges — a miserable lot altogether, fit to accompany the lonesome Mr. Black and the dead Sir John Moore. These "m" names do make a family, then: one that can be linked with the idea of black, as in "moor," or of fate, as in "moira," or of death, as in Latin and Romance words like "mors." Above all, these names can be connected with the biblical and traditional Mary, the woman of sorrows whose name some of them bear.[12]

*

As a convenience we can use the name "Mary" for the whole of this dark clan, and we can extend the clan itself to include figures without "m" names who have some evident kinship with its members. Now we should look more closely at a single member of it, picking one both typical and amply described. Myra in "Day of the Butterfly" has a name very close to "Mary," whatever its other associations may be. Appropriately she is a dark girl, perhaps Mediterranean though we are not told her family's nationality; and she is certainly a sad one. As ritual outcasts, Myra and her younger brother huddle by themselves at school recess, their faces "melancholy and discreet," their eyes heavy-lidded and "weary" (101); presently Myra is a victim of leukaemia, dying in childhood. At the same time there is a strange power in her suffering: it enables her to beat out the brash Gladys Healey as star performer of the class, even in a way to triumph over her betraying friend, Helen the narrator. Myra is not altogether different, then, from her mother, the woman who in handing you the produce of the family fruit-store mocks you with its price. And both, we find, have something of the ocean about them: Mrs. Sayla's hair is "crimped in black waves" (103), while Myra is believed to wash her own in cod-liver oil. Her little brother, we can also note, regularly wets his pants, creating a "big dark stain" (100) like Arthur Comber's pool of spilled ink.

It is easy enough to connect Myra with other figures in Munro's early writing. In "Changes and Ceremonies" the "never chosen" of the school include "the Italian girl who never spoke, and was often absent with kidney disease" (124) — a girl who dies in high school, to be remembered with "consternation, belated pride." In the same passage we find a lachrymose boy whose father runs a small grocery store; both these children, like Myra and her brother, pass their lives in "dreamy inviolate loneliness." Then there are the various Myras of "The Dangerous One," a fine early story never collected. At school the young narrator once befriended a delicate girl with the "sweet and barbaric-sounding" (51) name of Alva-Marie Skin — a girl not to be played with, since her father and elder brother were both in jail and the family thought to be contaminated. Donna, the narrator's darkly beautiful cousin, is another girl with a jailed father; and whatever may have been the case with Alva-Marie, Donna is a pathological liar and thief. At the same time she is frail, even morbid: her special games include funerals in which she herself plays dead and other children bring gifts — as the children do to Myra in her last stages. Indeed Donna's whole life is death, her world one of "final hostilities and loneliness" (51): behind her looms a mother who ruined her own life by an ill-advised marriage, died young, and looks out from a high-school photograph with a "small, mournful, bird-like" (50) face. To all of these we can add another figure from an early story, Harry Brooke's unnamed wife in "The Edge of Town." An expansive man himself, Harry is drawn to "anything tinged by the promise of Death" (370): he finds this in a still, remote, failing woman who dies in the course of the story and, Harry convinces himself, was never really alive at all.

*

And so Mary is, most obviously, a figure of darkness and sorrow — a sufferer or bringer of suffering. Appropriately, we often find her associated with night and rain, perhaps with sleep as well. In "Material," for instance, the forlorn Dotty sleeps "like the dead" (39) through a nocturnal downpour that has her neighbours squabbling upstairs. Eileen in "Memorial" likewise sleeps while others wake, during an important reception as in her life more generally; if she also wakes in the rain when others — notably her galvanic sister — have gone to sleep, this is really the waking of sleep itself, and the sequel a kind of dream. Nor is Eileen merely somnolent: she "is aimless and irresponsible, she comes out of the same part of the world accidents come from" (224). So does the fortune-telling neighbour in "Simon's Luck," who appears — again out of the night and rain — to presage the disappearance of Rose's lover. Rose herself, in her bitterness, throws over a job in Ontario to try her luck on the west coast; the "morose" Lydia Cooper in "Dulse" accepts a similar future after a similar shock; in "Red Dress — 1946" it is "Mary Fortune" who, scorning to chase boys, is going to try tobacco-picking. As for Dotty, she may not be one for fortunes — she knows all she wants to about her own, she says — but then Dotty is a prostitute, a woman whose very occupation means taking her chances.

If Mary's darkness and wateriness are the uncertainty of fortune, they are equally that of disease: and while this can be of any kind, certain forms of it are specially significant here. Often the problem is respiratory — Mary Agnes Oliphant, for instance, has her bronchial condition, as does Mary McQuade in "Images"; Franny McGill in "Privilege" cannot breathe properly and later dies of pneumonia; Dotty's woes began with bronchial pneumonia at the age of three. Lower in the body we find not only diarrhoea and nausea[13] but some more serious afflictions: it is kidney disease that proves fatal to the Italian girl in "Changes and Ceremonies," while Donna in "The Dangerous One" is kept out of school by a kidney condition called pyelitis.[14] The name of this last is suggestive in itself: it derives from a Greek word for the pelvis or, more generally, a trough or tray; the Latin "alvus" and "alveus,"[15] which we can perhaps hear in "Alva-Marie Skin," have about the same range of meaning.[16] I will be coming back to the image of the tray as we go on, but one thing already seems clear: the dark pool we have been encountering — produced in Jimmy Sayla's case by wetting his pants — is also the swampy inside of the human body itself. Myra's leukaemia, for that matter, belongs in the same region, being one of Munro's ailments of the circulatory system.

*

53

As a habitat external to her, Mary's pool takes such forms as the flooded basement where Dotty performs her great feat of sleeping. Mary Agnes Oliphant lurks in a storeroom filled with dim blue light and suggesting for Del an egg or womb; Mary Fortune's retreat, like that of some others in Munro, is a lavatory. Or a Mary's associations may be with the equally troublesome element of fire. In an earlier version of "Material" the faulty pump in the basement was not only a bad drain but a smoking furnace.[17] Mary Fortune has an illicit smoke behind the lavatory; old Mrs. Fullerton in "The Shining Houses" not only likes a cigarette, but at the end of the story emits smoke menacingly from her chimney. In "A Trip to the Coast," correspondingly, the grandmother does her smoking by the kitchen stove, another common piece of equipment in Munro.

No doubt there is something female about these stoves and furnaces, as there is about Munro's washing machines and dryers — all of them, that is, suggest the mechanics of gestation. So do factories: and while some of those in Munro produce gloves and hats, others produce musical instruments to be played on.[18] At the same time there is usually a male figure about, perhaps a proprietor, perhaps just a janitor. In "Half a Grapefruit" it is a janitor who tends the Kotex dispenser in the girls' washroom; Mary Fortune's lavatory leads to a janitor's room; and the lugubrious Mr. Malley in "The Office" is both a landlord and, at the end, the person left to clean up still another lavatory. Some such places, accordingly, are male rather than female preserves, like the room behind the men's changing room to which the manager and his cronies retire in "The Moon in the Orange Street Skating Rink." The air is smoky here, as we might expect, and it is even worse in the foundry in "Working for a Living," where the father has a job as night watchman. Men in fact get silicosis from such a place — for the male Mary has problems with his "tray" just as the female does.[19]

The basement or back room or factory thus makes a good architectural symbol for Mary's world as we have seen it so far. It may be down a hall or underground; it may be specifically at the bottom of stairs, like the janitor's room in "Half a Grapefruit" or Flo's kitchen in the same story (through which her stricken husband has to pass to get to the toilet). Sometimes we find people smoking on the stairs themselves, as Mary Fortune and the narrator do in "Red Dress"; we may also find them doing unpresentable things beneath the stairs — like the Three Jokers accosting Ruby Carruthers under the front porch in, once again, "Half a Grapefruit." And other "tray" places are similarly out of sight or out of bounds: accessory like a closet, screened like a stove, boarded up like some of Munro's lounges and factories,[20] or remote like the janitor's room in "Red Dress," to which only Mary Fortune knows the way.

*

If the person we find in this lowly place is a woman, she may well be a handmaiden — like the biblical Mary, of course. Alva-Marie Skin's mother takes in washing, as does Mary McQuade; Char Desmond, while more genteel, again labours at huge washings, being as we have seen a charwoman among other things. Other Marys are, or have been, factory-workers: Harry Brooke's ailing wife used to work in a hat factory, and the abased Lois of "Thanks for the Ride" has a job at the glove-works, making finery for her betters. Franny McGill, who could hardly keep such a job, nevertheless carries one of Munro's "gill" or "servant" names, appropriate to her sexual servitude in a school toilet. And when not servants, such women are at any rate outsiders, isolated in some way from ordinary human affairs. In this role they may be as forlorn as Franny McGill; or, like Mary in "The Shining Houses," they may be not so much abject as embittered, and alienated rather than alien — for this Mary's sympathies have turned from her prosperous neighbours to the despised Mrs. Fullerton. Others we have met show a similar disaffection: Eileen in "Memorial," Lydia Cooper in "Dulse," or, again, Mary Fortune. These last women remind us less of the New Testament Mary than of her prototype Miriam (the two names are really the same), since the Miriam of the Pentateuch, while a somewhat sketchy figure, is certainly an unco-operative one at times. It is Miriam who is cast out of the Israelite camp for insubordination,[21] and whose name has traditionally, if inaccurately, been linked with "mar-" words meaning bitter.[22] Miriam also, of course, sings a fierce paean at the crossing of the Red Sea, and we sense a like savagery in several of Munro's Marys. Char, usually a passive and brooding woman, not only smokes but is quite capable of ripping things up when her smoke turns to fire. The drooping Roberta of "Labor Day Dinner," while fearful of "something black that rises" (149), not only feels an urge to do violence to herself but chooses to bring a "raspberry bombe" (134) for dinner.

When such women misbehave openly they appear as sinners: an obvious case is Madeleine, the child-beating "tartar" in "The Flats

Road." With her illegitimate child, Madeleine is yet another Mary, Mary Magdalen; Aunt "Lena" of "The Ottawa Valley," while hardly a sinner, is again a child-beater — at least when not mollified, "an unthreatening dark shape" (238) holding one of the children on her knee. Other Magdalens add a note of contrition: Maddy in "The Peace of Utrecht," a tartar as a girl though later a determined conformist, smokes and flirts with a married man; she also bears the guilt of having abandoned her dying mother. Eileen in "Memorial" (whose name can, I think, be connected with "Madeleine" through "Lena"²³) is still another contrite adulteress. And with or without the contrition, all these Magdalens seem to meet in the erring Nora Cronin of "Walker Brothers Cowboy." Irish Nora is a wild alien in a Scots Protestant world; she has noticeably strong teeth; she is also a spirited and sensual woman who wants to dance with somebody else's husband.

Beneath their sporadic defiance and ferocity, however, Munro's Marys remain the sad figures we first found them to be: to follow their sadness where it leads, we can best return to the fact that the Mary complex includes janitors — servants again, tending another kind of visceral necessity. No doubt these men can be as jealous of their own as any Miriam, and as violently so — Joe Phippen, guarding his squalid basement, explodes with an axe — but they are also like Joe's whisky-drinking cat, which first leaps wildly and then sinks under the couch. Cats, in fact, make regularly companions for the likes of Joe: Arthur Comber in his decline has a cat sleeping at his foot, while the janitor's room in "Half a Grapefruit" contains, or is thought to contain, a cat's skeleton. And as if these cats were not black enough, some janitors favour "coons": Uncle Benny, a hired man living in a house filled with junk, has two pet "coons," "tamer than cats" (3), to which he feeds chewing-gum rather than whisky; "Coonie Box" (57), the janitor in "Monsieur les Deux Chapeaux," is evidently their human cousin.²⁴ As for Joe Phippen, he is implicitly a muskrat, still another hole-dwelling, water-loving animal: and the little girl who meets Joe learns from her father's traps what muskrats have to look forward to.²⁵

Arthur's cat, we should notice, is called "Old Tom"; Joe Phippen's is again a tom, as are some others. Perhaps they are Peeping Toms, for that is what Munro's janitors, male or female, seem in general to be. At the end of "Marrakesh" the aged Dorothy is explicitly called a "lady peeping Tom" (174), and with her schoolteacher's sharpness was that even before she took to watching sex on the neighbour's back porch. Dorothy, unlike kittens we hear about in "Baptizing," has had her eyes opened to the world: now she peers at it with relentless curiosity.

> It was not at all a peaceful, letting-go sort of feeling, such as old people were supposed to get; it was the very opposite, pinning her where she was in irritable, baffled concentration. (163)

With this kind of vision, Dorothy finds the world much like the pool of black coffee into which we find her gazing as the story opens; and as she gazes she asks "What is there to love?" (157). The sceptical observers we met in the introduction might all ask the same question; so might the insanely suspicious Joe Phippen; so might Marys of the more languid kind. For all are what Munro sometimes calls her janitors, "caretakers" — people, ultimately, in a state of despair. In terms of Christian typology, they are the Miriam who is unfaith under the Law; and while Peeping Tom comes from the Lady Godiva story, we can find a biblical match for him — the Doubting Thomas who asks virtually the same question as Dorothy.[26]

Nor is Thomas the only doubter among Jesus's disciples: there is also, notably, the Simon Peter who cannot walk on water[27] and who denies Jesus in the crisis. Simon of "Simon's Luck," who is like Peter in the way he gets out of scrapes, also fascinates Rose by his dark cynicism. And behind the biblical Simon we find Simeon: the son of Jacob who reappears in Luke's gospel as an old man, ready to pass away on seeing a new life into which he himself cannot enter. In the grandmother's dream in "A Trip to the Coast" it is at the "Simmonses' gate" (179) that a corresponding vision appears — to the sceptical grandmother this can only take the form of a black bird covering the sun.[28] Even more important here is Joe Phippen's namesake Joseph: the boy who falls first into a pit and then into the land of Egypt, with its furnaces, labours, and plagues. Myra, fading into death, is taken to St. Joseph's Hospital; in the hospital where the young Bobby Makkavala of "Accident" lies dying, his father remembers a "plaster St. Joseph . . . stretching out his arms ready to topple on you" (87). We may even, if we like, think of Joseph when Mrs. Jordan suggests what to do with Uncle Benny's junk: "you'd have to dig a pit to put it in" (13). Benny himself — Joseph's brother Benjamin, or, to give him his full name, Benjamin Thomas Poole — has the Grenoch Swamp to do his sinking in, not to say the underworld of Toronto; Joe Thoms in "Home" has sunk into the darker pit of blindness. And what both these men live in, for all their spasmodic leaps of faith, is the pit of their own minds: the darkness where Mary and Joseph must descend for a time, taking the hope of the world with them.

*

There is one further complex — partly of names, partly of roles — to which we should introduce ourselves, however provisionally, at this stage. The Joe who is a captive is also, in the person of a Joe Phippen, an effective jailer, arresting the Ben who ventures to the gate of his underworld. Etymologically a janitor is the same thing, a gatekeeper: Munro's janitorial figures regularly keep watch at entries, like the Mr. Malley of "The Office" who seems always to be at the door of the room he rents. Still another sort of doorkeeper, as we will find, is Uncle Bob Oliphant in "Heirs of the Living Body"; what we can note about him here is that he listens to programmes like "Police Patrol" (40). Evidently Uncle Bob has affinities with a bobby: in "The Photographer" we meet a "Bobby Sherriff" standing at another door, while "Robert Kuiper" in "Fits" has a surname suggestive of a keeper or copper[29] — in a story about perilous entry into the house of a shooting. At the same time, such men can be the opposite of bobbies. Bobby Sherriff, we will see, turns truant against the mother he serves, playing Robin Hood as well as Sherriff;[30] and if we listen to the name "Robert" again it may suggest "robber" — one of the burglars, perhaps, that we hear about in such stories as "Fits." It may indeed suggest "Robber" himself in "Heirs of the Living Body" — a specially interesting figure here since he is a tomcat.

Robber does very well for himself, notably at milking time; and yet we have seen what Munro's tomcats come to in the end. We may also notice that her characters called Bobby tend to have disastrous accidents — Bobby Makkavala in "Accident," Dorothy's son Bobby in "Marrakesh," and in a sense Bobby Sherriff himself, an inmate briefly home from a mental asylum. Remembering the tomcat who belongs to, and in effect is, Joe Phippen, we can conveniently use Joe to epitomize the situation here — one that will concern us at various points in this book. Joe peeps at the world from his hideaway like the Tom he is; he even bursts out to act as bobby against intruders. But that is because his own suspicion — his doubt, that is — has both stolen his mind away and consigned him to jail. And here we may think of some other figures: Robina in "Executioners," for instance, who plays bobby to the heroine while playing den-mother to thieves;

or Roberta in "Labor Day Dinner," the despondent, mutinous wife who in the end holds her husband captive.[31] With Roberta, moreover, we not only see Mary playing this dark double role, but being double in a way we have not yet considered: for to get the power she wants she ultimately turns cool and remote — like the bright moon shining above the end of this story.

*

So far we have found Mary and her kind to be a relatively simple phenomenon — uniformly dark and dismal. But now we should think of Myra again: for there is more to see in her than we first noted, more than just a pathetic victim with hints of a victim's special power. Myra at the end is an exalted being who solemnly "preside[s]" (109) over the ceremony in her honour; even as a pariah at school she was "set apart for legendary uses," an idol consecrated to "worship or magic" (101). And her name itself hints at a double status: it suggests not only "Mary" but "mira," "wonderful" as in "Miranda."

As this other Myra may remind us, the Mary of Christian tradition is more than a handmaiden and mother of sorrows: she is the queen of Heaven, the woman with stars for a crown and the moon at her feet.[32] In using or suggesting the name "Mary" itself, Munro generally brings out its darker associations, but it is a presiding Mary, like the presiding Myra, whose picture hangs on the Cronins' wall in "Walker Brothers Cowboy"; the Malleys in "The Office," correspondingly, have model "Queen Marys" to make their living-room look proper. "Bonny Mary of Argyle" (79), according to the song learned by Addie Morrison in "Princess Ida," is something more than proper — she turns the world back into Eden; and some Marys more immediately present in Munro have a similar calling. The unnamed heroine of "The Spanish Lady" may be a deeply humiliated woman at the outset, but later we find her high in the mountains, sipping a "pure and restorative" drink in an observation car while the sun makes "a circle of light on the white mat" (181). Now an airy visitant appears with the message that she is blessed among women — the same message that comes more obscurely to "Mary Jo," the secretary in "Eskimo."

Being thus chosen, it is not surprising that some of Munro's Marys should have names like "Donna." The Donna we have met in "The Dangerous One" has her faults, certainly, as does the Spanish Lady: yet she is a strangely sublimated being at the same time. She sings "My Blue Heaven" (49) and dances a "Highland" (49) fling; her

infirmity has taken her to "Mountain Sanatorium"; and as she enters
the story we hear the other children singing

> On the mountain stands a lady,
> Who she is I do not know. . . . (49)

Nor is Donna the only lady here: her mother Stella was another if
more pathetic one, and the "cool, implacable" (50) teacher Miss
Gilmar, whose name makes her an adherent of Mary, is a cosmetic
miracle in flashing glasses and a highland tartan. Even more impressive is the grandmother of the story: all purity and rectitude, a woman
who beats Donna at her own game of elevation. And if names like
"Donna" and "Stella" bring us close to the Mary of Christian
tradition, so, for instance, does "Clara" in "The Stone in the Field"
— where Aunt Clara belongs to a company of sisters who have not
quite "fall[en] into flesh" (27). Other saintly names include
"Thérèse," possibly the name of Mrs. Brooke in "The Edge of
Town";[33] in the same story we find "Grace," the mysterious girl who
in some sense replaces the lost Mrs. Brooke. A more surprising
member of this group is the brooding Char in "Something I've Been
Meaning to Tell You." Char was presumably christened Charlotte,
another name to which we can return; and I have suggested that she
is a charwoman — as, of course, is Mary the handmaiden. But we
have also noted that *cháris* is grace, and Char, whatever her more
ominous qualities, has the grace of a madonna.

Close to "Grace" again is "Dorothy," "the gift of God" — a notably
common name in Munro. Among others, the Lady Dorothy mentioned in "Changes and Ceremonies" is very much a genteel Mary, a
library-book heroine who ponders a mysterious message in a "rose
garden" (118). Dorothy in "Marrakesh," while seeming to lack any
outward or inward grace, receives a message of her own; so in a way
does the bedraggled Dotty in "Material," who is transformed by the
grace of Hugo's art. No such change is needed for "Lilla," to give the
flourishing grandmother in "The Dangerous One" her name; and the
world of Cousin "Iris" in "Connection" seems inexpressibly graceful
to the young Janet. Here as often "The Edge of Town" will help us
by being explicit: not only does it have a Grace and a Thérèse, but
Harry Brooke in a dream sees "*Madonna* lilies, half as big as your
face" (378), and links these with the Virgin. If, then, we meet a girl
in "Walking on Water" called Calla, and learn that she has a "large,
sweet white face" (89), we will not only think her *kalé*, "beautiful,"

and associate her with a flower (as Mr. Lougheed himself does), but feel that somehow she is Mary the queen, and her face the moon. We may even feel this in the end about Callie, the tough little heroine of "The Moon in the Orange Street Skating Rink."

*

Whatever else we will need to do with such names, it does seem that we have glimpsed a world of height, purity, beauty, perhaps sheer whiteness — the world, again, of "Patricia" (noble-born, as in "patrician") and "Gwen" (another name meaning white). And we can add male counterparts — "Patrick," "Clare," "Gabriel." What we will not find, though, is a Mary who is either bright or dark with no hint of the contrary. No doubt Donna impresses the narrator by her perfection — she is "so fine, so extraordinarily complete" (49). But this very perfection has something disquieting about it, like her "frozen-white" (50) face; and beneath it Donna is consumed by physical and spiritual corruption. In the case of some other Marys, white itself takes on a sickly tone: for as with Gladys in "The Turkey Season," a Mary in Munro is often an "Alva-Marie Skin" in the sense of combining intestinal disorders with pallor or skin trouble. Other Marys again are not immaculate but "dotty," and sometimes visibly so. In "The Edge of Town" Grace's white face is marked by "pimples along the jaw" (375); Calla's in "Walking on Water" is "white as chalk, dotted by many little inflamed pimples" (89)[34] — spots on the moon.

Often, indeed, we find Munro suggesting black and white in equal proportion and stark opposition: as far as names are concerned, this is a time to remember "Blanche Black," in whose company a name like "Myra Sayla" begins to sound as complex as "Del Jordan." If we are feeling the highness of "Myra" (encouraged by the suggestion of "mira," perhaps), then "Sayla" by contrast will suggest a sail as something merely aquatic. But if we hear "Myra" as "mire," then the "sail" in "Sayla" will sound less aquatic than airy — we will imagine something blown above the water by the wind. "Sayla," moreover, is close to the German "Seele" or "soul," as we are likely to notice in a story about a butterfly and a death. If, on the other hand, we feel "Myra" and "Sayla" as equivalent, we will be more aware of the Myra who is in some ways homogeneous, a constant melancholy presence in the changing, animated life around her. To return to colour imagery, this is the Myra who wears a single blue against the varying hues of the other children (blue, as we would expect with Mary, can take the place of black). And yet nothing can take away Myra's paradox — the paradox of the sacred victim cast out and glorified — and we find this paradox in terms of colour as much as other things: for the dark-haired and dark-eyed Myra also suffers from leukaemia, the mysterious disease of "white blood."[35]

Other Marys are dark and white even in outward appearance: Mrs. Brooke was in earlier life "a slight girl with dark-ringed eyes, and a skin slightly yellowed, but pure and smooth like old pearls; she wore a dark dress and one of the cobweb-lace collars she made herself" (370). Later she lives, first in the gloom and mustiness of the rooms behind the store, then in the uncurtained bedroom upstairs, where she gazes across the countryside with "light-dazzled eyes" (373). Grace, her successor, has "a long white face" (375), whatever the colour of her hair may be; she is also, we find, drawn to black and white in the form of chocolate marshmallow cookies. In Harry's dream Grace and her sweets reappear in a transfigured version — a city of white towers and lilies with a "dark fancy restaurant" serving "Peach Melba" (378); and while it may be fanciful to claim "Melba" as one of Munro's "m" words, the unearthly intensity reached by light and dark here is easy enough to feel. There is much of the same numen in "Something I've Been Meaning to Tell You," where the dark abyss opening beneath the story contrasts with an upper world of corresponding brilliance. At one point Et recalls summer in the great days of the hotel: "so much white it hurt your eyes, the ladies' dresses and parasols and the men's summer suits and Panama hats, not to speak of the sun dazzling on the water . . ." (6). Blaikie positively "shines in the dark" (14); Char, who wears a black-trimmed blue dress in an early photograph, appears as an agelessly white-haired beauty at the end. Even as a humble charwoman, for that matter, she does her white washings, and we can add that she once tried to kill herself by swallowing blueing — a dark substance used to make clothes white.[36]

*

One place to find the lady of contraries — the lady of the dark abyss and heavenly light — is where we have already found Donna in "The Dangerous One": on a height, perhaps overlooking an ocean. It is a city of towers that Harry Brooke dreams of in "The Edge of Town." Helena in "Executioners" — very much a little Mary in her navy blue tunic, white stockings, and hair-bow — craves safety and solitude, and so imagines herself living in a "small high-up room" (139). Mrs. Kidd, once young Marian Botherton in a similar costume,[37] would like to live alone in "a house on the edge of some dark woods or bog, bright fields in front of it running down to the sea" (175). In the same way again Willa Cather, as remembered in "Dulse," lives high above the ocean, Stella in "Lichen" near a lighthouse. "The Dangerous One" contains a reference to Portuguese exploration that may at first seem intrusive, but one of the Portuguese mentioned is Henry the Navigator, who managed to survey the ocean while living in a tower, and Donna is implicitly connected with him.[38]

Vasco da Gama, the other figure named in the same passage, did more than look from a tower: we can put him with the many others in Munro who descend into geographically nether worlds. In "Age of Faith" the melancholy Christ of a painting seems to Del Jordan "Mediterranean" (98), connected by his incarnation with a body of water and, more literally, with the middle of the earth. A number of Munro's other characters travel to the same region, both outside themselves and inside — for once again we are dealing with the soggy human "tray." In "Labor Day Dinner" a company at dinner chat about a Mediterranean trip: someone's wife, it seems, got through the whole enterprise with what is delicately called a "front-end loader" (154). On similar trips reported in "Marrakesh," one woman was doubled up in Spain by a "rending purgative" (168) while another had "stoopers" on the boat to Greece, learning as a result that, in the view of Cretan doctors, all women want abortions. Visceral preoccupations seem in fact seem to be a Cretan specialty. If you looked in Mrs. Jordan's encyclopaedia you would learn about "the plumbing in Knossos" (65): you would come close, that is, to the most Mediterranean and visceral of all places, the labyrinth.

Nor does Munro, any more than the Portuguese, limit herself to the Mediterranean. In "Marrakesh" the heroine's adventures take her on to Africa, where she is sexually challenged at knife-point; and Africa belongs with a whole geographical underworld luring or confronting Munro's northerners. It is worth recalling that Nellie Melba, the inspiration for Harry Brooke's Peach Melba, was from down-under Australia, which is also the scene of the affair in "Bardon Bus." Other travellers — Judith and Don in "The Moons of Jupiter," the Weebles in "Fits" — go on trips to Latin America; or they wear Mexican clothes, or make up stories about Aztecs, or think themselves reborn conquistadors. For the present we can simply link this

Iberian world with Mary, while noting that an exotic southern world can also be that of the United States — where Donna mistakenly locates Portugal and where her father has been doing his own kind of navigating. Here, too, we begin to see the potential richness of Mary's womb: in Munro the United States, and especially the southern part of it, tends to be a land of wealth and tropical pleasure, the place where people make money and marry well-to-do brides. And when Uncle Bill in "Princess Ida" comes back with a glamorous American bride called Nile, America becomes a still more suggestive land of plenty — as well as an African one again. We have already seen how Char's grace hints at the same land by hinting at Cleopatra.

Good Canadians should not, of course, trust grace from such a quarter: when Jerry Storey goes on an American tour he gets "gypped" (232), just as people get threatened in southern countries on the other side of the Atlantic. But it seems impossible to have Mary the star without encountering Mary the ocean, and this is equally what we will find if we return to her personality. As for the star, the Char who is Cleopatra not only lies in state at the end, but is type-cast earlier as a "statue-girl" (23) in a local dramatic production — a girl in white who stands motionless until a young man falls in love with her. We have met other statue-girls: the Myra who quietly presides in the hospital, the Donna who sleeps serenely after her wild adventure. All such figures have the iconic quality we noted first in Myra — Donna's eyelashes, for instance, are "still as delicate carving" (50); all excite the same almost religious wonder. Or it may be the worshipper who turns into a statue, like Mr. Stanley in "Dulse" keeping a vigil outside the house of Willa Cather — for the woman he is honouring has just the starlike fixity and assurance to make him do so.

The ocean is a different matter: it is what rises when, for instance, the "great wave" (16) of Char's passion threatens to overwhelm her. Even if a Mary keeps her poise, as she generally manages to do, we often feel the turbulence beneath it — the "something black" (149) welling up in the listless Roberta of "Labor Day Dinner" or the rigid grandmother of "Winter Wind" or, once again, the grandmother of "The Dangerous One" with her barely concealed "strain of weakness, wildness, desperation" (50). If the wave cannot be kept down, the result may be horrifying: women like Char and the Spanish Lady and Helena are prey to sadistic imaginings, while Madeleine and Aunt Lena actually beat their children. Mary, as we have already found, can be very cruel: it is not for nothing that the Madonna on the

Cronins' wall has a spiked halo. At the same time, the savage figure we have been seeing shares something essential with her remote and unmoving counterpart: the quality, once again, of unworldliness. This may seem a curious term to use — curious in one way for Madeleine, and in another for the resolutely coping and conforming grandmothers we have just noted. Yet the Mary in all these women never really accepts the world: she must have what her infinite longing desires. When she resigns herself to things as they are, she does so in a secretly self-defeating way; when she cannot put up with them any longer, she tries to escape or destroy them.

And so words like "fine" and "finish" echo around her, suggesting at once unnatural perfection and the making of an end. Donna, we have seen, is strangely "fine" and "complete"; the "Bardon Bus" narrator thinks of sexual consummation as something to "finish off everything you've been before" (111). In "Something I've Been Meaning to Tell You" Munro even introduces a "Finnish woman" (18) — that is, "finish-woman": a dressmaker or, as she prefers, "designer" who fails in business because she is "all style and no fit." Char is and yet is not treating clothes differently when she rips up Arthur's school gown — he tripped and "that finished it" (16). Later, of course, Char finishes herself, after all her efforts to maintain an ideal "figure" (19); Roberta in "Labor Day Dinner," another who fights to save her figure, feels the urge to throw herself off a truck. Indeed the Mary who cannot compromise, who needs to be "fine" through life or through death, turns life and death into a strange paradox. The dead Char is found "fully and nicely dressed, her hair piled up" (23): she looks like sleep, not death. The living Char, for all her violence, had a deadly coldness about her — it was Char, lying with Blaikie, who resembled her own drowned brother, and Char who misremembered "Death" as "Life" in "O Death, where is thy sting?" (12). Perhaps, like Mrs. Brooke, she was never really alive at all.

To this we can add that the Mary who is life and death and neither is young and old — and again neither. Always destined in some way for isolation, she remains an unincarnated soul, or a child who will never grow up to live on the world's terms. Donna the schoolgirl plays her endless games; Maddy in "The Peace of Utrecht," though older, has seemingly chosen "to live without time and in perfect imaginary freedom as children do" (196). Even the elderly Misses Marsalles in "Dance of the Happy Shades," being "marked in so many ways, *impossible*" (214), are "gay as invulnerable and childish people are"

— and we can readily sense the child in the old people made "free" by senility itself.[39] On the other hand, we not only find little Myra wearing an adult's dresses, but being put with two old women in the hospital because she "was not really a child" (108). It is in the same way that we must understand Mary's paradoxes generally: or we can say those of sensibility, for of course that is what Mary is — the condition in which contraries meet in their full contrariety, repelling and attracting each other. Perhaps we can typify her mystery by using the terms of wisdom that have always been associated with her. Mary cannot be ordinarily wise or prudent — Char, unlike Et, is content to say "We'll never know" (4); at the same time, Char knows in a way that the Ets of the world cannot fathom, even if her awareness of Blaikie's return is not strictly telepathic. The invalid Mrs. Brooke will not so much as talk or listen to the radio, but she seems aware of a great mystery, one that escapes her theorizing husband. Such a woman does not make a conventionally good mother, and may, like Madeleine, be a monstrously bad one. Yet if only in Benny's hopes, Madeleine is also the transcendently loving "lady with one child" (12) that he so deeply needs. And it is through this lady who is less and more that annunciation comes: a message from beyond the world.

III: ELIZABETH

Mary is Heaven and Hell: in a sense she comprehends everything. Yet between these poles there is a whole world that Mary in herself is not, and for which we are going to need a different representative. At the end of "Home" the narrator recalls a pair of cows: one of these, which died of pneumonia in a bad winter, was black and white, "large and shiny"; the other, which somehow got through, was smaller and "muddy red" (153). A shiny cow sounds rather like the high Mary, a muddy one more like the low; but then the first was both black and white, like Mary in her doubleness, and so the second would seem to have been something else again. Nor is the colour scheme here limited to farm animals: for a human counterpart, we can think of a pair of saleswomen encountered by the "Bardon Bus" narrator in a punk fashion shop. One "is spiky and has a crest of white hair surrounded by black hair, like skunk"; the other "is fat and gypsyish with a face warmly colored as an apricot" (125).

We can turn from these to some more central characters. Our "type" Mary was Myra; Myra's best friend and, obscurely, rival is a girl called Helen, whose name we can set aside for the present. Helen, like Myra, is something of an outsider and in that sense a Mary, but as contrasted with Myra she is more ordinary, more gregarious, and far more practical. Myra likes art and arithmetic — subjects that have to do with "truth" in Munro's sense, with ideal pattern entertained for its own sake. Helen goes in for "Social Studies and Spelling and Health"; she will no doubt be a very useful person in later life, and already feels "a great pleasurable rush of self-conscious benevolence" (104) at the prospect of befriending Myra. Myra's birthstone is sapphire, Helen's ruby: it is Helen, then, who at least emblematically has a colour like that of the fat, warm saleswoman in "Bardon Bus," with a personal expansiveness to match. If we turn to the two title-characters in "Mrs. Cross and Mrs. Kidd" we will find a similar pairing. Mrs. Kidd, the haughty woman who would like to live alone by the sea, is unmistakably a Mary. Mrs. Cross started out as the more plebeian Dolly Grainger (with "grange" in her name, perhaps), a girl with "a broad red face and a dress with a droopy hem, and thick fair braids, and a bellowing voice" (161); in later life as well she proves to be far more coarse-grained and straightforward than Mrs. Kidd — much like Helen, in fact. And like Helen she is a warm and ministering sort of person, if also a rather officious one with a distinct vein of slyness.

We can draw a similar contrast again between Del Jordan, whose aspirations call her beyond Jubilee, and Del's friend Naomi (not Ruth, that is): the girl who has a practical nurse for a mother, who takes Commercial in high school before going to work in "the real and busy world" (178), and whose more general task in life is domesticity. Char and Et — the tragic woman-in-love and the busy dressmaker — are still another pair of this kind: Et does not, it is true, make a career of marriage, but her outlook on life is in its way as circumscribed and businesslike as Naomi's. With Eileen and June in "Memorial" we have sisters again, the one withdrawn, ironic, and sensual, the other an enterprising doer of good works.[40]

Often the name "Mary" itself or a relative will appear in one member of such a pair — as with MaryBeth and Jessie, for instance. Again, the beautiful Marietta in "The Progress of Love" is a high Mary, sublimated beyond ordinary needs and appetites; her plain sister Beryl is much more concerned with worldly success. Even where the members of a pair are not clearly distinguished in themselves, a name of the Mary complex attached to one of them will make us suspect a pair like those we have been seeing: May and Julie, Lily and Marjorie.[41] We could easily go on with male pairs — Mr. Morey and Mr. Clifford, to judge again by their names, or the fatally romantic Blaikie Noble and the red-faced, virtuous Arthur; or we could pair men and women — the inscrutable Mrs. Brooke and her busy-minded husband. Once Munro has got us started we will see the same pattern all around us: if we are also projecting what we see, she has invited us to do so.

*

Mary thus has a regular companion, and we are going to need a convenient name for her: none suggests itself as readily as "Mary" did, but since Mary is a biblical figure, perhaps the Bible will show us her contrary as well. One obvious candidate is Martha, a practical woman set against a more contemplative Mary (who is our Mary just as Mary Magdalen and all the other gospel Marys are). But since "Martha" is not a prominent name in Munro, we will have to keep looking. In the Book of Exodus we find that Aaron the priest, the brother of Moses, has a wife called Elisheba or Elizabeth. While we are told nothing more about this woman, her name reappears in a story recorded by Luke, where again she is a priest's wife.[42] She is also the mother of John the Baptist: and that is just the point of Luke's story. John is being contrasted here with Jesus; Elizabeth is thus contrasted with Mary, Jesus's mother and Elizabeth's cousin.

If we look about in Munro for the name "Elizabeth" or some variant, we will find it fairly often. After his stormy marriage to the theatrical Rose, Patrick in *Who Do You Think You Are?* picks a much steadier second wife called Elizabeth. The practical and long-suffering narrator of "Material," who might well have been named Martha, was Elizabeth when that story was a third-person narrative. The more romantic narrator of "Winter Wind" has a friend called Betty Gosley, a girl rather like Naomi and later the wife of a stolid farmer. Flo is called Ella in drafts of *Who Do You Think You Are?* — and from Ella we can perhaps slide to Helen in "Day of the Butterfly," whose favoured reading matter includes "Betsy and the Boys." The tragic Maria in "Five Points" has the efficient Lisa for a sister; Aunt Elspeth in "Heirs of the Living Body" may be virtually the double of Auntie Grace, but their names serve to polarize them.

Apart from the indistinguishable Aunt Elspeth,[43] these Elizabeths behave rather like the other non-Marys we have begun to see: we have not only a name here but a kind of person, for which "Elizabeth" can serve as a type-name just as "Mary" did. We can of course expect great variety here, as with Mary; and for that matter only a very simple character will belong completely to one of the two types and not the other — a problematical fact that we will have to confront later. But Elizabeth does have a certain identity, and here we can concentrate on this in any characters who contain a good deal of it. We defined Mary formally by saying that she represents the diverse elements of our experience as polarized extremes; we also saw that the union of these extremes in a single subject has something extraordinary about it, moving or disturbing as the case may be. Elizabeth too brings diversities together (any unity can be seen as doing so) but seemingly in a much less paradoxical way. Where Mary is self-confounding, Elizabeth is single-minded — straightforwardly the thing she is. She is also entire and self-reliant: some Elizabeths, indeed, are marvels of self-sufficiency and aplomb. Others are marvels of sheer limitation, like the mother in "An Ounce of Cure" whose quotations have the "innocent pomposity and odour of mothballs" (76); but in any case Elizabeth does not favour disruption. Mary, being sensibility, makes trouble; Elizabeth, who keeps trouble under control, is sense.

She is thus a spirit of tidiness and togetherness. Elizabeth prevails in the house of the diplomatic Valerie in "Labor Day Dinner," or at Jenkin's Bend, where the aunts will go to any lengths to keep family relations harmonious. By the same token she is suspicious of outsiders or, in terms that concerned us earlier, of events that cannot quite be explained. Et, as we have seen, "was a person who didn't like contradictions, didn't like things out of place, didn't like mysteries or extremes" (7): her very attention to such things has the purpose of keeping them at bay. If, on the other hand, Et is no great reader, her view is like that of Irlma in "Home": "Irlma doesn't care for the sight of people reading because it is not sociable, and at the end of it what is accomplished? She thinks people are better off playing cards and having projects" (137). Other Elizabeths may be less averse to reading — Mrs. Jordan in fact joins the Great Books Club; but a club to her is very much a social institution, and reading is another project, not a way to imagine or transcend.

It is Elizabeth, again, whom we are meeting in Kay Stringer of "An Ounce of Cure": a seemingly wild girl but, as it turns out, a born arranger who grows "excited, aggressive, efficient" in a crisis, urged by "a great female instinct to manage, comfort, and control" (82).

The same ordering drive produces the enthusiastic Arthur Comber, "the moving spirit behind the Amateur Dramatic Society and the Oratorio Society" (15); or it produces June in "Memorial" with her various enterprises, or Mrs. Jordan throwing her intellectual party, "feverish with excitement and her voice full of organizing fervour" (73). Julie the back-packing librarian in "Hard-Luck Stories" actually likes meetings — "they make people feel everything isn't such a muddle" (186), she explains. And Julie's name, in one of its implications, indicates her success: July is the month when the year most fully recovers from the muddle of winter. As for June, she points us not only to a month but a goddess — another queen of heaven like Mary, but in this case a stickler for correct procedure.

Julie's occupation is a typical one for an Elizabeth. The mother in "The Ottawa Valley," with her taste for "sober bustle" (227), is an old schoolteacher; so are various others like her, women whose inclinations take them first to Normal School, perhaps, then on to the work of normalizing the world. And if Munro happens not to have social workers in her stories, June for one has studied psychology and sociology, while the Helen who eagerly befriends Myra is keen on social studies at school. Someone like Et may be less outgoing and benevolent, and hence farther from the official ministrations that a Mrs. Jordan delights in, but she has the same managing eye and the same appetite for work. When she brings these qualities to bear on Arthur, she becomes in effect a practical nurse — like Naomi's mother. Naomi herself is going to be a plain housewife, but by no means an inert one: Del imagines her "a bossy, harassed, satisfied young mother out looking for her children, to call them in to bed or braid their hair or otherwise interfere with them" (235).

It is thus Elizabeth, the priest's wife, who superintends the labours and rituals of the world, its endlessly ongoing activity. One thing she often is is a fosterer of life: Et keeps Arthur well fed, Prue (in the story of the same name) works in a plant shop, and Irlma can magically make all kinds of things grow — plants, animals, people. In "Labor Day Dinner," where Angela sees the country as a landscape to base dreams on, her enterprising sister Eva sees it rather as a place for breeding animals. The life fostered in this way must be continuous: Elizabeth is not a finish-woman but, so to speak, the incarnation of "et" — of line as unbroken movement.[44] By the same token, she does not want "figure" if that means consummation; instead, she seeks to bind life to its process. When the old woman in "Spelling" finds her way through words with "only the thinnest thread to follow" (183), the Elizabeth in her is keeping something together and something moving. If we multiply threads, we have the dressmaking of other women, notably Aunt Madge in "Winter Wind" and again Et — a seamstress who has the whole town sewn up and curtained. When, after the great fire in "Executioners," Robina turns Elizabeth, she becomes one of those in Munro who keep people from "going . . . into [the] ditch" — committing suicide or trying in some other way to finish themselves; and what Helena senses in Robina's manner is a kind of protective weaving:

> I had the feeling that if she could have moved all around me, been in front and behind and on both sides at once, that was what she would do. She would close me off. . . . (153)

Robina here is a circle as well as a line: she is much like another rescuer we have met, Kay Stringer, whose name makes her at once a string and St. Catherine, the saint of the wheel. When Patricia in "The Time of Death," resuming her singing career, adds "May the Circle Be Unbroken" (98) to her repertory, we may reflect that a cousin of hers, looking much like her, was once "Miss St. Catharines" (90); we may even feel it significant that, as Jessie explains to Mrs. Cryderman, "Peter the Great was connected to Catherine the Great" (174). Be this as it may, other Elizabeths use wheels to assert themselves:[45] the young Et copes with her brother's drowning by turning cartwheels, Flo restores concord at the end of "Royal Beatings" by revolving like the planet Venus. To add a further dimension, Elizabeth is a solid if unromantic building, often of red brick: she is the "square, useful, matter-of-fact" Jubilee Post Office[46] (as opposed to the more stately Town Hall across the street), or she is Jenkin's Bend, or Valerie's house, or — in a more up-to-date form — the shining houses in the story of the same name, with their solid construction and solid occupants. By the same token she is Naomi from Mason Street, or the June whose life seems to Eileen solidity itself — "built, planned, lived deliberately, *filled*" (214).

*

The neighbours in "The Shining Houses" are worthy people, as the disgruntled Mary in that story is forced to admit; Eileen has to admit the same thing about June. For if Elizabeth is no madonna, neither is she a monster: indeed she can be extremely nice. Valerie has an almost magical tact and kindliness; Prue, in spite of her sceptical views, cheers people up — "they say of her that it is a relief to meet somebody who doesn't take herself too seriously, who is so unintense, and civilized, and never makes any real demands or complaints" (129). In homelier versions Elizabeth is no less good-humoured, a comic muse like Aunt Dodie in "The Ottawa Valley" or "hefty and jovial" (216) like Caddie McQuaig the butcher's assistant in "Baptizing." Brian's peacemaking wife Phoebe in "Who Do You Think You Are?," while more insipid than these others, is by the same token nicer than the bullying Brian or the histrionic Rose. Aunt Madge in "Winter Wind" is nicer than the formidable grandmother, Mrs. Cross nicer than Mrs. Kidd. At times, no doubt, this niceness is on the rough-and-ready side, as with Caddie McQuaig; other Elizabeths are more winsome, even coquettish like the gentle Aunt Annie in "The Peace of Utrecht" — whom Munro contrasts with the stern Auntie Lou.

But something more than niceness may be needed to keep the world in order. The biblical Elizabeth is connected with Aaron the priest and Moses the lawgiver; and Munro's Elizabeths, appropriately, are often vigorous moral guardians. If a Mary like Aunt Lena "lays down the law" (233), she does so out of impulsive rage; Mrs. Jordan, on the other hand, is a highly principled woman who has deliberately chosen her array of causes. Her counterpart Flo is less of a theorist and a crusader, but she too has settled views, especially about sex; and many other Elizabeths are equally sexless — including June, who can absorb any amount of sexual experiment in her Growth Group and yet retain an innocence like that of the "brisk and hopeful and guileless" (81) Mrs. Jordan herself. Some Elizabeths, again, are all for health, like the Helen who is contrasted with Myra, or the "young and optimistic" (38) red-suited Health and Guidance teacher in "Half a Grapefruit." Mary may at times have an unearthly purity, but Elizabeth is squeaky-clean.

Thus shielded, she is proof against embarrassment. Mrs. Jordan, as she herself explains, has no time for shyness or self-consciousness: indeed she stuns her opponents by sheer bluntness, as do Flo and Irlma. Et's weapon, her sharp tongue, is used with more discrimination; the aunts in "Heirs" are more subtle again; and with these last we notice something that we also find in Flo, the gift of mimicry. In a way this is the opposite of Mrs. Jordan's straightforwardness: it holds a sly mirror up to pretence, including, in the case of the aunts, the pretence of Mrs. Jordan herself. Yet these various methods need not differ in their end, and Eva in "Labor Day Dinner" shows how they can work together: for Eva is an Elizabeth in all the disconcerting ways, "puritanical, outrageous — an acrobat, a parodist, an optimist, a disturber" (135). If to Eva and her like we add the more concerting kinds of Elizabeth, we will see what a wide spectrum we have covered: everything from Eva's rampaging to the poise and diplomacy of Valerie in the same story. In appearance, again, we have everything from the meaty Caddie McQuaig — or her fellow-Baptist Holy Betty, "big-busted, raw-faced" (216) — to the cameo-like Prue. But to the extent that all these are Elizabeths, they are secretly allies: they work together to neutralize the Mary in things, to keep the world safe and sanitary and in running order. Without them it would be a terrible place.

*

"Elizabeth" is of course not the only name that such people carry: in fact, certain others are rather more common, such as "Margaret" in its various forms. In "Changes and Ceremonies" the undertaker's daughter Gwen Mundy is paired with Marjory Coutts, whose father is a lawyer and MPP, very much concerned with the world's running order. In "Princess Ida" the corresponding pair are Margaret Bond and Pat Mundy — inconsistently, if Munro intends the same girls,[47] but giving us a form of Margaret once again. Etymologically, "Margaret" means a pearl (hence also a daisy): it is one of a number of names in Munro derived from precious stones. These have no simple attachment to either Mary or Elizabeth, and indeed a shining pearl suits the high Mary very well; but when we contrast a pearl with a ruby or garnet — jewels that Munro sometimes associates with low or sensual Marys[48] — then it may well suggest Elizabeth's qualities of brightness and self-sufficiency. It is rather like a diamond, perhaps: "Kimberly" in "Labor Day Dinner" is a very controlled and controlling girl who manages to hold her boyfriend against the more alluring Angela. Still another light-coloured gem is a beryl, found in the reliable Beryl Allen of "Postcard" as well as Aunt Beryl in "The Progress of Love" — a much flightier and shinier woman, but set over against a strict rural Mary in the person of her sister Marietta.

Margarets in Munro, if not always as hard to cut as Kimberly, generally share her durability. Jerry Storey's mother, coping with the world in the most no-nonsense way, is a Greta; Jack's quasi-mother in "Hold Me Fast, Don't Let Me Pass" is the monumental Margaret Dobie. A worthier counterpart appears when the demoralized narrator of "Home" introduces her step-sister Marge, the woman whose hard farm life has not defeated her:

> She comes into town combed and lipsticked, fresh and laughing, from her desperate work. She surfaces joking ... and full of what I can't describe, except so inadequately as high spirits, or good humour, or human kindness. (152)

Marg Honecker, the friend of the Spanish Lady, is another "great girl" (178), and for her own ends a resourceful one: while gawky, thrifty, cautious, and shy (these being the Spanish Lady's own words for her), she manages the pluck and skill to steal her friend's husband.[49] Aunt Madge in "Winter Wind," a more simple-seeming woman, is set against the tragically passionate grandmother of the story; and Aunt Madge is unmistakably an Elizabeth, "understanding what suit[s] her" (194), perfectly fitted to a world in which she plays the same seamstress role as Et Desmond.

A striking thing about these variously named Elizabeths, when one begins to see them as a group, is that they are often daughters or younger sisters or subordinate friends. Naomi's function in *Lives of Girls and Women* is to be Del's best friend; Betty Gosley's in "Winter Wind" is much the same. Et Desmond is a younger sister, as are various others with appropriate names: Eileen's sister June, for instance, or Janet's briefly mentioned sister Peggy in "The Moons of Jupiter." Similarly we can set brash little Eva in "Labor Day Dinner" beside her older sister, the aloof, dreamy Angela;[50] or the "blunt and stocky, blonde and candid" Judith in "The Moons of Jupiter" beside the "sly and solitary, cold, seductive" (223) Nichola. In other cases it is daughters that we find: Helen's Margaret in "The Peace of Utrecht," Eileen's Margot in "Memorial," Mrs. Gannet's Margaret in "Sunday Afternoon."

What is equally striking, these secondary Elizabeths are often supplanters. We have seen the unprepossessing Marg Honecker driving the Spanish Lady from her husband; in the same way, Et progressively takes over Char's husband Arthur, and has a role — whatever it may be exactly — in the removal of Char. Aunt Madge in "Winter Wind" may seem altogether different from Et, even if both take good care of their men; and yet her elder sister is a trapped and raging woman much like Char, and the narrator has seen an old family photograph in which Madge appears to be in cool control. In "Postcard," we can add, a stout woman named Margaret supplants the heroine in the intentions of her lover; and in "Hard Luck Stories" Julie the librarian robs the more sensitive narrator in a similar way. In other cases the supplanter is merely a second wife, acquired after a death or divorce. The unobjectionable Elizabeth replaces Rose as Patrick's wife in *Who Do You Think You Are?*; long before this the more objectionable Flo had replaced Rose's delicate mother; and Irlma in "Home," as we have seen, is Flo again — blunt but efficient, a far cry from the sickly, bookish mother who remains only as a troubling ghost. But in one way or another the Elizabeths and Flos and Irlmas are all successors: an odd fact if we reflect that the biblical Elizabeth, being under the Law, is the forerunner rather than successor of the Mary through whom the new dispensation comes into the world. The implications of this situation will take more than the present chapter to work out; more immediately, the idea of succession and especially usurpation can lead us to a larger context in which Mary and Elizabeth are no longer private individuals.

IV: COUNTRIES

In a writer like Munro the Marys and Elizabeths we have been surveying are sure to point beyond themselves. We have in fact seen something of their biblical origins already; but they come from other regions as well, and it will be important to have some idea of these. In the first place we can pay a visit to Scotland, as the heroine does in "Hold Me Fast, Don't Let Me Pass," and as we can do simply by considering the remarkable frequency of Munro's Scottish names. No doubt this was to be expected — in particular, Munro's south-western Ontario is a region of heavy Scots-Irish settlement. What is more noteworthy is the sense she often gives us of a chivalric Scotland. "Blaikie Noble," for instance — the "Scottish ballad singer" (9) in his stage version — sounds both Scottish and lordly. And Blaikie is more than lordly: he is also a born loser, an heir who ends up driving a tour bus. If we go on to connect him with things like Black Watch tartans, Muir Park, and Munro's assorted Murrays, it may occur to us that Scotland is connected with her imagery of misfortune and death — in other words, with the dark Mary.[51] If so, then a house on Murray Street, as in the early "The Idyllic Summer," is a house on the street of death. "Material," the story that descends into Dotty's flooded basement, is set in a house on Argyle Street, which looks like a variant of Murray Street. We can even, perhaps, hear a dark along with the bright resonance in "Bonnie Mary of Argyle" (79), the last of the songs Addie Morrison is taught in "Princess Ida."

We must of course distinguish the aristocratic and tragic Scotland from that of practicality and Calvinism. Both these Scotlands, it would seem, are present when Naomi goes husband-hunting and, after experimenting with the royal-sounding Stuart Claymore, settles for a mere lineman called Scott Geoghegan. For that matter, the royal Scotland does not have to be a dark one: in "Day of the Butterfly" Myra's sad blue is set off by other girls' bright plaids — the most impressive being "Royal Stuart" (102). And yet Munro's Scotland seems well represented by "Heather Sue Murray," the proud little miss in "A Trip to the Coast." Heather Sue makes herself up and does highland dances in competitions; she does not, of course, fancy anything as low as death, and is horrified at the thought of playing in the cemetery. But her surname belies her: and we may be reminded of Donna in "The Dangerous One," who also wears a tartan and does the highland fling — and in all her parading of life is secretly intimate with death.

For all her airs, Heather Sue remains a very minor Scot. A major one, and a haunting presence in Munro's stories, is Mary Queen of Scots herself, the most splendid and tragic of all royal Marys, the epitome of everything Catholic and grandiose and ruthless and pathetic. In an article Munro admits to weeping at the thought of Mary's execution.[52] Del Jordan might well do the same thing — at all events she wallows in history as provided by her mother's Encyclopaedia, where Mary and other great losers go to their deaths in the most romantic ways imaginable. Later we find Del reading a book about Mary during Household Science, not to say dreaming the decapitation of her own family.[53] In "Dance of the Happy Shades" it is again Mary who gazes from the wall behind the doomed Miss Marsalles; and if we recall the "Queen Marys" in Mr. Malley's living-room, we may now sense a more ominous suggestion in them than we did before. It is not just that ocean liners have been known to sink: Mr. Malley is another figure of prosperity ending in failure, with the same dark queen behind it all.[54]

But if history provides us with such a notable Mary, it also provides us with a red-headed Elizabeth to counter her — a queen we can conveniently imagine as everything Mary is not. The England imbued with this Elizabeth's spirit can similarly be contrasted with Mary's kind of Scotland — we can see it as industrious, shrewd, united, successful, Protestant. We sense such an England in someone like Marg Honecker, the bony English teacher in a rose wool dress (she does not want to look like a courtesan, she says) who efficiently steals the husband of her glamorous rival. We sense it in ruddy Arthur Comber and busy, calculating Et, as opposed to Char in blue and white wantoning with Blaikie Noble. And in the church to which the rivals come at the end of "Hard-Luck Stories" Munro gives us two explicit, as well as readily applicable, national emblems: a cross of St. George for the zealous, usurping Julie and a cross of St. Andrew for the fallen narrator.

*

Scotland was not the only country to be taken on by Elizabethan England. There is the Catholic Ireland implicit in Nora Cronin of "Walker Brothers Cowboy" (with Mary the Virgin on the wall rather than Mary Queen of Scots); and any non-Protestant region can, for our purposes, be substituted here. To specify an important one, we can note that Donna dances not only in a highland tartan but "Spanish skirt and castanets" (49): she is thus linked to Munro's "Mediterranean" and especially Iberian world, which has the same aura of glory and cruelty and final downfall as Mary's Scotland. The "Alva" in "Alva-Marie Skin," for instance, can be taken not only as hinting at the human inside but as naming the great general of Philip II, who ferociously put down the Protestant resistance in the Netherlands.

A more veiled set of allusions occurs in "Something I've Been Meaning to Tell You," where we encounter a pair of ventriloquist's dummies named Alphonse and Alicia, groomed to look like Vernon and Irene Castle. "Irene" will concern us in a later chapter, but "Alicia" is the Spanish (if also Italian) form of the high "Alice"; "Castle" here suggests "Castille" as well as castles; and "Alphonse" is a Spanish royal name. Indeed it was largely the Alfonsos who, in days of Spanish expansion, broke the Moorish power in the peninsula. The Spanish out-thrust to the New World and the Pacific Ocean — the name of which, incidentally, means the same thing as "Irene" — brought a further putting down of "Moors": the dark-skinned Indians of Latin America, with their own splendour and cruelty.[55] We can sense both victories in "The Spanish Lady," with its repeated indications of fields of honour, *autos da fe*, and, more explicitly, conquistadors. And yet the same story shows us a Spain that, like Scotland, must fail: the Spanish Lady loses out to Marg Honecker the English teacher, just as Char and Blaikie lose out to crafty Et.

One other country of a Mary nature is perhaps the most important of all. Mary Stuart was not only the queen of Scotland but the wife of Francis II, and the alliance of Catholic Scotland with France was for long a very close one. Equally close was the rivalry between France and England, with results specially significant for Canada. In Munro we find this rivalry coming to the surface, most notably, in "The Edge of Town." Harry Brooke is a great man for ideas and projects, a British Israelite, a connoisseur of scandals in the Catholic Church; the wife he cannot accord with is the silent, mysterious woman we have already met — a woman, we can now add, who is French-Canadian and sends cryptic notes in her own language. While few other characters in Munro are actually French, a couple of those who are — Eugene in "Dulse" and Allen Durrand in "The Ottawa Valley" — have the same air of fatality about them as Mrs. Brooke. Eugene, for all his success with women, "hollers" (49) in his sleep and is afraid of drowning. Allen, before making himself into a successful English tory, is one of Munro's luckless hired men — like his counterpart in "Heirs of the Living Body" he is mercilessly tricked by his employer's daughters. The relation of modern France to England, at least in a Canadian context, has been similarly fated: France is another fallen glory, a country whose empire was first contained by the Peace of Utrecht and then humbled by the rise of England in the following century.

When we assemble Munro's French names, as well as characters with French associations, what is most striking is the way they show us the very high and the very low. All we know of a woman called French in "Dance of the Happy Shades" is that she is a Rosedale patrician; Mr. McLaren in "Wild Swans" teaches French and is therefore — if we are to trust Rose — "a perfect autocrat of indulgences" (61). But since these indulgences would be those of the senses, Mr. McLaren could be said to combine pride of spirit with descent into flesh; and we could certainly say the same thing of the tyrannical and sensual Métis on the plane in "Eskimo." As for the Frenches of Jericho Valley in "Baptizing," they are not patricians at all, only a despised tribe from the wilds. Garnet French himself may be a jewel, to judge from his given name, but as one of the Frenches he is just the opposite, like the wood of the lumberyard where he works. In "Executioners" the son of a rather similar family is, once again, connected with a valley, since he bears the curious name of "Duval." Frank Wales[56] in "Changes and Ceremonies" is an unprepossessing youngster who later becomes a delivery man, Frank

McArter in "Walking on Water" a mad farm-boy. At the same time, none of these low Frenches is simply abject. "Pride and submissiveness" (214) alike are what Del Jordan reads in Garnet's face; earlier she had sensed these qualities in the even more reserved Frank Wales. Duval, an illiterate delinquent on bad terms with the police,[57] is proud enough to suffer sunstroke and a fall from a high roof for refusing to wear a hat. Even Frankie Hall in *Lives of Girls and Women*, a mere idiot, manages to wave "with a royal negligence" (246) on his free rides at the fair. We can begin to see, then, why the new homes in "The Shining Houses" might feature both "Murry's Glass" and "French's Hardwood Floors" (23). Either "Murry" or "French" can be either high or low here; together they give us glassy lighting and wooden footing — and Mary in her French connection.

*

To feel the full resonance of Munro's France, however, we will need a couple more royal names. One of these, "Charles," is nothing less than imperial, since the "original" Charles — the one we imagine as establishing the name — was the emperor Charlemagne, lord of the Frankish west. Charlemagne himself and his male counterparts will have to wait for a later part of this book: here we can deal with some female forms of the name, which in fact are more prominent in Munro. In the first place there are the Carolines,[58] notably the aristocrat of "Hard-Luck Stories" and the high-born if erratic heroine of Del's novel in "The Photographer." Then there are assorted Carols, one of whom is paired with a humbler Eve in "The Found Boat"; and there is someone else whom we have seen from various perspectives already: Char Desmond. Among other things, I have noted that Char's baptismal name must be "Charlotte," which sounds distinctly royal and is given to a curiously royal woman in "Mrs. Cross and Mrs. Kidd" — a Charlotte as doll-like and, in her way, queenly as any Char or Caroline. On the other hand these female Charleses have the lowliness we now expect. Charlotte is a slave to Mrs. Kidd before becoming a mistress to Jack. The Carolines not only suffer from severe mental distress — "Caroline the neurotic" (52) is one of Duncan's girlfriends in "Dulse" — but express this by playing waif to the men they also consume. We have even seen Char the mortified charwoman, "purging her sins" (20) as Et likes to put it.

And there is a more special kind of recurrence that we should note here. Even allowing for the affinity of Charles with Mary, it is remarkable how often names of the two kinds are paired in Munro.

Caroline in Del's novel, for instance, is a more gothic version of the real-life suicide Marion Sherriff, while the glamorous victims in the Encyclopaedia include "Charlotte Corday on her way to the guillotine, Mary Queen of Scots on her way to the scaffold . . ." (66). In other cases we have only the bare names. "Thank you, Mary Louise, thank you, Carol" (109), says Myra as she opens her schoolmates' gifts; Naomi acquires two girlfriends at the creamery called Molly and Carla. Charles and Mary, it seems, rove at will through Munro's world: and one should add that Charles's associations, like Mary's, are not limited to the specifically French. Carolina and Charleston were named for an English Charles, though a Stuart with French sympathies. When Del thinks of Charlotte Corday and Mary Stuart, she also thinks of Laud blessing Strafford as the latter goes to his death. It is an impressive scene that she imagines here — the black robes and the white faces, "composed, heroic" (66) — and it brings us fairly close to another and even more romantic Charles Stuart: the proud, foolish, and doomed Charles I, whose consort, as it happens, was the French Henrietta Maria.

Myra, we have just seen, thanks a "Mary Louise" as well as a Carol; Frankie Hall, we find, has a brother named Louie. Louis is the other French royal name we must note here — in modern history a grander one than "Charles." In "A Trip to the Coast," for instance, the son who has made good on the west coast is a Lewis — in this case a triumphant one. For his more tragic counterpart, we can think of the two old aunts in "The Peace of Utrecht": not only the ingratiating Aunt Annie but the grim-faced Auntie Lou. Or we can think of a more explicitly tragic figure, Lois in "Thanks for the Ride." Lois is only a factory girl and an easy pick-up for the boys from the city; yet she too is royal in her own way, with a decapitated father to match. There is something cold and supercilious in her very acquiescence — she speaks with "great gravity," in a "clear, stilted voice" (49); and she is one of Munro's tragic queens in her passionate surrender to love. Helen in "Postcard" seems just the opposite — someone who does not give herself even in the sex-act — yet she is "Helen Louise," a woman who aspires to high rank, and in the end a figure of rejected longing as pathetic as the stranded Lois.[59]

*

To put Charles or Louis in a still larger context, we can turn to one final name here with very different associations and a different sort of pairing. Duval, the boy who falls off the roof in "Executioners," has a brother and partner called Jimmy. In general these two are no more clearly differentiated than Aunt Elspeth and Auntie Grace, but perhaps Jimmy's name, as contrasted with Duval's, can tell us something about him. As royal it would suggest England rather than France; if we pursue it, it will take us beyond either country. We have seen how Garnet French, a counterpart of Duval, comes from "a farm out past Jericho Valley" (215). To make a further biblical connection, we can first note that a garnet is a red stone — like some others in Munro, such as the ruby for which Blaikie Noble is imagined searching at the bottom of the ocean. We have already seen how red brick and ruddy complexions go with Elizabeth and thus England; here we need to see how the same colour — perhaps in a deeper tone — can carry other suggestions as well.

Later we will meet a red figure pointing to Herod, the foreigner king hated by the Israelites. Specifically Herod was an Idumaean, or Edomite: the Edomites had in fact been enemies of Israel from the days of their eponymous ancestor Edom, better known to us as Esau. Here we find the same colour red, for Esau is presented in the Book of Genesis very much as a red man[60] — indeed "Edom" has been taken to mean "red earth," like "Adam." It is Esau, I suggest, who looms behind Munro's Garnet French, the boy from the wilderness beyond Jericho. And remembering Garnet's sexual rage at the crisis, we may also think of the dark Arab who accosts Jeanette in Marrakesh, famous as a city of red earth. But while we remember the biblical Esau as just such a rough and violent figure, like the Garnet who once mutilated a man, Esau is equally like Garnet in having deep feelings — a sense of loyalty and a sense of injustice. What he suggests to the imagination is a primordial self put down by a younger and more calculating one.

In Genesis this younger self is Jacob, the mother's favourite and the usurper:[61] since "James" is the same name, Jacob is the original Jimmy and, in Munro's world, the original "Englishman." As the Lord explains to Rebecca, in what looks like a preview of Canadian history,

> Two nations are in thy womb, and two manner of people shall be separated from thy bowels; and the one people shall be stronger than the other people; and the elder shall serve the younger. (Gen 25:23)

Jacob is as shrewd and successful as any of Munro's Elizabeths — often younger siblings, we should remember; and his success is in one way desirable, since it means that birthright is not everything. At the same time it shows that something older, something like the "French" world in Munro, can be cheated and deprived. In one context this former thing is only law or necessity — including the necessity of sex — requiring to be succeeded by a gospel of spirit; in another it is feeling, having claims of its own against any gospel that is less spirit than cleverness.

However we interpret the fact, Jacob is the winner and Esau the loser. Or at least that is what they are in principle: in practice, and for reasons we will partly have to come back to, Munro's Jimmys do not usually seem winners at all. We have already met Jimmy Sayla in "Day of the Butterfly": a troublemaker but also the frightened boy who wets his pants and clings to his older sister in the schoolyard. Jimmy Saunders in "Something I've Been Meaning to Tell You" is a maimed veteran; and here we have a Jimmy who cannot attach himself to the female world, since its curtains have been closed against him. Uncle James in "The Ottawa Valley," again, is not only poverty-stricken but married to the most unapproachable of wives — which may be why he sings wistfully about the adventure on a mountain that drove him to drink.

The plight of these Jimmies expresses something that, if present, is less apparent in the relation of Mary and Elizabeth themselves. Esau the heir of the father and Jacob the mother's boy belong to a world that has already fallen into division: within such a world each must try to supplant the other. At one stage, as we have seen, Allen Durrand in "The Ottawa Valley" was a poor French hired hand serving Uncle James's family — a subordinated Esau, we can now say; he was also very effectively tricked by two of the family daughters. Through the years, however, Allen has turned into a prosperous dairy-farmer and prospective MP, while Uncle James has gone on sliding into poverty; we even find Allen at the climax snubbing the woman who once tricked him. Esau, in other words, has now overtaken Jacob. And if we read "The Ottawa Valley" more deeply, what it shows us is not the final victory of either side, but a principle of retribution whereby the world's Esaus and Jacobs have devoured each other throughout history. What makes this stranger is that they have also acted in collusion. Jimmy and Duval, brothers in a family of pariahs, may "play-fight" (147) but also stand together — like Myra and Jimmy Sayla, or Harry Brooke and his French wife. This brings us to a problem in interpretation that so far I have kept on one side.

V: RELATIONS

We began our exploration of character types and their names by noticing the figure I called the dark Mary. I do not think it was mistaken to see such a type (though we could have started with a different one) — Munro's stories really do invite us to take a step of this kind; and having taken it, we naturally found ourselves going on first to distinguish a bright or high Mary, then an Elizabeth. But this procedure, however valid in itself, gets us into serious difficulty in the end: for as we ponder them our distinctions look less simple than we had supposed.

Let us take a single clear example. We have associated Mary with the colour blue — the colour of the sky and the ocean, deepening into black — and Elizabeth with red. In "Red Dress — 1946" the narrator's friend Lonnie is clearly an Elizabeth, a wonder of social acceptability. We would expect her, then, to have something red about her: yet Lonnie started life as a Blue Baby and goes to the dance of the story in blue, while the awkward and mutinous narrator, having tried to escape by making herself "blue with cold" (151), has to wear the red dress of the story's title. We could of course say that Lonnie is really a Mary, like the successful girls at the dance looking "bored, aloof, and beautiful" (153) — as much so, in fact, as Char Desmond. Yet we must also remember how Lonnie specializes in tact and conformity, whereas the narrator falls into an alliance with "Mary" Fortune, the great misfit of the story. And so there is a perspective in which Lonnie with her social skills is Elizabeth — a blue Elizabeth — and the narrator a Mary in red. There are other such Marys: red, as we have seen, is the colour of Esau as well as the various Garnets descended from him — a deeper red, perhaps, than that of a carrot-haired and pink-cheeked Elizabeth, but red nevertheless. Blue, in a more agreeable tone than that of Mary's darkness (or intense paleness), is the colour of the ordinary daytime sky, the colour that goes so inappropriately with Miss Farris's death in "Changes and Ceremonies." And if we can have a blue Elizabeth, we can have a high one, or a fine one;[62] we even discover in "The Shining Houses" that one member of the local community — a great collection of Elizabeths — bears the name of Mary Lou.

To have a model for our newly complicated situation, we might imagine an axis of which Mary and Elizabeth were the opposite poles; to this we could add another axis for the colours blue and red. In a simple relation, these axes would be positively aligned to each other, and might as well be considered the same; but if one axis reversed itself or its polarity, we would find ourselves with red Marys and blue Elizabeths. And our troubles would not stop there: whenever we distinguish one pair of elements from another, the second will have a way of reversing in relation to the first. If we isolate a red-blue axis, we soon find that Myra, for instance, has two blue dresses (or two blues in a single dress) — a light one like the sky and a more ominous one in "dusty turquoise crepe" (106). In other words, we now have an axis of high and low, or of bright and dark; and these last pairs themselves could separate and reverse their alignment.

*

One form of our problem — the problem raised by any such scheme as that of Mary and Elizabeth — is the question of other names: for in principle these always belong to, or constitute individually, axes of their own. Nor are we dealing with a mere abstract principle here. While it might be possible to find one name that invariably corresponded to another — "Margaret" seems generally to go with "Elizabeth" in Munro — there are names that are a good deal less co-operative, as we can see from a single important example.[63] Munro has various Helens — are we to say that they are Marys or Elizabeths? The original Helen was of course Homer's (as we are pointedly reminded in "Executioners"), and we accordingly expect any subsequent one to be rather alluring and dangerous. We also, perhaps, expect her to be a traveller: not only did the first Helen fly away to Troy but, according to a well-known tradition, flew off more literally afterwards to be a queen in Egypt. Aunt Helen in "Heirs of the Living Body," we may notice, is no spinster stay-at-home: she has gone all around the world and married a wealthy man on the west coast, from which she sends a blanket of lilies for Uncle Craig's coffin. The same motif of the escaping sister occurs in "The Dangerous One," where Aunt Gladys — a "glad" woman, evidently, as Aunt Helen also seems to be — has married a well-to-do husband and now lives in the city. We even find that her husband's name is "Wesley" (with a hint of "west" again, perhaps) and that the two of them, like Aunt Helen again, have sent home an expensive gift.

After these two cases we may be able to guess why the narrator of "The Peace of Utrecht" would be named Helen, since this narrator ran away from a sick mother, leaving her sister to stay on at home; she is now married as well, possesses some means, and lives in an unspecified but evidently more sophisticated place on a coast. The Helen here does not radiate gladness, nor does the abased and frightened Helena of "Executioners"; but the latter does flaunt herself royally when visiting Robina's family, and, more obscurely, flirts with Howard Troy. It is even hinted that she arouses the men of the two families to the story's great quarrel and fire, while keeping herself at a safe distance. Lastly we can think of a Helen to whom we have already given a fair amount of attention: the narrator in "Day of the Butterfly." This one is like the others in that she is able not only to attract a friend but, in the end, to abandon her. At the same time she is gawky and tomboyish, quite different from the iconic Myra. Munro's Helens, in other words, may range all the way from a Helena in her blue and white outfit or an Aunt Helen with her lilies — both of whom have much of Mary about them — to the very Elizabeth-like Helen in "Day of the Butterfly." Simply as Helens, however, they are neither Mary nor Elizabeth: they belong to an axis by themselves when we start putting them together.[64] Some, like Aunt Helen, seem as delighted and delightful as we would expect. Others, like Helena, are notably oppressed: the complacent Helen of "Postcard" becomes one of these when her lover himself flies away to Florida and a different wife.

*

As this last comparison suggests, a single name in Munro can always turn out to contain an opposition by itself. Mary, we have found, is two kinds of people poles apart; so for that matter is Elizabeth, though Elizabeth's talent for moderation and compromise hides the fact. If we follow a hint here, we can reduce our cumbersome model of axes to a more compact one of simple units — units that, as our more expanded model has shown, will and will not be brought together. What we have here, it would seem, is a general principle of the human imagination; and in Munro this principle offers itself in a specially tantalizing form, as we can perhaps see by turning briefly to a different context — the relation of her stories to each other and to other versions of themselves. In studying drafts and earlier published forms of the stories, we find that characters we know from a single name may have had others in the course of their evolution — Rose has had a good dozen. Munro herself has remarked that, while the names may change, the characters do not; but true as this is (the contrary, by the way, would be equally true), it hardly explains her need to fuss with her names as much as she does, nor could any such explanation dispose of similar variations within her work in its final form. Munro's writing is in this respect very different from, say, Faulkner's. In some of her unpublished early material, where the influence of southern regionalism is very strong, we find something like his way of maintaining the same characters through a range of interconnected narratives;[65] but in her mature work this has disappeared — except in the novels there is no simple continuity from one story to another. And yet we often feel that two stories (an earlier and a later one, perhaps) are in some sense the same story. By the same token, Ben Jordan in "Walker Brothers Cowboy" is not quite the same person as Ben Jordan in "Images," either in circumstances or personality; nor is either quite the same person as the Mr. Jordan of *Lives of Girls and Women* — and yet all these Mr. Jordans ask to be treated in some sense as one.[66] Within a single story, for that matter, we have seen how play-fighters like Duval and Jimmy also work as partners and virtual twins.

We find the same thing within various of Munro's individual characters. Mary McQuade in "Images" is one of her practical nurses, and coarse-grained and bossy to match — decidedly an Elizabeth. Or at least that is one picture we have of her:

> Out in the daylight, and not dressed in white, she turned out to be freckled all over, everywhere you could see, as if she was sprinkled with oatmeal,[67] and she had a crown of frizzy, glinting, naturally brass-coloured hair. Her voice was loud and hoarse and complaint was her everyday language. (31)

But in the bedroom of the narrator's dying grandfather we find someone very different: a silent and motionless presence, white against the surrounding gloom and smelling of "dark spice" (32). This other woman is "implacable, waiting and breathing" (30) — a cousin, evidently, of the dark god in Eliot's *Dry Salvages*; thus she is very much one kind of Mary, as her name indicates. And there is something disturbing about this doubleness, as we can see from its effect on the child who tells the story. Mary McQuade does not simply combine the qualities of Mary and Elizabeth: she is the one and the other in a way that remains a mystery.

A much more central character, Flo in *Who Do You Think You Are?*, is not unlike Mary McQuade. Certainly she has a great deal of Elizabeth to her (a similar figure, as we have noted, is called Ella in one version of the material): for Flo is a dauntingly prudish and forthright woman, all opinion and challenge, and in this way contrasting sharply with her more reflective and ironic husband. She contrasts with the Marys about her as well — most obviously with Rose, the flamboyant actress, but also with Rose's mother, a gentle woman who (like Mrs. Brooke in "The Edge of Town") painted china and died early. Yet there is something about Flo that, as Rose later feels, might have made her very different — something more than monkey-faced defiance and relentless ability to cope. "If she had thought it worthwhile, and had the resources, she might have had a black-and-pale, fragile, nurtured sort of prettiness" (9): Rose, in fact, senses in her an "extraordinary softness and hardness," a mystery of two-in-one. And after what we have seen in this chapter, we will feel the same mystery again when we come on characters whose very names make them Mary and Elizabeth at once. MaryBeth in "Jesse and Meribeth" is the most striking example, but in one of Munro's first published stories, "The Widower," we meet an all-enveloping woman called Ella Marie; and for what it is worth I will suggest that "Irlma" in "Home" is an associative scramble of two such names. In "An Ounce of Cure," similarly, we encounter a Mary Bishop who nevertheless plays Elizabeth in the school production of *Pride and Prejudice*.

*

When Janet in "The Moons of Jupiter" goes on a planetarium voyage through the Universe, she finds herself daunted by its "innumerable repetitions, innumerable variations" (231). Janet's concern is not academic: she is going through a crisis at this point in which the father and daughter to whom she feels deeply attached are also being separated from her by the approach of death and the estrangement of adult life. In its own way this study's voyage of interpretation has arrived at the same crisis, perhaps that of all relation between things distinct from each other — or between plurality and singleness as such, or (as Janet experiences it) between the varied and the repeated. Whatever our terms, we have seen things strangely splitting apart and drawn together — in its most general form, the paradoxical unity we call the world. The world is a large subject: all I will attempt here is a few observations arising from the microcosm of Munro's stories.

In first taking note of Munro's Marys and Elizabeths, we dealt with their variety in the most obvious way. Some of her characters, we found, have the qualities she associates with Mary, others those that go with Elizabeth; if Mary and Elizabeth themselves have some common features, we can set both — in the form of "MaryBeth," perhaps — against someone different like Jessie (to enlist her for the purpose); and in any case Mary, Elizabeth, and Jessie are all human beings. Differing elements thus come together into groupings large enough to contain their variety, while conversely groups divide into smaller ones, perhaps as minute as the syllables of "Yew-gene."[68] The narrator of "The Ottawa Valley" sums up this way of experiencing when she associates her mother with a department store: what she has especially in mind is "plenitude" (227) but we naturally think as well of the neat arrangement of things in their departments (her later word for her mother is "categorical" [227]).[69] And yet this solution has not fully solved our problem, for Munro's world does not always seem so well-managed: looked at more closely, the department store turns out to have problems just as we have found plausible stories to do.

For all its plentitude, an everything in general is nothing in particular — only a featureless Being. This in fact is what the "Ottawa Valley" narrator comes to feel about her mother, who in the end seems less a department store than a glacier: "she weighs everything down, and yet she is indistinct, her edges melt and flow" (246). The particular, on the other hand, might be called nothing in general. It is like the collection of faded snapshots that the same narrator is left with — for in trying to "bring back all I could" (246) she cannot find what holds it all together. It seems, in other words, that we can only achieve the universal by sacrificing the particular, and the particular by sacrificing the universal. Nor does it make any real difference if we choose not to go all the way in one direction or the other. If we refuse, say, to generalize beyond the character of Elizabeth, we have still given up the concreteness of Munro's varied Elizabeths and settled for some highest common factor. And to do this is to go against what we know by our deepest experience. In a way opaque to ordinary logic, though implicit in it, we know that the one and the many, like truth and reality, do not ultimately shut each other out. We are our fully individual selves; we are also members of one another — participants in a humanity that is no bare abstraction.

*

To arrive at a fuller sense of the mystery we have invoked, we can start with particulars — the atoms, or galaxies, in a universe that is everything and nothing — and distinguish kinds of relation into which Munro shows them entering. Our first relation, the one we began by taking for granted, is that of classification, which sees only simple likeness when not seeing simple difference. If we imagine Mary and Elizabeth as standing for two in general, we can say that, while not requiring each other in order to be themselves, they are just the same ("it never mattered which" [91], as Del Jordan says of her Aunt Elspeth and Auntie Grace), and could coalesce into a simple identity that would be no different from what each is separately. Yet this would only be possible if they had no characteristics at all — nothing of Mary or Elizabeth about them. When we come to feel this, we start to imagine not a bunching together of the simply like but a joining of the different. And this new way of thinking will force itself on us if we dwell at all on our earlier one.

What regularly happens when one studies Munro is that apparently self-contained things or classes turn out to shade into others. From a certain number of similar characters we form the idea of, say, Elizabeth, and start innocently to collect further examples of her. Our original idea might have come, for instance, from Munro's prudish mothers, especially those who have been or wanted to be schoolteachers — the mothers in "Boys and Girls," "The Ottawa Valley," and "An Ounce of Cure." We now note, say, that Dorothy in "Marrakesh," a mother though hardly thought of as that by her fellow-townspeople, is another old schoolteacher, and one who still makes her former charges think of "maps, percentages, spelling bees" (158). She is like her counterparts in other ways as well: apparently sexless, rather naïve about the world beyond her limited experience, straight-laced enough to be shocked when she finds her granddaughter making love with the neighbour. But if Dorothy belongs with the schoolteacher-mothers, so does the grandmother in "The Dangerous One," not actually a schoolteacher but someone with the same ageless toughness and prudence and sexlessness. Then there is the grandmother in "Winter Wind," more austere perhaps but no less able to keep her life in order and her eye on the family. And there are other women like this last: severe old Auntie Lou in "The Peace of Utrecht," for instance, not to say ancient Mrs. Fullerton in "The Shining Houses," who has the same gritty power of endurance, or Mrs. Kidd, consigned to the County Home but still independent and very much in command.

But by now we may be feeling puzzled: where did these Marys come from? For the last four of these women at least are certainly Marys, being clearly contrasted with Elizabeths in the stories where they occur. And we can see the same shift within a single figure, where we have enough material to go by: Mary McQuade, as we have found, is a Mary who turns into an Elizabeth when she leaves the grandfather's bedroom. This changeableness in people's natures is one of the things that dismay Munro's more conscientious narrators: in both "The Moons of Jupiter" and "Miles City, Montana" we find mothers who label their daughters and then admit contritely that the labels will not always stay on. Mary and Elizabeth, in our earlier metaphor, refuse to be separate departments; and if we had chosen a series of, say, Marys who still seemed to be that at the end, we would find that they had shifted in some other respect (blue Marys, for instance, might have turned into red ones). In either case there would no doubt be something that did not change: Mary and Elizabeth are both human beings, just as the ends of a line are both points. Yet we are now seeing something beyond simple classification, in which things completely forfeit what makes them individual.[70]

*

If we think more intensely about Mary and Elizabeth as the ends of a line — what we can always see two differing units as making — we will find our sense of relation changing once again. We will be impressed by the fact that these ends are extremes, that is, opposites, which as such exclude rather than shade into each other. But by the same token we will see them as having something special in common, the fact of being ends. In less abstract terms, we will now feel our two parties to be both more stubbornly themselves and more deeply interinvolved than before: each, in being what she is, implies the other. If, then, we find Mary turning into Elizabeth, we will now feel her to be a woman with a strong identity of her own entering somehow into a contrary identity. One useful way to project our new sense of the situation is to imagine Mary as playing an alien role — one from which she might at any time revert to her own. The most suggestive, and challenging, form of this change of roles is interchange: the trading that we have already seen, for instance, in the careers of Allen Durrand and Uncle James. Sometimes this seems only virtual, as when the serious Mr. Lougheed in "Walking on Water" dismisses Eugene's enterprise as a joke, while the laughing Mr. Morey and Mr. Clifford insist on its seriousness. Elsewhere, though, we find overt barter: the Spanish Lady and Marg Honecker exchange books; Helen gives Myra a butterfly, later getting a dressing case in return. We notice too a sense of contract, especially between these latter two girls — something is being required as well as given.

In a more mysterious way, Aunt Madge in "Winter Wind" once made the ill-fitting dress that, in effect, her sister must wear even as a grandmother. Madge made something more elegant for herself at the same time: she seems indeed to have forced an exchange in which each sister took on a self more properly the other's, just as she once traded dresses (only for a joke, she says) with a girl who later became much like the grandmother. The enforcing here, moreover, seems to be of a reciprocal kind. The grandmother appears at first to be pure victim, and yet Madge, like many a younger sibling, may well have become what she became because of having the sister she did. Et Desmond is a seamstress who, as the narrator puts it, keeps her sister Char well dressed; she is even a ventriloquist, with Char for her dummy. On the other hand, an older sister with Char's looks might well make a younger sister into an Et, and once again there seems to have been an exchange — Char's role of faultless constant would in a way suit Et better, while Et has stolen Arthur from Char. In this light we may want to think again about "Red Dress": can we say of the narrator and Lonnie that each, simply by being the person she is, has made an inappropriate dress for the other to wear to the dance? More simply, is each what she is by virtue of the other?[71]

*

But by this time we may have started to see in yet a further way: for who are these girls? It is not just that they shade into one another, or play one another's parts: in a strange way they seem to *be* one another in being most themselves. In "Day of the Butterfly" Helen's birthstone is sapphire, Myra's is ruby; but Myra likes sapphire better — are we to say then that her colour is red or blue? The Spanish Lady, who on one occasion dresses in "peacock" (179), urges the modest Marg Honecker to buy herself a dress of "heavy dark green cotton with gold and silver embroidery" (177) (green here, as sometimes elsewhere, replaces Munro's more usual blue[72]). Marg, we have seen, settles for a plain "rose-coloured wool" to avoid looking like a courtesan: but when the two have traded gifts, they proceed to trade roles as well, with Marg stealing the Spanish Lady's husband and the Spanish Lady becoming the outsider. Which, then, is the courtesan?[73] Other characters may reveal different identities in different relations: Ewart in "Memorial," for instance, is an Elizabeth as June's ally against Eileen, but a Mary as Eileen's ally against June. Or it may be a matter of an observer's viewpoint: Miss Farris in "Changes and Ceremonies" looks like a romantic Mary beside the workaday school principal, but compared to people who fall in love the normal way she appears all spinster bustle and briskness — an Elizabeth.[74]

In such a world the inhabitants themselves may understandably get confused. Helena in "Executioners" likes Robina's family because "with them I was not who I was" (146): another temporary change of identity, no doubt, but then we wonder from Helena's larger story whether she knows who she is in any case — the abject schoolgirl or the queening, flirting guest of honour. "Wild Swans," in which an adolescent Rose tries out new roles in new places, tells of Flo's old friend Mavis doing the same thing: once, it seems, Mavis pretended to be the movie star Frances Farmer pretending to be someone else in order to be recognized as herself. In Rose's own story we have the minister on the train, if that is what he was:

Was he a minister, really, or was that only what he said? Flo had mentioned people who were not ministers, dressed up as if they were. Not real ministers dressed as if they were not. Or, stranger still, men who were not real ministers pretending to be real but dressed as if they were not. (64)

In "The Spanish Lady" the possibilities are no less confusing: in picking the rose dress, Marg Honecker is trying not to look like a courtesan, but equally not to look "like somebody trying to look like a courtesan, which is worse" (177).

It will help us here — to see our own confusion, at least — if we think of two of Munro's favourite images. One of these is the mirror that I invoked earlier, and that appears as Myra's reflective gift to Helen; the other is the photograph — a mirror again, in a way, with the added suggestiveness of dark and bright, negative and positive. For present purposes we can note a single strange effect that such devices tend to have in Munro. In "The Dangerous One" we are shown an old high-school picture of Donna's mother Stella, at the time a girl with black hair. Accounts of Stella in later life differ: according to Donna she was white-haired at twenty-five, whereas the grandmother insists that her hair stayed dark until her death. The suggestion here of reversal connected with a photograph occurs more eerily in Del Jordan's secret novel. Caroline, a straying woman like Stella, has appropriately black hair and — one supposes — the dark eyes that normally go with it; yet in the class picture taken by a mysterious Photographer her eyes are white. As for authorial intention, "I had not worked out all the implications of this myself, but felt they were varied and powerful" (247). Whatever they are, the same curious reversal of negative and positive — or subject and photographic image — appears again in "The Turkey Season": in the group picture taken by Herb Abbott, the narrator sees her old comrades both with selves she knew and selves she did not.

> I am stout and cheerful and comradely in the picture, transformed into someone I don't ever remember being or pretending to be. I look years older than fourteen. Irene is the only one who has taken off her kerchief, freeing her long red hair. She peers out from it with a meek, sluttish, inviting look, which would match her reputation but is not like any look of hers I remember .... Marjorie and Lily are smiling, true to form, but their smiles are sour and reckless. ... (72–73)

Beyond any such product of modern technology we have found Munro hinting at more ancient things: the white moon at night in "Walking on Water," the white glacier in the northern gloom in "The Ottawa Valley," not to say the leprous whiteness of the transformed Miriam, or the whited sepulchre echoed, for instance, in the "White Brick Church" of Uncle Craig's family history.[75] We have also seen the serious Mr. Lougheed asserting a joke and his laughing cronies asserting seriousness: in "The Edge of Town" we could even have found a laughing old undertaker paired with a serious young doctor. What we are seeing now is the coinherence, as I am going to call it, of all such opposites — something that, felt to be unsettling, is the condition of sensibility. When we look hard at Elizabeth's department store, what looks back at us is the world of the unaccommodating Mary.

*

Sensibility, like sense, may give us one image of a more genuine form of coinherence; but as belonging to a series of complications it cannot do more — mere complications cannot lead to anything different in kind from their starting-point. Sensibility, then, cannot reach a vision of true unity, only that of opposites joined in bizarre intimacy, to use Frances's phrase in "Accident" once again. This strangest of relations

— which we can call metaphoric in the most paradoxical sense — is what puzzled us in the previous chapter when we had to see Art Chamberlain as David; now again it has thrown our whole procedure into question. Yet, as I have argued, Munro's world really does offer us groups of characters like the "black" complex, and having taken notice of such a group, we were bound to arrive where we did. The relation we arrived at, moreover, is what all worldly relation in Munro proves to be when looked at hard enough, whether we see it as joining classes, individuals, aspects of a single self, parts of a single name, or any other two things that make a double identity — as two things will always do when put beside each other.

An important context here is that of meaning: this appears plainly when we consider something we have already glanced at, the way allusions behave in Munro. As the simplest kind of relation, allusion joins things that for the purpose are completely like each other; as the most complex, it has all the irony of Art Chamberlain's being David, or of Mary Queen of Scots hanging on the wall behind Miss Marsalles. It is not just that the regal adulteress is the opposite of the simple old music-teacher: Miss Marsalles in her very innocence is made up like "the feverish, fancied-up courtesan of an unpleasant Puritan imagination" (217) — and Mary's abandonment, by the same token, might well have its own kind of innocence. Munro's allusive names bring us to the same irony. When paralleling "Something I've Been Meaning to Tell You" with the Arthurian legends, I noted things like Arthur Comber's chivalrousness, but I did not point out that in some ways the implied connections here are strange ones. Not only is Arthur an extremely ineffectual version of his own archetype, but he chooses to be Galahad in the game of "Who Am I?"; at the same time Blaikie, surely the Lancelot or (better) Tristram of Munro's story, has his heart set on a kind of Holy Grail. Elsewhere Arthur is pointedly called a Fool; Et is something of a Vivien, Char something of an Elaine. The inappropriateness here naturally bothers Et: when she compares her sister's tragedy to *Romeo and Juliet*, she immediately notices how the parallel confounds itself, since Blaikie has abandoned the part of Romeo. And Et might be no less bothered if she turned her attention to Munro's naming: for Munro has names as obviously suitable as the "Gladys" in "Gladys Healey," and as perverse as the same name when attached to the dismal Gladys of "The Turkey Season." Other names in Munro are used in the same double way, as we have found; and when a name is itself a double one, its parts take on the baffling variety of roles we saw with "Del

Jordan" and "Myra Sayla" — a variety we can now see in its full complication.

*

The problem we have just been concerned with — or more generally the problem with which this book began — has intensified itself without solving itself: we still do not know how to save both this and that, or many and one. If we were to do as we did earlier and add a medial third party, our problem would remain essentially the same: in the end we are left with an extreme paradox that, in various forms, is familiar enough in contemporary critical thinking. Perhaps one principle is everything — in the terms I have been using, truth or reality or the name between them. If all are in some way allowed, they remain isolated from each other; or, if we do away with margins, they turn into a general blur more like Munro's glaciers than any more adequate kind of unity. Sense suppresses the problem by dismissing or rationalizing the evidence, like Et Desmond dismissing the kinship between her dead sister and Juliet. Sensibility becomes sharply aware of the problem but goes no farther — it sees genuine unity as finally impossible. But then sense and sensibility are only reflections of one another. Beyond both, as a word like "drumlin" has suggested, we might find an identity that neither by itself can adequately show us; and in spite of everything, stories like Munro's make us feel that identity is there for the finding.

We cannot, however, appreciate this identity until we have done some more exploring: for we have yet to follow the path that we chose against in setting out to explore the world of Munro's names. We have noted that Elizabeth is often a daughter or younger sister, one with a knack of supplanting, perhaps by surviving, the older Mary. Beyond Elizabeth's victory, we could have added, there may be some resurgence on Mary's part: Char and Myra triumph in death itself, Donna steals from her grandmother, Eileen secretly possesses the husband of her more successful sister. And we have seen the same kind of thing with Allen Durrand and Uncle James in "The Ottawa Valley" — Esau getting his revenge on the thieving Jacob. The pattern, as usual, is getting more complex as we look at it, but even in its simplest form is enables us to make an important observation: the relation between opposites can take the form of a story. In fact the metaphoric relations we have been examining seem increasingly to demand temporal expression as they get more complex: things do not just sit on shelves in the same store, but go out to each other, take and relinquish each other's parts, even become each other in a way that can best be imagined from the experience we associate with time.

More speculatively — though this is certainly to go beyond the scope of the present book — we can say that if space, the category of names taken as static, has got us into trouble, time may help us to get out of it. It will not seem to do so at first: indeed we will reach the same crisis of sensibility with temporal forms as with spatial, and in a more complex way we will reach it with temporal and spatial forms working together as parts of a larger situation. But the fact of seeing our problem in other and bigger versions will not only show us its universality: it will also point with greater insistence to a solution — one that, if we have begun with a dilemma imagined spatially, will by contrast have the character of a temporal happening. Accordingly, we can now turn to a series of relations in time matching those we have seen in space: to the ordering, that is, of Munro's stories.

NOTES

1 For a discussion of Munro's love of words more generally, see Michael Taylor's very suggestive "The Unimaginable Vancouvers: Alice Munro's Words."

2 The phrase itself ("a serious kind of joke") occurs in "Walking on Water" 74.

3 In her interview with Hancock, Munro has said that, while the names in her stories "might" (110) be a clue to characters, she chooses them merely for their sound. As often she is stating the claim of reality, in this case the reality of the name in itself as opposed to its meaning. But when Del, for instance, feels "Caroline" to be just right for her heroine, there can be no doubt that the name means something to her.

4 Hoy, dealing with Munro's paradoxical wordplay, mentions oxymoron (102), though she is not concerned with names.

5 This combination will appear more plausible if we consider the associations of the "initiatory" world and of Diane in particular. See below, 187, 231.

6 In "Postcard" Clare MacQuarrie's gift to Helen is another Morris (142).

7 The poem is quoted in "The Ottawa Valley" 245.

8 Blaikie himself, returning to Mock Hill in later life, is forced to live in a "hole" (3).

9 For Murray Street see "The Idyllic Summer" 106; for Murray Heal see "Changes and Ceremonies" 128 and "Baptizing" 228; for Pierce Murray see "Changes and Ceremonies" 130; for Heather Sue Murray see "A Trip to the Coast" 176. We also find Murry's Glass in "The Shining Houses" (23).

10 These directions are not all dark ones — May in "A Trip to the Coast" must take her name partly from her youthful hopes; but it is also true that these are shattered in the end.

11 Mack in "Boys and Girls" is black as well as dispirited: "an old black workhorse, sooty and indifferent" (119).

12 In "Lichen" David thinks of "Rosemary" — oxymoronically, it would seem — as "a sweet dark name" (53).

13 At a time when they are behaving very much as Marys, we have Jeanette in "Marrakesh" caught short on her visit to Crete and Almeda Roth in "Meneseteung" running to the privy (Almeda is combining diarrhoea and menstruation). Cf. Jimmy Sayla wetting his pants in "Day of the Butterfly." The most spectacular case of nausea is Cam in "Forgiveness in Families," who succeeds in throwing up on his sister's wedding-cake.

14 "Inflammation of the mucous membrane of the pelvis of the kidney" (OED).

15 "Alvus" means "belly," both "as containing the parts of the alimentary system" and "as womb" (also "a hollow cavity"). "Alveus" is a "trough, dish or similarly shaped vessel." "Pelvis" itself is, in Latin, "a shallow bowl or basin" (*Oxford Latin Dictionary*).

16 "Alva" in "Sunday Afternoon" is a robust girl, but comes to sense a "tender spot" (171) in her that will prove humiliating. In what I take to be a corresponding story, "Eskimo," the heroine both goes to a washroom and dreams of one, experiencing humiliation in both cases. See below, 383–84, 499–501.

17 Tener 37.8.8.

18 For an illuminating instance of the same imagery, see "Something I've Been Meaning to Tell You" 17. When Arthur squeezes Et's waist, "she felt afterwards the bumpy pressure of his fingers as if they had left dents just above where her skirt fastened. It had felt like somebody absent-mindedly trying out the keys of a piano." Char, when disturbed about a sexual matter, habitually plays the piano.

19 See below, 196, 214.

20 For examples of such places, see "Accident" 82; "Thanks for the Ride" 49; "The Ottawa Valley" 227; "Walker Brothers Cowboy" 2 (where we also have a locked-up lumberyard). For the imagery of the closed door, see below, 235–36.

21 Num. 12:15.

22 Cf. the bitter waters of Marah (Exod. 15:23 ff.); also a figure like Mara in George Macdonald's *Lilith*, with her "House of Bitterness."

23 The Eileen of Margot's tale in "Wigtime" is "Lana."

24 See also below, 203, 310, 392.

25 However pampered some of Munro's cats may be, we also hear of one tomcat killed in a dryer and another mutilated; we also find a shot racoon, shot groundhogs, and an agonized ferret. (It is worth noting that ferrets, like groundhogs and muskrats, operate under the earth.)

26 Cf. Mr. Lougheed's response to Eugene's proposed walking on water: "Until I see with my own eyes that wastepaper basket rise and float over my head . . . I will believe nothing of the kind" (76). Eugene doubles allusions by answering "Road to Emmaus." See John 20:25, Luke 24:13 ff.

27 The biblical matter of walking on water appears, not only in the name of

one of Munro's stories, but more elusively in "Material," with its motifs of inundation, sleep, faith, and the giving of life. In an early version (Tener 37.10.24) the hero we know as Hugo was Simon. We also find a Peter falling from space at the end of "White Dump" (309); another Peter — the Pierce Murray mentioned in "Changes and Ceremonies" (130) — is killed in the Air Force.

28 See below, 148 (and 159 n60), 428.

29 "Kuiper" strictly means a cooper — see below, 449–50 n31.

30 "Robin" in "Circle of Prayer" may not seem related here, yet perhaps she is: the story hints that she is her mother's rival — someone ready to steal her father as Trudy herself once did. In "Oh, What Avails," Joan's son "Rob" sends her a threatening chain letter as a joke when, as it happens, she is launching on her affair with John Brolier (202).

31 Cf. Robert or "Roberta" (6) in "Royal Beatings," whose manhood has somehow been stolen — perhaps when hoodlums broke in to lynch his father.

32 See Rev. 12:1.

33 The notes Mrs. Brooke leaves at her death repeat the word "Therese" (sic): in some way it names her, though it is not, to Harry's knowledge, her name in the ordinary sense.

34 In "Real People" (Tener 37.8.8) the house occupied by Dotty was owned by "Mrs. Fleck."

35 In material closely related to "Day of the Butterfly" we find the same sort of contrast. In "Changes and Ceremonies" the Italian girl, whom one naturally thinks of as dark, is matched in her isolation by an albino boy. In the unpublished "Ole Man River" (Tener 37.13.10–13) the highly-named and highly-placed Patrick (who, in spite of his connections, serves as the pariah of the story) is another albino, not to say a victim of severe eczema — "Alva-Marie Skin" again.

36 Barbara in "Oranges and Apples," a Char crossed with a Fern Dogherty, has white skin and black hair (107) — which in later years becomes a fringe of white hair like "veiling" (112) around the face. To her adoring husband she seems "a bold black-and-white lily" (108).

37 A dark-haired girl, Marian Botherton wears in school a "pinafore sticking up in starched wings" (160), white no doubt; for ice-skating she wears "sky-blue trimmed with white fur" (173). A more lugubrious counterpart is Gladys in "The Turkey Season," imagined by the narrator in "a navy-blue dress with a kind of detachable white collar you can wash at night" (64).

38 Henry the Navigator reappears in "Fits" (109), again as someone who stimulated exploration without engaging in it himself.

39 See "Winter Wind" 194.

40 There are any number of such pairs in Munro: the frail, elegant MaryBeth and the tomboyish Jessie, "robust and sweaty and ill-clad" (165); the baroque Spanish Lady and the lanky Marg Honecker; Angela and Eva, Nichola and Judith, Cynthia and Meg. See respectively "Jesse and Meribeth," "The Spanish Lady," "Labor Day Dinner," "The Moons of Jupiter," "Miles City, Montana."

41 See the unpublished "The Green April" (Tener 37.15.4) and "The Turkey Season." We could add Mattie and Hattie ("Who Do You Think You Are?"), Maddy and Helen ("The Peace of Utrecht"), Mack and Flora ("Boys and Girls"), Marie and Beatrice ("Baptizing"), Grace and Vera ("Visitors") — though some of these figures carry other suggestions as well.

42 Exod. 6:23, Luke 1:5.

43 Not quite: Aunt Elspeth will confront the jumble of the storeroom, while Auntie Grace — to whom it suggests a tomb — is afraid to go in.

44 Stella in "Lichen" (more a "sunbeam" [50] than a star in the dark) ends thinking of "the flow of the days and nights as she keeps them going" (55).

45 The word "wheel" itself appears in "Mrs. Alf Wheeler" of "The Edge of Town." Since there is also a Stanley Wheeler in "Pastime of a Saturday Night" (Tener 37.15.52–53), "Wheeler" seems to be one of the floating names in Munro's early work — as is "McKay."

46 See "Princess Ida" 69.

47 In "Lives of Girls and Women" (157) we again have Marjory Coutts and Gwen Mundy.

48 Cf. Ruby Carruthers in "Half a Grapefruit," Garnet French in "Baptizing." In "Something I've Been Meaning to Tell You" it is a ruby that Et imagines Blaikie Noble searching for at the bottom of the ocean (3).

49 Peggy Goring in "Home" uses similar fortitude to regain and hold Joe Thoms. Greta in "Accident" is no doubt very different — a meek and artless woman who seems to give up Ted Makkavala with no real struggle. We notice, however, that she is physically solid — "big bones, long bones" (99) — and that she again contrasts with a Mary: she is Ted's sober wife, not his passionate mistress Frances.

50 We have a rather similar pair in "Friend of My Youth": the mysterious (though by no means aloof) Flora and her younger sister, the "Ellie" who is, or begins, as brash as Eva.

51 Blair King in "Marrakesh," the suffering radio-man whose given name is Scottish, was "Blakie Bennett" in a previous form of the story (Tener 37.8.3–5). Blair also proves a passionate lover — like Blaikie Noble again. Others in Munro, successful or unsuccessful but always with something fated about them, may again have Scottish names — Duncan in "Dulse," Douglas in "Hard-Luck Stories," Stu Sherriff in the early "The Idyllic Summer" — or may actually be Scottish, like Dudley Brown in "Hold Me Fast, Don't Let Me Pass." Mr. Black, the hapless Austrian in "The Stone in the Field," was or was thought to be a Scot in an earlier version (Tener 37.14.1).

52 "Remember Roger Mortimer."

53 This dream, she says, must have come from English history (114): but Mary belongs at least generically with such a dream, and her execution is part of English history as well as Scottish. In "Connection" (8) there is a curious bit of interplay as to whether Mary Queen of Scots was English.

54 In "Hold Me Fast, Don't Let Me Pass," surrounded by the history of Scottish bloodshed, we find "Antoinette" — another beheaded Queen Mary. In her present form Antoinette is more of a self-possessed Elizabeth, but she once had a more romantic and unfortunate self, and the narrator knows it is still there beneath the surface.

55 For the glamour of the Latin-American world we can turn to Mr. Torrance in the early "A Basket of Strawberries," who falls in love with the name "Goldora" because it reminds him of "Spaniards and the Fountain of Youth, baroque palaces and small white churches in the desert, garish and gilded saints" (32). For the other side of the matter we should remember Nora Weeble in "Fits," who chatters about Mayan sacrifices (106). In "Boys and Girls" young Laird names one of the foxes "Mexico" ("he did not say why") (115); he then takes part in a slaughter.

56 For "Wales" as a different "other country" see below, 340 n47.

57 While I am concerned here primarily with the Frenchness and the literal sense of "Duval," see also Martin, *Paradox* 190, for the famous Restoration highwayman Claude Duval.

58 See below, 386, 419.

59 In the early "How Could I Do That?" the socially aspiring heroine, strongly contrasted with her humble mother, is another Louise.

60 See Gen. 25:25.

61 See Gen. 25:26, 27:36.

62 For an example of "fineness" see "Providence," where Rose's daughter Anna is passed from her histrionic mother to Patrick's more acceptable new wife Elizabeth: a "fine and stable person" (150). Anna has insistently declared herself "fine" (151) in letters instigated by Rose, but now she takes on a "demure and satisfied" appearance — fine in Elizabeth's way, evidently. In "Simon's Luck" we hear of Anna's "fine gold chain . . . so fine you had to look closely to make sure it was a chain" (159). The question remains whether this elegant girl, "so silent, so fastidious, so unforthcoming" (at least with Rose), is not a Mary after all in the very intensity of her Elizabeth's composure: in fact that is just the kind of question that needs raising here.

63 We might have chosen other names: the gifted Dorothy, the circling Catherine, the flowery Lily, the bright Clara, the astral Stella, the precious Pearl, the priestess Anne — to mention names often associated with grace of some kind, which can have either Mary's transcendence or Elizabeth's worldly presence.

64 In the early and unpublished "Pastime of a Saturday Night" (Tener 37.15.52–53) we actually find a pair of Helens. The heroine of the story — a bony, sexually shy girl — lures the schoolteacher hero, Stanley Wheeler, into having sex with her by pretending that she is already pregnant. Stanley's fiancée is another Helen, a very noble and correct one according to him.

65 The same thing happens — to a mild degree — with the Fordyces in *Friend of My Youth*: these get a story of their own in "Oh, What Avails," but Morris

and his enterprises also turn up in three others.

⁶⁶ See above, 15, for the different Del Jordans in *Lives of Girls and Women*. Speaking of her stories generally, Munro has said that she often writes about the same heroine, varying only the name and occupation and background (Hancock 85; Struthers, "The Real Material" 30); but I would question whether this is entirely true. Janet and Rose, for instance, may come from the same matrix, but as we now have them they are distinct personalities.

⁶⁷ Connection with oatmeal seems a sure sign of an Elizabeth in Munro. "Run-of-the-mill" farm people eat a great deal of it ("Baptizing" 209), and in an unpublished Simon story a mistress gets replaced by "Mrs. Rolled Oats," one of Munro's practical supplanters (Tener 37.11.23–24).

⁶⁸ See above, 49.

⁶⁹ Flora in "Friend of My Youth," closely related in some ways, is imagined by the narrator as working in a department store. The mother in "The Peace of Utrecht" "spent a lot of time sorting things. All kinds of things" (202).

⁷⁰ The shifting here can be found in forms of the same name or complex of names. If we start with "Helen" and shift in one direction, we come, I will suggest, to Eileen, Lena, and Lana — Mary Magdalen. If we shift in the other direction, we move through Ella to Ellie and Elizabeth.

⁷¹ Something of the kind is suggested more expressly at the end of "The Ferguson Girls Must Never Marry," where the astute Bonnie notices a change in Ted and Uncle Deevey: "the strange thing was how Ted, now, had come to look something like Uncle Deevey, then, and how Uncle Deevey, in what was surely the last decade of his life, had come to resemble the younger Ted" (63). At the end of "The Dangerous One" the obsessed Donna, now asleep, shows "no flush, no sign of reckless necessity" (51) on her face, whereas her enemy the grandmother, who displays the same poise more habitually, has turned "cold and cross." Donna has stolen her enemy's composure as surely as her porcelain figurines, leaving a turmoil of her own in exchange.

⁷² This happens with Donna, for instance. Nurse Atkinson in "Friend of My Youth," another who flaunts herself, not only has a green car but a house, or half a house, in "cream with dark-green trim" (17). In "Jesse and Meribeth," however, we can discern something like the "Spanish Lady" episode in blue and red. MaryBeth, while wearing a spectrum of colours, has a blue winter coat; when offered a choice of her scarves, Jessie picks the one that is "pink shading into rose" (166). The result is an abortive exchange: MaryBeth "cried admiringly, 'Oh, that's the very prettiest!' So I tried to give it back. We had a pretend-argument, and I ended up keeping it."

⁷³ The Spanish Lady gives Marg "Lala Rookh" and gets "The Princess" in exchange. As subsequent events show, it is a good question which lady is Lala Rookh and which a princess. We cannot settle the matter simply by noting which is the giver and which the recipient of either book, since a gift says as much about the one as about the other.

[74] We might of course say merely that Miss Farris is half-way on a spectrum between the principal and the lovers, but we can see the situation as something more paradoxical.

[75] "Heirs of the Living Body" 61.

Stories

I: INTRODUCTION

In speaking of Munro's "stories," I have so far been using the word in a very general sense, referring to her individual units of writing taken in any way whatever. Now we will need to limit "story" to its purely narrative sense, by which I mean here the events themselves, and as having some degree of structure. If we define a story in this way, and come to it from a consideration of metaphor, we can call it a metaphor in time: a connection of two things, or more intensely their identification, by means of a process. In the simplest narrative structure that we can imagine, then, a hero moves to his goal; his quest may of course fail, but that failure itself, as I will be presenting the matter, is an arrival of a tragic kind.

Before viewing Munro's stories even in this simple way, however, we had better ask whether the events in them make any structure at all — to separate this from the order of their presentation. If we were considering a standard quest narrative, the obvious answer would be yes, but when we turn to something like "The Ottawa Valley" it may seem a decided no — compared to well-made plots, as we noted earlier, some of Munro's stories seem mere jumble or flux. And yet our question is like the one that we raised at the beginning of this book: can an Ontario town be far-off Marrakesh? This also meant asking whether Art Chamberlain, for instance, could be the hero of a distant story, that of the biblical David; now we are asking the question about narrative structure as such. In "Something I've Been Meaning to Tell You" Et Desmond finds that "the qualities of legend" (6) can haunt the world of reality: and legends have shapes, even if accommodation to ordinary life takes away their shapely appearance. The events of this same story may look as formless as the humps and hollows of a moraine, but behind them loom the careers of Juliet and Cleopatra and Arthur and Napoleon — great arches of glory, reversal, and downfall, as tradition has made them; and in our most intense awareness we can see that Munro's story *is* those stories. What makes this hard to see is that, to go on thinking in sensibility terms, the events have seemingly estranged themselves from the story as structure.

Apart from such a complicating factor, the forms of stories can be complex enough in themselves;[1] and yet the simple quest we began with also makes a simple scheme. Somebody, as I have said, seeks something; to find it he journeys, literally or figuratively, from a home to another place. Or perhaps the story is one of homecoming: in either case we can imagine a figure made from two points — a line, in the geometrical metaphor I will be using in this chapter. And since we have already met Home and the Other Place in a different context, we may well expect the opposites joined by the quest to be, or at any rate correspond to, others we have already talked about. A story, let us say, arrives at a point where reason and order prevail. It has come, then, to the condition of sense or "Elizabeth"; in actual space it may, like "Images," have reached the family home, with its warmth and comfort and tidiness — to see in this limited way a story we will certainly be seeing in others. Can we, then, speak of Mary and Elizabeth phases in a story? Yes, I believe, but we need a qualification here just as when we added sense and sensibility to truth and reality: the narrative phases we are introducing will also need selves of their own. The conclusion of a story may remind us far more of Mary than of Elizabeth; we cannot, then, simply associate an end as such, or a beginning, with either woman. Nor, for that matter, can we simply associate Elizabeth and Home: the ordinary human condition that we think of as our Home is in one view not "ordinary" at all, but as chaotic as Mary's ocean. The pairs of categories here — beginning and end, Home and the Other Place, Elizabeth and Mary — may have a common origin, ultimately that of opposition itself; but like pairings we have seen before, they lead separate lives as well.

Whether they always lead these as ends of a line — by which I will generally be meaning a straight line — is a further question: for of course there is much in a story like "Images" that our simple linear model cannot represent. We will in fact meet a series of models in this chapter, increasing in complexity as we go on; to make some preliminary considerations easier, I will add one further model here. In a way "Images" begins with one state of affairs and ends with another; yet it also begins and ends at the same family house, and with much the same régime there. In the middle lies the wild Other Place inhabited by the mad Joe Phippen; and to think of the encounter with Joe — especially the terrifying moment when he suddenly appears with his hatchet — is to see a definite central point before the return homeward. Thus we have a figure with not just two points but three; not simply a straight line but one that curves back from a turning-point to end where it started. In other words, we have a circle.

A circle has one more dimension than a line: that is why it can have the special features — the turning-point, the coincidence of beginning and end — that a line cannot have. Thus a circle has more meaning than a line, in the sense that it expresses a greater degree both of differentiation and of identification. A movement from one point to another identifies these points only to the extent of simple connection; but if movement returns to where it began through a distinct medial point, we feel beginning and end to be not only more separated but more integrated. Other figures will prove more meaningful again; at the same time any figure, simply as such, makes at least an emblem of full identity, and we will need to remember this possibility as we proceed.

With the line and the circle as a basic repertory of figures, we are ready for some preliminary questions about stories and figures in general. We will need, in the first place, to think further about the relation between the two — between a story, that is, and its own figure or shape. When we say that a story "is" a line or a circle, we cannot mean simply that: the figure is idea where the story is thing, truth where the story is reality, space where the story is time. On the other hand, figure and story do not simply exclude each other. Any story, apprehended as that, is also a figure; and conversely any figure can be imagined as having a story of its own — a line, for example, "runs" from one point to a different one.[2]

To see this inter-relation more clearly, we can ask how figures themselves turn into one another. A line connects points, and thus makes a certain unity out of them — another point, in a sense, and a higher-order one since it is a point made of two points. A circle, having a further dimension, can be thought of as bringing two lines (or axes) together: it is thus a higher-order line, or for that matter a still higher-order point. And in each case the lesser not only precedes the greater, but implies it: I remarked earlier that the ends of a line have in common the fact of being ends, and if we dwell on this fact we find ourselves with a circle, the figure whose ends are different and yet the same. The same kind of transformation, it would seem, occurs to give us form in the first place. In principle we first experience a story directly, as sheer content (not that we could ever quite do so in actuality); we are then ready to grasp the whole at once, and now it recreates itself as a form. (For clarity, I am going to say "form" for stories and figures alike taken as shape rather than as story in the sense of content.)

Any such movement — of story to figure, figure to higher figure, story to higher story — is essentially the same movement. In the present chapter it will appear mainly as a sequence of figures; and this sequence will of course need its own figure, the most convenient for our purposes being the line. But if this sounds like an infinite regression into the abstract, we should remember that we are also dealing with experience: and to see — if still in fairly diagrammatic terms — what recreation actually feels like, we can think again of the narrator in "Images." At the stage of life where we first meet her, she already as it were understands change in a single direction: she knows you can go for a walk. But the walk she does go on, while moving continuously onward, ends where it began:

> "Whose house is that?" my father said, pointing.
> It was ours, I knew it after a minute. We had come around in a half-circle and there was the side of the house that nobody saw in winter. . . . (42)

In circling around, the narrator has also moved from the line to the circle; and what she feels is the confusion leading to enlightenment that accompanies transcendence — in our deepest transformations as in this little girl's homecoming.

*

So far the terms in which we have been imagining forms have been serial ones — a story becoming a figure, one figure following another. Yet we have already found contexts in which we had to see them as it were simultaneously, and for this purpose we will have to bring in a new consideration, that of scale. We may notice that the less complex forms we have been seeing fit inside the more complex: the outward path of father and daughter in "Images," which we can imagine as a simple line, also bends to become the larger path — a circle — that brings them home again. If we wanted to compare the structure of two such forms independently of their size, we would of course have to imagine them on the same scale. It might, however, be just their size that we wanted to compare, and if so we would have to ignore their difference in structure — treat the line as a smaller-scale circle or the circle as a larger-scale line. Thus we need ways of transforming both scale and complexity of figure to suit our purposes. We must be able to imagine a form as, on the one hand, remaining on a single scale while changing its complexity, and, on the other, keeping its complexity while changing its scale. This will mean seeing figure as changing against story, and story as changing against figure.

I am going to use the term "reduction" for the process by which we bring a form down to a convenient level of complexity while leaving its scale unchanged. Without reduction the present argument would at times find itself embroiled in figures of several dimensions: this would be intolerable since we cannot imagine spatially in more than three of these, or put more than two into a diagram on a flat piece of paper. And since we most often think of a story as a line — that is, a line with separate ends — we may at times want to reduce even a circle, especially if we are comparing it to something else that we are imagining in a linear way. The converse upward process can be called "inflation": without it we might at times be stuck with a model inadequate for the differentiations we needed to make within even a small segment of a story.

The process I will be calling "concentration" (or, going in an opposite direction, "distribution") changes not complexity but scale. Here a circle, say, remains a circle; but we can imagine it as having various sizes in relation to another form against which we are matching it. These two kinds of alteration — reduction and inflation on the one hand, concentration and distribution on the other — appear in different contexts, and yet are really complementary: the more we treat some larger pattern in a story as only a distribution of a smaller one, the more we are reducing its complexity from what it might otherwise be; the more we inflate some smaller pattern, the more we are concentrating a large story into a little one.

*

An elementary form of distribution — to see distribution as its principle — is simply the coexistence of smaller versions of the same form with larger ones. If a whole story can be a line or a circle, then any unit making a line or circle can be a whole story: and we generally find that an episode within one of Munro's stories, where we can see enough of it, tends to be organized on the same structural principles as her stories taken as wholes. We have not yet gone very far with these principles, but at least we have seen that a story can be analyzed in terms of two points, if it is like a line, or three if it is like a circle. The central episode in "Images," taken by itself, shows us the linear movement very clearly: Ben has caught an "old king rat" (36) and swings it triumphantly in the sun; then Ben falls victim to Joe Phippen, and becomes a prisoner in his underground den. The same episode looks more circular if we see both Ben the victor and Ben the prisoner as, in their different ways, well off. It is in the middle that there is a point of real danger: Joe, not yet pacified, suddenly advances with his hatchet. Then the crisis passes, and by the end of the episode the two men are drinking whisky together. But whether line, circle, or some other figure, this central part of the story has a completeness of its own: it is an integral structure on a small scale.

On either side of such a central unit, initial and concluding ones tend to become structures of their own in the same way. In "Images" we first see an encounter between the narrator and Mary McQuade, perhaps noticing a shape in the former's unsuccessful attempt to challenge the latter. At the end there is a complementary encounter, with Mary as the one who now challenges and fails. If we look outside "Images" it is easy enough to think of other initial episodes having a clear shape: Uncle Benny's wooing, or the early affair of Char and Blaikie Noble, or Helena's first confrontation with Howard Troy. Closing episodes — the events following Blaikie's return are an obvious example — can be even more self-contained. Nor need we limit ourselves to the scale of episodes: we have seen forms in Munro as miniature as sets of names or the syllables of "Yew-gene"; in more narrative terms, we will be seeing presently how any event at all has a whole story implicit in it. Going in the other direction, we will see how any finite story makes part of a larger one. The stories of Del's association with Bert Matthews, Jerry Storey, and Garnet French, for instance, are complete in themselves; they also go to make up the larger story Munro calls "Baptizing."

But if the same form can co-exist on different scales, this becomes more significant when the form's different versions have a common orientation — a common centre, as I will be imagining it here. In "Images" Joe Phippen first appears as an attacker, but if handled properly turns into a kindly host: as I have suggested, the central episode of this story makes a little story in itself, circular in form if it returns to some kind of security. But there is further return in the homecoming that ends "Images" as a whole: thus we have two circular movements here, concentric but different in scale, each concluding in company, jokes, and refreshments. Another story might emphasize such movements on other scales again. There is a point on the way home in "Images" when the child recognizes her own house: this corresponds to scenes in both "Bardon Bus" and "Simon's Luck" in which the heroine, having passed through an ordeal, gets some refreshment in a restaurant and finds herself coming back to ordinary human life and society. We even find moments in Munro's stories, perhaps coming after their action altogether, when ordinary society hints at something beyond itself. When Trudy in "Circle of Prayer" has weathered the various crises of the story and settled down for a quiet game of cards with Kelvin, she senses a mysterious companionship beyond any of her normal ones. What we need to see here is simply that these various homecomings occur at different but corresponding points in their stories. The same form, in other words, can occur in less and more distributed versions, like rings going out from a common centre.

There is a corollary whose practical importance will become clear as we go on: except in relation to something external it is impossible to say how much of a story is "the story proper." In "An Ounce of Cure," for instance, are we to identify this with the events at the Berrymans' house? If so, "An Ounce of Cure" is rich in prologue and epilogue, as indeed Munro's stories tend to be. Or is the story proper the whole tale of the heroine's infatuation with Martin Collingwood, leading to the point where she manages to fall out of love with him? In "Images," once again, is the story proper the trapline expedition by itself, or is it the larger story beginning and ending with Mary McQuade? We can suit our convenience here, but we often need to remember different possibilities, and a general principle is becoming more insistent: scale is another relative matter, and like any variable can only be determined in relation to something that does not vary.

If, moreover, there can be varying both of scale and of structure — the latter having effects that we will come to shortly — the result is a doubleness of experience that we should also note here. When we look again at the different points of return I have mentioned, ordering them according to their distance from the centre in their respective stories, we notice a remarkable range of tone. Each return has a reassuring quality, even the one to Joe Phippen's strange home away from home; but Joe's den is so wild as to be home only in a paradoxical way (it reminds the narrator of a play-house). Return to the home at home is something else; and strange moments of communion like that of Trudy and Kelvin, with their suggestion of a home beyond home, are something else again. When we take an experience like homecoming as a constant (ignoring its varieties for the moment), we find it matched against a variable: the structural position in which returns of some kind occur. But when we give return a fixed position (ignoring its different distributions), it is the experience of homecoming that we will tend to see varying.

*

Before taking a closer look at Munro's particular temporal forms we can pause for a last observation, now on precisely their temporality. A story is of course something that moves in time, and even the figure by which we interpret it, while spatial by comparison (and appearing when the story is reflected on as a simultaneous whole), can be thought of rather as trans-temporal — something arising from the story as experienced temporally, and only detachable from it by abstraction. No doubt we are being spatial when we speak of a narrative point that coincides with another point on the circumference of a circle. But we should remember that a later event, as an event, cannot simply occupy the same temporal "position" as an earlier one. Refreshment with Joe Phippen in the woods may, in some sense, be the same thing as refreshment with Mary McQuade back home, but it cannot be the same thing in time. Later I want to return to the relation of space and time in stories: here we can consider their world simply as a temporal one.

If we do so, it will be easier to deal with a correspondence that suggests itself and is at least worth proposing here. It would seem that we can use the same figures to imagine relations in the temporal world of stories and the quasi-spatial one of metaphors. To start where we started in distinguishing kinds of relation between Mary and Elizabeth, we can make the simple observation that events belong to stories in the same way that static particulars do to classes. But we have also noted that two kinds of story can be imagined as a line and a circle. If we go back to our static relations again, we will find a line there too: that of connection between a Mary and Elizabeth who differ and yet pass into one another. I did not explicitly use geometrical figures for other kinds of metaphoric relation, but we should think again about the third one: that in which Mary cannot simply shade into Elizabeth and yet implies her, so that Elizabeth is Elizabeth by virtue of Mary's being Mary. I imagined Mary in such a situation as able to go out to Elizabeth and yet — potentially at least — return to the Mary she has not really ceased to be. In a circular story, correspondingly, we go out to an Other Place that is the opposite of Home, but that as a turning-point directs us homeward again.

If we thus have two correspondences, it looks as if we are going to find others: narrative counterparts of both simple identity and the double identity of coinherence. For in both of our worlds we are dealing with the same process: an increasing identification of members as themselves which is also, paradoxically, their increasing identification with each other. To see this process in the world of stories, we can now follow a series of narrative figures; and at the outset it is worth recalling something we recalled about allusion in an earlier chapter. We are likely to wonder what is "there" in our text and what is "here" in the reader's mind, projected though it may be onto the text; yet as we have just seen, the differentiation of elements that we find in a text depends partly on the interpretative model we bring to it — a narrative line or a circle, for instance. On the other hand, a sensitive reader is not just choosing arbitrarily: the story by its presentation invites some figures more than others, even if these also vary with the reader's purpose at a given time.

II. SIMPLE FIGURES

1. Point

We could begin our series of narrative figures[3] with the line, but perhaps it would be better to start with a more limiting case. Narrative being a process, we can first try to imagine a story, or the germ of one, in which this process is reduced as much as possible. Our static relations began with simple identity — of a thing as just itself, or of two things as having no difference; and we imagined this identity in a spatial way as a point. What we can start with in the world of narrative, then, is a temporal kind of point, or what takes place "at" it: in other words, with an event, the counterpart of the simple "thing" in space. Spatially or temporally, a point is not much to be: like any limiting case, in fact, it is strictly nothing. Yet Munro can show us how a point implies everything: to speak as before, an event simply as such is a miraculous "happening." And if we think of the point as arrived at by reduction of the narrative circle or line, we can see that, in one view, it is not simple at all: it is beginning and end, going out and returning. The point, that is, holds in itself all the contraries that will separate themselves out in more extended figures. Its limitation lies in the fact that these are only aspects, bound in a self-mirroring without real division: a point is all potentiality.

*

To see both the point's nothingness and its power, we can think here of some specially pure happenings in Munro. Earlier we saw how her stories tend to gather around distinct epiphanies. At that stage we were concerned with the cognitive aspect of these: now we must consider them as events, and for the purpose we can recall again how "Images" first came into her mind. Standing on top of a bank, a little girl watches a stranger with a hatchet advance toward her father. While it must be a few seconds before the father manages to calm his attacker, for the child these seconds are like a single moment: time is reduced to a point. This point, moreover, stands out sharply from everything else in her life. In terms of one pair of contraries, she experiences an intent Joe Phippen engaged in pure action — action that is his everything — while she herself responds with pure inaction: for instead of trying to stop Joe, "I saw him and just waited" (38). In "Monsieur Les Deux Chapeaux" there is a similar moment, or more precisely a moment of sheer action followed by one of inaction that we can take here simply as its complement.[4] A gun in Colin's hand goes off, his brother Ross falls to the ground more or less simulta-neously; then Colin climbs to the top of a bridge and sits motionless.

To confine ourselves to the second of Colin's moments, what is it like to sit there on the bridge? Once again, it is like nothing and everything. Most obviously it is a great blankness: Colin is not thinking of what he will do next, because the movement of life — of before and after, cause and effect — has stopped, and he cannot imagine it starting again.[5] The child in "Images," likewise, experi-ences Joe simply as an apparition, an uncaused something out of nowhere. As such Joe is pure happenstance, not a determinate person doing something for a reason; and by the same token he is meaning-less. In Colin's case meaninglessness is that of his own name and his shooting of Ross. It is merely silly, he feels, to see this last as "a *difference*"; it is silly even to see it as "sharp and separate, an event" (82) — an event, that is, with any meaning. Climbing the bridge is the same: it has no ordinary reason, is accompanied by no ordinary thoughts, does not matter in any ordinary way. Hence it is also without emotion: Colin feels no guilt, for instance, just as the child in "Images" feels no fear. Life has "split open" and revealed "noth-ing" — the nothing that was before any ordering of experience, and, we can add, before any comedy or tragedy.

Yet Colin has also had his moment of action, as Joe is having his; and this action is of crucial importance in the stories of both. For that matter, even Colin's time of indifference makes an enormous differ-ence. He sits on the bridge knowing, or at any rate believing, that he has shot his brother; the rest of his life will be what this moment already is, an attempt to separate himself from that event. In "Images" the child who takes Joe for granted is at the same time having the most intense of experiences: she calls it "recognition" (38) (which we must take as a kind of event here), the acknowledgement of a sheer presence standing apart from all the continuities of her life. And the manifestation of this presence is more than an accident: it is a fatal accident, a great necessity, something that does not surprise her because she has always secretly known it was coming. On this side (and, as we will see, in this structural position as opposed to that of Colin's retreat to the bridge) the epiphanic experience is not of nothing but of everything: the girl may not feel any particular emotion, but she does feel as if she had been struck by lightning.

Here we can briefly consider some questions that will arise again with each of our figures — and will have less paradoxical answers as these figures become more extended ones. First there is the question of characters, not as the timeless personalities we dealt with in the last chapter but as functions of narrative. What characters do we find in a story that is only a point? In a sense, none at all: only "character" as such, since the point is the simplest kind of identity. Thus the child in "Images" knows Joe Phippen most intensely not as another human being outside herself but as a sheer numen for which inside and outside make no difference. By the same token a story as point has no structure: once again it is sheer experience, like Colin's sense of occurrence without past or future. Nor do we find any mean between self and other, before and after, as we will do in more complex figures, since there can be nothing "between" what are only aspects rather than distinct entities, unless in a form as latent as their own potential distinctness. Taken as a point, then, a whole story is a single epiphanic happening. For Munro the central moment at which the child notices Joe was able to represent the whole of "Images"; and when we find the same child at the end sitting dazed and silent, simply watching again, centre has become circumference.

*

When Colin's world "splits open" he thinks of it as "a photograph split and rolled back" (81), using an image that Munro's critics have often noted and that we have already considered in more than one context. The same analogy, we found, occurs to the girl in "Images" (or her remembering adult self): seeing Joe with the hatchet, she says, she was "like a child in an old negative, electrified against the dark noon sky, with blazing hair and burned-out Orphan Annie eyes" (38). Once more, then, we are in the presence of "images," here as the kernel of narrative; and as our two protagonists show us, images have their own polarity of nothing and everything. Colin is thinking of the former: a photograph already taken — and no doubt old and dried — that cracks to reveal the emptiness it already suggests. The narrator of "Images" is thinking rather of the way a photograph (or negative "pre-photograph") continues to express its own coming into existence; and she imagines the moment of this as one of infinite intensity — light entering darkness so sharply that the two change places, and to see is to be turned blind. When Munro in an interview speaks of people as living by "flashes," she means not only that we experience our lives in special and isolated events, but that (to use her own word again) these are "snapshots" — the same image-making encounter of light and dark.[6]

It will be easier to understand the reality of such an experience if we have some truth, in our special sense, to go with it. To find this in one quarter, we can let the phrase "dark noon sky" (38) echo in our minds. Although the time of Joe's appearance is actually mid-afternoon, Munro is thinking of darkness at noon,[7] and not only for the blind Samson: here as elsewhere she is hinting at the Exodus and Crucifixion, the great times when there is darkness over the land and a veil or some other barrier breaks open.[8] Colin's cracking photograph points to a later counterpart of these events as well, the rolling up of the Heavens like a scroll.[9] "Images," moreover, seems haunted by Paul, especially the Paul of the Damascus road: we find the motif of blinding caused by light, the curious thought of "Annie," and later the irruption of the "Silases" (39) into Joe Phippen's own darkness — for like Paul's conversion, this is the story of a trapper trapped.[10] What can stand for all such shattering events is the image of crossing: the epiphanic moment in "Images" is the one at which Joe crosses the little girl's path, and we notice that the hill around which the travellers move is a kind of Golgotha, with "bare trees in wintertime that looked like bony little twigs against the sky" (37). The bridge in "Monsieur les Deux Chapeaux" is a device for crossing water: Munro elsewhere associates the same image with the Crucifixion, and as we will also see, "Monsieur les Deux Chapeaux" belongs with a group of stories specially linked to the crossing of the Red Sea and the desert. Any event, it seems, resonates with these supreme events.

Scenes of crossing raise a further question: where more generally are we to locate our picture-taking? Physically, the no-man's-land in "Images" and the bridge in "Monsieur les Deux Chapeaux" are open situations, yet they are also places of confinement in the sense that the figures we see are frozen there. Still photography of course requires its subjects to be "caught," inside the camera itself if not always inside a studio; elsewhere Munro often provides a camera for her happenings in the literal form of a chamber. In her Marrakesh story Jeanette first tells of having her camper robbed, with all her dresses and jewellery taken "as well as my camera naturally" (169). Presently she finds herself in a different sort of camera, for on accepting help from the two Arabs she is taken to "a little bare room with a couch and a bright bulb" (170); the ensuing sexual confrontation suggests a happening in a smaller chamber again.

There are others in the same story — a hot rented room in Toronto, a glassed-in back porch, the schoolroom with blackboards that is old Dorothy's eye. And if we look about in Munro we will find a remarkable number of such chambers, or cameras, typically either with a single interior light or with external light coming through some particular aperture. In "Who Do You Think You Are?" Rose meets Ralph Gillespie in the Legion basement, illuminated by the last sunlight; Del Jordan in "Heirs of the Living Body" is drawn into the stifling front room at Jenkin's Bend, "pierced with stray shafts of light" (58), to see her uncle exposed in his coffin. In "Images" itself we find, not only Joe Phippen's cellar with "a little grimy light" (40) from the windows, but the shuttered sickroom where the narrator's grandfather lies dying in the summer heat — along with other rooms in the same house where the brilliant sunlight makes "lightning cracks in the drawn-down blinds" (31).[11] Cameras come in many varieties: they may, for instance, be as empty as the room in Marrakesh or as junk-filled as Uncle Benny's house in "The Flats Road." But in one way or another, an impressive meeting of light and dark takes place in each of them.

When this occurs, the final result may well be a sense of composition, of something "held still and held together";[12] on the other hand, we have seen how the meeting itself can come as a blinding flash, and indeed it can come as an explosion. For this is the point where experience comes into "focus," to use a significant word in Munro;[13] and just as the child in "Images" feels electrified, so the same imagery of released power is often to be found elsewhere.[14] It may be associated with the sun, as in "Images"; it may come as the "dark flash" (159) of the unlit car at the end of "Labor Day Dinner"; or there is the great fire in "Executioners," not to say the lightning, thunderstorms, and forest-fires in the notes left by Rose's father. In a more displaced form we have glinting metal like Ben Jordan's skinning-knife or Joe Phippen's hatchet — metal of the kind we linked with the high Mary in the last chapter.[15] And to all these we can add Munro's currants and currents, which may take the deceptively sweet form of berries (growing on thorny plants, perhaps),[16] or be directly electrical or otherwise potent, like the mysterious current of the river in "Images":

> The river . . . was high, running full, silver in the middle where the sun hit it and where it arrowed in to its swiftest motion. That is the current, I thought, and I pictured the current as something separate from the water, just as the wind was separate from the air and had its own invading shape. (36–37)

To mention one more of Munro's favourite words, this power comes as a "stroke": the stroke of light or lightning, the stroke of paralysis, also perhaps the stroke or stroking of love — for when Dorothy watches the love-making in Marrakesh, the "stroke" (173) she fears is like all of these.[17] Understandably Dorothy finds it as much as she can take, and in fact the light in the camera, like the force Del Jordan senses in her dead uncle, might inflame the camera of the whole world — "flare up, in an instant, and burn through this room, all reality, leave us dark" (59). Yet the same meeting of light and dark constitutes everyday events, just as the meeting of Blanche and Black constitutes Blanche Black — in her everyday self as in anything more.

Even the most ordinary of these events is, once again, a "happening": a little miracle that, in any but its most neutral sense, is impossible in a world of mere physical cause and effect. And from the miraculous single event, the point by which all else can be oriented, the imaginative recreation of time begins.

*

In treating Munro's happenings I have not dealt with their placement in the stories where they occur, since that would have been to introduce the question of structure prematurely. But we will understand these happenings better in themselves if we imagine a place for them, and we can think of this first as a central one. A centre is a point of reference for a whole figure; and when we look at the centres of Munro's stories (how to identify these centres is a question I will come back to), we often find some event in which opposites meet in a specially clear way. It is at the centre of "Images" that Ben and his daughter encounter Joe Phippen: for a timeless moment reason faces madness. Or we can say that the sacrificed faces the sacrificer, whichever way we choose to assign these roles; and at the centre of other stories we may find a sacrament in which such figures seal a bond — by taking drink together, for instance, as in "Half a Grapefruit," or having sex together, as in the Garnet French story. In "Images" the meeting is one of the photographic flashes we have seen; elsewhere, to stay with flashing of one kind or another, we find the sudden flash of a nude photograph at the centre of "Lichen" or, in "Baptizing," the "white gleam" (227) of Garnet's buttocks signalling consummation both to Del and — she fears — people on the street.

Not all core events, as we can call them, are flashes in so manifest a way as these, nor need they be so distinct from their surroundings; but to the extent that they are, we sense something at the heart of a story that is at once its essence and not part of it at all — everything and nothing again, now in a structural context. In Shakespeare's plays, to look briefly outside Munro, we often find specially charged moments just as the action is definitively reversing itself. Between stoic posturing and the other madness of self-abandonment, Lear can see with complete simplicity that he has neglected his people's need; between pride and self-surrender again — capitulation to Nature in the person of his mother — Coriolanus sees for one clear moment what is at issue and what his surrender will mean.[18] While more "focal" than Colin's experience on the bridge (which, as I have suggested, is structurally not the centre but its complement), these points of detachment are like it in that the natural cause and effect impelling the story onward are momentarily arrested: the protagonist stands outside himself, knowing his choice and his fate, before events reclaim him. At the centre of Milton's Nativity Ode, to have a more schematic example, time seems to have stopped — the gate of Heaven is about to open. Then Fate insists that time go on: and yet for a moment the experience of being outside the world has met that of being bound to it. In about the same structural context as Colin on the bridge, the Rose who has had a royal beating and withdrawn into a private world hears Flo on the stairs with treats to lure her back: it is "the moment . . . that contains for her both present peace and freedom and a sure knowledge of the whole down-spiraling course of events from now on" (18). Beyond this return to separation there will be a final point, one I will deal with later in this chapter, at which the proleptic central meeting of opposites becomes, comically or tragically, a full union.

But if our narrative point can be located at the centre or end of a larger story, there is another location even more significant for our immediate purposes: the beginning. We have imagined a series of narrative figures "beginning" with a story seen as a point, and an awareness of coherent time "beginning" with the isolation of a single event. If we also imagine — not very scientifically, perhaps — the first consciousness with which a child knows a parent or a pet animal, we will have this beginning as one in actual time; and we can feel the simplicity or innocence of it when the little girl of "Images" simply recognizes Joe, neither fearing nor questioning.[19] It is not that this girl belongs to a myth of innocence: she is not Eve in a garden but a helpless child meeting a demon in the wilderness; for that matter even innocence, as we usually understand it, arises within a world that is finite and in that sense already fallen. But that is just what we need to imagine here: our narrative point as a simple first step within a chaotic world, where it will lead to implications no less complex than those we saw in the previous chapter.

To have an analogue outside Munro for much that we have been seeing, we can turn to a work I am going to mention repeatedly — Eliot's *Four Quartets*, with their remarkable richness, clarity, and concentration of scheme. In particular we can think here of the first of them, *Burnt Norton*: for if the estate of that name is a mere ruin, it is nevertheless the place where we step into "our first world." The way we do so, moreover, is associated with a point: the pool at the centre of the garden into which light suddenly strikes as it does into one of Munro's cameras. Even the poem's later world of unconcentrated process is imagined in terms of points — points on the London Underground, bits of paper, "twitterings" corresponding to the evanescent gleams and bird-calls in the garden. To play on the word "point" as Eliot himself does, we can say that all these points, however pointless in one aspect, point to a "still point" of pure life or death — of everything or nothing. But while this still point is timeless, there remains a sense in which it is a beginning: for in *Burnt Norton* it is experienced as an isolated moment, not yet integrated with life as a process. It is thus like a story apprehended as pure epiphany: it announces a fuller entry into time and all that time brings.

2. Line

Our second figure (or first, if we think of dimension as essential to a figure) can be dealt with much more briefly than its predecessor, partly because I have already introduced it, partly because it is less problematical as a figure. We started with the point: an event experienced in its own integrity, however paradoxical this might be. As finite such an experience transcends itself, for a something implies a something else, a here and a there — in narrative terms, one time and another. Since we now have two points to be related, we have arrived at extension and connection; temporally, we have arrived at process. Our new figure is of course the line,[20] moving in its single dimension between these points. A narrative movement seen in this way is, I have suggested, like the static relation in which Mary and Elizabeth shade into each other.

Certain emblematic forms of linearity, some of them very common in Munro, can serve us as labels here. Whereas the idea of a point makes us think of her isolated flashes and strokes, or currents imagined in the same way, we can think now of currents as having a more continuous kind of existence. The Wawanash River in "Images" not only gleams in the sun but flows forward; and its effect is even more linear when, as in the Garnet French story, the flow suggests something steady and irreversible, like the passage of summer or youth. Munro's many roads and railways suggest the same irreversibility (as, accordingly, vehicles like cars and trains may also do); and this is especially true when a "trip to the coast" implies a journey to death.

In "The Ottawa Valley," where a similar journey underlies the whole story, it is interesting to find, along with train-rides and car-rides, a procession in a church. Imagery of this sequential kind is even more pervasive in "Who Do You Think You Are?," with its assorted parades, line-ups, seats in rows in a classroom, slides in order in a slide-show, and pictures ranged along the wall at the Legion. Elsewhere in Munro we find various sorts of threads and cables, including means of communication such as the telephone lines in stories like "Winter Wind" and "Dulse." There are characters who make it their life's work to keep such lines unbroken: I have dealt with some of these under the general name of Elizabeth, and we can recall as well that individual Elizabeths may have names like "Flo" and "Et." Harry "Brooke" is in some ways very different from these last, as they are from each other, but when we find him rushing from one salvation to the next, and compare him with his mysteriously static wife, we can see where he gets his surname.[21] And of course there is Del Jordan: a much more comprehensive figure, but suggesting among other things one — or two — of Munro's rivers.

The point, we found, was in itself sheer experience with as yet no distinct object or distinct emotion: with the separation of points, object and emotion begin to crystallize as themselves. At the linear stage they are still very simple — we are drawn from one point to the other by sheer desire, which we can readily divide into the will that thrusts and the attraction that draws. Recognition, which is also beginning to crystallize here, is an awareness of process, and more particularly of setting out and arriving: it is this vision of onward movement with which Eliot is concerned in *East Coker*, the second of his quartets. There can be no greater vision in linear experience merely as such — the protagonist or reader learns only that one thing comes to or turns into another. The genre of a linear story is thus the simple quest or progress (or regress): *The Pilgrim's Progress*, for instance, simply as Christian's journey to his goal. When we read Munro's stories in the same way, what we notice is that people set out for destinations and get there — the Spanish Lady gets to Vancouver, Mary Jo gets to Hawaii in "Eskimo," Rose gets to Toronto in "Wild Swans."[22] Mrs. Jordan's adventures are less simple geographically, but equally linear if we feel them as pure onward drive. Or we may feel stories as simple change: the heroine of "Images" ends as a self-possessed young woman after beginning as a frightened child; the love at the beginning of the Garnet French story becomes anger at the end of it. Understood in this way, a story has no distinct turning-point: its centre is only part of the extension between its ends. Such a story is comic or tragic, where the point was neither; but comedy or tragedy here is that of a sheer success story or sheer fall from prosperity.

Apart from the protagonist as such, there are two characters belonging to a linear story. We can call them the Initiator and the Finisher (though we will hardly need such simple roles for later discussions): the person one leaves behind and the person one comes to. In linear experience these will be different people, or at any rate a person who reappears as someone else. Edie in "How I Met My Husband" goes out from both her immediate and her secondary family, especially the solicitous Dr. Peebles; in the end she makes a new family with a new acquaintance, the postman she marries. In "Something I've Been Meaning to Tell You" Char's love-life starts with a dashing and wealthy young man and ends with a seedy, white-haired failure; or if we are thinking of the person Char is rather than the person she meets, the alluring girl of the first affair becomes the old woman of the end. No doubt there is more than change here — both lovers are Blaikie Noble, both women are Char; but at the linear level it is change that impresses us, not the way the lovers keep their simple identities or the way their elderly selves come back to the younger again.

3. Circle

The old selves do come back, of course, after the central interval of Char's marriage to Arthur Comber: "Something I've Been Meaning to Tell You" is a story not only of progression but of return. And while this return could be imagined as the direct retracing of the line back to its source, we will do better to see it in two-dimensional terms: once again, a continuous line in two dimensions is a circle, or temporally a cycle. For an emblem we can again look to the Wawanash River, which we have seen both flashing and moving onward but which we also find, in "Images" and elsewhere, to have a curve to it — perhaps a "Big Bend."[23] Realism will not quite allow Munro to say that the river comes full circle, or that the travellers in "Images" follow it all the way home, but when, in "The Peace of Utrecht," she speaks of "the golden, marshy river that almost encircles the town of Jubilee" (209), she is getting as close as she can.

In a later chapter we will have to think further about circulating waters;[24] for the present we can simply note how circles, like lines, are omnipresent in Munro's writing. Often we find them embedded in her wordplay, as with the "Sexual Revolution" (186) that seems to have come full circle in "Hard-Luck Stories," or, in "Baptizing," the view of all such matters taken by Mr. Buchanan the "turn-of-the-century cyclist" (208). At the great party in "Simon's Luck" we find not only "turn-of-the-century advertisements" (154) but a juke-box in which the music presumably goes round and round; we are also told about a clothes-dryer in which Rose's hapless cat did the same thing. The party itself is much like May's dream in "A Trip to the Coast," which features "people in coloured hats going round and round" (180); "Home" has a song about the same thing, "all those people / Going roun and roun" (146). It is "as if we were all wound up a long time ago," muses the Spanish Lady, "and were spinning out of control, whirring" (190–91). "We were going round and round forever" (167), recalls Jeanette in "Marrakesh" about a roundabout on a British motorway: and here Munro is implicitly contrasting a circle with a straighter route, as also when she locates the Jubilee railroad station beside the circling river (not, by the way, where one would find it in the actual Wingham).[25] What people experience in such a roundabout world is not shocks or propulsions but "turns":[26] indeed some of Munro's characters are virtual turns themselves, marked perhaps by suitable emblems. An encircling type like Mrs. Sherriff may choose to wear a "turban" (108);[27] as for names, we have already met Munro's Catherines with their wheels, and with these we can put the Miss "Farris" of "Changes and Ceremonies" who wheels both on the ice and off it, as do the principals in "The Moon in the Orange Street Skating Rink." Where names make a set, this may be the "Sunshine, Boylesbridge, Turnaround" (3) through which Ben Jordan peddles his wares in "Walker Brothers Cowboy."

As I have already noted — and as the trio of names here may suggest — there is something ternary about circles. A line has only two real points, its beginning and end; a circle has not only these two (coinciding, of course) but a third, since the middle of its course has the distinct identity of a turning-point. Thus we begin to experience reversal in a cyclical story: comedy and tragedy are more complex than in their linear forms, being either a movement from prosperity through adversity to renewed prosperity or a corresponding movement starting and ending with adversity. There is no irony unless this is irony, but we do have the sense that things have finished where they began when they might have finished somewhere else. Cyclical stories include all those in which that happens: a hero is drawn into an alien experience and comes back to being more or less what he was to start with. There are for instance all the cautionary tales in which someone makes a mistake and, like Chaunticleer in Chaucer's *Nun's Priest's Tale*, is spared from permanent consequences. If the hero does not fall into error, a cyclical story may be that of a successfully undergone test, once again of an untransforming kind: to the extent that, say, Captain McWhir in *Typhoon* is confirmed in his stolidity by the ordeal of the story, *Typhoon* is cyclical. In Munro's own work a story like "Red Dress — 1946" becomes cyclical when read in the same way. While the heroine nearly gives in to a tempter, she comes back to herself just in time, and at the end is left reflecting on her success after near-failure. In "The Office," similarly, the narrator is tried by the ingratiating and accusing Mr. Malley, and is finally able to extricate herself from him — to see no more in the story than that. More tragically, a cyclical story is one of ascent and fall on Fortune's wheel; in a less allegorical form it is something like Hudson's *Green Mansions*, in which we can see the hero as finding a treasure and then simply losing it. The Del of the Garnet French story can be seen in the same way, and so, more definitively, can her mother: for the thrusting Mrs. Jordan, like her own stories, is doomed to go "round and round" (79) without really getting anywhere.

A remarkably common form of the cyclical story in Munro is the visit: again and again we find her characters physically going to an Other Place and returning. This happens in "Images," of course, and we find it equally in "Walker Brothers Cowboy," "The Photographer," "Labor Day Dinner," and "The Stone in the Field," to mention only a few obvious examples. Conversely, we may have a visit from rather than to the Other Place, as in the story actually called "Visitors"; somewhat more complex is the return visit to an original home, as in "The Peace of Utrecht" or "The Ottawa Valley," where the old home takes on the role of Other Place. All such stories may remind us of a comparison I have already suggested, between narrative cyclicity and a static counterpart in the world of metaphor. If we can say that Home is what it is by virtue of the Other Place, like Mary being herself by virtue of Elizabeth, we might say in more narrative terms that Home is a place we know when we have gone to the Other Place for a visit.

After such a visit there will be a homecoming, something we have already considered in a different context. A less spatial term that I will be using for this experience is "normalization": since the place we are coming back to, even at its most uncivil, is by definition Home, the return always means a renewed homeliness after whatever was glamorous or uncanny or simply unknown about the Other Place. In "Images," for instance, homeliness is the plain supper in the family house after whisky in a madman's den; in "Age of Faith" it is the mundane Flats Road after the thrills of religion in town. Often in Munro the thrills have been sexual, and so we find Rose, after her affair with Simon, sitting in a roadside café and seeing the world again without its temporary erotic glamour; or we have the lovelorn narrator of "Bardon Bus," sitting in a bakery and noticing the ordinary people whose world she is now going to rejoin. Disillusioned but reassured, these protagonists are always in a sense returning from truth to reality: they are like Del coming back to "real life" (242) after the enchantment of Garnet French, or, less sexually, Del's mother doing the same thing after her wild attempts to sell encyclopaedias to the farmers. And as Mrs. Jordan comes back, tired and acquiescent, she murmurs lines from "a poem about going in the same door as out she went" (69):[28] the cyclical recognition, while something more — and more surprising — than the linear awareness of sheer arrival, is not more than the awareness of being back where you started.

We will need two new characters for a cyclical story. At its centre, where we now have a definite Other Place, we will have in a personal form the figure I am going to call the Stranger: not necessarily someone strange in himself, but deriving a quality of strangeness from his location if nothing else. We will soon be seeing how, for reasons having to do with our next narrative figure, the Stranger tends to come as two contrasting characters, but it is not impossible to find cases in Munro where a single if ambiguous person has this role to himself. A good specimen, and a stranger in the ordinary sense as well, is the mysterious clergyman whom Rose meets on her train-ride in "Wild Swans." Chris Watters in "How I Met My Husband" is a single Stranger again: someone who appears in the middle of a story only to disappear later — and, like the clergyman, an object of wonder for an inexperienced adolescent.

Polarized against the Stranger is the figure I will call the Neighbour: someone in whom the Initiator and the Finisher of the linear story are combined. In "Images" Joe Phippen plays Stranger, representing the wild Other Place; an obvious Neighbour is Mary McQuade, the presiding figure at home from whom the travellers escape and to whom they return. In cyclical experience there is no difference between such a figure as found before and after the encounter at the

Other Place. What matters is simply that the narrator's experience of the Neighbour be interrupted: Blaikie Noble, seen in this way, reappears as the same Blaikie after a long absence. It is the Stranger's role to provide, in one way or another, the means by which this return comes about. The encounter with Joe Phippen prepares the child in "Images" for her return to Mary McQuade, and in a more than merely physical way: after Joe the child can accept Mary, though Mary herself has not changed. The third among Eliot's quartets, *The Dry Salvages*, is a poem about going out to strange worlds, associated with a strange god whom we have found echoed in Munro.[29] It also shows us that we cannot go anywhere at all: in its own way it takes us back to the world of our Neighbours.

III. TYPOLOGY

The figures we began with — point and line — were simple ones, and instructive for just that reason; but it is not very remarkable to find them in all narrative, and this book will not spend much time noting that a Munro story is always a unit or always gets from its beginning to its end. If end and beginning coincide, that is rather more noteworthy; and if we now proceed with our series of figures, we will arrive at something that needs to be considered at some length, both because we will have to satisfy ourselves of its presence in Munro and because it is more complex in itself.

We can best start with some concrete examples. In "The Flats Road" Del Jordan — to take the story as her story here[30] — goes out as it were from the reliable world of her family to the chaotic one of Uncle Benny, with its great marital convulsion. She then returns home again; at the end she is tucked safely into bed, and the disturbing adventure she has watched is starting to fade into legend. Yet even as this is happening, something else happens: the strange and the familiar become one. Reflecting on Benny's homecoming, Del has seen his world as the opposing mirror-image to her family's: "lying alongside our world was Uncle Benny's world like a troubling distorted reflection, the same but never at all the same" (25). Now, as she lies in bed on stormy nights, the two worlds which are not the same impress her by their sameness — the Jordans live where Benny lives, in a tiny vessel on a dangerous sea.

What comes here as an unsettling intimation within a general movement of cyclical return and reassurance may come much more insistently in other stories. In "Age of Faith" Del has an Anglican church for her Other Place and, when she is done with God, the Flats Road house again for Home. This last is much less domestic than in "The Flats Road" itself:

> The house . . . was so dirty that it no longer had to be a house at all; it was like some sheltered extension of the out-of-doors. The pattern of the kitchen linoleum was lost; dirt itself made a pattern. . . . The whole place smelled of fox. There would be no fire in the stove till evening and the door stood open. (111)

And so it is a strange place to be after the house of God — except that the particular house of God selected by Del was curiously similar. The shabby little Anglican church has no furnace; a bleak sky looks in through plain windows; the only floor-covering is a little brown matting; the pulpit banner is threadbare; there is a smell of "mould or mice" (100). Above all, there is an air of sacrifice about the dark Christ over the communion table, just as there is in the Flats Road house where foxes are skinned: for all its beauty of ritual and air of remote sanctity, the church is not really a different place. Del herself may not be as distinctly aware of this as a reader, but there is something else that forces itself brutally on her awareness. The God who finally horrified her in the church is like her mild father at home — both are revered, both are killers.

Now we can go back to "Images" again. The "no man's land" (43) of Joe Phippen is much like the world of Uncle Benny: a savage region of hunter and hunted, of men without families, of loneliness and apparitions. Home is of course the family house, tidy and safe with a warm supper waiting. And yet Home here is not just homely: it is a house of death, associated with the doomed grandfather and more immediately with the mysteriously ailing mother and the fearsome Mary McQuade. In fact the little girl of the story finds Mary's strictness as formidable as Joe's savagery. Or we can see the situation the other way around: Joe's hospitality, however primitive, is like the ministrations of Mary the efficient practical nurse. Both Joe and Mary are terrors; both are providers; both, as the child learns by watching her father, can be teased and placated and deceived. And there is a still more fundamental way in which their worlds can be seen as the same. When the returning child looks at her house from a new angle, she sees a door sealed against the winter wind: the house has been shut for fear something will get in. Mary's tough good housekeeping is rooted in the same fear; so, the child has just discovered, is Joe's fierce defending of his filthy burrow. Mary has no use for Joe, needless to say, and yet the two are really a match — as Ben sagely observes. The opposites, in other words, are one in their very oppositeness:[31] that is why the child learning not to be afraid of Joe is also learning not to be afraid of Mary. By the same token, Home is the Other Place and the Other Place is Home; the Stranger is the Neighbour and the Neighbour is the Stranger: we have reached a narrative counterpart of the static coinherence whereby Elizabeth in being herself is also being Mary.[32]

We are coming, then, to see an intensely paradoxical kind of identification as something reached through a series of events. When I tried at the start of this book to show that an Ontario small town might also be far-off Marrakesh, I treated that fact simply as implicit throughout Munro's story — which it is; but now we can review what happens in that story. Jeanette has arrived for a visit, feeling as wilted as her hostess Dorothy; Dorothy impulsively invites the next-door neighbour for an evening drink, and in the resulting exhilaration Jeanette tells her Marrakesh anecdote. A tale about a geographical Other Place, that is, appears in what is also an Other Place in the narrative structure. Later in the night, when things have circled back to normal, Dorothy sees her two guests making love: and at this point the identity of the opposite worlds becomes clear — emotionally for Dorothy and more conceptually, perhaps, for the reader. The enclosed room in the desert city is a glassed porch in Ontario; the dark and passionate Arab is the stricken Blair King; and, to stay with the events of the foreground story, the nervous chatter of the central episode was the same sexual reaching out that Dorothy now sees in a more manifest form.

And this is amazing, in a way that none of our previous ways of reading has shown us.[33] Beyond any cyclical experience of surprise in homecoming, it has the full irony, tragic or comic, of getting what you bargained for and discovering that it is something else — or getting something else and discovering that it is what you bargained for.[34] As various touches in "Marrakesh" indicate, Dorothy wants something to happen; she is left unsatisfied by the gin-and-tonic flirtation during the evening; then, when the matter seems concluded, something does happen — and not at all what she had consciously planned. The irony here is not essentially different from that when, say, Oedipus gets to the cause of the Theban plague only to discover that it is himself.[35] And while in Munro's world it may not lead to physical self-mutilation, it can produce Dorothy's wild arousal at seeing the lovers on the porch, or the dismay of Del in "Age of Faith" on discovering the kind of God she has invoked. Elsewhere in Munro the experiencer may be less susceptible — all that Stella consciously feels at the end of "Lichen" is irritation — or, as always, the experience may be left mainly for the reader; and yet its basic character remains the same. "Images" can as usual serve us as a model. The little girl — as her narrating older self remarks — is like a fairy-tale heroine returned from "marvellous escapes" (43) to resume her former life "with humility and good manners": she has come full circle, in other words. But at the same time she is "dazed and powerful with secrets" — dark secrets that, paradoxically, are the source of a new self-possession. For she knows now that "our fears are based on nothing but the truth": she has gained freedom from what she dreaded, not by avoiding it but by meeting it.

*

Unfortunately there is no convenient word for a story that expresses what we are made to feel here, the differentness of the same and the sameness of the different. If "historical," for instance, carries some of the right meanings, it carries more of the wrong. It naturally suggests that the story is factual or at least based on fact: but fact is not a literary category, even if an effect of factuality can be a literary phenomenon. "Typological," while still unsatisfactory, may serve us better. Not only does the traditional idea of typology point more strongly than that of history to the relation we are now concerned with, but it can more readily be taken in a literary sense: there is no reason why one event in a story cannot be the type of another independently of their historicity. The difference between typology and "myth," in the sense of "eternal return" without the uniqueness of historical events, is for our purposes simply the difference between two narrative figures, since the eternal return is a repeating version of the circle. Typology might seem rather to be the line, proceeding as it does from one point to a different one, but it is actually a relation that combines two relations: a later event recapitulates an earlier one, and yet the two remain unique, even opposite. In a typological reading of the Christian Bible, the coming of David is recapitulated by the coming of Jesus, but on very different terms: Jesus is King of the Jews in being a King of Sorrows, executed in the end as a criminal.[36]

If we want to stay with our model of geometrical figures and their dimensions here, we can perhaps proceed as follows. When the figure of the point became that of the line, we found ourselves with two points, and a one-dimensional axis. Our circular figure brought these points together; at the same time it introduced another point and another axis, since we now had a distinct Other Place at the opposite pole from Home. It seems that at each step in our sequence the same kind of thing is going to happen: and now we find Home and the Other Place themselves to be identified, while by the same token the identity of Home as itself is more paradoxical than ever. Our model now has three dimensions, of course, allowing Home and the Other Place to be the same point in spite of their being in opposite positions in a flat projection. For our geometrical emblem, then, we seem to need a three-dimensional sphere or cube: but by now geometry has become more of a hindrance than a help. No doubt spheres and cubes make good images for the entirety of a world, which is what our new kind of story constitutes relatively to the earlier kinds: when, for instance, the visitors to the churchyard in "The Ottawa Valley" find "a large cube of dark blue granite, flecked white" (239), we are reminded of the starry universe itself. But when Munro uses such images, or similarly global names like "Mundy" and "Desmond," they are not associated with any particular narrative structure; and the reason is easy enough to see. Once again, our basic sense of narrative is linear — a story is a succession of words or events — and if a circular line is more complex than a straight one, it is hard to imagine a sphere as having anything linear at all about it, since with three dimensions we lose all sense of a line on a plane.

*

We may fare better if we shift to a different sort of figure, and in any case we will come to another important feature in the landscape of Munro's stories. When thinking of circles and spheres and cubes, it is easy to ignore a figure composed of dimensional axes themselves, the cross. Yet we associated the cross with the figure of the point, where all narrative structure seems to be implicit; and now that more complex figures have arisen, we can see their structures in terms of crossing as well. A line crosses in the simple way that a railroad crosses the continent; a circle encloses two crossing dimensions, expressed in the fact that, as a continuous perimeter, it is turned back on itself. What would be a crossing in three dimensions?

As often, we can best start with some emblems: we can think of Christ, for instance, not merely attached to the cross's intersecting arms as they lie on the ground but "lifted up"[37] by it; or we can remember the more abstract image of the *axis mundi* rising vertically out of the circling world. To see the same figure traced in time, we can go back to "Images," where I have already noted the hint of a Golgotha on the hill above the river. I have noted as well that Joe Phippen crosses the path being taken by Ben and his daughter: but the movements here are rather more complex than I indicated earlier. In the first place, we have already seen that the river takes the travellers around a curve: it has begun to do so even before Joe's arrival, so that the child loses her sense of direction — of clear onward progress, in effect. In the second place, there is a marked verticality about what happens here. First Ben reaches a high point, metaphorically and in a way literally. He has trapped a muskrat, the creature that lives in the water and burrows under the bank: in his exhilaration he swings his dead victim in the air, and his daughter sees its eyes, as well as her father's knife, gleaming in the light. Then, after more such muskrats, the light darkens and the terrain gets wilder; and suddenly Joe comes down the bank, confronting the pair and drawing them off to his dim cellar — only after this unexpected detour will they be able to resume their horizontal journey. Nor is this the only place in Munro where we have the sense of verticality impinging on a horizontal cycle. The accident in "Memorial," for instance, is no less schematic than the Joe Phippen episode: Douglas's car climbs the roadbank while going around a curve, then kills Douglas by toppling on him. Elsewhere such crossing may reduce itself to two dimensions, even two horizontal ones — in "Executioners" Howard Troy moves to cross Helena's path, in "Labor Day Dinner" the unlit car crosses in front of George's truck. But wherever the effect of shock is strong enough, we will feel what we feel when Joe Phippen attacks: a sense of movement not just turned back on itself in the cyclical way, but crossed more incisively. Or if we prefer to imagine an unbroken "story line," this will be deflected sharply off its course for a time.

Where in a story does this happen? — for we will have to see it as a function of the story's structure if it is to be more than the "flash" of the point experience by itself. Douglas's accident cannot help us here: since it occurs before the main story of "Memorial," its circumstances have a symbolic rather than structural importance. Other great crossings, though, are strongly associated with Home and the Other Place, the points at the beginning, middle, and end of a complex story. Howard Troy's accosting of Helena belongs to an opening episode; the passage of the unlit car in "Labor Day Dinner" belongs to a final one — like Dorothy's near-stroke in "Marrakesh" or the "downflash of a wing or knife" (91) in "Princess Ida." The great disruption in "Images," on the other hand, is central; and with or without imagery of vertical movement, or movement at all, something like this disruption happens constantly at the centre of Munro's stories — it is as characteristic of them as the final identifications I have called typological, and can for our purposes be associated with the same level of structural complexity.

To have a sense of its importance, we can think for a moment of great vertical shifts at centres elsewhere in literature. The most striking is no doubt that in *The Divine Comedy*: in the middle of his life's path Dante must descend to Hell and ascend to Heaven before he can complete his journey.[38] Or to enlist Eliot again, *Burnt Norton*, after its opening intimation of the timeless, takes us upward (in this case) to the top of the world-axle and then downward to its base before bringing us back to the world of more ordinary communication at the end. Such undisplaced extremes of experience are not, of course, what we expect in realistic fiction, but in their own way stories like "Images" are showing us the same central axis connecting heights and depths. If, then, we want to imagine a "three-dimensional" story as a two-dimensional story-line, it seems we will have to incorporate this axis into it. Most simply, we can reduce any two-dimensional figure to a straight line (so that the coincidence of the two Home points, and the resulting complexity of meaning, is not actually represented); then we can imagine this line as having a deviation that takes it upward from its horizontal course, abruptly downward, then back upward again to finish on its original plane. (We could have the down first and then the up, as in Dante, but the other arrangement is more appropriate for Munro.) It is this zig-zagging line that I am going to use as my main model in what follows.

Before we proceed any farther, some provisos seem in order here. Not only may we find Munro expressing the force of the "three-dimensional" in terms reduced to the two-dimensional,[39] but these levels of experience can always be felt in their continuity more than their opposition, just as a typological identification at the end of a story may be implied or diffused within a cyclical one rather than breaking into it more overtly. By the same token, we should not suppose that there are neatly "cyclical" and "typological stories," with each variety having just the appropriate features on display.

Cyclical and typological readings apply in principle to any story, since the simpler figures imply the more complex ones; and while some stories invite one reading more than another, we cannot assume that complications co-ordinate in a given explanatory scheme will stand out together in actual presentation. A different proviso has to do with the ambiguity of any centre, and of its relation to ends. In one way the centre of a story is nothing, or only the type (as we can now say) of a later realization; and in a number of Munro's stories it is this final realization that is overtly decisive, while the centre is remarkable for its unremarkableness. But if this produces a very different effect from that in "Images," the effect is an ironic one, in ways and for reasons that I will try to explain later: something is always going on at the centre.[40]

*

We are ready now to look more closely at the central axis in Munro's stories. First we come to an Other Place that seems all we could desire — or at least this is what we will come to if the reversal at the centre is going to be a descending one. At the same time we are likely to come to a new character. We have seen the Stranger appearing at the turning-point in our cyclical figure; if that point has now become an axis, there will be two Strangers here — like the two Neighbours with whom they are identified in the end. The first of these we can call the Primary Stranger: one of Munro's high and gleaming characters in this function, whether of the Mary or Elizabeth sort. If such a figure appears as an object — desirable, of course — we will have Madeleine as the lady of Uncle Benny's need, or God as the lord of Del's in "Age of Faith," or any of the various men who feature in Rose's love-life. Or the Primary Stranger may represent what one wants to be rather than possess: what Rose wants in "The Beggar Maid," for instance, is less to have Patrick than to be a queen. In other cases again, a protagonist's desire is for self-assertion, as with the writer wanting privacy in "The Office" or Rose wanting to say something forbidden in "Royal Beatings"; desire may for that matter be for escape more than attainment. But all these are plainly variants of the same thing. There is always a going out in some kind of hope: the same hope with which Ben Jordan goes to check his muskrat-traps, or Del to find God at the Anglican Church. And there is a brief time when it seems fulfilment is being reached, even (where the experience is of typological intensity) fulfilment beyond expectation.

132

Munro has some vivid evocations of this favoured time: any of her cycles, large or small, can be of use to us here, whether or not strictly central in a story. What would it feel like to be Jeanette, having a drink with the attractive Blair King and finding him so easy to talk to? Or the Spanish Lady having her own drink in the dome car high above the world and then listening to the flattering Rosicrucian? Again, what it would be like to walk on water — as, for a euphoric moment, it seems Eugene is really going to do? We even hear of people floating to the ceiling, or looking down from it like Callie above the Orange Street Skating Rink; and if most of us have never been in quite such a situation, we have all had a holiday — even, like the couple in "Bardon Bus," one "without the holiday feeling of being at loose ends" (113). As children we may have gone for a triumphant ride in a fixed-up rowboat, or been in a school operetta; later, like various of Munro's characters, we may have been happily in love.

In any such experience we seem to have one side of life without the other, an elating truth without a depressing reality: for we have entered a separate world, or half-world, as the couple in "Bardon Bus" do literally by having their affair in another hemisphere. Hence the glamour that suffuses the experience, often appearing as light; hence also a sense of rarefaction, as in the Spanish Lady's intimation of purity, or the "holiday of lightness of spirit" (113) in "Bardon Bus." And with this comes a sense of clear understanding, though this has its own mystery about it: to quote the thoughtful "Bardon Bus" narrator yet again,

> In such a short time everything seemed remarkably familiar and yet not to be confused with anything we had known in the past. . . . This familiarity was not oppressive but delightful, and there was a slight strangeness to it, as if we had come by it in a way we didn't understand. (112–13)

To think more in terms of cause and effect, there is a great feeling of luck here, even of blessing: a "flood of luck," as the narrator of "Tell Me Yes or No" puts it, "unqualified, nearly unbelieved-in" (113). At the same time there is complete reliability, as on the wonderful nights at the Orange Street Rink when "nothing went wrong, nothing could go wrong, triumph was certain" (156). With this certainty goes liberty — "we lived without responsibility, without a future, in freedom" (113), says the "Bardon Bus" narrator of her lover and herself; and they live without a past as well, since their

Canadian entanglements cannot reach them in Australia. In the terms we have been using, this can be an experience of sheer point, the moment at the top of the wheel when time seems to stop. Or, in a complementary way, time seems endless: the narrator of "Tell Me Yes or No" has only to "float upon the present, which might stretch out forever" (112). During her summer with Garnet French Del Jordan feels the same privilege, since discovery or even pregnancy is somehow out of the question — "everything we did seemed to take place out of range of other people, or ordinary consequences" (231). And so this is an experience of magical pleasure: Del's happiness on her day at the Frenches' and, from one perspective, her sense of "glory" (227) in the act of sex with which it concludes. In such a state characters may become generous, like the "Bardon Bus" couple, or forgiving, like Miss Farris on the great night of the operetta. Even if their exhilaration comes from a successful trapping, as in "Images," or speaking the unspeakable, as in "Royal Beatings," it keeps the same enchanted quality.

*

Then comes the great reversal. Making love standing up, Del and Garnet French work themselves to a fine climax: and at the moment of it they collapse helplessly. It takes longer for their affair itself to collapse — they spend some weeks in a trance-like present as summer passes by[41] — but when the further crash comes it is again violently sudden, and the whole affair seems swift enough in the light of Del's plans for a career. Felt as part of our present figure, any central reversal in Munro has the same air of swiftness, for the axis it takes us down is not so much a section of time as an intersection of it. There may, as we have seen, be a distinct core at which light and darkness are held together, but then we quickly find ourselves at the bottom of the world: on the ground like Garnet and Del, in a den like Joe Phippen's prisoners, or in the basement of the Storey house like Del again — whom Jerry Storey shoves down the cellar steps after inspecting her in the bedroom upstairs.

And so we have been thrown, most simply, from truth to reality: the thing we forgot or dismissed or imagined away, but to which we are all the more committed as a result. This is what has to be learned, for instance, by various characters in the chapter "Lives of Girls and Women" who grasp at sheer pleasure or glory (high in my present sense, though the more misbehaving of them think of it in terms of moral fall), only to find themselves with the opposite:

Perhaps nowhere but in daydreams did the trap door open so sweetly and easily, plunging bodies altogether free of thought, free of personality, into self-indulgence, mad bad licence. Instead of that, Mr. Chamberlain had shown me, people take along a good deal — flesh that is not overcome but has to be thumped into ecstasy, all the stubborn puzzle and dark turns of themselves. (174)

In "The Photographer," where she will not take the real Jubilee into her imaginary novel, Del is again confronted with what she has left behind: "It is a shock, when you have dealt so cunningly, powerfully, with reality, to come back and find it still there" (251). No doubt such a return can be found in distributions well beyond the centre of a story; but as a fall along the central axis it does not lead directly Home or beyond: it belongs to the Other Place. In the same way the character who appears at this stage is part of the more general presence that I have called the Stranger: we can call him the "Counter-Stranger" to contrast him with his Primary opposite.

First Ben Jordan exults in the sun; then Joe Phippen, the tormented earth-dweller, takes over. In "Age of Faith" God the loving Father is replaced by God the victimized Son — or more precisely, the experience of having one's prayers answered is followed by the spectacle of someone whose prayers are not. When the narrator of "Red Dress — 1946" is dropped by the athletic hero with whom luck has matched her at the dance, she is promptly scooped up by Mary Fortune, the girl we have found lurking in the washroom. For in story after story figures of the same kind appear at the point we have reached: the lonely fortune-telling woman in "Simon's Luck" who comes out of the night when Rose is expecting Simon; the dark and accosting Arab who replaces his gentler companion in Jeanette's Marrakesh story; the gloomy Eileen in "Memorial" whom Ewart encounters in the absence of the buoyant June; the Cassandra-like Nancy who comes to claim Ross in "Monsieur les Deux Chapeaux." We are already familiar with such figures, of course. Those I have just mentioned can all readily be seen as inflections of the low Mary — spirits of calamity and isolation and unbelief, people we shun as bad luck when we are feeling on top of the world. Now we are meeting them at a certain point in a story; in particular we are seeing how they beset the Other Place, drawing the visitor from its heights to its depths. And they do so outside Munro as well — figures as varied in other ways as the despised Magwitch who reappears from an underworld in *Great*

Expectations, the mysterious Mariana who replaces the angelic Isabella in *Measure for Measure*, or the aptly named Poor Tom who receives Lear on his fall from assurance.

*

And so the Stranger has split into a pair of opposites; if distinction, moreover, leads to identification, we can expect that to happen here as well. To draw once again on "Images," we can note that Ben the muskrat-trapper is not so different after all from his adversary, Joe the trapped rat. Not only is the turning of the tables equally the trading of their roles, but both roles seem already to belong to each. There is an air of failure about Ben's very competence: he has escaped to the river — for the last time, perhaps — because, like similar men in Munro, he feels increasingly trapped at home.[42] Conversely, Joe is a king-rat with all the wiliness of one, or the greater wiliness of human paranoia. As he makes his lightning attack, the narrator at first sees only a head, then "clever" (37) legs: Joe the holed-up animal is also a man galvanized by an obsession. There is duality, again, in the two Neighbours we expect at our present level of complexity. The ominous Mary McQuade of the beginning is plainly different from the more manageable one at the end; but the early one has a second self — the outdoors Mary without the white uniform and the dark smell, the lumbering woman who, while bossy enough, wheezes and complains of overwork. Nor does the Mary of the end simply lose her frightening quality: rather, as we have seen, the narrator learns how not to be frightened. In "Something I've Been Meaning to Tell You" there are two Chars: the young one whom Et sees lying with Blaikie, and the much older one whom Et finds dead. On the other hand the first Char looked strangely pallid, inert, and repulsive, while the second is a queen in her glory; and in fact both are the same corrupted and incorruptible beauty.[43]

But if this is so, the world is getting very complicated. It is as if we were being drawn toward yet another narrative figure in which we would have two distinct Primary Strangers, two distinct Counter-Strangers, and so on, all demanding to be made into one. With each step we took, there would be more characters to be identified; at the same time we are coming to see individual characters as containing more and more, so that — to take one view of the matter — a single comprehensive figure is starting to loom ahead of us. The Ben Jordan of "Images," for instance, has the capacity to be many people. He is a good fellow and a killer, a family man and a loner; he is a protector against both Joe and Mary yet also an alien threat, as his daughter senses from his boots:

> His boots . . . had an expression that was dogged and uncompromising, even brutal, and I thought of that as part of my father's look, the counterpart of his face, with its readiness for jokes and courtesies. (36)

It is worth noting that the brown god of Eliot's *Dry Salvages*, whom we have found echoed in Mary McQuade, is also present in the Ben whose boots are "temporarily discarded, waiting" (36). And of course Joe Phippen is waiting — the unpredictable savage who lives by the swollen river. Among Munro's papers[44] is the sketch of an epilogue for this story: Ben's daughter visits him years later, after the death of the mother, and finds him living in lonely squalor. The Ben we knew primarily as a decent married man has turned into someone manifestly like his old antagonist Joe Phippen — or, if we want, into someone who unites Joe's union of wildness and domesticity with the same union in the family Ben still represents.[45]

By now the most dauntless reader must be feeling a sense of crisis, like Janet in the Planetarium faced with the "innumerable repetitions, innumerable variations" (231) of the Universe. The identity expressed by our successive narrative figures, as by our successive static relations, is one in which a person is increasingly someone else in being himself, with the result that we seem lost in an endless complication of splitting and fusing. To have something more concrete to imagine, we can suppose a troupe of actors taking various roles from which they remain distinct at the same time. Munro's company are an extremely versatile lot: they trade and double and divide their parts to the point where we might as well say that any of them can play any part or parts whatever — that we are watching a metamorphic sort of theatre in which forms endlessly take new bodies and bodies new forms.

*

We have seen how the casting is done for an individual story like "Images"; it may also help us, or alert us, to note the same procedure as applied in the company's larger repertory. At the risk of anticipation, we can compare "Images" here with two closely allied stories, one of which I have been drawing on throughout this chapter. In "Age of Faith" Del goes for a time to the Anglican Church in town, where she enters into dealings with God; later she finds him, typologically, in the house on the Flats Road. But in the first place we can note the ambiguity of roles in this story taken by itself. Even within the Other Place of religion God is two persons, a Father and a Son, and these trade roles in a way we are now becoming familiar with. The Father is supreme and unbending — indeed merciless at the crisis; the Son is a lowly sufferer. At the same time, the Son looks "regal" (98) enough as depicted over the altar, whereas the Father, as we will be seeing, is terrible because he is secretly helpless. And if God is thus double and self-mirroring, he also mirrors Del's father. Mr. Jordan, in spite of his rough surroundings, is a "luminously sane" (108) man; when he shoots the family dog, he does so for utterly reasonable reasons. Yet in a dream he appears to Del as the same homicidal maniac she has found God to be: it is this God and man, victor and victim, sane and insane, who dismays Del at the end even more than when she saw him simply as God during the Good Friday service. If we look more closely at Del herself we may feel a similar dismay: for she herself plays God to her younger brother Owen, forcing him to do and believe as she wills. Owen, for that matter, plays God to his cutout hockey players — who themselves play to win, of course.

Now we can compare "Age of Faith" with "The Time of Death." In the latter God the Father is not directly a member of the cast: his role is taken by the talented Patricia, who at the central reversal scalds her trusting younger brother to death. But while Patricia is fully adequate to such a role, she is a very different player from her counterpart: not a lofty sky-god but the daughter of a poor family on the outskirts of town. In this way she is more like Del in "Age of Faith," as she is in other ways as well: Del at times plays patrician with Owen, Patricia at the end is dismayed like Del. But then Patricia is far from being dismayed in the central incident — it is her mother Leona who takes Del's role of shocked spectator here, turning from her daughter as Del turns from God. Benny, the innocent victim, is reminiscent of the unsuspecting Owen; but Benny would never act God the Father as Owen does with his hockey players — it is the other children, George and Irene, whom we find "playing their cut-out game, cutting things out of the catalogue" (92). If we compare the endings of the two stories, we will again find simple correspondence eluding us. What disturbs Del is, primarily, a serene killer and a helpless, duped believer. What disturbs Patricia is neither of these, but old Brandon with his "crownless felt hat" (98) and mournful call:

someone, in other words, like the suffering king pictured over the altar — though Brandon's association with sharpened blades suggests a killer as well as a victim, even someone like the butcher Mr. Jordan. Patricia herself, who has in effect skinned her younger brother, now turns into just what a blade might be used on, "a wretched little animal insane with rage or fear" (99). (At the same time the animal mentioned is a ferret — a hunter.)

If we go back briefly to "Images" with these variations in mind, the first thing that may occur to us is that the central killer here is someone most like the Son in "Age of Faith": the miserable Joe Phippen, who pursues Ben Jordan the triumphant Father. Since Joe also lives in poverty and attacks because he feels oppressed, he is much like Patricia — except that in other ways he is her opposite, having no desire to be a star and no aversion to dirt. It is Mary McQuade, rather, who plays Patricia's role of bossy, short-tempered housekeeper; it is Mary who at the end wants the slovenly and the socially inconvenient put out of the way — Joe himself in this case. The narrator of the story plays the role of bewildered spectator, and yet at the end she is neither the crazed Patricia nor the embarrassed Del: she has learned what a high God knows — the power that lies in concealment and restraint — and calmly takes up her new weapons. If we turned from all these stories to "The Flats Road," we would again find a Benny, a brutalized child, a mad attacker, animals who are doomed to the skinning-knife, animals who kill their own young: but we would find the roles distributed and combined in another way again.

One can protest that these are very different stories, and of course they are; but there is reason to feel that there is a single story here as well, and the varying of the same that we have just found meets us whenever we put Munro's stories side by side. (One result, for anyone studying them as they appear, is that each new arrival seems both familiar and surprising.) In the rest of this book I will have to ask readers to note Munro's multiple casting for themselves: to remain aware of it even where my business is to bring out her stories' other aspect of likeness. For we will be needing to live with multiplicity for some time; on the other hand — to return to our narrative figures — the degree of it we reached with the double Ben and the double Joe can stand well enough for any beyond itself, and there seems no point in expending ingenuity on hypothetical complications. What is more important is to return to the mysterious Counter-Stranger: there is something to be learned here that may show us where narrative complication is leading.

IV. THE COMFORTER

In our typological story we have been drawn off our main course onto a different path, which has led us to a strangely elevated sort of Other Place in one direction and a strangely abased one in the other, inhabited by Munro's losers and doubters and bringers of bad luck. But we have just been finding something very double about these Counter-Strangers, and this doubleness has implications we will need to consider further. It is not just that Joe Phippen is a victor as well as a victim. He is content, even proud, to be living in his snug Lair — to use a word I will be applying to the habitat of any Counter-Stranger; and if you make terms with him, he comports himself there not only as a captor but as a host. So does the Mary Fortune who invites her new acquaintance for a friendly smoke and a talk: indeed all Munro's janitors and bobbies and fortune-tellers might reveal an agreeable side if we knew them better.

No doubt we should be wary of their agreeableness, since the reasons for it may be unsavoury ones. Mary Fortune wants to lure the narrator away from her normal role in life; Nora Cronin, taking Ben Jordan in after the humiliations of his sales-round,[46] is equally a temptress; shelters at corresponding points in other stories, such as the room in Marrakesh, often turn out to be traps of various kinds. Behind Nora's excitement, moreover, it is easy enough to sense something else, a Counter-Stranger's desperation. The festivities in Bert Matthews's hotel room, while no doubt different in style, have the same *Galgenhumor* about them: something not too different from the leap of Joe Phippen's drunken tomcat. Other such carryings-on may not be so clearly fated, but they can have a similar air of defiance. An important complex of images in Munro shows us revelling in places that, in one way or another, are really jails of necessity. In "An Ounce of Cure" and "Oh, What Avails" we hear about dancing in an armoury; other stories — including "Red Dress," of course — have a dance at a school, perhaps "the stone school."[47] This last as we find it in "Walking on Water" offers a related form of entertainment as well, since there is a sex demonstration at the entry to one of the toilets, as also in "Privilege." From here the complex loses itself in more general manifestations: there are the high-jinks, for instance, to which the children in "The Found Boat" dare each other in an abandoned railway station (and which include urinating and taking off their clothes); or in "Walking on Water" there is the love-making at the foot of the stairs — a common location for a Lair in Munro.

Perhaps all this is just bravado: perhaps it is Mary Fortune making the best of her unacceptability and wanting another failure to keep her company.

But we need not always, or only, see Counter-Strangers and their hideouts in such an unflattering light: once again, their offer of comfort can be quite sincere. Mary Fortune and Joe Phippen are both acting as friends, whatever else they may be; and if we want a clear case of negative and positive combined in a single character, we can think of Eileen in "Memorial," the woman whose embrace is for Ewart that of darkness itself but also of someone genuinely "hospitable" (223). The Suicide Woman at the party in "Simon's Luck" who says "Wake Up" and offers Rose her "sly intimacy" (157) is, within the structure of the party, offering a comparable hospitality.

In these last cases we have the offering of death itself: but now we will need to see a displacement of one aspect from another that, as we go along, will increasingly prove a displacement in time as well. In the first place we should notice that a number of Munro's Comforters, as I shall call them, are like Joe Phippen: captors first but then helpers. Indeed we often find the Counter-Stranger splitting into two separate and successively dominant figures. The Finnish woman, a more emblematic counterpart of Eileen or the Suicide Woman, is soon finished — the vigilant Et drives her out of town; Et herself then cares for Arthur when the antics of another finish woman, Char, have delivered him into her hands. Nor is Et the only rescuer of this kind. Mrs. Peebles rescues Edie from the onslaught of Alice Kelling; in the funeral episode of "Heirs of the Living Body" Del is rescued from the onslaught of Mary Agnes Oliphant by her aunts as well as her mother. And in cases like these it becomes especially clear what kind of shift we are dealing with. If a first Counter-Stranger is usually a dark Mary, Mary is now giving way to Elizabeth, just as she does when Munro's bustling second wives and younger sisters and practical nurses take charge. For these regularly play Comforter (generally within a larger story containing the immediate one, as with Mary McQuade), after death or illness has brought a reversal.[48]

In this light we can better understand the individual Marys who prove — perhaps first at this point, perhaps at the corresponding point in their own earlier stories — to have an Elizabeth in them waiting to burst out. This is true of Kay Stringer in "An Ounce of Cure," as we have already seen.[49] If Kay, like Eileen, is a wild girl who appears "by accident" (82), the accident seems not only fatal but propitious: for Kay turns out to be a Comforter looking for someone to comfort. Mary Fortune may be a loser, but she again refuses to lose. "Here was someone who had suffered the same defeat as I had — I saw that — but she was full of energy and self respect. She had thought of other things to do" (157), including, of course, the gathering in of the narrator. Even Robina in "Executioners," the Mary who strikes Helena down in a fit of mania, promptly turns into the restoring normalizer who is her other self. She does so more grumpily than Kay Stringer, no doubt; Mrs. Malley in "The Office" is simply listless tidying up after Mr. Malley. But to the extent that they do tidy up, these Marys all have the spirit of Elizabeth inside them, refusing to let the world fall apart.[50] To mention one male counterpart here, they are like Buddy Shields in the final episode of "Postcard" — the bobby who first rounds up the crazed Helen and then turns guardian, plying her with comradely advice as his name suggests he would.

*

Buddy does this in the squad car that is his own kind of lair — even, we could say, his stone school: but now it seems that stone schools can be something more than prisons, with or without riots. Earlier in the same story it is a Comforter who is named Alma Stonehouse, and in "Labor Day Dinner" the owner of a "little stone dairy house" (142) is the all-comforting Valerie. In other words, the Counter-Stranger's special place is as ambiguous as the Counter-Stranger. A Lair, we often find, can take on the glamour of a play-house: Joe's den almost does so for the child in "Images," while Valerie's dairy is a secluded and charming place that it would be fun as much as work to turn into a "studio." And if comfort separates even further from necessity, we may have not only a Lair but a distinct place that I am going to call a Refuge.

One form taken by separateness here is that of an underworld divided into compartments. Munro often shows us not just a single space like Joe Phippen's, but a whole sequence of rooms and passages — suggesting its own miniature story. In "Heirs of the Living Body," for instance, the storeroom where Mary Agnes awaits Del is down a hall and through a door, in an old part of the house that seems a different building "tacked on" (53). This Lair is already a Refuge as well: Del has fled from the parlour at the front door where her dead uncle is lying, and now she finds herself in a kind of "doll's house"

(54) crammed with old implements and furnishings. When she passes from Mary Agnes — herself a Comforter in one aspect — into the hands of rescuing elders, she is taken to a further sort of Refuge: Uncle Craig's office off the hall, the room in which she is left to recuperate. In "Red Dress — 1946" the washroom to which the narrator makes her retreat belongs again to a whole complex of rooms: beyond it lies "a dark closet full of mops and pails" (156), beyond that again the janitor's room. And here we find a complex within a complex, since beyond the janitor's room itself there is a partition, a flight of stairs, and finally a closet on the next floor.

Perhaps we can generalize about such places by saying that there tends to be a relatively public antechamber, a passage, and a more secluded place beyond that. In "The Moon in the Orange Street Skating Rink," for instance, the rink can itself be seen as an interior world; within this world there is a more special one, the manager's hot and smoky retreat "beyond the men's toilet and changing room" (140). There are any number of variants — the toilet, closet, or stairs, for instance, can function as any of the chambers we have distinguished; but in one way or another an underworld is showing itself to be a bower "beyond" being a prison.[51] The janitorial figure inhabiting this place is similarly a king beyond being a prisoner or a servant. His own room may be any of the various compartments here (no doubt the most Janus-like of these is a medial closet with doors on both sides, as in "Red Dress"): but in any case the underworld, with its secret rites and privileges, belongs to him — it is like Mary Agnes Oliphant's "place of her own" (45), revealed to Del at an appropriate point in "Heirs of the Living Body" (45). When Lear descends to Poor Tom's hovel, we can recall, the two presently make their way to a somewhat kinder place, where they set themselves up as the world's rulers, not victims.

What happens here, in a subterranean version, is the meeting we have seen in other cameras: coming here is also coming together. In fact this is already true of the entry into the Lair, but when Lair is distinguished from Refuge, it is the latter that will be the place of union, and certainly of conviviality. The manager's room in "The Moon in the Orange Street Skating Rink" serves as a gathering-place for an inner circle; and while one sex, as often, is getting away from the other here, it may also be the two sexes themselves that do the uniting. We have seen un-comforting and un-recessed versions of this — the public fornication at the entry to a toilet in both "Privilege" and "Walking on Water." But the sex glimpsed under the stairs in the latter story seems more agreeable for both parties, and when Eileen in "Memorial" has sex with her brother-in-law in the back-seat of a car (having proceeded from a bathroom through a kitchen to a garage), she is being not only private but welcoming.[52] In other cases the hint of sexuality is mainly in the arrangement of the rooms themselves: in "Red Dress," for instance, we find movement through a mop-and-pail closet and a partition to a flight of stairs. It is not that the narrator's relation to Mary Fortune is sexual in any immediate way — simply that an encounter in the more privy parts of a building can always be associated with sexual union if one wants. And in any case it is union: we reach a kind of consummation on underworld terms when we have failed to do so on those of a higher world.

In the last cases I have mentioned, an exclusive and intimate meeting takes place in a confined recess: what is more remarkable is that the same place can suggest a whole world, physical and social. A specially rich example occurs in Munro's non-fictional "Working for a Living," where, at the bottom of one of the story's reversals, her father takes a job as caretaker and night-watchman in a foundry. As usual Munro wants us to know the layout: there is a caretaker's room off — or perhaps on — a passage from the office into the main building, and beyond that the foundry proper opens up, equally "my domain" (39) the way the father presents it. This is of course still a prison — the place where men work for a living, a dark, tomb-like world of iron and sand; and the work itself is a "never-ending time-consuming life-consuming process" (41). Yet this place is also one in which the father feels "serious pleasure," not to say solidarity with his mates. And for all its interior quality, his domain is a very comprehensive one — at first resembling a forest or a town, Munro says, with lights like street-lamps at the meetings of its passage-ways. In fact lights above the darkness can suggest something larger again, a Virgilian underworld provided with heavens of its own. Certainly this foundry, with its clutter of apparatus and blue-painted windows, is much like another of Munro's Lair-Refuges, the storeroom at Jenkin's Bend that for Del is at once a womb, a tomb, and a great egg filled with blue light. If we take the hints offered us in some other stories, the Universe itself may be such a Refuge in one aspect — just as it is a stone school in another.[53]

V: RECOGNITION

The foundry in "Working for a Living" can epitomize much that we have been seeing. It is a kind of jail but also a sanctuary; its denizen is a Mary-like caretaker but also one who feels an Elizabeth's pride and pleasure in his work. We even have an inkling of someone more presidential — recalling Janet's dying father at a corresponding point in "The Moons of Jupiter," seated at his ease in a hospital room, or the dream-Flo in "Spelling" enthroned in a cage and uttering "clear authoritative" (184) words. It befits such a dignitary to be gracious — Janet's father is an "affable host" (232) — and in "Working for a Living" there is the bottle that, on Friday nights, the men at the foundry often share in the caretaker's room, just as there is Joe Phippen's whisky and candy or Mary Fortune's cigarettes. But along with this shift to comfort comes a greater shift. We have found social sacraments occurring at the heart of a story: as we move outward they become less decisive and more diffusive. Food and drink, if they appear at this stage, are a matter of relaxation, and in any case what we have here may be something less physical: the play and talk that often develop at a meal or follow it.[54] People get into games; or they recite poetry or tell tales or simply chat; the chat itself, perhaps starting with immediate practicalities, drifts out to more universal matters — fate, fortune, ghosts, religion, happiness.[55]

Rose lying alone in her bedroom can hardly get into conversation, any more than Del in her uncle's office, but we find each of them expatiating to herself in much the same way, happily or unhappily. Del arrives at something like a "mystic's" (57) vision of the imprisoning flesh; Rose, more at peace, has a vision of freedom — she is going to die, or perhaps she will kill herself or run away from home, as she pleases, but in any case she need never go back to her hated elders. Mary Fortune's plans for a career, if more realistic in themselves, have much the same imagining quality: another loser is floating free of her immediate predicament.[56] And it is significant that Mary describes her plans while sitting part way up the stairs, for at this stage of things characters often find their way from the depths to some such elevated place. We have just seen Rose lying in an upstairs bedroom; the children in "The Time of Death" do the same thing after the great crisis in that story; so does Lydia Cooper in "Dulse" after her evening at the guest-house. And all such characters feel as Rose does: having had to face a crisis, they now pass to a detachment in which they can reflect more freely on their experience

— even perhaps on all experience. Some of them, we find, have a room with a view.[57]

*

As we move out from the heart of the Other Place, then, we enter a region of vision: a region, we can add, with rather uncertain affiliations to the one we are leaving. Vision may see, and share, the failure shown to it by a pure Counter-Stranger; it may see something quite different, a restoration shown perhaps by a distinct Comforter; it may even turn away from whatever is limited in the Comforter's own view of things, as when Almeda Roth in "Meneseteung" turns from Jarvis Poulter to her vision of the river. In cases like this last especially, we begin to feel that we are in territory foreign to the Other Place altogether, if also to the Home we will soon be re-entering: this seems to be a country in its own right, a distinct phase of our story.[58] Such countries can be found in various structural positions, for action and vision repeatedly alternate as a story ripples out from its centre. Phases of vision may be peripheral ones — typological late recognitions, for instance, or simply homecoming visions in a cyclical model. Inside a story they will of course be transitional, but just how many transitions there will be for them to occupy is a further question, its answer depending in principle on the complexity of our structural model.[59] In practice, however, it seems best to imagine four main locations for vision, each with a character of its own.

Since the two peripheral visions will concern us in later chapters, we can be brief in dealing with them here. What we can call the commencing vision — as contrasted with that on the way to the Other Place — fixes the world of the story in the first place, at once pointing back before that world and defining the conditions of any action within it. At the beginning of "Images," for example, the child is recalling the death of her grandfather and with it the establishing of "my grandma's house" (30); we also hear of the invasion, now repeating itself, of the dreaded Mary McQuade. Answering this first vision is a story's final recognition — what is usually meant by recognition generally. Often in Munro this comes in a distinct epilogue, and if that does not quite happen in "Images," the return to Mary from Joe Phippen, as we have seen, does bring with it a new understanding. Most intensely, the child sees typologically that the world of the story is that of Joe and Mary acting as one: seeing this, she is ready to go on to a further world. But she has also had her vision at Joe's — typologically, a sense of two Joes as one — and this is a more interior affair. It is also, structurally, a concentration of the final vision, and the same thing, in an opposite way, is true of the vision preceding rather than ending a central complex. Both cases, in other words, show us the problem of "the story proper" again — does it begin, in the case of "Images," when Ben invites his daughter on his trap-round, or with her mother's illness and Mary's second arrival? At any rate, we may well feel the visions flanking the centre of a story as interior, and in being that they have a special character that needs describing.

*

Preceding the centre, there is what we find in "The Peace of Utrecht" when Helen, having made the long trip from the coast to Jubilee, arrives with her children outside the family house — the house she has not seen since before her mother's death. No doubt this arrival is more closely attached to the following visit than to their earlier setting out — a transitional experience is readily pulled one way or the other — and yet the arrival remains something on its own: the travellers cannot yet feel the reality of Jubilee, and so experience the same double awareness that we have found in Rose turning back (in her case) to the world. For Helen's little daughter, this is the doubleness of the imagined and the real, "the flatness and strangeness of the moment in which is revealed the source of legends, the unsatisfactory, apologetic and persistent reality" (197). For Helen herself, coming to a Home that is now an Other Place, the house like its neighbours seems familiar and unfamiliar, "plausible but unreal" (196). It is of course the house she once knew, but looking "closed, bare, impoverished" (197) from the fact, mainly, of its being empty — for her sister Maddy is at work, no-one being now required to look after the sisters' dying mother. When Helen goes to enter, signs cluster at the threshold: there is a note from Maddy with an ominous secondary meaning; there is a bouquet of "phlox," suggestively enough in this story about an outer and inner heatwave. Above all, there is the image that confronts Helen when she absently-mindedly turns to listen for her mother's voice: for she finds herself looking into a mirror, facing a woman — and a mother — where she had once faced a girl. Helen is seeing as she has never seen before, and will not see again once an old notebook has re-naturalized her in her former world.

Helen's experience may recall others of the same kind — what we can call approaching visions to distinguish them, if only in context, from commencing ones. As Ben Jordan and his daughter, having left their house, cross the field leading down to the river, she becomes distinctly aware of his boots. And vision here is again double, for the child has a sense both of her father's mildness and of the roughness that the boots suggest to her; it is this latter, of course, that is coming to the fore as they near the river and the trap-line. There is the same premonitory quality about Chris Watters in "How I Met My Husband," standing dark against the light at the kitchen door.[60] Other such apparitions belong more overtly to journeys: for the family on its trip in "Miles City, Montana" there is a dead deer and a children's song, unsettling if one thinks of what it says; for the youngsters in "The Ottawa Valley" there is "Bob Hope" (228), a soldier on a train who throws out a dead-pan challenge. In some cases — Del Jordan entering the Gay-la Dance Hall in the Bert Matthews story, or the writer in "The Office" mounting Mr. Malley's stairs — there is a sense of sheer unreality, perhaps accompanied by foreboding as in "The Turkey Season." Experiences of this kind correspond to the preliminary visions and tests (often the same thing) confronting heroes of legend on their way to central actions. And they readily make whole stories of their own: in Munro "Wild Swans" and "Eskimo," to mention two specially clear examples, both have as their main subjects dream-like encounters (and an actual dream in the latter case) on the way to an unfamiliar world.

In Munro, however, the approaching vision tends to be less elaborate than that on the other side of the central action: what a heroine sees on her way home. Since we have already introduced ourselves to this in relation to Munro's Refuges, it may be enough here to mention a few cases where the sense of transition is specially strong in itself. "The Spanish Lady" as a whole, concentrating on an odd meeting and revelation during the retreat from a failed marriage, can be thought of as a returning vision. Episodes like this occur inside stories as well, though they are less likely to contain meetings than to make vivid the emptiness in which strange meetings might happen. In "The Ferguson Girls Must Never Marry" Bonnie walks by herself across town: the funeral, with its shattering reversal of plans, is over, but her final encounter with Ted Braddock is yet to come. Along with the sense of the familiar turned strange that we found in "The Peace of Utrecht," what Bonnie experiences is at once numbness and unusual awareness: as she goes along, listening to her own footsteps, she realizes the total indifference to which her life has brought her. Walking home through the cemetery after her quarrel with Garnet

French, Del Jordan feels a desolation of much the same kind.[61]

At the other extreme a heroine may experience a sense of freedom and renewal, like Rose after her royal beating: Del in the Bert Matthews section of "Baptizing," having escaped from a Refuge that proved to be an imprisoning Lair, walks home with an almost rapturous — if residually alcoholic — sense of illumination. In less realistic kinds of literature, the positive returning vision — which may not be clearly distinguished from a Refuge vision — gives us all the Delectable Mountains and Houses of Holiness in romance, to which the hero comes between an exhausting, perhaps failed, central ordeal and the final action toward which he is still bound. It is here that he is restored and re-enlightened — perhaps disciplined as well, like Spenser's Redcrosse. At this stage we may even find an anticipatory vision of glory, like Redcrosse's sight of the New Jerusalem; more tragically, the experience will continue and intensify that of the Counter-Stranger's Lair — as in distinct literary encounters with Despair, or Hamlet's bleak musings between his return from the underworld of England and his duel with Laertes.

*

As the elaborateness of some of these examples would suggest, returning visions, like approaching ones, can easily expand to become stories — or counter-stories — in their own right, with all the structural possibilities we have seen in more primary stories of action. I have been speaking of Munro's returning visions mainly as if they were simple experiences of something like Hell or Heaven: often, however, they are of both — one after the other in succession, perhaps. Rose after her royal beating may be more aware of Heaven — of floating and liberation — where Del in the office is more aware of Hell; yet in each case we find the one kind of awareness, whichever it may be, following the other. Elsewhere awareness can become a whole story in miniature: a vivid example is Robert's night walk over the snow in "Fits," evidently both an escape from a recent shock and a chance to reflect on it. Robert heads for the diner on the highway, then abruptly changes his mind (while changing it about the situation at home as well): in other words there has been a reversal, in his plans if not his actual direction. Continuing on, he now comes to an unnerving vision that will concern us later in this book; but, it suddenly occurs to him, what he is seeing is not really so grim — just a pile of old cars. And so he is like the child in "Images" realizing that the strange house is a familiar one: he is now ready to go home and be normal, even if a thought remains to trouble his normality and possibly transform it.

In the corresponding part of "Bardon Bus" we find a set of fragments, presented with so little continuity — cognition is strongly impinging on narrative here — that its sequence may seem hardly to matter. Yet if we simply take the narrator's experiences as they come, the result is very suggestive. To begin with she has had her wonderfully easy and satisfying affair in Australia, and supposed herself content to leave it behind. When she finds herself to have unknowingly fallen in love, the charming X is replaced by a Counter-Stranger — his desiccating friend Denis, a philosopher of world-renunciation. And now the heroine passes into a returning phase of visions and dreams — dreams all the more dreamlike when experienced as events in the outer world. First she tells us of a fantasy in which, after a lovers' quarrel, a man and woman reach a state of intense happiness, "brimming with gratitude and pleasure" (124). What follows is a virtual descent to an underworld: in a crazed preoccupation with dress she is drawn to a "spooky" (125) clothing shop, that of the punk Mary and Elizabeth we saw in the last chapter; and here she finds the two decking out an effeminate boy as a ladylike woman — one of Munro's sexually reversed Counter-Strangers, similar in his way to Mary Fortune. Now comes a phase more specially visionary. Having reached what she knows to be "a low point" (126), the narrator begins to feel an unreality comparable to the desolation of other protagonists we have seen at this same stage. In her case it is not indifference but obsession — as she explains, "I can't continue to move my body along the streets unless I exist in his mind and in his eyes." Such a feeling is at once desperate and, to her devouring self-consciousness, trivial; to make things worse, she remembers once treating a man as she herself has been treated by X. And yet she passes here to an opposite experience (again seemingly banal, for she remains self-despising throughout this part of the story): a dream in which she and her lover reach an ethereal communion, their embraces "transformed, by the lightness and sweetness of our substance, into a rare state of content" (127). Then at last she is back in Toronto — sitting in a Queen Street bakery with the inevitable coffee, watching ordinary human life, feeling tired and grateful. Like Robert, she has come home again.[62]

*

We must not exaggerate the shapeliness of these visions — things would be different if "Bardon Bus" were as schematically presented as Dante or Spenser. It does seem clear, however, that the cognition we have associated with the ordering of space can also have that of time, and that a phase of detachment from a story's action can itself be a story. In this way as in others, then, it constitutes its own world, set apart like the foundry in "Working for a Living"; indeed we may find it assimilating the other world of action to itself. Even if we prefer to think of it as a single point, a point can be a microcosm: legend and allegory, after all, frequently show us a single dream containing a whole series of adventures. And cognition can be far more than a point: conscious reflection may, as in "The Spanish Lady," take up the major part of a story; or, as in "Wild Swans," the experience of learning may give it its dominant flavour.

In moving to the more complex ways of seeing narrative structure, we have found action and cognition behaving much like the Mary and Elizabeth who trade dresses or coinhere in each other.[63] In fact, this coinherence was implicit even in the experience of the point as we saw it earlier in this chapter. While for narrative purposes I stressed the point's character of event, we also saw it as recognition — that of the child in "Images," for instance, meeting the spectre of her fantasies.[64] If we prefer to see point simply as action, we must add that action here is its own kind of cognition. Del Jordan in the storeroom, biting her cousin in blind desperation, is not simply blind: this is the moment of "thinking I had done the worst thing that I would ever do" (55), the moment of existential engagement that is also, as the saying goes, the moment of truth. Conversely, reflection is action: during the crisis in the storeroom Del gets some protection from her shame — her aunts and mother are very reassuring — but lying by herself afterwards she feels it in a great spasm, no less a happening than the explosion of action that preceded it.

Where there is such ambiguity between action and cognition, there will be the same ambiguity between the places in a story at which we specially find them. Munro often gives us the inside-out phenomenon that I will call the "hollow" story: one in which the most conspicuous and overtly significant events come at the ends, while nothing much — or nothing essential — seems to be happening in the middle. Such a story is secondary if we think of action in narrative as primary: but it is a common enough phenomenon in literature. Dante's experience *nel mezzo del camin* is a virtual dream, dreamed when he cannot go directly forward with his active life; in a romance with a more active quest but still hollow structure, the knight may similarly encounter dreams or other spectacles, perhaps temptations, on the way to an achievement at the end. "Images" with its dramatic central action may seem very different, but from one point of view it is not really so, since the central incident, as we have noted,[65] takes place while a larger action is suspended. The narrator has fled from her home to an empty no-man's-land, where she meets the visionary figure of her fantasies; on her return she is able to use this brief experience to cope with the more solid and continuing monster investing the family house. In the funeral episode of "Heirs of the Living Body," the meeting of Del and the "demon" (55) Mary Agnes comes while Del is avoiding another meeting, that with the corpse in the front room; and in a story like "Something I've Been Meaning to Tell You" there seems nothing whatever in the middle — only a humdrum marriage, with the presence of two sets of sheets in the wash to hint at a reversal of its fortunes. In other stories something more overtly cognitive may happen here: in "Marrakesh," for instance, we have seen how the uneventful evening preceding the story's eventful night consists mainly of talk; in "Labor Day Dinner" talk and reflection expand to fill almost the entire story. At times during this talk there is the ominous awareness of "something black that rises" (149): but there is so sense of immediate practical crisis. Only in typological retrospect do we identify the apparent absence of happening in the middle with the fateful happening at the end — just as we do in, say, James's "The Beast in the Jungle."[66]

*

When we think of the importance cognition has taken on in the last pages, it may occur to us that we have been coming back to metaphor — in my special sense of different things united in a static rather than temporal way, by detached vision rather than engaged experience. And if this is so, then we are starting to see metaphor and narrative as begetting each other. The farther we pursued kinds of metaphor in the previous chapter, the more we felt a mystery pointing to a story for its solution. Now we have been seeing how stories point the opposite way: our developing forms of narrative, while showing us more and more about experiences in time, have also come to require an experiencer — within the story or without — who can see what events mean, and without whose comprehension the story could not be itself. A way to illustrate this process is to ask of our successive narrative figures what kind of knowing they call for. The point, taken as a narrative principle, is sheer experience, with no knowledge distinct from participation. The line, however, requires a bit more detachment: we not only have to move from one point to another, but know the two at the same time, since recognizing the end as an end also means remembering the beginning, and thus knowing their connection as something other than sheer presence. If the place where we arrive turns out to be the place we started from, this takes further knowledge: the place in itself is single, so that only for someone who has left and returned is it a beginning and end identified. And at the typological level the things identified are not physically the same at all. Their oneness is "there" — we are still dealing with what is felt to be objectively the case — but it is there only because of someone's ability to see a meaning or, in our most paradoxical sense, a metaphor.[67] In "Age of Faith" the Anglican Church and the Flats Road house amount to the same thing, but only as Del — or the reader — is able to understand them.[68]

If metaphor and story are transformed in the way we have been seeing, each might be seen as the other's salvation. Metaphor, which as static can only represent a fixed situation, is set free in becoming a story; narrative, which in itself can only represent the flux of things, is crystallized as metaphor. But if the two can only metamorphose into one another without overcoming their fundamental opposition, we are caught in a vicious circle, unable to escape the condition of this and the other with which we have been plagued all along. We have, of course, seen a mediating element between opposites: in considering the relation between ideas and things, for instance, we thought of signs — especially names — as bringing each to the other, and in Munro's stories as narratives the same principle has appeared as that of temporal conveying and linking. But we are also coming to see that mediation is a great trickster and trouble-maker — which is certainly curious, since by rights he ought to be an obedient servant. He is only a go-between, after all, subordinate — one would have thought — to the parties who use his offices. But while he has always seemed co-operative at first, enabling us to establish a spatial or temporal world, in the end he has come out not servant but master. In narrative, for instance, he is first a linear mover who gets us from one end of our journey to the other; in a more ingenious way he brings us back home as well; and yet he increasingly reveals a will of his own — we do not arrive at the place we intended, or not in any way that can be called ours. At the typological level, we found, we get what we expected, but on terms we did not expect — terms which are really the trickster's own, and generate a recognition turning narrative inside out.

And so this trickster is a great nuisance; might he also be something better? He does seem to lead to places that would be hard to reach without him; perhaps, if we bear with him, he will help us find our way to a place beyond trickery itself. What he has done for us in the world of narrative is to produce meaningful forms: the line with its message of arrival, the circle with its message of return, the typological figure with its message of arrival in return. And in the end he will produce another figure still — or something other than a figure, expressing something other than the mere coinherence that typology in a limiting sense cannot transcend. To illustrate this greater figure I will eventually be drawing on the stories with which Munro ends her various books — a distinct group of their own, as I will argue. These, however, conclude a development that we have so far considered only in a preliminary way; and if they make a group, we must deal with the problem raised by the very notion of such a group. We have seen how a complete story can be present in miniature within the larger one we call "the story" — in an episode, even in the merest fragment. But so far we have only glanced at the opposite phenomenon: the way a whole story can implicitly fit inside a larger one. A simpler way to suggest the step we should now take is to note that Munro has written a couple of novels. A novel, even a loose *Bildungsroman*, is an integral story in itself: perhaps it has the same constituents as other stories. Perhaps, then, a good way to group the chapters of Munro's novels, as well as her stories more generally, will be to associate them with the various phases of action and recognition that we have discovered in the present chapter.

NOTES

1 Complexity of structure is not the same thing as proliferation of material. A loose adventure-story like *The Pilgrim's Progress* admits any amount of amplification, duplication, and digression while retaining a clear basic shape derived from the romance and morality traditions — the same shape as in, say, Book 1 of *The Faerie Queene*.

2 See above, 106, for the way a story, simply by continuing on its own principle, reaches a point where it must become a figure.

3 It will be evident that I am not going to assign these figures sexes. We may choose to associate the "linear" form or reading of a story with thrust and the "circular" one with containment, and so call them male and female. But such

forms, I have tried to show, are readily inflated or reduced into one another; as complexity arising from simplicity they are not connected with either sex; and the kinds of experience they represent are everybody's. To say that form as such is male is again to have a handy emblem, but nothing more; and there is as much truth — in principle and in Munro's practice — to the idea that form is female and what disrupts or escapes it male. See also below, 543–44 n110.

4 Structurally we can separate the two events as a central reversal (see above, 131) and a returning vision (see above, 145–46, 148–49); these belong, of course, to the background story for which the foreground one in "Monsieur les Deux Chapeaux" is considerably more than a frame.

5 In her interview with Hancock, Munro says of Roy Fowler's accident in "Wood" that it brings Roy "out of the ordinary world of control and inquisitiveness and into a completely different world" (90).

6 See Hancock 89.

7 See below 155 n8 for the history of "noon." Milton's "dark amid the blaze of noon" (*Samson Agonistes* line 81) is itself an allusion to the crucifixion, Samson being a type of Christ.

8 At the Crucifixion darkness comes at the sixth hour (noon); Jesus dies at the ninth hour (mid-afternoon, though the word "nones" or "noon" came to mean the time leading to this and eventually the sixth hour itself); the veil of the Temple and the graves open at the same time (see Matt. 27:45–53). For the Exodus see Exod. 12:29 (the Passover takes place at the complementary hour of midnight — see below, 372–73).

9 Rev. 6:14: "And the heaven departed as a scroll when it is rolled together."

10 See Acts 9, in which Saul (the future Paul), pursuing Christians, is himself struck blind by a light from heaven. He later receives his sight from Ananias, whose name also calls up those of Hannah (1 Sam. 2ff.) and Anna (Luke 2:36ff.). Silas is Paul's companion in the preaching of the gospel, resisted much as Joe resists his imaginary invaders.

11 To see the counterpart of blankness rather than intense happening, we can note that the lighting in Munro's cameras may be diffused rather than focused. The light coming through Joe Phippen's grimy windows would make a general dimness in the room. The storeroom at Jenkin's Bend, with its windows almost completely blocked, seems to Del "filled with blue light, that did not need to get in from outside" (54). Cf. Munro's "temples" (below, 470–71).

12 "The Photographer" 253.

13 See below, 426.

14 Carrington, concerned with times when the surface of life is violently broken open, deals extensively with this image and other related ones in Chs. II and III of her study.

15 See also below, 242–44.

16 Et Desmond and Arthur Comber keep "raspberry canes," somewhat ominously, during their peaceful life together (23); Rose's father leaves the note

"Scald strawberries to remove acid" (3). It is worth noting the title of an early story here, "A Basket of Strawberries"; for Mr. Torrance has found the fruits of life acidic enough. For berries and upheavals, see below, 207–08.

17 See "The Photographer" 253; "The Ottawa Valley" 243; "Marrakesh" 173–74.

18 Cf. the reappearance of the ghost in *Hamlet*, the appearance of Banquo's ghost in *Macbeth*, etc. We can expect similar "cores" within subordinate parts of a story — Lear's experience on the heath, for that matter, could itself be placed within the fallen condition to which he reverses after the over-confidence of his earlier retirement.

19 This is a central event within its own story, of course; Joe is also "something final, terrifying" (38). The important thing here is simply that any "happening" can be seen as a beginning.

20 Linearity and especially its disruption have interested critics like Orange and York (" 'Distant Parts of Myself' "). Where I will be differing from them is in seeing this disruption not just as forcing us back to the figure of the point but as sending us on to the more complex cyclical and typological figures.

21 In her reading of "A Basket of Strawberries" Carrington (19) has made a similar suggestion about Mr. "Torrance" (torrents), who is certainly precipitous on more than one occasion. The mother in "How Could I Do That?" is again a Mrs. Brooke.

22 Just as I am treating all stories as forms of unification, even when the parties fail to unite, so I would treat all stories in which sequence is emphasized as linear, even when the protagonist fails to get somewhere. What we have in the latter case is the hope of arrival leading to disappointment.

23 We hear of the curve of the river in "Images" (37) and "The Flats Road" (6). In her article "Everything Here Is Touchable and Mysterious" Munro speaks of "a loop known as the Big Bend" (33) in the Maitland, the river flowing through Wingham.

24 See below, 314–15.

25 In "Princess Ida" the Jordans rent a house "down at the end of River Street not far from the CNR station" (69). In "Baptizing" (194) Del can see both the river and the tracks from her bedroom window. The family house in "The Peace of Utrecht" looks out on the CPR station and the river.

26 Edgar in "The Moon in the Orange Street Skating Rink," having been as a boy one of the skaters circling round the rink, later has a stroke that Callie refers to as "a little turn" (158) — and sits watching figure skaters on television.

27 Loony Buttler in "Oh, What Avails" is a turbaned woman (185) not unlike Mrs. Sherriff. In "The Spanish Lady" (182) another turbaned woman "turns around" to address her flock of children.

28 I.e., lines from Fitzgerald's version of the *Rubaiyat* of Omar Khayyam.

29 See above, 86.

30 Del is more an observer than an actor in "The Flats Road": there is a story

of her own here to the extent that she feels concern for Uncle Benny's story and ultimately senses it as involving herself. There are various other "observer" stories in Munro; their full implication will become apparent in the final chapter of this book (see below, 503–05).

31 The new identity here can be seen in more than one way. In a sense it is *neither* of the opposites — as a single self, or self returned to; in a sense it is *both* the opposites; and in a sense it is *either* as being also the other. A given story may ask primarily for any of these readings.

32 In relation to Eliot's other quartets as representing our previous figures *Little Gidding* belongs here, with its vision of opposites "united in the strife which divided them." I will later deal with *Little Gidding* as showing us more than "coincidence" in my sense. See below, 466.

33 We have seen that our first figure, the point, can be experienced as a shock, and this shock can stand for all further ones. But the point is ambiguous — everything and nothing — and if we are trying to see the way figures progress we should think of it as just a happening in a minimal sense.

34 In the Hancock interview Munro emphasizes not only the experience of the unattached "point" but the feeling associated with it: in fact the "event" itself does not matter (81) even if "surprise endings" do occur (82). This is being paradoxical: if people's feelings are occasioned by events, then the events and their structure do matter. What Martin sees in Munro's mature stories seems much like what I mean by typology: a "dynamic interplay" of the familiar and strange, producing "a different mode of seeing or being that may be quite unexpected, but is certainly new" (*Paradox* 18), in fact "both surprising and probable, new and natural" (*Paradox* 37).

35 For a differing view see Orange, "Alice Munro and a Maze of Time," and Mathews, "*Who Do You Think You Are?*: Alice Munro's Art of Disarrangement."

36 It does not matter whether we think of a first event — the kingship of David in this case — as "Home," the beginning of the story, or as "the Other Place," an event in the course of a larger story that began, say, with the promise to Abraham. In the latter case the movement to Jesus from David will of course be simpler than that from Abraham — if the one is a line, the other is a circle. But either can be inflated to the typological complexity we need here.

37 John 12:32.

38 Once again we have to reduce, since Dante's horizontal path is treated as linear, not cyclical. Note, however, that the vertical axis appears when he cannot go forward and must not turn back — which is what circling amounts to. In other words, a new dimension is needed.

39 I do not think there is any absolute correspondence between three dimensions and the experience of getting what you expected in a way you did not expect: if, for instance, "ordinary" experience, including returns, is felt as a simple path of life, then it will take only a second dimension, as in a circle, to suggest

some extraordinary impingement on it.

40 I would like to disclaim any competence in higher mathematics. I find the analogy between narrative structure and geometry suggestive; nor is there anything silly in principle about this analogy, as one can see from the ready way lines and circles represent basic facts in our experience of stories. But it is the facts themselves, and especially as I perceive them in Munro, that I am concerned with here: someone else might be able to put these in geometrical terms more cogently than I have done.

41 We can compare the situation here to that in "Images" when Ben has discovered the first muskrat. Other muskrats follow as he works his way methodically along the river, so that it is actually some time later when Joe Phippen appears. But homogeneous process here amounts to arrest, and we feel Joe's attack as a response to Ben's initial triumph.

42 The most obvious examples are the other Ben Jordan of "Walker Brothers Cowboy" and Roy Fowler in "Wood."

43 Char does not simply play Neighbour in this story, of course, but the living-dead face Et is compelled to see in the opening episode is what she sees again at the end.

44 Tener 37.6.17.

45 Conversely, Munro has said that she would like to drop the last paragraph of "Postcard" and other stories (Struthers, "The Real Material" 9). In effect this would reduce a story's level of complexity.

46 A chamber-pot is dumped on him from the upper storey of a more legitimate house.

47 The stone school is mentioned in "Heirs of the Living Body" (34) and "Winter Wind" (70). Such places are not necessarily mentioned after central reversals: they may be simply emblematic, or occur at low points in other cycles. Indeed the two armouries are "Primary" (suggesting that the whole world of a story may be a larger Lair) in that the heroines are excluded from the dances there, and proceed to meet, or be, Counter-Strangers elsewhere. We do, however, find comparable surroundings at central low points: the old station where the children cavort in "The Found Boat," for instance.

48 Mary McQuade is of course a complex example: a Mary presiding over illness and at the same time a hearty Elizabeth saying "Come on now, raise up" (33). See above, 86.

49 See above, 71.

50 We sometimes find both principles at once. The Fortune-Teller in "Simon's Luck," for instance, has both Mary's role of announcing misfortune and Elizabeth's "hearty and practical" manner (165) — as for that matter does Mary Fortune.

51 This generalization, while having a special relevance here, needs to stay general. For one thing, Munro's compartmentalized underworlds are related to a wide range of imagery in her work (see above, 97 n20, for a few kinds and

examples). And when not simply emblematic, these withdrawn regions can be found at various points in a story (we should remember the principle of distribution here).

52 Eileen and Ewart can both be seen as Counter-Strangers here, each in relation to the other.

53 See below, 464. An actually subterranean "world of its own" (47) is the mine beneath the lake-bed in "Five Points."

54 For some important examples see below, 371.

55 In the opening cycle of "Oranges and Apples," after reversal at a disastrous dinner-party, Victor continues to visit the Zeiglers and is soon sitting out with them on summer evenings, chatting and listening to the neighbourhood sounds. "There was a sense of people's lives audible but solitary, floating free of each other . . . just as people in the same room, talking, float free on the edge of sleep" (123). In this "meditative, comforting" atmosphere the friends play Oranges and Apples — what the entire story is about, but here represented as a detached and speculative game.

56 "Meneseteung" offers an enormously expanded form of this vision after a crisis. "Labor Day Dinner" belongs structurally to a special class of stories in Munro (see above, 151–52, and below, 160 n66), but if we see its "Primary" point as the cheery arrival at Valerie's house, followed by subsidence, we can find a Refuge and a visionary conversation in the little brick-walled patio behind the screened porch. Valerie and Roberta drink wine together, have a heart-to-heart talk, and in the course of it make some very general observations on life.

57 For an opposite version of the same experience, we can note that the section of "Meneseteung" in which Almeda sees her vision has for its epigraph lines from one of her poems: "I sit at the bottom of sleep, / As on the floor of the sea. / And fanciful Citizens of the Deep / Are graciously greeting me" (68).

58 I am not sure how such phases are to be integrated into the geometrical kind of model I have been using, though the empirical fact of them seems clear enough. (The handiest diagram here is a line repeatedly cut in half.)

59 Rose's time of serenity in the bedroom, for instance, comes as a transition, but its end is itself a smaller transition: Rose hears Flo on the stairs, and for a moment knows both her independence and her impending surrender.

60 Garnet French, who within a smaller cycle does the same thing, first appeared to Del in a complementary though no less mysterious way — as a sharply observed figure standing out against a crowd. See below, 428.

61 Another powerful example occurs in "Hold Me Fast, Don't Let Me Pass." On the rainy drive back from Miss Dobie's house Antoinette, stricken with migraine, rouses herself just long enough to point to a sodden brown field and say "This is Cathaw" (98) — meaning "That's what happens to girls who give themselves."

62 For reasons of space I have omitted the fullest of all Munro's returning visions, and certainly a story of its own, Almeda Roth's laudanum experience in

"Meneseteung." A more compendious "vision story" is that of Del's walk home from the Brunswick Hotel in the Bert Matthews section of "Baptizing."

63 Crawling through the bush after the great central reversal in "Wood," the normally unreflective Roy Fowler finds various thoughts occurring to him. These "go through his mind as if they were going to link up somewhere, but they don't" (54). If they did, they would transform Roy's story.

64 At the turning-point in the river scene of "Baptizing," to add one more example, Del Jordan sees the real nature of her relation to Garnet — and sees that he sees it — just as their playful scuffling is turning into deadly earnest. (Like the child in "Images," she is too astonished to be afraid.)

65 See above, 14.

66 In a hollow story there will obviously be little to distinguish the central phase from visions flanking it, so that we may find a single central section with as much the character of vision as of muted action. The location of the centre, we should also note, depends partly on the reader's projection. I have mostly kept this complicating factor out of the present book, but we might take the long dinner scene in "Labor Day Dinner," for instance, as the story's centre — in which case the talk and recreation preceding it would simply be a phase of vision (an approaching one in this case). For a different projection see above, 159 n56.

67 By the same token, this recognition of meaning may be increasingly disjunct from the end of the story as such. Reaching the end of a linear path and knowing you have done so usually go together, but when the child in "Images" comes full circle, it takes her a bit of time to grasp the fact. Typological recognition can be even more detached — Del's in "The Flats Road" comes to her fully only on stormy winter nights, whereas Benny's drive to Toronto takes place in spring.

68 A parallel development can be found in the forms of metaphor — for which I have used the same geometrical analogy. But it is also true that metaphor is cognitive to start with, and if we are *contrasting* it with narrative we will notice how, in evolving, it increasingly takes on the latter's characteristics. See above, pp. 95–96.

The Other Country

PART II

Books as Stories

Lives of Girls and Women has existed in more than one version. Its roots go down into a mass of early draft material for which Munro seems to have envisaged a Faulknerian kind of unity; and even when the work had arrived at something like the form we know, she was prevailed on to recast it as a "proper" novel. This last, still surviving as a manuscript, is a disaster: reading it has the value mainly of throwing the book we do have into relief — of clarifying its own structural character. In the published *Lives*, as we have seen, the material conglobes around certain special events occurring at well spaced intervals (we will see later why "The Flats Road," possibly, and "The Photographer," certainly, make exceptions to this spacing). Intervals of a different kind are indicated by the book's title, with its suggestion of the lives of many girls and women. Yet these lives, while lived by others like Mrs. Jordan and Fern Dogherty and Naomi, are also those of Del herself, who contains and transcends them all; and the work itself, for all its spacing and multiplicity, is as united as it is various.

It is this unity, and specifically narrative unity, that we need to consider here: the single story in which Del grows up, is baptized into direct sexual experience, suffers its tragedy, and decides for the womanhood of "real life" beyond adolescent illusions — to all of which is appended an encounter of a different kind, in which she receives the vocation to be an artist. To appreciate the kind of story we are dealing with here, we can do as before and align it with some others. For one thing, we have seen how *Lives* belongs to the same literary family as Joyce's *Portrait of the Artist as a Young Man*, which follows the hero to the sexual crisis of his adolescence and ends as he is preparing to leave youth and home, having received the same artist's vocation as Del. While of course different in manner, an earlier work like Wordsworth's *Prelude* tells much the same story: the hero reaches the tragic crisis, sexual among other things, of a revolution outside and inside himself, then discovers his true calling.[1] In a still earlier convention *Lives* might have been a pastoral work like, say, Spenser's *Shepheardes Calender*, centring on the vain passion and minor poetry of youth, and concluded or followed by a summoning to the greater achievements of maturity. But there is a particular work, less special in its genre, to which *Lives* connects itself by repeated allusions: the Bible. We have already seen the matter of David; more generally, *Lives* is the story of "Del Jordan," the girl from "Jubilee," who at the crisis of her story falls in love with a boy from "Jericho Valley," gets baptized, and in the end seeks an everlasting city. It is thus, if in a less overt way, what Joyce's *Ulysses* is in relation to the Odyssey: a profane story having a continuous analogy to a culturally sacred one as found in a particular recension.

If we are going to invoke such an analogy, we will have to be clear what it means and does not mean. Once again, it does not mean that Munro is writing a *roman à clef* or a substitution allegory: the way in which the Bible haunts her novel is much more elusive than that — much more a matter of sensibility. And it does not mean that the Biblical analogy is something that Munro deliberately worked up. There is, for instance, nothing in her papers to suggest any conscious biblical scheme (although her drafts do show us some interesting allusions to supplement the ones in the work as finally completed); I have already argued that allusion does not depend on conscious intention. Munro herself, as we have seen, has said repeatedly that she does not consciously put symbols or patterns into her work: this applies, presumably, to large-scale structural allusion as much as to anything more local, and indeed a general structural parallel is less likely to be noticed by a writer than the resonance of a name like "Del Jordan." On the other hand such a parallel, deliberate or not, has nothing unlikely about it. If we think again of Joyce or Wordsworth — not to mention forebears like Milton — we will find exactly the same parallel. Joyce's *Portrait*, especially its last chapter, alludes endlessly to the Passion; *The Prelude* points us unmistakeably to — among other things — the frustrated vocation of Samson, the Messianic hope of a righteous kingdom on earth, and the Transfiguration as re-enacted on Mount Snowdon. The fact is that the Bible affords a very complete and well-articulated structure of events and metaphors, and that it has had a special status in our own literary tradition: while the present book was being completed, Northrop Frye published his great two-volume study dealing with just this, as so much of his earlier work had already done. We need not be surprised, then, if a *Bildungsroman* like *Lives of Girls and Women* reveals a definite parallel to what is for us the "original" of all *Bildungsromane* — the story of the formation of Israel.

*

To see this parallel more clearly, we should first consider Munro's novel chapter by chapter, though at this point I will give only brief indications of what will be treated more fully later. "The Flats Road," to begin with, is a Book of Genesis: it takes us into the chaos of Uncle Benny's swamp and Uncle Benny's mind. Appropriately, we find him pointing fiercely to a rainbow while asserting, as the Lord does to Noah, that there will be no more Flood; and at the end we find Del recognizing that her parents' world is itself the Flood. "Heirs of the Living Body" introduces us to a much more solid and prosperous world, something like a land of Egypt with its intensely corporate and familial society, its ritual and stock-taking, its god-king worshipped in a mummified form at the climax of the story. "Princess Ida" suggests Egypt once again — more explicitly, in fact, since we find a character called Nile, and at the end the goddess Isis herself (next to an annual flood). But the Egypt of Addie Morrison and her brother Bill is a failing one — a land of famine even when it manages outer abundance. Both sister and brother, in their respective ways, spend their lives in a desperate attempt at exodus: the chapter begins and ends with Mrs. Jordan "out on the Jericho Road" (65).

Next we find ourselves in a wilderness: the God of "Age of Faith" is not at all the serene Egyptian deity embodied with his land of plenty, but the remote and formidable being to whom the twelve-year-old Del turns from what has come to seem an empty and hostile universe — the God of commandment, in other words; and we are made to see the same god in still another assertion of power, the abandonment of his Son in a later version of the theophany at Sinai. With the following chapter we enter a country where Law has become accepted routine — that of children plying their tasks at school; at the same time these children engage in other rites of friendship and enmity, and show a keen consciousness of the difference between insiders and outsiders. It is just these ceremonies that make changes possible, for something more romantic is afoot within the tutelage of Law — an operetta about the Pied Piper. In other words, this country is looking to a saviour, even a king: we will be seeing later how figures like Frank Wales and, more farcically, Dale McLaughlin, correspond to the Gideons and Samsons of the Book of Judges. Next comes opera itself, given in a private performance by Fern Dogherty and Art Chamberlain and a more public one by the whole of Jubilee, with its institutions and festivities and media. This, as we have found, is the Kingdom, the world of David and Solomon; it is in the same world that, at the climax, the Temple opens its gates for a king of glory. Yet again Del is unsatisfied: there is no genuine king or genuine opening here, and the outer show of glory only leads to forsaking and exile.

"Baptizing" brings us to what seems a truer uniting and a truer revealing: to simplify, Del is finally baptized into sexual experience by a lover from Jericho Valley. Yet this too is a story of failure: its ecstatic first baptism only leads to a second in which saviour and bride angrily reject each other. And so Del is left to be "grave and simple" (242) — to face adult life without the grace of love. Only one hint of something else accompanies her on her way: in "The Photographer," set in a world of empire and looming destruction, Del receives an invitation from the curiously gifted madman Bobby Sherriff, who emerges from a kind of tomb, blesses her, and poises as if about to make an ascent, leaving her to seek the eternal city that she soon finds herself craving. In this special "epilogue" (243) a revelation is finally made — even if, in Munro's epiphanic genre, it can only come as something fleeting and ambiguous.

*

The biblical parallel I am suggesting may or may not be convincing as merely sketched here, but if the reader will suspend disbelief for the present, we can pass on to the structural question that the parallel raises. Assuming that *Lives of Girls and Women* bears a continuous analogy with the Bible, so that both can be said to tell the same overall story, what shape does this story have? It is a *Bildungsroman*, as I have suggested, but that term does not in itself imply much about structure. What does seem clear is that, if we are dealing with a story, this story should respond to the same analysis that we have been applying to stories on a smaller scale: that is, it should show us the same levels of line and circle and so on, and the same relation of Home and Other Place and transition between them. Since the Bible displays its shape more openly than a realistic novel, it makes sense to consider the Bible first.

It can be misleading to speak of "the" structure of the Bible: what can be said, I think, is that some varying ways of structuring it are allotropes of one another. To give ourselves an orientation, we can begin by asking "What is a Jew?" After the general fall of the human race in the person of Adam, the Jews are the children of the Promise — the children of Abraham and Jacob; more specially, they are the nation which, on being led out of Egypt, covenants with God for the Law, and on its terms achieves a kingdom in a Promised Land. The failure of this kingdom in its more limited form engenders the hope for its restoration under a greater Messiah, or "anointed," who in a Christian version is Jesus the *christós*. And while Jesus is rejected by the Jews themselves, those who accept him become a new Israel and inherit the kingdom in its true form.

Since Munro's allusions so often point us to the New Testament, and to the New Testament's reading of the Old, I am going to take the Christian version of the story as the norm here. What are we to see as its shape? As a single comic cycle, the Bible moves from an original Fall of Man to the final coming, or return, of the Messiah. But if this is what we see when we stand well back, any closer view reveals some interior cycling as well — as with all stories of any length. The most obvious cycle within a cycle here is the rise and fall of the Israelite Kingdom: a lesser tragedy within the greater comedy. One might object that a good deal happens in the Bible before the calling of Moses, or for that matter the calling of Abraham: but with the model we are considering at the moment, this early material must be assimilated either to the general Fall or the formation of the Israelite people. In "Royal Beatings" Munro presents Rose as "a baby in a basket" (2) taken over by a stepmother: her mother, a much gentler woman, has left only some egg-cups "with a pattern of vines and birds on them." The mother is vaguely the unfallen Eve, the lady of the Garden; Rose is vaguely Moses, floating in the Egyptian swamp; and that is not unlike floating in Noah's ark — to use an image from another, and similar, opening story, "The Flats Road." In other words, a great deal can be concentrated into a simple experience of fall and, associated with Moses among others, reascent into a more firmly mundane existence. At the other end of the story, Christ as King of the Jews within a still fallen world must, according to our present model, be assimilated to his forebears the Kings of Israel: and so Munro can fill her Davidic stories — "Jesse and Meribeth," for instance — with allusions to the Christ who is David again. Conversely, she can put Davidic material into stories alluding to Christ: in our present view the two kinds of material appear as much the same. Where David and Christ are differentiated, it will be as the victorious king at the top of the cycle and the king of sorrows on its downward slope; correspondingly, any predecessors of David — Abraham, Moses — will appear in contrast to him as figures of promise and covenant. What we have thus remains a single interior cycle with its initiatory, central, and terminal phases, as I will be calling them.

On our principle of distribution, however, we could also see the biblical pattern as having not one but three cycles (within the more general movement of fall and return); and while it would be easy to get lost in comic and tragic here, we can again say simply that any cycle within a fallen world will in one aspect be tragic. In this tripartite scheme a pre-legal cycle begins with the calling of Abraham, passes through the sojourn in prosperous Egypt, and ends with the Exodus: Egyptian prosperity collapses, while the Israelites escape from Egyptian bondage. Once again we have to say that any earlier cycling will appear only as an aspect of the present cycle. To follow another allusion in Munro, the Fleming family in "The Stone in the Field" are, as we shall see, Egyptians of a kind; if they also live close to "Mount Hebron," (24) then an earlier haven is being combined with a later one. What we can call the legal cycle, a more limited version of the single interior cycle in our first scheme, begins with the calling at Sinai, moves through the new prosperity of the Kingdom and ends with its collapse and the Babylonian exile. Now comes a post-legal cycle, if we think of Christ as putting away or transforming the Law: Christ appears, is acclaimed by his followers, and then dies tragically. There is still a good deal of unfinished business before the Apocalypse, but this can be assimilated to the cycle of Christ himself. It is part of his tragedy, then, that the Church experiences its own rise and its own fall into tribulation and inner betrayal. In the end, however, it will be cleansed and permanently established with the Second Coming — the fulfilment of the larger comedy containing the three tragedies of our present scheme.

This scheme, like our series of narrative figures, could be developed still further, but it would remain the same in principle; and it would still fit the normal Christian view of history. What would fit this less well would be a reading that changed the principle itself: and yet, as I will be arguing, that is what Munro in effect gives us. In the last stories of her collections especially, we find some very suspect worldly establishments with echoes of the Apocalypse playing about them. Perhaps these establishments are only parodies of the Apocalypse, but perhaps they indicate that the Apocalypse itself, on its stated biblical terms, is something of a parody; and since Munro lets us see glimpses of an apocalypse different in kind from any given establishment, we shall need to take the second possibility seriously. It may be, then, that there is something false or incomplete about the whole story we have developed, including its unfallen beginning and victorious end: not false in the view of its participating characters or even the St. John who seems to take it all in, but false in the eye of a further seer. This seer would have to interpret the innocence of Adam as part of an already fallen world: he would note that a chaos preceded it, and if he were reading Munro he would also note that in her work imagery suggestive of Eden can also be suggestive of Egypt. At the other end of her world he would note how arrangements that meet with general satisfaction are nevertheless resisted by certain characters, who find ways to elude them and live by visions of their own. For such characters, or for readers who see as Munro invites them to see, yet another kingdom is failing: and a truer revelation waits beyond the official one. Only in this way, perhaps, can the Bible be at once rejected in any carnal form and recreated in its eternal one.

*

To see the Bible as a system of cycles within a larger cycle[2] is not only to reduce its historical humps and bumps to a manageable pattern, repeated in different contexts, but by the same token to see its internal correspondences more clearly. If, using the final version I have given of our model, we think of the chaos that precedes creation or calling — the primordial waters, or the wilderness into which Adam is expelled — and if we then think of the second of our interior cycles, it will be apparent that the sea and wilderness through which the children of Israel make their way are really the same chaos in a different context — as the psalms themselves often imply. If we turn to the beginning of our third inner cycle, we will find wilderness again: that of exile, and later that of John the Baptist. John himself, as Jesus points out, has the role of Moses or Elijah — for once again a prophet has appeared out of the wilderness. And this again means a calling: in the first cycle Abraham is called out by prophecy to cross a desert; in the second the children of Israel are called out to cross another;

and at the beginning of the third we find John crying that the paths of Lord are to be made straight. At the same time, of course, John is enacting the crossing itself by his baptizing in the Jordan.

The high points of these three cycles correspond in a similar way: there is the rich kingdom of Egypt in the first, the Israelite kingdom itself in the second (not to say wealthy neighbours like Tyre), and in the third — as we have it in our triple model — the "reign" of Christ as a king already acclaimed in his earthly life. If we distribute further in the way I have suggested, his kingdom becomes that of the Church in the world and even of the apocalyptic Church announced by John. In a tragic view, of course, such a kingdom, and its king, are still subject to failure. The corresponding failure in the first cycle is that of Egypt, accompanied by the flight of the enslaved Israelites; in the second cycle we have the fall of the Israelite kingdom and the exile of its people; with the failure of the third cycle — the death of Christ, in one version — the Bible again gives strong indications of an Exodus.

The scheme I have been developing, one that combines a basic simplicity with an acceptance of variations, can help us to find in Munro's novel the shape we have been finding in her individual stories. We will need to make one modification here, though only an apparent one: just as Munro's stories tend to distinguish a late epilogue of recognition more than an initiatory counterpart (which is generally worked into the first part of the story proper), so *Lives of Girls and Women* has an "Epilogue" in "The Photographer," but makes "The Flats Road" do duty for prologue as well as for the story of original calling. If we are willing to lump prologue and first phase together in this way, then our scheme, with the ultimate transformation I have suggested, becomes a matter of three plus a somewhat special fourth: this will on the whole be the most convenient model for analyzing *Lives*. Its correspondence with one of our narrative figures is obvious: this is like a typological story with a setting out from Home, a visit to an Other Place (in the course of which there is a great reversal), a Homecoming, and a late recognition. And we might remind ourselves that it is like some other simple things: our basic experience of beginning, middle, and end, or temporally of past, present, and future, with the intimation in either case of something "after" these that was also before them and that transcends their separateness. The story of *Lives of Girls and Women* can, I think, be resolved into something as simple as that; and while we could perhaps have done this resolving without the aid of the Bible, the structural reinforcement afforded by our biblical parallel will be an important aid as we go on.

This is not to say that the chapters of *Lives of Girls and Women* provide one-for-one correspondences with the phases of our biblical scheme in any of its forms. To give labels that I will be using generally from now on, *Lives* has Genesis, Egypt, Exodus, Wilderness, Judges, Kingdom, Passion, and Apocalypse chapters. The first three of these render neatly enough the three phases of our first biblical cycle (in the more extended scheme, that is). The beginnings of the second cycle, however, are represented by two separate chapters — a Wilderness chapter for the desert itself, a Judges chapter suggesting settlement in a new land. Then comes a Kingdom chapter, leading directly to the third cycle; and this last is represented by a single story, followed by the book's apocalyptic epilogue. This may seem to be short-changing some parts of the Bible, but then the Bible does much the same thing: to be very simple-minded, the Old Testament is more than twice as long as the New, and the divisions we are concerned with — Genesis, Egypt, Exodus, and so on — do not get anything like proportional amounts of its space.

Yet when we think of the general movements in *Lives of Girls and Women*, especially with Munro's biblical allusions in mind, we do find something suggestively like three cycles and a special fourth. In the first of these (expressed, like the others, partly in what Del overtly is and partly in what she sees) we find a Genesis, an Egypt, and an Exodus, all imagined as the experience of a child before puberty. The high point of this cycle is Del's early security as an "heir of the living body": a member of the solidly established family at Jenkin's Bend. This security is not without its underside; and with its collapse comes the violent exodus that, in "Princess Ida," Del watches in her mother and knows to be her own need as well. Then we have Del the adolescent: in the first place the girl who finds herself alone in the wilderness of "Age of Faith," and turns to a God of sheer being and power for support, just as Uncle Benny had turned to "the Lord" (11) in the earlier cycle. Soon we follow Del into the more settled world of her school, with its dependable routine and regulations; and here we find her turning not to God but to boys for the first time. By the time of "Lives of Girls and Women" she has grown into a highschool girl revelling in an imagined kingdom of sex, with all the trappings. With the collapse of this kingdom, and the sense of transformation that pervades the long conclusion of the chapter, Del moves on to her third cycle — concentrated in a single story, "Baptizing," but then

"Baptizing" is really three stories in one. Del has passed the brazen pseudo-confidence of her second world, and must now attempt less imaginary relations with the other sex, especially in the last of her adventures here, the intimacy with Garnet French in which she seems at last to find a kingdom of love. When this too fails, Del's girlhood is finally over (to choose this interpretation of the novel's title): she will now, she believes, live a bleak "real life" (242) as a disillusioned, soberly adult woman. But as this is happening something surprises her: an intimation that the life to which she is called may be different, not only from her adolescent fantasies, but from ungraced "real life" as well.

*

In *Lives of Girls and Women*, then, Del's larger adventure is like the smaller ones of the individual chapters: the book as a whole has a shape, reflected back to it from a biblical mirror. But Munro has written other books, including a second novel. *Who Do You Think You Are?* takes its heroine to the threshold of old age rather than womanhood; biblical allusion is much less continuous and prominent here than in the earlier work: and yet the two books, as I shall try to show, have essentially the same story to tell. And this brings us to the question whether Munro's other books may not also tell this story. To say that they do is to step onto much more treacherous ground than with either of the novels: I am going to take the step, but I want to make clear at the outset both the kind of claim I am making and the qualifications it demands. It should already be clear that I would not claim any simple numerical correspondence of parts. We have not found one between *Lives of Girls and Women* and our biblical scheme; nor is there one between *Lives* and *Who Do You Think You Are?*, though the general parallel in structure here seems clear enough.[3] What interests me is rather the way certain kinds of story tend to come in the same relative position in the two novels: and I find them occupying the same position again in Munro's collections of separate stories.

A further question, of course, is that of how the collections come to have their orderings in the first place. Here I can only say what I have said elsewhere, that I am not concerned with deliberate intentions. For one thing, the ordering in these collections is not necessarily Munro's alone. She works with editors and publishers, and no doubt the shaping spirit to which I am giving her name is to some extent that of a collaboration — as is the case with most books. On the other hand I doubt whether Munro would approve much that the creator in herself really did not want,[4] and in any case the pattern I am concerned with is an archetypal one, known to the creator in all of us. This does not necessarily mean that an author likes to be sharply conscious of the creator's workings. To judge from an interview like that with Geoff Hancock, Munro is less comfortable thinking of structure than seeing people's lives as collections of "flashes" (89) — evidently the epiphanic moments we have found so important in her individual stories. Yet even here she is arguing as well for a typological as opposed to a merely linear understanding of life;[5] and we have seen how her individual stories are far more than sets of isolated epiphanies. The same thing might be true of the collections into which these stories are arranged.

Whether it is true in fact is of course another matter. In a limiting case a collection of stories might have no organic ordering at all: it might simply follow the order of composition or that in which manuscripts happened to lie on somebody's desk. If we can discern a more literary kind of sequence in Munro's collections to date, it is still quite possible that some stories are not "in place" or are not as characteristic of their places as others. And in any case we cannot merely say that a given story is "of" a particular phase in a scheme. As we saw from the complexities of mirroring in the previous chapter, stories can have multiple correspondences to show us. When we look inside them as we have done, we find cycles within cycles; we also find ends mirroring each other and ends mirroring the middle, not to mention points between these points, until structure, like the relation between Mary and Elizabeth, collapses on itself if that is what we want it to do. If we now look outside these stories to the greater one that I believe them to constitute, we can expect them to behave like their own parts: in other words, they will become less and less "of" any particular position in the larger story as we bring out the complexity of their inter-relations.

Conversely, we should remember that any individual story contains the larger one in itself. Some of Munro's later stories (if also an ambitious early effort like "The Edge of Town") give us a particularly strong sense of just this comprehensiveness: they may focus on particular happenings, but they also make us feel that they could easily have been novels. "Images," the story we have used as a type for all Munro's stories, shows the same universality in a more compendious form, for while closely connected with several of

Munro's phases, it is hard to limit to any one of them. Inevitably, then, there is something arbitrary in the choice of particular stories to illustrate particular phases of a scheme, and readers who want to consider the assignments I will be making as random ones are welcome to do so. Yet when we set out the contents of Munro's different books side by side, what we see is as intriguing as her family of Marys:[6] it would be wilful blindness to the evidence not to look further, even if, in the nature of the case, the result cannot be a plain and simple one. What we will have to settle for at the moment is a few preliminary observations on a few of the stories.

*

Perhaps the most salient feature of Munro's collections as collections (and we can include her novels with these for present purposes) is that they generally end with "epilogues" like that in *Lives of Girls and Women*. Just when her affair with Garnet French is nearing its end, Del happens to meet Bobby Sherriff, the young man temporarily home from an asylum, and finds herself invited to cake and lemonade. Bobby is not Del's lover or even an ordinary friend — Del finds him a bore, in fact — and yet he gives her something that none of the other boys and men in her life has given her: a mysterious blessing and commission. If we set this story beside "Dance of the Happy Shades" the correspondence is striking: Miss Marsalles, the failing and deluded yet invincibly genteel old music teacher, magically calls up an Elysian dance that stays with the narrator as a "communiqué" (224) after Miss Marsalles herself is gone. Ralph Gillespie in "Who Do You Think You Are?," the disabled non-lover who is somehow closer than any lover, communes with Rose in the same mysterious and healing way; Janet and her father in "The Moons of Jupiter" feel a similar communion as he gets ready for the operation he is not likely to survive. Two other concluding stories, "The Ottawa Valley" and "White Dump," may seem at first unrelated to those I have mentioned (though much like each other in ways we will find): even here, though, we can note times of magical fellowship associated with art and play.

There is a great deal more that could, and to some extent will, be said about these stories and others in their neighbourhood. We seem justified, however, in positing a distinct group here; and judging by our biblical scheme as well as what we have seen of late recognitions within individual stories, we may already have some idea why such a group would come at the end of Munro's collections. If we turn to these books' beginnings we find another group, hardly less definite than that of the epilogues: for the collections regularly open with "Genesis" stories like "The Flats Road." These peer back into a dim and legendary past; or they ask aetiological questions — how, for instance, did royal beatings begin? The answer to such questions seems to be that things began as they still begin: in the foreground of these stories we find not only the royal beating of Rose but that of Diane in "The Flats Road," and with outright beaters like Rose's father or Madeleine we can range such figures as the brooding Char and the dangerously energetic Nora Cronin. The typical story here seems to be that of a calling — Madeleine, for instance, the "lady with one child" (12) advertised in the paper, calls to Uncle Benny; and the result is always a betrayal, perhaps a mutual one. Thus we have stories about the wounding of innocence — of the trust that is the most primal of creaturely needs — often set against a background of wars and falling empires and uprooted refugees.

Special placement of stories is most likely at the beginning and end of a collection: it gives the whole a linear form of organization, if nothing more complex. But what about the middle? The title-story of *Lives of Girls and Women*, as we have seen, brings us to something like the world of David and Solomon, a world of glory and philandering: the local counterpart in Munro's novel is the public glory of Jubilee and the private carrying-on of Art Chamberlain and Fern Dogherty, truants against the town's values who nevertheless share its taste for splash. In "Jesse and Meribeth" a similar carrying-on is watched by another susceptible teenager like Del Jordan; and the relation of this teenager to a counterpart of Art Chamberlain is much as in the earlier story. At what I take to be a corresponding place in *Dance of the Happy Shades* we find carrying on yet again — the affair of Helen and Clare MacQuarrie in "Postcard" — and as in "Lives of Girls and Women" the result is a cruel jilting. In "Mischief" the great love-affair is never quite staged at all, but the pursuit of illicit thrills is the same here as in the other stories; in "Oranges and Apples" we see this pursuit through the eyes of a jealous spouse.

And so, it would seem, we have not only ends but a middle — the Other Place that, in the biblical analogy, is a splendid but uncertain worldly kingdom. I will not try at present to sketch the other groups in Munro's books, but I will state the claim that they are there: groups we can associate with Egypt, Exodus, Wilderness, and the other phases I have already linked to the chapters of Munro's novels. What I have said so far about these groups is certainly not offered as adequate explanation, and has made no attempt to account for all stories or all variations even within the groups I have briefly presented. It may, however, win provisional indulgence as we turn to examine both Munro's individual stories and their family ties. Here, though, a further word is necessary concerning organization. The following chapters will use a reduction made possible by a parallel we have already noted: all the interior cycles in our biblical scheme — whether in its simpler or more elaborate forms — can be seen as rising and descending tragic arches, or more basically as having a beginning, middle, and end. The first three of the following chapters will deal respectively with these three aspects of any tragic cycle (rather than with the various cycles as distinct from each other). The apocalyptic "cycle," or transcendence of cycle, will then have a chapter of its own. This procedure will avoid a good deal of repetition; it will also help us to see correspondences that I find important. But I am going to modify it in a couple of ways, following Munro's handling of the material in *Lives of Girls and Women*. What we must note here is two anomalies that we have already seen in the work — anomalies, that is, if we are coming to it from our biblical parallel. The first of these lies in "Baptizing": there is only a single chapter here to match our terminal cycle, though a triple one in which Del's successive adventures clearly suggest such a cycle. Since these adventures can best be kept together, and because the last of them — her involvement with the passionate Garnet French — looms so much larger than the first two, it seems appropriate to reserve the whole of this story for my chapter on the terminal phase. More generally, the initiatory and central Christs — the baby in the manger and the leader acclaimed in his own earthly life — will not figure very prominently in my first two chapters.

The other anomaly is that material suggesting the movement from the world of the Kingdom to that of Christ — the Babylonian exile, the anticipation of a Messiah — gets no chapter at all in *Lives of Girls and Women*, but is contained within the title piece (mainly a Kingdom story, I would argue) as well as, to a lesser extent, within "Baptizing." When we examine Munro's other books, we do find distinct stories at this stage — making what I am going to call "Exile" and "Annunciation" groups; and as we would expect, these transitional groups show notable similarities to those connecting the first two cycles. But whereas Munro has a definite group of Exodus stories to be dealt with in my third chapter, there is nothing so distinct at the end of her Kingdom group. The most powerful story of willed exodus here,

"Goodness and Mercy," is also the most ambiguous and difficult, and it seems advisable simply to treat the "Exile" stories as a late sub-division of the Kingdom group and the somewhat different "Annunciation" stories as an early sub-division of the Passion group — though the Annunciation stories might logically have been put with the Judges stories, which bring their own annunciation of a Kingdom at hand.

Whatever my ordering may lack in strict consistency, it represents, I feel, the best way of combining justice to the surface of Munro's books and to the structure underlying this. On the one hand, it will show us how her chaotic Genesis world reappears in that of the Wilderness; how Egypt and Kingdom are much the same worldly city; and how the Exodus and Passion make closely related terminal crises. On the other hand, it will where convenient allow Munro's books to do what we have seen *Lives of Girls and Women* to be doing: to follow something like the steps of the Bible in their chronological order. And whether we proceed by cycles or phases, we will be dealing with a single structure, the one we have also found in Munro's individual stories. For on whatever scale of presentation, it is the same human experience that she shows us: a leaving of home and a coming back to it, with a glimpse in the coming back of a greater home we might also return to.

NOTES

1 In Wordsworth's case, of course, this is a matter of homecoming rather than exile, but that is only to say that this work has a cyclical rather than linear emphasis.

2 In the rest of this book I will have to use the terms "cycle" and "phase" more or less interchangeably. I would have preferred to keep "phase" for the parts of a cycle (initiatory, central, and terminal): the problem is that a cycle is itself likely to be a phase within a larger cycle, while its own phases may well be little cycles of their own.

3 The simplest way to put the numerical difference is to say that *Who Do You Think You Are?* has two "extra" chapters: "Providence" and "Spelling." The structural comparison I am concerned with here is between the two novels in the form that finally satisfied Munro.

4 No doubt exceptions are possible. See Struthers, "The Real Material" 29–32, also Martin, *Paradox* 100, for the publishing history of *Who Do You Think You Are?* Munro has also told Geoff Hancock that Janet in her *New Yorker* version became a painter because stories about writers were not wanted (Hancock 75–114, 85). Even in these cases, though, Munro ultimately chose for herself: at

considerable financial sacrifice she made the decision to turn *Who Do You Think You Are?* into the book that satisfied her, and for the collected *Moons of Jupiter* turned Janet back into a writer.

5 Munro seems to me to be saying two things in this part of the interview: that we understand only in isolated flashes, and that — in Hancock's words — "something happens in the gap between the scenes" (89). This does not mean simply linear progress in either life or understanding ("I don't see that people develop and arrive somewhere"). What it does mean is that there is an ironic difference between "what we think is happening and what we understand later on" (102): in fact "we think we've got things figured out and then they turn around on us." This is what I would call a cyclical and even typological way of seeing human experience. For a different view see York, *Other Side* 48. See also Munro's remarks in Slopen 76; Rasporich, *Dance* 28.

6 I mean what I myself see, inevitably, though my way of grouping the stories does not have to invalidate those preferred by other critics. See Carrington, especially 39 ff.; Martin *Paradox* 101–27, 131–32; Hancock 80. Rasporich (*Dance* Ch. 2) advances an interesting — though to me somewhat forced — argument that the sequence of Munro's whole books, up to *The Progress of Love*, makes a single typological story (to use my term), complete with an epilogue (for which see following paragraph, also below, 485ff.).

The Foundry Disease

I. CHAOS

The snow around our house
Lay in drifts, like whales asleep.
You could make caves underneath.

At night I thought of my caves
Making them large as Ali Baba's,
Domed, perfect, secret rooms under the snow.
Lamps hung from their carved snow ceilings
And they were warm, though white.

Winter surrounded us
   like a solid fantasy,
Built preposterous landscapes
   one on top of the other like the city of Troy,
Brought out for our night's entertainment
   real Furies, ancient barbaric storms. . . .

(Tener 37.4.26)

While Munro does not have the way with poetry that she does with stories, this fragment of an early poem makes a good introduction to her initiatory world: a world of snow that is equally one of sleeping whales, waking furies, and ancient barbarism. Winter has its positive side, no doubt — the poem shows it to be a time for dreams, and according to Del Jordan it is even a time for love;[1] but in the first place it is chaos, what we find at the opening of the Book of Genesis and indeed throughout its course. It is equally what we find in Munro's Genesis group of stories, as I have called it. Later we shall see how the Wilderness stories, and in one view the Judges group, belong to chaos as well: in fact the closest analogy in Munro to the poem I have quoted comes at the opening of "Boys and Girls," primarily a Judges story. The attic where two children lie in bed, or more precisely their own songs and fantasies, make a warm refuge in a cold season:

> the time of year when snowdrifts curled around our house like sleeping whales and the wind harassed us all night, coming up from the buried fields, the frozen swamp, with its old bugbear chorus of threats and misery. (112)

I have already assigned certain stories in Munro's collections to the various initiatory groups; with these we can put some special cases and uncollected pieces that, in one way or another, have the same flavour. "Winter Wind," something of an initiatory story within a later group, is one of these; another is "The Stone in the Field," a second-phase story in some respects and coming after "Connection" (with which it is paired) in *The Moons of Jupiter*, yet so much a mirror of its companion that we can easily reverse phases here, or take the two stories as showing us complementary versions of the initiatory world alone. "Wood," still uncollected at the time of the present book, shows us the same world in a number of ways. In multipartite stories we can expect the first part to have an initiatory character, as with the Bert Matthews section of "Baptizing" and — more obviously — "Deadeye Dick," the first section of "Oh, What Avails." And we can expect the same thing with the first section of any story: "Working for a Living" contains a specially good example. For the present, however, we can limit ourselves to Munro's Genesis group proper, which of course means the opening stories in her books: "Walker Brothers Cowboy," "The Flats Road," "Something I've Been Meaning to Tell You," "Royal Beatings," "Connection," "The Progress of Love," "Friend of My Youth." Some of these are more initiatory than others, but all share a distinct quality — in all we can hear Munro asking, more insistently than anywhere else, "What was in the beginning?"

*

If we think of the world as originating in chaos, what was in the beginning must have been like the Flats Road — a place that belongs neither to town nor country, has no order of its own, and in general is best described by negatives. Here the houses are "more neglected, poor and eccentric" than in town:

> Half a wall would be painted and the job abandoned, the ladder left up; scars of a porch torn away were left uncovered, and a front door without steps, three feet off the ground; windows could be spread with yellowed newspapers in place of blinds. (6)

Munro already shows us such a world in an uncollected early piece, "The Edge of Town," and with minor alterations it continues to appear throughout her work: as West Hanratty in "Royal Beatings," the Jordans' run-down street in "Walker Brothers Cowboy," the scruffy road outside Dalgleish in "Connection," the "haphazard" (196) old Logan of "Deadeye Dick," and the Ottawa Valley of "Friend of My Youth" — "a scrambled, disarranged sort of country" (4–5).[2] Chaos can also, of course, be larger than a neighbourhood: the cousins in "Connection" exercise their bravado against the whole "prodigal, and dangerous, world" (6), full of "accidents, proposals, encounters with lunatics and enemies" (5). Benny in "The Flats Road" manages to cover an even greater area. Not only does he have his ramshackle little house (containing its own "wealth of wreckage" [4]) but in some sense Grenoch Swamp itself is his; when he makes his desperate foray to Toronto, Toronto promptly turns into a larger swamp again — a confusion of "factories, dead-end roads, warehouses, junkyards, railway tracks. . . . all kinds of clogged or barely floating waste" (25). And behind his house insects whirl in "galaxies" (2): where Benny is, chaos is universal.

Being a fisherman, Benny owns not only the swamp but the Wawanash River itself. Ben Jordan in "Walker Brothers Cowboy" similarly has a song about the Rio Grande; at Dalgleish we find "Father Maitland,"[3] and it is interesting to see Munro drafting a story called "Ole Man River."[4] If these various parental waters remind us of Father Nile, the name "Benny" has the same effect; so, in "Royal Beatings," does Flo's adopting of "Rose in the basket" (2) — and here we must see Egypt, not as a land of plenty, but as the primaeval river-swamp that surrounds Moses and from which, according to Egyptian mythology, the world first arose. Still another form of the original waters is the lake in "Walker Brothers Cowboy" or "Something I've Been Meaning to Tell You," paralleled by the ocean elsewhere. We should be in no doubt about this lake's potential for wildness: placid in "Walker Brothers Cowboy," with a "safe swimming area" (2) for good measure, it nevertheless has "all kinds of weathers" (18), like Father Ben Jordan himself.

If we want other elements for our chaos, Ben's Rio Grande song can tell us about "plungin' through the dusky sand" (7) — sand which, like the legendary quicksand in Grenoch Swamp, gives no firmer footing than water. And as he sings, Ben is taking his children with him to the inland country, "flat, scorched, empty" (7), a dry desert to match the wet one of the lake. The same desert, wet or dry, appears on a smaller scale whenever Munro points down to the footing of her pioneer towns, such as the "unpaved streets full of dust or puddles" in the old Logan.[5] One way or another, then, we are looking at an abyss — the same that Mary's world showed us in an earlier chapter. We have already seen something of the deep seas and grand canyons in "Something I've Been Meaning to Tell You"; Grenoch Swamp has its own great hole, attested by Uncle Benny, while the Wawanash River contains holes twenty feet deep.[6] Nor are these the only kinds of depth: the eyes of the blind mother of "Walker Brothers Cowboy" show "no shape of the eyeball, just hollows" (12), and as for the eyes of Mrs. Fullerton, a very initiatory presence in "The Shining Houses," "things sank into them and they never changed" (20).

*

As these eyes may suggest, chaos is people as well as places. For one thing, the inhabitants of Munro's Flats Roads are a rag-tag lot: shabby tradesmen, keepers of bizarre livestock, eccentrics, bootleggers, prostitutes, and idiots, to take the Flats Road itself as representative. Moreover, these people seem to have no real homes. Often, to be sure, they have habitats, and never venture far from them — a drive to Toronto is more than Uncle Benny can cope with, a ride to town too much for the aunts in "The Stone in the Field," not to say hermits like the Mr. Black of the same story.[7] But then Mr. Black is only a squatter, allowed to have his shack in a corner of the Flemings' farm; the same term can be applied to the others, even when, as in Mrs. Fullerton's case, time has given their squatting-places a curious fixity.[8] And many of the characters in these stories are not fixed at all: the sedentary Mr. Black at one end of "The Stone in the Field" is mirrored by the itinerant Poppy Cullender at the other; "Working for a Living" tells us about the trappers who once roamed the bush, living the life to which Munro's father, like the Ben Jordan of "Images," reverts for a time before surrendering to domesticity.[9] Ben Jordan the travelling salesman, the touring cousins in "Connection," the seasonal Blaikie Noble, all roam in much the same way; and when such people do settle down, there tends to be something unstable about the occupations they pick — they are like Mr. Jordan the fox-farmer, who likes the Flats Road because it tolerates odd and uncertain pursuits. Uncle Benny is even less stabilized, being only Mr. Jordan's hired hand; he is also a collector of junk, material with no place of its own, while Poppy Cullender in "The Stone in the Field" deals in antiques — junk to the farmers who sell them. Benny lives in the clutter of his junk; as for Janet's family, associated with Poppy in his business, "we were living in a warehouse" (19).

This world of wandering and provisional settlement, of hunting or primitive herding and cultivation, can suggest various analogues. Anthropologically there is something neolithic, even palaeolithic, about it. In white North American history it has a special connection with the pioneers or pre-pioneers: "The Stone in the Field," for instance, has Janet's father telling about the family's immigration to the new world.[10] Then there is the biblical analogy that I have already suggested. For one thing, the Flats Road is much like the Mesopotamian background to the Book of Genesis — a world close to flood and subject to amoral and capricious deities, the world in which Gilgamesh undertakes his wild adventure. We are equally in the Book of Genesis itself here, for among other things I will mention, we find Uncle Benny referring explicitly to the Flood, and Del to the Ark.[11] In "The Stone in the Field" "Mount Hebron" (24), located near the family farm, points us to a later part of the Book of Genesis, but still in one view to a chaos: a world of wandering and sojourning before the more settled residence in Egypt, not to say the Israelite kingdom.

*

In the story of an individual human life, genesis is the phase of gestation. This again can be put into different contexts: we may think of a state before any "falling into flesh" at all,[12] or of the uterine flood that precedes birth; and often the Genesis stories show us childhood itself, the undetermined world before the more definite one of maturity. "The Flats Road" features children of all ages — the youngsters, of course, but also the Madeleine who is "a child" (16) in spite of her seventeen years (itself not very old for a mother), and the Uncle Benny who, while as old again, is no less a child. It is Benny, in fact, who shows us most plainly what childhood means, for he cannot manage the abstracting by which other adults fix and distance their world.[13] He collects facts the way he collects junk, but has no means of ordering them; he cannot understand a telephone or a map or a traffic-light. For the same reason he shies from anything "public and official" (21), clinging rather to the immediately personal — directions from a man in a field, human-interest stories in his newspaper, the Heaven that goes on forever because "the Lord is there" (11). And if Benny is an extreme case of adult innocence, the shy Fleming aunts, the giddy Chaddeley cousins, the funny-man Ben Jordan, the guileless Arthur Comber, even the brash Blaikie Noble all have something of his simplicity. All respond as they can to a world they are unable to fathom; all, we should note, evade mature sexuality.[14]

Along with the children, there are the parents or quasi-parents: the elders whom the children spend so much time watching, as the girl in "Walker Brothers Cowboy," for instance, watches her father's adventure with Nora Cronin. One of these elders is Benny himself, who here again can show us something with special clarity. Benny has a very parental way with babies and animals — even Diane sleeps trustingly on his shoulder — yet also responds to the appeal of a "lady with one child" (12): a sexual object, perhaps, but certainly someone who arouses the child (if also the parent) in himself. To play either of these roles, in other words, is to have an aptitude for the other: the Genesis world is a beginning and end, the world both of those coming into the present life and of those leaving it. Conversely, it is the world of children finishing their prenatal adventures and old people preparing for such new ones as lie beyond death — in both cases the wrecked survivors of a previous life and the pioneers of a further one. In sum, we are in the world of "pop," a word we are going to meet with some frequency. Pop is what children want from their parents; it is what elders like "Pop" in "Thanks for the Ride" have for sale. It is also what happens in "Royal Beatings" when flash-bulbs "pop" (22) at the nonagenarian Hat Nettleton.[15]

Sometimes we find the parents in the Genesis stories to be as ineffectual — and as boyishly so — as Ben Jordan in "Walker Brothers Cowboy." But if Benny is a similar figure, he can also be a good deal fiercer in the way he orders the Jordan children around; the father in "Royal Beatings" may be a gentle man but beats his daughter with rage and pleasure. And some of the parents in these stories are tyrants pure and simple: there is Edward Tyde, for instance, according to the anecdote passed down in "Royal Beatings," or the Chaddeley patriarch as recalled by his grand-daughters. The authority of such fathers is not of the constitutional kind we will find in the central world, but that of sheer power, and personal power — for patriarchs as much as children live by personal relations. As a result they can be as high-handed as the god they believe in: in this respect the "powerful fathers" (23) remembered from pioneer times in "Working for a Living" are initiatory figures, concerning themselves with the "subjugation" (23) of a new world. The women attached to such men may be as "drained, flattened, bleak" (23) as the wife in a pioneer photograph — or a stretch of newly cleared farmland.

They may also be formidable in their own right: and while we can return to these women in a larger context, we need at least to acquaint ourselves with them here. The priggish Mrs. Jordan of "Walker Brothers Cowboy" is very much concerned for her own superior status in the world, very much against alcohol (she is sure her husband never touches it), and very much against obscenity — the dirty words, for instance, that laugh at her from the sidewalk. She has allies in various other women who take a hard line on drink and dirt, such as the Mrs. Jordan of "The Flats Road," or the Flo who has Rose trounced for saying filth and later keeps whisky away from Brian.[16] The other woman in "Walker Brothers Cowboy" is as formidable in an opposite way, for Nora Cronin brings out whisky and invites Ben to dance. Nora, we should add, makes this invitation very forcefully: in her more sensual way she is a cousin of Madeleine the "tartar." Becky Tyde in "Royal Beatings" invades with her tongue; Char Desmond may be far more statuesque and silent, but under the silence there is the same rage as Madeleine's, and with her smoking and her backless evening dress Char is no less scandalous than Nora.

One feature that connects the uncollected "Wood" with the Genesis stories is the presence of a similar figure in Roy Fowler's niece Karen[17] — not the Karen who has grown fat and sloppy but Karen the orphan and red-jacketed going concern, always "in such high gear" (48). And Karen can alert us to another important strain of imagery in these stories. Bursting into Roy's life as a girl, she impressed him by her talent for "twitchy" (48) lettering; the fact that this lettering was Old English may suggest the propriety of an Elizabeth, but "Old English" can have more Mary-like associations that we have not examined so far. The nation of that name started as barbarian raiders, and if we go far enough back Angles turn into angels — the star-angels who made war in heaven at the beginning of the world.[18] Similarly, "the Norwegian" of a projected novel was the original of Chris Watters in "How I Met My Husband" — an airman who flies in menacingly low, as planes also do in "The Flats Road." No doubt a later Germanic world can have more comfortable and burgherly associations, and for that matter characters like those I have just mentioned are domestic enough in some ways; but what concerns us here is the hint of barbarians[19] irrupting from a world of snow or the heavens themselves. Nor has barbarism come to an end: both "The Flats Road" and "Something I've Been Meaning to Tell You" are war-stories, set against a background of Germanic invasion.[20]

*

The Genesis world is thus one not only of victims but of oppressors: perhaps law-dealing tyrants, perhaps disruptive tartars, but in either case wielders of naked force. Such a world makes no sense — it is one of sheer necessity; and by the same token it is a matter of sheer happenstance, as Benny well knows:

> In that world people could go down in quicksand, be vanquished by ghosts or terrible ordinary cities; luck and wickedness were gigantic and unpredictable; nothing was deserved, anything might happen. (25)

All one can do in a situation like this is take one's chances, which is exactly what Benny does. He concocts schemes for selling turtles to Americans while talking about money from chinchillas and budgies; he gambles his personal happiness on a bride advertised in a tabloid. Above all he fishes — and gets hooked in the process, for like every trickster Benny is also a dupe. When we look about in the Genesis world we see many of his kind: these people who are so old and so young, so shrewd and so simple, are all cousins of the gambler Abraham and the trickster Jacob. One should be very careful with Ben Jordan, the salesman who uses his luck and his patter to sell dubious medicines; or the even more charming Blaikie Noble, who tries phoney guided tours and matrimonial ventures after squandering the family money; or the oily Poppy Cullender, who wheedles farmers out of their antiques. The Mr. Jordan of "The Flats Road," if not a trickster, is no less a gambler than these others: he is out to get rich on foxes. Less commercially, we have the bravado of Rose daring to sing her Vancouver song; we have the game and terrified cousins in "Connection," and for that matter we have their patriarchal grandfather, to whom they have attached a romantic tale about gambling debts at Oxford.[21]

A gambler is not simply a winner or loser, but a loser obsessed by a distant vision of winning: what excites fox-farmers and their like is "something precarious and unusual, some glamorous and ghostly, never realized, hope of fortune."[22] In other words, a gambler belongs to Mary's world of sensibility, in which contraries are experienced in their full contrariety; if the phases of a story cannot simply be identified with either Mary or Elizabeth, it is nevertheless in Mary's terms that Munro's initiatory world, seen for its uncertainty, asks to be understood.[23] Foxes themselves make a striking emblem here, since in addition to being untamable they seem always to be of the silver variety.[24] What this means, as she explains in "Working for a Living," is that they are silver on black. For it is Mary's black and white — the colours before all colour — that best represent the primal separation of light from darkness, sky from abyss, and that endow the Genesis stories with their special tonality.[25]

This tonality is readily apparent in Uncle Benny's house — the house that might as well be Benny himself. On the exterior it is unpainted and "silvery," standing out against the "black" (2) bush behind it; the dark inside, conversely, "swallow[s] light," (4) represented here by a single bulb. The buildings encountered by the Ben Jordan of "Walker Brothers Cowboy" during his salesman's tour are much the same — an unpainted house near some "black pine-shade" (7), then the Cronins' house itself "dried to silver in the sun" (10), with black-haired Nora and her "very white" teeth inside; and no matter how black things may be looking for Ben himself, he wears for the occasion "a white shirt, brilliant in the sunlight, a tie, light trousers belonging to his summer suit (his other suit is black, for funerals . . .) and a creamy straw hat" (6). In "The Flats Road" the emblematic Irene Pollox is an albino; when, on the other hand, we find her "crowing and flapping" (7), we think of something black — like the crow's feather picked up by the white-faced Diane (15), or Arthur Comber in "Something I've Been Meaning to Tell You" flapping the "crow's wings" of his black academic gown (15–16).[26]

*

Light will always suggest spirit or thought; in a sensibility world we can expect ideas and things to be both as distant from each other and as interinvolved as the whites and blacks we have just been collecting. We see this, for instance, in the curiously uncertain status of what people do and say in the Genesis stories: for the crises here have a distinct air of make-believe about them. When Madeleine threatens Del with a stove-lid lifter, there is no doubt that she would really use it; at the same time her rage appears "calculated, theatrical" (17), as if she were watching herself; and at the end of the story her audience will relegate her to the status of pure fiction, something to be applauded. The great set-to in "Royal Beatings" is prepared with the same care for effect: first Rose with her "theatrical unconcern" (13), then Flo getting "amazingly theatrical" herself, and finally the father drawn in to play his own role. The royal beating proper is a fine melodrama of crime and punishment, with Rose howling "Forgive me" (17); as for the father, "he is acting, and he means it" (16).[27] "The Progress of Love," in the same way, looks back to a crisis in which Phemie's grandmother was acting, according to Aunt Beryl, and meant it, according to Phemie's mother; "Friend of My Youth" raises similar doubts about Flora.

Performances like these take place in a world that, for all its litter of material objects, is itself strangely unreal: "life is but a dream" (18), sing the Chaddeley cousins, who do not share the hard materialism of the Flemings. Strange things occur in this dream — a poltergeist, a miracle, an airship lit by ten thousand light bulbs. On his trip to Toronto Benny descends like a shaman into a region of the weird and dangerous; Blaikie Noble, as Et imagines, seeks something equally fantastic, a jewel at the bottom of the ocean.[28] And even without such marvels this world is strange enough — the place of "emptiness, rumor, and absurdity" (223) in which "A Queer Streak" begins, and in which the bizarre hoax of that story's opening section becomes possible. Phemie or Euphemia in "The Progress of Love" prefers to call herself "Fame" (7) — the old term for rumour — and the neighbourhoods of these stories offer plenty to keep her busy.[29] Nor does rumour confine itself to the present and the living: raconteurs like the Chaddeley cousins and Flo all have their tales of a horrific or glamorous past. The father in "Royal Beatings," meanwhile, is scribbling speculations on scraps of paper, and as always we can point to Uncle Benny, with his repertory of wild tales, not to mention wild schemes and a wild newspaper. Even the level-headed Jordans live in this house of rumour: they are dependent both on Flats Road gossip and on the radio, with its unreliable news of a world "out of our control, unreal yet calamitous" (30).

To inhabit such a world is paranoia: we cannot know what is there, and by the same token we cannot know what is inside our heads and what outside. Madeleine is evidently an extreme case, brandishing weapons and snarling "dirty little spy-bugger" (17) at an innocent visitor, but she is by no means unique. One thing we notice is that several characters in these stories have the need and ability to draw things into themselves. Benny may not be able to cope with a map, but he can make his own — "a map of the journey was burnt into his mind" (25). Poppy Cullender in "The Stone in the Field" "must have had in his head a map of the surrounding country with every house in it" (20); Roy Fowler in the closely related "Wood" wants to get every tree in the district into his head, safely under his control. Roy's story also shows us the result. Believing a local gossip's tale, he is sure that a contractor is out to steal his trees, and feels greatly relieved when it occurs to him that the contractor is "nobody but himself" (54). The reader is left to wonder what difference that makes: in trying to forestall the contractor Roy has got into a very dangerous accident, harming himself as he feared someone else might. The man, that is, who wanted to get the material of the world into his head has turned a notion in his head into something material. He is thus like Sandy Stevenson in "The Flats Road" with his poltergeist, or Rose in "Royal Beatings" with her "filth," which must come out of her head into the real world where it can be punished. In the words of the poem with which we began, the initiatory world is a solid fantasy. Its landscapes, like those formed by the winter snow, are preposterous ones, and yet real Furies materialize here, ready to present their bizarre entertainment.

II. IN THE BEGINNING

"The royal beatings. What got them started (11)?" — how did the solid fantasy come about? Munro's opening stories ask this question not only with special insistence but in a way that takes us deep into the past. For while the question about royal beatings naturally makes us think of recent ones — those in Rose's childhood — the story tells us of more remote disasters as well, just as other of Munro's opening stories tell of the beginnings of families or towns. And we are taken farther back again: Blaikie Noble has a tour-guide's routine that includes Indian graves and limestone; Ben Jordan explains to his daughter how the Great Lakes came into being, ages ago; and Uncle Benny, pointing to a rainbow, proclaims the end of the Flood. Even a casual phrase like "our lost starting-point" (12), ostensibly referring to a particular quarrel between Rose and Flo, takes on a much greater resonance in such a context.

This does not mean, of course, that we can simply equate the main action in one of these stories with the origin of the world: if "Royal Beatings" imagines a beginning for Rose's story, it also makes clear that this beginning was not that of things in general, or even royal beatings in general. When, moreover, we go any distance into the history of beatings, we come to a world quite unlike our own — "present time and past, the shady melodramatic past of Flo's stories, were quite separate. . . . Present people could not be fitted into the past" (8). In Rose's early childhood, we learn, people called the First War the Last War, suggesting for one thing what Munro spells out in an article on Dickens's *Child's History of England*:

> There is no doubt in the mind of a good Victorian that the Dark Ages are past. That is another time and another kind of reality; it goes without saying. . . . (37)[30]

Benny is being a good Victorian when he insists that the Flood is over and done with. So is Ben Jordan when he tells his daughter about the Ice Age — long ago, it seems, a mighty hand pressed down into the landscape, but great depressions do not happen nowadays. The effect of such dissociation is clear from the same passage on Dickens: "the whole story has the charm and recklessness and exaggeration of a spell-binding fairytale" (37). The quarrel between Rose and Flo is itself "like a dream that goes back and back into other dreams" (11); and if we go far enough back we arrive at the dream time in which fact turns into myth — not just Flo's fabled days of working at the Toronto Union Station but "a life Flo seemed to have had beyond that, earlier than that, crowded and legendary, with Barbara Allen and Becky Tyde's father and all kinds of old outrages and sorrows jumbled up together in it" (10).[31]

And yet the mythical past and factual present are not just opposites. Things were different in the early days, says old Hat Nettleton in "Royal Beatings" — and indeed they were, from what we are told in this chapter. But in one form or another royal beatings still occur, as well as provocation to them (Flo at this stage is in the County Home biting the nurse); and in fact what we are dealing with here is projection — or retrojection, if we prefer. In "Something I've Been Meaning to Tell You" Et Desmond looks at a past spectacle — an attractive one in this case — that seems, and is, very different from anything present: in an old photograph her family sit grandly before a "pillar and draped curtain, a scene of receding poplars and fountains" (6). Yet the recession in the picture is illusory (the grandiose background being only "a dusty, yellowing screen"), and so is the temporal recession separating the picture from the Et who later studies it. This has a double implication: on the one hand, there is nothing to Et's vision of beauty; on the other, there is more to it than she can be comfortable with. For as she senses, "the qualities of legend ... [are] real": not only did beauty once exist in the world, but it was that of a girl who sits before the receding view in the picture — Et's own sister Char. For that matter, this sister is not just the girl who once posed for a photo: still beautiful, she is in the next room doing the washing.

In "The Progress of Love" there is a similar intuition, for the reader and to some extent at least for Phemie herself, when the latter goes back to the house of her childhood. What she finds on the bedroom wall is a naked couple, yellow-haired and blue-eyed, their skin "a flat beige pink" (27) — painted, evidently, by the commune that came along after her parents' death. Nothing seems left of the cornflower wallpaper that Phemie once helped her mother put on, paper that looked like the flowering fields outside the window. But then Phemie does find a bit of it: all the layers of experience represented in the room are still there. And implicitly they are one with each other, for Phemie's old-fashioned parents were in their way the same Adam and Eve as the hippie couple on the wall. Whatever the tensions in their marriage, they too were beautiful though poor, and on one occasion Phemie — who like most children has little distinct awareness of her mother's appearance — noticed her smiling a strangely radiant smile, a smile with the quality of legend. As something projected in time a story cannot be pure beginning or pure aftermath, nor can the two things be entirely unrelated. Not only is there a linear connection between them, but each contains the other, so that a story of beginnings already embodies the conditions it explains. The quarrel of Rose and Flo, to think of fall rather than innocence, "has been going on forever" (11); it also begins on the day when Rose gets her royal beating.

*

If things do and do not change, we will now have to limit ourselves to the first side of this paradox: for the only way to deal with the start of royal beatings is to contrast their presence with an earlier absence, as we have already begun to do. And so we must picture either a long-ago innocence or the present of the Genesis stories at its most gratifying. Del Jordan as a little girl walks barefoot over the stubble, smells Uncle Benny's smell of fur and fish, or watches him stick gum on his fork. These are all pleasant experiences — the world is full of a number of things; and the world even has a glory about it. "All things are alive" (3), Rose's father writes in one of his philosophical notes; in Uncle Benny's more practical wooing letter a ramshackle house and unkempt property become a paradise full of delightful and friendly animals. So, for the narrator of "Walker Brothers Cowboy," does the local Woolworths store, with "live birds singing in its fan-cooled corners and fish as tiny as fingernails, as bright as moons" (4).

The wildflowers along the Flats Road are taken more for granted, yet Munro has written an essay about her own Flats Road in which she speaks of the plants there with all the wonder of the child in the Woolworths store.[32] Perhaps Phemie feels something of the same wonder when she looks out, in a specially happy mood, at the summer milkweed and wild carrot and mustard. In a more cultivated form the unfallen countryside becomes the England to which the Chaddeleys look back, an "ancient land of harmony and chivalry . . . all fresh and rural, ceremonious, civilized, eternally desirable" (10). Rose's father dreams of a more urban paradise, the city with cloud-capped towers and gorgeous palaces; and in Benny's "The Lord is there" we have the name of the holy city itself.[33] But whether ordered or simple, all these Edens share the same grace: the grace that, as remembered in "Walker Brothers Cowboy," once suffused even a plain fox-farm. That was in a more "leisurely" (5) time, like the "far gentler and more ceremonious time" (2) preceding the arrival of Flo in "Royal Beatings." In those days Rose's mother did fine work with upholstery; the Chaddeleys were impeccably genteel; the dinosaurs in "Walker Brothers Cowboy," if not genteel, had a primordial richness of energy that was itself a grace.

But the dinosaurs are extinct; England is far away, as is the Chaddeley gentility; and graces that are more present in a physical sense are elusive in other ways. The treasures of Woolworths are not only downtown but unavailable, since the Jordans could hardly afford them. The flowers of the field may be there for anyone to see, but the gift of seeing has itself become an uncertain thing: Phemie has to peer out through a "mesh of screens and . . . wavery old window glass" (7). It seems that innocence is never fully or steadily here in the world we now know — always something in an Other Place or Other

Time. In "The Moons of Jupiter," a story of ending that returns to the matter of beginning, Janet's father tells a suggestive tale about running away from home. In his flight, he says, he came on a quince tree — not what one would expect in Huron County — and while he did not quite eat the fruit, he did feel that he was in "a new part of the world" (220). But he could never find the quince tree again.

Where a marvellous first world did not vanish, it collapsed: there was "a great comedown, a dim catastrophe."[34] Once, says Ben Jordan, there were the dinosaurs, but "then came the ice, creeping down from the north, pushing deep into the low places" (3). And so a cold hand passed over, leaving its "fingers" in the land; these fingers became the severing lakes, and now there is only the flat and exhausted topography through which Ben and his daughter make their way. Elsewhere in "Walker Brothers Cowboy" the same story appears in less focused versions. We have already heard Ben's song about plunging through the sand of the Rio Grande; we equally hear of "ragged, dissolving" children's games, and the children themselves separating into "islands of two or one" (2). Everywhere, it seems, things fail and disintegrate, or an abyss is opened by a force that is itself now enervated and listless.

At the same time, something more violent is going on: if the ships in the harbour are merely "ancient, rusty, wallowing" (2), we also find that the roots of trees "have cracked and heaved the sidewalk and spread out like crocodiles" (1) — or like the grimmer sort of dinosaurs, or the fingers of the glacier. In more historical terms, we have encountered upheavals such as the two World Wars and the various other conflicts echoing through "Something I've Been Meaning to Tell You." Like Abraham called out from the fertile crescent, with its own history of war and displacement, people are driven to make the dangerous passage across the ocean, to move on into the heart of the new world, even to reach its far coast. And the final result is a population of refugees: for in the context of war that is what the flotsam and jetsam of these stories are — the immigrants and the cast-offs, the wanderers and the washed-up losers. War or depression, war and depression, war that is depression — in one way or another a flourishing world is replaced by a great ruin.

*

But if, as we have seen, the present is implicit in the past, Munro can also show us the opposite of this collapsing innocence: an outwardly unfallen world in which the agencies of the Fall are already at work.

Eden seen in this way will have a latent corruption about it, as well as something "hectic, unsure":[35] a grace asking for its own failure. Such a rickety paradise will be like what we may or may not choose to distinguish from it, an early (or, for that matter, later) greatness within the fallen world to which it gives way. The Book of Genesis not only speaks of Eden, but of subsequent giants and angels and lost civilizations; on a more modest scale it shows us the prosperity and longevity of an Abraham or Jacob — still a matter of fabulous luck and favour rather than anything more mundane. In Munro's Genesis group we often find something comparable: an early world — earlier, perhaps, than the main action of a story — which is neither innocent nor as settled as we suppose our own world to be, but rather has the glory of a flash about it. We can think of such a world either as original brightness not quite lost or as frontier splendour; in either case what it often is is cavalier — careless, festive, not to say raffish. In "Something I've Been Meaning to Tell You" we have "Mock Hill" in its palmy days, the lakeside resort town with the dazzling light and grand hotel. It is here that Char and Blaikie have their fine and reckless love; and the Cleopatras and Lancelots and Napoleons whose legends hover about them appear as romantic gamblers of the same sort.

They all lose, of course: similarly, the partying Fordyces of "Dead-eye Dick" lose their easy-come-easy-go affluence, and Nora Cronin's brief flirtation with Ben Jordan is a last vestige of earlier high times. For the world of such people has really been under judgment from the start. The Cronins have always been considered by their Protestant neighbours to "dig with the wrong foot" (14); the carryings-on of Blaikie Noble or Char have been equally scandalous to the local townspeople, and Char in particular has had the all-seeing eye of her sister upon her since childhood. In "Connection" Cousin Iris boldly lives her creed of "movement, noise, change, flashiness, hilarity, and courage" (16), but she too is under a shadow, that of her domineering grandfather: her very giddiness, as Janet comes to see, is that of someone "brash and greedy and scared." Char is more than brash — when not in her abject phase, she can be visibly wrathful, even cruel. Indeed the whole of the cavalier world has the same cruelty about it: a royal beating, as imagined by Rose, would be "an occasion both savage and splendid" (1), and there was a fine savagery, if less of royalty, in the great age of horses recalled by Hat Nettleton.

We can also reverse our perspective here. A burgeoning early world can itself be a judging one — a royal beating, after all, is an act of punishment. It was a legendary gentleman whose high-handedness and snobbery crippled the Chaddeley cousins. Edward Tyde in his heyday was another gentleman of sorts, living in a fine house "before the neighborhood got so downhill" (6) — and it was Tyde whose assaults on his daughter left her no less giddy than Cousin Iris. Nor is the world of immigrant prosperity always cavalier. Tyde, for instance, is not free-and-easy at all, but notoriously tight-fisted. The pioneer town in "Meneseteung" — to draw for a moment on a different initiatory group — is remarkable not for lordly stylishness but puritan enterprise.[36] We hear of shysters and bravos, of course, but this is a respectable community. Even the central beating of Queen Aggie by hoodlums is its own kind of law-enforcement, like the beating of Tyde, and the local paper, which objects strongly to Queen Aggie, has nothing to say about the beating itself.

If we take more than a simple view, then, the world of early swashbuckling and, in a specially intense form, the world we associate with later sense and compromise have both been there all along. To turn them into individual people, we can say that Mary and Elizabeth have always been fighting their battle, and that this is what the cosmogonic war itself amounted to. In the very comprehensive "Labor Day Dinner" we find a pair of sisters with the suggestive names Angela and Eva — the seductive Angela, like the mythical Lilith, being the elder. Of the two it is Eva who belongs to a world of law and license. Angela was, as she herself says, the "pre-permissive child" (153), whereas her sister not only is explicitly "puritan" but gets away with being "outrageous" (135) — outrageous, like Flo, in her very puritanism. If Munro had written the story from another perspective, Eva's wildness might have been vested in Angela, who resembles Char in some ways, and the name "Eva" might have belonged to someone more like the poised Angela we have. As it is, we find an Eva rambunctious, optimistic — and in danger of being left "smashed and stranded" (152). "I am not a relic" (157), she proclaims loudly, yet the thoughtful Ruth imagines her as the Bride of Lammermoor, and near the end we see her with her veil askew and her face "a patchy flower" (157).

If we compare these emblematic sisters with more central figures in "The Progress of Love," we find the same situation — with, of course, the variations we expect in Munro. Marietta, the older of two sisters, has the cool beauty of Char or Angela, as her name suggests she might. The younger Beryl, like Et or Eva, is the plain one; she also sports a white-and-red outfit no less outrageous than Eva's. The two

stories differ in that here it is the elder who is the Puritan, though in
a staid rather than outrageous way, while the younger — whose outfit
is more fashionable than Eva's — lives a life of easy virtue in
boom-time California. Eventually the two confront each other, and
Beryl is left smashed on learning what her sister did with their father's
money. Nor is this the end of the feud: in the next generation
Marietta's daughter Phemie will run away to live an unpuritan life
with no regrets. Perhaps, as Phemie supposes, peace has come when
she has no daughters of her own, but in a larger sense the war will
go on as long as time. Only when Phemie notices her mother's
gracious smile at the heart of the quarrel do we glimpse the true Eve,
the greater woman whose loss left only a pair of spatting and
negotiating sisters.[37]

III. THE FALLING TITAN

As we have watched a disintegrating world, our picture has concentrated itself into that of two persons having a quarrel — two women,
as we have mainly found them, though we will be seeing other
possibilities.[38] If we go on concentrating, we arrive at one rather than
two: a single life that has somehow failed. The stories we are
concerned with often mention accidents that leave people mutilated;[39] and while such figures occur in various contexts in Munro,
from the initiatory point of view they are all, so to speak, First War
casualties, like Jimmy Saunders the one-legged veteran in "Something
I've Been Meaning to Tell You." And if an accident still suggests
something happening from outside, we can move further inward. A
number of people in Munro, as we have seen, suffer in the "tray" of
their bodies. Among specially initiatory figures we find that Uncle
Benny, for instance, has respiratory trouble; in "Royal Beatings"
Munro tells us more pointedly that Rose's father coughs because his
"lungs took in a whiff of gas in the War" (3) — the First War again
— and that other men who cough are dying of the "foundry disease"
(3). If, accordingly, we go back to Munro's accounts of foundings and
founderings, we will now notice that Edward Tyde died of pneumonia
after his royal beating and that Rose's mother died of a blood-clot in
the lung. Somehow an original life lost its power to breathe: the
shadow-life succeeding it breathes a more poisoned kind of spirit if
it manages to breathe at all.

The self with the breathing problem rules a whole world of infirmity. Wheezing Uncle Benny is king of Grenoch Swamp, having dominion over every living thing there and especially the fish.[40] At the same time he is only a fisher king, a king in ruin — not to say Benjamin, a captive in Egypt. In his background stands a more purely iconic figure: the Charlie Buckle whose store is located at the beginning of the Flats Road. "Buckle" is suggestive enough in the context of a fall,[41] and "Charlie" can introduce us to another wasteland empire — a specially important one in Munro. To begin with this empire's imperialness, we have noted[42] that the "original" Charles, the one who made the name familiar, was Charlemagne: the "great Charles," in other words, even though "carl" or "churl" simply means a human being and has come to mean a peasant. As the first Holy Roman Emperor, Charlemagne buckled the world together in various ways.[43] Ruling the west, he contemplated marriage with Irene, empress of the east;[44] in alliance with the Pope he tried to found a universal theocracy. For inspiration he turned to *The City of God* — in other words, to the city whose name we have already seen in Benny's "The Lord is there" (11). Elsewhere in Munro we find "St. Augustine" itself as a place-name, applied in one instance to Harry Brooke's heavenly city in "The Edge of Town," with its stained glass and Madonna lilies. Charlemagne's great claim was to rule over such a city on earth; Charlie Buckle suggests an even higher claim, for "we could see him through the dark screen like a figure partly hidden in a mosaic, and bowed our heads" (7). Charlie, it appears, has installed himself in a sanctuary.

Munro's Charlies include still another impressive patriarch, as we learn when the Jubilee radio plays an anniversary piece for "Mr. and Mrs. Carl Otis" (149). "Otis," "son of Odo," comes from a Germanic root meaning prosperity; it also, of course, suggests a way of going up in the world. And not only is Carl Otis elevated in himself: he and his wife have an impressive progeny in "their foundry son George and wife Etta, and their three grandchildren, Lorraine, Mark, and Lois." We can return to "George" presently; George's wife Etta is problematical. I feel more confident about the Otises' grandchildren Lorraine, Mark, and Lois: the successor states to the Carolingian empire were precisely Lotharingia (that is, Lorraine), Germany (ruled by a line of Ottos and including the "march" or "mark" of western Christendom), and France — the land not only of Odo but of Louis, as elsewhere in Munro.[45]

With such descendants the Otis family certainly does honour to its founder; and yet he may not warrant it as much as he seems to do. "Otis" also suggests words like "otiosus," and if we turn again to Charlie Buckle, we can see signs of going down rather than up in the world — for Charlie's store is creaky and squalid, marking the transition from the order of town to the anarchy of the Flats Road. When we think of it, Charlemagne's establishment was not dissimilar: only a flash in a dark age following the collapse of a greater civilization. In anything like its original form, it proved as flimsy as other cases of refugee prosperity we have looked at, and what it bequeathed to later Europe was the long shadow of its failure.

*

If a Charlie is a fallen titan, great only in ruin, there are various others implied by the names in these stories — titans, again, who may not really have been very titanic. One close to Charlemagne in many ways looms behind "Something I've Been Meaning to Tell You": as we have already seen, there are various touches of Arthurian legend about the love of Char and Blaikie, and the king himself appears in the person of "Arthur Comber." This is an invalid Arthur, of course, and his surname, while no doubt suggesting someone who comes romantically from the deep, inevitably suggests an encumbrance as well.[46] King Arthur reappears suggestively in the last story of the same collection, "The Ottawa Valley": in particular we find the narrator's mother quoting (or misquoting) the lines with which Tennyson's Arthur sets off for "the island-valley of Avilion" (245) to be healed of his wound.[47] The book thus ends with both the passing of Arthur and the hint that he has been asleep throughout its course — that a greater Arthur will rest in the valley "Until the Day Break"[48] at the end of time. All Munro can show us as flourishing within the world is the likes of "Art Chamberlain": the Arthur whose mastery is servitude, and who looks as inert as we have imagined Carl Otis to be.

While we are considering masterful lovers, we should also think of the mysterious "X" in "Bardon Bus," whose name seems to be Alex Walther (that is, "wielder of power") (128); Duncan in "Dulse," whose present name will concern us later, was an "Alex" up to the New Yorker version of that story. Here is another emperor, then — one, moreover, with several incarnations in "Something I've Been Meaning to Tell You." There is the maimed war veteran Jimmy "Saunders" whom Et keeps screened away from the ladies; in an earlier and longer form of the story Blaikie Noble himself played Alexander the Great in "What's my name?"[49] Above all, the story's world is contained by the drowned brother "Sandy" — the form of whose name links him not only with Alexander but with the Ben Jordan of "Walker Brothers Cowboy" and others who plunge "through the dusky sand" (7). Once again we have the hint that worldly rule is only the shadow of something lost — a house built on sand, as we will now want to say. It seems fitting, then, that in "The Flats Road" the hapless adventurer who wins and loses an eastern bride should be called Sandy Stevenson; and later we will have to consider his sandiness again.

We can deal with some other related names more briefly. I have already remarked that "James," while originating with the winner Jacob, usually adheres to losers in Munro's world, such as the ineffectual Uncle James of "The Ottawa Valley." If we go back to "Jimmy Saunders" again, perhaps we will better see why: this is a maimed Jimmy, one who has gone the way of a Sandy — ironically if we think of God's promise to make his descendants like the sand of the sea.[50] Perhaps we have here, too, a clue to the dead "Jimmy Poole" mentioned in "Heirs of the Living Body" (53); we can add both that Jimmy Poole must be a kinsman of Uncle Benny — Benjamin Poole — and that in Munro's early draft material a boy named Jimmy drowned in Grenoch Swamp.[51] One further royal name, as well as a member of the "Ad-" family, appears in the "Uncle Ned" of a song sung in "Boys and Girls": "Oh, there's no more work, for poor Uncle Ned, he's gone where the good darkies go" (120). The Ben Jordan of "Walker Brothers Cowboy" has his own wistful song to explain the result:

Old Ned Fields, he now is dead,
So I am ridin' the route instead. (7)

"Fields" here may remind us of a desert or of Eden — there may even be a faint echo of the word "Eden" in the "Ned" that is also "Ed": in any case a kingly figure has passed away, and only the hapless Ben is left to carry on.

*

Another of Munro's Neds can help us to see our figure of a buckled Charlie more plainly. The sullen and miserly Edward Tyde in "Royal

Beatings" has, in the first place, a surname suggestive both of "tide" (and thus an ocean) and of what "tide" more basically means, time. Tyde, in other words, indicates the collapse from eternity into mere temporality. What he does not yet seem to be in his day of pride is time as split into past, present, and future, for when he has the great fall we are told about, this is the work of three younger men:

> Jelly Smith, a horse-racer and a drinker; Bob Temple, a ball-player and strongman; and Hat Nettleton, who worked on the town dray, and had his nickname from a bowler hat he wore. (7)

Leaving the names and activities of these three to speak for them-selves, I will suggest an association between the trio as a trio and the three aspects of time: in any case the very fact of their number means something, for this is not the only place in Munro where we will find three contrasted with one (we have, for instance, just met Lorraine, Mark, and Lois, the three grandchildren of Carl Otis). In "Walker Brothers Cowboy" there is no such arrangement, but there is the family name itself to consider, since "Cronin" sounds like not only "crone" but *chrónos*. And there is a further connection worth suggesting here:

> "We've taken a lot of your time now."
> "Time," says Nora bitterly. "Will you come by ever again?" (17)

In this exchange it seems that not only Ben but time itself is unlikely to return, even that in some sense Ben *is* time. So perhaps is Nora's dead father, who can hardly return if the front door has been shut ever since his funeral (11). The Greeks conflated *chrónos* with Kronos or the Roman Saturn: the titan who castrates his father Uranus is himself overthrown by his children the gods, and leaves the present world-order to be established under a triumvirate.[52] Once again, that is, we find fathers set against children and one against many — Kronos and the three gods in this case, like Jupiter and his moons elsewhere in Munro. Kronos with his sickle, moreover, can alert us to something else about Edward Tyde's story that will need ponder-ing. Tyde is a butcher, and turns into "Butcher's meat" (8) himself when he gets his timely beating from the three young men.

There are various butchers in the initiatory world. Fox-farmers like Mr. Jordan and hired men like Benny butcher their foxes and horses (including old Mack, the "Uncle Ned" of the song); Charlie Buckle slices meat in his back room; even the gentlemanly grandfather in "Connection" turns out to have been a butcher's apprentice before emigrating to Canada. Some of Munro's initiating butchery can best be saved until later, but there is a figure in the background of "The Flats Road" who needs to come forward at this point, one who will show us that butchery is not limited to meat. This is the mysterious older brother who dangles Madeleine before Benny's eyes: we are told very little concerning this "Mason Howey," but taken with what we have just seen about butchers, his name itself can tell us certain things. To begin with, "Howey" sounds like other names in Munro such as "Howie," "Hugh," "Ewart": a difficult complex to derive etymologically (among other things "Ewart" may be connected with "Edward"), but having various associations with loftiness or spirit.[53] And there seems a further association to be made for forms like "Howey" and "Hugh": they suggest the verb "hew" or its German counterpart "hauen," as in "Fleischhauer."

Mason Howey, then, would seem to be another butcher, or at any rate cutter. At the same time he is a mason: and this means for one thing that he is connected with some very unlofty things in Munro. There is the despised farm-girl Muriel Mason in "Half a Grapefruit"; there is Mason Street in *Lives of Girls and Women*, where we find the down-to-earth Naomi;[54] most suggestively there is the Mason jar in which Joe Phippen keeps his whisky — a material container for spirits. The name "Potter," we can note, has comparable associations: a lowly Potter girl works in the glove factory in "Baptizing," and here again we find a connection with spirits, since the Potter boys are among the bootleggers on the Flats Road. On the other hand, both a "potter" and a "mason" are makers, and in Munro a Hugh can be the same thing: both Hugo in "Material" and Ewart in "Memorial" devote themselves to producing works of art. A "Mason Howey" must be creator and butcher at once — like the biblical God, then, the potter who both makes and breaks his pots.[55]

To draw the same process of making and breaking from historical allusions, we will have to return to figures like Charles and Alexander. Alexander conquered a world; it promptly split into warring successor states, including that of the Ptolemaic Cleopatra. At the time of the latter's liaison with Antony, conversely, Rome was in the throes of civil war, after which it became a monolithic empire. Charlemagne's empire began as a single construction, then gave birth to all the wrangles of church and state, church and church, state and state, that have plagued Europe ever since, starting with the fateful division of "Lorraine, Mark, and Lois." Nor was this Charlie the only butcher of modern Europe. The Anglican parish in *Lives of Girls and Women* includes a butcher named "Dutch Monk," whose name in such a context suggests an imbroglio of Erasmus, Luther, and Catholic tradition — that is, it suggests Reformation squabbles and a butchered mediaeval Church. And perhaps we can detect a similar squabble if we turn to Billy Pope, the butcher in *Who Do You Think You Are?* The "original" Billy was William the Conqueror, with his associations of secular might and victory; the particular state instituted by William was eventually ruled by the most anti-papal of all heroes, William of Orange — a King Billy whom we will find making some conspicuous appearances in Munro.[56]

We have come on various other historical breakings — the two World Wars, the American Civil War, the struggle of English and French; we have also seen the makings that can come of them, such as the United States. And in one way or another, the same linking of consolidation and division meets us everywhere in Munro. If Flo goes to work in the Union Station, she is sure to see a man sliced open like a watermelon. If, on the other hand, we start along the Flats Road, Charlie Buckle the butcher is followed by Louie Hall the watch and clock repairman — a mender of time. Rose's father is a repairman, as is Uncle Benny at least in principle. Rose's mother works with upholstery, Flo trims and fits linoleum, and the mother in "Walker Brothers Cowboy" seems especially thorough: she "rip[s] up" an old suit and dress of her own, then "cut[s] and match[es]," putting her daughter through "endless fittings" (1) to achieve what is aptly called her "creation" (5).

*

One other image and one other given name can help us to sum up all this cutting and fitting. In the first place, we have it on the authority of Uncle Benny's newspaper that a woman once sent "her husband's torso, wrapped in Christmas paper, by mail to his girl friend in South Carolina" (5). Carolina is of course the world of Charles, with its founder Charles II and its city Charleston. Later in *Lives of Girls and Women* North Carolina makes an appearance (166), and without labouring the matter we can recall Munro's general sensitivity to North and South — ultimately, to a whole world of divided united states. As for the Christmas paper, we can say at this stage that it is a material, if sanctified, container, and that in the circumstances the gift of life it should contain can only come as that of shock. In a general sense it is thus like the Mason jar with the whisky inside; or if we want to stay with paper, we can go back to "Walker Brothers Cowboy" and watch Ben Jordan make a cigarette. Having noted the link between a butterfly and the soul or spirit in "Day of the Butterfly," we will now sense what is happening when Ben "shakes tobacco out carefully on one of the thin butterfly papers, flicks it with his tongue, seals it . . . (3)."[57] Now it is ready to be set on fire.

The given name we need at this point is "George": specifically a vine-dresser in Greek, but etymologically something more suggestive here, a "worker of the earth." One thing this can mean appears in the George of "Labor Day Dinner," a house-maker and, when he has the time, an artist specializing in "pop sculpt" (143).[58] Such a creator looks down on beings he regards as lesser, especially women with their creaturely vanities.[59] On the other hand "George Klein," a prospective engineer,[60] sounds like a humbler kind of maker; George in "Thanks for the Ride" is merely inept, in spite of his swagger;[61] and in "Spelling" Flo's response to an award-winning George is "Look at the Nigger!" (187). After all, the original worker of the earth, himself made from it, was Adam — traditionally "red earth" — and the name "George" itself has been taken to mean "man of earth."[62]

There is some question, then, about George's credentials as a maker. No doubt the George of "Labor Day Dinner" really does his sculpting (or would if he could finish recreating his house): working only in wood,[63] he claims to produce things as solid as a potato, not to say a two-headed baby. Yet the "wooden doughnuts" (143) in which he also specializes must have holes in them: they thus suggest other cosmogonic hollowings we have seen, such as the gouging of the earth that produced the world of "Walker Brothers Cowboy." We will also remember Ben Jordan's "Plungin' through the dusky sand" (7); and here we can note that Munro's "foundries," as represented by the one in "Working for a Living," produce heavy castings moulded in sand and clay — accompanied, of course, by dust-filled air, the source of the foundry disease. We can also note something that haunts Angela in "Labor Day Dinner": a memory, or dream, in which Munro's creation imagery appears with extraordinary concentration.

Angela has one picture in her mind of Eva before Eva was born. The three of them — Angela, her mother, and her father — are on a beach. Her father is scooping out a large hole in the sand. Her father is a gifted builder of sand-castles with road and irrigation systems, so Angela watches with interest any projects he undertakes. But the hole has nothing to do with a sand-castle. When it is finished her mother rolls over, giggling, and fits her stomach into it. In her stomach is Eva, and the hollow is like a spoon for an egg. (148)

Some of the imagery here — especially the mother who takes the place of the castle — will come back again: what matters at present is, on the one hand, the hollowing-out of a space in the sand, and on the other the father's making of splendid but baseless fabrications.

Now perhaps we can get the paradox of the last pages into focus. When first considering chaos, we noted that a sink of material might also be a grand canyon. In the hole of space, after all, something can only take the place of nothing; according to St. Augustine the world itself was made from nothing; and if this is so, something depends on nothing — in a fully metaphoric vision they are the same thing. This thing of nothing is also the kingly creator himself: a busy worker, perhaps, but also a Carl "Otis," or Rose's withdrawing father,[64] or the solid George who is less solid than he seems. Another of Munro's Georges, the Walker Brothers man expected by Nora Cronin instead of Ben Jordan, is called "George Golley" (10); and while this George's surname may hint both at Goliath (the source of the word) and more strongly at "golly" or "God," it also sounds suspiciously like "gully." The same name with a different spelling — "Gauley" — recurs in "Miles City, Montana," where it applies both to a boy who falls into the river and to the father who lets him do so. In both stories, then, we have not only a Golley but a man in charge who at a crisis is not there. If we now turn to a further cluster of stories parallel to the Genesis group, we will find a comparable figure: a god who says "I am," and is not, in the emptiness of a desert.

IV. WILDERNESS

When Del Jordan enters the Anglican Church in "Age of Faith," what she sees above the communion table is Holman Hunt's Christ, a figure "more regal and more tragic" (98) than her own church has prepared her for. Del reaches out to such a god: he is her only safeguard against "the strange, anxious pain that just seeing things could create" — her fear of "the dull grain of wood in the floor boards, the windows of plain glass filled with thin branches and snowy sky" (100).[65] Here, just as in the Genesis stories, we are at a threshold; here again we experience the world as naked existence, not really a world at all; and here again we find a deity associated with formidable power and formidable humiliation.

I have already suggested a reason for this parallel. Just as "The Flats Road" comes at the beginning of a first cycle, so "Age of Faith" comes at the beginning of a second: it belongs to a group of "Wilderness" stories, as I have called them, which we can associate with the crossing of sea and desert between Egypt and the Promised Land. "Age of Faith," while the clearest example of such a story in Munro, may be confusing here in that it is much concerned with the Passion; but what it shows at work there is the old God of Sinai in all his arbitrary power. If we turn to the other Wilderness stories we find a large and varied group. In the first place there is the chapter "Wild Swans" in *Who Do You Think You Are?* — with which we can associate the uncollected "Characters," a story about Rose in high school that would have had to come in roughly a Wilderness position if Munro had included it in the novel.[66] In the various collections we find three stories in *Dance of the Happy Shades* — "The Office," "An Ounce of Cure," and "The Time of Death"; "Walking on Water" in *Something I've Been Meaning to Tell You*; "The Turkey Season" in *The Moons of Jupiter*; and again no less than three stories in *The Progress of Love* — "Monsieur les Deux Chapeaux," "Miles City, Montana," and "Fits." In *Friend of My Youth* we can single out "Meneseteung" and "Hold Me Fast, Don't Let Me Pass." Another uncollected story, "The Dangerous One," seems to me to have a very strong Wilderness flavour, and "Wood" shows a strong affinity to stories like "Fits."

The Wilderness phase follows that of the Exodus, and, as we ought to expect, the boundary between the two can be hard to draw — "Half a Grapefruit" and "Dulse," for instance, are best treated as Exodus stories with certain Wilderness features.[67] But it is easy enough to say what each of these phases is in principle. An Exodus story emphasizes the experience of escape itself; a Wilderness story deals more with what escape leads to, the lonely no-man's-land between an old world and a new. The figures we encounter in this emptiness are, again, best seen as proper to it: figures of solitude on the one hand and naked confrontation on the other. The Wilderness thus corresponds — in terms of the narrative structure described in the last chapter — not to the end of a first phase or cycle, but to the detachment between this and a central phase.[68] If we travel on, we find the Wilderness on its far border touching the world of Judges: we find, that is, increasing concern with entry into a new country. In *Lives of Girls and Women* this Judges world gets a chapter to itself; in some other cases it simply merges into the Wilderness phase preceding it or the Kingdom phase beyond. In the present chapter I shall make some use of what I consider Judges stories where they also show Wilderness characteristics, but leave discussion of their more special features until later.

As we approach Munro's Wilderness we can as elsewhere provide ourselves with some talismans: a good supplier is Miss Farris in "Changes and Ceremonies," whose list of operettas begins with *The Pied Piper*, *The Gypsy Princess*, *The Stolen Crown*, and *The Arabian Knight*. The first of these sounds like a Genesis story, being the tale of a lone wizard in motley; and for reasons that will become clearer, the next two can be associated with Munro's next biblical phases — *The Gypsy Princess* with Egypt and *The Stolen Crown* with the Exodus. When we come to *The Arabian Knight*, however, we have someone like the Pied Piper all over again: a wanderer of the desert suggestive of the "flawed and dark and lonely horseback rider" (119) whom Del has been daydreaming about in the containing story.[69] And there is something else here that seems odd if we are paralleling operettas and chapters: the operetta actually put on in "Changes and Ceremonies" is the first on Miss Farris's list, *The Pied Piper*, yet the chapter itself comes not first in the novel but fifth. It would seem, then, that the Pied Piper and the Arabian Knight are interchangeable, and a reason readily suggests itself: so are the phases they represent. For *The Arabian Knight*, with its desert rider, sounds like a Wilderness operetta — or, more precisely, like the operetta of Wilderness and Judges phases both, to go by the rest of Miss Farris's list and the fact that "Changes and Ceremonies" itself is primarily a Judges story.

No doubt the evidence here is rather shaky in itself (though the presence in Munro's novel of a new phase like the Genesis one seems clear enough). It is interesting, at the same time, to find that emblems similar to the Pied Piper or Arabian Knight occur in other lists as well:[70] we notice them in "Simon's Luck," for instance, when we are being told the kinds of hospitality Rose might find congenial. The first of these is haphazard enough for Uncle Benny, consisting as it does of "parties in rooms hung with posters, lit by lamps with Coca-Cola shades, everything crumbly and askew" (152). If we jump to the fourth we find a setting like that suggested by "The Arabian Knight" — a world of "lurex-threaded sofas under hangings of black velvet displaying mountains, galleons, polar bears. . . ." (Here again we cannot separate Wilderness from Judges, since the next party strongly suggests the Kingdom.) And this world of dangerous adventuring may remind us of another image, not part of a series but part of a Wilderness story — or at least belonging to the Wilderness end of one. In "Boys and Girls" the narrator describes the picture-calendars supplied by the Hudson's Bay C_____ y and the Montreal Fur Traders: "against a backgr_____ ky and black pine forests and treacherous n_____ venturers planted the flags of England and Fr_____ bent their backs to the portage" (111). It see_____ entered an Age of Exploration: an old world has been left behind and we are not yet at home in a new, but move through an unknown region of wonders and perils.

*

Some of the images we meet on our journey are distinctly biblical ones; and while Munro's elusiveness will make any account of these somewhat tortuous, they can help us to see more clearly what for her lies at the heart of the Wilderness experience. We can begin with the apprehensive Nancy in "Monsieur les Deux Chapeaux," who arrives in "a top that was like a bag with holes cut for the head and arms, the whole thing dirt-coloured" (68). Munro does not quite say that Nancy is wearing sack-cloth and ashes, but she comes very close, and elsewhere the word "ash" itself appears in curious ways. For one thing, Munro changes the actual township-name "Wawanosh" to "Wawanash," the name in *Lives of Girls and Women* for the river on which Jubilee is located, and in "Wigtime" she locates the origin of Margot and Anita specifically in "Ashfield" Township (a real township, as it happens). The ominous implication of "ash" comes to the fore when Del returns to the Flats Road in "Age of Faith": for not only does she see the same river but she finds her brother Owen virtually hanged, "swinging on the rope under the ash tree" (111). When, moreover, we hear how Del once fed Owen "mountain-ash berries" (104) — poisonous for all she knew — this ominousness takes on a more special character. To see what this is, we can also turn to one of the notes left behind by Rose's father: "Dark Day, 1880's, nothing supernatural. Clouds of ash from forest fires" (3). Another note reads "Aug 16, 1938. Giant thunderstorm in evng. Lightning str. Pres. Church, Turberry Twp. Will of God?" (3). Noting how "ash" and "berry" have appeared together again, we should also follow the suggestion of a god who proceeds in darkness and fire against erring worshippers. Munro's mountain ash, it seems, comes from the fire-storm on Sinai, the mountain of Law.[71]

Elsewhere we find the mountain itself. Along with "ken-" or "holy" names in the Wilderness and Judges stories — the name of Mr. McKenna the dour school principal in "Changes and Ceremonies," or of the severely inhibited Cela McKinney in "Wild Swans" — we can think of "Kilakenny Mountain" in "The Ottawa Valley," associated as it is with firewater. Still another complex of imagery appears if we note that the fourth of Flo's mementoes in "Spelling" — the one in the Wilderness or Judges position, if we like — is "a Blue Mountain pottery vase" (176). We are familiar now with Munro's potter-creators; Blue Mountain overlooks the town of Collingwood, which among other things is the name of the jilting lover in "An Ounce of Cure"; and Collingwood lies on a body of water mentioned frequently in Munro, Georgian Bay. After "George Golley," a meaning for "Georgian Bay" readily suggests itself: the holy mountain, in other words, is coupled with an abyss.

We should also remember here a detail from the end of "Wild Swans": Georgian Bay is where Flo's old friend Mavis once went on a holiday. Since this holiday was implicitly parallel with Rose's victory trip to Toronto, we can connect Georgian Bay at least indirectly with what Rose secretly carries on that trip, "the little bag with the ten dollars" (64). This bag has in fact been provided by Flo, who worked in the Union Station "coffee shop" when Mavis was working — more graciously, no doubt — in the gift shop. In later years Flo still has the art of wrapping things in "heavy-duty" (56) paper, and also attaches the secret bag to the strap of Rose's "slip" (55): it seems, in other words, that the ten dollars, or dolours, are being associated with the Ten Commandments. Their location here — next to Rose's skin, which also interests the clergyman on the train — is of course an appropriate one: the Law controls the world of the senses. And the number of that world, not to say multiples such as ten, occurs in various significant contexts in Munro. In "The Office," for instance, the writers of the washroom graffiti supposedly come from a coffee house called "Numéro Cinq" (71); in "Walking on Water" outhouse sex takes place on the Fifth Line; and in "The Peace of Utrecht" old women are said to hand out "five-dollar bills" (28) — the bills that are for, and that are, the five dolours of the sensory world.[72]

*

Setting allusions aside for the present, we can now explore the terrain of Munro's wilderness a little more extensively. When Robert in "Fits" does just that on his night walk, what he discovers is a wild "congestion of shapes," looking for one thing like a city of "jumbled towers" (130). Mr. Lougheed's dream in "Walking on Water" shows the same jumble in the form of a crumpled bridge; in a more human version it is the raw mix of employees in the Turkey Barn, or the poverty-stricken families on the outskirts of town in "The Time of Death," or the social detritus encountered by Mr. Lougheed in Victoria. The wildly named Sylvia who gives birth to the world of "Monsieur les Deux Chapeaux" is a jumble all by herself, a typical initiatory figure in her confusion and childlike eagerness to gamble. Looming behind these figures, as we learn in "Age of Faith," is a universe much like Uncle Benny's swamp, a whirl of "atoms, galaxies of atoms" (100); or if we want holes rather than sand, there is a great void here, a universal Georgian Bay. The sign on Mr. Lougheed's door has a "black hole" (74) at the centre of it, and the strange shapes in "Fits" have "black holes" (130) of their own — like those in the universe, if the same shapes conjure up a "space-age" city.

In the Wilderness phase, rather more than the Genesis, this void appears as a certain kind of weather or season. As I have already noted, the poem about winter that the present chapter began with strongly suggests the winter at the opening of "Boys and Girls." The season in which Del Jordan goes to the Anglican Church is winter again, as is the time of Helen and Myra's friendship in "Day of the Butterfly"; both "The Turkey Season" and "Fits" take place during winter cold snaps.[73] Other stories come at times that in a way are even emptier: the main action of "The Dangerous One" occurs in "the cold, late time of fall" (50), while "An Ounce of Cure" is set in very early spring.[74] Leona Parry in "The Time of Death" can explain for us how such an in-between season feels — in this case, the time immediately before the coming of snow:

Just as I took the hook off the gate something stopped me, I thought, *something's wrong!* . . . No cars comin' one way or the other and the yards all empty, it was cold I guess and no kids playin' out — And I thought, My Lord, maybe I got my days mixed up and this isn't Saturday morning, it's some special day I forgot about. (90)

There is no life on a day like this, no movement, no time — only the ominous "time of death." Mr. Lougheed's dream in "Walking on Water" takes us into the same time, the "gray weather, not disclosing much" (82) through which a child makes his frightened way. The narrator of "The Office" recalls looking out the window "on long spring evenings, still rainy and sad" (60), even feeling a strange need for loneliness — "loneliness too harsh and perfect for me now to bear" (61). And to find this loneliness inside as well as out, we can visit the bare little Anglican church in "Age of Faith" or the Berry- mans' living-room in "An Ounce of Cure" — the latter not a small or shabby space but certainly an empty one, a "big softly lit room, . . . an uncluttered setting for the development of the emotions" (79).[75] The passage into such a space, like the in-betweenness of the in-between seasons, has an uncanny quality of its own: that of the "little cold entry" (97) into the Anglican church, or the stairs in "The Office" where for a moment the narrator feels "complete unreality" (61). Peg Kuiper in "Fits" feels something no less uncanny as she starts up the Weebles' stairs, knowing somehow that "there wasn't anybody but me alive in the house" (125).[76]

If Peg is venturing into the nothing of death, she is also going to encounter the terrible something of it. When Robert goes on his similar venture — not into a silent house in his case but outward over the snow — we see, conversely, how something is nothing: for the snow that makes its own landscape, hard as marble or cement, is bound to melt as soon as the weather changes. In various ways, then, we have come to a world where something and nothing meet: just as in the Genesis stories, we experience a sensibility paradox of the intensely material and the immaterial, with illusion ready to spring up in the midst of vacancy. It is in this world that the baby-sitter in "An Ounce of Cure" has her wild hallucination — one, we can add, corresponding to an actual situation that itself depends on the illusions of love and in turn corresponds to a play. It is in the same world that the "show" (85) of Eugene's walking on water gets put on, as do various other exhibitions. Even the Anglican Church gets into the act, keeping what more Protestant denominations have nervously thrown away, "the theatrical in religion" (99): its central prop is "a cross which looked as if it might be cardboard covered with silver paper, like a stage crown" (98).

Patricia in "The Time of Death" may seem alien to all this, since "she did things the way a grown-up does; she did not pretend things" (92); but then Patricia herself is an entertainer. So is Donna in "The Dangerous One," and here we can see clearly how pretence and deadly earnest go together, for Donna is a compulsive liar who also witnesses, even in lying, to facts the narrator's grandmother does not want to know about. Or rather, Donna leaves us wondering what the facts really are — as we also do in other stories of the group. What really happened between Walter Weeble and his wife in "Fits"? What happened in "Monsieur les Deux Chapeaux" when the gun in Colin's hand went off? What, in the same story, are we to make of the allegedly dangerous car? There is no getting a straight answer from the non-committal Eddy, nor can Colin tell whether to believe Nancy when she issues her warning "in that phony-sounding voice he had to believe was sincere" (71). Perhaps it is all just a joke, like Eugene's walking on water; but then it may be a "serious kind of joke" (74), as Eugene remarks, which suggests that something may come of its nothing. For in the Wilderness world, no less than the Genesis, fancies have a power of materializing. Mr. Malley in "The Office" entertains notions about his tenant that turn into visible obscenities on the wall, while in "Walking on Water" Mr. Lougheed finds the notional world even more substantial than the physical one.[77]

*

To understand this power better, we should first ask what sort of heroine, or in some cases hero, appears in these stories. Typically we have an innocent: not quite a child, like the Rose and Del of the Genesis group, but perhaps a girl on the verge of adolescence, undergoing the second birth of puberty. Del is twelve in "Age of Faith";[78] Patricia and Donna must be about the same age. The narrator of "The Turkey Season" is a bit older, fourteen, and Rose in "Wild Swans" must be older still;[79] but these older girls share the same inexperience as the younger — Rose has never ridden a train by herself, and the narrator of "The Turkey Season" will think for years that rye and coke is the drink to ask for. The teenage narrator of "An Ounce of Cure," similarly uninformed about alcohol, offers her tale expressly as a case-history of innocence; even grown women like Peg in "Fits" or the narrator of "The Office" have something of the same quality to them. It is true that, on the whole, these heroines are a precocious lot, and that Donna in "The Dangerous One" can even make some claim to worldliness; but then Donna remains ignorant of just the things that other girls know.[80]

An adolescent, no less than an infant, has just separated from a parent, and accordingly seeks a replacement. For Del this is God; for the narrator of "The Turkey Season" it is Herb Abbott; the heroine of "An Ounce of Cure" falls in love with Martin Collingwood, at least a high-school senior, and is later unsettled by Mr. Berryman. Rose has a larger repertory again: having been attracted both to her French teacher and the breadman, she has her first direct sexual experience at the hand of a middle-aged clergyman on a train. What the father craved by all these girls must have is power — he must be like the god who "chastens, and hastens, His will to make known."[81] In "Age of Faith" this makes him primarily the god of being — the god who can say "I am": in the nothing where she finds herself, Del's greatest need is that such a being be there. This god will of course assert himself by creation, the imposing of something on nothing; and, as we have been seeing, he can equally be imagined as imposing nothing on something — idea on matter. If we turn to his creatures as we have them in these stories, we find them playing God in turn: Eugene believes in mind over matter, and the imaginative babysitter in "An Ounce of Cure" practises what Eugene preaches (her job in the school production, we may notice, was to have been "Makeup" [76]). Most suggestively of all, perhaps, we find the children in "The Time of Death" playing with their paper cutouts, and Owen Jordan playing "godlike games" (105) with the hockey players he has cut out of cardboard. Owen himself, as it turns out, is God's hockey player.

*

If God here is what we can call the Upper God — a deity of directly manifested power and being — there is another and very different god to be met in these stories. The figure Del sees in the Anglican Church may be regal, but he is also "tragic" (98); and after the bland iconography of the United Church his world seems "gloomier and richer, more pagan somehow, or at least Mediterranean" (98). From what we have seen elsewhere about Counter-Strangers, this Under-god, as I will call him, is already a familiar figure: what we must examine here is his place in Munro's Wilderness. Being Mediterranean he is of the earth — a dark, fleshly presence; what he is not is the abstracted Creator in whose mind the whole universe is a thought. Or to reverse terms as we did before, this lower god is nothingness — mortality — compared to the transcendent god who is being.

To find this Undergod we do not have to go into a church. Benny in "The Time of Death," for instance, is the helpless victim of his clean-minded sister: and Benny turns almost mythical when, in effect, he returns as the wandering Brandon. This latter is old where Benny was young, but he too is a sacrificial figure, wearing a stained brown overcoat and "crownless felt" hat (98),[82] singing a crazy lament, and offering himself as a scissors-grinder — with the result that the children run for knives. In a more comic version the Undergod is Mr. Malley of "The Office," once prosperous but now a caretaker and professional loser, swathed in flesh and carrying his burden of "troubling humility" (64) and "matriarchal discomfort" (63–64). "Matriarchal" is just the right word: along with the Mediterranean dying god we sense — here in the same person — the sorrowing mother whom we see more directly in "The Time of Death." In "Fits" there is no-one quite as lugubrious as Mr. Malley, but there is certainly Kevin, the dark and ailing son who passes the crucial morning of the story in the basement; we find, too, that Kevin wraps himself in a table-cloth as if in a shawl and spends much of the story whining at his mother. Ross in "Monsieur les Deux Chapeaux," though the opposite of a whiner, is still another fleshy mother's boy given to lying in bed. As for the young heroines of the Wilderness stories, they positively revel in the part of underling. To be sure of God's power Del is eager to humble herself — to be like the "nuns in the snow" (100) of her imaginings.[83] In a more directly sexual way Rose wants to be "pounded, pleasured, reduced, exhausted" (61): in a word, "to be somebody's object."[84]

Mr. Malley the caretaker can also introduce us to a more special group of figures, and a very important one here: what we can loosely call the Hired Men. A sizeable number of these are called Henry — Henry Bailey in "Boys and Girls," Henry Streets in "The Turkey Season," Harry Crofton in "Home," Harry Sherriff in the early "The Idyllic Summer," as well as the Harry that Rose's repairman father was in the penultimate version of "Royal Beatings."[85] The Henry Bailey of "Boys and Girls," who can stand well enough for all of these, is much like Uncle Benny: a man who works for another man on a fox-farm. Both Benny and this Henry, again, are to be found doing their work in a basement, and to judge from the name "Bailey" or prison, this is Henry's kind of place. It is true that — much more than

Benny — he is a man of boisterous good nature, like his Chaucerian forebear: in other words, he is the Counter-Stranger on his affable side, as is a related figure like Ross. And yet there remains something sad about all these men, a sense that they have never quite come into their own. For one thing, their relation with women seems as unsatisfactory as that of Chaucer's Harry Bailey with his wife: Benny runs into marital disaster, several others are bachelors, and a related figure, King Billy in "A Queer Streak," is decidedly henpecked. Again, several of these men suffer from physical affliction — Henry Bailey, for instance, shares Uncle Benny's bronchial trouble — and often we find them associated, however ambiguously, with sacrificial animals.[86] We may even wonder, considering the incidence of "Harry," whether these are not hairy men, allied with Munro's Esaus as well as with her Joes and Bens. It is at least worth recalling that Allen Durrand, the Esau of "The Ottawa Valley," is another hired farmhand.

Others whom I would class as Hired Men are not necessarily that in a narrow sense and may not at first seem to be that at all: Martin Collingwood, the narrator's god in "An Ounce of Cure," is a future undertaker; the Mr. Berryman who virtually replaces him is a plant manager. But an undertaker sounds like an "under-taker" for one thing, and in any case goes with a "bury man" to suggest the same world of sickness, sacrifice, and death that we have started to see in the Harry Baileys.[87] In fact Mr. Berryman descends into "Baileyville" (78), if for the purpose of having a Henry Bailey's good time — we are very close here to Munro's janitors in their foundries and stone schools. And more directly than the Hired Men proper, Mr. Berryman is one of the fertility figures of the Wilderness stories: for this bury man is also a berry man — a plant manager in a different sense — connected with the same berries that we have found in the neighbourhood of ashes.[88] We can thus set him beside "Herb" Abbott, the foreman in "The Turkey Season"; and in other of these stories we will find still further hints of the cycle of vegetation. The Mary Bishop who succeeds the narrator in Martin Collingwood's affections combines "big vivacious eyes" with a "sallow complexion" (77); Mr. McLaren, the alluring French teacher in "Wild Swans," is similarly "quick and sallow" (61). "Sallow" of course means willow, with its funereal as well as vegetable associations: the Lloyd Sallows recalled in "Visitors" appropriately disappears into a swamp.

*

As we continue to assemble Upper Gods and Undergods, our picture as usual complicates itself; and once again we will have to follow this process for a certain distance, since there is no other way to understand the game that is being played in the various Wilderness stories. In "Wild Swans" the man who sits beside Rose on the train is no doubt an Undergod, using underhanded tactics; at the same time he seems a confident and healthy person, and certainly he is an affable one — as we have found various Hired Men to be. If, as he claims, he is a minister, then he is not only a servant but a figure of authority: and when we think of it, there is the same ambiguity of status about all bailiffs, foremen, and managers — not to mention "servicemen," a group with their own glamour in Munro.[89] Indeed some of Munro's Undergods are positively distinguished. Martin Collingwood plays the aristocratic Mr. Darcy in a school production, and will still look rather like him when wearing his undertaker's finery; Mr. McLaren, as we have seen, is a "perfect autocrat of indulgences" (61). Even Henry Bailey, with his Chaucerian connection, is in some sense a man who presides; and "Henry," we can add, is another of Munro's royal names. It seems that kings without crowns may be kings after all — as is the tragic but regal Christ of the Anglican Church.

If we go back to the dark and pallid Kevin in "Fits," we may now see him in a new perspective as well as the old. When he sits in his basement playing a "Billy Idol" (112) tape and watching a televised "game show" reminiscent of Owen's hockey games, Kevin is no doubt an Undergod attending an Upper God's orderings from a distance; but Upper Gods themselves, as we have seen, are sports fans, and Kevin, while having to obey his mother, seems to be the reigning idol of the local high-school girls. If we turn to the corresponding figures in "The Turkey Season" it is even less easy — as the narrator herself remarks — to know who is in charge, Morgan Elliott the boss or Herb Abbott the foreman. As for the first of these, a "Morgan" belongs with Munro's dark Marys, while "Elliott," I will suggest, points to "El" or "God" as in various biblical names. The second, Herb Abbott, is at once a plant and an abbot — which means a father; and in fact it is the capable and self-possessed Herb who seems to have "the efficiency and honor of the business continually on his mind" (62), where Morgan is hopelessly distracted and moody.[90]

Our picture becomes more complicated again when we imagine this double figure as a creator with creatures: and yet the very complexity here can bring us back to simplicity. God plays Upper God to the human Undergod because he plays truth to human reality; at the same time we should be prepared to see the tables turned — to see God as what we ourselves make and destroy. And with this we can return to the simpler notion of a being — god or man — who wants to gain power over whatever is not himself. What we can also say of such a figure is that he works most effectively by a combination of means. God impresses Del by his strength, yet also by his weakness: if his cult has faltered, he calls even more unanswerably from a distance — from "His old times of power, real power" (100). And as the dark god of Holman Hunt he is unanswerable precisely because of his sad face and crown of thorns.

The same doubleness appears in various other ways. God commands; he also charms like the bell of the Anglican Church — a "lovely thing for a church to have" (95). He draws others; he also finds a way of going to them, and we will see him doing both things if we look again at the opening of "Age of Faith." Del at one time supposed the Flats Road house to be watched by "melancholy dedicated" men with a talent we have already met — that of "holding in their minds the most exact knowledge of our house and everything in it" (92). These are burglars, the thought of whom is at once disturbing and curiously appealing: "their knowledge, their covetousness, made each thing seem confirmed in its value and uniqueness" (93). And while burglars are not mentioned again in the story, the craving they represent does not go away. Del is sure that God must be there, omnipresent though invisible, holding the universe in his mind, validating it by knowing and wanting it; when she enters the church, what she sees is a melancholy and dedicated god standing at a door, trying to get in. Del in turn is a burglar at a door here, venturing alone into a place not hers; so is the writer who climbs the Malleys' stairs, or the Peg who climbs to the Weebles' bedroom.[91] As for stowing booty in the house of one's mind, we should remember Glenna in "Monsieur les Deux Chapeaux." Glenna is in some ways a central-phase figure, yet there is something initiatory in her compulsion — and uncanny ability — to imagine: to "hold in her mind" (81) just the things she wants her house to have.[92]

A compulsion like Glenna's is an awesome thing. If we see figures like Del and Peg again as victims being lured or invaded, what may now strike us is the extraordinary power at work here: the attraction, for instance, that draws Peg up the fatal stairs, or draws her husband Robert for miles into the dangerous cold.[93] The narrator of "The Office" experiences the same attraction when she looks out the window and is shaken by a "fierce and lawless quiver of freedom"

(61) — the urge that drives her to seek out her grey office. The narrator of "The Turkey Season," feeling the same overwhelming need to prove herself, takes a Christmas job at a turkey barn. She walks to work at dawn, as the morning stars dance in the sharp cold and the "pine" trees lift their arms in supplication; and the place of sacrifice before her is as compelling as any Childe Roland's Dark Tower:

> There was the Turkey Barn, on the edge of a white field, with a row of big pine trees behind it, and always, no matter how cold and still it was, these trees were lifting their branches and sighing and straining. It seems unlikely that on my way to the Turkey Barn, for an hour of gutting turkeys, I should have experienced such a sense of promise and at the same time of perfect, impenetrable mystery in the universe, but I did. (101)

V. STORIES

Putting the Genesis and Wilderness stories together now, we can ask a more essential question than we have done so far: if something happened to begin the world we know — something that happens again in the main narrative of any initiatory story, or of any story seen in its initiatory aspect — what is at the heart of such an event? What is it that draws life apart and packs it together to start any train of worldly experience? The best way to answer this question is to follow the course of the initiatory story more sequentially than we have done hitherto; and in the first place we can note the event that begins — and, in a larger relation, is — any such story. This is a calling: biblically, the calling forth of a patriarch from Ur or of Israel from Egypt. And we have to say at once that, within the larger fallenness that contains all finite stories, this calling must be something of a trick. A Wilderness story, we have just seen, typically gets under way when an innocent — the narrator of "The Turkey Season," for instance — is drawn to a place of sacrifice. In "The Flats Road," similarly, Uncle Benny answers an ad in the paper with fatal results; nor is he the only one in this story to get hooked. He is himself a fisherman, of course; the Jordan children help by catching frogs for bait — "we squished them tenderly in our hands, then plopped them in a honey pail and put the lid on" (1); and more generally the story's world seems an endless array of traps, pens, and spring-doors that abruptly snap shut.[94]

Traps need baits, and the Book of Genesis can again provide some suggestive examples: the fruit in the Garden of Eden, of course, but also figures like Rebecca and Rachel who, whatever else we may want to say about them, appear as distinctly alluring and chancy. The latter beckons repeatedly in Munro's initiatory stories: "Rachel" face powder appears in two of them, and in "The Dangerous One" the biblical Rachel is the object of yet another allusion — a very pointed one.[95] If we turn from Old Testament to New, we find not only the Woman of Samaria[96] but someone specially important for Munro: Mary Magdalen, a prototype of both Nora Cronin and the "Madeleine" of "The Flats Road." What is extraordinary in the face of all this enticement — and will need some later commentary — is that the initiatory calling also has an unearthly innocence about it. When Frank Wales in "Changes and Ceremonies" acts the Pied Piper, he sings in "a still-unbroken soprano, unself-conscious, in fact hardly human, serene and isolated as flute music" (125). Uncle Benny is hearing the same voice as he reads of a "lady with one child" (12): someone who, as I have suggested, arouses both the parent and child in himself. And so Benny writes his letter.

In doing this he enters into a covenant. In Book of Genesis terms he is like Abraham, or Noah before him, or for that matter Adam; in terms of the Canaanite cycle he is Moses, covenanting at Sinai.[97] The parallel here may seem strained if Benny's letter expresses no more than a noncommittal interest, but Munro has a keen sense of the way people covenant without formal consent, even without conscious desire. The narrator of "The Office," who in a formal way consents only to a monthly payment of rent, really consents to much more: she never quite has the assurance to face Mr. Malley down, and in any case finds him rather intriguing. Rose in "Wild Swans" is much the same, allowing the minister gradually closer without being clearly aware that she wants to. As for Benny, he is laying himself open to marriage from the start; and the significance of his step will appear if we set him beside Munro's other "undertakers," whom we can now see as covenanters. We will recall how Martin Collingwood in "An Ounce of Cure," the first boy to give the narrator a proper kiss, later becomes an undertaker by profession, perhaps because that is what he was from the start. Del Fairbridge, the first of the Three Jokers in "Half a Grapefruit," is another future undertaker, his present undertaking being to have sex with Ruby Carruthers. More exotic is the undertaker in the background of "Wild Swans": a man who, according to local rumour, lures women into his plush-lined hearse with smooth talk and chocolate-bars. Figures like Benny or Rose are of course the lured rather than the luring, but the difference is ultimately less important than it seems: it takes two to make a covenant.

*

One of the anecdotes drifting about the Flats Road is that of Sandy Stevenson: the man who gets a bride from the east, complete with $2000 and a Pontiac. In the circumstances Sandy's given name — Alexander — seems natural enough, and we will also be seeing how he is someone who builds on sand. "Stevenson" has a somewhat different implication: it connects Sandy with the proto-martyr Stephen, the deliverer of an impassioned diatribe on the faith of his fathers.[98] The main exemplars given by Stephen are the patriarchs and Moses, figures whom we have just seen as covenanters; and perhaps this fact can help us to understand what lies at the heart of all covenanting. A covenant is an act of faith: it asks readiness to perform and to believe in another's performance. Appropriately, Sandy Stevenson is a fore-echo of Benny, the man who believes fiercely in — among many other things — the Lord's promise concerning the Flood; and in fact the typical figures in Munro's Genesis stories are all believers of one kind or another. For some this means belief in a special person — the belief of a patriarch or a child or a bridegroom. For others it means trusting in the more diffuse way one trusts luck: the immigrant, the gambler, the travelling salesman, the antique-dealer, the brash and terrified aunts in "Connection," are all heroes of faith in this sense. Then there are all those who try to walk on water or snow or sand — like "Moses at the Red Sea" (85), as we are explicitly reminded in "Walking on Water." To add one more element, "Walker Brothers Cowboy" gives us not only the name "Walker" but a farmhouse with "a door upstairs opening on nothing but air" (7) — a handy feature "if you happen to be walking in your sleep and you want to step outside" (8).

For a euphoric hour or so Ben Jordan does walk on air, or at any rate rides high over the back roads — unlike the *alter ego* who plunges through the dusky sand, or the sin-laden Baptists down in the lake. Eugene, similarly, seems about to walk on water; Robert in "Fits" is made "buoyant" (117) by the bright winter day — just as later, during his night stroll, he walks magically over the crusted snow. We have arrived here at the triumph of faith, along with which we find an eagerness to keep whatever laws faith may impose. Winter having settled on Huron County like the ancient glacier, the townspeople in "Fits" are "watchful, provident, fatigued, exhilarated" (110) — proud to be meeting demands, like Robert himself in the new life he has chosen. Del Jordan in "Age of Faith" may not connect religion with virtue as such, but she is willing to go to church "on wet windy Sundays, snowy Sundays, sore-throat Sundays" (96): anything to be "saved by faith" (101). And now comes crushing reversal. At one emblematic point Del's faith seems to be achieving a miracle; then she has to give up:

> I would shut my eyes . . . and say to myself — frowning, praying — "God. God. *God.*" Then I would imagine for a few precious seconds a dense bright cloud descending on Jubilee, wrapping itself around my skull. But my eyes flew open in alarm; I was not able to let that in, or me out. (106)

It is the same with the structure of these stories. The high-spirited Robert stops at a favourite diner for lunch, and hears terrible news; Eugene goes under the water. Sandy Stevenson comes to his own version of the same crisis: reaching out for his windfall bride, he gets the poltergeist of her former husband as well, and in the end has no choice but to send his bride back home. His counterpart Benny marries a woman who is something of a poltergeist herself — in fact he meets his Waterloo in "Kitchener," with its hint of war.[99] What makes these disasters the more overwhelming is the abruptness we have noted in typological reversals generally. Rose's father in "Royal Beatings" is a mild-tempered man until his explosion on the story's fatal day; the quiet Walter Weeble has given no sign of intending to kill his wife and blow his own head off. Nor can anyone think of a convincing reason: what we do know is that, after a world of godlike games, we have suddenly arrived at a world of smashed playthings. Robert's night walk brings him to a jumble of derelict vehicles in the snow; the bridge to which Mr. Lougheed comes in his dream looks like "a toy someone had stepped on" (90).

*

Someone, then, has trusted, and been cruelly betrayed; an undertaker has failed to carry out his undertaking — that, in the simplest terms,

is the central event of the initiatory tragedy. And since it is the child in us that trusts, we should not be surprised if this is the point where we most directly see children molested or abandoned — Diane, Rose, Benny in "The Time of Death," the boy in Mr. Lougheed's dream who is left by his father to cross an unsafe bridge alone. For now we are seeing in its most concentrated form what typifies initiatory parental figures at all times. Benny in his parent's role habitually looks after the animals of his little world, but also gloats over their doom — and in the event abandons Diane to hers. In "Age of Faith" his attitude to Major the family dog is much the same; and even Del's father, whose decision to shoot Major seems more disinterested, appears in her dream as an insane killer.

As we would expect in Munro, the precise allocation of roles differs from story to story. In "Boys and Girls," a close cousin of "Age of Faith" though with a different point to it, the shooting is of horses not dogs, and the duplicity the narrator senses is not in her father but her mother:

> My mother, I felt, was not to be trusted. She was kinder than my father and more easily fooled, but you could not depend on her, and the real reasons for the things she said and did were not to be known. She loved me . . . but she was also my enemy. (117)

In "Miles City, Montana" we again have a father who is straightforward, in fact indifferent: the father of the drowned victim in this case. It is the narrator's own parents — the two of them — who are not to be trusted; and in later life it is the narrator herself in consort with her husband. But the same betrayal is taking place in both stories, and in the latter especially its meaning is made explicit. When little Meg reaches trustingly for a beautiful object in a swimming-pool and falls into the water, her parents show remarkable determination in saving her; yet the narrating mother knows what undependable saviours they are. It is not just that they might arrive late another time: simply by producing children, they have brought them into a world treacherous in its very principle. The "natural, and particular, mistakes" (105) of which parents are guilty are contained by the greater mistake of "sex and funerals" (104) — the mistake that is process itself, in which being is given and taken away. Under the circumstances, any lesser reliability is the same thing as deception.

Nor is it only adults who play parent — for one thing, both of the young heroines in the two stories about animal-shooting have mothered younger brothers in their time. Del, we remember, once fed mountain ash berries to the trusting Owen, and now we can note that she was as deceitful as any parent about it: when it occurred to her that the berries might be poisonous, she said nothing in the interest of her "prestige" (104). The narrator of "Boys and Girls" is less reserved — she runs crying for help when her younger brother has climbed a high ladder — but she does not let on that the climb was her own idea. As a result "nobody ever knew the truth" (122–23): in other words, this girl is not very different from her inscrutable and unreliable mother. There is even a further reversal of roles here. These children who play deceiving parent remain children — and are deceivers as precisely that, since a child, like a parent, can only be what it is by denying its contrary. In betraying their younger charges, the girls we have just considered also betray their parents; elsewhere we find two girls robbing their grandmother directly and a boy suddenly killing the parents he has been caring for.[100] Equally treacherous again are the trusting children, or adults with a child's need to trust, who in the event do not trust. For all his ready assurances, Benny remains as shy and unco-operative as the foxes; if he puts his faith in gambles, he also has the gambler's secret need to lose. Del, putting her faith in God, needs to test him, and will not stop until he fails the test.

If children thus betray as they are betrayed, we have come to the vision that an adequate reading of Munro always brings us to: we are seeing not just what is done to someone but what opposite parties do to each other. To generalize in cyclical terms, we can notice all the table-turning in the initiatory stories. When the writer in "The Office" snubs Mr. Malley, the latter not only turns her behaviour into "another betrayal of trust" (74) but even manages to capture the role of an Upper God — "the eyes almost closed, nostrils extended to the soothing odour of righteousness, the odour of triumph" (73). "Age of Faith" reveals a whole world of parents and children — or others in essentially the same relation — stealing from and punishing each other like the cops and robbers we met earlier. God the Father and God the Son behave in the same way, playing each other's burglar and judge: for the Son's Cry from the Cross is in its way a terrible judgment, as was the forsaking that prompted it. And if we continue to look at this imperfect but intensely imagined story, what we see is a coincidence of roles going beyond mere reciprocation. Mr. Jordan plays the "true believer" (108) — gently by day, fanatically in Del's dream.[101] The same Mr. Jordan shoots the family dog; and this dog is itself both a trusting innocent of sorts and "Major" — a godlike ancient with a godlike habit of killing sheep and taking their wool "for form's sake" (112). Owen plays Upper God with his hockey men and then turns into a whimpering suppliant at the prospect of Major's death. Del herself, as we have found, plays Upper God with Owen in the very act of playing Undergod with God.[102] The more we think of all these superiors and inferiors, the more we see a single "God . . . really in the world" (115), and when we do so, we see betrayer and betrayed as contained in this god. If, as we saw earlier, the original Fall was the failure of a single identity, this failure must have been self-betrayal, the denying of a faith greater than anything we usually mean by the word.

*

For a simple picture of self-betrayal, we can draw as usual on an early story. We have seen how Patricia, the heroine of "The Time of Death," is a very grown-up young lady — the "Pint-Size Kiddie with the Great Big Voice" who travels with the Maitland Valley Entertainers. The same young lady, we find, plays reprimanding parent to her siblings, and at the climax consummates this role by scalding the youngest and most helpless of them to death. The final scene of the story is very different: here Patricia behaves like a child herself, screaming with fear and rage at old Brandon the scissors-grinder. Yet Brandon used to be a favourite of Benny's and, as I have suggested, *is* Benny — it is the same vulnerability in both that Patricia cannot bear. To take a further step now, this vulnerability is Patricia's as well: what she experiences as an intolerable threat is her own natural feeling, whether as parent or child. And that can only be because a greater Patricia — one who does not fear, and in whom the more vulnerable feelings are held safe — has been untrue to herself. Now a broken successor is left to play one or all of the roles as the same betrayal reenacts itself.

We are brought to a similar picture in the much more mature and subtle "Monsieur les Deux Chapeaux." Here again we find siblings — a pair of brothers — and once again these function much like a parent and child. As brothers, Colin and Ross are look-alikes and contraries; they are also rivals — a joke, it seems, is going the rounds about a black man and white man who somehow collide at a urinal. To see what this last amounts to, we will have to consider the female element in the story as well. Ross, the younger and more boyish of the brothers, still lives at home with his adoring mother Sylvia; he also expresses the wish that he had got to Colin's wife before Colin; and there is a third woman, Nancy, who says placatingly "I love you all" (71). Whether we believe Nancy or not, it is plain enough that Colin resents Ross even in protecting him, while Ross, a lowly groundsman and Colin's trusting junior, also "wants the power" (80), as Colin at one point expresses it. Ross's urge to have a respectable car for once, the source of the trouble in the story, is thus an implicit challenge to his brother's role in the world; even as Undergod, for that matter, Ross has things about him that suggest an Upper God, such as his passion for "car-wrecking and combo-building" (63).

The danger is that Ross will put too powerful an engine into a small body. "It can take the whole car over. It literally flips it over" (70), warns Nancy — in fact it may "break the universal" (75). We are not told what actually becomes of the car, but another great upset did take place when the brothers were adolescents. Colin took up a gun to keep Ross from getting it,[103] fearing it might go off, and somehow it did go off — Colin in some sense shot Ross, then sat in blank indifference on the "Tiplady" (78) Bridge.[104] And if in this story it was the older who shot the younger, a bit of archaeology will show that the reverse is also possible: Munro here is reworking one of her earliest motifs, and in a previous form of the story it was the younger brother who did the shooting.[105] What matters most, in other words, is not which brother kills which — nobody is killed in any case, as it turns out — but the fact that, like Cain and Abel,[106] the brothers are a threat to each other simply in being brothers.

What we have, then, is Monsieur les Deux Chapeaux: two hats on one head, two natures in one Ross, two sons of one Sylvia — an amicable arrangement, as it often seems, but we should also remember the gun. When Robert in "Fits" looks at the jumbled vehicles, it is really the same brothers that he is seeing — "armed giants half collapsed, frozen in combat" (130). In seeing these giants, moreover, Robert is seeing a single mass of collision and wreckage, the same buckled god whom we first found in the Genesis stories. The "black holes" (131) here are really the "gutted insides" of the vehicles; if for vehicles we substitute the gutted royal birds of "The Turkey Season," we will see a stricken god somewhat more clearly. The whole universe as we have it, matter and space alike, is the dark cavity — the "tray" — that has opened within this god: and now we are in a position to see what this cavity means, the same self-abandonment that we sensed in a figure like Patricia. To use a complementary metaphor, the god was left with a big engine in a small body, and the result was a universal crash.

Having lost the faith that is life or identity itself, the fallen god now plays games with a lesser kind of faith: he affirms his prerogative by answering prayer or — as Del Jordan senses — by not answering it, as he pleases. The creatures of this god must not murmur, for he is not to be tested or tempted, as the Israelites learn to their cost. Yet he himself can only be what he is by doing what he forbids others to do, since in creating a world of "sex and funerals" he is luring the beings of that world, with their creaturely needs, to commit an offence against him. Thus he himself, as one kind of Undergod, is a serpent suggesting crimes that, as Upper God, he will have to punish. We should think here again of the Mason Howey who brings man and woman explosively together, or the Mr. Berryman who, having left his babysitter alone to do something wrong, judges her for doing it. Patricia puts it very neatly: after scalding her trusting brother to death she adds a new piece to her repertory, "It Is No Secret, What God Can Do" (98). For in all such tricksters we can sense the greatest trickster of all — one who became what he is by tricking himself, and now can only exist by tricking others.

We will see the same figure again in what follows the reversal in his story: the despair of a Counter-Stranger. This despair can be a simple sense of failure; often it appears more specially as the shame that goes with either the concealing or revealing of failure. In "Age of Faith" shame is what Del Jordan imagines in missionaries, and what we can imagine in a local counterpart, the preacher trying to explain God's abandonment of his Son at the Good Friday service. It is equally what the narrator of "The Turkey Season" senses in Herb Abbott when Morgan Elliott has attacked young Brian with a meat-cleaver. The narrator of "Miles City, Montana" felt shame as a child watching her elders at Steve Gauley's funeral; as an adult she feels it watching herself. The disgrace here is at once that of a fallen idol and of the idol's victimized worshipper; and with peculiar intensity it is that of the idol's minister — his Hired Man — obliged to put a respectable face on the business. When, in "Walker Brothers Cowboy," a chamber-pot is emptied out of an upstairs window and Ben Jordan gets hit by the splash, Ben is certainly a victim. He is equally a disgraced, though not cruel, father ("Pee, pee," sings his son in delight [10]); and he is an employee of Walker Brothers, trying loyally to make sales. Like Herb Abbott he has no choice but to do his walking in another direction, keeping whatever poise he can manage.

The disgrace of such men often shows itself as that of the merely physical: in Ben Jordan's case, the spirit that is only urine, hitting him as he stands on a "bare, slanting slab of cement" (9). In "An Ounce of Cure" the mortified babysitter turns to a more rarefied kind of spirit — whisky, etymologically the water of life; in the anecdote of Sandy Stevenson we find a more rarefied kind again, a poltergeist. But whether material or immaterial or some explosive combination, such spirits can only show us what the babysitter sees under the influence of one of them: a world "playing with me a game full of enormous senseless inanimate malice" (81). Such a world is not truly spiritual at all, only the "solid fantasy"[107] that we are now seeing as that of unbelief. "You do always resist the Holy Ghost," says the biblical Stephen:[108] if Sandy has done so, no doubt that is why he is bedeviled by the other kind of ghost. It is not that he lacks ordinary belief, as we can see from his counterpart Benny. Benny believes all kinds of things: he is sure, for instance, that Sandy's story is true — after all, he saw the bruises with his own eyes.[109] But in the first place, so did his biblical namesake — his middle name, we will remember, is Thomas — and in having material evidence for a returned spectre Benny is seeing only what a Peeping Tom can see. If he is also able to believe without any such seeing, it is only in the sense that he is able to make up the evidence, like Joe Phippen in "Images." The latter, as it happens, does a trick of his own with spirit: he plays the godlike game of giving his tomcat whisky, with the result that it first makes a great leap, then collapses and hides under the couch. Meanwhile Joe himself hides in a hole in the ground; so, as we have seen, does God.

*

We can tell the rest of the initiatory story — a distribution of its central reversal, if we like — much more briefly. First we may find the vision in detachment that often comes after a Counter-Stranger's lair: that, for instance, is what Uncle Benny's descent into Toronto amounts to, in this case a confirming vision of chaos. Rose's vision in "Royal Beatings" is lighter and brighter — up in the bedroom after her ordeal she lies at peace, feeling her very hopelessness as freedom; but in either case the ordinary world now begins to draw the visionary back to itself. Giving up on Diane, Benny comes wearily home; Rose goes back to the parents who have beaten her. And this sad conclusion is, in the cyclical way, a relief at the same time — perhaps even something more pleasant. As Rose sits in the evening with the parents she was never going to forgive, there is "a feeling of permission, relaxation, even a current of happiness, in the room" (20). In the same way life on the Flats Road recovers its normal equanimity — or at least it recovers the kind of craziness it is used to rather than the kind it is not.

What does this ending amount to in the more cognitive terms we have also used — those of knowledge or its expression? In one way it is like waking up; for Del it also means falling asleep, reassured by her parents' sanity, and we may recall the girlhood incident in which Et Desmond saw her sister making love — like Del, Et coped by falling asleep. In a sense she remains asleep through all her later feats of vigilance: for the achievement of normal awareness is also the putting away of an awareness greater than normal — what the little girl in "Images" calls "falling asleep with my eyes open" (41). We have already seen characters like Et and Rose dissociating themselves from the far-off origins of the initiatory world; by the same token there must be a dissociation from that world itself if life is to go on. We notice Madeleine lapsing into "blankness" (17) after her fits of rage, and Benny looking "blank" (3) when you remind him of some failed scheme a few weeks later. In the same way, Colin in "Monsieur les Deux Chapeaux" cannot remember — his conscious self refused to know even at the time — what happened when the gun went off. Or it may be the wonderful rather than the terrible that gets forgotten: Janet in "Connection" forgets the idyllic "first England" (10) to the point where the news of Joseph Chaddeley's real origins finds her indifferent. And along with the simple separation of conscious from unconscious that is forgetting, we find various other kinds. One can for instance detach fact from fiction, perhaps attributing everything to the latter — for it seems Diane did not really get beaten at all, the whole business having been made up by Benny. Or it may be fact that one prefers: in "Fits" the chaos Robert sees in the snow is just a pile of cars — no cause for alarm, then, nor is there any at home. Benny has his own way of using fact, since in all the piled-up detail of his Toronto story he conceals from us, and himself, the real object of his quest: not Diane at all, but proof that she was impossible to find.

We can notice, too, how Benny runs on and on in his "meticulously remembering voice" (25): he is showing how speech, like silence, can serve as a covering.[110] The initiatory crises themselves, to be sure, as well as the acts provoking them, may be highly verbal affairs — the royal beating is brought on by Rose's "terrible tongue" (14), matched by Flo's. Et Desmond is even more "terrible" (19), and indeed Et can be said to have the gift of tongues itself: she gets the "inspiration" (21) to invent a widow for Blaikie to court, and uses the complementary gift of ventriloquism to speak through her own creatures. Or the people of the initiatory world may be as withdrawn as the *deus absconditus* we met earlier — Edward Tyde is said to have been as tight-lipped as his daughter is the opposite.[111] But this strange world of dumbness and tongues is succeeded by one of more ordinary reticence and more ordinary communication — as is beginning to happen in Benny's Toronto story. Robert, while turning his night vision into marital small-talk, says nothing about the odd discrepancy between Peg's story and the constable's: Colin, it would seem, is going to say nothing about Ross's car. Et may at times feel an unwonted urge to rip matters open, yet she never tells Arthur about the rat poison.

And as something is forgotten, someone is left behind — someone who may lag as others go on with their lives or may literally cease to be there. In "The Flats Road" Del begins to grow up, but Benny will always be a boy fishing in the swamp, and Madeleine simply disappears. At the end of "Something I've Been Meaning to Tell You" Et and Arthur settle down peacefully, but Char and Blaikie are gone like Madeleine. Long before this, of course, Sandy disappeared into the lake: in Munro we often find that, of a group of siblings or other associates, one died before the story proper began at all — died, that is, in an even more initiatory initiation. A recurrent figure of this kind is the young man killed by a falling tree at a time of settlement: one such young man gave Jenkin's Bend its name in "Heirs of the Living Body"; another is mentioned in "The Stone in the Field," and in "Working for a Living" we learn that there was such a person in Munro's own family.[112] In "Deadeye Dick," the initiatory opening of "Oh, What Avails," Morris does not die young, but he loses the sight of one eye at the age of four after an accident with a rake: the remarkably self-possessed and capable Morris of later years is secretly the boy to whom that happened.[113]

It is no less suggestive that, about the time when Morris himself lost his eye, his father died in a car accident — the wounded child here is doubled by one of Munro's mutilated, dead, or vanished elders. Often, like Sandy, they have descended into water. Herb Abbott, having lost a young friend, walks off into the snow by himself; and as he does so, we see him "rolling slightly, as if he were on the deck of a lake boat" (76) — he is in fact a sailor when not living above the "poolroom" (62). Then there is the roaming salesman and "pop" Poppy Cullender, the antique-dealer: a queer old man in all ways and among other things an acquatic one again, since in his risky business he barely manages to keep "his head above water" (20). Poppy is a leaky colander, doomed to sink, not to say a "cull-ender" in at least three senses; when, accordingly, he stands outside houses pleading "Ith anybody h-home?" (20), respectable people bolt the door. The boyish and weary Ben Jordan gets a similar reception when he calls "Hullo there!" (9); old Brandon, as we have seen, is greeted with knives and scissors. The strange thing is that, in one way or another, these outcasts are all men who return: they are like Blaikie Noble, the diver for gems who comes back to "haunt" (5) — or like the revenants from death itself we have been meeting. Their return may of course be what generates the initiatory adventure in the first place; but it also persists in spite of any later safeguards. In passing away, then, the initiatory world does not pass away: this is what we will now have to consider.

VI. AT THE DOOR

If our first world within the world has ended and yet has not, how can this be? To deal with such a question, we will first have to go back again to our linear, cyclical, and typological levels of reading, and ask ourselves where we have arrived in terms of each. (In doing so, it will be simpler for the moment to stay with the initiatory world by itself, ignoring its relation to any other.) As seen in a linear reading, the initiatory story simply takes us from one point to a different one: temporally, to the end of the day on which a royal beating has taken place, or — in "Something I've Been Meaning to Tell You" — to Labor Day, the day of Char's funeral which also marks the end of a season. In a cyclical reading, however, we return to our starting-point — with a hint, as we saw in the previous chapter, that the movements out and back lead to each other, so that we might go around indefinitely. In "Royal Beatings" the family explosions and the times of mutual acceptance alternate; in "Something I've Been Meaning to Tell You" not only is Labor Day a holiday that leads to work, but the work itself will lead to another holiday, and then more work again.

If we continue to bring out implications, circularity becomes typology: while we return Home from the Other Place, not only might we go back again, but the Other Place we visited and the Home we have now returned to are essentially the same place. There is something very paradoxical about a holiday called Labor Day; and we notice how Arthur and Et in their peaceful retirement — that at least is what it looks like on the surface — do things like cultivating raspberry canes and playing "rummy" (23). In fact there have been rummy goings-on all through the story: rest and labour, doing nothing and being up to something, are really the same thing here. "The Flats Road," as we saw in the previous chapter, is typological in a more explicit way: Uncle Benny comes back from the swamp of Toronto, but continues to live in the same swamp at home — his world of wild heights and depths, luck and misfortune; and as Del senses on stormy nights, her dependable parents are living in the same uncertain world. We must even say, in the terms of "Age of Faith," that the terrible God who was supposedly left behind has not been left behind at all — he is really in the world in this sense as in others. The old horse-whipper is there in Hat Nettleton the affable senior citizen, just as he proved to be in Rose's affable father.

Some of the later initiatory stories, such as "Fits," take rather more explanation. Robert, we saw, dismisses the chaos he comes upon as something ordinary and harmless, and it is left for the reader to connect his vision with another, recalled at the very end: Peg's sight of the chaos that had been Walter Weeble's head. If the terrible is the ordinary, it seems that the ordinary is also the terrible. Similarly, we have to see that the two facing houses of the story are the same house, the two facing marriages the same marriage; and when Peg's son says that an earthquake is just a "periodic fit" (126) like those that trouble all marriages (that of Robert and Peg excepted, of course), we have to see what is implied in Munro's typical play on the word "fit." A fit in the sense of what Et Desmond produces for a living is something tidy; a fit in the other sense is a disruption. Such disruptions occur in all sensible arrangements — after this same conversation, for instance, Robert needs to get away from the house for a while — but more than that, disruption is the other side of order itself. A "periodic fit," after all, is at once a disruption and a regular part of a cycle. The two sides fit each other, just as the houses of the Weebles and the Kuipers fit each other; seen typologically, they are the same thing — and we should remember that the Weebles when alive were no less equable than the Kuipers.[114]

*

Now we can enlarge our frame of reference. If to come to the end of the initiatory world is to go back to the beginning, it is also, because of the ongoing nature of time, to approach a more central world — or at least this is true for the self that goes ahead rather than the one that is left behind. Seen in a linear way, the relation between the two worlds is one of simple continuity: as a settling down, the end of the initiatory world merges with the more settled state that comes after it. In our more adequate models what we have rather is return or something more complex. This confuses our picture, of course: perhaps the matter will be easier to deal with if we resolve all the movements we are considering into a few familiar emblems. And this is what we must do in any case if we want to make some important inner and outer connections for Munro's work.

A convenient way to think of typology here is to use an image that has served us before, the mirror. When a person looks in a mirror, his linear perception is of another person, but typologically this person is both other and himself. In a more complex way we can imagine him as being between two objects reflecting one another, so that in looking at either he will see its opposite. To think first of vertical rather than horizontal mirroring, we can note that upward and downward attraction within the initiatory stories is really the same thing. When coaxing Diane to say "dink watah" (15) Benny is setting her on the ground (where she picks up a crow's feather). Later on we find her moving up and down the stairs as the men skin foxes in the cellar below; Benny in fact worries that she may "climb up places and fall" (18). But typologically it is the same whether we think of Diane as climbing too high or descending too low, and it is the same whether we imagine Benny himself as reaching up to a moon-goddess or coming down like the sons of God to the daughters of men.[115] In more horizontal and temporal terms, we can say on the one hand that Benny, reaching forward to sexual experience, gets an innocent instead — Madeleine the helpless child; on the other we can say that, reaching backwards to an image of innocence, he gets Madeleine as a violent form of experience.

There is something of the same going back and going forward in any passage into a further world, as we will perhaps see better by stepping outside Munro for a moment: a useful analogue is again Eliot's initiatory *Burnt Norton*, the first of the *Four Quartets*. In the opening section — an initiation of its own in relation to the rest — we find the speaker visiting the garden of an estate long since destroyed by fire. Within this garden he is drawn forward: he moves toward the centre, where he sees "them" before him — the owners of the estate, no doubt. But these owners died long before; and while he sees them ahead they are really behind, reflected in the water, or seeming water, of the pool that he is approaching. We can see the situation in an opposite way as well. The garden has a childlike innocence about it — the hosts are in some sense Adam and Eve — and in being there the visitor is going back to Eden. At the same time, his vision is a "requiring" thing: it sends him out into the world, the "birth and death" with which the following quartets will concern themselves — and now we are clearly dealing with the relation between his initiatory world and further ones. Eliot here is like the boy Wordsworth, called into the future by the reflections or echoes of a world before birth. It is as if he had heard the instrument played by Frank Wales in *The Pied Piper*: for this is not a flute, as we might expect, but a "recorder" (130) — the same remembering instrument, in fact, that can be heard in "Walking on Water" as Eugene steps forward to walk across the ocean.[116]

At the ends of the Genesis stories the mirror hung most prominently is a cosmic one: the sunset as we see it in "The Flats Road," "Walker Brothers Cowboy," and "Royal Beatings." Movement toward the sunset occurs whenever Munro's characters travel west, as they regularly do, and is built into the very topography of the Genesis stories, since the Flats Road, for instance, arrives at what Mrs. Jordan calls the best place in the world for seeing the sunset (23). Stories like "Walker Brothers Cowboy" add water to a final western view, and "Royal Beatings" tells us about land across the water, in this case the state of Michigan. It is because of this prospect, or something like it, that such stories conclude in the glow of contentment we have already seen. The Jordans of "The Flats Road" admire the sunset; those of "Walker Brothers Cowboy" come back to the calm lake; even Et Desmond stops her labours long enough to sit out on summer evenings, while inside the house Arthur watches "television" (22) — the "far vision" or "final vision" that so often appears at the end of a Munro story.[117]

In "Royal Beatings," similarly, Rose's family enjoy the evening inside the house while some old men enjoy it outside; and presiding over the tranquillity of both groups is the same pacific goddess — Venus the star in the west, gleaming above the lake.[118] Or, as the old-timers think, the bright object may be an American airship, lit by ten thousand light bulbs and floating in "the miraculous American sky" (20): but this amounts to the same thing, for if Venus is an object of wonder and desire, so is the affluence of Americans themselves, living in their peacefully united states and challenging the heavens. What we must do here is to understand all such visions in temporal terms, as a projection onto the future of a happiness remembered from the past — the peaceful world before the Flood, perhaps, proclaimed again by Benny when he sees a rainbow. The present world is something else (as, in reality, are those of other times): after all, the Rose who enjoys the evening has just received a royal beating. Yet as experienced between the mirrors of an idealized past and future — or, more simply, as reflected from a single such mirror — the present seems agreeable enough. And as a result it really is so: while the men outside take pleasure in Venus, the family inside take pleasure in Flo, the instigator of the royal beating, who at this point is amiably rotating on her own axis. She belongs with Munro's "tipladies," evidently,[119] but is one who can contain her own tipping, and thus keep her world at peace no less effectively than her counterpart in the sky.

The vision in the homecoming scene of "The Flats Road" is very similar: here the role of America is played by England, the distant land of hope and glory that the children sing about while their elders enjoy the view. The local world is not so glorious, of course, nor for that matter is the distant one: an immediate war may be won, but the sun is setting rapidly on the British Empire. And yet a charm like that of Venus is operating here too. Once again we are seeing reality not as itself but as truth coming back from a screen — the same screen in fact that we found at the beginning of "Something I've Been Meaning to Tell You," with the difference that it is now showing us a future. And if having such a screen to look at gives us normal contentment — the ability to be reasonably happy in the here and now — it also gives us confidence to continue on.

*

Another sort of mirror will bring us to the ocean rather than the star above it. When Del lies upstairs on winter nights, frightened by the darkness and the wind, her parents seem "a long way away in a tiny spot of light" (26). This light has a remarkable origin: we have found chaos to be a black hole, usually filled with water, and yet the reassuring image of Del's parents comes from just such a source — it "winked at me from the bottom of the well as I fell into sleep." A well works a bit differently from a mirror in that it draws us beyond a surface rather than repelling us from one, but in either case we are lured by an image of one thing only to find ourselves with something else. I have already noted the occurrence in Munro's initiatory stories of biblical women like Rachel, and we can note here that such women are often associated with wells: even Diane seems to belong with them if the one sentence she knows is "dink watah" (15). Another version of the same siren figure hovers in the background when Nora Cronin puts on cologne — not to say "floating sheer crepe" (12) — to dance with Ben Jordan, or when the cousins in "Connection" sport cologne along with their rachel powder, their tortoise-shell combs, and their themesong, "Row, row, row your boat" (4). We are not far downstream from the Lorelei here: perhaps we can sense her presence again in the parting gift of a mirror and comb offered by aquatic Myra in "Day of the Butterfly."[120] And we should not be surprised if the beautiful Matilda in "Oh, What Avails" not only has something "fishy" about her[121] but brings a nautical Deadeye Dick to shipwreck.

The word "well" by itself is curiously insistent in Munro. It is common enough in ordinary English, needless to say, and often appears in Munro's stories without any special implication; but for one thing we may notice the H.G. "Wells" whose philosophy impresses the "Combers" and whose *Outline of History* is Mr. Jordan's way of "putting himself to sleep" (231). We may sense the same wordplay when we read of the Duke of "Wellington" in "Something I've Been Meaning to Tell You" — a story with drowning, waves, and a ruby at the bottom of the ocean. We are less likely to sense anything out of the ordinary when people merely say "well," but it is worth pointing out that Dorothy in "Marrakesh," who says or thinks it with great firmness (161), is also to be found staring gloomily into a cup of coffee. It is old Mrs. Cronin again, the woman with dark hollows for eyes, who says "Well" (12) on hearing of Ben Jordan's ailing wife. Mrs. Cronin says it more sympathetically than Dorothy, of course; and when Del in bed, dropping off to sleep, thinks the reassuring thought of her parents, she is evidently being drawn by something that is "well" (26) in more than a drowning sense. On the one hand she is falling, like Carroll's Alice, into an underworld — in "Fits" we even hear of virgins thrown down wells for sacrificial purposes. At the same time she is being calmed: like Munro's Venus-watchers, she is sure that all is well.

*

For good measure we can connect our typological mirror and well with a third image; "Deadeye Dick," a virtual epitome of the initiatory stories, is specially interesting here. When Morris Fordyce crosses the street from his mother's house to the facing one of Loony Buttler, intending to invite the latter's daughter Matilda to a dance, a Peeping Tom is on the watch — Morris's sister Joan is secretly looking through the glass in the front door. As she looks, Joan begins to have a Peeping Tom's doubts: hitherto secure in her mother's house, she now feels "the dimness, the chilliness, the frailty and impermanence of these high half-bare rooms" (193). She also feels the danger of Morris's adventure — we might say that she is sensing both a bare Wilderness space and the unsafe bridge of Mr. Lougheed's dream; but the image of looking through a door is significant in itself here. This door, as it happens, has two windows, of which one is boarded up while the other still has its many-coloured glass. Joan has picked the "red view" (192), for if she is like Munro's various doubters she is also like the trusting people who watch sunsets. It is true that the red here is "a dark red, like blood" (193), so that Morris (whose mission is unsuccessful) comes back across the street showing a "pink, blood-eyed face." But what this suggests is that the glass, like the combination of glass and boarding, is an ambiguous thing, and it is just this ambiguity that we are concerned with at present — what we have already seen in mirrors and wells. Joan, for that matter, is looking into a mirror even here: at another point in the story we find someone else — Loony Buttler herself, in fact — staring through the same glass in the opposite direction, as if reflecting the Fordyces back at themselves.[122]

We will have to consider "Deadeye Dick" further, but first we should follow the image of the strange door where it leads: and to begin with, we can recall some other kinds of situations in which doors play an emblematic role. "Walker Brothers Cowboy" includes a front door that was closed permanently after the funeral of a father; another in "Visitors" was opened only for a mother's coffin. In both these cases we have a door associated with a dead parent, shut long before the opening of the story and remaining shut throughout it — like the door of the family house in "Images" that stays shut all through the cold weather.[123] Elsewhere we have doors that open in the course of a story; the Wilderness stories, moreover, have shown us the explosion that can take place when thresholds are crossed. In "Royal Beatings," similarly, "the screen door hasn't yet been hung, and the storm door is standing open" (14): what follows is of course a human storm. After this the door is closed, literally or metaphorically, and presumably the screen door is soon in place (the story is set in early spring). If a screen door itself opens at the conclusion of "The Flats Road," not only is this door well in place already, but as Owen swings on it we hear "the old, remembered sound of the spring stretching, then snapping back" (22) — the house, in other words, is another of this story's traps.

Meanwhile a Flats Road sunset is taking place: a door in the west stands invitingly open. If it is also closing, both on the day and on a world, what we must say is that it is opening and closing at once — that it is a door we go through and do not go through, just as it is a mirror that draws us forward but also turns us back. To have still another related image here, and a more obviously double one, we can say that any such door resembles a "stoplight" (193) — what Morris's sweater, seen through the door, looks like to Joan as he crosses the street. A stoplight gives the signals (alternate, of course) both to advance and to hold back: appropriately, a stoplight is what baffles Uncle Benny in his pursuit of Madeleine, confronting him with the dilemma of red and green, stop and go. Red and green, we may recall, are also the colours he wore to get married in.[124]

*

Doors, windows, even stoplights all present areas — surfaces or apertures; now we can go on to a different and potentially opposed form of the same image. A sunset may be nothing more than the red rift in the snow-cloud described at the beginning of "Winter Wind": less an extended surface than a band, even a streak. When, in "The Office," we encounter a "thin line of bright lipstick" (62) on Mrs. Malley's face, or for that matter lipstick scrawls in the ladies' washroom, we have the same image again — Venus's mirror has become Venus's cosmetic, and in the process the mirroring surface has turned into a one-dimensional line. A line is in a way trickier than the surfaces we have been seeing, since we readily imagine it either on the same transverse axis as a mirror or on an axis leading forward (and backward); we may even imagine lines on two axes crossing one another. Yet Munro's lines are like her mirrors, and we will need to see them that way in the present context. "Winter Wind," closely allied to the initiatory group, comes to focus on the tragic death of Susie Heferman: during a blizzard Susie gets lost on the way from the house to the barn, having failed to tie a clothesline to the door.[125]

Here we have the image of a forward-and-backward line, as well as an interruption of it; while we may not think of the blizzard itself as a crossing line or even surface, it is certainly a barrier, and when the narrator sees nothing but snow through the window this barrier is blocking an opening. When, in "Visitors," Wilfred's drive to Owen Sound is blocked by a "wall" of snow, the snow also comes as "skids and drifts across the road" (206) — something closer to the crossing lines we are beginning to see elsewhere. It is over just such a drift that Robert in "Fits" crosses the fence on his perilous midnight walk.

In cases where it appears as a streak of red hair or lipstick, the crossing line is taking on a sexual character. When, similarly, Frances and Ted in "Accident" first enter the closet behind the science room to make love, their legs get smeared with fresh paint from the door frame — no warning signs are up because "nobody was expected to get in" (84). And with the world of sex we can put that of funerals: there is a touch of both when, for instance, the men in "Boys and Girls" shoot a horse called Flora, and young Laird proudly displays the "streak of blood" (126–27) on his arm. We find both again when Peg Kuiper in "Fits" gets something on her coat that looks like "a long crusty smear of reddish-brown paint, down to her hemline" (118): the reddish stuff comes from a bedroom — or perhaps, her husband thinks, its door frame — and is in fact the blood of a man who has shot both his wife and himself. But the full paradox of the threshold appears when we compare the red of either sex or death with the white that we have been finding as well. Munro is emphatic about the whiteness of the snow both in "Winter Wind" and in "Visitors" — Wilfred, for instance, has to drive through repeated "whiteouts" (198). Moreover, the dress once worn by the dead woman in "Fits" — "pale gray" (106) to complete her "silvery-blond" (107) look — has "a fine, shiny stripe in it" (106). Peg herself is a "pale and silky and assenting" person, "hard to follow as a watermark in fine paper" (126): there is a white line, it seems, as well as a red one.[126]

It is appropriate enough that Peg would suggest white: she is an innocent Wilderness heroine, as in a different way is the sexless and outspoken Mrs. Weeble. This is just what makes it so hard for Peg to cope with the world of blood that she is compelled to enter. At the same time it is what makes her attractive to her husband — and we can add that if there is something winning about Peg with her stillness and propriety, there is something flaunting as well as candid about her counterpart across the street. Elsewhere we find things like a clean-minded Health and Guidance teacher in "a dashing red suit that flared out over the hips," not to say the puritanical Mrs. Jordan wearing a "semitransparent red dress" at a party or hurriedly putting on a "haphazard streak of lipstick" at the approach of Bill Morrison.[127] Of course this last is only token femininity, yet there is something more mysterious here — something tantalizing in Mrs. Jordan's very refusal to tantalize. The untantalizing Uncle Benny, when feeling stress, reveals "the red streak across his sweating forehead" (14), and his throat always shows "a V of tough red skin with a tender edge of white" (1): somehow innocence in Munro always hints at provocation or sacrifice or both. I will even suggest that this fact has something Canadian about it: at any rate Uncle James in "The Ottawa Valley," brought up on the old Ontario school readers, knows what happens when winter snow is on the way.

> Along the line of smoky hills
> The crimson forest stands. (245)

One more type of image will enable us to make an all-important connection here. The child Becky Tyde, in the local tale that has her accosted by her father, appears as a "white streak at the window" (8); in the story of her father's royal beating she is watching from the same window, declining to go and help him because she has only her nightgown on.[128] There is an evident kinship between the antics here and those of Sandy Stevenson's poltergeist: "his wife's best nightgown was ripped from top to bottom, and knotted in the cord of the window shade" (9). In cases like these the screen that does or does not hold is a gown, a piece of cloth: we will recall that Munro's Marys would like to rip such a cloth apart where her Elizabeths prefer to sew it tight. A shade is still another fabric — one that, like many others in Munro, may have cracks in it. And with the wording Munro chooses for the Sandy Stevenson anecdote we have arrived at a crucial biblical analogue:

> The veil of the temple was rent in twain, from the top to the bottom; and the earth did quake, and the rocks rent; and the graves were opened; and many bodies of the saints which slept arose.[129]

If we follow the events of the Crucifixion back to their Old Testament types, we come among other things to the first Passover, which we can consider here as an initiatory entry into the Wilderness. The children of Israel go free when the Lord smites the first-born of Egypt; the Israelites themselves are untouched because of the lamb's blood smeared at their doors.[130] Here, then, is one biblical version of the red streak at the threshold; and there is another when the Israelites reach a mirroring threshold, for at the destruction of Jericho the harlot Rahab, having assisted some Israelite spies, saves herself by putting a "scarlet cord in the window."[131] Still another biblical threshold echoed in Munro may at first seem very different. When Eugene in "Walking on Water" has performed his successful or unsuccessful experiment in walking on the ocean, Mr. Lougheed goes to look for him in his room. " 'Eugene's door is unlocked' " (91), he reports to Calla in alarm, though both know the door is always unlocked. Mr. Lougheed is even more alarmed by what he sees inside:

> Eugene was not there and neither were his wet clothes. . . . The window was all the way up now. . . . Eugene usually put it down before he went out, for fear of rain getting at his books or a wind coming up. There was some wind now. Papers had blown off the top of the bookcase and were scattered on the floor. Otherwise the place was tidy. The blanket and sheets were folded at the end of the mattress, as if he did not intend to sleep there any more. (88)

Once again we have something like a poltergeist; we also have an empty tomb, for Eugene has somehow managed a resurrection and ascent.[132]

We can note other of the Resurrection motifs echoed here as well: the earthquake, the alarmed visitor, the sheets lying about like Eugene's papers, the napkin tidily "wrapped together in a place by itself."[133] As far as we are told, Mr. Lougheed does not actually go into Eugene's room, and we find the evangelists' accounts quite sensitive on just this point — in John's account Mary does not go in, while of the two disciples one enters and the other only peers in from outside. When Peg Kuiper investigates at the Weebles', it is not clear just how much she sees or how far she goes — Walter Weeble's shattered head, lying in the hall, is what she "would have to step over, step through, in order to go into the bedroom and look at the rest of what was there" (131). Here we can note simply that what Peg does have to see has nothing tidy about it, for in this story there are two tombs and two open doors, situated on different axes: the door of the "clean and empty" (114) bathroom that she sees straight ahead when she goes up the stairs and, at a right angle to it, the door of the room containing the remains of the dead couple.

Now perhaps we can epitomize our typological situation in the biblical terms that Munro has suggested for us. As we have noted, an initiatory story — or any story seen as leading beyond itself — brings us to a threshold that can and cannot be passed. And this is just what we find with each of the biblical thresholds we have seen. At the Passover the children of Israel go free, but this is because their doors have, as it were, been sealed — it is in fact this sealing that divides them from the first-born of Egypt. Later the walls of Jericho fall down and the Israelites enter, all because of a woman who seals her window in the city wall — the window from which she has also let down the Israelite spies on a cord. When the veil of the Temple is rent at the Crucifixion, a different veil remains intact: Christ's seamless garment, which we are going to meet again. The entry into the tomb goes with a shrinking back; the tomb itself is both foul and empty.

As Munro's red streaks indicate, the figure of Rahab is specially suggestive here, for Rahab seems the very spirit of ambiguous passage — it is no wonder she has always had such a mixed press. Munro shows her most notably where we might least expect her: in Del's maiden aunts Elspeth and Grace in "Heirs of the Living Body." Presently we will see the Egyptian connections of these ladies, but we can locate them on the other side of the Wilderness as well by recalling two of their practical jokes. Once, it seems, Grace brought a young man home from a dance, perhaps at "Jericho" (34). The two tried to sneak in, "as quiet as a pair of lambs,"[134] but Elspeth had had the foresight to tie a line of tin cans — shiny white ones, no doubt — over the door, and "*down* they came" (34), like the walls of the city itself. If this was the trick to play on Grace, Grace knows the trick to play on Elspeth: many years later, she lifts a quilt from her sleeping sister and ties her ankles together with a red ribbon.

VII. THE LOONY LADY

While Rahab appears in only one biblical story, her ambiguity is that of a far more universal figure — universal enough, in fact, to vie with the god of being himself. One thing to be observed about Aunt Elspeth and Auntie Grace is the way they come into their own at milking time; a number of people in the initiatory stories could make a similar claim. In "Deadeye Dick" what the gentle Matilda suggests to Joan is "'the milk of human kindness'": "there was something milky about the blue of Matilda's eyes, and her skin, and her looks altogether" (186). Blaikie Noble not only has a voice like cream but reappears in town white-haired and creamy-suited — as Et remarks, "I knew either it was you or a vanilla ice-cream cone" (5).[135] The same dairy imagery is everywhere in Munro. If, for instance, Ben Jordan is a "cowboy" in the service of Walker Brothers, Bert and Clive in "Baptizing" are two more "cowboys" (191), and take a lively interest in Naomi, the girl at the creamery. In "The Ottawa Valley" Allen Durrand the "big Holstein man" has a related line of work; so does Susie "Heferman" with her cows in "Winter Wind"; and so, it would seem, do the "Grazier" boys in "The Moon in the Orange Street Skating Rink." Looming behind these is the provider of all sustenance: Nature herself. It is Nature whom Munro is suggesting not only in a carefully displayed phrase like "the milk of human kindness," or in the wealth of cattle and dairy products, but more subtly in other motifs that she puts in sensitive contexts — the colour green, for instance — or simply in a certain kind of vocabulary. Del takes other people's offerings no more than "naturally" (254); Rose and her parents return to a state of "geniality" (19) while the old men outside find the thought of Venus "congenial" (20).

What is most natural and genial is of course procreation, which also means succession — one life following another in the line of birth and death. Here we can bring in another of Munro's dairy products, and one that takes harder forms than milk. When dying, Rose's gracious mother feels something like "a boiled egg in my chest, with the shell left on" (2); and this mother has already accommodated such a thing in another way — by purchasing some egg-cups, delicately painted with "a pattern of vines and birds."[136] The tough egg invading her space is in some sense Flo, who later claims to have had fifteen gallstones removed from her own body, one the size of a "pullet's egg" (188); Flo in turn is challenged by Rose, whose "nature," we are told, grows like a "prickly pineapple," (5) cased in pride and scepticism, until it too is ready to break out.

There is something here, moreover, that goes beyond individual organisms or linear succession. Flo is positively global: her legs are "marked all over with blue veins as if somebody had been drawing rivers on them" (13). In other words she is the earth itself; and when she demonstrates this by rolling over, Rose thinks of the "elongated transparent bubble" (20) of the airship in the west — the same figure, it seems, in an ethereal and diaphanous guise rather than an earthy and opaque one. It is not that airships normally roll over: rather, Flo returning in her course is like the Venus who is an alternative version of the airship. And she is like Nature more generally: for Nature renews herself in the same cyclical way, or is identical with herself in a typological way — this is why she is ultimately such a hard egg to crack. To go back to the land of hope and glory at the end of the Flats Road, Nature is the goddess to whom the children sing

> How shall we ex-tore thee
> Who are bo-orn of thee? (26)

All the tearing and beating and impregnating in the initiatory stories is an attempt to get in that is also an attempt to get out — to escape a mother who cannot be "ex-torn," but keeps us trapped in her womb of birth and death. We may hymn her as "Mother of the Free,"[137] but freedom is just what cannot be found in her carnal city.

*

In a chapter like the present one, the idea of Nature as a container will make us think of something beyond — a chaos surrounding her cosmos: and to understand what is finally in question in the initiatory stories, we will have to see how Nature also is, or belongs with, this chaos. It will be useful here to go back to our distinction between white and other colours, or — what amounts to the same thing — between two forms of white itself. Some of the whites we first noticed in the Genesis stories were shining and "silvery": they had an inorganic quality alien to Nature as we ordinarily think of her. "Tin Roof" (10), a kind of sundae favoured in West Hanratty, suggests an economy version of the same silver; West Hanratty itself has a tin flower over its one street light, and its houses are patched together with "sheets of tin" (5) — as well as tarpaper, to give the appropriate black-and-white effect. It is in this climate of silver and tar that Del Jordan confuses quicksand with quicksilver, imagining it as "shining, with a dry-liquid roll."[138] Mrs. Fullerton's unfathomable eyes, while "black as plums," have "a soft inanimate sheen" (20); one of the hollow eyes of Nora Cronin's blind mother emits "a drop of silver liquid, a medicine, or a miraculous tear" (12). In other cases inorganic light appears as fiery or electric, even explosive. When Hat Nettleton gets popped at in his old age, it is with flash bulbs; Flo manages to get flashed at, not only by a young man exposing himself, but by a priest with a cigarette-lighter; her husband meanwhile keeps notes about lightning striking the Presbyterian Church. We have met this flash before, as the self-asserting point with which all narrative begins; now we are also seeing it as the beginning of the world, and we will need to know its relation to the milkier sort of brightness that the world has to offer.

Sometimes Munro indicates a sharp opposition. The name "Matilda," to Joan's way of thinking, sounds silver "but not metallic" (187): it has more the softness of satin or, as we have just seen, the blandness of milk itself. Elsewhere silver may not be milky at all — settled "kindness" is being more completely differentiated from earlier chaos. This remains so whether we think of chaos as darkness before all light or as light and darkness locked in a cosmogonic war; in the latter case we will assign to it all Munro's flashers and tin roofs and metallic tears — to which we can add redder things like an under-sea ruby or a "Mrs. Carbuncle," the mineralogical old woman who precedes the kind Matilda. But, like other distinctions we have made, this division of cosmos and chaos, or the milky and the metallic, also confounds itself.

Since wood in Munro often suggests the whole world of organic matter in its basest form,[139] it is strange in a way to find a wooden house sunbleached to silver, or signs for "Silverwoods" ice cream posted at the beginning of "Walker Brothers Cowboy": but that is what we do find, and we find the same strange combination in things that are white to begin with.[140] In "A Trip to the Coast" the ageless grandmother sits in one of Munro's country stores "beside the ice-cream freezer, under a big baking-powder sign that had a background of glittering foil" (182): if both the ice-cream and the "foil" belong to this grandmother, they belong with each other as well, and for that matter there is something oxymoronic in the notion of ice-cream itself, the milk that comes out of a freezer. The woman who presides here is no less oxymoronic. We have found her sweetness in old Mrs. Cronin; we can find her more chilling aspect in the present grandmother or in someone like Mrs. Fullerton, the old egg-woman with black-and-sheeny eyes whose order is that of disorder. In other words, a more contained and nourishing world — the world of seedtime and harvest, milk and honey — and a more primal world of cold and darkness and glitter reflect each other because they are the same world: both belong to the Mrs. "Cronin" who is time itself.

And we need to take a further step here. If the bounds of this woman's empire are set so wide, where does that leave God — that is, the god of creation in chaos and law in wilderness whom we have met in this chapter? This god, of course, concerns himself with being and nothingness beyond the mere becomings of Nature: in "Labor Day Dinner," to give ourselves an image of him, we find the creatorial George scything the grass around Valerie's stone dairy, cutting Nature down to size as he does throughout this story. But George does not cut down the dairy itself: in fact Valerie is thinking of renting it to him as a "studio" (143) — which makes it one of Munro's stone schools. George, moreover, is acting as a servant, another of the Hired Men; here as elsewhere he is far more dependent than his pop sculpt would suggest on the various females he tries to dominate. More adequately, there is a mutual dependence here, even a coinherence.

In spite of his occupation, the Ben Jordan of "Walker Brothers Cowboy" would find such a thing hard to imagine — he has never, he says, known anything like the green "poppies" (12) on Nora Cronin's dress.[141] But then, as Nora points out, there is a lot Ben does not know. If he had looked about him in town, he would have seen not only milk in bottles but, not far from the Venus Restaurant, the Woolworths store that we have found to have "fish . . . as bright as moons swimming in its green tanks." (4) Under the influence of whisky, the babysitter in "An Ounce of Cure" has her own vision of green poppies: she sees the space she is in as a great becoming and passing away of "green blobs" (80). The curious exhibit near the exit (or entry) of the Toronto Art Gallery in "The Ferguson Girls Must Never Marry" sounds more cosmogonic or apocalyptic — a "room full of flashing lights and pieces of metal descending from the ceiling" (35)[142] — but when Nola identifies the metal as flying saucers, we remember how the baby-sitter saw the ceiling "spinning like a great plate." (80)[143] We may also remember the disc of petals painted on Mr. Lougheed's door, with its red circle and black hole in the middle, or the shapes seen by Robert in the snow, again looking like petals and containing black holes. If God is the god of the black hole and the tray, it seems he is the god of the flower as well, the circle of organic process. When a father in "Labor Day Dinner" makes a hole in the sand, a pregnant woman immediately fits herself into it.[144]

For a principle of being is ultimately the same thing as a principle of becoming — if God is mere being, that is what he became when he ceased to be a life greater than either being or becoming. Now he is only a cowboy, a god of nature: perhaps this is why Spinoza, the philosopher of *Deus sive Natura*, gets confused by Flo with an eggplant.[145] At any rate, we regularly find this god in similar company. He has his ministering and "matriarchal" underself, for one thing, perhaps with a name like "Berryman"; and as the august Mr. Carl Otis he shares his anniversary with Mrs. Carl Otis (it is their twenty-eighth, in fact — the lunar number).[146] Perhaps Mrs. Otis's given name is Mary: for the combination of Charles and Mary, as I have noted, is oddly common elsewhere in Munro. It is true that this couple, like others, are not always on the best of terms — in "The Shining Houses," for instance, Carl the successful real-estate man heads a confederacy opposed by the recalcitrant Mary through whose eyes we see the story. But even such a Mary is more a confederate than she knows: the squabbling alliance of Charles and Mary — of man and woman, state and church, Nature and God — is not easily put asunder.

*

If we now add one more biblical threshold to our collection, we will be able to see clearly how the initiatory stories take us into the world of Charles and Mary; the Charles we will need for the purpose will be Charlemagne's chief predecessor, Caesar Augustus. When we were dealing with the coverings of sleep and silence, we might have noted a more special kind: among the various "woolens, quilts and comforters" to be taken out in late fall, the finest is no doubt the "Star-of-Bethlehem quilt,"[147] the comforter that is Christmas. This appears at various places in Munro: in "Boys and Girls" the song by which the frightened Laird puts himself to sleep is (at any time of the year) "Jingle Bells" (113); the candy used by Joe Phippen to lull the trapped child in "Images" is Christmas candy; and here we should note as well that Joe's cosy lair is compared to one of the play-houses made by the child under snowdrifts. The present chapter started with a poem about magic caves under snow, and we have encountered snow again as we went along: after the bareness of the Wilderness stories, for instance, it arrives at the end of both "The Time of Death" and "The Turkey Season." In the former it is at least a covering for the frozen earth; in the latter it is pretty as "a Christmas card" (75) — just what, in "A Trip to the Coast," we are told that the grandmother's shiny foil looks like.

After the various conjunctions of kind and unkind that we have been seeing, we will readily feel something strange about a comforter of snow. Snow is no less cold than ice cream, and comes as the crystallization of winter itself. It is thus like the various materializing notions or invading ghosts we have met, the most overpowering of all being the glacier that once blanketed the world of "Walker Brothers Cowboy." And Munro has other hard and cold things linked with snow or snowy whiteness: in "The Turkey Season," for example, three women become "three kings" (76) who dream of a "White Christmas" (76), and produce one of their own by gutting various unfortunates — turkeys, husbands, even perhaps foremen — into impotence. In "Wild Swans," with its snow of various kinds,[148] we have seen the hint of Law in Flo's "heavy-duty white paper,"[149] what she uses to wrap candies with: and we might have noticed the other compulsion of "white slavery," to mention still another recurrent notion in the Wilderness stories.[150] If it is this coldness that swaddles the Christmas child, he may not be really be protected at all — he may be more like the innocents at Bethlehem or a Christmas turkey. We have noticed the woman who wraps her husband's torso in Christmas paper, and in "Boys and Girls," where we find the men skinning foxes before Christmas, Henry Bailey produces some gift-wrapping of his own: he swipes at the narrator with a sack of bodies and says "Christmas present!" (111).

Christmas, then, means different things in Munro: winter, protection against winter, winter itself as a protection like numbness or forgetting. But for this very reason Christmas in its initiatory aspect — we will be meeting others later — can well represent what it is to be at the door of the world. In the poem I have quoted, Munro imagines the caves under the snow as "doomed, perfect, secret." "They were warm, though white," she adds: so is the paradoxical mother and virgin into whose womb Jesus enters with his incarnation. Nor is this Mary with her sealed cave — to see her here as confining rather than delivering her son — finally different from the other bright figure we have met, Venus holding her lamp in the endlessness of the sunset: the virgin with her white band and the woman with her red lure are the same containment, surrounding and beckoning.

If we look again at "Deadeye Dick," we will see a still more comprehensive figure. Let us ask ourselves once more what is going on as Joan peers through the coloured window and finds herself looking at a stoplight. On a day like others we have noted — "gray sky and an iron frost" (189) — a Christmas dance is in the offing; so is a Christmas concert, for which Joan has been practising "Jesu, Joy of Man's Desiring" (190), a hard piece. Across the street Matilda Buttler, who has not been invited to the dance, is preparing to spend the evening in the coal-shed — the Bethlehem Inn of the story, if we like — since Mrs. Buttler is determined to have her out of the house. Morris is accordingly prevailed on by Mrs. Fordyce, much against his will, to invite Matilda himself; yet when he goes across to the Buttlers' door he is driven away. We are not told whether snow comes, or has already come, but in any case the snow in which fallen life began is coming again to initiate the world of adulthood. Matilda and Morris both do well enough in this world, but they cannot really be lovers, and their later habit of escorting each other only hides a need that can never be fulfilled.

Why can the two not come together? At the point when they might have done so, a crazy old woman got between them — a janitor guarding her door. Or, turning our image inside out, we could imagine the woman and her lair as all-inclusive, with Morris and Matilda as fellow prisoners who cannot escape just as they cannot unite. For Loony Butler is the whole world in its initiatory aspect: while she may not seem much like Mary or Venus, her "looniness" — she is the moon — really contains both, and we have found the same looniness in the ever-changing ambiguity of light and dark, reality and illusion, Upper God and Undergod. As we enter the more reasonable world of Munro's central phase, we will be putting such things behind us; yet we should pay our respects to the loony lady as we do, for we will not really have got beyond her power at all.

NOTES

1 See "Changes and Ceremonies" 140.

2 What Joan remembers of the old Logan in "Oh, What Avails" is "the shabby houses, the long grass, the cracked sidewalks, the deep shade . . ." (196). Cf. the "old wilderness city" in "The Shining Houses" (24). In "Oranges and Apples" the untameable "Barbara" comes from the local version of the Flats Road: "Shawtown," "a rackety half-rural settlement on the edge of Walley" (107), apparently inhabited by "Swamp Irish" (108).

3 See "The Stone in the Field" 23.

4 Tener 37.13.10–13.

5 "Oh, What Avails" 196. In "Meneseteung" the main street of the town is gravelled but the others are "dirt roads, muddy or dusty according to season" (54).

6 So, according to oral belief passed on by Munro, does the actual Maitland at "Loretown" ("Everything Here Is Touchable and Mysterious" 33). See also "Meneseteung" 70.

7 The Grieveses in "Friend of My Youth" are not quite so daunted, but they make the trip to town seldom (8), and live very much apart from the world.

8 We can say the same thing of the Flemings themselves: while they are far from squatters in the ordinary sense, and will give us one of our images of "Egypt" in the next chapter, their life of unremitting work is so barren humanly that their farm in one view can hardly be called a home at all.

9 An important cousin is Jack Curtis in "Hold Me Fast, Don't Let Me Pass," who likes to stay at Margaret Dobie's rough hill-farm, surrounded by "pails and implements and guns, fishing rods, oilcans, lanterns, baskets" (89).

10 We are similarly aware of the Chaddeleys' old-world origins in "Connection." In "Friend of My Youth" the Grieveses belong to a Scottish sect which remains very much that, as long as it remains at all; and it seems natural that Robert Deal would stay with his fellow-Cameronians when immigrating.

11 See "The Flats Road" 2; also "Princess Ida" 70, where Del is remembering the Flats Road. In "Everything Here Is Touchable and Mysterious" Munro remarks of the annual flooding of the Maitland that "we did refer to it as the Flood; it came upon us with a Biblical inevitability, and got respect" (33). (In a given context such a flood can sound more like the Egyptian kind than Noah's, but Munro may still emphasize its destructiveness.)

12 "The Stone in the Field" 27.

13 Monaghan in "Confinement and Escape in Alice Munro's 'The Flats Road,'" similarly treats Benny as a child, unable to cope with the adult world when he lets himself be trapped into it by marriage. I am not sure that Benny's freedom is otherwise as simple as in Monaghan's view.

14 Rasporich, in the words of her article's title, discusses Munro's "child-women and primitives" (11), putting them rather in the context of female subordination but also connecting them with life "on the edge of civilization" (11). The article in question developed into Ch. 2 of *Dance of the Sexes*.

15 See "Walker Brothers Cowboy" 6; "Thanks For the Ride" 44; "Royal Beatings" 22.

16 See "Half a Grapefruit" 50.

17 Karen, while another waif like Rose and Madeleine, may seem unrelated to Munro's Magdalens as such; in the case of others like her the connection is clearer, at least if we link Mary Magdalen with the woman taken in adultery. This can readily be done with, say, Nora Cronin, though here the clearest echo takes an oddly reversed form: it is Nora who makes "an unintelligible mark" (17) in the dust on Ben Jordan's car (cf. John 8:3 ff.), and Ben who drives off, leaving her comfortless. Much the same thing happens with "Karin" in "Pictures of the Ice" (see below, 326). "Karen Adams" in "Fits" is an ordinary enough woman, yet she too wears a red coat, and on seeing the bloodstained floor asks Peg "Was that me or you?" (115) — Peg being an innocent involved with a terrible act of violence.

18 The "Anglican" church, at least as pictured in "Age of Faith," has similar

associations; we can also note here that one of its pillars is a butcher named Dutch Monk, and that for her descent on Uncle Benny's place Mrs. Jordan arms herself with Old Dutch Cleanser. Sophie in "White Dump," if neither a tartar nor a prig in any ordinary way, is nevertheless an "Old Norse" (280) wielding the full power of restriction, and we have seen how she is a bringer of fate.

19 The pitiless "Barbara Allen" (10) of Flo's song haunts Rose's imagination. The meaning of "Barbara" is clear, but it is at least worth noting that "Allen" derives from the Germanic tribe of the Alans — Allen Durrand being a barbarian to the family in "The Ottawa Valley." See also below, 536 n16.

20 In "Royal Beatings" (3) the father was gassed in the first World War.

21 In "Deadeye Dick" none of the family difficulties is important — what matters is "jokes and luck" (183).

22 "The Flats Road" 4.

23 Macdonald, 200, has a good sketch of the initiatory world (as I would call it), noting the allusion to the Ark in "The Flats Road"; he contrasts this world with Jenkin's Bend the "bastion of order." Macdonald's article, while structuring *Lives* in a different way from my own, seems to me one of the best written on Munro.

24 See "Walker Brothers Cowboy" 4; "The Flats Road" 3; "Working for a Living" 24.

25 Other colours, no doubt, can have the same effect when sharply contrasted — Rose's imagined royal beating, for instance, is a scene in red as well. We may also find black and white with associations opposite to those I am taking as standard. In "Monsieur les Deux Chapeaux" it is the neat and domestic Glenna who imagines her house with a black and white tiled floor (81); it is the no less orderly Peg in "Fits" who insists on staying in her old house with its "white aluminum siding, narrow black shutters, black trim" (111). Yet both Glenna and Peg have an initiatory intensity under their surface composure — both come near to breaking down, for instance. For black and white see also Rasporich, *Dance* 179.

26 For the archetypal black bird see below, 428, 458 n145. We have already seen a few of the whites elsewhere in the same story; in "Royal Beatings" we can note, not only the colours of the beatings themselves as imagined by Rose, but Flo with her "black-and-pale" (9) potential prettiness and her imagined enjoyment of "Black and White" (10) sundaes. In "The Progress of Love" Phemie's father is black-haired for the whole of his life, her mother white-haired for most of hers (in spite of her black straw hat); we are also surrounded by things like the black nights and the all-white interior of the Wildwood Inn, with the black and white cat (13) serving as a kind of focus. In "Oranges and Apples" wild Shawtown produces Barbara the "bold black-and-white lily" (108).

27 In "Meneseteung" the street-fight, belonging as it does to wild Pearl Street with its swamp, has much the same character. Nothing could be more real and yet, as Almeda notices, "it is always partly a charade with these people . . . . As

if anything they did — even a murder — might be something they didn't quite believe but were powerless to stop" (63–64).

28 The illusoriness of the initiatory world is evoked very vividly in "Hold Me Fast, Don't Let Me Pass" when Jack Curtis recalls his war adventures (88).

29 When strangers appear in "Meneseteung," we are told, "speculation surrounds all of them — it's like a cloud of flies" (55). It also descends on the locals, as we can see from the Vidette's comments on Jarvis and Almeda (or from "Winter Wind").

30 "Remember Roger Mortimer" 37.

31 It is especially in Munro's initiatory stories (though again in the Apocalypse group at the other end of the world) that we find attempts either to reconstruct or mythicize an indistinct past. A narrator may engage in imaginings, as in "The Progress of Love" or "Friend of My Youth" or "Royal Beatings" — where the phrase "Suppose a Saturday, in spring" (10) also gives the main incident a tinge of fantasy, like the beating of Tyde itself (which Flo asks Rose to "imagine" [9]). The narrator of "The Stone in the Field" both imagines and researches; in "The Progress of Love" and "Friend of My Youth" two versions of the past are brought into conflict. It is as if the true and false of the world had not yet sorted themselves out, or could not be sorted out in later accounts.

32 "Everything Here Is Touchable and Mysterious" (33).

33 Ezek. 48:35.

34 "Connection" 8.

35 I am taking this phrase from a corresponding but different context; see "Memorial" 218.

36 The Grieves in "Friend of My Youth," by local standards a prosperous family on a good farm, are at the same time strict, hard-working, and thrifty Cameronians.

37 Mutatis mutandis, the two sisters in "Friend of My Youth" make a clear parallel. Flora, the elder and stricter, is also strangely beautiful; the younger Ellie is an "impudent, childish girl full of lolloping energy" (9). While at first there seems no rivalry between the sisters (nor is any apparent on the surface later), Ellie does steal Flora's fiancé. It is Ellie, though, who is smashed as a result, while Flora keeps her mysterious composure.

38 For the struggle between male figures, see above, 223–24. No one form of the story is standard in Munro.

39 "Meneseteung" for instance, with its strong initiatory flavour, offers a list of "hands caught in the wringer while doing the washing, a man lopped in two at the sawmill, a leaping boy killed in a fall of lumber at the lumberyard" (55).

40 See Gen. 1:28.

41 In "Deadeye Dick" the disastrous Loony Buttler is known to the Fordyces as, among other things, Mrs. "Buncler" and "Buncle" (185). We seem close here to both "buckle" and "bungle." (A butler is also a servant, not to say someone who puts things in bottles.)

42 See above, 79.

43 In this context the name "Grieves" in "Friend of My Youth" becomes curiously like "Buckle": it suggests both "grieves" and "greaves" — grief and a piece of armour. In "Connection" the Chaddeley grandfather turns out to have married "Helena Rose Armour" (10).

44 The Empress Irene, in spite of her name, was one of the most ferocious figures in Byzantine history. The equally ferocious Irene Pollox in "The Flats Road" seems a parody — with the hint of a "pole-axe" in her surname, perhaps — of the more pacific figure who inspires men elsewhere in the Genesis stories (see above, 232–33). The mythical Pollux protects seamen.

45 In "Five Points" the two children of Cornelius and Brenda Zendt are Lorna and Mark (30). (Cornelius is *otiosus* of necessity: an accident-victim unable to work more than part-time and sitting down.)

46 For Arthur from the deep see Tennyson, *The Coming of Arthur*, line 358 ff. and 410. The name "Comber" properly means someone living in a combe or valley: "Arthur Comber" would be oxymoronic in this way as in the others.

47 *The Passing of Arthur*, 427.

48 See Song. Sol. 2:17.

49 See Tener 37.8.23.f23.

50 Gen. 32:12.

51 See Tener 37.14.21.1.

52 In "Eskimo" the magisterial Dr. Streeter is strongly opposed by his wife and daughter. The latter, Rhea, gets her name from the wife of Kronos, who conspires against him with her sons, including Zeus. Sexual mate and daughter are very close in this story (the Eskimo woman complains to the Métis man "you're not my father" [199]).

53 Several derivations may be at work in such names, the one most commonly mentioned being from the Old Germanic "hugu," meaning mind or heart. All or most of these make the name a high one: we can think of Hugo in "Material," the man who lives in his head. "Howard" and "Ewart" may or may not be etymologically related to "Hugh." It is interesting to note the progress of the name in "Memorial": Eileen's former husband, "Phil" in earlier versions, later became "Howie"; June's husband, originally "Hugh," became "Ewart."

54 We also find the airy Miss Farris, but this seems more paradoxical.

55 See especially Jer. 18:1–6 and Rom. 9:21. The same metaphor occurs in various other OT passages (e.g., Isa. 64:8).

56 See especially "Who Do You Think You Are?" 191; "A Queer Streak" 209; the name appears more incidentally in "Boys and Girls" 114. In "Red Dress — 1946" a lordly "Mason Williams" discards the heroine rather as Mason Howey discards Madeleine.

57 See also below, 426, 427, 429.

58 For "pop" see 184 above. George and Irene in "The Time of Death" cut a human race out of paper (92).

59 "George" is also a royal name, of course. The king whose picture is displayed all over Jubilee in "The Photographer" (250) would be George VI, and perhaps Georgia in "Differently" gets her name from a queenly composure that she never quite loses.

60 See "Baptizing" 228.

61 In the same way Scott Geoghagen, in whom we can hear (or see) the same "geo-" as in "George," is a humble enough husband for Naomi after the lordly-sounding Stuart Claymore. (The latter's surname, by the way, has its own interest in the present context.)

62 See *The Faerie Queene* 1.10.52, 61 (following the *Legenda Aurea*). A similar name is that of Neil "Bauer" in "Five Points": an earthy peasant as well as a builder (in his case a construction worker).

63 Wood in Munro seems associated with organic matter, or simply matter, in general: it is thus what the creator of a material world works in. Roy Fowler's obsession with it gives the story "Wood" its name, and Roy has much in common with falling creators we are concerned with here. Not surprisingly, woodworking and woodcutting have the same ambiguity in Munro as working in the earth. In "Oh, What Avails" the now shabby Fordyces once owned a lumbermill (Morris will later go into construction); yet Mrs. Fordyce airily dismisses the family patriarch as "just a woodcutter who got lucky" (182), and the lowly Garnet French in "Baptizing" is the employee, not owner, of a lumberyard. Cf. "French's Hardwood Floors" ("The Shining Houses" 23). The last of Miss Farris's operettas in "Changes and Ceremonies" is *The Woodcutter's Daughter* (130). See also below, 258 n140, 428.

64 Father-figures, including creators, who retreat from public activity or communication are very common in Munro. Rose's father and Roy Fowler both retire to their sheds to work; George in "Labor Day Dinner" prefers solitude for his "self-sufficient, remote, productive life" (140). Others turn into readers who keep silent about what they read — Del's father in later years, for instance — or keep their thoughts to themselves like Mr. Lougheed in "Walking on Water."

65 Averill in "Goodness and Mercy" is like Del here in feeling the Twenty-third Psalm to be "a barrier set between the world in her head and the world outside, between her body and the onslaught of the stars, the black mirror of the North Atlantic" (169).

66 See above, 37–38. "Characters," with its opening directions for killing a chicken and its main theme of head-on confrontation, can readily be taken as a wilderness story. "The Turkey Season," with the same theme of confrontation, also has the onslaught on turkeys and human beings by means of what is expressly called a cleaver, as well as the figure of the sexually isolated instructor.

67 This is also true of "Princess Ida," where the old Morrison farm as imagined by Del (75) — the bleak late-fall weather, the grim and empty house, the mother's fanatical worship of a distant god — would fit perfectly into a Wilderness story. But "Princess Ida" is primarily a story of attempted escape, and in that perspective

even the farm is best seen as Egypt or counter-Egypt — an Egypt of famine, in other words.

68 There is thus a parallel between Wilderness and what I call Exile stories: a group set in the no-man's-land on the other side of the central phase, separating it from the terminal one. See below, 323–24.

69 I give the operettas in the number and order set out by Miss Farris on p. 130 and repeated at the end of the chapter (141). In draft versions of the story the order is different (see for instance Tener 37.5.8, 11), as it is in the short list of operettas given by Del (124). To complicate matters there is an inconsistency in an account given later (127): if *The Gypsy Princess* were put on in 1937 as part of the cycle Miss Farris describes, *The Pied Piper* would come round in 1942 and 1948, too early and too late respectively for the events of the chapter. What remains is the order firmly stated by Miss Farris and repeated at the end of the chapter, and this order seems to me a significant one.

70 The list of Almeda Roth's poems in "Meneseteung" (52), like the list of operettas, presents a problem: we cannot simply correlate the poems as listed and as used for epigraphs of the story's different sections, since the two orders clearly differ. Yet in the list at any rate the first poem, "Children at Their Games," seems distinctly initiatory; the second, "The Gypsy Fair," suggests *The Gypsy Princess*. "A Visit to My Family" (a cemetery poem) is concerned with the death of the parent, an Exodus motif; "Angels in the Snow" puts us in the same world as the devotees in the snow of the Wilderness group. "Champlain at the Mouth of the Meneseteung," obviously a poem with special relevance to "Meneseteung" itself, would be Wilderness or Judges — like the calendars in "Boys and Girls."

71 For another connection we should note that the young Ted Braddock in "The Ferguson Girls Must Never Marry" appears with a black mark on his forehead for Ash Wednesday (43). Also see below, 266, 488, 494: characters in Munro with such marks often suggest Cain.

72 In "Five Points," for instance, the "dollars" (38) obtained from Maria by the boys she has sex with go from one to two to five, then upwards in multiples of ten — Neil gets to forty. For the dolours of Mary Agnes Oliphant at the hands of five boys, see below, 316–18.

73 "Meneseteung" seems very different, being set in a heat wave; but in a treeless frontier town midsummer is as brutal as midwinter. The wilderness of the Bible is of course hot, not cold.

74 "An Ounce of Cure" differs from other Wilderness stories in that life is clearly on the way — for all but the narrator, trapped in her obsession with the distant Martin Collingwood. See also below, 336 n2.

75 In "The Dangerous One" we have a similar situation: two girls roam through an empty house while their strong-minded grandmother is away.

76 In "Hold Me Fast, Don't Let Me Pass" Hazel enters a very foreign world, misty, eerie, and haunted by earlier feuds and atrocities; she finds it strangely "enthralling" (85). She also enters the gloomy and empty upper lounge of the

Royal Hotel, and later visits a woman who has lived most of her life on a "large, cold, neglected house on a hilly farm" (77) — a place that, as recreated in Hazel's imagination (89), sounds much like the Flats Road farm at the end of "Age of Faith." (For Miss Dobie's later surroundings see below, 337 n17.) Hazel's feeling, especially at dusk, is the same panic of emptiness as in other Wilderness stories, articulating itself as "Why am I here?" (75).

77 Similarly, when Rose first feels the clergyman's hand in "Wild Swans," "her imagination seemed to have created this reality" (61). Dahlie (*Munro* 36) argues that the reader cannot be sure whether the clergyman is fact or fancy. See also York, " 'Distant Parts of Myself' " 37.

78 This is in fact about the age of Rose in "Royal Beatings" ("nine, ten, eleven, twelve" [10]), but — after the earlier chapters of *Lives* — the Del of "Age of Faith" does not strike us as a child encountering the world for the first time.

79 Rose enters high school before her father's death, which occurs some time before "Wild Swans" (in its final version).

80 Almeda Roth in "Meneseteung" is thirty-nine, but very much a cloistered innocent, on her own for the first time after her father's death. Hazel in "Hold Me Fast, Don't Let Me Pass," a woman in her fifties, has made herself the opposite: shrewd and self-reliant. Yet she was once quite different, and as she ventures for the first time into a strange otherworld — that of her dead husband's wartime experience — her now customary assurance deserts her.

81 "Walking on Water" 85.

82 In "Mrs. Cross and Mrs. Kidd" Charlotte gives the haughty Mrs. Kidd a "red felt" purse (174), and various of Munro's unfortunates have hats to match.

83 The breezy Mrs. Weeble of "Fits" seems quite different, but the grey of her stockings "made [Robert] think of a nun" (121); she talks about sacrificial virgins (106); and in the event her mild husband proves a formidable enough "Walter."

84 The highschool girls in "An Ounce of Cure" feel much the same thing about Mr. Darcy as played by Martin Collingwood — another figure of "arrogance and male splendour" (76) in black and white.

85 *New Yorker* 14 Mar. 1977: 40.

86 Some of these men kill foxes (Benny, Henry Bailey), some kill turkeys (Henry Streets, Harry Crofton). Benny also keeps various animals whose "unpleasant destinies" (3) he enjoys; but in his case especially it is clear that the Hired Man is himself a sacrificial animal.

87 Seen in this light, the name "Patricia Parry" (Patricia ap Harry) may be more oxymoronic than it looks.

88 Mr. Malley in "The Office" presents the narrator with a potted plant that "thrive[s] obscenely" (67).

89 For the darker implications of "serviceman" see below, 392.

90 In "Frazil Ice" Morris, a flourishing local entrepreneur by this time, looks like a "foreman," "a man who is competent, even authoritative, but responsible to someone else" (193–94). The captain in "Goodness and Mercy" is like Herb

Abbot — responsible and dignified but not the owner of the ship he commands. Such figures in Munro can function either as Wilderness paradoxes or as central-phase figures of establishment, depending on which of their aspects is being emphasized. See below, 300–01.

91 Peg is sure there is no-one like a burglar around ("somebody up there with a gun"): "I knew there wasn't anybody but me alive in the house" (125).

92 Like black-and-white, the ability to hold things in one's mind can point two ways. Glenna is like a central-phase god in the composure of her imaginings. Uncle Craig in "Heirs" similarly knows all the facts of the township's history, Morris Fordyce the cash value of everything in the Logan neighbourhood. But there is something initiatory about such feats to the extent that they are performed compulsively: Glenna "overdoes things" (80), pushing herself to near-suicide at one point. We sense the same compulsiveness in Roy Fowler's ability to remember every tree, or Benny's to remember every detail of his drive to Toronto. Uncle Craig on the other hand, while "voracious" (253), plods slowly away at his history.

93 Peg's first husband was lured all the way to the Arctic, where he ended "driving trucks to oil rigs across the frozen Beaufort Sea" (107). At the same time, as Robert reflects, there must have been some "wrenching and slashing" in his marriage with Peg (129): the strange attractiveness of wintry distance and emptiness in these stories always has a very present violence for its other face.

94 "Come over, come over," call the children in the first of the poems described in "Meneseteung": they are playing a game in which the two sides "try to entice and catch each other" (52).

95 When the girls go into their grandmother's bedroom they are surprised to find some very feminine things, including dark "Rachel" face-powder. Donna proceeds to steal two expensive figurines and hide them in the under-drawer of her crayon box. In Gen. 31:19, 34 ff. Rachel steals her father's household gods, conceals them under her saddle, and escapes by the pretence that she is menstruating and cannot get up.

96 Martin (*Paradox* 83) connects Edie's offering of water to Chris Watters in "How I Met My Husband" with the story of the Samaritan woman (John 4).

97 The Cameronians in "Friend of My Youth" descend from the Scottish Covenanters (see 26), who also loom behind "Hold Me Fast, Don't Let Me Pass" (see 86).

98 Acts 7; cf. Heb. 11. "Stephanos" in the literal sense of "crown" or "garland" reinforces "Alexander." "Steve" Gauley in "Miles City, Montana" is a counterpart of the drowned "Sandy" in "Something I've Been Meaning to Tell You."

99 The name "Kitchener" has its own military associations; as a town-name it was also substituted for "Berlin" at the time of World War I.

100 See "The Dangerous One" 51; "Walking on Water" 81. Cf. the child-molesting Edward Tyde and the three young men who bring him down.

101 More adequately, Mr. Jordan neither believes nor does not believe (see

below, 524): but his sensible acceptance of the world is its own kind of belief — and appears in Del's dream as insane fanaticism.

[102] In the same way, the God of the story's late recognition — the God Del sees at the end — is at once Upper God and Undergod, a serenely indifferent judge and an uncatchable burglar "not contained in the churches' net at all" (115).

[103] Colin here is no arbitrary destroyer, but someone taking responsibility like the parents in "Miles City, Montana"; yet this itself is a dangerous thing to do, whether the resulting explosion comes from Colin or Ross himself. Note that the boys, while refusing to give their elders' world "credit for existing" (76), are very interested in its artefacts, which sound like a list of stage-props for Munro's initiatory stories: cars, shovels, traps, guns, and forbidden magazines.

[104] I can offer only suggestions about this striking name. In "Fits" the derelict vehicles are "tipped over one another" (131); but perhaps the primal disturbance this hints at is also what sets things in their fallen rotation. We hear of Angela's mother "rolling over" into the hole in the sand made by the father in "Labor Day Dinner" (148), and also see Flo as a rotating planet (20). See above, 233.

[105] See Tener 37.13.10–13.

[106] Carrington (67) proposes, not only that the Ross who lies bleeding echoes the Abel whose blood cries from the ground, but that "Colin" echoes "Cain" — ironically, since Colin spends his life as his brother's keeper. I will add that Ross has his own mark of Cain — "purple bruises along the side of his face, a cut over one ear" (65) — and that, lying with his arms flung out, he is one of Munro's Crucifixion figures as well. One may or may not be happy with all of these suggestions, but there can be no doubt about the explosive situation of the two brothers.

[107] See above, 179, 189.

[108] Acts 7:51.

[109] On the other hand, Benny hiccups dubiously when advised to see some prospective scars (10); and when he says "I sure will," as he regularly does, we know he is not going to. Cf. the Ben Jordan of "Walker Brothers Cowboy" saying "I will if I can" (17) when Nora asks him to come back.

[110] We have already seen this burying — by speech or silence — as pervasive in Munro's stories, and we will see it in a specially intense form when we come to her Exodus group. Here we have it as a way of making ourselves an endurable world in the first place.

[111] It is thus appropriate that Mr. Black in "The Stone in the Field" finally dies of cancer of the tongue — whatever the physiological cause of this may have been.

[112] A variant is Phemie's dead younger sister in "The Progress of Love"; see also "Goodness and Mercy," where a young man died and was buried at sea some time before the main story.

[113] Someone as seemingly complete as Uncle Craig in "Heirs of the Living

Body" is blind in one eye (29). The manager of the rink in "The Moon in the Orange Street Skating Rink" is called "Blinker" (140). Such a man may be sharp-sighted in a worldly sense, like the "lock-headed fathers" I have referred to; or he may be as imperceptive (if also as knowledgeable) as Uncle Craig; but in any case he is missing a greater kind of sight. His mythological counterparts are gods like the Norse Odin, who acquired worldly wisdom at the cost of an eye. See also below, 425, for important figures in the Passion stories.

114 There is a useful analogue to this situation in the early "At the Other Place," where the narrator's decently harmonious family is put in contrast with that of her savagely feuding aunt and uncle. The narrator does not suspect the two couples to have anything in common, any more than Clayton does in "Fits."

115 Gen. 6.

116 This is also the instrument played by Hugo in "Material."

117 The "tele-" in "television" is derived from the Greek prefix "tel-" (eta), "far." Given the settings in which Munro tends to put the word, one also thinks of "tel-" (epsilon), "final," as in *télos*.

118 "Connection" has Cousin "Iris" — the rainbow — who in an earlier version (Tener 37.14.1) was "Myrtle," sacred to Venus.

119 Cf. the Tiplady Bridge in "Monsieur les Deux Chapeaux" (78), and see above, 256 n104.

120 In "Miles City, Montana" little Meg is lured, not by the reflection of a pool, but by a comb — the Lorelei's again, no doubt — inside it; yet the principle of deceptive brightness, here that of the clear blue water itself, is the same.

121 See above, 186. She also has "long, waving, floating light-brown hair."

122 The nickname "Mrs. Carbuncle" makes Loony Buttler a red stone among other things; her turban is many-coloured as these door-windows tend to be.

123 Since this door is "stuffed with rags . . . to keep out the east wind" (42), Munro may possibly be remembering the eastern door of the sanctuary in Ezekiel's temple vision (44:2), passed through once by the Lord, now shut to all but the prince, and — we may want to say — waiting for the time when all doors will be open (see Rev. 21:25).

124 Red and green are also Christmas colours (see above, 245ff.). In "Accident" we find Christmas "ropes of red and green stuff" (95), also "red and green Christmas rainbows" (105) playing on Ted when he comes into Mrs. Wright's living-room to claim Frances.

125 For the motif of Elizabeth holding a line, see above 70–71.

126 As always, the colour scheme complicates itself if we dwell on it. Red can be contrasted with either white or black (see above, 249 n25); and what is contrasted with these can also be multiplicity of colour, as in Loony Buttler's turban or some of Munro's door-windows. This multiplicity, as distinguished from the absoluteness of black and white, can also be the characteristic of Munro's central world. See below, 295, also 342 n83.

127 See "Half a Grapefruit" 38; "Princess Ida" 71, 81. Cf. Miss Farris's "rash,

smiling line of lipstick" (122) in "Changes and Ceremonies." We can add Munro's red-coated Karens and Madeleines, especially those who streak by (see above, 185, also 248 n17).

¹²⁸ Cf. Tyde's own "bloody progress through the snow" (8).

¹²⁹ Matt. 27:51–52.

¹³⁰ Exod. 12:21–23.

¹³¹ Josh. 2:18.

¹³² See Martin, *Paradox* 84.

¹³³ The earthquake is in Matt. 28:2; the discoverers are in all the gospels; the sheets are in Luke 24:12 and John 20:6–8. In Luke Peter sees "only the grave-cloths," translated in the AV as "the linen clothes laid by themselves"; in John we have "the linen clothes lying," whereas the "napkin (*soudárion*) that was about his head" is "wrapped together in a place by itself." Perhaps we should see Calla as a parody of the reassuring angel (a youth in Mark 16:5).

¹³⁴ See Exod. 29:38 for the two lambs of the Temple sacrifice associated with the Exodus and thus with the lamb of the Passover (Exod. 12:21 ff.).

¹³⁵ In "Walker Brothers Cowboy" Ben Jordan wears a "creamy straw hat" (6); as for the world around him, not only does our first view of Tuppertown include ice cream signs, but Ben's children repeatedly beg for ice cream and sometimes get it.

¹³⁶ For Roberta in "Labor Day Dinner" as a cosmic egg see above, 203–04. Cf. the name Jarvis Poulter in "Meneseteung."

¹³⁷ Cf. Gal. 4:21–26, especially 26.

¹³⁸ "The Flats Road" 2; cf. 26.

¹³⁹ See above, 252, n63.

¹⁴⁰ For both forms of the combination, see "Fits": "Very fine flakes of snow, fine as dust, and glittering, lay on the crust [of snow] that held him. There was a glitter, too, around the branches of the trees and bushes that he was getting closer to. . . . It was as if the wood itself had altered and begun to sparkle" (130).

¹⁴¹ Nora's dress is "green and yellow on brown" (12). Cf. among other things the "green and leaf-brown colours" (79) of the Berrymans' living-room, where the babysitter has her vision of the natural world. In "Thanks for the Ride" Lois combines important motifs by appearing in "a dress of yellow-green stuff — stiff and shiny like Christmas wrappings" (51).

¹⁴² For the war in Heaven see above, 185–86. Cf. Callie's store as described at the beginning of "The Moon in the Orange Street Skating Rink," with its "jittery electronic noise and flashing light" (132). At an earlier date such a place would merely have had "faded tinsel ropes, old overlooked Christmas decorations."

¹⁴³ More euphorically, the boys in "Five Points" get the same sort of vision from drugs — a flux of "flowers, towers, birds, and monsters" (33), not to say "sweet streams of atoms" (40). Note that the flowers are projected onto "the old pressed-tin ceiling, which the Croatians had painted white" (33): Flo's tin roof again. Et Desmond, incongruously as it may seem, is another who watches

flowers against a tin ceiling, "all her own" (18).

144 Note that in the account of the foundry in "Working for a Living" Munro lays some emphasis on the use of "green sand" (40).

145 See also below, 384, 452 n62.

146 Eugene in "Walking on Water" is 28; Bert Matthews, one of the "cowboys" in "Baptizing," is 28 or 29 (182) (it could be relevant here that there are 28 chapters in Matthew's gospel).

147 "The Dangerous One" 50; "The Time of Death" 92.

148 "The Beggar Maid," still close to a Wilderness story, has a white goddess and a god who is to "kiss the snow" (79). This story also shares with "Wild Swans" the presence of Yeats — a matter of direct quotation (of "The Stolen Child") in the one case (80) and allusion (to "The Wild Swans at Coole") in the other (60). Carrington (127) is right, I feel, in sensing "Leda and the Swan" here, even if Rose's feelings are not quite the same as Leda's. What is interesting for our present purposes is the cold, compelling world of the inhuman in Yeats — "the brute blood of the air" — and the fact that, as Yeats sees it, the Leda myth mirrors the Christian story of the virgin birth.

149 "Wild Swans" 56; note that Flo's "heavy-duty white paper" makes things look "something like presents."

150 See "Wild Swans" 55; "An Ounce of Cure" 76.

The Shining House

A. INTERLUDE: THE PIED PIPER

The poem of Munro's which I used as an epigraph for the previous chapter starts in winter, the time of caves in the snow. Then comes a different season:

> In March the yellow icicles
> Crashed from the kitchen eaves, it rained all week.
> The yard appeared, the pump, the lilac tree,
> The broken barberry hedge. . . .

With the final dissolution of winter, a new world emerges, including not only a useful-sounding pump but a yard with a living hedge, even a flowering tree inside the yard. The closest analogue in Munro's stories — for this part of the poem as for the wintry one before it — is to be found in "Boys and Girls," where the "fantastic landscape of winter" dissolves both to reveal the familiar shape of the earth and to provide "a great feeling of opening-out, of release" (120). A similar release constitutes the story's main action: of two horses destined for death, the stolid Mack gets shot as straightforwardly as Major in "Age of Faith," but the more spirited Flora is set free — for a time at least — by a girl who is feeling the first stirrings of her own sexuality. At the corresponding point in Munro's other books we find stories like "Forgiveness in Families," with its miracle of revival; "Changes and Ceremonies," with its school operetta that "[bellies] out like a circus balloon" (123) in the dreariness of late winter; and "The Beggar Maid," in which a poor girl ventures on unheard-of riches.

Another way to sense the presence of a distinct group here is to consider the scheme of chapters in Munro's two novels. In the first cycle of *Lives of Girls and Women* we proceed directly from an initiatory chapter — "The Flats Road" — to the central-phase "Heirs of the Living Body." We might expect to go just as directly from "Age of Faith" to "Lives of Girls and Women" in the second cycle, but instead we find the intermediate "Changes and Ceremonies"; in *Who Do You Think You Are?* we similarly find "The Beggar Maid" between "Wild Swans" and "Mischief." Once again a biblical parallel can help us to orient ourselves: if in "Age of Faith" we move through a wilderness experienced as such, confronting its god of naked power, in "Changes and Ceremonies" we begin to make a home in a new land. In spite of, or even because of, the unrest that goes with a *landnama*, there is an incipient turning to something other than sheer obedience and discipline: a desire for milder relations, even with Canaanite enemies, and for a human glory that will in time be that of the Kingdom. In various ways that we will be seeing, we have come to the Book of Joshua and especially the Book of Judges, with its quarrelling, its revelling, and its chosen leaders who are not yet kings.

To isolate a "Judges" group of stories is to make a distinction that elsewhere I make only within groups: special care will thus be necessary with it. Munro's collections, as opposed to her novels, do not in most cases have distinct Judges stories; and where a story exhibits her Judges world, we can expect this world to share something of the Wilderness on the one side of it or the Kingdom on the other. The operetta in "Changes and Ceremonies," to take it as an emblem, is not unlike various apparitions in the Wilderness, while also making a curtain-raiser for the grand opera of "Lives of Girls and Women."[1] In particular, various stories at corresponding places in Munro's other books seem — when looked at as we are now looking — to be half Judges and half Wilderness: "Walking on Water," for instance, or the more recent "Hold Me Fast, Don't Let Me Pass." "Monsieur les Deux Chapeaux," a Wilderness story to go by its location in *The Progress of Love*, has in Ross someone much like the incorrigible and wonder-working Cam of "Forgiveness in Families"; Ross's spring burst of automechanics, moreover, is not unlike the operetta in "Changes and Ceremonies." On the whole, "Monsieur les Deux Chapeaux" had better stay where we originally put it, not so much because of its position as because of its central concern with a great explosion, once and possibly future: but it does indicate the flexibility we need here. So does "Meneseteung," which again features a central explosion — the royal beating of Queen Aggie — but also a vision of life treated so fully, and positively, that we feel close to the Judges world: closer than in, say, "An Ounce of Cure," a corresponding story in several ways and itself having something of a Judges flavour.[2] After any such fussing with assignments — a somewhat arbitrary business as always — it remains true that stories like "Changes and Ceremonies" or "Forgiveness in Families," to mention the two most typical members of the family, have a quality of their own worth describing. What this is, we can say, is the quality of transition itself (or transition from transition, to give the Wilderness in its own transitional character); and we will be finding, as we have found before, that mere transition has some special privileges.

*

"Age of Faith" deals with the strange attractiveness of desolation or of a god found only within it. As part of this experience, any attraction to a Calf of Gold must have the same sterility: its result can only be a revel in a Janitor's Lair. If we treat, say, "Changes and Ceremonies" as a Wilderness story — a tale of barren winter infatuation — we will see its operetta as a performance of the same kind. On the other hand we have seen that a Lair can be a Refuge, and that the comforts there can prepare one for return from a lonely Other Place: in the same way, the operetta in "Changes and Ceremonies" is preparing the children for the sexual world that now lies before them.[3] Just how far such a story takes them into this world varies a good deal: at the beginning of "Boys and Girls" the narrator's songs on winter nights may be leading her toward her later outburst of femininity, but she has no conscious sense of herself as a girl yet. Del during the winter production of the operetta is enough of a girl to long for a real boy, however disembodied; Rose even becomes a bride. At the same time Rose remains the "White Goddess" who orders Patrick to "Kiss the snow" (79): and it is symptomatic that these stories vary a good deal in their seasons. As the coming of life, the Judges experience may be set definitely in spring — the main action of "Boys and Girls" affords a clear example. But as pointing to a life still unrealized, the same experience always remains something of a dream in winter — the time for love, according to Del, where spring can only lead to prosaic factuality. Or a Judges story may belong to an in-between time, like a Wilderness story itself: and yet the meaning of in-betweenness is shifting here. Del's operetta takes place in March, and a snowy March at that; but this March is equally the herald of spring, and there is a feeling here not just of emptiness but of anticipation.[4] More paradox-ically, there is a feeling that winter itself is fostering the spring that will succeed it.

For if winter is the time for love, Law — to use the biblical term again — is encouraging its own subversion: perhaps Law has a side to it that we have not fully appreciated. In the previous chapter we saw the declaration on Sinai as that of a God not to be bound by conditions, even those of his own covenant; but while the dealings of an absolute ruler must always have some of this arbitrariness, the very idea of law — of commandments to be obeyed as long as the law-giver wills — also implies repetition, the "ceremony" of "Changes and Ceremonies." And this makes it something reliable: not just an eruption in a wilderness, but the protection of a known land where something more positive than obedience can germinate. The school in "Changes and Ceremonies" is certainly a place of Law; but Law here, as administered by Mr. McKenna the "dusty brown-trousered" (129) principal, is not a wonder and terror — rather, it is the daily routine of students with intelligible rules to follow. And while routine can be dismal enough — like the "blurry, snowy afternoon, when we were half-asleep, copying from the board" (123) — it is in Mr. McKenna's world that the operetta bellies out.

We can think here again of Wilderness opposition, the "giants frozen in combat" (130) that Robert sees in the cold night. Donna in "The Dangerous One" may introduce revelry into the legal regime of her grandmother, but the narrator comes to see that this is not ultimately play. For all her look of serenity, Donna remains in her world of "final hostilities and loneliness" (51): she will never make her peace with her great enemy, nor will the criminality inside her make its peace with her own innocence. As "Changes and Ceremo-nies" opens, we are in a very similar environment. Looming in the background is a war; conspicuous in the foreground is a struggle between authority and resistance in a primary school. We hear the sounds of the *1812 Overture*.[5] We meet Mr. Boyce, the Englishman wrecked with the *Athenia*; we also meet Miss Farris, the local woman who plays the *Turkish March* — the march, that is, from *The Ruins of Athens*. Outside school we find Del and Naomi reading *Kristin Lavransdatter*, with its Viking feuds and raiding;[6] and above all, we find the war between girls and boys, the latter riding their bicycles like war-chariots "as if they wished there were knives on the wheels" (117). If, to go back to the biblical analogy such an image can suggest,[7] the Israelites are entering a new land after the desert, the entry means heavier fighting than ever — not to say squabbling among the Israelites themselves to match the warring with their neighbours.

Yet the hostility of boys and girls, in becoming more intense, also becomes "ritualized" (133); then we see it starting to break up. In the school, with its firm rules, there can be a "truce area, where neutral, but hidden, communication between boys and girls [is] possible" (125) — where, in fact, they can start to fall in love with each other. In "The Beggar Maid" the school is a university, and especially a library: a baronial pile with casement windows that "might have been designed for shooting arrows" (72), but also a place where Rose has a regular job to do, and where in due course she meets the gallant rescuer who will become her husband.[8] Libraries can be settings for romance. Along somewhat the same lines, a dingy waiting-room in "Forgiveness in Families" is the place where a dance restores a woman to life; in "Changes and Ceremonies" it is in the no less dingy teachers' room that the Peasants' Wedding Dance is rehearsed — the dancers even see the back parts of Mr. McKenna, descending through the ceiling with a box of treasures. And for the public performance of the operetta we are taken to the dark Town Hall, in which boys and girls not only dance together in full costume, but have glimpses of each other half-undressed in the Council Chambers. In the same story "Naomi" the down-to-earth town-girl and Del the pensive Ruth from outside come together; so, in "Forgiveness in Families," do brother and sister; so do rich Patrick and poor Rose.[9] "We come from two different worlds," as the latter sums it up (75): yet these worlds find a way to meet.

*

If all such meetings have a certain secrecy to them, some special situations can show us the value of secrecy. Del's school maintains a strict if unspoken division between the always chosen and the never chosen, the latter being outcasts who spend their lives in "dreamy inviolate loneliness" (124). The ambiguous "occasionally chosen" are typified by Del, who with one side of herself likes to be lonely too. For years she has been withdrawing into the town library, where she reads *The Winning of Barbara Worth, A Prince of the House of David*, and later, *Kristin Lavransdatter*, all tales of romance in a world of dangers. Rose in "The Beggar Maid," older and bolder, prefers to read Mann and Tolstoy and to imagine herself as a flamboyant actress, but she too is retreating into a world of her own here. The narrator of "Boys and Girls" has her songs and fantasies on winter nights; even Val in "Forgiveness in Families," with no conscious yearnings, has her library books. "Flow Gently Sweet Afton" (125), sing the children in Del's school: a Mary is asleep and dreaming, not yet to be wakened. And yet a "mysterious communication" (118) may come in her dream — the same that the Lady Dorothy of Del's library book ponders in her enclosed garden.

For once again a call is sounding. "Come away" (80), call the fairies to Rose as she reads Yeats' "The Stolen Child"; in "Changes and Ceremonies" Miss Farris sings "The Minstrel Boy" (131); in "Boys and Girls" it is "Danny Boy" (113) with which the narrator soothes herself. In a song like this last, moreover, it is not just the pipes that are calling — a returning lover is going to say "Ave," even if his sweetheart is sleeping the sleep of death. In other words an annunciation is going to take place: and that is the wonder here. The obscure, sequestered Marys of these stories may also, it seems, be the chosen.[10] Anyone, Del tells us, may turn out to have a good voice and get a part in the operetta, regardless of effort or station. Rose has her "lucky day" (72) when, skipping the scholarship students' meeting, she finds herself chosen by Dr. Henshawe; later, of course, she is chosen by Patrick himself — a thing she has "dreamed of" (77), a "miracle" unrelated to anything she knows about herself. And at the heart of "Changes and Ceremonies" Del is chosen by Frank Wales, the boy who would be happy to take her home. Frank plays the hero in the operetta — the Pied Piper who is all the lone, calling lovers of Del's fantasies.

*

The Pied Piper is in many ways a very initiatory figure: a solitary from a distant country who combines a habit of wandering, a talent for getting betrayed, and a way with animals and children. His piedness itself can be an initiatory thing — in its starkest form it would be the opposition of black and white — and it is by no means limited to the colour of his clothes. Like the dark horseman whom Del fantasizes from *Kristin Lavransdatter* or, presumably, the Arabian Knight of another operetta,[11] Munro's Pied Pipers all seem both chivalrous and "flawed" (119), a motley combination of graces and disabilities. There is no mistaking the latter: Frank Wales has boils worthy of Job; Patrick, the Pied Piper of "The Beggar Maid," sports "a long pale-red birthmark, dribbling like a tear down his temple and his cheek" (65) — our red streak again, now looking much like the mark of Cain. While not reminding anyone of tears, Ross in "Monsieur les Deux Chapeaux" appears at one point with similar "purple bruises along the side of his face, a cut over one ear" (65), the result of collision with a bathtub. Cam in "Forgiveness in Families" takes us more in the direction of the human "tray," since along with the stomach flu that once had him vomiting on his sister's wedding cake, he suffers from chronic asthma and talks picturesquely about "hereditary fatal kidney disease" (97). Ross goes Cam one better: as a boy he was or seemed to be shot dead; later, not content with driving one car into the bathtub, he rolled another in the ditch. At the time of the story, we find, he is working as groundsman for a janitor.

The Pied Piper, then, is clearly a loser — "everywhere that boy hits turns into a disaster area," as Cam's mother puts it (96). And his tendency to be singled out for trouble accords with a more general singularity: he is what Munro (and Cam's mother) likes to call an "idiot," literally someone who does things on his own. This naturally makes him comic as well as tragic — even Frank Wales has the face of a sad-sack comedian, while Ross is a clown outright.[12] Cam, if not exactly a clown, shares to the full Ross's inability to work at a serious job; and in strictness we have to add that he is a wheedler, a liar, and a cheat. Frank Wales is different, of course — tractable enough and by no means dishonest — yet to Del there seems a downright perversity in his bad spelling, as if it were "a furious stubborn joke" (125). In any case, idiocy seems to be illegitimacy: the Pied Piper will not fit into an Upper God's world of Law, and is bound to pay the price that Law exacts. Yet there is another element to his piedness, or another aspect of the whole of it: he is strangely gifted and giving. For one thing, he has the gift of coming back from his own fall — "I ain't dead" (82), says a Ross who has in fact "risen up" (83) from the ground, later to walk away from the rolled-over car without a scratch. And this rising Undergod has life for others as well: when Cam in his hippie phase does a dance, his dying mother somehow revives. To perform such wonders, the Pied Piper does not labour in the ordinary way. Cam educates himself by, in effect, playing hookey; he "works" for his dying mother by praying, as he puts it, or we might say by imagining — for that is what he has been doing in all his movie-watching, his story-telling, even his fibs and "creative life-style" (95). And the effect is magical — Cam is what Del calls Frank Wales, an "unteachable speller" (132).

*

This brings us to the most remarkable thing about the Pied Piper: his charm. Frank Wales calls with his flute-like voice — matched in a way by the "very thin, sweet voice, all on one level" in which Cam likes to repeat "ve-ery ni-ice" (97).[13] Ross, whatever his vocal qualities, has his brother and sister-in-law "sort of hypnotized" (64) — joining in spite of themselves in a hobby that, like the operetta in "Changes and Ceremonies," lures them from serious work while taking on a play-importance of its own. Ross's effect on his mother is even more hypnotic, and here there is a very marked parallel with "Forgiveness in Families": though a much soberer woman than the free-wheeling Sylvia, Cam's mother makes her own endless excuses for a son whom, to the chagrin of an elder sibling, she sees as the "centre-of-the-universe" (94). Needless to say, the Pied Piper of legend calls to another group of people as well: the children he leads spellbound into a far country.[14]

Among such charmers Patrick Blatchford is a limiting case: in a way that we will have to return to, he is almost a demonstration of what a Pied Piper is not. Patrick is anything but underprivileged, and if he has been feuding with his wealthy father, engagement to Rose brings about reconciliation and a renewed cash flow. Nor does Patrick subvert established order in any other way: indeed he later turns into a marvel of blustering conservatism. He is a hard enough worker, and far from being a comedian, seems to have no sense of humour whatever. He equally fails to exert much attraction — if he has good looks, Rose has to keep reminding herself of the fact. And yet she cannot refuse him: "she believed that she felt sorry for him, that she had to help him out" (77). With all his conceit he remains the most vulnerable person Rose has known, and in a paradoxical way he has his own irresistible quality. Patrick is a knight worthy of any operetta — a dauntless champion of maidenhood in distress, with a sense of honour proof against mere common sense. If he does not quite match Burne-Jones's King Cophetua — the kind of man who could "make a puddle" (77) of Rose — he too offers a gift that she finds hard to turn down.

The other exemplar of chivalry in these stories is Frank Wales himself, and in Frank's case there is an allusive resonance to be brought out. His name suggests not one but two "other" nations, both less fortunate in Munro's iconography than the English;[15] in a story full of war-time patriotism it is equally notable that he does not take off his cap for "God Save the King" (139). In other words, this quietly independent boy does subvert an establishment (as his defiant spelling suggests he might), and perhaps this is because he is really a Prince of Wales — a potential king himself. On the other hand he is not given to putting on airs, and in real life ends as a polite delivery man with a "dutifully crooked elbow" (140). It may be, then, that Frank is neither a king nor an heir apparent in the way of ordinary succession, but someone chosen for a more special role in the world. Biblically, this makes him like one of the judges, and in particular it makes him like Gideon, the divinely chosen deliverer from the border country of Manasseh. Gideon stars in his own kind of operetta — with the support of his picked company, he overcomes the Midianites by a noise of trumpets and jars. What is more important, he refuses kingship.

It may even be possible to connect the more laughable side of the Pied Piper with the Book of Judges. Frank Wales, while sober enough himself, has a comic side-kick in Dale McLaughlin, the Ross of the story: a cut-up with the girls who has reputedly taken the frail Violet Toombs to the bicycle-shed and gets the willing Alma Cody for his partner in the operetta. Without attempting precise identifications, we may feel an affinity here with the Judges world of raped concubines, abducted daughters of Shiloh, and randy Benjamites;[16] and at the climax of the story there may be a more definite connection to be made out. After the triumph of the operetta, the down-to-earth Dale takes over from the courteous Frank, teasing Del, pulling her to the floor, and disarranging her veil. Dale is bringing down a Philistine temple here — in his own way he is a Samson, another extroverted lady's man. If he ends cutting grass on a golf course, this too seems appropriate for a lady's man — wryly so, in fact, for the Samson who himself gets mown. And we may think of Samson again, or the kind of god who sponsors him, when Dale gets associated with a mysterious object in a hanging light: not a French safe as expected, but an old "sock" (140).

Not much weight can be put on any of these specifics, nor do we have anything here like the well-advertised presence of the Kingdom in "Lives of Girls and Women." It is important all the same that, like the heroes of the Book of Judges, the Pied Piper — serious or slapstick — frees something. And in doing so he meets a response that can remind us again of the biblical liberators — betrayal. For that is what Del imagines when she imagines him: "No treachery could really surprise him; battered by the world's use of him, he kept, like Humphrey Bogart, his weary honour" (132). But here our plot thickens, for the Pied Piper is a betrayer himself, whether from irresponsibility or malice or indignation or even a strangely "tender" quality that Del senses in him. It seems, in other words, that he is pied in more ways than we have yet seen.

*

To go deeper into the Pied Piper's mystery, we should first consider a figure in these stories whom we can call the Patron. The leading example is Miss Farris in "Changes and Ceremonies": a manically bright and eager woman who devotes her life to the fostering of make-believe, and whose pretty house[17] and skating costume seem make-believe themselves. It is Miss Farris who puts on the operettas at the school, challenging the rule-bound Mr. McKenna and conjuring up the festive world in which boys and girls can come together. She herself, on the other hand, does not quite come together with Mr. Boyce, her elegant male complement: what interests her seems to be not men (nor is Mr. "Boyce" really interested in women) but the endless production of romance as such. This is clearly hard work — Miss Farris even reaches a crisis of "despair" (131) as performance approaches; but on the great night itself she dissolves into "bountiful acceptance" (136) before the inevitable putting away of costumes and return to drab reality. Nor are the costumes simply discarded, for the cycle of operettas goes round and round. So does Miss Farris herself as she circles on the ice or swirls in a stage-cape: evidently she has her name for a good reason.

Miss Farris has her darker aspects as well. She breaks her cycle by jumping into the river at the end, and we also hear of a protégé who — as she mentions in a curiously absent way — was killed in the War. This was "Pierce Murray" (130): the hint here, not only of a Murray, but of a Mary whose soul has been pierced[18] suggests that beneath her bustle and gaiety Miss Farris is one of the doting mothers of these stories — indeed a *mater dolorosa*. And she has yet another role to play: she is not just a victim but a victimizer, inviting her charges into a world of delight that is also a snare. Miss Farris's counterpart in

"The Beggar Maid" is the admirable Dr. Henshawe: again an age-lessly bright and busy woman detached from the world of normal sexuality, again one who encourages learners, taking university girls to live with her in a house no less artful than Miss Farris's. And there can be no doubt that Rose finds this house a snare, since Dr. Henshawe will not hear of her dating boys, much less marrying one. Miss Farris does not go so far — in fact she introduces children to romance — and yet she is a Dr. Henshawe all the same. As Del puts it, she wants to "set free" operettas in which children will nevertheless be "trapped forever," their selves at once "transformed" and "child-ish" (141), as if they had answered the call of the fairies in Yeats's poem.

It is a Patron like Miss Farris, then, who stage-manages the Pied Piper: and in fact Miss Farris *is* a Pied Piper — a colourful impresario who both frees from a curse and lures into a trap. It may seem stranger to say that Frank Wales is a Miss Farris: in many ways the undemon-strative, unpretending pupil could not be more different from the histrionic teacher. Yet they have similar effects on Del, for both awaken her, arouse in her a need for something, then quickly disappear. And in his own way Frank is another lover who cannot be a lover. He is an unchanged treble, said on expert testimony to be unready for real sex, and clearly he is not in love with Del in the usual sense. Del for her part does not quite know what she wants from Frank: nothing as incarnate as physical love-making, certainly, rather the enactment of one of her library dreams or simply an ethereal presence. In the end Frank does not walk her home — partly because of a mistake about its location but also because they live too far apart in a deeper sense.

The Pied Pipers of the Judges and Wilderness stories are all like the elusive Frank, better at patronage than at more direct forms of love. The minister in "Wild Swans" may come to mind here: the courtly, blarneying man who touches Rose sexually — and of course does so more directly than Frank — but then vanishes, leaving her with only the intimation of a new life. Ross in "Monsieur les Deux Chapeaux" touches Glenna in a less specific way, and would not, Colin is sure, try anything beyond that; Cam in "Forgiveness in Families" gets as far as a wedding proposal, then uses an alleged family malady to back out. With Rose and Patrick things go farther again, yet in their wooing, more clearly than anywhere else in these stories, we see just how chimaerical love can be. Rose begins as something of a dreamy loner like Del; then, under the inadvertent patronage of Dr. Henshawe and Patrick's family, the curtain rises on the operetta of the Beggar Maid. Rose plays the blushing bride in true style, with Patrick co-starring as the lavish and adoring King Cophetua — nor can there be any doubt that Patrick for one is really in love. Yet it is a Rose of his fancy that he loves; and certainly Rose does her own fancying here. In "Changes and Ceremonies" the children spellbound by Miss Farris and Frank Wales have a similar talent, and, we can add, a talent for turning the tables on their patrons: Frank becomes a figure in Del's imaginings, while Miss Farris and Mr. Boyce, like so many teachers, have to star in a romance fabricated by their pupils.

*

If we take one more step here, the significance of patronage may become clear — as well as the significance of the Pied Piper himself. Our first Patron was Miss Farris, the woman who produces operettas in the midst of a school's world of Law. But if we substitute Dr. Henshawe for Miss Farris, we will have a hard time deciding whether it is Law or operetta that we are looking at: on the one hand Dr. Henshawe has her jewel-box house and cycle of pretty girls, on the other she believes in the working class and is given to saying "You are a scholar, Rose" (66). In "Changes and Ceremonies," no doubt, the sides are more definitely opposed: there is a clear difference, even hostility, between the giddy Miss Farris and the dour Mr. McKenna. Yet Miss Farris both practises and inspires "fanatical devotion" as she prepares the operetta — devotion, as Del observes,

> to the manufacture of what was not true, not plainly necessary, but more important, once belief had been granted to it, than anything else we had. (131)

This would make a remarkably apt — if sceptical — formula for the Israelite attitude to Law itself.

And so we come back to the curious relation between Law and license that we considered in setting out. Law, we found, seems to foster its own subversion: in a more negative view, subversion can only work for Law. The Pied Piper, with his ambiguous appearance and behaviour, calls to freedom and yet is himself an oddly legal figure — most obviously, someone who makes a contract and then enforces it to the letter, even if this means the sacrifice of a race of innocents. The Pied Piper does this, moreover, by leading the children in a dance:

he is administering Law even when producing an operetta.[19] It is in this context that we can best understand the stiffness and intolerance of a Patrick, even or especially when he is in his Pied Piper's role. We may also recall Miss Farris's retrograde cry of "Back-back-back! . . . Begin again from the beginning!" (135) — and feel that her own final leap takes her in the same direction rather than on into freedom. We may even be able to see why these stories persistently link romance with an outright violence beyond any settled form of law. The operetta is a play-war, with its internal rivalry for partners and roles, its external campaign waged by Miss Farris and her "allies" (131) against a Philistine enemy. When, similarly, Miss Farris sings "The Minstrel Boy" or the narrator of "Boys and Girls" puts herself to sleep with "Danny Boy," they are singing of young men who join the ranks of death — like Pierce Murray, the operetta captain who died as an airman. In this last instance, of course, play gave way to grievous reality, but that is just what is in question here. Directly or indirectly, the operetta calls to the reality of physical love, and this, as appears from certain warnings, is to call to battle as well — what Del apprehends when she listens to Naomi's pronouncements on sex and wonders about "the anarchy, the mysterious brutality prevalent in that adjacent world" (134).[20] It is no wonder that at times war and romance seem hardly different:

Just as during the war you could not imagine what people thought about, worried about, what the news was about, before there was a war, so now it was impossible to remember what school had been like before the excitement, the disruption and tension, of the operetta. (129)[21]

*

We can epitomize the Judges situation, seen in this gloomy light, by noticing how the Pied Piper's piedness lies in his "cloak patched with various colours, predominantly blue" (135). Miss Farris, we find, has some similar cloakings: the dark blue skating costume in which she circles to show the sky blue lining, or the black cloak, once worn by the dead Pierce Murray, in which she swirls to show a lining of fiery red. The cloak settles again, of course, just as the "ancient dark blue" (131) curtain of the Town Hall opens and then shuts on the parti-coloured operetta. Earlier in the story Del had learned from Naomi about another kind of covering: for it seems that "babies born with

272

cauls" (119) turn into criminals — or perhaps scholarship students, since Rose sees a "pall" (71) on these as well. Naomi knows further that babies conceived out of wedlock will be malformed, and again we may be reminded of Rose, who at one point begins a poem,

> Heedless in my dark womb
> I bear a madman's child. . . . (80)

Rose later wonders if she had meant "headless": in any case, something is being held in a deforming container here. If we think of the egg, silver but crushingly heavy, that she imagines Patrick wanting her to share, we will have another version of the same container; the more delicate bubbles in which Del imagines Miss Farris trapping her pupils are another again. And this container is that of the Pied Piper himself — the Frank Wales who, throughout his acting career, goes on wearing his smoky blue sweater.

The Pied Piper is equally one of Munro's watchers at a threshold, "guarding the door" (66) as Dr. Henshawe says ambiguously about Patrick. And here we see his victim's side again, for he is a sentry who will never pass through the door himself: he is like various biblical figures including the Gideon we have noted who foreshadows a kingdom yet will not be a king himself. Frank Wales's destiny is similar: quitting school after the operetta, he goes to work for Jubilee Dry Cleaners, and is soon indistinguishable from his "exhausted, bluish-looking" (140) employers. Frank is thus one of the young people in Munro held back where others go on — such as the never chosen Italian girl who dies while still in school.[22] As for Miss Farris, she passes away by water rather than dry cleaning.[23] No-one knows what happened: the woman whose whole life has been exhibition finally exhibits only a closed curtain — or what amounts to the same thing, a "clear blue sky" (141) like the lining of her skating outfit, which is ultimately no more revealing. And this means that, like her fairytale house in which there seem "no secrets, no contradictions" (127), Miss Farris is all contradiction: nothing can connect her show and her reality, just as nothing can connect the shooting in "Fits" with the known facts of the case. The Judges operetta, which was to bring contraries together, seems only to have increased the distance between them.

But while this tragic view of the situation is valid enough, it is not the only one that can be taken, or the one with which to leave these stories. However fruitless it may be in itself, the operetta does point to the fruit of sexual maturity; and it points to something less dubious which we should at least glimpse here. To do so, we can best look beyond the specific kinds of law and license we have been seeing. If Mr. McKenna is a school principal, there are various people in the Judges and Wilderness stories whom we can describe more generally as responsible — the blighted scholarship students in "The Beggar Maid," for instance, or the mother in "Forgiveness in Families" trudging up the hill in the winter dark. And as we can see from the sober Colin in "Monsieur les Deux Chapeaux" (as opposed to the happy-go-lucky Ross) there is something about responsibility that breeds compulsiveness and anxiety: for Colin is a great worrier, and his wife, the reliable Glenna, invariably "overdoes things" (80). In "Wild Swans," again, a Mr. "McKinney" — almost "McKenna" — chooses to restrict himself permanently to his house, while his wife understandably turns "odd and nervous" (59).

A worrier may also, to be sure, appear as a figure of play like Miss Farris: in "Monsieur les Deux Chapeaux" we have the affected Nancy in her costume (sackcloth to go with her premonitions), not to say Glenna again, who for her wedding performed a Miss Farris's prodigy of dress-making.[24] But the dress-making also led to a Miss Farris's desperation, for people like these take their playing very seriously; and the most illuminating figure here is someone who does not play at all — Val in "Forgiveness in Families." Val is pure responsibility, someone who finds the shiftless Cam unbearable for just this reason. And the result is the exasperated and rancorous woman that she is — a person not unlike the "muddled and tearful, sourly defensive" (117) girls of Jubilee at the outset of "Changes and Ceremonies."[25] In the crisis of the story, moreover, Val comes to see something else about herself. She does not really want her mother to get better: she would rather feel vindicated in her belief that the world is unfair.[26]

To say "Ve-ery ni-ice" like Cam may not seem much of an alternative to Val's sulkiness. But we know that Cam is concerned in his very unconcern, and we may also notice that he has a curious partner in Val's husband. Haro, while a dutiful and considerate man, sleeps normal hours through the crisis of the story, reminds Val that Cam has never really hurt her, and above all has the gift of persuading her. This brings us back to Frank himself, the boy who does without strain what the anxious Miss Farris does, or tries to do, by exhausting labour. It is Frank who — beyond any mere truce or treaty — brings Del "peace and consolation" (135): and in the echoes of this phrase, taking us back through *Samson Agonistes* to the Song of Simeon,[27] we can hear something greater than either anxiety or facile optimism.

The Frank who calls Del to peace is for the most part remarkably unremarkable: indeed all of Munro's Pied Pipers seem to have unprepossessing selves behind the glamorous ones they or their worshippers invent. Patrick is only a "timid scholar" (75), Cam a drop-out, Frank a middling student with a knack of singing. Yet in Frank's case especially we are made aware of something more: an "ordinary, reticent, and mysterious" (132) boy whose ordinary self is not detached from but identical with an extraordinary one manifested in his music. This Frank, Del observes, "[does] not need either to efface or call attention to himself" (132); he remains "unself-conscious" (125) even in playing a role. And so he has an integrity that Miss Farris's paradox can only appeal for, a sincerity that is equally itself in art and in life. By the same token the boy who is only a forerunner is also a leader whose authority does not come from carnal succession at all, the herald of a more than worldly king. It is this greater authority that Del hears in Frank's "serene and isolated" (125) singing, and even more intimately in "the unheard music of his presence" (135). Somewhere in the theatrical Miss Farris there is the same authority and the same sincerity: the "undefeated, unrequited love" (141) that Del finally senses in her, forever calling to her children — or her lost lover. Her Refuge, then, is not just another room of Mr. McKenna's Lair, or part of the way home: it is like all transitional places in affording, between one world and another, a communication from a world beyond both. We will hear from this world again when the drowned Miss Farris reappears along with the abandoned Frank in a new company of saving messengers: for the present we can let their calling — like any heard in time — draw us into a more immediate world, where winter with its dreams gives way to earthly summer.

B. THE CENTRAL PHASE

I: Kingdoms of the World

As the Pied Piper fades back into his loneliness, we enter the world of Munro's central phase, corresponding to that in any story where — in cyclical terms — outward movement reaches its farthest point and turns homeward again. The general qualifications necessary in linking stories with phases apply here, of course; so do others more specific to anything we see as being in a centre, for a central point is at once a place of concentration and a source of distribution. On the one hand we shall be finding the central world a remarkably tiny and self-contained one, a point defined against all the expanse around it. On the other hand, it has its own expansiveness: we will see it swelling to take in everything that stretches out from it, or, to imagine in the opposite way, absorbing into itself the whole of its sphere. Yet if the centre is only that of a finite universe, there may be a perspective in which it is not central at all.

In the Judges stories we found winter moving toward spring: new life, and also new definiteness after the season of storms and imaginings. Among the reappearing items in the poem I have quoted is a "Slab of cement in front of the kitchen door" (elsewhere Munro plays with "concrete"[28]), and the movement here from the fantastic to the substantial is a familiar one in literature. *Burnt Norton*, to use Eliot again, gives us the airy fancy of a paradise we never knew; *East Coker* plants us in an earthier world, that of heavy-bodied farm-labourers and a family unchanging through centuries. In *Lives of Girls and Women*, similarly, the world of "The Flats Road" — the morass haunted by intimations of wild success or failure — is succeeded by that of Jenkin's Bend. This latter, after its own swampy beginnings and the death by accident of the eponymous Jenkin, is a substantial house on a well-established farm, with an orderly, hard-working family in charge. From generation to generation this "solid, intricate structure of lives" (31) keeps itself together: its members can thus claim to be "heirs of the living body,"[29] and the family itself can be called a body if we use the word to mean any enclosure by which we define ourselves within chaos. In this sense a body is what we take on when we enter, as it were, the containment of the womb — to see the womb now as a container rather than a flood; or the body is any physical or other incorporation that we find for ourselves in later life. The rewards, as seen at Jenkin's Bend, are enormous — health, prosperity, even something more: for if Aunt Elspeth's name suggests the practicality of Munro's Elizabeths, Auntie Grace's suggests beauty and privilege. There can be no doubt that Jenkin's Bend is a favoured place, able to count on its luck and exempt from any need to take chances. This is no world of risks and dreams: it is the real thing, and a sure thing.

Before proceeding, it will be helpful to locate this solid establishment in our biblical scheme: a particular complex of imagery can help here by taking us to a biblical locality. In the first place, we will remember how "Heirs of the Living Body" includes a barn cat called Robber, a "striped tom" (35) at whom the aunts squirt milk; it also includes the idolized Uncle Craig, described by the aunts as "the cat that licked up all the cream" (29). In "The Flats Road" there is someone oddly similar: Frankie Hall the idiot sits in the sun "beside the dirty store window cats slept in" (7); and if not idolized, Frankie at any rate looks like an idol — "fat and pale like something carved out of Ivory soap." Rose's dying father in "Half a Grapefruit," who again resembles "the animals they had once carved at school out of yellow laundry soap" (50), has an authority that makes him still another idol, if a falling one. There are of course differences here — on the face of it Uncle Craig hardly seems a robber, or an idiot, or dying — but it is the similarities that we should notice if we are to follow these images where we now need to go.

In "The Flats Road" Munro does not make clear which of two windows Frankie Hall sits beside — perhaps that of the clock-repair shop run by his brother Louie, perhaps that of Charlie Buckle's general store next to it. The second of these seems more likely to have a cat in the window: at any rate, a cat is what we will find if we turn to Harry Brooke's store in "The Edge of Town."[30] Harry's store further resembles Charlie's in that its window has a perennial display; and appropriately enough in an almost parabolic early story, there are strong hints as to where the display comes from. Flanking the sphinx-like cat are "two modest pyramids of Kleenex and cereal boxes" (369): pyramids suggesting the land of paper and grain, the land of Egypt.[31] In an even earlier story, "The Widower," we find much the same store and pyramids.[32] Once again, there are provisos to be made — we have already met Charlie Buckle as an initiatory emperor in ruin; but it is his imperialness and his bounty, such as they are, that concern us at present.

Without as yet taking these motifs further, we can now go back to Jenkin's Bend for a closer look. What we find does indeed have something Egyptian about it. There is the rich farm — a marvel to Del and very different from anything on the Flats Road; and to water this farm there is a co-operative river, running in a "cool trough" (43) between the sun-beaten grainfields. The master of the land is the godlike Uncle Craig: not a remote and unpredictable power like the initiatory god but a dependable presence, incarnate as it were with the fruitful body of his world. This god is equally a scrivener amassing annals — a Thoth as well as a Re, under whose supervising eye the family live a life of "intricate formality" (37), of "work and gaiety, comfort and order." In particular we notice that he has two female guardians, the sisters who once flanked him in an old family photo, attend him in his later life, and continue to do so all the more vigilantly after his death.[33] For it is death that calls forth the full powers of the family: the story reaches its final climax in the great ceremony, complete with a banquet, in which the mummified god is celebrated and made ready to "pass on" (61).

In such a world it seems fitting that there should be a tomb: that is the way both Del and her Auntie Grace imagine one part of the farmhouse, the storeroom at the end of the corridor.[34] Like King Tut's, this tomb is very cluttered: among other things here we find implements, chests, a bed, and "a baby carriage clumsy as a galleon, keeling drunkenly to one side" (54) — an echo, possibly, of the tipped-over boats in Tutankhamen's tomb or the solar boat of the god Re himself.[35] At the time of the funeral the house's parlour makes another kind of mortuary chamber, a shut-up room pierced with "shafts of light" (52),[36] adorned with jewel-like tiles, and of course containing the coffin itself with its satin and lilies. Nor are such motifs linked with death only: the numinous water-lilies of another episode can remind us of the Egyptian lotus or lily rising from the primal waters to produce the world's life. The blue light pervading the storeroom resembles the waters themselves, while the great egg suggested to Del by the room itself is like the cosmic egg they bear. For this place seems to contain everything, in space and also in time — in Del's mind it is both womb and tomb.

In the order and abundance of Jenkin's Bend we have Egypt's version of itself. A story like "Images" reminds us that Egypt can also be a place of bondage — the prison where Rachel's sons Joe and Ben are held captive. Other stories show us an Egypt no longer flourishing: "Princess Ida," as we will see in the next chapter, is set in the failing land of a dying corn-god, and for that matter the world of the Jenkin's Bend aunts in their declining years is already a failing one beneath its carefully preserved surface. But it is a land of affluence and security that mainly presents itself in "Heirs of the Living Body," and for convenience I am going to say "Egypt" for all such expansive worlds in Munro.[37]

*

These worlds can regularly be found in a distinct group of stories coming after the Genesis group in Munro's various collections. We may as well use our term "Egyptian" for the whole of this second group, though once again we will have to make qualifications. "Heirs" itself is the only story here to allude strongly to Egypt;[38] the group itself, moreover, is less definite than any other in Munro — or more precisely, stories that are plainly Egyptian in my sense are outnumbered by others that are so only in special ways we will have to return to. Yet as with her Wilderness, one can easily see what Munro's Egypt is in principle, and a story like "The Shining Houses" displays its general features as clearly, if not as richly, as "Heirs of the Living Body." Here again we find a world moving from primitive disorder — that of the obsolete Mrs. Fullerton — to solid incorporation. The admirable new homes of Garden Place have a "soundness and excellence" (23) like that of Jenkin's Bend, and the social body we find here is no less sound. For as the disgruntled narrator has to admit,

> these are people who win, and they are good people; they want homes for their children, they help each other when there is trouble, they plan a community — saying that word as if they found a modern and well-proportioned magic in it. (29)

Stella's house in "Lichen" — at least partly an Egyptian story — is somewhat less solid, and Stella herself, while solid enough in one way, lives a more helter-skelter kind of life; yet both house and life are in their own way "pleasantly in order" (55), and Stella is a match for the Garden Place community in her "overwhelming sociability" — the comprehensive way in which she "gather[s] everybody in" (53).

The same packaging instinct makes Egyptians of some families less modern or outgoing than Stella. I will have to come back to the problem posed by the two sections of "Chaddeleys and Flemings," where the mirroring of initiatory and central worlds is specially noticeable;[39] but while either of the two families in this compound story could be seen as Egyptian, it is the Flemings of "The Stone in the Field" whom Munro's positioning invites us to see in that way. These are no doubt very Israelite Egyptians (among other things, we have found them living near "Mount Hebron" [24]): and yet they seem to Janet "perfectly encased in what they had and were" (29) — as immoveable and self-contained a body as the Jenkin's Bend family, or of course a stone in a field.[40] They too live ritually ordered lives centring on a revered male figure; they too keep outsiders at bay — in their case the nomadic Austrian whom they find no less foreign than the similar Austrian in "Heirs of the Living Body."

In "The Stone in the Field," then, we find an Egypt of a paradoxical kind, and the same thing can be said *a fortiori* of "Privilege," the second chapter of *Who Do You Think You Are?* — for the brutal squalor of Rose's school could hardly be more different from the order and grace of Jenkin's Bend. Yet even here, one can argue, there is an Egypt of sorts: the school is another self-contained world, and one with a wild order of its own that Rose considers "unchangeable" (24). The story's central incident, moreover, contains two motifs very reminiscent of "Heirs" — the sumptuous body of Cora and the playing of a funeral game. We find similar motifs in two unpublished early pieces of a more directly Egyptian character: "The Funeral-Goer" — a very fine story whose title explains it — and "Liberation," the story of a protective woman who spends her life folding bandages. In "Material" we find the bandage-folding once again, and — to introduce this complex story as briefly as possible — we more generally find material. The volatile Hugo may not be much like the solid Uncle Craig (though Gabriel, the narrator's second husband, is considerably more so), but Hugo too is a writer, and in the end manages to fix the wavering Dotty in the permanence of his prose.

In more commercial terms Hugo has made a "paying investment" (43) of his experience. All good Egyptians appear to have the same knack — to use the metaphor of several stories, they all do well in real estate. Reality here is not of the mysterious and unmanageable kind: it is truth in a worldly incarnation, the assured possession that seems ours in a Primary Stranger's world. In the case of conservative farmers like those of "Heirs" or "The Stone in the Field," assurance means clinging to inherited property; for others it means something more adventurous, and yet, to see its Egyptian aspect, no less certain in the end. In "The Progress of Love" Aunt Beryl, whose Egyptian qualities we will be seeing presently, puts her money into California real estate — "you can't lose" (28), she confides; and if we watch Phemie's own progress from the farm to the real-estate business, we will see that the material and the speculative kinds of real estate are ultimately the same. One way or another, then, we have come to the domain of Carl, the real estate man in "The Shining Houses"; indeed, as his name suggests, Carl's domain may contain the real estate of the whole world. Nor is he a mere Charlie Buckle: this is a "stocky, earnest, successful" (26) man, well able to manage things.[41]

*

If Garden Place can be called Egypt, there is a similar locale to be found in a group of stories well separated from the Egyptian. In "Sunday Afternoon" Alva the maid stands at the window of her employers' house and contemplates its well-to-do neighbourhood:

> The houses were set far apart, far back from the street, behind brilliant lawns and rockeries and ornamental trees. . . . In spite of the heat, there was no blur on the day . . . ; everything — the stone and white stucco houses, the flowers, the flower-coloured cars — looked hard and glittering, exact and perfect. There was no haphazard thing in sight. The street, like an advertisement, had an almost aggressive look of high spirits. (166–67)[42]

We are in the same spanking world here as Garden Place; and we will find ourselves there again if we explore the stories leading up to "Sunday Afternoon," or look in the corresponding parts of Munro's other books. To stay with architectural imagery for the moment, we will find the imposing public buildings, present and future, in "Lives of Girls and Women"; in "Postcard" we will find the Queen's Hotel, and on the other side of Clare MacQuarrie's life the dignified old MacQuarrie mansion; in "Jesse and Meribeth" we will find the Steuer house — no less fine if somewhat more whimsical. Valerie's house in "Labor Day Dinner" may have been less impressive to start with, but it has been refurbished in triumphant good taste, and George is hard at work on his own place a couple of miles away. Patrick and Rose in "Mischief" move into a house that even Patrick is proud to show visitors: not the family mansion, to be sure, but by no means a "dump" (88).

Along with these fine buildings we again encounter fine social bodies: Carl the real estate man, we can say, meets his match in the Mr. and Mrs. Carl Otis mentioned in "Lives of Girls and Women," at least as these would be honoured in a family celebration.[43] Other redoubtable families include the MacQuarries in "Postcard," the Makkavalas in "Accident," and — more gracefully — Valerie's family in "Labor Day Dinner," whose delicate harmony is a more casual, or seemingly casual, version of the "intricate formality" (37) at Jenkin's Bend. These families share the Jenkin's Bend solidarity, as Frances learns from Ted Makkavala's unsettling references to "our family" (99), and Helen in "Postcard" even more painfully. The funereal kind of body is here as well, since Fern Dogherty and Art Chamberlain have a joke about "dead livestock" (149), and in "Accident" Adelaide discourses fondly on the laying out of corpses — which, as in "Heirs," seem almost interchangeable with food.

And as if to declare the value of their shining world, our present group of stories makes extensive use of the media. Art Chamberlain is a radio announcer; so was Ted Forgie, Helen's former suitor in "Postcard"; Eric Cryderman in "Jesse and Meribeth," the lover in "Tell Me Yes or No," and Joan's husband in "Frazil Ice" are all journalists. Others are communicators or performers in different ways: Ted Makkavala, like George in "Labor Day Dinner," is a teacher who likes to put on a show for his pupils; Fern, Frances, and Clifford are musicians, while the Grazier boys in "The Moon in the Orange Street Skating Rink" start out as acrobats. It is true that not all declarations here are public ones, for Lady Dorothy's strange message in "Changes and Ceremonies" seems to have touched off a spate of letters and postcards — one that must keep Fern Dogherty busy in the post office. Not only do we have Clare MacQuarrie's postcard itself, but all the letters in "Tell Me Yes or No" (a story that itself is a real or imagined letter), and in "Lives of Girls and Women" the letters present and absent in Fern's bedroom. Other kinds of message, while not necessarily private, are decidedly cryptic — especially in "Lives of Girls and Women," where we find the code between Del and Art Chamberlain, the secret name in the chain letter, and the parable read by Naomi's father, not to say Del's "babble" (158) as a paralytic or her barking as a seal. Some of these declarations, again, are anything but celebrations — we have only to think of Art Chamberlain's parting note to Fern. What we can say, nevertheless, is that all belong to a world of communication, and that, on its optimistic side, this world has a single message to proclaim: that of glory. Sometimes this is a glory fully present, like the wealth of the Gannetts in "Sunday Afternoon"; elsewhere it may be just arriving or about to arrive — as Del Jordan explains in "Lives of Girls and Women," "it was glory I was after, . . . not sure from what direction fame would strike, or when, only convinced from my bones out that it had to" (144). But Del anticipating is much like the Gannetts possessing: it is because of the confidence they share that we can provisionally connect our new group of stories with the Egyptian.

*

We saw earlier how "Lives of Girls and Women" points to the Israelite Kingdom, with its David and Solomon, its cedars, apes, peacocks,

glory, wisdom, and whoring. We need not expect other stories in our
new group to point as definitely in the same direction, but these do
have the strong family likeness we have begun to see, and if "Lives
of Girls and Women" can be called a Kingdom story, the same term
will do for its companions. The most typical seem to me to be
"Postcard," "Mischief," "Accident," "The Moon in the Orange
Street Skating Rink," and "Jesse and Meribeth." With these we can
readily class "Frazil Ice," the central part of "Oh, What Avails."
Other stories in the Kingdom area of Munro's books belong here in
more special ways;[44] and two that I shall be using at times — "Lichen"
and "Five Points" — are not located in this area at all, but come after
Genesis stories in their respective collections. Later I shall be treating
these with the Exodus group; but since that group grows out of the
Egyptian, and also parallels the Kingdom group in certain ways, these
two stories can be of use to us here.

As soon as we put the label "Kingdom" on the present group,
certain correspondences offer themselves — not necessarily ones that
are "there," but ones that readily occur to us when Munro has
suggested a context for them. The fine buildings of Jubilee, to remain
for a moment with "Lives of Girls and Women," begin to remind us
of Solomon's house and temple; and when we hear the children's
"clear, devout" voices singing

> On the mountain stands a lady
> Who she is I do not know[.]
> All she wears is gold and silver . . . (158)[45]

we think of Jerusalem herself, the lady who stands on Mount Zion.
In spite of her gold and silver this lady needs "a new pair of shoes"
(158), as the children's song goes on to tell us: along with Zion's
splendour goes her degradation. And since Fern Dogherty embodies
the same contraries, she can play Bathsheba or Jezebel for us — in
one of Munro's drafts an earlier version of Fern goes so far as to call
herself the Witch of Endor. In another draft the woman who, like
Fern, sits smoking in her bathrobe at the breakfast table is called Aunt
"Esther":[46] not a Jezebel, certainly, but a woman queenly enough to
wear Fern's kind of bathrobe. And so we could go on: all these women
come from the same part of the Old Testament as David and Solomon,
and all point to the story of the Kingdom — which, as a name like
"Esther" reminds us, ends as a story of exile.

The finery here may remind us of something else as well: how greatly the Israelite kingdom depended on, and came to resemble, its neighbours. The cedars and apes and peacocks in "Lives of Girls and Women" came to Solomon from Sheba and Lebanon; in other ways Munro's Kingdom recalls the wealthy coastal cities of Phoenicia. We see an old photo of Fern and Art Chamberlain "in a strange city, walking under the marquee of a movie house where *Anchors Aweigh!* was showing" (165); we are told about various expeditions to Tupperton, with its Lakeside Pavilion. When Fern recalls that only "Ransom's" (172) of Tupperton could fit Art with suits, we may even think of the rates charged by Hiram of Tyre for building the Temple; or we can move farther around the coast to note that the seals mimicked by Del originally performed in a "turquoise" (161) pool. One can please oneself about such details or others we will come to; but throughout "Lives of Girls and Women" we encounter a worldly display which, in relation to the biblical Kingdom, was primarily that of the sea-cities. In more recent stories like "Five Points" Tupperton becomes Walley,[47] a port-town that in summer turns into something of a lakeside resort; and if we go to other Kingdom stories, or correspondingly central-phase elements in Munro generally, we often find the same glamorously marine world as in "Lives" — Clare MacQuarrie sending his postcard from "Coral Gables Florida" (137); Austin Cobbett in "Pictures of the Ice" retiring, supposedly, to a palmy seaside resort in Hawaii; the narrator of "Tell Me Yes or No" pursuing her lover to an imagined pleasure-city by the ocean, having already made love with him in a similarly decorated motel room. In "Mischief" even the stiff-necked Patrick gets into the spirit of things, putting a Neptune in an illuminated fountain to glamorize his back yard.

*

We have, then, something like the Kingdom and its neighbours here; we have found the King himself, of course, in the form of Michelangelo's David, who disports himself for all to see in "Lives of Girls and Women." There are also, I think, more subtle hints of David and Solomon, some of which I have already noted. An impressive image in the same story is that of the peacocks beside Pork Childs's oak-trees, a "glory in the cold spring, a wonder of Jubilee" (159). With their gorgeous colours, intense male sexuality, and "kingly" heads, these are royal birds indeed — not just the Queen of Sheba's gift but its recipient. Finest of all is the pure white bird perched in a tree, its tail "falling down through the branches" (159): and here we also sense, among other things, the long-haired and perfectly beautiful Absalom, caught by the head in an oak while battling his father in the forest of Ephraim.[48] A father and son in conflict will be familiar by now — we have seen the same motif in our initiatory phase (and will see it again in the terminal one); but here we are sensing it beneath the peace of the central phase — which, as the historical books of the Old Testament show, was not always so peaceful.

To find this conflict in a more directly warlike form, we can first recall that David himself, doubled by his bosom friend Jonathan,[49] began his career as a threat to the jealous Saul — not to mention a more monstrous father-figure, the giant Goliath. This David fits readily into "Lives of Girls and Women": Art Chamberlain is very much an overgrown boy, slinging stones at the whole parental world of the authoritative, the famous, "the people who 'took themselves seriously' " (167). The same oedipal David suggests himself in "The Turkey Season," a story that I have treated with the Wilderness group but which also indicates the beginnings of the Kingdom itself.[50] Brian, the friend and suspected lover of Herb Abbott, is a handsome young man with "taffy hair, bright-blue eyes, ruddy skin, well-shaped body" (69). "Taffy," in the sense of Welshman, is a version of "David," and Brian does in fact sound much like David as chosen by Samuel — the David who "was ruddy, and had beautiful eyes, and was handsome."[51] The word or idea of "ruddy" occurs at other appropriate points in these stories as well:[52] the most important here, if we recall Art Chamberlain's Davidic penis, is the account of Ted Makkavala's "ruddy cheerful penis, upright and workmanlike" (86). Indeed these last terms contain a further echo, since in parts of the Bible associated with the Kingdom they are repeatedly used for the just man or his God — the man, for instance, who is fit to abide in the Lord's tabernacle because he "walketh uprightly, and worketh righteousness."[53] Such a figure in Munro is the captain in "Goodness and Mercy," to whom the heroine feels drawn in the course of a glamorous ocean cruise: and what this worthy man suggests to her is the twenty-third Psalm, a paean of victory as she imagines it.

We are not yet done with "The Turkey Season." In our present context, Morgan Elliott, whose name I have already commented on,[54] assumes a special role: when, in a fit of rage, he takes a cleaver to the handsome Brian we may again be reminded of Saul, now in all his gloom and violence.[55] And there is a further image to remember here, as the narrator herself does — that of the dead turkeys:

I saw them hanging upside down, plucked and stiffened, pale and cold, with the heads and necks limp, the eyes and nostrils clotted with dark blood; the remaining bits of feathers — those dark and bloody, too — seemed to form a crown. (61)

Pork Childs's peacocks have been stripped of their splendour and hanged like Absalom — or, more royally, like Saul himself.[56] If we cannot add David here, we should at least remember his association with the threatened Brian: for Munro's characters with David's name or associations make a whole cycle of greatness and fall. The most kingly is perhaps David in "Labor Day Dinner," who displays the self-possession and receives the ritual deference we would expect, while his dark hair, like his relation to girls, hints at a latent Undergod. A more abandoned side appears in the philandering David of "Lichen"; "taffy" Brian makes a philanderer, or at any rate exhibitionist, of a more initiatory sort; the neglected and aggrieved David of "Simon's Luck" belongs to Munro's terminal world.[57]

*

Along with David, there is an all-important later counterpart to be noted, in the Kingdom stories as elsewhere. In "Jesse and Meribeth" — another central story with peacock feathers, luxurious dressing gowns, an ornamental house, and a dashing lover calling himself "Barnacle Bill the Sailor" (174) — two girls change their names from "Jessie" and "MaryBeth" to the forms given in the story's title, with the result that their teacher sarcastically asks for "a boy named Jesse" (166). The notion of a boy tells us something about Jessie's role in the girls' friendship; it also calls our attention to an implied bit of biblical typology. In the proximity to "MaryBeth" "Jesse" suggests "Joseph" and more strongly "Jesus" (we shall see in a moment how roles are in fact distributed); but Jesse was also the father of David, Jesus's ancestor.[58] Jessie's change of name reminds us that David and Jesus are of the same house, to which we can add that they have similar callings, since both in their ways seek to establish the Kingdom.[59] For Jesus, of course, this Kingdom is to be something other than worldly: but there is also Jesus the "son of David" acclaimed by the world, and that is the Jesus who belongs here.

We should not be surprised, then, to find Jesus a pervading presence in Munro's central world. "The Turkey Season" is of course a Christmas story; in the Kingdom group proper, as I define it, not only is "Accident" set at Christmas, but the word "Christ" (as well as "cross") seems to be floating free, leaving its mark on an odd variety of names — Chrissie, Kress, Cross, Cruze, Kruberg.[60] We can think as well of all the music to be found in these stories, and notice that Fern Dogherty is not only the leading songstress but the leading case of a bride pining for a bridegroom — or at least that is what she becomes when we consider her songs. These last tend heavily to the yearning and hopeful — "O Promise Me" (145), "Because" (145), "I Wonder as I Wander" (149); and in the end "Where'er You Walk" (176) takes on a special pathos from the fact that Fern's lover has just walked out on her.[61] At the same time we find her repertory and that of the Kingdom stories in general to be strongly biblical, ranging from "The Voice that Breath'd O'er Eden" or "He walks with me and he talks with me" to "The Holy City."[62] In fact some of the numbers here have directly biblical texts, and it is worth noting that, whatever their original meanings, all of these refer to Christ in their musical versions. "He Shall Feed His Flock" and "I Know that My Redeemer Liveth" are both from *Messiah*;[63] in "Bardon Bus" it is the narrator's imagined gospel hymns that point the Old Testament to the New:

He's the Lily of the Valley,
The Bright and Morning Star.
He's the Fairest of Ten Thousand to my Soul. (111)

Naomi's father, accordingly, is not out of place in this setting when he reads the Parable of the Wise and Foolish Virgins. We are in a world of prophecy, looking to the advent of a king who will also be a consort: and that is just what Jesus himself is predicting when he tells the parables of the Kingdom.

In such a world we also find the Eric "Cryderman" of "Jesse and Meribeth": when, indeed, we reflect that this lively if "sallow" (174) lover is thirty-three years old, that he quizzes Jessie about *The Brothers Karamazov* (she has skipped the "Grand Inquisitor" (175), which also means skipping Christ), and that in the scene leading to the summerhouse encounter she is looking at a bus from the "Calvary Tabernacle" (181), we may be inclined to place this story with the Passion group. Yet it is also closely related to stories like "Lives of Girls and Women" and "Tell Me Yes or No" in a way that can at least be summarized here. As I have suggested, the involvements of Eric and Jessie on the one hand and of Jessie and MaryBeth on the other are to be identified in a typological or Stranger-and-Neighbour way:

Eric plays "Jesse" in our general sense to Jessie's Mary (or Mary and Elizabeth together); Jessie herself plays Jesse to MaryBeth. We can even reverse the roles as so often in Munro, and say that Jessie plays Mary to MaryBeth's Jesse: we find her, that is, not only as a dominant male but as someone "astonished, almost dismayed, at being chosen" (162) when MaryBeth first approaches her.[64] All these relations lead to betrayal: most obviously MaryBeth disbelieves Jessie's story, but Jessie herself withdraws from MaryBeth, and at the climax Eric Cryderman first accosts and then withdraws from Jessie herself — who for her part is feeling a new coldness toward Eric. If we look beyond the main action we find betrayal again, connected with names like Beatrice and Evangeline. And that is what we have found with Art Chamberlain and Del, or David and his Kingdom: in one view at least, their story of these last can only repeat itself when Christ comes as a worldly Messiah.

II: The King and His Realm

Now we can go back to the David we need most for the present chapter: the king of the world's central kingdom, the peacock in the oak-tree. Since that is the kind of Pharaoh we need here as well, we can conveniently unite these rulers, together with their realms, as marking two high points in our biblical scheme. For Munro, however, we will need kingdoms outside the Bible as well. A story like "Heirs of the Living Body" makes us see the central realm as British — not, as in "The Flats Road," the British Empire in its death-throes, but rather as viewed through the eyes of Uncle Craig, a continuing city for which a World War is only a temporary nuisance. Wherever we turn at Jenkin's Bend, this Empire announces itself: in Uncle Craig's official functions, of course, but also in the flags on the porch, the coronation picture in the office, even details like the "London Pride" (36) that the exasperated Mrs. Jordan cannot quite "yank up."

The Yanks, for that matter, have their own empire. Del's aunts, whose cookie tins display Queen Alexandra on the lid, also provide Martha Washington cake; and the motif of an expansive southern land comes up repeatedly in the central stories, or corresponding parts of non-central ones. Since the pioneer prosperity that we found to be a form of Eden, or of Eden's successor-state, can easily be seen as a central phase within an initiatory world, we can draw here on enterprising characters like Blaikie Noble and Aunt Beryl: and when we do so we find ourselves hearing of golden California, all sea and real estate. If we return to the Kingdom stories, we find an ornamental city on the American west coast (or perhaps a balmy Victoria) in "Tell Me Yes or No";[65] Florida, on the other coast, lures Clare Mac-Quarrie; Hawaii, more distantly American, seems to be having the same effect on Austin Cobbett in "Pictures of the Ice."[66] But in the Kingdom stories as in the Egyptian it is British rule that stands out (we can pretty well assume that royalty in Ontario names is British). Fern Dogherty studied, while morally worthy, at the Royal Conservatory of Music. Helen in "Postcard" works at King's Department Store; Clare MacQuarrie passes his days at the Queen's Hotel, which is also where he courts Helen. It is in another Queen's Hotel that Miss Kernaghan locates the birth of Callie; it is in another again that George and Roberta in "Labor Day Dinner" have their great night out.[67]

Other empires are suggested more obliquely. One associated with wealth and beauty rather than military power comes to the fore when Mrs. Jordan enthuses about Florence (including, of course, Michelangelo's David); in "The Progress of Love" the escort who shows up with Aunt Beryl from California is again a Mr. Florence, a cousin of the limply hedonistic Art Chamberlain.[68] A sturdier sort of prosperity is suggested, at various points in Munro, by the Low Countries: in "Heirs of the Living Body," for instance, we have the "Orange Hall" (46) at Blue River, a place said elsewhere to be inhabited by "industrious Dutch" (209).[69] A further realm will take a little more exploring. The aunts in "Heirs of the Living Body" like to invite people to come in off "that dusty road" (32); a person who once did so was the hired man, an "Austrian" (33) on whom Aunt Grace proceeded to play a ruthless trick. A dusty wanderer from the east is appropriate enough as a servant in Egypt, and an Austrian, needless to say, is merely an alien savage in the eyes of the Jenkin's Bend family. In "The Stone in the Field" the same view is taken of the Austrian Mr. Black who camps on the family's border. But there is a good deal of mirror reversal here, as we will be seeing later: the realm of the Flemings, however sturdy, is not a particularly aristocratic one; Aunt Grace masquerades as a "darky" (33) for her trick. Conversely, things Austrian or Austro-Hungarian can indicate a far more civilized or established alternative to things local.

It may not be very remarkable that the music for skating in two Kingdom stories should be "Tales from the Vienna Woods";[70] it is a little more so that the aristocratic Mrs. Comber in Lives of Girls and

Women should be unpronounceably Hungarian. In "White Dump" Munro goes out of her way again to give a Hungarian name (as she notes it to be) to Magda, the Englishwoman who becomes Laurence's second wife. Magda's name suggests that she may be a closet Madeleine, but what matters here is something else, her queenly serenity. Gabriel, the narrator's engineer husband in "Material," is less royal but no less serene, as his angelic name suggests; and here Munro chooses to bring in yet another nationality — Gabriel is a Romanian. Romania, as it happens, appears as well in Del's account of her mother's Encyclopaedia: Bucharest, rather oddly, has stuck in her memory along with Amsterdam as representative of solid factuality — including "diagrammed insides of engines" (66)[71] — rather than the swashbuckling pageant she sees in history.

Aristocratic or bourgeois, "Romania" will sound estimable enough if we recall that the word was originally used for the whole Roman (in particular Byzantine) world: Romania is thus the same universal city as the Holy Roman Empire of the west, and in this sense Munro's Romanians belong to the same family as that of Mr. and Mrs. Carl Otis — a multi-national one, as I have already suggested.[72] We have also seen this family to be a church as well as state: in Munro's small towns this appears as the protestantly catholic United Church, where Fern Dogherty sings and Frances Wright plays the organ.

> This was the church the Legion attended, uniformed, on a certain Sunday; also the Lions Club, carrying their purple tasselled hats. Doctors, lawyers, merchants passed the plate. (95)

And so the whole temporal and spiritual order appears as a single hierarchy, with one law and one god: both an empire and a sound piece of engineering.

*

What of the central ruler in himself? If, in a male form, he ranges from Uncle Craig to Art Chamberlain or Eric Cryderman, he is evidently various enough, and in Munro we can expect his central characteristics to shade into peripheral and opposite ones; but we can first look at his primary nature as we have already glimpsed it in someone like Uncle Craig. We started with the idea of a god solidly present: noting that "Craig" is the same word as "crag," we can observe that Uncle Craig is as present as a pyramid or the rock-like god of David.[73] This need not mean that his contours are hard ones, for he was once "a blond, plump, self-satisfied adolescent" (29), and in later life is no less fleshy: "his face was square and sagging, his body stout." Others share the same plumpness along with the same imperturbability, such as the "substantial, calm" Gabriel (26), or the round-faced, round-shouldered Morris Fordyce, or a figure we can link to these for present purposes: Herb Abbott in "The Turkey Season," "a tall, firm, plump man, . . . smooth-faced and benign" (62).[74] With these we can put several of the lovers or hoped-for lovers in the Kingdom stories, such as the "fat, comfortable, sleepy-faced" (144) Clare MacQuarrie as Helen finally sees him. Art Chamberlain may not be overweight (the overweightness has transferred itself to Fern Dogherty in this case[75]), but where others are flesh he is clothes — "he might have been shirt and tie and suit all the way through" (150). And like the others, he seems in this version of himself not to know what excitement is. He is "always tired," or perhaps it is just that he has nothing about him that "predict[s] chance or intended violence." Gabriel, to his wife's amazement, placidly enjoys life; the lover in "Tell Me Yes or No" pictures himself as "tired and lazy" (114) — and the narrator comes to see that this may be the truth. Once again we are seeing Carl "Otis," unstriving now in his very plenitude.

As always, simple identities confound themselves if we press them: several of the godlike men with whom we have to do here are not lazy or even especially placid. Mr. Chaddeley (to take "Connection" on its Egyptian side) has a talent for invective and put-downs; Mr. Fleming, the patriarch of "The Stone in the Field," goes for his son with a pitchfork. For that matter these last two cases — the gentleman of leisure and the hard-working farmer — are opposites of one another as well, though in ways that take both in the direction of the initiatory world. What they share with Uncle Craig is their assurance: we must see them here as patriarchs, not of the desperately believing and chancing kind we met in the last chapter, but of the kind that takes its competence in the world for granted. And that is what all these gods have in common. Uncle Craig issuing licenses or presiding at the cream-separator is not more assured than Clare MacQuarrie in "Postcard" telling Helen to go home. George in "Labor Day Dinner" uses the same assurance to disparage the antics of his family; Stella's father in "Lichen" uses it to disapprove of his flighty son-in-law. Others, like Herb Abbott, are much more forbearing and courteous, but wherever we meet such figures in Munro (and they may be found anywhere, in their element or out of it) they carry the same central kind of authority — that of the world's order.

*

Suggestive as it is in itself, the fleshiness of the central god becomes more so when connected with carnal amplitude in other forms. The robe in which Fern Dogherty comes down to Sunday breakfast is "a ruby-coloured satin dressing gown, a gorgeous garment, fruitily molding, when she sat down, the bulges of her stomach and thighs" (144); the same swelling, set off by a similar wrapping, appears on the pregnant Mrs. Cryderman. The central world, it seems, is not only a land of milk and honey but one of ripe fruit. More particularly, it often seems to be a land of peaches and apricots — fruits that are the colour, at least in Caucasian races, of glowing human skin.[76] In "The Progress of Love" we find both that Aunt Beryl's version of the ubiquitous gown is "peach-colored" (16) and that she comes provided with "Apricot Delight" face powder (like a dessert, thinks Phemie), kept in another curved and quasi-organic container, "a celluloid box shaped like a shell" (17). The same fruit is on display in "Heirs of the Living Body" when Aunt Elspeth and Del, fetching the cows one summer evening, spy a deer at the edge of the bush. Holding out her stick "like a monarch" (35), Aunt Elspeth is able for a moment to arrest change — the deer does not move, nor does the light in its Egyptian swaddling: "It was a hot and perfectly still evening, light lying in bands on the tree trunks, gold as the skin of apricots" (35).

Another round fruit, coloured much like a peach or apricot, is equally significant here. In "Oranges and Apples" the "oranges" of Barbara's game seem by themselves a mere counter — the point of the title is difficulty of choice — but they become rather more when we notice the same fruit in related stories. In "Heirs of the Living Body" Del learns that her Uncle Craig has just died in "the Orange Hall, at Blue River" (46), a place I have already noted for its Dutch connection. Del knows that the hall is not really orange-coloured, and presumably that "orange" in this context is not the kind one eats; yet orange is being juxtaposed with blue, and shortly before this Del compared a dead cow's eye to "an orange stuffed in a black silk stocking" (44). "Orange," then, really is a colour and a fruit here; and we can say the same thing when it becomes a street name emblematic enough to go in another title: "The Moon in the Orange

Street Skating Rink." The "moon" in this case is a "yellow bulb" (140) in an open tin can: the can is jerked to suggest "shifting light" (160), other lights are turned off, and the skaters circle beneath, or within, a kind of night sky. A comparable effect, or its light-for-dark counterpart, is later produced in the apartment decorated by Callie: having created starry heavens of white and gold, she enthrones a resplendent Edgar in the centre — like the planet Jupiter in yet another story. "He had a little turn" (158), she says to explain Edgar's immobility: for the "orange" is the hub of a turning world, or even that world itself.

It is also the human body: the Orange Hall is David's ruddy flesh, the brick of Egypt, and ultimately the red earth that is Adam, here seen in his pride rather than his mortality. To these we can add other noble structures in the central stories. We hardly expect the buildings here to be orange-coloured (except in pictures on motel walls[77]), but we do find a number that are white or red, colours of healthy flesh. Thus the shining houses of Garden Place are predominantly white; the Jubilee post office is red brick; the Steuer house in "Jesse and Meribeth" and Valerie's house in "Labor Day Dinner" are both pink. In "Material" the same container is a more inward one: the rain-beaten house on Argyle Street where Hugo and his wife pass the winter is of "sad gray stucco" (31) on the outside, but the bathroom — its heart or bowels — is painted "a deep orange-yellow" (like a cheese, as Hugo remarks), and the bedrooms are blue and magenta for contrast. With the Orange Hall at Blue River, on the other hand, it is the whole building that is like a heart, situated on the blue river of the circulatory system: and it is here, appropriately, that Uncle Craig suffers his fatal heart attack.

These Orange Halls, to take the expression in the broadest sense now, are often places of supply, as seems natural: they may for instance be the grocery stores where we have noticed pyramids and sphinxes in the windows — together, we should now say, with other fruits and vegetables including oranges or even "oranges and apples."[78] Or they may be what one sees at Walley: grain elevators beside pyramids of salt.[79] Alternatively, such places may look after the world's needs in less material ways: as offices for mail or licensing, even as churches such as the White Brick Church opposite the General Store in Uncle Craig's history.[80] Callie's variety and confectionary store in "The Moon in the Orange Street Skating Rink" is hardly a church, but it does have video games, and upstairs Edgar — glorified as we have seen — is watching television itself, with the implications usual in

Munro. While rather scattered, these examples may for that very reason help us see the wide range of goods carried by the world's emporium: for it seems to offer both the carnal and the super-carnal, what was and is and will be. Soon, according to Mrs. Jordan, it will take more grandiose forms than a mere store or house — more grandiose even than the Jubilee post office, which appears in a newspaper photo as a tower rising in honour of communication behind an arch of snow. The world of the future, she tells her daughter, is going to consist of "domes and mushrooms of concrete, with moving skyways to carry you from one to the other"; any remaining countryside will be "bound and tamed forever under broad sweeping ribbons of pavement" (143). And yet beyond all such change the world will still be the living body that is the Orange Hall. The most eagerly awaited of the erections in this chapter is also the most organic: that of Art Chamberlain's penis, which is red like the post office tower and no less a mushroom than any skydome.

*

This penis is, to be precise, not orange but "reddish purple" (169) — a colour between, or fusing, red and blue. We have just been seeing some of the reds of the central world, and we have seen a fair number of blues in the process: Blue River, the blue inside of the house on Argyle Street, the turquoise pool and blue peacocks in "Lives of Girls and Women." In "Sunday Afternoon," again, blue seems omnipresent: the heroine finds herself wearing a blue uniform and working in the blue kitchen of a house decorated extensively in blue tones. Appropriately enough, the rooms of this house seem "floating in an underwater light" (163), beyond which we find bright summer sky and a lake. The same blue expanses form the background of the central world generally, as with the "hot blue sky" (128) of Clare MacQuarrie's postcard and the lake or ocean in other stories — perhaps with Catherine in "Lichen" posed as a mermaid in the foreground. Catherine's eyes are of course a "watery blue" (34), and other eyes in this world are much the same: Del notices of Art Chamberlain, for instance, that "his light blue-green eyes had no expression, just that colour, so pretty you would want to make a dress out of it" (149–50).[81] Even more impressive — and less exclusively central — is the grandmother in "Working for a Living," one of whose eyes has a blue "window" in its brown, so that she is often made to "sit with her eyes wide open, being looked into" (32). We are not told what people find there: we can, however, sense a strange sort of infinity. The window in the grandmother's eye is so tiny that you would have to come very close to see it; yet what you would see would be distant, for the blue is "pale and clear without a speck of other colours in it, pure as the sky." And when Del imagines the storeroom at Jenkin's Bend as an egg filled with blue light, blue is not only near and far but a pervasive medium, like the watery light in "Sunday Afternoon."

In a context where we are also finding Davidic and Levantine motifs, blue naturally recalls the Tyrian purple or the "royal purple" descended from it — that of Violet's coat in "A Queer Streak" (235), for instance, worn during her queenly days of living over the Royal Bank. Since the words translated as "blue," "purple," "crimson," and "scarlet" frequently appear together in the Old Testament, and in any case do not indicate quite the same points on the red-blue spectrum as our own terms, it is fair to say that the "royal blue" (14) of Mr. Florence's car comes to much the same thing as Violet's purple.[82] For a more organic version we have Bugs's "aubergine" ("dark-purple") (170) dress in "Goodness and Mercy," for which Averill exchanges her own green as she moves towards womanhood. More delicate, perhaps, is the purple of the lilacs so often mentioned in Munro — those at the end of "Lives of Girls and Women," for example. But in its bluer range especially, this most prized of colours remains something absolute: "essential" (159), as Del says describing the hue of the royal peacocks. One way of imagining more ordinary red and blue, the warm and cool shades we have associated with Elizabeth and Mary, is as opposites separating out from this essence. These are the colours we found contrasted, for instance, in the red and blue dresses of "Red Dress — 1946"; they seem to diversify themselves even more in the "red and orange and purple" of the "famous gardens" (115) found beside the waters in "Tell Me Yes or No" (for Tyre and Sidon are not the only worldly cities in their part of the Bible).[83] Differences like that between the Orange Hall and Blue River represent the same polarization again, as do more intense contrasts like that of the "orange boats, dark and orange buildings, reflected in blue-black water" (113) in the motel in "Tell Me Yes or No."[84] In "Lichen" Stella's two summer outfits, one flamingo and one turquoise, seem to be her own way of celebrating the same kind of contrast, and in "Who Do You Think You Are?" the true-blue Orange Parade displays banners of "blue and gold, orange and white" (192).

Once we step into the world of reds and blues, its variations seem endless. Either colour, for instance, can have associations of the exalted or abased: red may be that of Adam's passion or simply of his daily labour, ruddy David's sensuality or just his bumptiousness.[85] Again, we can have blue making a contrast of dark and light, as in the tones of Del's peacocks, or of icy cold shades and tropically hot ones, or of garish and discreet. As we would now expect, any simple polarity of colour and colour, or of a colour and the same colour in another shade, or even of the opposite associations of a single shade, soon metamorphoses into a chaos of multiplying dimensions. But there is a polarity that can perhaps represent all these others for us: that of colour in general with whatever essence is something other than colour, or a colour beyond colour itself. If we resolve what often seem the rainbow hues of the central world into the essential blue of Pork Childs' peacocks, we can now set this itself against what Del calls "pure white, pure blessing" (159): the radiance of the single peacock that sits high above the others, its tail cascading like water through the branches. And we can notice that, in more everyday forms, the contrast of blue and white appears repeatedly in central stories and episodes. Brenda in "Five Points" can give us a full demonstration: for her tryst with Neil Bauer she gets herself up in "tight white pants and turquoise top and low-slung white belt" (36). She even has "blue shadow and liner" (89) around her blue eyes — Brenda does nothing by halves.[86]

In its most dynamic form the blessing of white expresses an energy so pure as to draw all colour into its own brilliance; the same can be said of blue itself if it is that of Art Chamberlain's presence in Del's fantasy — "essential" again and "humming away electrically like a blue fluorescent light" (155).[87] Flowers, Florida, Florence, fluorescence — we seem here to be at the very heart of an unfolding, many-hued world; and we may even see this world changed from glory into glory. When the narrator of "Tell Me Yes or No" speaks of "dazzling sea-light" (115), a city by the ocean becomes that of a carnal apocalypse — not surprisingly in this world of beryl and pearl and ruby and emerald and turquoise and "jewel-bright waves."[88] And when the clouds open above Garden Place on its mountain to reveal both light and a triangle of blue sky, we have a hint of the Transfiguration itself, the central high point in the life of Christ. After all, this is a story about "white and shining houses" (23), as Mary thinks of them — though it also contains an incongruously black and recalcitrant Mrs. "Fullerton" for us to consider in due course.[89]

There is one further connection we should make at this point. Aunt

Beryl likes to appear in white with red accents — either the "red-lined frill over the hips" (18) of her stepping-out dress or the "flaunting red ribbon" (16) of her sun hat: in other words, she enjoys displaying the red streak we are now familiar with. And since we are associating red and blue, we can also recall the "line of turquoise blue" (134) where the lake meets the horizon in "Oranges and Apples." Such images have their central context, as a related one can perhaps show us. In the central episode of "Working for a Living" Munro's enterprising mother, like Aunt Beryl, appears in glory at a summer hotel, wearing "a cream-coloured dress with a pattern of little red flowers" (33) not unlike Beryl's white and red satin. In this hour of triumph, moreover, her hair resembles a "coronet"; at a similar hour in "Five Points," Brenda's hair is described as "catching the sun like a crown of petals" (36).[90] We can also recall here Munro's royal peacock in the oak-tree, along with her crowned turkeys; and we can think of Edgar Grazier's hair in his final enthronement "glistening like the angel hair on Christmas trees" (158). Whatever qualifications may be necessary, an appropriate image for Munro's worldly consummation would seem to be that of the sun meeting the tree — or flower, or lake, or crown of human hair — just as light meets colour or reflection. Later in this chapter we will find a whole world seated proudly upon the waters: what matters here is that at the heart of time, no less than at its beginnings and endings, we encounter Nature's "well" — the gleaming surface where contraries touch, be the result what it may.

*

The colour-schemes of the central world have shown us some vivid contrasts; but in this world, taken as it wants to be taken, differences are not in principle hostilities — the tones into which light refracts itself, like those of Garden Place, compose a peaceful harmony, emanating as it were from a pure source and gathered back to it again. In mythological terms this source is a sky-god like Atum or Re, a giver of seminal light; we have seen the same god in the many-coloured fruitfulness of the world that is his body. We have thus reached a beautiful and, as we have found it so far, reasonably simple economy: but even on these terms we can sense that something is wrong.

The unity of this world can be imagined as that of a god and his creation; in a more mundane form it is the amity the creatures enjoy among themselves. And in either version there is something ununiting in unity itself. We have imagined the central world both as a tumescent male and as a woman swollen in pregnancy: in both cases a "living body" with an expansive self-completeness, in spite of its obvious connection to a sexual opposite. There is the same quality about the familial living body at Jenkin's Bend,[91] yet we should also notice something very different here: not only do brother and sisters there continually tease and belittle each other, but their domesticity is of a strictly celibate kind, and their work strictly divided between the sexes. Things are essentially the same with the widowed Mr. Fleming and his spinster daughters in "The Stone in the Field," matched by Mr. Chaddeley and his spinster grand-daughters in "Connection"; and in one form or another this adhesive celibacy seems the condition of the central world generally. Even where we find marriage, it remains — in the case of the Jenkin's Bend world — within a larger version of the family; and the solidarity of such families can also act as a positive hindrance to marriage. Roy and Lila in "Wood" are man and wife, but Lila's large and gregarious family drives Roy first to the shed and then to the bush. Ben Jordan's family in "Images," ably represented by Mary McQuade, likewise disrupts a marriage, carrying Ben triumphantly back to itself — or, again, driving him to the bush.

A more paradoxical form of celibacy can be marriage in itself, which in the central world may be unitary in the dismal way of "Ron-and-Mary" (49), to quote David's formula in "Lichen," or may show an opposite face. At Garden Place, as at Jenkin's Bend, men and women have almost nothing to share except when they make league against a common enemy. The marriage of Hugo and his wife in "Material," while a trick played by two, is essentially the same: the couple have their laugh at the world, yet they share little else, and certainly not each other. Joan's marriage in "Frazil Ice" may be far more normal — Joan has married a good-looking man, "intelligent and trustworthy" (199), a successful journalist; their union seems no less successful. And yet Joan feels dissatisfied:

> Her marriage seems to her commodious enough — she and her husband have twined together, developing a language, a history, a way of looking at things. They talk all the time. But they leave each other alone, too. (198–99)

If the partners of a marriage can be as separate as this, the one flesh they make only is another form of united celibacy — not to mention more perverse forms of this celibacy, such as prostitution and incest, that crop up at times in the central stories.[92] Uncle Craig is wakened from one of his naps by an old man and woman wanting a licence to get married; but the old man and woman are really Elspeth and Grace, the spinster sisters, having one of their jokes.

To see the celibacy of the central world at its most revealing, however, we should consider what we might call non-marital marriages. There are various affairs in these stories — a matter that will concern us again presently — and some, such as those between Helen and Clare MacQuarrie or Fern and Art Chamberlain, are as settled as marriages while they last. They may also manage a good deal of the sexual excitement that affairs are for: and this makes it all the more striking that they are such matters of routine. Fern and Art play their endless game; Clare uses Helen while Helen puts up with Clare. To think of "Frazil Ice" again, such affairs are not unlike the alliance of Morris and Matilda, the two who did not go to the Christmas dance in "Deadeye Dick." Matilda, having run off to a brief marriage or non-marriage with a moustached bigamist, reappears disillusioned by love but needing a periodic escort — a man who will understand and not "get ideas" (204). "Which is me," explains Morris, who never ventures to be Matilda's lover or husband.[93] The two might be Maddy and Fred Powell in "The Peace of Utrecht" with their endless "unconsummated relationship" (194) — something that the narrating Helen of that story finds typical of Jubilee.[94] The "tender, loyal, boring friendship" (162) of the schoolgirls Jessie and MaryBeth is a different version of the same thing — as, in effect, is its echo, the comic-opera marriage of the Crydermans.

On these terms people do well enough. When Joan thinks of Morris and Matilda, she imagines a good deal of awkwardness; then she changes her mind. After all, she reflects, they dance very well together — "they are so terribly, perfectly balanced, each with stubbornly preserved, and wholeheartedly accepted, flaws" (205). It is just this balance, constituted by separation and opposition themselves, that makes the central world. To use the term that the narrator seizes on at the end of "Material," this is a world of "arrangement" (43) — the "cohesive tact" that, as we are told elsewhere, keeps the United Church united.[95] In another metaphor it is diplomacy: the "Peace of Utrecht" agreed upon by Helen and Maddy, or the system of "delicate checks and balances" (139) that is Valerie's household in "Labor Day Dinner." It is even, in "Jesse and Meribeth," the "feuds and alliances and fits of not speaking" (164) that maintain *concordia discors* in a boarding-house, just as "everlasting negotiations" (188) maintain it in the Cryderman household. Curious as some of these arrangements may be, they can be seen as ways of making relations work, and in that way can all be put under the heading of sense: for that is what we are dealing with here. If we see the story of our fallen experience as originating in a chaos of sensibility, sense is the cosmos we make within that chaos.

*

We can see the curse upon such a world, even while it remains inviolate, by going back to the very sensible arrangement we began with, that of the Jenkin's Bend family. As Del's aunts get older and more withdrawn, their household appears increasingly as "a tiny sealed-off country, with its own ornate customs and elegantly, ridiculously complicated language" (59). A country like this seems utterly self-sufficient; its inner relations are of the most decorous kind; yet it is also shrunken and shut up — human possibility has limited itself to a "decent narrowness of range" (51), to quote "Lichen." For the central world is that of the "contractor": not the maker of dubious covenants we met earlier, but the more domesticated man (or god) who has got himself into a solid contract and is thus contracted in the other sense — bound and constricted by his agreement. Munro actually has a few contractors in the professional sense: Horse Nicholson, for instance, the second of the three jokers in "Half a Grapefruit," or Lawrence, the second of the three workmen in "Dulse." The Morris of "Frazil Ice," again, has become a real-estate and construction man, and in "Five Points" we learn that his company has the "contract" for the breakwater on which Neil is working. All three of these men succeed in the world, Horse Nicholson even continuing on into politics; all have the assurance that goes with their success; and yet Morris is oblivious to any world beyond his own, and Lawrence in particular can show us the condition to which the success of such a world is bound.[96]

In building his no doubt shining houses, Lawrence must often have to remind his clients of their contract and its terms — that, at any rate, is what Lydia Cooper senses he would do as her lover. And for all his brashness he seems disturbed by the terms of his own larger contract with the world, for there is something not only oppressing but oppressed about him.[97] In one way he hardly seems to be running things at all: he is like Morris, the boss with the air of a mere foreman.

We have already, of course, looked at the complicated relation of master and servant — Upper God and Undergod — in a less settled world. We saw, for instance, how in "The Turkey Season" it is Morgan Elliott the boss who seems a Hired Man, and Herb Abbott the foreman who seems in charge (Herb, for that matter, has turned out to share some qualities with Munro's calm and fleshy Egyptians). In a more plainly Egyptian setting, Uncle Craig's duty as clerk of Fairmile Township is to issue licences, documents which restrict as much as they permit; he himself is at once a boss and a hired man — a minister's minister.[98] The last scene of "The Moon in the Orange Street Skating Rink" seems typical here: while the godlike Edgar sits in state, pleased with the glamour of a TV show, the prudent Sam attends to a tax regulation on the news.

Sam's concern can also help us with "Jesse and Meribeth," perhaps Munro's most evocative presentation of a contracted world. It is true that the Steuer house hardly suggests such a thing at first, being a charming affair in pink and cream; and no doubt it really is a playhouse compared to the more earnest buildings around it. No doubt it also has a fine central sturdiness that appears when we compare it to something even more whimsical, the neglected little summerhouse behind. The name "Steuer," on the other hand, does not sound either sturdy or playful. If we anglicize the pronunciation it comes out rather like "Stuart" (not to say "steward"): in this sense "Steuer" fuses two things often paired in Munro, a house and a Scottish name for its street — Argyle or Murray. And since such names have gloomy along with their lordly overtones, they can be related to a further association of the Steuer house, one that will take us back to Sam again: "Steuer" is the German word for "tax." A house of taxation, moreover, should remind us of a different context we have already established for this story. It is in the Steuer house that "Eric Cryderman" presents himself to the former "Evangeline Steuer." In the summerhouse at the back of the garden he then presents himself to "Jessie": allowing for the displacement in the name, a conception or annunciation is occurring here in a *hortus conclusus*. In the larger story, indeed, a birth is about to take place: but we should not forget the restricted quarters into which taxation forces the biblical Mary and Joseph. It is here that their son is confined in bands, his later sojourn in Egypt being another version of the same confinement. In Munro's story the scene of pride or pleasure is really one of constraint all the time. The birthday-cake Steuer house is like her Stone Schools; Eric in the summerhouse is teaching Jessie a lesson.

And the Dr. Steuer looming behind it all is one of Munro's domineering fathers — men whose daughters often turn out as frail and flighty as Mrs. Cryderman.

We must ask ourselves, then, why the central Kingdom has bound itself in this way. Why must human relations be contracted ones? In more Egyptian terms, why must the ornate and elegant country be sealed off? Why, to go back to our definition of Egypt, must we incorporate ourselves in bodies? The answer that presents itself is fear: outside the cosmos waits chaos, outside the well-guarded borders of Egypt waits a terrible enemy. It is this larger situation that we will now need to consider.

III: Pranksters and Barbarians

In the last pages I have been speaking as if two types of character in the central-phase stories were hardly distinguishable: the Uncle Craigs and the Art Chamberlains. We can indeed describe both these men in the same terms if we like — both are complacent, inscrutable public figures much admired in their respective spheres. But there is a world of difference between the king's loyal representative — the man "who really believed in the world of public events, of politics, who did not question he was part of these things" (30) — and the man whose whole life is truancy and undermining. There is an equally great difference between Del Jordan's aunts or mother — women who in their different ways believe very firmly in the world — and the shrugging, pliant Fern Dogherty, with her frivolous dressing gown, sleazy documentation, and general readiness to have a good time.

Art and Fern, of course, have their good times together; nor are they the only ones in the Kingdom stories to do so. In "Mischief" we find Clifford and Rose; in "Postcard" there are Clare and Helen, in "Accident" Frances and Ted. In "Frazil Ice" again — more a Kingdom episode than an Egyptian — we find Joan turning to John Brolier, rejecting both her marriage and the kind of bond chosen by Morris and Matilda. The "mischief" of these characters, to call it after one of Munro's titles, is perhaps the most salient single feature of these stories: in a way that seems strange at first, it is what most obviously makes them a group (with some elements in the Egyptian group corresponding, as we would expect).[99] Joan, in spite of her thoroughly acceptable husband, rebels against the years "of accumulation, of acquiring and arranging, of padding up the corners of her life" (202); others have been rebels from the start. As a result marriages are broken, propriety flouted, the whole central-phase establishment shaken: in biblical terms, Art Chamberlain plays David the adulterer, assisted by Fern Dogherty as one of the associated figures of whoredom. It is as if the high-mindedness and optimism of the official Kingdom had been challenged by a more sceptical voice — one like that of *Ecclesiastes*, for instance, saying "Smoke goes up the chimney" (132) as Rose and her friends prepare for group sex.

The world of mischief is naturally a more heterogeneous one than that of conformity: we have only to think of the wide assortment of Art Chamberlains in the central stories. Of these the one who comes closest to Art himself is Eric Cryderman, a romantic soldier and journalist who strings his official partner along while secretly groping a teenage girl. Faster and flashier is Clifford, the supple lover from whom Rose expects "tricks, a glittering secret" (112). Ted Makkavala of "Accident" is the same lover in a more directly pugnacious way, Clare MacQuarrie of "Postcard" in a more unperturbed, Victor of "Apples and Oranges" in a more mettlesome. Others are different again, and yet all these men can be thought of as David out of his official role, David the sexual truant. Their truancy, for that matter, extends to the way they play the more official kinds of David. Art Chamberlain is a veteran, as is Eric Cryderman, but Art remembers his battles simply as subversion — escapades against his own side as much as the other. As for David the musician, we find Art Chamberlain singing about "pretty pea-cocks" (160), just as we find the David of "Lichen" giving an accomplished rendition of "O Mistress Mine" (39). Anything that takes itself seriously can be mocked, and mockery is what all these men have in common.

*

Once we have isolated mischief from the establishment it undermines, we can give a first answer to the question I raised in the previous section: mischief, it seems, is the threat to the central world, the alien thing that must be guarded against — which is certainly not untrue. Here, however, we will have to launch into deeper waters: for apart from the fact that our proposed answer leaves us with a smaller picture than we are going to need, it also leaves us with a dangerously simple one. To see the kind of problem that arises, we should first notice that our collection of male figures makes something more than an assortment: as we look at them we start to see polarization, running along various lines but for one thing repeating the opposition between mischief and establishment itself. Clifford is almost as volatile as Hugo in "Material," whom he also resembles in his relation to his intellectual wife; other philanderers are less so, and we will even be meeting the "large and benign and civilized" (44) Duncan in "Dulse," a match for Gabriel in his sedateness.[100] In more ethical terms, some of the men we are concerned with here are simply loose and cynical — Clifford again, or Art Chamberlain; others are notable for their strong will and high principle, the latter often expressing itself in disapproval of the other sex. George in "Labor Day Dinner," if not currently a philanderer, is an important figure here, connected in various ways with the no less opinionated Ted Makkavala. Ted Forgie, Clare MacQuarrie's predecessor in "Postcard," may have been less strong-minded, but seems to have been principled enough in the course of deserting Helen; even Hugo, a "moral idiot" (41) according to his wife, is principled when he upholds the honour of his art, or expresses his intolerance of Dotty. And if we look still more closely we see how these men can make strange combinations even within themselves. Art Chamberlain is a rebellious boy doubled by a proclaimer of the local institutions; the David of "Lichen" is similar, an irresponsible youngster yet also a middle-aged civil servant — and a "simple serpent" (38) altogether.[101] A mischief-maker, then, is a very slippery figure. He is no Uncle Craig, and that may be what chiefly impresses us; yet he always seems to have something of Uncle Craig about him at the same time — something we feel in his portliness, or his ease of manner, or his assured opinions, or his sense of superiority to lesser minds and kinds. This is just what the astute narrator of "Material" comes to realize: Hugo and Gabriel, she sees, are not so different. Compared to her disaffected self, both are Egyptian — for both have made arrangements, neither is "at the mercy" (44).[102]

What about the mischief-making women? No doubt these are more difficult to reduce to formula than the men, since they tend to be the experiencers in their stories, or intimates of the experiencers; but for this very reason we are in a better position to look inside them — to ask what they want, or think they want. A number of them, certainly, want sheer mischief. Fern, the adolescent Del who spies on Fern, the Rose of "Mischief," Jessie in "Jesse and Meribeth" all delight in the thought of playing Jezebel. Other women, however, not only take their mischief less seriously but can be curiously unmischievous about it. Mrs. Cryderman in "Jesse and Meribeth" is plainly a close relative of Fern Dogherty, but with an important difference: she is brazen not so much because she defies propriety as because she hardly notices it. And if we still sense something of naughtiness here, the narrator of "Tell Me Yes or No" has none of it at all — no sense or relish of misbehaviour, though a considerable relish of theatre. We can even connect this last woman with some who are the opposite of the Ferns and Roses.

It is worth noticing that the heroine of "Tell Me Yes or No" looks rather slovenly when courted, and that this seems not to make much difference to her. We can go on to connect this unsexiness in sex itself with an unsexiness more simply unsexual: someone like Jocelyn in "Mischief" is not only sloppy — and deliberately so — but remarkably innocent. She has no affairs that we are told of, no suspicion of what her husband may be doing with her best friend, and more generally no sense of the "weariness, suppleness, deviousness, meanness" (111) that for Rose is the mark of her own kind. And from Jocelyn we can take a further step. Though we last see her engaged in the group sex I have mentioned, she is oddly like Mrs. Jordan: another great despiser of things outdated, one who never suspects what her boarder and indeed daughter are up to, and one whose old kimono, pyjamas, and mukluks make a striking contrast to Fern's luscious dressing-gown.[103] Jocelyn and Mrs. Jordan may be truants — both defy conventions of the society around them, and Jocelyn for one is self-consciously impish about it; and yet they are also high-minded women determined to maintain order and reason in the world. Their strength is essentially the same in each case: a renouncing of the knowledge of good and evil, particularly sexual good and evil. In being thus "whole and predictable" (111), Jocelyn is rightly bracketed in Rose's mind with Patrick, a rebel against his father who turns out as an upholder of the establishment. Matilda in "Frazil Ice" enters into a platonic alliance with Morris that to Joan seems, once again, "innocent"; it is left for Joan herself, about to leave husband and children for another man, to feel a conflict with which Matilda is unconcerned:

> She feels compunction, certainly. . . . this is genuine — her grief and guilt at this moment are genuine, and they'll never altogether vanish. But they won't get in her way, either. She is more than glad; she feels that she has no choice but to be going. (206)

All the ambiguity of mischief, male or female, seems to find expression here. Joan has regrets; she also feels a determination that seems at once brazen and curiously moral — and her morality in turn seems half the counter-morality of mischief itself and half the morality of the society it rebels against.

*

If mischief and what it flouts are on such intimate terms, this need not surprise us: we have already seen central-phase affairs as being oddly matters of routine — of desire contracted by Law. There is more to the matter than that, no doubt: Law arouses desire as well, producing the need for thrills typical of the mischief stories. And yet the great affairs here always have the character of charades — these are not really love stories, however intense things may get — and the affairs always collapse back into what they have challenged. For Munro's Uncle Craigs and her Art Chamberlains take essentially the same view of life: all, in the terms I have used for the central phase generally, enjoy or expect a present glory. It does seem, however, that the world we at first saw in terms of its solid corporeality is also a more volatile one. Nor need we restrict this volatility to its more mischievous forms: the central world has a pervasive character of spirit that we will need to explore before we can embark on a more far-reaching exploration.[104]

One sort of central imagery that we are already familiar with is that of flowers and pastels. Names like Flora, Lila, and Iris,[105] while scattered throughout Munro, go in this context with the flowers of the pleasure-city in "Tell Me Yes or No" or the "blanket of lilies" (52) sent by the charming Aunt Helen for Uncle Craig's funeral; in a more focused way there is the lilac at the end of "Lives of Girls and Women" or the waterlilies at the centre of "Heirs of the Living Body." "Fern" Dogherty, though somewhat wilted, obviously belongs with these graceful plants; and among Munro's empires, one I have not yet mentioned is no less aesthetic than flowers or Florence. The tea-cup to which Egyptian Nile is compared in "Princess Ida" would naturally be of china, the material that is too precious to risk at the funeral in "Heirs"; and preciousness or preciosity, always with something of ancient grace about it, is just what we sense in the *chinoiserie* collected by the ladies of the Kingdom stories. Helen has an embroidered Chinese dressing-gown, a gift from Clare; Mrs. Cryderman, more extravagantly, has not only a Chinese gown but Chinese furniture and incense among her other curios.[106] When we think of it, the forbidden, elegantly ritualized country to which Del's aunts retire suggests China or Japan as much as it does Egypt,[107] and we sense China again in the various fine fabrics of the central world.[108] It seems that there is an empire of porcelain and paper and silk to set beside the empire of grain and brick — not that Egypt wants for its own refinement with its cotton and linen, alabaster and, once again, paper.

Chinese or Egyptian, our spiritous new world seems very much a kingdom of art. It is represented effectively — if in the dreamy style of a left-over hippy — by Catherine in "Lichen": a woman who teaches art, seeks out the Book of Kells, and is also, we can note, commented on for her "filmy" (39) dress, a tissue of "cobwebby cotton" (33). "Art" Chamberlain, the veteran of Florence, has something of the same style about him, with his slack politeness, self-conscious grooming, and textile appearance. In a somewhat different vein, the Chaddeley aunts in "Connection" (a "pre-Egyptian" story, as I have suggested) can be put here as well, having as they do the same lightness of taste — the same eagerness for fun and make-believe and party treats. The world of Del's aunts, while much more stay-at-home and down-to-earth, has it own tea and cakes, and proves in the end to be altogether a work of art, "frail and admirable and inhuman" (60).

But ethereal as all this may be, it wields its own form of Egyptian power. Hugo in "Material," as we have seen, is the most rarefied of artists: all nerves, games, tall tales, and in later life a fake "image" (31); yet the narrator eventually learns his potential, and we should see the same thing about rarefaction elsewhere. This is not hard to find: the art of Del's aunts includes a crocheted injunction in the bathroom to "freshen the air before you leave" (60), and it is remarkable just how much in the way of improved or improving air there is in these stories. For one thing there is perfume — Auntie Grace has her eau de cologne, Mrs. Cryderman her incense, Cora in "Privilege" the smell of her "talcum and cosmetics" (31). To be sure, Cora's world is also one of toilets, chemical and other, and Auntie Grace's includes Aunt Moira with her rubbery "gynecological odour" (40). But here too the odours are or should be sanitary ones, like that of the burnt match in the bathroom: they are the smell of something preserved in the face of corruption. And this is equally true of a different kind of odour, a dark version of the white peacock's "pure blessing" (159). Cora's essence as imagined by Rose creates "the sense of a glowing dark spot, a melting center, a smell and taste of burnt chocolate" (34).[109] To this we can join dark sweets like Del's breakfast molasses in "Heirs of the Living Body"; closer to Cora are the chocolates brought by the aunts in "Connection," and in their case what we smell is not only the chocolates themselves but an odour of "artifice and luxury" (3) given off by their wrappers.[110] All these smells, in effect, are artificial ones: Auntie Grace's own "fresh and healthy" (40) smell is carefully maintained; the smell of Cora's "warm dark skin and hair" (31) becomes in Rose's mind that of a confection. So does the smell of Cora's nail polish, which is "like bananas, with a queer chemical edge" — a combination of fruit and chemistry that we also found in Beryl's Apricot Delight face powder.[111]

In all this an artful spirit seems to be performing a work of transmutation. If at Jenkin's Bend even cow-pats look like "hand-made lids of clay" (43), that is because the August heat has baked them, as it also bakes the mud along the river into "cake icing." The same process results in the "crusted scalloped potatoes" and "fat roast chickens, looking varnished" (52) of the later funeral reception; and just as Cora has her banana-scented nail-polish and Stella her endless blackberry jam, so the funeral feast is all pickles and aspics and preserves. The aunts in "Connection" help out not only by producing "marvellous molded salads" (4)[112] but by moulding themselves as well: thanks to the art of girdling, they can boast "firm curves and proud slopes" where they would otherwise have been "wobbly as custard" (1). Fern Dogherty, while wobbly enough, is at any rate "fruitily mould[ed]" (144) by her luxurious gown; Mrs. Cryderman is "Jelly" (172) to her friends. The professional artists in these stories work to the same end: Catherine in "Lichen" produces pictures in which "tiny figures [are] enclosed in plastic bubbles" (41), Hugo in "Material" encloses the all too fleshly Dotty in his own "marvelous clear jelly" (43). And above all there is the Egyptian art of arts — the art of embalming. It is embalming that turns Uncle Craig himself into a confection, while Stella's "post-human" grandfather in "Lichen" is not only "preserved" but "transformed" (51): vitrified like "a smoked-glass vase." Even more remarkable in its way is the transformation in "The Funeral-Goer," where Miss Hobden, the hero's "guide to the world of funerals," exudes

a complicated chemical odour, in which dry-cleaning fluids, deodorants, talcum powder, and Yardley's Funeral Perfume were all so involved that he could hardly recognize the kindly kitchen-smell of a heavy woman sweating on a hot day. (Tener 37.15.10–13)[113]

Spirit has power — a power to change body, and in that way to keep it from change.

*

Another form taken by Munro's solid-and-spiritous central world is of special importance here since it involves the word "Egypt" itself. In "A Trip to the Coast" we hear about the town of Kinkaid, evidently a place of some pretension with its Royal Dance Pavilion: but the "Queens of Egypt" (178) at the Kinkaid Fair would be not ladies but gipsies, Romany rather than Romanian; and of course they would be mischief-makers, not at all what we find at Jenkin's Bend.[114] Now we should take another look at what we do find there. Del's aunts, while unquestionably ladies, have a distinctly frisky side: at milking-time especially they put on "all sorts of ragged patchwork garments" (35) and behave in a highly spirited manner. This in fact makes them much like the dairy-farming Aunt Dodie in "The Ottawa Valley," a "gypsy" (243) who works in alliance with the stately Egyptian mother of the story. And if we think of the tricks played by the Jenkin's Bend aunts, we will notice that one of these especially is rather like the trick played on Allen Durrand by the "Ottawa Valley" pair: Auntie Grace, it seems, once humiliated a hired foreigner by hiding behind a tree and then jumping at him with a knife.[115]

To remember this foreigner's particular origin is to see how completely Egypt and its counter-self mirror one another. Munro makes him another Austrian: in fact her eastern European and particularly "Finno-Ugrian" (97) peoples, as they are called in "Accident," can for our purposes all be assimilated to the same stock — a wild one, in this context, and likely to produce just such types as the irascible and superstitious hired man in "Heirs." Two of the more major central-phase figures belong here as well. George in "Labor Day Dinner" is a peasant Hungarian from wild northern Ontario, Ted Makkavala a peasant Finn from the same area; and not only are both what Munro twice calls the Finns, "magyar," but both have much the same abrasiveness that Auntie Grace is able to bring out in the Austrian. That at least is one side of the matter: on the other, not only do these wild peoples have their own pride, but when Auntie Grace guys the hired man, a costumed gipsy is hoodwinking an Austrian, which in Munro's iconography can mean hoodwinking an imperial Romanian.[116] Egyptians and gipsies trade and combine roles:[117] we should not be surprised to catch the very Egyptian heroine of "Prue" pilfering one of her lover's amber cuff-links — itself both a treasure from Russia and an Egyptian jelly like Uncle Craig's lost eye or that of the dead cow.[118]

*

In exploring the wilderness outside Egypt's borders, we first travelled from a primary Egypt to a livelier region that, on investigation, has turned out to be only an Egyptian province. But as we watch Munro's gipsies in action, we may sense that we are nearing more definitely foreign territory — not that the border itself is very definite. In "The Shining Houses" the heroine is drawn to someone we will now want to see as a gipsy, the smoky old egg-woman Mrs. Fullerton: at any rate Mrs. Fullerton is as "slatternly-gay" (20) as any gipsy, with a mouth forever twitching as if to conceal a joke. At the same time she represents something other than gipsy mischief as we have conceived it, just as she represents something other than Egyptian good house-keeping. Her eyes are not amber ornaments but dark pits; nor is she in any ready sense an agent of Garden Place, which will go to great lengths to be rid of her. We can also go back to the Austrian in "Heirs of the Living Body," like Mrs. Fullerton an underling who gets driven away. Auntie Grace's trick on the Austrian is only a practical joke, of course, and she is happy to see him come back, suitably cowed; yet she shows a deeper malice here than when teasing her sister or brother, and the reappearing Austrian looks correspondingly grim — "gloomy as Satan" (34). In "The Stone in the Field" another Austrian from the road is called Mr. Black and set in implicit parallel to Poppy Cullender, the black-clothed itinerant trader. Mrs. Fullerton is a black-eyed, black-haired woman with a black-cherry tree and, at one stage, a pet "coon" (21). Auntie Grace herself has to put on the blackened face of a "darky" (33) to cope with the Austrian.

One thing to notice about these variously black characters is that, apart of course from Auntie Grace in her brighter phase, they tend to have disreputable locations: Mr. Black in his hut, Mrs. Fullerton in her unsightly warren, Poppy in a house full of cast-off litter not unlike Uncle Benny's. There are many other such habitats in these stories: storerooms, basements, dumps, the "old wilderness city" (24) of which Mrs. Fullerton's property is a vestige. And these unsavoury places are associated, if not always with unsavoury people, at any rate with a descent to unsavoury kinds of experience. We are familiar with this descent, of course: once again we have come to a Counter-

Stranger's Lair, with denizens who, to the extent they are that, belong among Munro's black janitors. What makes this fact stand out here is the central phase's special position in Munro's larger story: this is where we suddenly fall from a shining upper world into a dark lower one. Beneath the proud ramps and pyramids at Walley there is an underworld of noise and danger and "the darkness people on the surface of the earth never get to see" (47): the underworld, that is, of the saltmine proper, a great hole dug from the remains of an ancient ocean. To go into that world is like going into the ice-cave of the poem I quoted earlier — it is to find "caverns and pillars, miles out under the lake."

It is also to find the endless toil that we have seen in Munro's foundries. If the dwellers in the upper world are Egyptians, the barbarians of the lower are tolerable to Egypt, if at all, only as scavengers like Percy Marshall in "Wood," or native traders like Mrs. Fullerton, or bond-labourers of one kind and another. Often, we discover, social class is distinctly at issue: Rose turns from her wealthy husband to someone she considers lower-class like herself; Helen is abandoned in the crisis by the genteel MacQuarries. Thus we have stories about masters and servants, about "privilege" and what is excluded from it, about the "connection" that means denying baser connections, and certainly about "material" — an opposite of spirit that may be got into some more presentable condition, but that may also be simply used and repressed.

It cannot be held down permanently. The barbarians may be kept decently out of sight in their lower or outer world, but as we will see by returning to the emblematic Makkavala family, they are waiting all the while for their chance to strike. We have seen the Finnish Makkavalas as, in a sense, gipsies; there is also something more deeply alien about a long-pagan and (in the eyes of their neighbours) barbarous race lurking in a northern fastness. When driven from their original wilderness, the Makkavalas first find themselves another in the new world; then they invade a more cultivated region with all the swiftness of Counter-Strangers. What gives them their opportunity is an accident: a son of theirs has been killed going down a hill. In fact we can say of the Makkavalas, as of any Counter-Stranger, that they are accident itself, reclaiming whatever has presumed to rise above it. And this accident is "finish": of all barbarians, the most deeply threatening to the living body of Egypt is of course death.

*

The extraordinary thing about Egypt is that it can absorb even this barbarian: Egyptian life is to be identified not only with counter-Egyptian liveliness but with mortality itself. In the first place, we should go back to the two invaders in "Images." Joe Phippen is much like the Makkavalas: a wild hermit from no-man's-land who suddenly invades with a hatchet. Mary McQuade, we have seen, is a match for Joe — which means here that she is an uninvited nurse looking for illness and indeed bringing it on. Even before "the time of her power" (31) Mary is fearsome enough: she bosses, she scolds, she "twitches and rumbles" (34), her very breathing is an "old, indefinable complaint" (30). Still another such invader is dark-clad Aunt Moira Oliphant in "Heirs of the Living Body," who has a fatal version of "Mary" for a given name and a surname suggesting a romance giant. Aunt Moira is altogether a woman of complaints, both in the sense that she suffers everything flesh can have wrong with it and that she is as seismic as Mary McQuade — we find her hissing and trembling when aroused "like a monument about to explode" (56). And yet Aunt Moira is not an outsider at all. She may live in wild, outlying Porterfield, from which she journeys as if "across the Sahara" (39), but she regards Porterfield as completely alien, greatly preferring to come back to her kin. This is equally true of Mary McQuade, who is a returning member of the family she invades, and in fact Munro has various such figures: the grandmother in "Working for a Living," for instance, who comes "magnificent with foreboding" (31), sweeping up the family during the mother's absence much like Mary. Auntie Grace, we are seeing, is not the only Egyptian who appears like a black fate: it is quite an Egyptian thing to do.

If, moreover, Auntie Grace's barbarian victim is in the same plight as respectable families elsewhere, we can identify the Egyptian and barbarian worlds from the other direction as well. There is something strangely impressive about the domain of Mrs. Fullerton:

> When Mary came out of this place, she always felt as if she were passing through barricades. The house and its surroundings were so self-sufficient, with their complicated and seemingly unalterable layout. . . . Here was no open or straightforward plan, no order that an outsider could understand; yet what was haphazard time had made final. The place had become fixed, impregnable, all its accumulations necessary. . . . (22)

In spite of the chicken-wire and the wood-pile, it would be hard to imagine a better description of Egypt: even as a labyrinth, for that matter, Mrs. Fullerton's place is like the "maze" (50) that is Jenkin's Bend at the time of Uncle Craig's funeral. No doubt it is a rude Egypt that we have here, but we have the same thing in the Fleming farm or Miss Kernaghan's boarding-house, not to say the school in "Privilege" — which again has its own paradoxical order, incomprehensible to outsiders like Flo. It seems that there are not only Egyptian barbarians, but barbarian Egyptians, or an Egypt that manages to be both barbarous and civil at once.[119] I introduced the Makkavalas simply as wild invaders; yet apart from being a cohesive family, they are something more than barbarous, and not just because they prove to be respectable Lutherans. Finns, we learn, have a strange doubleness in their make-up. Ted is dark, Greta blond:

> he told [Frances] that there were two kinds of looks in Finland, the Magyar and the Scandinavian looks, dark and fair, and how they did not seem to mingle but kept themselves distinct, showing up generation after generation unaltered, in the same district, in the same family. (99)

There are two interweaving strains here, dark and light, one associated with shamanic forest-tribes, the other with the rulers they stubbornly resist:[120] and yet the two strains make one people.

To generalize in the spatial terms that we have been using, our paradox is that of centre and periphery. Nothing could be more central than a fair, or a fair-haired dominant race, or Uncle Craig's own Fairmile Township, or Jenkin's Bend itself, especially during a fair like Uncle Craig's funeral. Yet a fair is precisely where we find gipsies, and certainly Del's aunts are in their gipsy mode when they sing "Meet me in St. Louis, Louis, meet me at the fair!" (35). Fairgrounds, moreover, are located on the edge of towns, and may look as marginal as they are: for however lively during the fair itself, no places could be more out-of-the-way, even forlorn, in the off-season or in decay.[121] Crossings have an ambiguity of the same kind: if Jenkin's Bend looks like "a crossing point on a border," that is precisely because it is "an official, semi-public sort of place" (28). We are finding here, once again, is the coinherence corresponding to narrative typology,[122] which we have imagined in diagrammatic terms precisely as the identification of a centre and a periphery. What we must continue to do at present is to see this coinherence in the centre itself — as we did in noticing the curious likeness of a level-headed Ben Jordan and a savage Joe Phippen. For we have still to imagine the self-sealing middle kingdom in temporal as well as spatial terms — as an organism subsisting by its internal cycles and the oneness of life and death that they imply.

IV: The Living Body

We have already imagined an atemporal emanation and return in the relation of Egypt to its god: but Egypt is equally notable for circulations like that of water and alternations like that of wet and dry. The Wawanash River has its big bend, of course, and when Del and Mary Agnes go for their walk, they find both the waterlilies growing out of the river and the dead cow lying on the dry bank.[123] Lilies and cow in this sense belong together, as we can also see from the connection of both with the dead muskrat in "Images"; we can note, moreover, that waterlilies like muskrats are amphibious creatures — static emblems, as it were, of a life that moves between land and water, upper and lower worlds.[124] A more human emblem is Catherine in "Lichen," who poses like a mermaid on a breakwater; on a grander scale, the Kingdom stories have cities that sit upon waters and empires that rule the waves,[125] not to say a patched-up rowboat for which names are proposed like Sea Horse, Flood Queen, and, again, Water Lily.[126] The wheeling of skaters in the Orange Street Rink can gather all this imagery together, being at once a kind of watery circling and a pleasure to be enjoyed in the dome above.

If the waters of time circle in the same way, the central world must so to speak be Finnish and never finished: what Catherine is in fact thinking as she sits by the lake is that, like the rays of a daisy, "the waves never, ever come to an end" (45). It is the same cycle that is half concealed and half proclaimed at Jenkin's Bend: we "pass on" (61) from life to death, and if, as Del senses, womb and tomb are the same place, we pass on to life again — or at any rate the "we" that matters does, the family that contains both life and death in its unbroken continuity. Poor Maitland Kerr is dead; Uncle Craig is in the front room and he looks very handsome; Mrs. Fraleigh managed to get herself buried before the freeze, so she is "all right" (53): the dead are regularly spoken of as if they were no different from the living. Mrs. Jordan, who scorns the family's religion, is being more up-to-date but not really different in her rhapsody on organ transplants. We are all heirs, all members of one body, she explains in noticeably Pauline terms;[127] death will soon be done away with, and in any case we only "change" — pass into other forms of life. Mrs. Jordan is equally trying to be monistic where the family's idea of body and soul is dualistic (as if a principle of natural change did not bring the dualism back); but what she really describes here is a world that remains one by passing between two — the temporal version of the united and divided central world we saw earlier. Passage of this kind is just what Stella, Catherine's hostess, is there to ensure: a "flow of the days and nights" (55), each giving way endlessly to the other.

There remains, to be sure, a weak spot in the cycle of life and death: the point, or points, of crossing between its contrary arcs. If nothing is to pass in or out, these will have to be carefully guarded. Rumbling Aunt Moira Oliphant has for her husband Uncle Bob, the unflappable man who listens calmly to "Police Patrol" and "Boston Blackie," and whose name, as we have seen, connects him with a family of "bobbies."[128] Uncle Bob seems well posted in rough Porterfield, and if we want we can also think of the pass where Roland sounds his oliphant, or of Elephantine, the city of the southern gate where the first cataract of the Nile bursts into Egypt from black Nubia. At any rate Uncle Bob guards another cataract, for as Aunt Moira erupts in childbirth he soberly covers her with his hand, preventing haemorrhage.

To see again what is really the same act of prevention, we can consider the strange tale told by Miss Kernaghan in "The Moon in the Orange Street Skating Rink." One wild winter's night in the crossing-town of "Stratford," a desperate couple bursts through the door of the Queen's Hotel; when the woman goes so far as to have a baby on the spot, Egypt must leap into the breach. The Uncle Bob of the situation, far from being unflappable, is a hot-tempered French-Canadian driver, a cousin of Munro's peppery Austrians: but we have seen that barbarians can be federates of Egypt, and it is this driver who, while swearing a "blue streak," stops the flow of blood, cuts and ties the umbilical cord, and kicks a dog away for "getting too interested" (150). A less forthright bystander (with the lofty-but-natural name of "Louie Green") provides some snow, and while the driver curses her for not bringing more, the two between them save the day. The central incident of "Material" makes yet another tale of the same kind. Here both a baby and a play are approaching birth: not only is Hugo's wife pregnant, but as a writer Hugo himself has reached "the point where this play *lives or dies*" (34). On the rainy night of the story's crisis, he turns off the pump in the basement to get some rest for his labour. His devious wife does not simply turn the pump on again, but neither does it occur to her to have faith in her husband (we can feel the story of Christ in the storm here[129]), and the next morning she cleans up the mess with sombre relish. While the pump was off there had been a real danger that something might happen: if the frail Dotty, "sleeping like the dead" (39) in the basement, had touched water and a light switch at once, she — like the wife — might have got a shock. But the danger has luckily been averted and the world passes on; or as Dotty puts it, "The things that don't happen to me, eh?" (40).

The other danger-point in the cycle is defended with the same efficiency. Just as a pump stops in "Material," so does Uncle Craig's heart, and once again the disturbance proves only temporary — dead or alive, he is soon back in circulation, looking as unperturbed as ever. And so nothing can break the Egyptian circling, or the Egyptian coinherence. The Orange Hall on the Blue River is life — the living heart or more generally the living body, with its internal circulation; we have also seen how this is a body of death, the flesh of Adam; and in fact it is both at once, for the life-and-death that we saw as the condition of the world in its beginning is what we are now finding even when the world has reached its greatest fullness. Whether coffined like Uncle Craig or burgeoning like Cora in "Privilege," such a world is always the same; and the celebration of it is a funeral game both solemn and festive.[130]

*

If the single self that is Egypt is maintained in life and death alike, what kind of self can this be? "Didn't he think he was somebody!" (37) cry Grace and Elspeth: one must not be that. Mary Agnes Oliphant, born under the hand of Uncle Bob, is deprived of oxygen in the birth-canal; later she is taken to the "fairgrounds" (42) by five boys who proceed to strip and molest her. In consequence she is "blunted" (39), though in a way Del finds hard to formulate. Callie, the result of the scene at the Queen's Hotel, is more functional: here again, though, we have the sense of someone who may be a slavey or a queen — someone who may even display Edgar the way Grace and Elspeth display the embalmed Uncle Craig — but who can never quite be somebody, an individuated human being. Del may notice the particular configuration of the dead cow's hide, but in the hot sunlight of Jenkin's Bend she equally feels the meaninglessness of all such particularity; and when she finds herself an object of special interest to Mary Agnes, the reason turns out to be that her own particularity — her desire to stand apart from the funeral — is about to be sacrificed. Uncle Craig's particularity may seem less threatened, since he is in every sense the heart of the family: and yet for this very reason there is a special danger of his becoming somebody, as in fact he tries to do with his exploding heart. This worshipped being, accordingly, must also be humiliated and rendered powerless; and the Uncle Craig who lies helplessly in the casket can remind us of some other hints of martyrdom. In "Images," as we have seen, the bending river encloses a hill with bare trees looking like bones. Mr. Burns in "Privilege," another hapless object of attention, sings a hymn about a different hill, far away and without a city wall: yet that green hill is the same place again, the fairground or crossing at the heart of things where somebody is crucified.[131]

Another martyr in these stories is of course Mary Agnes herself, the Mary who is a lamb: and here we see all the infirmity of Egypt, for Mary Agnes cannot do anything on her own, but must always remain part of her mother; and after what happened in the fairground she must never catch cold. Mary Agnes takes us back to what we might not have expected in Egypt, the various ailments of the "tray" that plague Munro's dark Marys. The central world has others like her: Franny McGill, with her smashed face and hence breathing trouble, who gets publicly raped by her brother just as Mary Agnes gets molested in the fairground; Dotty the spied-on prostitute, with her history of bronchial pneumonia. More self-reliant women may not really be different, for Aunt Moira is a "cautiously moving" creature with varicose veins — as well as bandages that have to be let "breathe" (40) from time to time; Mary McQuade not only suffers from a bronchial condition but has drainpipe legs needing to be regularly soaked. And in fact the Egyptian life-and-death is infirm even at its firmest, since natural firmness is itself an infirmity. To be born naturally is to fail a greater birth, and a greater breathing. It is to become the prisoner of one's own circulation, the blue river that is also a "river of blood" (39)[132] resisting any exodus; and it is to be wrapped in the swaddling of flesh itself. Uncle Craig lies blanketed by both lilies and his own beautified face; Mary Agnes is covered both in protective underwear and, once again, her own body — "her skin was dusty-looking, as if there was a thin, stained sheet of glass over it, or a light oiled paper" (39).[133]

It is hence the obscenity of flesh itself — of being a soul and body separate and yet fatally involved with each other — that Del is forced to learn as she lies in her uncle's office. More iconically, the Mary Agnes who has been covered in so many ways is tormented by the five boys that are her own five senses; to say that she cannot feel things is the same thing as saying that she can only feel them. By the same token we can say that Uncle Craig's functioning eye and its blind double are the same eye: and in fact an unseeing eye can stand for all the lifeless life that we need to be aware of here. Del looks uneasily at the eye of a dead cow, a "smooth, sightless bulge" (44). Mary Agnes would express Del's feeling by binding and exposing, as when she hugs and tickles or, significantly, covers her cousin's eyes. Del, on the other hand, likes stepping through a crust of mud; in a crisis she bites; in the same way she would like to poke through the cow's eye, "to show what contempt I had for its being dead" (44). But it is not easy to break the surface of Egypt; or we can say that it hardly matters whether one does or not. Under the surface of the jelly-like eye there may be more of the same jelly or there may be the opposite, corruption; under Uncle Craig's mask-like face there may be something or there may be nothing; people may, like Cora, seem all flesh, or, like Art Chamberlain, all clothes. But we can never get to a heart or mind beneath such wrappings:[134] Egypt's heart was taken away in the process of mummification.

V: Stories

Having seen Egypt draw so many things into its capacious body, we are ready to do some separating again, but now along narrative lines: for the central world has a story, and its various forms correspond to the phases of this story. We have imagined Egypt, counter-Egypt and anti-Egypt in a spatial way: as regions increasingly remote from a metropolitan centre. Thus the established land of Egypt is the navel of the world; the place of mischief seems more marginal, peopled as it is by borderline types like gipsies; beyond this again are the barbarians in their remote wilderness. To stay with spatial terms for the moment, we can imagine the cast of "Heirs of the Living Body" in the same general way: Uncle Craig, we have seen, is the heart of the family, whereas Mrs. Jordan — a barbarian by Jenkin's Bend criteria — is kept on the edge of it. In terms of the character-types we distinguished earlier, we can say that Uncle Craig is a Primary Stranger (Jenkin's Bend being a place that Del visits) whereas Mrs. Jordan is a Neighbour, waiting at home for her return. Mary Agnes seems still more barbarous than Mrs. Jordan, but then she is the barbarian member of the family proper, not a mere in-law. When she accosts her cousin, Mary Agnes proves to be a Counter-Stranger — Uncle Craig's opposite, but still in the middle of things.

If we turn our spatial terms into temporal ones, what sort of narrative shape does "Heirs" assume? Here we can best begin with the distinct and highly articulated episode that, in one projection at least,[135] comes at the centre of it. This is Del's walk by the river with Mary Agnes: not something that much affects the general course of events, but then "Heirs," for reasons we will come to, is a somewhat "hollow" story, with nothing overtly important happening in the middle. In the earlier part of the chapter Del has found Jenkin's Bend attractive on the whole; it becomes so in an intense and focused way when she sees the waterlilies lining the river, "pale, tranquil, and desirable" (43). Wading out, she manages to pick some of them, appropriating their glory for herself — and then gets a surprise. "Brought to shore, the flowers seemed coarse and rank and began to die immediately": there has been a typical central reversal, and now Del puts the lilies out of her mind, just as she will avoid the dead cow in the concluding part of the same episode.

The whole of "Heirs" is like this little adventure. Del moves towards full enjoyment of Uncle Craig's world and its riches; then she is confronted by the underside of the same world, represented by the Mary Agnes who acts as a harassment during the river scenes. In the elaborate funeral episode, we are shown in a further way what we have already seen with the cow: Del trying to detach herself from an Egypt she has come to find repellent, summed up now in the deceased Uncle Craig himself. Finally there is the retrospective epilogue, with its own tale of the bequeathing and demise of Uncle Craig's manu- script, and its own further recognition of what Egypt means. "The Shining Houses," while much more concentrated on a single incident, has essentially the same shape, rising to the high point of the birthday party (with its accompanying burst of sun and blue sky), reversing itself with the collapse of party high spirits, gathering itself for the crisis of Mary's hopeless stand against her neighbours, and ending with her private reflections on their world.

We could analyze other stories in the same way, but the central group is larger and more varied than its initiatory predecessor, and here it will be best to make some further divisions. As we can see from a specially rich example like "Heirs," a central story (like any other) contains phases that readily evolve into fully structured little actions of their own; if we see complete stories in the group as associated with one or another of these actions, the result will be manageable sub-groups within the diverse central complex. This does not mean that we can expect anything tidy: while in some cases our sub-groups will have whole stories for their members — the sub-group, for instance, that contains both "Postcard" and "Lives of Girls and Women," with their tales of sudden jilting — in others we will be dealing only with certain aspects in stories that have other aspects as well. Nor can we lay much stress on the ordering of stories in a given collection — though even here there is at least some degree of correspondence between placement and affiliation. At any rate we can explore the stages of our general story by bringing together stories in which these are, respectively, well represented; and when we have done so we will be able to consider the central dilemma once again, now as the outcome of an action which expresses it and is summed up in it.

*

When Del responds to the serene beauty of the waterlilies, she is feeling the longing with which stories begin — directed in the central world to something substantial and at hand rather than a far-off gleam. In some central stories our sense of this longing is very strong, even if there is nothing so definite as an initiatory sub-group. We can think, for instance, of the fatal day in "Accident," when the school has settled into routine and Frances senses something about to break from its legal shell:

> Along with all this order and acquiescence there is a familiar pressure, of longing or foreboding, that strange lump of something you can feel sometimes in music or a landscape, barely withheld, promising to burst and reveal itself. . . . (79)

"Accident," moreover, is filled with something we have already seen in the initiatory world: the symbolism of Christmas. Years before the affair with Ted Makkavala, Frances was already wondering how she could be confused with a girl called Natalie;[136] and as the story proper begins, the school glee club are singing the Christmas pieces she herself has taught them. But it is when events reach their climax that we are most pointedly reminded of the season. Ted, resolved now to leave his wife for Frances, comes to sit in her mother's living room, where "Christmas rainbows" (105) play over him and *The Angelus* hangs on the wall: and it is here that he makes his great annunciation.[137]

"The Moon in the Orange Street Skating Rink" covers a more extended range of time, yet in one view it is a Christmas story again. Its most striking action takes us to the Orange Street Rink, with its initiatory light — to see it as initiatory — in the darkness of winter. Even more initiatory is the trick by which the three conspirators get in: the rink, a world unto itself, is also rather like the human person, and an ingenious young trickster is able first to slip through the roof into the head, then to unlock the snow-door beneath. After this spring can come, and with it a mischievous central-phase affair; yet we have not really left the rink or its season behind. When Sam, almost a lifetime afterwards, calls at Callie's variety store, he may not find the Christmas decorations he expects, but the flashing video games make a fair substitute; in the apartment upstairs televised skaters whirl in "twinkly outfits" (159), and Edgar himself, suitably decorated by Callie, sits as we have seen like a shimmering Christmas tree. It is not just that we are in the same building as the grocery where the boys once bought jam tarts: Edgar is in effect where Callie first attended to him, the house of Miss Kernaghan[138] And he is once more in the Orange Street Rink — a whole Egyptian world of turning and returning is being seen as an entry into one of Munro's ice-caves.

*

Unable to resist the waterlilies, Del wades out and picks them. As she does so she no doubt experiences a moment of fulfilment: if we fix this moment we have the condition of the securely established Egypt, or the Kingdom celebrating the presence of its king. Contained by such an establishment, "Heirs of the Living Body" can serve as a type for an important group of central stories. The river episode here is itself contained by the triumphant family visit going on all the while at the house; and in one sense this visit never quite ends — Auntie Grace and Aunt Elspeth will forever be telling their stories, forever rejoicing in their superior status, forever thinking of ways to put down luckless outsiders. Problems may arise — Uncle Craig may try a heart attack, age may interfere with family rituals — but even in their final disintegration the aunts are "not radically exposed or damaged or changed" (60). In their own way the Flemings of "The Stone in the Field" have the same pertinacity, lasting into the years of cataracts and arthritis; and once again we have a story centring around a family visit, whatever the sentiments of the visitors may be. The immediate action of "Lichen" (to treat it as Egyptian) takes in a much briefer time-span, nor do we feel the same family solidarity, but we notice the presence of the ageless father, immobilized but still presiding in the County Home; and in the story's foreground we find someone hardly less durable. Stella, as David teasingly suggests, is older than anything; and in spite of divorce or such irritants as David's reencountered photograph, she is still very much in control at the end. "Labor Day Dinner," though with a much stronger sense of looming trouble, can be read as the same kind of story: the admirably wise and hospitable Valerie receives her guests into her beautiful house, and in the end they get safely back to their own. Prue, again, enjoys Gordon's dinner (as a guest, to be sure, though she has been a hostess in her time), retaining her composure even when Gordon's wife makes a brief ruckus.

A story of this kind, or taken in this way — an "Establishment story," as we can call it — is often "hollow": and like any family visit or holiday dinner, it may be not so much an action as a symposium. In this case the not-quite-disruptions we have just seen will often be relegated to the periphery, while a change in the centre may be not only muted, but hardly an action in the usual sense at all. The bedding of Callie by the Grazier boys and the resulting upheaval in their lives mark an obvious reversal, embodied in definite physical events; but we hardly feel such a thing in "Labor Day Dinner" as the lively arrival scene gives way to various kinds of relaxation, followed by leisurely talk at the supper table. If Stella in "Lichen" lives in a breezier style, she does so with such aplomb that the story's central reversal — David's flashing of the photograph — barely ruffles the surface of their conversation. What may seem quite unlike such graceful leisure, or cheerful bustle, is the fight for survival as carried on in the savage world of "Privilege": yet if Rose's school is a paradoxical Egypt, the adventure here — mainly taking place during recess — is not unlike Del's in "Heirs of the Living Body." "Come on up, honey" (32), sings the beautiful Cora as she sits painting her nails in the first warm weather; presently she reveals herself in full bloom, decked with flowers as part of the story's funeral game; and even later, when Rose's attempt at ingratiation — not in this case disruption — has failed abjectly, Cora herself remains serene, still a water-lily. She does, however, reveal a water-lily's brevity: for unlike the ageless-seeming Jenkin's Bend aunts, Cora soon loses her beauty and her poise, while the school itself goes on to lose its old bravura. In another set of stories this loss will provide the central action itself.

*

The downfall of central glory is specially marked in the case of mischief — what the Kingdom falls into and what the Kingdom may already have been. Munro, as we have found, has a clearly marked group of stories dealing with collapsing affairs,[139] some of which may have gone on long enough to be virtual establishments but all of which come to their end with dramatic suddenness. This is not, of course, what the mischief-makers expect, any more than their established counterparts, since in the central world at its most euphoric there seems "no possibility anywhere of a mistake" (29), to quote "The Shining Houses."[140] Along with this confidence goes complete reliance on luck — what Del counts on, for example, for her imagined encounter with Art Chamberlain. Life as we usually know it, of course, is not like this at all. Del imagines Art Chamberlain coming like a bolt of lightning, a "breakthrough" (162): she can no more connect this with the ordinary world than she can connect her idea of a prostitute with the woman reading the *Star Weekly* in Mrs. McQuade's front yard. And yet the breakthrough may seem really to be happening. Frances in "Accident," who has worried about the transition between the two worlds, reaches a magical assurance — "there was no chance in the world they would not make the switch. It was already made" (83). Then comes the news of Bobby Makkavala's death, and with it the end of the whole affair, at least as an affair.

And so we have the most striking phenomenon of the Kingdom group and the essential of a "Mischief story." In its simplest form, the heroine of "Postcard" or "Mischief" or "Oranges and Apples" prepares for glory and then, at the point of it, is rejected by the man in question.[141] Now we come, biblically speaking, to a Book of Lamentations. Once Jerusalem was a lady on a mountain, but now her Lord has rejected her, and we find her sitting desolate or, in the form of her people, gone into exile.[142] Fern Dogherty plays this Jerusalem in both ways, since she grieves in her fashion at home and then sits by the far-off waters of Windsor, with excursions to the pleasure-city of Detroit. We learn all this, to be sure, only from the end of "Lives of Girls and Women" (and a detail in "Baptizing"); where a heroine's dejection is less peripheral we have one of the Exile stories, as we can call them. In "Bardon Bus," for instance, the affair in Australia reads almost like a prologue, and what really matters is the heroine's suffering afterwards; in "Tell Me Yes or No," the other main Exile story, the heroine's affair is entirely in the past — we know of it only through her reminiscences. Nor does the present simply make a frame for these. The narrator is acutely concerned with the desert her heart has now become, "dry and cracked like a bare bit of landscape marked with gullies" (117), and her account of the situation — the letter she writes, or imagines herself writing — comes to focus on a journey thought of as present or even future. "Lives of Girls and Women," we can add, starts to read like an Exile story as a whole if we emphasize the way Fern has been grieving all along, singing absently about a lost lover more mysterious than Art Chamberlain.

In the larger story of which there is yet to be a phase corresponding to the coming of Christ, stories like these are intermediary between one kingdom and another.[143] Since transitions, as we have seen, tend to be phases of vision rather than action, it is not surprising that an Exile heroine is more engaged in seeing than in doing. What she sees may be reality in all its bruteness — the desert of "Tell Me Yes or No"; but since disillusion has illusion for its other face, Exile heroines are given to strange fantasies — fantasies that can swell to become stories of their own, as we have seen in "Bardon Bus." In "Tell Me Yes or No" the narrator's imagined journey to the city of her lost lover is itself the main story: and this seems appropriate enough for a heroine in whom fantasy so readily overpowers fact — whose dream-self, for instance, does not know the real one or its double, the mysterious Patricia. Other heroines prefer activity to brooding, but act in ways so hysterical that their reality is itself a kind of fantasy. Fern Dogherty at the end of "Lives of Girls and Women" does not mourn directly for Art Chamberlain: she chatters and puts on weight and has a good time. Helen in "Postcard," recovered from the first shock of her loss, proceeds to yell in the middle of the night outside her lover's door; the heroine of "Bardon Bus" goes through an obsession with clothes. The same kind of thing is happening when the heroine of "Tell Me Yes or No" haunts the bookshop of her dead lover's widow — to take her fantasy as the actuality it virtually becomes.

*

The Mischief and Exile groups have quite definite identities in Munro; along with the latter, however, we find an assortment of other stories before the main Passion group, and among the endless cross-connections to be made, certain links seem specially important here. In the first place I am going to bring together two stories that in some ways are not much alike. In *Who Do You Think You Are?* the chapter called "Providence" comes between the main central- and terminal-phase adventures in Rose's life; as we might expect, it can be read as an Exile story, if a rather special one. Having lost Clifford in "Mischief," Rose has now separated from her husband Patrick as well, and must find her own way in the world: her Exile experience, though, is of the manic rather than the depressive kind. She gets a job in a snowy mountain town that, after the mud and rain of Vancouver, makes a cosy hideaway, not to say a kind of play town in which it seems no-one could ever die. In other words, it is like the places of temporary safety that we have seen as settings for "returning visions" — including upstairs recovery rooms. But while Rose's mood in this haven is almost giddy, moods from elsewhere also make themselves felt. Anna, Rose's daughter and the object of her own providence, may share in the giddiness, but she also cries for a lower world — that of her former playmate "Jeremy" with his hint of human lamentation.

Rose herself does not cry for Patrick: she puts her hope in one of Munro's Toms, a civilized and elusive historian who can best be compared to the lover in "Tell Me Yes or No." Dorothy, a neighbourly Comforter, reminds us of the same story: she has a current lover of her own in Seattle and once made a desperate and unsuccessful attempt to meet another in England. When we think of it, the world Rose finds and makes for herself, complete with hanging plants, fish in orange and blue and black, and a very colourful Woolworth's, is itself not unlike the glamorous city in "Tell Me Yes or No," though set high on a mountain rather than by the ocean. The godlike Tom is essential to this world, for it is Rose's connection with him that "[holds] her new life in place" (143): her only fear is that, like the new world itself, he may exist only in her imagination.[144] What she gets from Tom, or from an even more teasing Providence, is heavenly silver — the fall of snow that prevents her from joining him, the shower of coins that comes out of a pay phone at the same time. Properly received, this might be a genuine blessing; Rose, however, finds it insubstantial, and in the end returns from her rarefied exile to normality. In a later dream she sees Anna as a "botched, heavy-headed idol" (133) covered with wet clay and garlands of dead leaves: the reality beneath Rose's false silver.

Another somewhat special story, the touching "Pictures of the Ice," is like "Providence" in ways that go beyond their common winter setting and imagery. Karin is again a woman embittered by the failure of a marriage, and again one who would like to ensconce herself in a high refuge — an apartment like Rose's, if more genteel, so that she could "turn and floor anybody trying to intrude" (149). Then, she feels sure, her bitterness would go away. What Providence sends in this case is not silver coins but ice-pictures taken by Karin's employer Austin Cobbett: the aged minister who, having announced his retirement to a house and wife in Hawaii, secretly goes to die in a lonely charge in the north. Only Karin finds out; she senses, moreover, that he has intended her to find out, and to know that he knows she has been robbing him. As this device suggests, Austin is something more than a superior and elusive Tom. He is making Karin see frazil ice, the vanishing show that her intended refuge would be; he is also letting her see that his vanishing self is a sacrifice, not just a show. And in doing this he is offering her a new kind of life — it was Austin who founded "Turnaround House," later renamed "Lazarus House." In fact this story takes us toward a distribution of the returning vision in which life will appear in death itself: what needs saying at present is simply that Austin brings Karin back to earth. Where this story differs from "Providence" is in emphasizing the latent grace, not just vanity, in the vision that leads to such a return.

*

In feeling "approved of" (155) — freed of her bitterness, though by different means than she expected — Karin is rather like Val in "Forgiveness in Families," a Judges story; and if the Judges stories showed us the coming of a new cycle of life, "Pictures of the Ice" can be seen as leading to another again, pleasant or painful. We are in fact close here to the "Annunciation" stories that I will be dealing with in the following chapter: first, however, we have some unfinished business in the central world, since — like distributions of it that we will be seeing — it proves to be a kingdom not readily left. We will need a more complex model now than in the last paragraphs, for while we have simply treated exile stories as falling between central and terminal phases, we must now think of the central world as having its own complete story.

Stories like "Providence" and "Pictures of the Ice" end in returns; so do Exile stories, as for that matter Mischief stories themselves. One thing we notice about these latter, with their crashing heroines, is a number of Comforter figures: in "Postcard," for instance, we have not only Helen's mother but the brisk and officious Alma Stonehouse, not to say Buddy Shields the friendly policeman. And if Helen is not completely restored even at the end, other Mischief stories show us Fern going back to her good times or Rose going back to normal life. "Heirs of the Living Body" shows us something different. Sceptical of Jenkin's Bend from the start, Del is disillusioned by the water-lilies and horrified by the funeral: and as a result she runs away to the storeroom — she is not an exile from her world but a prisoner attempting escape. So far I have treated the movement away from the centre more as glory lost than as confinement fled, yet we can easily learn from, say, "Images" that exile in one view may be exodus in another, though the relation between them may be a complex one. We may even find cases where — to appeal to "Heirs of the Living Body" again — one view follows the other, with loss of central glory turning into rebellion against it.

The flight from a world no longer accepted will be a main concern of the next chapter, where I will be dealing with the Exodus group that follows Munro's Egyptian stories. A "Disaffection story" within the Egyptian group itself would be one concerned throughout with resistance to Egypt, though a resistance that did not fully materialize as rebellion or escape. In one view "The Shining Houses" is such a story, perhaps, dwelling as it does on Mary's continuing if unavailing refusal of her neighbours' values; and refusal here goes deeper than mere mischief, for Mary is allying herself with the barbarian Mrs. Fullerton. The neighbours, to be sure, never stop smiling — Garden Place, like Jenkin's Bend, prefers to see deserters as erring members of the family; yet Mary keeps her "disaffected heart" (29) all the same. In the world of the Kingdom, "Red Dress — 1946" is similar in some ways. While not averse in principle to social success, the narrator is trying from the outset to avoid the school dance; when calamity strikes during the dance itself, her story becomes very much that of abortive escape from the whole world of normal sexuality — to see normality here as calling her back rather than forward. In the end she does go back, of course: a rescuing boy draws her "from Mary Fortune's territory into the ordinary world" (160), where she accepts her duty to be "happy" — ordinarily so, that is. Edgar Grazier is drawn back to Callie, altogether happily in his case; more sullenly,

Del in "Heirs" returns to the Egyptian life-in-death of the funeral. Once more, then, and now in terms of narrative structure, we are learning the central world's ability to contain and neutralize dissent. In "Labor Day Dinner" a worldly kingdom shows itself to be in grave jeopardy, as we will be seeing later; but at the end that world is still intact, and the disaffected Roberta has relapsed into indifference. Mary in "The Shining Houses" may not be indifferent, but for the time being she puts her hands in her pockets.

*

Here we are seeing containment in cyclical terms; to see it in a subtler form, at whatever distribution from a story's centre, we can first go back to the fortunes of Del Jordan in Egypt. Del's aunts, unlike Mary Agnes, do not try to keep her there by force: they forgive her for biting her cousin, excuse her from having to look at the corpse in the parlour, even leave her to herself with cake, tea, and a blanket. And it is just this forgiveness that brings on Del's mystical experience of humiliation, for she has been freed in a way that binds her; we find the same ingenuity at work later when, armed with cookies and flattery, the aunts manoeuvre her into taking over her uncle's history. In the case of the Grazier boys it is the consequences of mischief that are to be escaped from, with Edgar in particular expecting a liberating "explosion" (153): and as their train leaves town, they discover that the person sitting across the aisle is Callie. She does not seem to be bringing them back — indeed she is running off with them; yet it is as if the blank fence they have just been staring at were a mirror, since going forward and going back are the same thing here. Fifty years later we again find Edgar sitting between a mirror and a false window; he is also, as we have noted, virtually in the place where he once skated fast and free, the Orange Street Rink — except that now he is also the paralyzed victim of his "little turn" (158).

For a specially rich treatment of the irony of liberation — rich because of its scope and the heroine's gift of reflection — we can go back to "Accident," where Frances wants the freedom to possess Ted Makkavala. The sudden death of Bobby, while cutting short the lovers' affair as such, initiates the series of events leading to marriage: here we have a little typological story already, a comic one since marriage suits Frances perfectly well. But the irony of the situation goes farther, since in the first place she quickly feels a concern she did not expect: "the weight, the disturbance, the possibility of despair"

(107) that comes with her freedom — the sense, that is, of a constraint in accident itself, or of the inevitability of danger, that makes her say "We will have to be careful." When she reflects, many years later, on the difference the accident of the story has made in her life, she is confronted with a deeper form of the same concern: a voice from inside her asking "What difference?" (109). The Frances who has wanted change — who has seemed always to be getting her car started or forcing it out of the snow — has finally driven off to a new life; in doing so she has felt mired by change itself; and in the end she comes to see that change may be no change at all.

VI: Mummies

When someone inside Frances asks "What difference?" she is astute enough to know it is her mother: a self-indulging, self-absorbed old woman for whom all the happenings of the outside world are much the same. In fact this mother's attention can hardly be kept on the outside world at all, since she quickly goes back to her meals and her library books — which she forgets as soon as she has read them. Her house is thus like that of Del Jordan's aunts as we find them in the end: the sealed place "where true news of the outside world was not exactly forbidden, but became more and more impossible to deliver" (59–60). We have already seen how the vital and expansive central god — the god who is presence in the world — is at the same time Uncle Craig in his coffin. If we are now seeing such a figure as the end of a story, we should also see him in cognitive terms, as someone who does or does not bring final knowledge. In the central phase, we have found, we often seem on the verge of revelation: at the end this is vested in a "terrible, silent, indifferent" (59) dead man — someone no less remote and unresponding than the god of "Age of Faith." Or the bearer of knowledge, if in some sense living, may be the reclusive old woman who asks "What difference?": one way or another, the only revelation seems to be that of no revelation, for these figures tell us nothing, and take in nothing we say to them.

And this is as we might have expected, since it fulfils something we find at the heart of central stories, especially Mischief stories. Just before her central reversal a Mischief heroine regularly visits someone else's private quarters;[145] these may belong either to her consort in mischief or to his own consort — in other words, either to the self she would like to unite with or the self she would like to supplant. At this stage she finds the experience primarily a thrill, and yet there is always something distasteful about the visit or the place itself or both[146] — as the heroine would see if the glamour of adventure disappeared, and may already see sufficiently to be disquieted. Del, having fantasized about Art Chamberlain in her mother's bedroom, sneaks into Fern's; and what she sees is spilled face-powder and dried make-up. Rose, babysitting for Clifford and Jocelyn, is so dismayed by the latter's undone laundry and unwashed dishes that she tries to clean up the mess herself. In her infatuation with Clifford, she also searches for "traces of his presence" (124), even drinking from what she takes to be his cup: but a dirty mark on an empty cup is the only trace she finds. All Frances sees in Ted Makkavala's supply room, apart from a science-teacher's chemicals and Bunsen burners, is bottles of pickled "organs, or maybe organisms" (82), as well as something else that we should find noteworthy — a cat's skeleton. And there is no communication to be found in such a place. Del ransacks Fern's bedroom for Art Chamberlain's love-letters, but while she comes on old pictures and papers, the letters are not there: the great announcer is silent. So, at a later stage of his story, is the glorified Edgar in his apartment, not to say the glorified Uncle Craig laid out in the parlour.

We have seen something complacent, even indolent, about the central god: to this we are now adding the inscrutability that, for instance, baffles the narrator of "Material" contemplating her placid husband. "How are we to understand you?" (124) cries the narrator of "Tell Me Yes or No": indeed one heroine after another finds her man to be what Helen calls Clare MacQuarrie, "unexplaining" (146).[147] Strangely enough, each of these enigmatic figures is in some way "public" (131), to use another of Helen's formulas for Clare MacQuarrie. Helen means by this that Clare hangs about the main street, but she also remarks that he could run successfully for office — he is that important. Clare does not run: the trouble seems to be that he is not "serious" (131) enough. Uncle Craig is of course utterly serious and official, yet he too holds back from politics, the stated reason in his case being pride. Gabriel performs a public kind of work, but in an "anonymous" (27) way, and he finds Hugo the performer totally alien.[148] All such men, we might say, are like the Neptune in Patrick's fountain, a god who allows himself to be viewed but never takes off his fig-leaf.

Art Chamberlain, to be sure, makes a more open sort of god: "inner curtains" (169) part to reveal the holy of holies, and out comes "the real whitish stuff, the seed" (170), a manifest blessing like the white of Pork Childs' peacock. Yet Del can only stare in dismay: the dancing king before her looks "blunt and stupid,"[149] and she has no sense of revelation at all. In more ethical terms, this farewell performance makes a baffling combination with an earlier message: not long before, Art wrote "Del is a bad girl" (164) as a sample of his handwriting. Two other crucial messages, Art's farewell note to Fern and Clare's postcard to Helen, say in effect the same thing — "be a good girl"; and we find various other forms of this double play (that of Upper God and Undergod, as we have seen in another context).[150] Jessie wants Eric Cryderman as a suitor; what she gets in the summerhouse is a man who reproves her in canting tones while feeling his way up her leg. Another of Munro's vanishing letter-writers, Ted Forgie in "Postcard," sends not exhortations but assurances of his esteem, in a style almost as unreal as Eric Cryderman's; the same Ted Forgie, in Helen's account, "said he wanted to put his head down in my lap and weep, but all the time what he *was* doing was something else" (134). In the face of all this, a woman understandably wants clarification: "Tell me yes or no" (122), begs the narrator whose lover, after an earlier declaration, has evaporated as a correspondent.

And so the bridegroom never comes to speak fulfilment. What Art Chamberlain displays is not a spiritual body but only material spirit; nor is the more rarefied kind of spirit in this world anything more, unless in a ghostly or diabolic way. When Del looks at her uncle displayed in his coffin, what she sees is a carcass haunted, as she senses, by a spectral energy; Art Chamberlain himself, for that matter, seems "possessed" (170) as he writhes in front of her. As for the Mary Agnes Oliphant whom we have seen to be another version of Uncle Craig, she is a numbed body driven by a "demon power" (55); and to see the reach of this imagery we can add the mysterious Callie — a leathery body even in her maze-like insides, though a "demon worker" (133) at the same time. Such figures are once again mummies, if galvanized ones: as she moves along the birth-canal to normality, Del learns to see them as she must, with provisional forbearance tempered by detachment. She is in no danger of poking her dead uncle; she keeps her distance from the frenzied Art Chamberlain — whose demonstration, she realizes, is just the self-squeezing of a flesh that has nothing to do with her.[151] Now she can take on the strength that detachment always brings in Munro.

*

But there remains a further question — one that, like others with which Munro's phases leave us, might draw us beyond our present world or any distribution of it, but which needs to be raised here. Del has learned to be on her guard against a world of mummies: in the process, though, has she not turned into a mummy herself — enclosed herself away as surely as her aunts or Mary Agnes?[152]

Del is far from thinking so: she for one is going to be free. At the end of "Lives of Girls and Women," similarly, she separates herself from her mother — an independent woman, but not sufficiently so for her daughter. A key word here is "respect" (141): what, according to Helen's mother in "Postcard," a man feels for a girl who holds back. At the end of "Lives of Girls and Women" it is "self-respect" (176) that we hear about — Mrs. Jordan triumphantly has it, Fern Dogherty does not have it, and Del, in her mother's opinion, needs to cultivate it. Once again this means holding back — avoiding entanglement — and Mrs. Jordan is sure the task can be managed: with a little strength of character "the burden" can be escaped, and for that matter change is coming,[153] a great liberation for women on condition that they detach themselves from men. Fern does not want quite this kind of liberation, but she knows that marriage puts an end to your good times, and she stocks birth-control information. Del intends to be the boldest of the three: self-respect for her will mean respecting her own desire for experience while rejecting the burden carried even by her mother, that of "carefulness and solemn fuss and self-protection" (177). In fact Del is going to be like men themselves, who it seems can "go out and take on all kinds of experiences and shuck off what they [don't] want and come back proud."[154]

"Lives of Girls and Women" is specially illuminating here — if also specially complex — because of its splitting of roles. In our simplest version of a Mischief story we had only a single heroine, rejected by a man who walked away; but we may also have two women, differing in their attitudes both before and after the great reversal. Fern in "Lives" takes her position for granted to begin with, even while starring in the opera of it; the younger Del, taking nothing for granted, is beside herself with excitement. After the reversal, on the other hand, Fern is plainly crushed, however she may cover the fact, while Del is merely disillusioned — Art Chamberlain has turned out to be a curiosity, nothing more. And so Fern is trapped, Del free to do her own walking away. The situation in "Jesse and Meribeth" is obviously much the same, though with certain variations: for here the official Mrs. Cryderman seems never to learn of the carryings-on, and when Eric Cryderman leaves town, she sells the house and leaves with him. It is MaryBeth, rather, who is crushed, who grieves — openly and desperately — and who is left at the end to put on weight like Fern Dogherty.[155]

In Mrs. Cryderman's inner room, at an earlier point, Jessie learns of a book Eric Cryderman has never written, and from the sound of it will never write. When Del searches Fern's bedroom, as we have seen, Art Chamberlain's letters are similarly missing. But in the latter case at least, the woman in question is part of the problem. In Fern we have someone who wants and does not want to know: who is keen to have the good times of life, yet remains curiously inert and neglectful at the same time.[156] And while she may preserve and codify information — her three bundles, in fact, make up a sort of scripture — she has mislaid or discarded a more crucial kind of scripture, the letters in which a man offered his love. Fern, in other words, is a foolish virgin like those in the parable, and like them she finds herself repudiated. Meanwhile the man in the situation, having shared the good times, is doing his best to suppress the same letters. Fern and Art, that is, are two of a kind: and to connect mischief with establishment, Fern is oddly like someone else in the central world, the Uncle Craig who compiles the annals of Wawanash County while discarding the lost Jenkin — the evidence, in other words, of human vulnerability.

Del perceives Fern's negligence, and the burden it leads to, but she cannot apply her perception to herself: in spite of seeing that people "take along a good deal" (174), she is sure at the end of "Lives of Girls and Women" that she need not. No doubt there is an immediate sense in which she is right — she can have some experience without getting hurt; and we will later find a sense in which she can enter into life far more deeply while keeping her freedom. What matters here is the sense in which she is fooling herself: still living in the kingdom of domes and mushrooms where, even in the last scene, we find her reading *Arch of Triumph*. Jessie's taste in fantasy may be somewhat different — a love affair full of suffering, guilt, and once again a "burden" (179): but fantasy is what this is, and when MaryBeth challenges the fantasy MaryBeth is discarded, along with her anguished letter. Jessie's view of burdens is thus like Del's:

I saw MaryBeth shut in, with her treats and her typewriter, growing sweeter and fatter, and the Crydermans fixed, far away, in their everlasting negotiations, but myself shedding dreams and

lies and vows and errors, unaccountable. I didn't see that I was
the same one, embracing, repudiating. I thought I could turn
myself inside out, over and over again, and tumble through the
world scot free. (188)[157]

Helen in "Postcard" is no doubt different from Del or Jessie — she
clearly intends to be a faithful wife to Clare MacQuarrie. But
"Postcard" is a simpler organism than "Lives of Girls and Women,"
and if we apply the terms of the latter story to Helen, we will see her
as combining the woman and the girl. Like Fern, she keeps mementoes but throws out a love-letter (not to say a memory of having once
played "Josephine");[158] she takes her privileged status with Clare
MacQuarrie for granted; and she is a constant mistress on whom the
burden of misfortune descends. On the other hand she is more like
Del in her naïve expectation of glory at others' expense, not to say
her eager inspection of a rival's treasures — at one point we find her
going through the drawers in Mrs. MacQuarrie's dining-room. And
in her very acceptance of Clare there is the failure to respond that we
have found, first in Fern, then in Del and Jessie themselves:

I looked back and thought am I a heartless person, just to lie
there and let him grab me and love me and moan around my
neck and say the things he did, and never say one loving word
back to him? I never wanted to be a heartless person and I was
never mean to Clare, and I did let him, didn't I, nine times out
of ten? (135)

Such a person is not fully human, nor can she apprehend the human
reality of others — only projections of her own making. Indeed, the
whole central phase, as we are now coming to see it, is a more
carefully constructed form of what its predecessor was: a solid fantasy
on the part of someone who has forgotten something better. It is
symptomatic that mischief figures (not to say their exile successors)
are at once very physical in their preoccupations and great imaginers,
making up both feelings and their objects.[159] In this respect the
dancing puppet in front of Del is her own puppet: "Jesse and
Meribeth," in fact, features a lecture on this subject by Eric Cryderman, who may not be in a strong position to lecture but does say
things Jessie might take seriously. Certainly the narrator of "Tell Me
Yes or No" does so, for as she acknowledges to her distant lover,

I invented you, as far as my purposes go. I invented loving you and I invented your death. I have my tricks and my trap doors, too. (124)

This woman is not, of course, complacent about her stagecraft; and even in that of the naïve adolescents we can sense a confused attempt at something different. What is harder for them is to realize that others are making the same attempt. Del cannot see that the foolishness of Fern's bedroom, or Fern's life, is a confession of need; nor can she see her mother's need, or Art Chamberlain's. She cannot, then, form any real bond with another: and the result, as always, is going to be bondage. The heroine of "Tell Me Yes or No" knows this already; Del will know it fully, perhaps, when she finds herself possessed by the spirit of Uncle Craig — whose manuscript she once forgot like an unwanted letter.[160]

Beyond such bondage there might be a different kind of love. When Helen, having lost Clare, sees him for the unexplaining man he is, she wants — for the first time, and briefly — to touch him. Perhaps she is only like Del, looking at the dead with the mixture of repugnance and fascination that is closely akin to the sexual response. But there seems something else here — a desire to touch Clare more humanly. If she could do that, Helen might reach his own humanity, and find her real lover there. It is her tragedy, and that of the central-phase heroines generally, not to be quite able to let that happen. When, at one point, Del sees her father embracing her mother in genuine affection, it is more than she can take:

I wanted to shout at them to stop and turn back into their separate, final, unsupported selves. I was afraid that they would go on and show me something I no more wanted to see than I wanted to see Uncle Craig dead. (49)

And so man and woman are not to come together; nor is a child to be born. The Crydermans may produce a baby ("quite normal, as far as anyone knew" [186] in spite of its mother's age), but as Munro hints, this is only a forerunner leaping inside a sealed womb.[161] Fern Dogherty may have been thrown out of the Royal Conservatory for having a baby of her own, or so the rumour goes; but she does not want one now, in spite of the "pregnant curve" (146) of her stomach. Nor does Del: Art Chamberlain wipes away the seed that has touched the hem of her garment, and the lady on the mountain stands alone.

NOTES

¹ In *Who Do You Think You Are?* the contrast between "Wild Swans" (or the rejected "Characters") and "The Beggar Maid" is less sharp than that between "Age of Faith" and "Changes and Ceremonies." But "The Beggar Maid" does have important resemblances to the latter, and relative positioning in a book can itself imply contrast. Thus "Wild Swans" appears less of a Judges story when followed by "The Beggar Maid"; it would have appeared more of one if preceded by "Characters" (for which see above, 37–38). The lonely Mr. Cleaver invites Rose into a different world, and leaves her with a magic token; but this is almost in spite of himself — he prefers to "cleave" like a Wilderness god.

² In both "Meneseteung" an "An Ounce of Cure" an isolated heroine experiences a chemically produced hallucination; otherwise the two stories differ considerably. "An Ounce of Cure" looks like a Judges story if we emphasize "the huge sweet winds of spring" (79) and the fact that the dashing Martin Collingwood chooses the narrator, amazing her and awakening her sexually. But Martin Collingwood plays not so much a Pied Piper as a mastering, black-and-white Mr. Darcy; and if others go on to spring, the narrator remains trapped in her lonely winter obsession with this god of being. In her hallucination (itself the central collision in this story) she accordingly sees the universe as filled with "enormous senseless inanimate malice" (81). In "Meneseteung" we can note in the first place that Almeda's lost father, with his "appreciation, his dark, kind authority" (60), is a much more venerable figure than Martin Collingwood or Mr. Berryman — the local executive who is in some ways rather like Jarvis "Poulter." And Almeda's poem is a celebration of life, not a vision of malice. Another story close to "Meneseteung" is "Boys and Girls," in which the heroine's release of the doomed "Flora," corresponding to the release of spring, is a less profound counterpart of Almeda's release of the flora and fauna in herself.

³ This is to make the movement between Egypt and kingdom — two high points in our ternary biblical scheme — a story in itself, with its own structure.

⁴ "Meneseteung" shows its kinship with the Judges group in that, after a day in summer no less oppressive than one in winter, a refreshing breeze is blowing as the story gets under way.

⁵ "I suppose it doesn't make you think of anything" (122), says Mr. Boyce. Yet he himself is probably not thinking of the local war of 1812 — which in a sense is beginning again in the lives of his students.

⁶ "Laughlin" ("lakeland"), as in Dale "McLaughin," is the old Celtic word for a Viking.

⁷ Cf. for instance the story of Deborah and Barak in Judg. 4:3 ff.

⁸ In "An Ounce of Cure" the school dance is again held at the "Armouries" (78), as also in "Deadeye Dick" (189).

⁹ So — to put "Day of the Butterfly" with the Judges group — do the very different Helen and Myra. The betrayal in this story can be paralleled with that

of, and by, the Pied Piper in "Changes and Ceremonies."

¹⁰ Del and Naomi's version of a conversation between Miss Farris and Mr. Boyce is virtually a parody of the Song of Solomon, a wedding eclogue with a chosen bride and a *hortus conclusus* ("I am not painfully skinny I am incredibly beautiful. . . . O you are so romantic, O my beloved" [126]). (The allusion here is noted by Blodgett [49].)

¹¹ See above, 206.

¹² Dudley Brown in "Hold Me Fast, Don't Let Me Pass" is another lonely and wistful comedian.

¹³ Cf. Dudley Brown reciting "Tam Lin" in a "warm, sad, splendid male voice" (101). Patrick as always is something of an exception here, his high voice being mentioned repeatedly (e.g., 74). Evidently it is not a charming voice, yet Patrick, as we will see, has his own kind of charm.

¹⁴ Cf. here the mysterious "Ellis Bell" in "Forgiveness in Families" (98): the "heart man" whose role is taken over by Cam, making Cam himself in effect the Ellis Bell. While "Bell" may remind us of the calling bell in "Age of Faith," the presence here of Emily Brontë (who used "Ellis Bell" as a pen-name) is certainly curious. We can note, though, that Munro's Pied Pipers are closely related to her "Messengers" (see below, 487), always in some sense artists and apt to have names like "Milton Homer."

¹⁵ For "Wales" and related names, see below, 340 n47.

¹⁶ See Judg. 19 and 21. On the subject of abduction we can note that in "Forgiveness in Families" Cam's favourite movie is "Seven Brides for Seven Brothers" (95).

¹⁷ Margaret Dobie in "Hold Me Fast, Don't Let Me Pass," having spent most of her life in a grim and uncared-for farmhouse, is living at the time of the story in a quite different house, "stuccoed, with stones set here and there in a whimsical suburban style"; her sitting-room is "full of patterned upholstery, brass and china ornaments, pampas grass, peacock feathers, dried flowers, clocks and pictures and cushions" (91). Whether or not these come from the unfrequented parlour of the older house, they suggest less a wilderness god than the producer of an operetta — as does Miss Dobie's recitation in the style of "the best scholar's offering at the school concert" (95).

¹⁸ Luke 2:35.

¹⁹ Note that Dale McLaughlin's partner is "Alma Cody" — pleasant but pertaining to "code" or law.

²⁰ We should also remember the line about "doing it" in *Kristin Lavransdatter*: "Was this ill thing the thing that was sung of in all the songs?" (120).

²¹ When she goes to the town library, Del never opens books that might suggest the more legal and adversarial side of the Jewish frontier romance — *Forty Years a Country Preacher* and *The Queen's Own in Peace and War*. Yet perhaps these are not really so different from the books she does read. We can also note "Bella" (117) Phippen the librarian, who presents Del with children's romances and

brides-to-be with kewpie dolls. The latter are of the kind in which a skirt conceals a pincushion — once again someone is to pierce or be pierced.

22 We may also think of Myra in "Day of the Butterfly," another strangely alluring figure in blue doomed never to be an adult. Like Miss Farris Myra comes in lighter and darker shades: "she glimmered sadly in sky-blue taffeta, in dusty turquoise crepe" (106).

23 Almeda Roth is similar: she catches her death of pneumonia in the Pearl Street Swamp. She may have been chased there by "urchins" (72), though otherwise she suggests a Pied Piper's withdrawing side rather than his role as betraying or betrayed leader. In any case she is a drowning virgin with a lost man in the background; she has her poems for operettas; she helps with the festivities of others (weddings and Sunday School picnics), while drawing back from marriage for herself. In an early version of "Changes and Ceremonies" Miss Farris's name was "Joynt" — Almeda's middle name.

24 "The next day, she was angelically pretty, showing no ravages, drinking in praise and wishes for her happiness" (80): this is Glenna's version of Miss Farris's "bountiful acceptance" (136).

25 Note Patrick's voice is not only high but "rather aggrieved, and tremulous" (74) — at once the voice of a Pied Piper and of someone like Val.

26 Once again we are very close here to "Material," with its virtuous narrator who wants her husband's downfall more than a successful marriage. I have treated "Material" as an Egyptian story, but its epilogue is "Forgiveness in Families" in little: if only briefly, the narrator is shaken out of her bitterness by Hugo's life-giving magic.

27 See *Samson Agonistes* line 1757.

28 E.g., the "domes and mushrooms of concrete" anticipated by Mrs. Jordan in "Lives of Girls and Women" (143). See above, 226; below, 426.

29 In legal terminology an "heir of the living body" is one by physical descent.

30 In "Five Points" the candy store in Victoria was formerly run by a woman who "let her cat sprawl in the sun in the window" (34).

31 It seems appropriate, if less clearly diagnostic, that the same display includes a fan-window, bushels of onions, and some rubber boots. Onions and cucumbers (cf. Num. 11:5) occur in some suggestive locations in Munro: see "Princess Ida" 76; "Half a Grapefruit" 51.

32 In "Characters" Mr. Cleaver has a way of knocking over "a pyramid . . . of boxes" in Flo's store (77).

33 To be precise, the flanking Egyptian goddesses are Isis and Nephthys (perhaps with Neith and Serket as well); Nekhabet and Wadjet, the goddesses of Upper and Lower Egypt, have a similar function. See Desroches-Noblecourt 74, 259 ff., for the presence of these pairs of goddesses on the nested coffins and the shrines of Tutankhamen's tomb.

34 This location suits Tutankhamen's tomb well enough. Even more suggestive is the underground part of the mine in "Five Points" (a "world of its own" [47]

like the foundry in "Working for a Living"). When pieces of equipment are worn out, as Cornelius explains, they are "piled into a dead-end passage that is sealed up — a tomb for these underground machines" (47).

35 The tomb of Tutankhamen contained among other things a folding bed (Desroches-Noblecourt 184–85), a dismantled chariot (64–65), a number of boats (83), and various chests. The solar boat itself is depicted as well (261). The storeroom at Jenkin's Bend is not of course what the family would wish to be represented by, but neither would Egypt wish to be represented by the hasty jumble of Tutankhamen's tomb; and in a perspective we will come to, the storeroom as much as the parlour is Jenkin's Bend.

36 This is true of a syrinx built perhaps for Tutankhamen (though not of the tomb where he was actually buried), as of one built for Akhenaten (Desroches-Noblecourt 216).

37 See my article "The Shining House." Some of Munro's Egyptian motifs have also been noticed by Rasporich (*Dance* 46–47, 108–09).

38 Conversely, it should already be clear that Egyptian allusions are not limited to "Egyptian" stories. To give only a couple of further examples, we have the pseudo-Egyptian lettering put by a commune on the wall of the house in "The Progress of Love" (24), and in a different key there is "Egyptian" Auntie Lou — a virtual mummy — in "The Peace of Utrecht" (203).

39 See above, 311, for the world of "Connection": an initiatory one, but this in the form of wild civility rather than wild barbarism, hence having distinct central features (as does the Mock Hill of "Something I've Been Meaning to Tell You").

40 The family of Munro's grandfather in the uncollected (and non-fictional) "Working for a Living" make a clear counterpart. They have learned "how to work till they dropped, but not how to take any risk or manage any change" (23); and as with the Flemings, their work is a ritual, done for its own sake.

41 Another highly successful real-estate man is Morris Fordyce as we find him in "Frazil Ice," the central part of "Oh, What Avails." Clare MacQuarrie in "Postcard" is a real-estate man among other things.

42 Cf. postwar Logan in "Frazil Ice": a greatly "spruced-up" place, all "deliberate arrangement," where eccentrics like Loony Buttler seem "not to be possible any more" (196).

43 Fern Dogherty at one point is preparing to sing at "Donna Carling's" wedding (160).

44 "Sunday Afternoon," with which we began our view of the Kingdom, is actually moving from the present group of stories toward a further one: see below, 384.

45 Children sing the same song as Donna, formerly of the "Mountain Sanatorium," approaches in "The Dangerous One." The lady on the mountain, if we emphasize her isolation, can evidently be a more "Wilderness" figure than I am suggesting for "Lives of Girls and Women." What characterizes the central phase

is that here she seems close to worldly union with her bridegroom.

46 For the proto–Fern as Witch of Endor, see Tener 37.4.30 ff. For Aunt Esther, see Tener 37.14.21.2.

47 "Walley" is like "Wallis," the name of a doctor in "Lives of Girls and Women" (173) who thrills Naomi; the name is of course like that of Frank "Wales." "Welsh" means "foreign": I suspect that Munro's Wallises and Walleys seem wonderfully foreign to her Naomis and Jubilees.

48 See II Sam. 18:9: Absalom is "taken up between the heaven and the earth." For his beauty, charm, and thick hair, see II Sam. 14–16.

49 In "Five Points" the dashing Neil has a younger and similar brother called Jonathan.

50 If what we emphasize in "The Turkey Season" is the lure of the remote and inscrutable, with a violent confrontation at the climax, then it is a Wilderness story. The more we feel the equitable Herb Abbott to be one of Munro's eligible sailors (with male dash shifted to the younger Brian), the more we feel ourselves in the central world. Certainly the narrator's attempts to pry into Herb's sexuality remind us of stories like "Lives of Girls and Women."

51 I Sam. 16:12.

52 We can add the lover of the Song of Solomon, who is "white and ruddy, the chiefest among ten thousand" (5:10). (Cf. the hymn recalled by the narrator of "Bardon Bus" [111].) To complicate matters, "ruddy" can have associations as unglamorous as those of the brick post-office in Jubilee: Del, for instance, looks at her "ruddy" (165) face in the mirror of the school washroom after applying strong soap, thus connecting herself with other girls who, if not actually ruddy, are as "stout and cheerful and comradely" (72) as the "Turkey Season" narrator in the group photo or Jessie contrasting herself with MaryBeth (165). The paradox here is really that of glory in the flesh: Art Chamberlain's penis, when actually seen, looks as plain and innocuous as these girls.

53 Ps. 15:2.

54 See above, 215.

55 For Saul and his javelin, directed both at David and at Jonathan, see I Sam. 18:10–11; also 19:9–10, 20:33.

56 I Sam. 31:10. In Del's poem the crying in the trees may be that of the spring peacocks, or it may be "the winter's ghost" (162). Austin Cobbett in "Pictures of the Ice," whose name suggests a cob or male swan, is also very much a "rooster" (138), with "neck wattles" (146) like a turkey: but these last are a sign of old age, and he is in fact preparing for a very wintry kind of self-sacrifice. We can note as well the muskrat in "Images," whose tail first appears "waving at the edge of the water, like something tropical, a dark fern" (36). Since the dark spots on the peacocks look like "soft vegetation under tropical water" (159), we again have the association of splendour and sacrifice (and, incidentally, the word "fern" for the muskrat). For muskrats see also above, 314.

57 Maureen's lover in "The Ferguson Girls Must Never Marry," very much

one of Munro's Passion figures, is the gentle and sickly Dave. Set against the whole of this cycle of Davids — or of Sauls or Absaloms — we may have one hint of the prophet who questions the whole business of monarchy. This is "Sam" in "The Moon in the Orange Street Skating Rink": not a prophet in the usual sense, but a critic with disturbing intimations and misgivings.

58 To go back a step, the name "David" makes two suggestive appearances in the Judges stories. In "Changes and Ceremonies" Del has been reading *A Prince of the House of David* — a children's novel about Christ — and in "Forgiveness in Families" Cam tells Val about a soap opera containing "Gee Gee and Papa David" (94).

59 The association here is made much easier by the post-exilic reinterpretation of the royal psalms as messianic.

60 See respectively "The Moon in the Orange Street Skating Rink" 143; "Postcard" 139; "Lives of Girls and Women" 146; "The Moon in the Orange Street Skating Rink" 136; "Postcard" 128. We can add that MaryBeth's surname is "Crocker," that Patrick has a housekeeper called "Mrs. Kreber" ("Providence" 137), even that the very central-phase Mr. Florence in "The Progress of Love" arrives in a "Chrysler" (14). Then there is the mysterious lover "X" in "Bardon Bus" (really an Alex, it seems, but X nonetheless). With a vague complex of names like these it is impossible to know just when to blow the whistle.

61 When introduced in "Princess Ida" Fern is singing "What is life without my lover?" (73) — seemingly Orfeo's "Che farò senza Euridice?" In "Lives of Girls and Women" she croons an aria that, as Munro renders it, goes "*Do — daa — do, da, do,* da do-do" (145). My guess is that, if anything in particular, this is "Un bel dì" from *Madama Butterfly* — an aria sung by an abandoned bride.

62 See "Lives of Girls and Women" 145; "Accident" 78; "Accident" 77.

63 See "Accident" 77; "Lives of Girls and Women" 145.

64 For "Jesse and Meribeth" as an "Annunciation" story, see below, 382.

65 In "Providence" the city is Seattle, where Dorothy has her lover. Victoria — a less ornamental but not less euphoric Victoria — is also the setting of Neil's story in "Five Points." (It appears in other moods in "Walking on Water" and "Differently.")

66 More distant still, in "Bardon Bus" we have Australia; in "Jesse and Meribeth" again Eric Cryderman comes from Australia, or a more generally East Indian world.

67 Royal hotels abound here: the Brunswick Hotel in Jubilee, for instance, is the preferred place to have Sunday dinner, while the Regency Hotel in Tupperton is a more exotic counterpart.

68 This is so in spite of the fact that Art Chamberlain professes no interest in Florence.

69 "Baptizing" 209. Cf. the "Flemings" in "The Stone in the Field," sturdy if not wealthy, and the similar Cornelius Zendt in "Five Points." (Here, of course,

Dutch strictness is made to contrast with the high spirits of Neil and Brenda.)

70 See "Accident" 106, and "The Moon in the Orange Street Skating Rink" 139.

71 Engines appear repeatedly in related stories. In "Frazil Ice" Joan gives Morris a history of machinery, feeling it an appropriate gift; in "Five Points" Cornelius tells Brenda of the machines in the mine that have replaced human beings like himself.

72 See above, 197.

73 See II Sam. 22, as well as various of the psalms.

74 Herb Abbott is much like another sailor, the portly captain in "Goodness and Mercy" with his air — for Averill at least — of "peaceable authority" (167).

75 Clare MacQuarrie has a sister called "Porky" (129). We should note, though, that central figures come in both thick and thin varieties, like the domes and towers they resemble. Valerie in "Labor Day Dinner," for instance, is a "tall, flat-chested woman" with a "long, plain face" (138); Callie is "so thin her hip-bones stood up" (146). Clifford, a "mischief" figure (see above, 302–03) ff.), is similar; so is Eric Cryderman. Conversely, a terminal-phase hero may be as fleshy as (at times) Dane in "A Queer Streak" (see below, 440): once again two polarities (central-terminal, fat-thin) are resisting a single alignment. In general, however, the central world is fleshy where the terminal one is haggard; and central health and terminal infirmity make a very plain contrast.

76 In June, when the world seems "rewarding enough," the evening sky itself is like a "peach skin" ("Baptizing" 186).

77 See "Tell Me Yes or No" 113.

78 "The Widower" n. pag.

79 See "Wigtime" 273. Neil and Brenda are drinking vodka and orange juice, as well as watching the lake, throughout the framing conversation of "Five Points."

80 In "Postcard" we have the MacQuarrie mansion itself, compared to a church by Helen (132).

81 Clifford's eyes in "Mischief" are "very light in colour, a bright gray-blue" (105); Victor's in "Oranges and Apples" are "light, bright blue" (115); the closely related Mr. Florence has "very light-colored eyes" (14) — to which we can supply blueness by adding his blue car and the "pale blue" he wears on festive occasions. Neil Bauer in "Five Points" has "deep-set light-colored eyes" (48).

82 Cora in "Privilege," the reigning beauty of the school, has "royal-blue velvet with a rose of the same material" (30) in the middle of her cycle of colours.

83 Cf. the "red and pink and gold flowering trees and bushes" of the Hawaiian town in "Pictures of the Ice" (141) or the "fresh and vivid" pastels of the houses at Garden Place (23) — not to say the "flower-coloured cars" (167) in "Sunday Afternoon."

84 Barbara in "Oranges and Apples," a central-phase flirt with an initiatory intensity like Char Desmond's, wears for dinner "a polished-cotton skirt of

yellow and orange and copper colours, a tight black belt, a low-necked black blouse, and large, cheap hoop earings" (119). For her fatal interview with Victor she sharpens to black and white.

85 See above, 340 n52.

86 Two others among the many examples are the "milky lotion, ice-blue astringent" (16) in Aunt Beryl's beauty kit and Miss Farris's fairytale house, "white with blue shutters" (as well as "scalloped" boards [127]) — an operetta preview of the opera to come.

87 Cf. the effect, both electric and organic, of Neil Bauer on Brenda: an intense "energy," though "even to call it energy is not exact — it's more like the sap of him, rising from the roots, clear and on the move, filling him to bursting" (48).

88 See "Pictures of the Ice" 140. Along with Aunt Beryl, there is the "pearl gray" (14) interior of Mr. Florence's car, the ruby of Fern Dogherty's dressing gown, the emerald of the parlour tiles in "Heirs of the Living Body." Turquoise, which we find repeatedly, is not only a colour but an ancient stone used by the Egyptians — for some of the funerary ornaments in Tutankhamen's tomb, for instance (Desroches-Noblecourt 64).

89 See Mark 9:3: "And his raiment became shining, exceeding white as snow; so as no fuller on earth can white them." Peter proposes to erect three tabernacles. "Fullerton," of course, also suggests "fuller town" — something less limited than Garden Place.

90 Magda, a very central-phase presence in "White Dump," has "a lovely, floating crown of silver-gold hair" (275). Mary McQuade in her outdoor role as queen of life has "a crown of frizzy, glinting, naturally brass-coloured hair" (31).

91 "The Funeral-Goer" (Tener 37.15.10–13) features a similar arrangement: an unmarried look-alike brother and sister, ensconced in an old family home.

92 Prostitution is of great interest both to Del in "Lives of Girls and Women" and to Hugo and his wife in "Material." "Privilege" features incest between Shortie and Franny McGill.

93 It is hard to say whether, beneath his compliance, Morris is feeling the "romantic" devotion to Matilda — "stern, unfulfilled, lifelong" (205) — that Joan fancies. If so, it lies deep: what is more evident is two people playing a charade of romance without the substance of it; and this is what, in various forms, typifies the central phase.

94 This is the Jubilee that, as we shall see, makes a subsidiary central world within that of Munro's fourth-phase stories. See Halvard Dahlie, "Unconsummated Relationships: Isolation and Rejection in Alice Munro's Stories." (Dahlie applies the phrase more broadly than I am concerned to do here.)

95 See "Age of Faith" 96. In "Frazil Ice" we learn that Joan during her marriage has come to "the time of accumulation, of acquiring and arranging" (202). " 'It's all arranged' " (208), announces the very central-phase June in "Memorial" concerning car-rides, having just phoned to "arrange" for a coffee-maker; the

brooding Eileen takes a dim view of all such "arrangements" (209). So does Cornelius in "Five Points" contemplating the "changing and arranging" (31) going on at the harbour. Arranging, I have argued (see above, 69–71), is a preoccupation of Munro's Elizabeths. Wallace (61) sees it as typically male, but while the narrator of "Material" is certainly speaking as an exasperated wife (though not general man-hater), Munro has plenty of arranging women.

96 Bailey (113), arguing in Jungian terms, notes that the persona of success in various of Munro's male characters (to which she might have added female ones) hides uncertainty.

97 Lawrence's name connects him with Laurence in "White Dump," another successful entrepreneur and another distinctly edgy one. "Lawrence" means "crowned with laurels" (the Lawrence in "Dulse" operates out of "St. Stephen" for good measure).

98 We can note a name like Art "Chamberlain" here.

99 The Egyptian stories generally have fewer of these affairs; in "Material," though, we find Hugo and his wife in a marriage that is more like a liaison, and we then find Hugo taking up with a series of wives and mistresses. Stories like "Dulse," "Five Points," and "Lichen," which I will later consider with the Exodus group, naturally contain Egyptian — that is, central — elements, and since a Mischief story can also be seen as representing a less distributed Exodus, it is not surprising that these stories should be so close in certain ways to the others we are considering here.

100 Cf. the "lazy" (114) journalist in "Tell Me Yes or No." Even Clifford is "weary" (111) (if also "neurotic-looking" [104]); and in a more padded way there are the "tired" (150) Art Chamberlain and the "sleepy-faced" (144) Clare MacQuarrie.

101 Cf. Matt. 10:16. Victor in "Oranges and Apples" is a clear case of a mischief figure who is both slippery and curiously innocent — in his case, simply amoral.

102 Similarly, Brenda in "Five Points" notices that "Neil" is much like "Cornelius" (43) just as her great affair is turning into something like a marital spat; and in any case there is a deep similarity between the two men — both, we might say, are "Bauers."

103 The ungirt Stella in her jeans and dirty T-shirt makes the same kind of contrast to her stylish and sexually adventurous guests as does the unabashedly homely Valerie in "Labor Day Dinner" — the woman who has chosen "sexual abdication" (156).

104 We can also note that if the more mischievous among the lovers like taking risks as the Uncle Craigs do not, these risks are not felt as the desperate gambles of the initiatory phase. Even Rose, at times fondling Clifford in public while at others going weak with fear, lives temporarily in a world where things cannot seriously go wrong.

105 To mention only a very few examples, "Connection" includes a Cousin

Flora, as well as an Iris who in a draft version was Myrtle and had a friend called Lila (Tener 37.14.1). In "The Dangerous One" the staid grandmother who nevertheless has cosmetics in the bedroom is Lilla.

106 We can follow Mrs. Cryderman in Munro's imagination back to an early version of "Heirs" (Tener 37.8.23) in which she was the wealthy and decrepit Miss Musgrave (now of "Walking on Water") living above Mrs. Oliphant (of "Walker Brothers Cowboy"): in this early story we not only find the incense, but Chinese pyjamas and a Buddha. In "The Beggar Maid" Dr. Henshawe's house has "polished floors, glowing rugs, Chinese vases, bowls and landscapes, black carved screens as well as little jade animals" (66–67).

107 At the Misses Milton's slide-show on China in "Who Do You Think You Are?" one sees the same sort of country, "all dry and papery-looking, fragile, unlikely" (197).

108 In "Lives of Girls and Women" the flowered "black . . . dressing gown" (151) of her mother's in which Del fantasizes about Art Chamberlain is rayon; Art's voice affects Del like "the touch of rayon silk" (153); a peacock's tail is "painted satin" (159). Two other examples of satin are Fern's ruby dressing gown and the lining of Uncle Craig's coffin.

109 It is important to note that the two kinds of chocolate, or "honey" (30, 37), in this story are closely linked.

110 The cousins also bring coffee — a dark beverage with an "unfamiliar, American fragrance" (4). Cf. Art Chamberlain's "dark chocolate" (149) voice on the radio, as well as Fern Dogherty being guzzled like "chocolate icing" (173).

111 Beryl also has "nail polish with an overpowering smell of bananas" (17).

112 Cf. the "cake and molded jellies and cookies with animal faces" (24) at the birthday party in "The Shining Houses."

113 Similarly Mrs. Gannett in "Sunday Afternoon" has "a look of being made of entirely synthetic and superior substances" (163). Antoinette in "Hold Me Fast, Don't Let Me Pass" is "sprayed and painted and preserved to within an inch of her life" (82) — a very different person from her human-smelling rival Judy.

114 In "Wigtime" Margot makes herself up "kind of Cleopatra-ish" (265) for her own mischief.

115 In "The Peace of Utrecht" Auntie Lou and Aunt Annie make another formidable pair. Auntie Lou, the dark and grim one, is explicitly "Egyptian"; Aunt Annie may have nothing quite gipsyish in her manner (though she does have something "coquettish" [203]), but she plays a sharp trick, intentionally or otherwise, in giving Helen her dead mother's clothes to wear. Of the two punk salesgirls in "Bardon Bus," one is called "gypsyish" (125).

116 In "Five Points" the store in Victoria was formerly owned by "a grouchy old woman with painted-on eye-brows" (34) — a hostile sort of gipsy from the sound of it — while Maria's respectable family are Croatians. Victor in "Oranges and Apples," who plays roughly Ted Makkavala's role, is aristocratically Polish, though he also takes a job as a night watchman.

¹¹⁷ Magda in "White Dump," with her Hungarian name, is the most poised of Egyptians; yet when she hums "Home to Our Mountains" (288) she is Azucena the gipsy from *Il Trovatore*. A woman much like the aristocratic Mrs. Comber of "Princess Ida" appears in one of Munro's poems (Tener 37.20.13) doing a wild gipsy dance.

¹¹⁸ We can expect contradictions whenever gipsies are mentioned in Munro. The second or Egyptian of Miss Farris's operettas, for instance, has a very oxymoronic title: "The Gypsy Princess." Almeda Roth's poem "The Gypsy Fair" (29), briefly, makes us wonder who the thieving gipsies really are — the wild kind or the enterprising nation-builders destroying the forest.

¹¹⁹ An important figure here is obviously "Barbara" in "Oranges and Apples," the leisurely "lily" (108) from the swamp. For a more terminal counterpart see "Lily Barbour" in "Mrs. Cross and Mrs. Kidd" (164), the woman at the end of the corridor in an Old People's Home. In "Tell Me Yes or No" it is not the passionate narrator but her lover's store-managing wife who is called Barbara, but this Barbara was once a "gypsyish" (108) dancer.

¹²⁰ Paradoxically for a barbarian, Ted Makkavala's given name was "Karl" as late as the proof version of the story, kindly shown me by Walter Martin, though "Makkavala" is certainly Magyar.

¹²¹ See both "Baptizing" and "How I Met My Husband" for marginal (and dilapidated) fairgrounds.

¹²² Note that the central world in its greatest intensity can take on the character of its contrary: in terms of colour, the blue of Del's peacocks becoming the black of "ink blots" (159), the blue of Neil Bauer's Mercury becoming "a pool, a spot of swampy darkness under the trees" (35).

¹²³ The cow seems to be coming from the river: cf. Pharoah's dream in Gen. 41:1–4.

¹²⁴ For the suggestion of a vertical cycling of water itself, we can think of the Wawanash River as imagined by the child in "Images," shooting up into the sunlight from a mysterious underground source to which one can imagine it falling back. (I suspect that Munro has "Kubla Khan" in the back of her mind here, as well as *Macbeth*.)

¹²⁵ Cf. also the saltmine in "Five Points," with its superstructure rising above an ancient sea; the posh River Inn in "Wood'; and the frazil ice that rises "magnificently" (199) over deep places in a river. This last, like the formations in "Pictures of the Ice," will remind us of the snowy landscape observed by Robert in "Fits" on his night walk: what is central about it is both its splendour and apparent stability.

¹²⁶ See "The Found Boat" 131.

¹²⁷ See Rom. 8:17, 12:5 — among various passages in Paul's epistles that could be referred to here.

¹²⁸ See above, 58–59.

¹²⁹ One of the hymns sung at the funeral in "Heirs of the Living Body" is

"Jesus call [sic] us, o'er the tumult / Of our life's tempestuous sea" (58): a hymn that goes on to refer to the calling of Andrew, but also alludes to Jesus's calling of Peter while walking on the sea (Matt. 14:22 ff.).

130 Cf. the love-ballad sung at the funeral in "Circle of Prayer": "Now, while the blossom still clings to the vine, / I'll taste your strawberries, I'll drink your sweet wine" (263).

131 In "Dance of the Happy Shades" the mongoloid children come from "Greenhill School." "Dolores" Boyle, the girl who plays the piano, is one of Munro's figures who assume a Crucifixion attitude, "her head hanging down" (222).

132 See Exod. 7:20.

133 Cf. Gabriel in "Material": "his face curves out smoothly and his eyes, set shallowly in his head, curve out too under the smooth pink lids. The wrinkles he has are traced on top of this smoothness, this impenetrable surface; they are of no consequence" (26). We should also note Munro's professional bandage-folders: the narrator of "Material" at one point, and more permanently Mrs. Gowran in a very Egyptian early story, "Liberation" (Tener 37.8.23–24).

134 In "Material" Hugo's wife would like nothing less than to "claw his head open" (42).

135 See above, 160 n66.

136 We may have here a further reason than Munro's usual one for the name "Frances": St. Francis is peculiarly the saint of Christmas — the saint who originated the crèche. Cf. "Gabriel" in "Material," the counterpart (as the narrator comes to see) of the Hugo from whom she receives a very annunciatory experience at the end.

137 As late as the proof-stage "Accident" came after "Bardon Bus" (see Martin, *Paradox* 137): in the transition to the terminal rather than the central phase, then, where we also find "Red Dress — 1946," a story about a Christmas dance and a girl's entry into the world of sexuality.

138 Miss Kernaghan is Callie's reputed mother and a specialist in "firm, flashy lie[s]" (138).

139 A story like "Five Points" is something of an Egyptian equivalent — see above, 344 n102.

140 A paradox here is that in a Mischief story downfall itself can be the great attraction. In "Five Points" it is what draws Brenda to the quarrel — "what a dazzling temptation ahead — destruction" (43); in a moral form it is even what Del Jordan expects as a high point with Art Chamberlain.

141 Since Barbara's marriage in "Oranges and Apples" survives this and other crises, the Mischief story here is contained by an Establishment story. What "Oranges and Apples" is not is a love-tragedy of the kind found in Munro's first and especially third phases. If, for instance, we set it beside the closely related "Something I've Been Meaning to Tell You," we see that the mischief between Barbara and Victor, for all its intensity, is not the passion that brings Char and

Blaikie together again after a lifetime. "Oranges and Apples" takes added intensity from the fact that Et's role of spy is played here by the wronged husband himself, but once again we do not have erotic passion: Murray's love (like Arthur Comber's, for that matter) is adoring but domestic.

[142] See Lam. 1:1, 5:22; Is. 64:10.

[143] We can have similar wandering in desolation as the "returning vision" of any individual story: see above, 148–49. I have also noted that Exile stories correspond to Wilderness stories — stories, that is, coming before rather than after the Kingdom. In "Tell Me Yes or No" the heroine wanders figuratively in a desert, has strange fantasies, and prays at the end to an unknown god who has total power over her while also being in some sense her own creature.

[144] This sense of needing another's knowledge or acknowledgment in order to exist is something we have already found in the wilderness of "Age of Faith" (see above, 212). In "Bardon Bus" the narrator comes to feel that "I can't continue to move my body along the streets unless I exist in his mind and in his eyes" (126). "Patricia" in "Tell Me Yes or No" is feeling similarly when she begs for a communication ("Please write to me or phone me, I am going crazy" [122]).

[145] As a matter of looking and thinking before the central action proper, such a visit is structurally an "approaching vision": see above, 147–48.

[146] Mrs. MacQuarrie's dining-room in "Postcard" is presumably not scruffy, nor are we told that Clare's bedroom is. What is scruffy is tiptoeing up the back stairs or peeking into the drawers in the dining-room.

[147] Rose, imagining at first that she understands Patrick, finds she cannot "get at" (108) the nobility she believes to be there, much less reveal it to anyone else. She has no better luck with Clifford, nor do others: when Jocelyn in a burst of psychotherapy supposes she can see "the great blazing truth" (127) about him, Clifford reminds her that this is not such an easy thing to come by.

[148] Various mischief figures are, like Hugo, not public in Uncle Craig's way but decidedly conspicuous: Neil Bauer as a striking man doing striking work in a public place, Edgar as a flashy skater at the Orange Street Rink, Art Chamberlain as an announcer, Clifford as a professional musician.

[149] Cf. 2 Sam. 6:16.

[150] See above, 216.

[151] Cf. John 2:4.

[152] We can even ask whether the perspective we just have been taking should not sometimes be reversed altogether. The power Del senses in her dead uncle might be not spectral but spiritual, that is, human: something "barbarian" that Egypt can never quite nullify, and that might consume the whole of its mummified world. It is the same with the gentleness Del senses in Mary Agnes — who puts her hand over the dead cow's eye "seriously, shrinkingly, yet with a tender composure that was not like her" (45). Del cannot bear such a thing: she immediately sees the same hand dark against the light, and is as troubled as the grandmother in "A Trip to the Coast" with her dream of a black bird covering the sun.

153 After the Pauline way in which Mrs. Jordan has talked about change in "Heirs of the Living Body" (see above, 314–15), I suggest the "we shall be changed" of 1 Cor. 15:51–52 here.

154 We have Munro's own word about the irony here (Hancock 103), but in any case it is present in the structure of the story. See Carrington 91; Keith 159, who also notes the parallel with the end of "Mischief." The same contrast between mother and daughter reappears in "Friend of My Youth" (23).

155 The situation is in fact more complicated. MaryBeth does her own betraying in disbelieving Jessie — who has in fact been partly telling the truth and partly lying.

156 Barbara in "Oranges and Apples" is rather like Fern: sensual yet inert, bitterly disillusioned, and left in the end to grow fat and self-pampering. She is also, like Jessie, a reader of "The Brothers Karamazov," though the parallel Victor finds between Barbara and Katerina Ivanovna is no simpler than the literary parallels in "Something I've Been Meaning to Tell You."

157 This illusion is not confined to adolescence: while an older Jessie is criticizing her teen-age self here, it is the lives of girls and women we are seeing. The middle-aged Rose of the end of "Mischief," having tried group sex with Jocelyn and Clifford, first means to drop them and then prefers to keep the connection for a while — "because she needed such friends occasionally, at that stage of her life" (132).

158 I.e., the heroine in H.M.S. Pinafore (133).

159 In "Oranges and Apples," the role of a "looker" (106) is a main theme of the story from the outset. In this case the most intense looker of all is Murray, the jealous husband. With a self-consciousness that is another form of looking, Murray watches Barbara and Victor at their game; then, needing to turn fantasy into reality, he throws the two together. The message "Don't disappoint me again" (135) — flashing in Murray's mind as she comes back to report on a tumour — might also be her own message to him.

160 At the end of "Heirs," when a spring flood has ruined the forgotten manuscript, Del seems free after all. Yet her feelings — "tender remorse" matched by "brutal, unblemished satisfaction" (62) — are very much like the tenderness and malice of her aunts: in this story's world of transplants they have managed to transplant their minds into hers, and later she will find Uncle Craig's obsessions there as well.

161 See "Jesse and Meribeth" 170, 180. Cf. Luke 1:7, 18, 41.

The Man in the Fire

A. EXODUS

I: Introduction

A centre is only a point, yet we can readily imagine it spreading out to fill a circle. The self-contained world of Munro's central-phase stories, we have found, is similarly capable of expanding to take in regions outside its borders. And while any phase in our scheme can be seen as a microcosm, the central one is special in the way its initiatory movement, for instance, adjoins and resembles the initiatory phase proper — which can thus be thought of as the first part of the central phase distributed to become a distinct phase with its own structure. Recently we have been seeing how the central-phase stories, while managing to keep their world intact, often have in their final sections matter of exile, escape, or rebellion.[1] Beyond the central world we come to a further one with just these concerns: a distinct terminal phase, in other words, on the same principle as the distinct initiatory one. After the Egyptian stories in Munro's collections we come to Exodus stories, as I will be calling them; after her Kingdom stories we come to what I will call a Passion group. (After this group, as I have indicated, we will come to an end beyond the end: but in an important sense "terminal" remains the right word for the point we are reaching.)

The Exodus group is fairly small, homogeneous, and easy to define:

since the Passion group is rather the opposite, the best way to proceed will be to take the former group by itself first, using it as a key to its more unwieldy counterpart. Among the Exodus stories "Princess Ida," "Half a Grapefruit," "Dulse," and "Lichen" are closely bound together by a common structure and common motifs (even if we can also use them, as I have done, to illustrate not just escape but the Egypt that is being escaped from). "Thanks for the Ride" and "How I Met My Husband," both as it happens early or rooted in early material, stand somewhat apart from these others; yet they show the Exodus pattern clearly enough, and in fact more simply than the later members of the group. "Five Points" is like them in many ways; "Images," which I have used as an all-purpose Munro story, is more distinct — so much so, in fact, that if it were not placed where it is in its collection, there would be no grounds for associating it with this group more than certain others. For this reason I shall not make much use of it in the present account, though it responds in a number of ways to the reading that its placement suggests.

*

What we saw in the previous chapter was, in various guises, Jenkin's Bend; and what we saw in Jenkin's Bend was the "living body," an incorporation bringing assured worldly plenty and grace. When we turn to "Princess Ida," the next chapter of *Lives of Girls and Women*, we find ourselves in a very different world, one which the continued (and scandalized) presence of Del's aunts only helps to define by contrast. Mrs. Jordan, the central figure here, is a woman haunted by famine: it seems that her whole life has been a flight from the hard land of her childhood, "where the rocks ... were poking through the soil like bones through flesh" (74–75). Once, as her daughter remembers, she painted a picture showing

> a stony road and a river between mountains, and sheep driven
> along the road by a little girl in a red shawl. The mountains and
> the sheep looked alike, lumpy, woolly, purplish-gray. Long ago
> I had believed that the little girl was really my mother and that
> this was the desolate country of her early life. (71–72)

Del had been right, of course, and not only about her mother's childhood. Mrs. Jordan will always be making her way through a wilderness, always "out on the Jericho Road" (65) as Munro pointedly phrases it. For she is the self in everyone that goes into chaos, as humanity did before the world and must do again after any Egyptian sojourn inside it — a sojourn that may prove famine rather than plenty. We can expect stories like "Princess Ida," then, to resemble those of the Genesis and Wilderness groups — the terminal third phase mirroring the initiatory first. But our new group of stories deals with going out rather than going in; and because it tends to be followed by a distinct Wilderness group, it does not deal very much with chaos itself. Instead, it concentrates on the departure — the exodus in a strict sense; or it presents the journey through chaos as something continuous with this departure.

The Jericho Road is not easy going: Mrs. Jordan only just manages it, coping endlessly with the perilous and unforeseen, urged on by a desperate hope. As little Addie Morrison — to go back to her early history and more precisely its own first cycle — she runs away from her parents' poor farm, finding refuge in town; but the refuge and a promise of financial help fail her, and she has no choice but to move on. After this first adventure she makes her way to a job in Owen Sound, but now comes another upset: a shadowy fiancé "did not turn out to be the sort of person I had thought he was" (79). Off she goes on her travels again, and even when she settles for the dependable Mr. Jordan, she has by no means reached contentment. The story of Flo's early years in "Half a Grapefruit" — years of drudgery and escape and wandering — is much the same;[2] so, in a more general way, is that of all the Exodus heroines. To take one further example here, Lois in "Thanks for the Ride," together with her *ad hoc* boyfriend, sets off for Owen Sound, a town that also figures in Mrs. Jordan's story. At the same time the two are setting off on a sexual escape: for if others can "go only a little way" (57) on that road, Lois is able to take Dick on a "headlong journey" (56) of lovemaking.

But here too there is a failure: after their seeming escape the lovers only "find our same selves, chilled and shaken" (56). In their own way, then, they are like Mrs. Jordan, who arrives not at glory but at being "just her, the way she was now, just my mother in Jubilee" (80). And this is where, in a tragic cyclical reading, all the Exodus heroines are doomed to end. At the risk of anticipating, we can note here how Edie in "How I Met My Husband," after her brief romance with an aeroplane pilot, is forced to settle for humdrum domesticity; how Brenda in "Five Points," having been on her sexual ride with Neil Bauer — and "come through some complicated adventures . . . and dangers" (37) — finds herself trapped in the affair itself. In this last case, to be sure, the result is not likely to be humdrum — Brenda knows that what you take for the end may be "only the start of a new stage" (49); Lydia Cooper, after her own adventure, accepts the fate of being "up and down" (59). But that itself is a kind of end: when Israel, in the biblical Exodus, is turned back from the borders of Canaan, it does not simply return to Egypt but is forced round the desert again, condemned to a circling that might go on until it reached exhaustion. Mrs. Jordan's stories are similar — they all go "round and round and down to death" (79), like the mouse's tail at the same structural point in *Alice in Wonderland*.

*

There are different ways in which this story of failed escape can embody itself in characters and places. Instead of imagining attempted flight from a land of hunger, we can simply imagine a dying person trying to avoid death. Alternatively death may be vested in a person external to him: someone he himself tries to kill or disable perhaps. Alternatively again, it may be life that he experiences as someone external to himself, so that death is like the loss of this person's favour or support. To go back to our biblical terms, we can say that Egypt resists its own dying, or that Israel turns against Egypt, dealing a parting blow to its enemy. We can even say that in a sense Israel has been cast out: this reading would correspond to a story of lost riches like "Dulse," though we would not expect an Israelite account of the matter to take such a form.

Egypt in turn has its own canonical story: that of Osiris, the fertility god whose death it tries to accommodate to its characteristic refusal of death. In the same myth we meet Osiris' consort Isis, closely associated with wisdom, who on the loss of her husband turns into an imperilled wanderer searching for his remains.[3] In Munro Mrs. Jordan makes a more floundering counterpart — "Isis," in fact, is Del's suggestion when her mother cannot think of a word for her crossword puzzle. Among the Israelites Mrs. Jordan bears some analogy, as we will see, to the feisty Miriam; more obviously like Isis is a figure we have already glimpsed in the central phase, the biblical Wisdom herself. It is Wisdom who brings Israel out of Egypt and through the Wilderness; later she can be found by the paths, calling men — successfully or otherwise — to accept what she can offer.[4]

It seems strange — and will have to stay that way for the moment — that Mrs. Jordan should have connections with both Egypt and Israel; but at any rate we may be prepared now to notice other

Egyptian and biblical resonances in a story like "Princess Ida."[5] If we return to the boarding-house in town, for instance, we may for one thing find certain echoes in the name "Grandma Seeley." We are close here to the "Sayla" of "Day of the Butterfly" — itself as we have seen a name with various suggestions — but "Seeley" sounds like the "selig" family of words (as in the German Beatitudes): this is a place of blessing, as, in another context, is the "Balm of Gilead Home" (50) in "Lichen." If "Seeley" sounds like "seal," that too is appropriate enough: Grandma Seeley hides Addie Morrison from the danger of her father. And some touches here are more specifically Egyptian: Addie is not only put to menial tasks but favoured by a gracious teacher called Miss "Rush," the Pharaoh's daughter of the story. On getting married this latter succumbs to an Egyptian kind of weakness,[6] dying in childbirth; Addie, as if in one of Munro's Egyptian stories, sees the dead mother with the child lying in her arms "like a wax doll" (79). When Grandma Seeley herself dies, and a nephew who knows not Addie repudiates a promised bequest, Addie passes on to Owen Sound: a lakeside city of the kind we met in Munro's Kingdom stories, so that in one projection we can see her journey as the continuing history of Israel, a larger Exodus.[7] We even find that "Princess Ida," like almost any of Munro's stories, puts us in the world of Jesus — the second Moses whose life closely parallels that of his predecessor. When the young Addie, running away from a tyrannical father, is sheltered by Grandma Seeley "till time had passed" (78) we are reminded that the child Jesus, no less than his ancestors, found refuge in Egypt. When the grownup Mrs. Jordan takes to distributing encyclopaedias (earlier, of course, it had been Bibles), we may in this context think of the New Testament version of Wisdom, the pondering Mary. By the same token Mrs. Jordan is a commissioned evangelizer. Her brother recalls how, when a butterfly broke out of its cocoon one Easter, their mother had seen this as a symbol of the Resurrection; and while no doubt there is irony here at the expense of brother and sister alike, we will be seeing how both, in their own ways, are seekers after salvation.

II: The Exodus World

Now we can sketch the world of these stories in somewhat greater detail — the world from which they set out, primarily, though also one at which they have a way of arriving again. To begin with the obvious, this is always in some way or other a dying world. Mission Creek in "Thanks for the Ride" seems at one time to have had or expected central-phase prosperity, judging by its fine town hall; now it is a faded and half-empty place, and in Munro's story the cottage season on which it is forced to rely has come to an end, as has summer in "Five Points." In "Dulse" it is the season of Duncan and Lydia that has ended, while the Maritime Provinces where the latter takes her vacation have fallen on hard times. In "How I Met My Husband" Edie hopes to escape from the old farm world of rural Ontario; so of course does Addie Morrison, and if in Addie's case there is no real evidence of earlier prosperity, she does spend her life re-enacting some great disappointment — one sustenance after another does not turn out to be what she had thought it was.

In the words of George in "Thanks for the Ride," this is the world of "All-a-man left" (45): in "Thanks" itself, for instance, the only man still visible is an old café-owner looming "huge and cynical and incurious" (44) behind his cash register. The name he goes by is "Pop": for as the prolific god of Egypt reaches senility, he shows himself again to be the ancient god of chaos, seen here in his impotence rather than his might. Cornelius, Brenda's middle-aged husband in "Five Points," is a cripple; Rose's father as we have him in "Half a Grapefruit" is a dying old man; and when the latter appears in his "brown wool bathrobe with a tasseled tie" (44) he is virtually Father Osiris the corn god, now nearing the end of his cycle.[8] Then there is the garnered corn of these stories — whether found in bread-boxes, storehouses, granaries, or mealbags. If Bill Morrison is compared to a young snake later buried in a bag of meal, he reminds us of yet another story about Egypt: he seems a refracted echo of Benjamin,[9] while the world of grain, with its god-providers and its famine, is more generally that of Joseph himself.

A failing god of plenty naturally turns from a protector into an encumbrance; by the same token his land turns into one of bondage. In a certain perspective Egypt has always been that, of course, but where Jenkin's Bend masks its coercion with courtesy and forgiveness, the world of "Princess Ida" is one in which we are intensely aware of servitude as servitude. Addie Morrison's domineering father expects his daughter to stay home and keep house until marriage; when she runs away to town we find her cleaning chamber-pots. In other stories we find Edie serving the Peebles, Lois serving in a glove-factory while sexually serving the boys from the summer cottages, Brenda chafing at the oppressive husband whom she gave up an earlier job to assist. "Dulse," in which Lydia has abased herself before Duncan, adds a male version of servitude with its three workmen; and more than any of these other stories, "Half a Grapefruit" shows us an entire world of subordination — not only of the poor to the affluent, but of West Hanratty to Hanratty, country to town, women to men, and more that we will come to later.

Those serving are not, in this phase, prepared to be merely servile about it. Mrs. Jordan's name, significantly, is "Addie" or "Ada" (the latter being what the aunts call her),[10] and we also find "Ida," "Edie," "Della," and "Adelaide" (the friend in "Thanks for the Ride" to whom the name seems displaced from the heroine); perhaps "Lydia" in "Dulse" is close enough to "Adelaide" to warrant inclusion here as well. Names of this type, we have seen, are associated with loftiness: all these women — as a psychiatrist suggests to Lydia — have a great fund of pride, even when their lot is one of humiliation. Rose may feel constrained to bow before parental authority, but she does not submit, any more than young Addie Morrison — or grownup Mrs. Jordan; and Lois especially is an unforgettable figure of abjectness combined with pride, even abjectness that is its own kind of pride.[11] The result, of course, is the great attempt to escape. Pop may disapprove — in his eyes people make fools of themselves "just by walking up and down, driving up and down, going places" (44) — but on all sides we see people trying to do just that. The teenagers in the same story make a literal example; so do Brenda and Neil in "Five Points," riding the van and the car, making love in the trailer, passing Brenda's daughter out for some joyriding of her own. And we can add here the very different Ben Jordan walking his trapline — making a temporary escape for himself and his daughter from a house of sickness and confinement — since this is the main reason for including "Images" among the Exodus stories. Not surprisingly, these stories are full of Munro's roads and gates: the town of Mission Creek, for instance, whatever we make of its name, also proclaims itself the "gateway" (44) to the wild Bruce, the holiday country to which some people at least manage to get away.

*

More elevated forms of road and vehicle play an important role here too. In "How I Met My Husband" Edie is going to make her escape by aeroplane; closer to the ground there are various bridges to use, such as the Jubilee bridge "hanging in the dusk" (68) in "Princess

Ida," or the bridge into Hanratty crossed by Rose to begin "Half a Grapefruit." From these and other images we often get the impression that we have passed into a world of air. Dick in "Thanks for the Ride," for instance, is once called "Dickie" (48) by his cousin, and since this sensitive boy is indeed more birdlike than the earthy George, it seems that Lois no less than Edie is going to be taken on a kind of flight. In "How I Met My Husband" again we meet Loretta "Bird," a woman who in her more blatant way is what all the women in this story are, someone who would like to fly away from depressing surroundings to more genteel ones. "Loretta," moreover, is itself a somewhat aerial name: it comes from "Loreto," the destination to which, traditionally, angels carried the house of the Virgin through the air.[12] And while Catherine in "Lichen," like others of her name in Munro, appears to be named after St. Catherine's wheel, it is at least worth mentioning that this saint's bones were air-lifted in the same way.

One thing we seem to be dealing with, then, is an air-house: a house that is airborne, or a destination for an airborne virgin, or perhaps the virgin herself, but in any case something suggestive of passage through an upper element. We have already, of course, found Egyptian domes rising above water, among which we can include Stella's house in "Lichen" perched on its cliff above Lake Huron. But there are things about this house that are not simply Egyptian: it is both "full of light" (36) and situated near a lighthouse — a tower for light associated with dangerous passage over water, just as "Stella" can be associated with the star of the sea. And it reminds Stella's guest of the island summer-house in Bergman's *Through a Glass Darkly* (in which, we are also told, "God was a helicopter" [37]).[13] Evidently, then, we are in the same world of get-aways that we have already noted; and Stella herself, whom we have seen as a solid Egyptian, is not only a lively mischief-maker as well but, we can now add, someone making a high-spirited exodus from marriage. We can see Brenda and Neil in "Five Points" in much the same way, since we find them looking down at the lake from Neil's trailer; and to come back as always to "Princess Ida," we find a counterpart of Stella's house in the one Mrs. Jordan rents on River Street. The grey paint and faded awnings of this provisional place make Del think of a beach: it may also remind us of the guesthouse on the sea-island in "Dulse," or the whole town of Mission Creek in its lakeside world of sand and wind.

With central reversals in mind, we should also see that the more ethereal forms of the half-way house are not the only ones. The Virgin's house is of course a place of incarnation — in one view a medial, even a low kind of refuge. The guest-house in "Dulse" is similarly medial, situated between the house of the virginal Willa Cather high above the ocean and "the Ocean Wave" (47) itself, the brothel down by the water. We are more likely to think of Grandma Seeley's boarding-house in "Princess Ida" as simply low, if by no means a brothel: Grandma Seeley herself is a down-to-earth woman, and for Addie Morrison at least her house is one of servitude. The Peebles' house in "How I Met My Husband" is similar in this respect, a place where another young refugee from a farm is taken in and put to humble tasks. At the same time there is great ambiguity of the high and low in both these houses, for along with their work Addie and Edie get a taste of something more elevated. Grandma Seeley's boarders are a refined class in Addie's eyes: if developed further in this direction they would match the ladylike Mrs. Peebles or the even more ladylike, and more snobbish, bishop's sister in Flo's reminiscences. At the same time Addie experiences the kindness of Grandma Seeley; and above all she meets the wonderful Miss Rush, the teacher who introduces her to a refinement that can better be called grace. Edie has no-one quite like Miss Rush, but she discovers kindness in Dr. Peebles and elegance in Mrs. Peebles: she even gets a chance to "play queen" (53) in the latter's dress, and to admire herself naked in the Peebles' bathroom surrounded by rosy light, flamingoes and a cloud of perfume.[14] Addie and Edie — similar for all their differences, as their names suggest — are going through much the same transformation. Each is at the end of one life and the beginning of another, knowing both the full hardship of a servant's position and a newly discovered promise of gentility. Presently Chris Watters will appear to invite Edie emblematically into his plane and literally into his tent; and if this latter is only a rude shelter on the ground, hot and stuffy as Edie finds it, it is also a place to "get some fresh air" (59) according to Chris — and one where he will offer her his own grace.

*

In this passage through a middle place, a separation of identities is occurring. Addie and Edie are both going away from the world of their parents; so is Rose, whether or not she is actually leaving home ⸱ this point; Del Jordan has not yet reached puberty, but is at the age ⸱ere she no longer feels comfortable with her mother's ways. All, ⸱nse, are getting born: and if this is to happen, an old self will ⸱ let the new one out. "Half a Grapefruit" is specially full of openings and emissions of one kind or another, often linked with life's various passages: we hear about a bleeding head and bleeding noses, not to say coughing fits, menstruation, stained underwear, and the sweating by which Rose expresses adolescent qualms. We hear as well about the wrappings and plasterings in which Egypt puts its trust — sheets, Band-Aids, Kotex, the "Mum" (39) Rose tries for the sweating, or simply the lump in her throat — some of these being now used with a desperation that indicates their failing effectiveness.[15] Other stories, if not quite as effluent, give us things like Mrs. Jordan's noisy stomach and unmanageable hair, or the tendency of Stella and others to break out of their corsetting; and in all the Exodus stories something is breaking out of verbal restraints. "Flo's voice climbed and hurried on, embarrassed that she had let that out" (52); Mrs. Jordan, proof against embarrassment, comes out publicly with things like the chamber-pots. Her chatter with Fern Dogherty, in fact, is "a river that never drie[s] up" (69): and after hearing Lois's mother in spate we can perhaps see why, of the two cushions in the family house, one would read "To Mother" (49) while the other would have a picture of Niagara Falls.

A remarkable violence goes with all this outwelling, something very different from the sheltering that we saw earlier in this chapter. In "Lichen" violence may not appear directly in the story's action — though we hear of Stella slapping the dinner meat about — but Catherine reminds Stella of an amputee ("not much cut off, just the tips of her fingers and maybe her toes" [44]), while Dina's pubic hair looks like "the dark pelt of an animal, with the head and tail and feet chopped off" (42): all this when Catherine is in danger of getting "the big chop" (43) from David. In "Princess Ida" the violence goes beyond imagery: a brother accosts or "torture[s]" (77) his sister, calves are butchered, a woman is cut open "on the table" (77), and in the end the consummating "downflash of a wing or knife" (91) can be sensed as an almost physical wounding. The biblical Exodus is of course a tale of violence throughout, full of beating and sacrificing, the cleaving of seas and rocks, the flow of blood and water: above all it has the dividing of Israelite from Egyptian, marked by the blood of the Passover. Nor does the violence in Munro's version point only to the Bible. What Del takes from her mother's Encyclopaedia is history, which to her means Charlotte Corday and Mary Queen of Scots and Lord Strafford, not to say battles — "all bloodshed, drowning, hacking off of heads, agony of horses" (66). When Mrs. Jordan joins the Great Books group, she puts her mind to things like *Hamlet* and *Antigone*. When Rose comes home from school in "Half a Grapefruit," she is carrying *The Merchant of Venice* with its pound of flesh, *A Tale of Two Cities* with its guillotine, and, needless to say, *Macbeth*.

Another cause of death, if no less sure than wounding, is less overt. Where Uncle Craig in "Heirs of the Living Body" dies of heart failure, people in the Exodus world often die of cancer. Cancer is what Rose's father succumbs to in "Half a Grapefruit";[16] so, in the same story, does Ruby Carruthers, and so does the bishop's sister in Flo's account of her own life — it is seeing the latter on her deathbed, in fact, that brings on Flo's epic nosebleed. In "Princess Ida," again, there are some very conspicuous cancer-victims: both Mrs. Jordan's brother and her mother. Etymologically cancer is a crab, which sounds like another kind of knife, but this is a knife with a difference. It destroys within, leaving the skin unpierced, and may for long work in a slow and unnoticed way — as Mrs. Jordan points out, one can be cut up under anaesthetic. There is no less remarkable a duality about cancer's victims, who may be either as gaunt as Mrs. Jordan's mother on the barren farm or more like her brother Bill Morrison, the skinny boy turned fleshy man[17] who not only reminds his niece of the snake in the bag of meal but talks about caterpillars growing "fat and sleepy" (89) from feeding on milkweed.[18] In other words, the wasting away represented here by cancer comes either from lack of sustenance or from too much of it: good years seem as perilous as lean ones, and shelter, for those making an escape, as perilous as direct opposition.

This is not to say that other characters in these stories are necessarily over- or underweight. "She was perfect" (83), says Del of Bill's wife Nile, a wonder of youth and beautification with skin "like a pink teacup" (84). Here again, evidently, we are seeing the glowing skin of Egypt (along with the gleaming porcelain of China), and we may notice that another fine lady, the bishop's sister in "Half a Grapefruit," takes no less care of her skin than Nile. What she uses for the purpose, in fact, is "Hind's Honey and Almond" (42) — a product that, among other things, can take us back *via* "hind" to the deer seen by Del and Aunt Elspeth suspended in a golden light. In the same connection we can note that the gift once given by the bishop's sister to Flo — the counterpart of the yellow scarf given by Miss Rush to Addie — was a pair of "fawn" (43) gloves. And yet, unlike the waterlilies at Jenkin's Bend, this perfection is out of its element here. Nile is a very foreign body in Mrs. Jordan's house, no less than in the arms of the shaggy Uncle Bill. Her beauty may seem as timeless as that of a deer poised in air, but the changes of life are not really timeless at all, nor can most of us manage them so gracefully. First there are the problems of adolescence, typified by the butterfly trying to get out of the cocoon. Then, beyond a brief maturity, comes the time of decay: just as fruit and cake moulder in "Half a Grapefruit," so do all the fading human figures in these stories — dying men like Bill Morrison, aging women like Alice Kelling, Lydia Cooper and, in "Lichen," both Stella and Catherine.

Once again, the trouble may lie beneath the skin, revealing itself in Catherine's gauntness or Stella's obesity; at the same time Catherine's skin is itself sickly, while Nile's in such surroundings is unnatural in its very perfection. It is the imagery of skin, in fact, that can show us more plainly than anything else where we are: no longer in an Elizabeth's world of wholeness but in that of a divided Mary, where purity and impurity keep a strange commerce. Skin here may be as "dotty" as we have found Mary's often to be: while the fawn gloves given by the bishop's sister would be free of a fawn's spotting, and Nile's skin is "without a mark" (84),[19] other creatures here are very different. The butterfly coming into the world was a "little spotty thing" (89); Uncle Bill himself at the awkward age was a "little spotted snake" (88); Lois's skin in "Thanks for the Ride" is pale and "dustily freckled" (49), necessitating heavy powder when she goes on a date. As for the aging, Fern Dogherty, while not showing her years as plainly as in a later phase, has skin that is both dusty and spotted — rather like the "spotty bananas" that (along with "small unpromising oranges" [39]) are the only fresh fruit allowed in Flo's store.[20] And in the end nothing is left but Lois's grandmother — a "collapsed pudding" with "pale brown spots melting together on her face and arms" (51) — or, in the case of Flo's once "tall smooth-skinned" mistress, a "bony and spotted" woman on her death-bed (44). Immaculateness, where we still find it, may be no more than deathly pallor: the scalp of Addie Morrison's dying mother, for instance, is "white as marble, white as soap" (75) — a whited temple, or sepulchre, as elsewhere in Munro.[21] And any vital gold remaining in such a temple is only the "yellowish" (88) cast of the failing Bill Morrison, or of Rose's father looking like something carved out of yellow soap. Soon the latter will be installed in a larger form of the same temple: a hospital with "yellowing curtains" (not to say "spotty basins" [53]), where decay and ritual purity share the same blood-lessness.

III: Pairs

The world we have just been seeing may be a place of contraries, but as imagined by Mrs. Jordan and the Book of Exodus it remains simple in one way, since its story is a straightforward melodrama of ferocious tyrants and fleeing victims. At the same time I have noted something odd about Mrs. Jordan: she is a typical Israelite in my sense, putting all things Egyptian behind her, and yet an Egyptian Isis as well. To deal with the paradox here we can best go back to our forms of narrative (tragic, as usual) and ask how an Exodus heroine fares in terms of each. If she did not manage any escape at all, even temporarily, we would have a linear story moving directly to death. Even Lois does better than that, as we have seen — she goes for her ride; so in a sense does Edie, and so, certainly, does Mrs. Jordan herself as she plunges along the Jericho Road. Yet these rides, bound for glory as they may be, only lead to returns, and the result is the bitterness that, in the end, consumes almost all the Exodus heroines. "Thanks for the ride!" yells Lois in a "loud, crude, female voice, abusive and forlorn" (58). In fact Lois has been a sulky girl throughout — like the moody teenage Rose or the "morose, messy, unsatisfactory" (52) Lydia Cooper, the woman who irritably dismisses Mr. Stanley.²² Even the jolly Stella proves venomous enough on the subject of Catherine, and is irked in spite of herself when she discovers the picture left behind by David. As for Mrs. Jordan, she comes wearily back from the hopeful sales trips, muttering lines about the door out that is also the door in; and at the end her sarcasm is worthy of Lois — she might, she snaps, spend Uncle Bill's token bequest on Bibles.²³

If we still have only a cyclical picture here, a typological one will show us even more fully how exodus can miscarry. The clearest example is perhaps that in "Five Points," where Brenda's summer affair seems to be ending in a quarrel: instead, the quarrel throws the lovers together again — and by the same token shows the affair to be like Brenda's marriage, just as the dashing Neil has come to remind her of her husband Cornelius. Other Exodus heroines, no doubt, seem more fortunate than Brenda. Mrs. Jordan, for all her rancour, would at least claim to have done as she wanted, and Stella in "Lichen" has an excellent right to such a claim: in a helter-skelter way not unlike Mrs. Jordan's own, she fixes up her house, turns literary, and is satisfied, even buoyant about her new life, "as if this was what she'd wanted to do all along" (33). But the more we look at this renovated Stella, the more we see a complacent Egyptian who has always been there — "Lichen" can be read as an Egyptian story for just this reason. When Stella comes on David's photograph, then, we do not feel simply that her exodus has failed, but that it has been compromised in its chosen goal: the new land she has wanted is an old one, as David's mockery attests. The case of another achiever, Mrs. Jordan's brother Bill Morrison, is different again. In the first place, Bill has some circling of his own to report:

> He began a long story, with complicated backtracking and correcting himself on details, about buying and selling houses. Buying, selling, buying, building, rumors, threats, perils, safety. . . . (88)

In the process he becomes an American success-story, complete with an expensive car and glamorous wife: there can be no doubt whatever that he has arrived. Where he differs from his sister, or even Stella, is in his overt choice of "Nile" for a bride and the United States for his Promised Land — an Egyptian one, as I have suggested, in the Canadian imagination. Bill, then, may not seem to be fleeing from Egypt at all: yet in his own way he too is escaping a failed land, seeking the freedom of a better one. And in its more deadly way Bill's nemesis is not unlike Stella's. The fat man who buys all the sweets in town remains hungry in the end — indeed his fatness is itself hunger, for the cancer destroying Bill is his own prosperity. We have seen him to be a snake dying in a mealbag, and we even find him longing for the poverty in which he was born, seeing it now as a blessing rather than a failure.

Bill can be set beside other successful men in these stories. We have just seen Neil the swaggering construction-worker; earlier we met Lawrence the hustling contractor in "Dulse"; Billy Pope the butcher in "Half a Grapefruit" has at least graduated from living in a slaughterhouse to living over the store, and is as proud of his new car as the other Bill of his new wife. George in "Thanks for the Ride" is somewhat different — he comes of a well-heeled family in the first place — but he has the same crude expansiveness as the others, and it is interesting to see how close his world-view is to Billy Pope's: girls as seen by George are "pigs" (47) hanging for customers. And yet George is not really a winner — even in his teens he is starting to show wrinkles, and for all his advantages he is easily "touchy and dissatisfied" (46), baffled by a sense of not getting what is coming to him. Lawrence has the same edginess; so in the end does Neil Bauer, while Billy Pope complains about the car. In other words, we are once again finding Exodus frustration in the midst of success; and to return to its leading representative, we can note that Mrs. Jordan is not really so different from her brother. The one may take the Jericho Road, the other the road to Egypt, yet both are desperate seekers who find and do not find, journey and get nowhere. In fact there is an even more intense link between them that we will need to understand as well.

*

We can turn briefly here to a very different Exodus pair, Dick and Lois in "Thanks for the Ride." In a way these two make a satisfactory couple: they go on the ride of love together, and Dick later recalls what "we" did and felt. They are opposites too, of course, since for one thing Dick has a middle-class boy's education and chance of getting somewhere in the world, while Lois is a factory-girl trapped in a dying town. And now we can ask a question that has not really come into focus so far: does their oppositeness amount to opposition? What do they feel toward each other, and, more actively, what do they do to each other? At first we see nothing more than indifference; then Dick makes a needling remark, Lois slaps him — and they kiss and make love. Since repulsion and attraction are like the otherness and sameness we have been considering, we have here a new form of our typological paradox: hate is also love. And while it may be ordinary enough for two youngsters on a date to squabble and then embrace, the Exodus stories have the same drama in more threatening forms, ones that societies generally hedge with strong taboos. Bill Morrison and his sister, once again, have been enemies from the days when he "tortured" (77) her in the barn, and yet they were never simply enemies: while her mother will not say quite what happened, Del comes to realize that it must have been sexual, love as well as hate. When, many years later, the dying brother comes to the sister again, we have no difficulty in sensing their old animosity; but as Mrs. Jordan listens to Bill's exploits, Del perceives in her "a mixture of disapproval and participatory cunning" (87). Bill and Addie are still intimates.

Another version of this intimacy is a strange bond between the old and the young. The earlier Exodus stories tend to be the simpler ones, in this respect as in others — in "Thanks for the Ride," for instance, the older people of Mission Creek are hardly more than obstacles. In

"Princess Ida," however, we will be finding matters more complicated, and in "Half a Grapefruit" the mutual engagement of different generations comes strongly to the fore: here, more centrally than in any other Exodus story, we see something that needs close consideration, the love-hate between a parent and child, specifically a father and daughter. In the first place, we had better remind ourselves just how high-handed the Exodus fathers can be. Addie Morrison's father forbids her to leave home; in her later history she meets the more refined but not less oppressive Dr. Comber, "very frail, courteous, and as it turned out, dictatorial" (73) — indeed her life and imagination are full of such men. Stella's father commands deference in his own way, still authoritative at ninety-three; Rose's is the kind of man before whom a daughter bows like the children passing Charlie Buckle in "The Flats Road." There is even a sense in which this father's power, like that of the initiatory god, increases as he grows more helpless. At the same time the helplessness is quite real: these father figures are aging men and some are like Uncle Bill, dying ones. If, as I have suggested, the death that brings the Exodus father down is the growing life of a new generation, what will this mean in our present terms?

When Rose's father is to go to the hospital from which he will not return, Billy Pope offers his car to "run him down" (46). Billy's sympathy seems genuine enough, and we might not sense any double meaning here were he not one of Munro's butchers — with a name, moreover, that we have connected with the dismemberment of a paternal order in church and state. What is plain in any case is the increasing defiance of the father on the part of both Flo and Rose, matched by the same kind of thing in other families — Addie Morrison's intense resentment of both her parents, for example, or Bill Morrison's need to break away from home. And while some of these situations may again be ordinary ones, we should reconsider the Great Books in the background of both "Princess Ida" and "Half a Grapefruit." *Antigone, Hamlet, The Merchant of Venice,* and *Macbeth* all have to do not only with violence, but with the violence of generational struggles in families; *The Republic* and *Das Kapital* have to do with the violent enforcing or unseating of a paternal kind of order. At Mrs. Jordan's intellectual party, similarly, one of the games involves Julius Caesar: a dictator like Dr. Comber and another victim of virtual parricide. When, accordingly, we hear of Rose reciting Lady Macbeth as the others prepare to run her father down, the implication seems clear. It seems equally so when we meet a woman wringing her "big red hands" (52) in one of Flo's anecdotes; and we can note that in "Dulse" Lydia Cooper's lover — middle-aged and seemingly well-enthroned — carries the name "Duncan."

Putting together one hint and another, then, we can form a picture of a father being cut down; and in "Half a Grapefruit" we can imagine his daughter as an assassin. In other stories we do not catch anyone quite so red-handed, but there are repeated indications that highly placed men, especially, are brought down by women, especially, in an attendant relation to them — daughters or mothers perhaps, or wives playing either role. Billy Pope himself complains about the unreliable service he is getting from "her"; and while he means his car, Bill Morrison's corresponding "she" is his wife Nile, who — in Mrs. Jordan's view at least — has married him for a meal ticket and is looking forward to his death. In "Dulse" the Lydia who once did homage to Duncan speaks sharply to the aged Mr. Stanley — in spite of the fact that she has put herself in a ministrant's role to him. And just as Lady Macbeth looms behind Rose, so behind Lydia there looms the formidable Willa Cather: "she sounds a proper bitch" (57), thinks Lydia, not meaning to mean herself as well.

The imagery of violent cutting open, typical as we have seen of the Exodus world, attaches itself closely to the women I have been mentioning. When a "wing or knife" (91) flashes at the end of "Princess Ida," the outraged Mrs. Jordan seems one of its sources as well as objects. Mary McQuade has a fork thrown at rather than by her, but she gives as good as she gets, and in Mary's case invasion takes a more insidious form as well, one that may remind us again of cancer. For Mary, as we have seen, is a "practical nurse" (32), and saps others' power as much by her attendance as anything else. Flo is an important counterpart, absorbing the strength and authority of her dying charge. Another is Stella, who comes into her own at her father's nursing home and formerly impressed David with her ability to feed and absorb parties; Alice Kelling is herself a nurse who absorbed Chris Watters while tending his ruptured appendix. And so we come in a yet another way to the Lady Macbeth of Rose's quotation: someone who in spite of giving suck — or, we can say, in the process of it — unsexes herself to do the opposite.

*

But such a formidable woman does not simply unsex herself. Behind Mrs. Jordan is the Mrs. Morrison who wept and prayed when her husband, not to say her god, stayed away; it is because the daughter is secretly like the mother that she plays Isis, the goddess mourning a lost consort. Wandering through the world, Mrs. Jordan has put her faith in a series of men and institutions, generally of a paternal sort: Dr. Comber of the Great Books Club, as we have seen, or for that matter Mr. Jordan, who if chosen as a "gentleman" (80) must be among other things an unthreatening kind of father. In Mrs. Jordan's brother this oedipal attachment to a parent is much easier to make out. While Bill Morrison's adventures have included a series of Callies and Niles, all no doubt as ornamental as such names suggest, it is his mother whom he talks about, compulsively and devoutly, when confiding his deeper thoughts. Once his mother nursed him back to life; now she remains his "she" beyond any mere Nile.

In "Half a Grapefruit" there is no natural mother, and not much is said about Rose's brother Brian; we do, however, hear strange things about Rose and her father. The latter disapproves highly of his daughter's unseemliness; at the same time he takes a secret delight in her, and Rose, somehow aware of all this, would rather not think what it means — "she was as uneasy as he was, about the way their chords struck together" (46). Brenda in "Five Points" chafes at the overbearing Cornelius but is thrilled by the masterful Neil — who, as she remarks, has the same name. Lydia Cooper loves the middle-aged and patronizing Duncan beyond all reason; and we may even detect a comparable situation when Edie in "Thanks for the Ride" stays in the house of Dr. Peebles. The doctor, a kindly man, is almost a father to the girl he has taken in — not unlike Chris Watters, her gentlemanly suitor; and while the Peebles' well-appointed house is hardly Chris's temporary shelter, the word "Peebles" in fact means "tents."[24]

Not surprisingly, sexual attachment to a parent never becomes overt in these stories: what may be more so is avoidance of — or mere flirtation with — the other members of that parent's sex. Mrs. Jordan as Princess Ida once pulled back from an engagement; in later years she turns against Dr. Comber, and she has equally hard words for such males as the minister, Hitler, and God. In her intellectual progress we find much the same attaching and detaching; and if we turn to the men in these stories, we will find a number of them flirting in a more standard way. Chris Watters shifts from Alice Kelling to Edie and beyond, while some others here are philanderers pure and simple — Duncan in particular boasts a list of women long enough for Don

Giovanni. Where we do find intense devotion it is often towards one's own sex, and here Mrs. Jordan can help us again. In the first place there is her curious loyalty to the mother she so deeply resents — for while the final knife-flash is among other things Addie Morrison cutting Mrs. Morrison open, the daughter has also, in effect, gone doggedly on with the mother's evangelism. More obviously there is her worship of the luminous Miss Rush, the embodiment of a femininity she cannot accept in herself. Flo, while unable to conceive homosexuality,[25] wants to say good-bye to the lady who gave her the satin gloves; Del at a gawky age dreams of the beautiful Pat Mundy in a similar role. In a rather different vein, "Dulse" reminds us pointedly that Willa Cather lived with a woman; and while Mr. Stanley, it seems, "wouldn't know what to do" (48) with the girls at the Ocean Wave, he not only venerates Willa Cather but has been devoting himself to a shadowy male figure — perhaps a brother or relative, but perhaps a lover.

One further step here will enable us to see this incestuous world with the complexity we are going to need. Attempting to destroy Osiris, the great adversary Seth always works with confederates. In one strange episode he is even helped by his sister Isis;[26] and while Munro may or may not have this detail in mind, Seth does seem to be the "Egyptian god with four letters" (91) whom Del Jordan confuses with Isis when her mother is doing a crossword puzzle — no other god in the Osiris cycle fits.[27] In any case she has known a Seth of her own in her brother Bill, the "evil, bloated, cruel" boy (77) who once did things she will not recall: and here too we have found a surprising confederacy.[28] Indeed Mrs. Jordan's world, full as it is of dictators, seems full of conspiracies as well — real or imaginary, against her or including her. The same thing can be said of the Exodus world more generally:[29] if, for instance, Rose's father must go to the hospital, we find Billy Pope, Flo, and Rose — allies whatever their resentment of each other — making joint plans to send him on his way. Elsewhere in these stories the opposition of one and many appears in an almost schematic form, for the harmony we found in the central world is giving way again to primal conflict. In the initiatory world we saw three young men attacking the patriarchal Edward "Tyde." In "Dulse," where Willa Cather makes a kind of rock of ages for Mr. Stanley, not only does Munro find a way to mention *Shadows on the Rock*, but Mr. Stanley himself is shadowed by the mocking alliance of three workmen, young, middle-aged, and old — to whom, as a group, we can add the brooding Lydia Cooper.[30]

IV: Stories

Having seen something of Exodus characters and their configura-
tions, we can turn now to what happens in these stories as stories:
and for simplicity's sake it will be best to take a single type of character
as central. At this stage the best choice is the failing and usually aged
man — the dying Osiris, we can say — partly because his story will
complement that of the younger refugee with which we began, and
partly because he helps us to bring together some of the most complex
stories in the group: "Dulse," "Lichen," and the Exodus chapters in
the two novels. Any Exodus protagonist is bound on a journey,
whether into life or death; any will stop for temporary refuge of some
kind; and in the case of the doomed man, whatever his physical
movements, refuge means the care of a nurse or nurse-like hostess.
Mrs. Jordan and Stella and the proprietors of the guest-house in
"Dulse" all offer hospitality, as does Lydia Cooper on her motherly
side. Flo of course plays nurse outright, and in the process can show
us all the nurse's ambiguity. If "safety [lies] with Flo" (45), the house
she now keeps is a refuge; if she is an assassin, safety lies in getting
out — if only to another house of the dying, a hospital.[31]

Within the nurse's containment, Osiris goes through the inflation
followed by collapse that we find in any Munro story. In "Princess
Ida" Bill Morrison first arrives in triumph and commandeers treats;
David in "Lichen" — a somewhat anomalous Osiris in any case[32] —
takes more explaining, but we easily recognize his manic exhilaration
as he nears the point of displaying the "lichen" photograph first to
the shockable Ron and then to the unamused Stella. Even Rose's ailing
father — or Rose's father especially — reaches a high point: ensconced
in his bedroom upstairs and calling out demands, he in one sense
reigns over his household as never before. In so doing he of course
unites it in his service; at the same time it seems that he is usually
alone in the bedroom. In other words, this man who rules others also
removes himself from them, becoming one of our single figures set
against many. Bill Morrison leaves his wife and sister to go shopping;
David leaves Catherine or has a lone interview with Stella's father.
This latter — of whom David himself is an unwitting counterpart —
makes an emblem for all the fated gods in these stories: obsequiously
attended in the Home above the lake, he is by the same token isolated,
his throne a solitary wheelchair on a back porch.

It is just this majestic isolation that puts the god in the power of his
enemies: Stella's father, strapped into his chair, is totally dependent

on helpers, as of course is Rose's.[33] Another iconic figure, Duncan in the background story of "Dulse," sits grandly in his high-rise apartment with its "one great, ugly armchair" (54) — and of course commands a whole company of enamoured women, not to say others who crave his society but are excluded from the apartment; yet we also have a glimpse of this tin woodman's own need,[34] and perhaps he is not as different as he seems from Mr. Stanley on his camp stool, worshipping Willa Cather from outside her house on the rock.[35] In the case of Rose's father there is nothing covert about the role of suppliant: things have come to the point where Flo answers his calls or not as she pleases. Meanwhile Flo — or rather the squabbling confederacy of Flo, Rose, and Billy Pope — is preparing his removal.

Now the god descends to the worshippers who are also his executioners. Rose's father appears in the kitchen at the bottom of the stairs, looking like one of Munro's sacrificial idols, an animal carved in soap. In our present terms we can see this appearance either as solitude yielding to community or as an attended god becoming an increasingly isolated victim: but in any case the earlier situation is reversing itself, as it does in each of these stories. In "Images," we will remember, Ben Jordan first brandishes the trapped muskrat, and is then himself trapped and taken off to Joe Phippen's den. What David in "Lichen" flourishes is a photograph of his girl-friend Dina, looking much like another furry and mutilated rodent; then David too is trapped, if less obviously than Ben. For not only is the earthy Dina a "witch" (42) after the airy Catherine, but David by his very flashing and confidentiality is surrendering to Stella — as is Bill Morrison to his sister when he confides in her. Later, we notice, David gives the photograph to Stella for safe-keeping.

Just at the point of reversal in "Half a Grapefruit" comes a core event that concentrates all this collapsing superiority: Rose's father drinks whisky with Billy Pope. It is a moment of trust and betrayal — for we are finding a third-phase counterpart of the initiatory story of covenant here; seen in other terms, it is a moment of intense communion in which we also feel the singling out of a scapegoat. We can sense the same yes-and-no in the details of the scene: the whole family are present, but girls like Rose are not allowed to have whisky. Nor is a boy like Brian — when he begs, Flo laughingly slides her glass (she has one too) behind her Egyptian bread-box. With a little variation and distribution, the same scene occurs in "Lichen": David, Catherine, and Stella share the latter's mead, but Catherine is quite happy to see David leave; and during the washing up Stella in turn

slips the leftover mead behind the blender, keeping it for herself and
away from the wobbly Catherine.[36]

*

And so we have descended into a Lair, with the usual dark associations; but Lairs can also be, or lead to, places of comfort. What we
find in the stories we are now concerned with, either as an aspect of
the central communion or in some more distributed form, is a last
supper — quite a sociable one in each case. At the same time we may
find what Munro's stories also tend to have at this stage, someone
withdrawing from sociability into private vision: and here again the
relation between the many and the one is crucial. After supper in
"Dulse" Mr. Stanley retires to his camp chair on the hill — the kind
of figure we have seen enthroned is now performing an intense,
solitary vigil which in the circumstances may remind us of Gethsemane. Later in the evening Lydia retires to her own kind of vigil, going
upstairs, locking her door, and lying alone in the dark with her
thoughts. Such a solitude can itself be a communion — Mr. Stanley
is with Willa Cather, Lydia is thinking of the various men she has
known and most keenly of old Vincent. In "Lichen" it is rather the
painful aspect of solitude that we are made to see: having left Stella
and Catherine to do the dishes, David endures an agony in a
phone-booth, trying desperately to get through to the elusive Dina.

Meanwhile — where there is no temporal distribution — the
company itself finishes its supper and turns to games. Some of these
have intriguing titles: in "Dulse" it is skat or "thirty-one" (45) —
three and one — that gets played; in Flo's kitchen, even more
suggestively, it is "euchre" (53). And along with the food and games,
in both cases, goes something else typical of this structural point, the
talk that is a feature of the Exodus world generally and is especially
prominent here. For a fuller sense of what is happening, it may be
useful to compare these stories with "Labor Day Dinner," closely
allied and coming at a corresponding if later stage in its collection.
Here too we have the account of an end-of-season visit leading, as its
title indicates, to an evening meal; here too the conversation during
and beyond this meal is reported at considerable length — we can in
fact make a whole cycle out of it if we want to. Notably it arrives at
the topic of love, complete with a quotation from Paul;[37] by the same
token it is suggestive of a Platonic symposium and — most important
for our purposes — the discourse on love at the Last Supper, though

the fine talk about long-suffering and cathedrals also conceals a sharp power struggle. Again we find someone who draws apart, if not by actually leaving the room: Roberta is watching and pondering, taking on a remoteness that soon turns her husband himself into a yearning worshipper. Rose in "Half a Grapefruit," while making a fourth at euchre, withdraws into her musings in the same way. Her father, like Mr. Stanley after his vigil, is dozing: perhaps a failure to watch and pray, perhaps its own kind of vigil.

For of course Rose's father is waiting for something. To invoke yet another story outside the Exodus group, in "Memorial" we hear of a "vigil with . . . biscuits" (221) — the night watch, at once intensely private and intensely social, kept by Eileen with her mother as the latter prepares to break the news of the father's death. It is the same kind of watch that is being kept by the company in "Labor Day Dinner": as they fall in and out of their chatter, what haunts them is "overpopulation, ecological disaster, nuclear disaster, this and that disaster" (157) — the "something black" (149) of which Roberta has already felt a premonition. The same black something, concealed in different ways yet always known to be present, looms for more special victims in "Princess Ida" and "Half a Grapefruit": those who are soon to die of cancer. And when Flo as a child hid with her playthings in the granary, as Rose remembers, the something was looming for her too — she expected "death to slice the day" (53). Munro's wording here not only points to the sliced grapefruit epitomizing the story, but establishes an important biblical connection that I have only touched on so far. In "Images" Joe Phippen slices with his hatchet, and darkness comes near mid-day — the darkness, Munro hints, of the Crucifixion.[38] The Last Supper (as John's gospel pointedly notes[39]) and the vigil at Gethsemane both take place in the dark of night, near the other extreme of the daily cycle; and behind all these lies the crucial event of the Exodus itself — the death-dealing passage of the Lord at midnight, preceded by the Passover meal.[40] The last suppers of Munro's Exodus stories are generally evening meals — Billy Pope in fact stays the night, as do Bill and Nile in "Princess Ida." It is "after midnight" (50), and so not very long after it, when Lydia locks herself in her bedroom.[41] We are not told exactly when Valerie's supper ends in "Labor Day Dinner," but it is certainly late when the conversation dies away, yielding to "the yawning, the pushing back of chairs, the rather sheepish and formal smiles, the blowing out of candles" (158). A children's rhyme about a candle followed by a "chopper" (155) has already floated into the conversation; then, as George and his family come to a crossroad on their drive home, an unlit car suddenly passes before them like a "huge, dark flash" (159).[42]

And so the vigil has led to a final encounter: that, certainly, is what we can call it when it takes a sexual form as in "Thanks for the Ride." After Lois's mother has slyly said "Night!" (52), and the riders in the car have shared some home brew from an old woman's farmhouse, Dick and Lois go off by themselves, do their quarrelling and kissing, and presently — at about midnight — make love with mystical fervour in a lonely barn.[43] The lovers in "Five Points" go through essentially the same process, though at the end of a season rather than a day: following a drink and a fight and a solitary walk for Brenda, they find themselves drawn compulsively together again. And there we will have to leave them for the present, as the story itself does. Later in this chapter I want to deal more adequately with the question of just what has happened, or whether anything has happened at all yet — the question, in effect, of what may be meant by "Thanks for the ride." But there is another matter that we must inspect more closely here: the endless conversing that goes with communing in these stories.

V: Wisdom

The talk that we have found around supper tables and elsewhere is much concerned with the curing of disabilities, the recovering of mislaid goods, the solving of world problems: it is Exodus talk, in other words, looking for ways out of loss and death. Wisdom will be needed to find these ways, but then wisdom is a preoccupation of these stories — an Exodus kind of wisdom, once again, in that its purpose is not to consolidate but to save and release. For a presiding figure here we can turn back to Isis, the seeker and the revealer of mysteries: as we have seen, Isis is explicitly linked with Mrs. Jordan, the woman who once dispensed "notions" (79) in Owen Sound and in later life offers her encyclopaedia for the salvation of the farmers. Nor is she the only Isis about, for other women here have mental powers that may be quite uncanny. Willa Cather is a wonder to Mr. Stanley, while "Madam Stella, the celebrated mind reader" (54) not only knows David's thoughts but somehow foresees the lichen that will appear at the end of the story. The "fey" (40) Catherine, who once found her way by a sixth sense to the Book of Kells,[44] has similar premonitions: in fact this latter seems to have learned what she knows from a fortune-teller, while her replacement Dina is for David a kind of witch. In "Half a Grapefruit" Flo takes the same view of a woman in the divination business — a clairvoyant.[45]

But while wisdom is everywhere in these stories — among the women especially though also a number of the men[46] — it takes a puzzling variety of shapes. Often it is a very intellectual or at any rate bookish affair. We think of Mrs. Jordan, of course — Princess Ida; but Mrs. Jordan's daughter can at one age recite presidents, countries, explorers, and much more without a hitch; Stella is a writer, Lydia Cooper a poet and editor; and rising in Lydia's background is the majestic Willa Cather herself.[47] Elsewhere we need to distinguish between the intellectual and the clever. In "Dulse" the high-brow writer Duncan is one thing, the contractor Lawrence another: as a self-made man without much formal education, the latter is closer to the shrewd, enterprising Bill Morrison, whose opinion of encyclopaedias is that there is not much money in them. Flo, while playing more or less a Mrs. Jordan's role in "Half a Grapefruit," makes no claim to education at all — "*I* don't know anything" (49), she snorts, contrasting herself with the learned doctors. What Flo does know (and it seems the doctors do not) is how to handle her husband: for this able and determined woman has her own way of being wise.

Now we need a further distinction. Intellectual or otherwise, the wisdom of a Flo or Mrs. Jordan or Bill Morrison is a matter of will — lacking in subtlety or sensitivity, perhaps, but by no means lacking in thrust. If people like Duncan or Lydia are rather more fastidious, they too have a way of trampling on toes; so, we hear, did Willa Cather. Others are much less forceful: the indolent Fern Dogherty, for instance, or the wispy Catherine. These last, as it happens, are also not very intellectual — the one can hardly remember which opera she is listening to, the other never reads a newspaper; and in fact there are characters in these stories who are simply unintelligent. The beautiful Nile is a dummy, a woman who can hardly get from the car to the house; Edie in "How I Met My Husband," if not so helpless, is the least intelligent in a grade-passing sense of all Munro's protagonists, a girl who wants out of school where Addie or Flo wants into it. Simplest of all, perhaps, is Ruby Carruthers in the Three Jokers anecdote, the girl who cowers uncomprehendingly under the porch. What is strange is that these too, in their own way, can be figures of wisdom. Nile may be the significant exception, the privileged woman who does not need to know, but Edie comes as she must to a sure if unreasoned sense of her situation: she knows that her airman has left her, and that she must choose one life over another. We could even say the same thing of Ruby, for when the Jokers have treated her more or less as another threesome treat Rose's father, she knows what she can claim as surely as Edie knows what she must do.

To simplify somewhat, we have been moving from a high wisdom of idea down to a low wisdom of experience or instinct — taking, in fact, a course like the one we took with establishment and its enemies in the previous chapter; and once again this movement has led from the honoured to the despised. In the Exodus world, however, the despised is much more closely linked with the "filthy" (63), to use Alice Kelling's word for Edie — with the intolerable and the unmentionable. As we have seen, this may be a matter of guilt: Lady Macbeth tries in vain to clean her hands of blood, and the clairvoyant in "Half a Grapefruit," wringing her own red hands, seems to know something more terrible than the neutral facts she reveals to her clients. But even deeper than guilt, perhaps, is shame, the witness to creaturely need and weakness that was before any law and that we have already considered in its initiatory context. Shame is what Rose feels for being Rose, a teenage abomination in her father's eyes; it inheres in her father's own stained underwear, or the used Kotex pad mysteriously displayed at the high school;[48] it inheres in poverty and in illness. When it speaks to Rose from under the bridge — in voices that are "wistful, so delicately disguised she could not tell if they were boys' or girls' " (39) — it does so to remind her that she knows these things.

*

What seems immune to this knowledge is something Del perceives in her mother, "her innocence, her way of not knowing when people were laughing" (81). It is "innocence" again, if in a somewhat different form, that Dick sees in the brash George, impervious to the "sly and sad and knowing" townsfolk with their "slovenly, confiding voice[s]" (51).[49] But such innocence is not wholly innocent: that is why it can be so embarrassing to watch, and why it can be parodied so lethally by the voices under the bridge.[50] Mrs. Jordan's "brisk and hopeful and guileless" (81) manner covers the fact that she has known what the people of Mission Creek know; and if she is ready to proclaim her origins, chamber-pots and all, there are things she does not proclaim, such as what really happened in the barn. In fact this woman who cannot afford "shyness and self-consciousness" (67) hides a good deal of both: she is like other bold people in these stories afflicted with "nerves" (52), as Flo calls them — Bill Morrison with his gnawing dissatisfaction, David with his compulsive womanizing, Stella with her irritability, Rose with her fits of brazenness and terror. The outrageous Flo was herself a frightened and bewildered girl once, not unlike the exploited Ruby or the abandoned Edie: if she waves her husband's underwear with no thought of Rose's distress, it must be because she has cut herself off from the same distress in herself.

We have already seen this cutting off in other contexts: what we can say now is that the cancer beneath the skin of the Exodus world is also hidden knowledge, and that what has hidden it is the more slicing kind of knowledge — or concealment of knowledge — that is the other killer here. For if Egypt maintains itself by a kind of oblivion, escape from Egypt demands ignorance in a more wilful form, one that suggests cloven rather than uncleavable fruit. There is no mistaking the Israelite puritanism of a Mrs. Jordan or a Flo; when Rose goes to the school across the bridge, she similarly finds an obsession with Health and Guidance, Canada's Food Rules, and above all segregation — of town and country, girls and boys, the clean and the unclean. She herself, in claiming to eat half a grapefruit for breakfast, is attempting segregation from those of supposedly lower tastes and incomes; she is attempting it again at home when she hides her adolescent uncertainties from Flo. And when we find Mrs. Jordan barking "What picture? *What picture?*" (71), knowledge is being concealed from the knower herself. Mrs. Jordan, it seems, has put the picture of the shepherd-girl out of her mind; she has equally managed to mislay the scarf given her by Miss Rush; she cannot recall the butterfly or produce the name of the Egyptian god, though like Del reciting presidents she knows she knows it.[51] Her "reckless, hurrying" (81) manner is a clue here: clutching at new pieces of knowledge, Mrs. Jordan gets rid of old ones the way she knocks ink bottles off the desk.

If we return now to the "vigil with the biscuits" (221) in "Memorial," it is the same concealment of knowledge that we will see there. When Eileen sits with her mother at midnight, the latter does not tell her terrible news — she will do so only later, like Mrs. Jordan blurting out the fact of Uncle Bill's cancer some days after his visit. And while Eileen's mother hides her knowledge by means of food rather than words, communion meals elsewhere, as we have seen, are symposiums in the verbal sense as well — feasts of talk and speculation. What is dished up at these is an extraordinary hodge-podge: a farrago of gossip, tales, forebodings, and theories, alternately malicious, wistful, paranoid, or simply frivolous. And in all of this something seems missing — the answer to the "crossword" (91), perhaps, that Mrs. Jordan cannot recall. Perhaps the talk here is what we have often found in Munro's stories: a telling meant to keep something from being told.

Concealment has its uses: in the form of sheer repression it gives Mrs. Jordan her unbeatable energy, and it makes cannier sorts like the child in "Images" "powerful with secrets" (43). Stella in "Lichen" is even better stocked: she contains not only her own secrets but David's, which in turn include an entire world of Exodus obsessions, "a weight not just of his sexual secrets but of his middle-of-the-night speculations about God, his psychosomatic chest pains, his digestive sensitivity, his escape plans . . ." (54). As a result Stella has David where she wants him — he will never again be easy in her presence — while she herself is free to be a sunbeam. Or she might be something else that insecurity wants to be or have or worship: an authoritative father, a sibylline Willa Cather, a beautiful Nile with no snow on her shoes. But even Stella cannot quite escape the thing that is tearing and devouring the Exodus world. There is the clean knowledge and the filthy, the knowledge that must conceal and the knowledge that rises from its concealment; and there is a deadly cleavage between the two. In a world where wisdom is essential to salvation, it also seems that wisdom is sick.

*

Where, then, is the wisdom that can heal wisdom? The Exodus world has a number of doctors, as well as links with others elsewhere; and yet these are often challenged. Flo, who bows to medical expertise, also has words about the "do-nothing doctor" (46). Lydia Cooper, having ranged widely in her meditation, ends by recalling a confession to a psychiatrist — indeed her meditation itself is virtually another such confession, and like the earlier one does not seem to do her much good. If we recall the various inset tales of the Exodus stories, we will find still other questionable authorities: not only the clairvoyant but a faith-healer and, in Bill Morrison's reminiscences, his own homilizing mother, the former schoolteacher. Rose's mind runs on her father: someone who has known her thoughts and called for repentance, but in the end is powerless and inscrutable — only a dying man.

We might characterize all these people by saying that their wisdom comes, as it were, from the Encyclopaedia; and we might characterize this latter by saying that its accumulation of knowledge is contained by a "sedate dark green binding" (65). Such bindings need not be old-fashioned: the school at the end of "Half a Grapefruit" gets its green walls from modernization, and Nile, who paints her nails the same colour — "Nile green" (87) in fact — is even more fashionable. But another institution with green walls, the Home in "Lichen," is a place for the dying, and Rose's father goes to his death wearing "a dark oily sort of green" (50) — the Osirian green, if we like. For green, as we have noted, is the colour of Nature in Munro as elsewhere, and death is what Nature leads to. The same thing can be said of the natural wisdom that a Mrs. Jordan finds in the Encyclopaedia — its limitations are like the "blind green" (53) walls of the school, which might as well be the green blinds elsewhere in Munro.[52] Yet there is something else to be said here. Del finds the Encyclopaedia a treasury of stories and pictures; and stories and pictures have their own kind of wisdom, if we can take them in the right way. When the butterfly worked its way out of the cocoon on Easter Day, Mrs. Jordan's mother urged her son to take the event as a sign: we can follow her advice without remaining in the cocoon of her own literal beliefs, or her daughter's.

The more usual way of understanding appears in a couple of the tales told in Flo's kitchen. In one of these a man gets his hearing back from a faith-healer; he then has it taken away again, since in answer to questions about hearing and believing he has replied "what in?" (51). Such a man, it seems, can only see belief as commitment to an objective "something": no doubt that is the faith-healer's under-standing as well, so that his horror only comes from the patient's ignorance as to which something to believe in. The subject of another anecdote recovers his wallet through the advice of Flo's clairvoyant, only to regret the whole business when he finds that the money inside has been chewed up by a dog. Here we evidently have a story about valuation rather than faith, yet the underlying issue seems to be the same again — paper money is all this man wants, just as other of the clairvoyant's customers want "rings and wills and livestock" (51). Bill Morrison, to return to Mrs. Jordan's world, wants real estate; Mrs. Jordan herself is less materialistic, but in the end her notions are much like his speculations. Both brother and sister see the world in terms of things to be acquired, both endlessly buy and sell in one sense or another — both, of course, knew as children what it was not to have things. Mrs. Jordan's children want things in turn: in a country store they might even get "bags of a certain golden-brown candy, broken in chunks like cement and melting almost immediately on the tongue" (68). We can remember here the manna gathered by the Israelites in the wilderness; we may even recall the body of the golden corn-god himself (a substitute, we note, would be "cold pop").[53] In its materiality any such body is going to break and disappear, as is any abstract idea; to take it as a sign, however, would be to recover the lost in a new form. It would be like joining the poor in spirit,[54] a group of whom Mrs. Jordan takes a dim view but who gain an inheritance that she does not.

Perhaps this inheritance is what is really being offered her in the bequest from by her dying brother. In itself Bill's gift is virtually nothing, like the gift of dulse left behind by Vincent or the "lichen" left behind by David. And there is more lichen in these stories: Rose is "bushy" (46), Lydia Cooper "messy" (52), Mrs. Jordan herself sprouts "little wild grey-brown tufts and thickets" (80) of hair,[55] while Edie according to Alice Kelling is a similar embarrassment, a "little rag" (63).[56] More ladylike tissues — such as the scarf given by Miss Rush — are ultimately the same rag again; so, in a stern view, are the Great Books, including the one on which Mrs. Jordan might spend her legacy. But perhaps one could find a better sort of text in these shameful things: a word that Mrs. Jordan cannot remember "to save my soul" (91). Lydia is strangely warmed by the dulse, an ancient form of life that has endured the sea; lichen, similarly, has endured the sun, "mysteriously nourished on the rocks" (55) like pilgrims in the wilderness. If rough-haired Mrs. Jordan lives in a faded beach-house, and Stella on a lake-side cliff exposed to the sun and wind, they too might be nourished in a way they cannot yet understand.[57]

B. PASSION

I: Introduction

Mrs. Jordan is not the only person to be found in the neighbourhood of Jericho. In the third part of "Baptizing" her daughter — another Jordan, of course — falls in love with Garnet French of Jericho Valley, a born-again Baptist, and proceeds to get a crucial baptizing herself. In the New Testament the rite of baptism recapitulates the Israelites' crossing of the Jordan, closely associated with the taking of Jericho; and since Jordan and Jericho at the end of the Israelites' journey echo the crossing of the Red Sea at its beginning, baptism is that earlier crossing as well. We are thus concerned with the Exodus again, now in its antitypical New Testament form; and in coming to the New Testament we can hardly stop with John the Baptist. John is the precursor of Jesus, the second Moses; John's baptism, like the Exodus itself, announces the greater baptism of — especially — the Passion, when a veil is broken and the dead walk free. In what follows I am going to use "Passion" as I have used terms like "Egypt" and "Exodus": as a term of convenience for a whole group of related stories, in some of which allusion to the Biblical Passion is very marked.

There is already, as we have seen, the hint of a terminal phase within the story of the Kingdom itself — a time of collapse and at least abortive departure: the Passion phase is in one view a repetition of this earlier one. Beyond the life of Jesus, the story of the Church and even the Apocalypse can be seen as further distribution of the same falling movement. Allusions to the latter event make an important element in stories like "Baptizing," "Simon's Luck," and "Executioners"; conversely, Munro's Apocalypse stories, as I will style them in the final chapter, have a certain amount in common with the Passion group, and where helpful I will be drawing on some of these later stories in the present discussion. Once again, the view we must take here is primarily the tragic one: just as the Exodus completes the death of Egypt, so the Passion phase completes that of the Kingdom — of Israel established in this world. In another view, of course, the coming of Jesus means a new kingdom, founded on better terms: but for the present we will have to see this recovery as a mere eddy in a downward-moving stream. And this will mean seeing, not only how the new kingdom has the distinctness that warrants our speaking of a new phase, but how it fails like its predecessor. If there is a sense in which Jesus's kingdom is not of the world, that will have to wait for a final chapter.

Since a Passion story can be so many things, it may also help us here to look briefly beyond our Israelite and Egyptian models. Since I have already compared our first and second phases to the first two of Eliot's *Four Quartets*, we can also note that *The Dry Salvages* is his quartet of the third phase. We find here the crossing of river, wilderness, and ocean; we also feel a presence new to Eliot's poem — the dark undergod who sometimes waits in patience and at other times breaks out in fury. We learn how all life comes to the judgment of the sea, a death of or by the same undergod; and watching this judgment we see another figure, whom we are going to find important, the *mater dolorosa* in her shrine on the promontory. In more general terms, the message of this quartet is one that we have already found in Exodus stories like "Princess Ida": we journey to escape, yet remain where we are. If we want to see the Passion phase more clearly as a story, we can turn to a couple of narrative epics. In Tennyson's *Idylls of the King* Arthur's great order is brought down by passion — here the adulterous love of Lancelot and Guinevere, the hate of Modred. Passion, accordingly, must be judged, being in itself a judgment on the world that has harboured it. Spenser's *Faerie Queene* has a much more elaborate structure, but again we find central books about the earthly empire that "Artegal" and his consort Britomart are working to establish; this is the world that, at least on its more instinctive level, is watched over by the smiling Venus, here the central goddess of natural concord and abundance. Then, and before the epilogue book of courtesy, comes the sombre book of justice, where both love and empire reach a crisis, and where everything that is merely betraying about natural love is judged in the person of the great whore Duessa.

*

I have just said that the terminal phase, while a downward movement as a whole, can contain its own cycle of awakening, triumph, and failure: we will need to be aware of this cycle immediately to make some necessary distinctions. For Munro's Passion stories present a much larger and more motley assortment than her Exodus ones, and we will accordingly have to do some sub-dividing as we did with the central group — or, in principle, could with any other. The major stories here can best be seen as forming a central cluster inside the Passion group itself: in their own way they show us the same "vigil with biscuits" that we saw at the heart of the major Exodus stories. Flanking this main sub-group are others somewhat less important for our present concerns. One of these makes an introduction to our new phase; the other contains stories of an elegiac character that not only complete the whole group's falling movement but merge with the phase beyond. A story like "Baptizing" poses a special problem, since its three parts take us through a complete cycle in little; yet since the longest and most terminal of its three phases — the Garnet French episode — is very much a "central" Passion story, I am going to put the whole of "Baptizing" with the main Passion group.

In my previous chapter we found the Lady "Dorothy" of "Changes and Ceremonies" receiving a mysterious communication in a rose garden, and Del receiving another from Frank Wales: the Judges stories, like an approaching vision in an individual story, herald the new life that will burst out in the central phase. Within the main body of that phase, we also found, a story like "Accident" has something of the same quality, with Ted Makkavala coming miraculously to offer himself to Frances. At the further end of the central phase we came to similar stories again — stories that, in a simple model, blend into the beginning of the terminal phase: and this onward tendency is what concerns us now. In "Pictures of the Ice," for instance, Karin receives her own mysterious communication, and from another vanishing Pied Piper. Even "Red Dress — 1946" manages in the end to be rather like "Changes and Ceremonies": a girl at a Christmas dance is one of the chosen after all, and gets a kiss of sorts.[58] We have seen this as repatriation — the heroine being brought back to normality — but there is another view to be taken here: for in these late central-phase stories as well a call to something new is sounding. Specially suggestive for our present purposes is "Jesse and Meribeth," in one view a reversing Mischief story ending with a rejected MaryBeth and a footloose Jessie; ironically, the same story echoes with hints of the New Testament, and particularly of the Annunciation and Nativity. Like Del in "Changes and Ceremonies" Jessie is a Lady Dorothy; what is more, the new life announced here is such as to draw us beyond the sheer worldliness of the central phase.

In "Lives of Girls and Women" Del ends no less brazen than the Jessie whom we have seen as a second-phase fall-back — Del's old world, I have suggested, is reasserting itself in the very way she lays claim to new ones. By contrast a strange gentleness appears in Naomi, who emerges from a bout of fever murmuring about the attentions of Dr. "Wallis" — another of Munro's "Wales" names, we can notice.[59] By the following chapter Naomi is Naomi again — her aspirations have been channelled in practical directions — but now Del herself is to take on a new seriousness; and this will have an uncertainty about it quite different from her old pseudo-assurance. The same change can be seen beginning in "The Found Boat," placed in its collection between "Tell Me Yes or No" and "Executioners." We have already noted the central phase here — in a boat called *Water Lily* or *Flood Queen*, in the brashness of the parading children — but now we should be aware of something else. The children ride their patched-up boat down the river to an outlying place, a derelict train station; and in the sexual uncovering that follows — with the naked Clayton squirting water onto Eva's breasts at the climax — we can sense not only an Art Chamberlain's exhibitionism but a new desire for intimacy. Earlier we find the girls putting away their pride — "relinquishing something, but not discontented" (129); we even find that Eva in a returning vision imagines Clayton as another Frank Wales, "speaking to her, out of his isolation, in such an ordinary peaceful taking-for-granted voice" (131).[60] No doubt there is a huge ineptness about the undressing itself, after which the boys run off and the girls league to deny the whole incident: yet the "pain" (137) at the end of the story — the girls' burden — marks both a humiliation and an awakening.

Something of the same kind is happening in "Sunday Afternoon," the story before "A Trip to the Coast" in *Dance of the Happy Shades*. An intelligent farmgirl called Alva gets a summer job as maid with the well-to-do Gannetts in town. It is not a very comfortable situation, for while Alva may be used to housework, her employers' opulent and consciously arranged world — one we have seen as typically central — seems strangely unreal to her. She feels uneasy, too, with both the high-flying Mrs. Gannett and the latter's husband, a more considerate but also more troubled and mysterious person; and above all she dreads the awkwardness and idleness of being with the family at an island summer cottage. Then a male cousin of the Gannetts kisses her, leaving her "grateful and expectant" (170): there is a reality here after all, if also a "humiliation" (171) like that of the girls in "The Found Boat." And the confidence Alva takes from this new knowledge is not that of a Jessie, though in some ways her story has been very similar:[61] rather, she is now more willing to go to the strange island, where she will give herself in ways she has never known.

A much later and subtler Annunciation story — to use that term — is "Eskimo," preceding "A Queer Streak" in *The Progress of Love*. "Mary Jo" is a hard-working secretary and mistress; the doctor she serves in both capacities is, as in "Sunday Afternoon," a conscientious, obscurely sad husband (if also a pompous one in this case) with another bustling wife. His Christmas present to his secretary, moreover, is a holiday in Tahiti — another visit to a strange pleasure-island — although Mary Jo, like Alva, would rather stay home. On the plane she sees something that disturbs her, a Métis man and an Eskimo woman first quarrelling and then reuniting in a sexual tenderness that shatters Mary Jo's tidy, busy little central-phase world. She is only an onlooker here: and yet, as becomes clear to the reader, she too is a cold "Eskimo" with a vocation of passionate love beyond any mere sexual arrangement with an employer. If her conscious mind does not quite recognize this vocation, we can see from her musings and her strange dream — to which we will have to return — that like Alva she is feeling the intimation of an unfamiliar new life. And like her earlier one, it has something to do with Dr. Streeter.

At roughly the same place in *Friend of My Youth* — between "Pictures of the Ice" and "Oh, What Avails" — we find the very suggestive and difficult "Goodness and Mercy." In some ways this is a story much like "Lives of Girls and Women" or "Jesse and Meribeth" again: a young heroine's fantasy about an intriguing older man proceeds, in a bizarre way, to realize itself. But here there is no accosting, much less rebuking, of the heroine; Averill's fantasy, moreover, materializes only as a story, so that at the end it is the fantasy again with which she is left. She is thus rather like Karin in "Pictures of the Ice," feeling "absolved and fortunate" (179) on receiving an ethereal gift. And like Karin she is able to take her place in the world, since — to invoke yet another story in the same neighbourhood — she now puts on the dress of womanhood: not exactly a red one, but of a related colour that we have met before, aubergine or eggplant.[62] Mary Fortune here is sharp-eyed, sharp-tongued "Bugs" Rogers: the mother who keeps Averill shy and restricted until the captain's annunciation liberates her.

What complicates this picture — in a way that I will try to deal with in the following chapter — is the extent to which "Goodness and Mercy" shows us the negative of its positive: all the ambiguity we have found in a threshold can be felt in this story about the crossing of a mirror-like ocean.[63] If we want to see Averill as escaping from Egypt, her mother no doubt makes as wily an Egyptian as the aunts at Jenkin's Bend, while in her official self she is none other than "June" Rogers the opera-singer.[64] The portly captain with his "peaceable authority" (167) may be something of an Egyptian himself, but for Averill he is also a liberating David blessed with "goodness and mercy." Unfortunately, these things are accompanied in her imaginings by "strenuous egotism, and straightforward triumph," not to say "a childish sort of gloating" (169). If the service of the Lord means this, Bugs's subversion starts to look appealing, like that of a Mrs. Fullerton; and her singing is something more — it brings "a revelation of kindness and seriousness" (168) in the light of which her relinquishing of the aubergine dress suggests an offering and a self-sacrifice.

"Goodness and Mercy" is thus in a way the contrary of "Eskimo," though both concern themselves with a mysterious stranger contemplated on a pleasure-trip. In the latter story, as I will argue later, Mary Jo is called to see what is kind and serious behind Dr. Streeter's high-handedness — or her own primness. Averill's captain, in himself a modest and decent enough man, seems fated to appear as the vehicle, or minister, of high-handedness itself, that of a God who does not care for *The Sound of Music* and in particular dislikes "Maria" (166). Conversely it is the recalcitrant — or plain nasty — Bugs through whose singing an annunciation of genuine goodness and mercy can be heard. One thing we notice in "Goodness and Mercy" is a Sandy or Jenkin — a young man who, as we learn from the captain, died and was buried at sea before the events of the story.[65] Since that time, we might say, nothing in the world has gone right: the captain in charge and the Bugs under his authority must be at odds, good must be lodged in bad and bad in good. When Averill, accordingly, opts for the captain by opting for normal maturity, she is also abandoning something precious, and will have to pay a price. In fact her later life seems jinxed: a love marriage fails, a second is to a man curiously like Bugs at her most objectionable. Yet — to return to our present concerns — Averill has heard a call; and if this is more ambiguous than the one heard by Karin, that itself can introduce us to Munro's Passion world, where we will find new life doomed by an old curse.

*

We can deal with the other two groups of Passion stories more briefly at this point. The next and largest contains stories dealing in a major way with the major Passion experience. Most typically this is a reaching out to life after all: following the collapse of earlier mischief, or even of love itself taken too much for granted, we find a shaken and deeply needy heroine seeking a deeper engagement — looking, as is said of one such woman, for "a messiah of the opposite sex."[66] The Passion chapters of the two novels belong here; the other stories that I will take as major are, above all, "Executioners" and "A Queer Streak" — about both of which I will have a good deal to say towards the end of this chapter. "A Trip to the Coast" is a bit different: certainly a story about life after all, but in a way that suggests a grim parody of "Goodness and Mercy." "May," wanting her own life, is held back by the ruthless grandmother who triumphs even in dying

— though in the meantime this grandmother has made her own attempt at life in the face of death, not only proposing a trip to California but even half-responding to a would-be saviour. Certain uncollected early stories can also be mentioned here: "The Idyllic Summer," for instance, which is obviously a fore-echo of the Garnet French story in "Baptizing." A much more important piece, "The Edge of Town," is too comprehensive to go easily into any one phase, much less sub-phase, but at the end it is clearly a Passion story, concluding with an unmistakable allusion to its biblical counterpart. In a way that Munro would hardly have allowed herself later, the hero directly quotes Christ's lament over Jerusalem; and when he suddenly leaves town his old store remains as an emblem of both Passion and Resurrection — "the boards were nailed crooked across the windows, and some of them have pulled loose in the wind" (379–80).

Other stories in this second group make a special little cluster of their own — what I am going to call the Caroline stories. The figure of that name makes her first published appearance as the wealthy, neurotic and sexually intricate heroine of Del's secret novel in "The Photographer." Much the same woman with the same name comes into "Angela," one of a projected series of Simon stories;[67] she then becomes the Caroline of the main anecdote in "Hard-Luck Stories" and advances into the foreground of "Differently" as Maya. "Mrs. Cross and Mrs. Kidd," written in a more parabolic vein, gives a crucial role to "Charlotte," a servant who proves a commanding lady — the other Carolines being ladies who play servant.[68] Often these stories do not seem especially typical of the Passion group — Douglas Reider in "Hard-Luck Stories" is not obviously a Passion hero, Georgia in "Differently" not obviously a Passion heroine. But the Carolines themselves are altogether of the Passion world. They are wealthy women, apart from Charlotte, with lackeying husbands on the one hand and lovers on the other drawn notably from the ranks of the unsuccessful and the artistic. Using their advantages to the full, they cause enormous mischief: and yet they are not simply Mischief heroines. As the Caroline of "The Photographer" will show most clearly, they are desperate — women driven wild by a need for love. Tragically, their need can hardly express itself except in reciprocal victor-and-victim games; and when they reach out more openly, they are crushed.

A last Passion group will recall the first one: in "The Spanish Lady" a journeying woman, very much a Mary, meets a strange man and receives — then and later — the annunciation of a new self and a new mission. But since the Spanish Lady, an older woman cast off by her husband, is living at the end rather than the beginning of passion, there is something to be said for keeping her story in a separate compartment. The other stories to be put here are those that, in their respective collections, border on the following Apocalypse group: assignment to one group or the other becomes, as often, somewhat arbitrary, and a good deal that needs saying about these late Passion stories can best wait for the following chapter. What is distinctive about them can be seen from "Rose Matilda" (the third part of "Oh, What Avails") in which the aging heroine surprises her long-term escort with a sudden bout of allurement and a supper invitation. This is the love-after-all that we will find typical of the terminal phase; it is also the last flicker of a woman about to collapse into senility. In "Marrakesh" we are shown another such flicker. Nearing her death — and, in this case, having gone far beyond the loss of her husband and son — old Dorothy finds love vicariously as a "lady Peeping Tom": in watching her grand-daughter have sex with a neighbour, she almost receives, or perhaps does receive, the "stroke" she thought no longer possible.

It is both their reminiscent or elegiac quality (shared to a great extent by the Caroline stories as these are presented) and their concern with a message at the end of tragedy that characterize the late Passion stories: they begin to suggest what we find at the end of an individual story, the late recognition coming as a mysterious extra from beyond its cycle. Whenever, then, a Passion story lays some emphasis on its final recognition, it will have some resemblance to this sub-group. "Anonymous Letters," the first part of "A Queer Streak," is clearly like the major Passion stories — a tale of tragic passion; its sequel, "Possession," can be read as simply parallel, yet here a sequel also has the quality of a late reflection, and the final revelation by and to the dying Violet connects this story with others like "Marrakesh." In "A Trip to the Coast" we again have an old woman with a threshold dream, though here the emphasis is more on the ability of the natural self to get the better of any such dream, as of any faith-healer's offering. Rose's final sense of a Simon reappearing from the dead is closer to what the Spanish Lady hears from the dying man in the station; so in its way is the wistfully visionary ending, solemn and foolish by turn, of "Hard-Luck Stories" — another treatment of an aging and already rejected woman.

Munro's Passion world is evidently a rich and various one, and will show itself even more so when we trace, in some degree, its origins in her early drafts. It also seems to be a world that has troubled her a good deal: we not only find her working and reworking early material, but saying very deprecatory things about both "A Trip to the Coast" and "Executioners." No doubt there is some ground for the deprecation — the main incident in "A Trip to the Coast" is an awkward and immature near-allegory, and perhaps Munro is nervous about a similarly allegorical flavour in "Executioners." Yet this last remains, for one reader at least, an extraordinarily powerful piece of writing, and other of the central Passion stories are among the most intensely thought and felt in all Munro's work. What we feel about "Baptizing" in *Lives of Girls and Women* is what the Passion group as a whole can make us feel: that beyond any central rise and fall we have arrived at the climax.

II: The Dying God

Now we can go back to the Passion world in its simplest tragic form, that of sheer fall. To put ourselves there we can think of the village in "A Trip to the Coast": a forlorn little cluster of houses with no river, no shade, and, beyond the rocky fields, only the blue ghosts of spruce and — again — "pine" (172). We have already seen such a place as the poor farm in "Princess Ida," to draw an obvious parallel; and "Black Horse" seems the right name for it, the apocalyptic black horse being that of famine.[69] Food can no doubt be had at the general store — as, for a price, in the apocalyptic famine itself — but the "sweet crumbling cookies, soft oranges, onions" (182) show that this is only another of Munro's Egyptian garners in decay. And if it is made of fading "red brick" (172), the store is what we have found the red earth of Marrakesh to be: the human body itself, seen now in all its mortality.

Black Horse is evidently a good place to get away from, and in fact something has already done so: the church has burned down, leaving a cemetery and empty livery shed. More modern vehicles are making their own escape, since the road is full of cars travelling to Muskoka — the counterpart here of the Bruce in "Thanks for the Ride." Black Horse, in other words, is a fringe place like Mission Creek, being located in the scrubby no-man's-land between the south and the Laurentian Shield; and for the same sort of place again we can turn to other of the Passion stories. In "Simon's Luck" Rose moves to a village in the juniper desert north of Kingston; the farm in "A Queer Streak" may be further north again, but still in poor country for farming. In "Executioners" both Robina's house and that of the Troys are similarly out-of-the-way, the latter being situated on a kind of Flats Road at the edge of a town. The early story of just this name — "The Edge of Town" — adds a bridge and a blasted tamarack; it also indicates the meaning of all such places with youthful explicitness:

> The tall, misshapen tree is like a sign saying: Here is an end, here is a difference. And here is an end, the end of town. The sidewalk does not go any further, there are no more street lamps, and the town policeman does not cross the bridge. (368)

And so we have come to a last border or river to cross: for our immediate purposes we can simply call this frontier death, meaning by that both the crossing and the place to which it leads. Death in this view is the "Third Bridge" at which the girls in "A Trip to the Coast" might swim, the alternative being to sit in the cemetery; it is at another Third Bridge that Del Jordan and Garnet French do swim, with near-fatal results.[70] Structures like this bridge tend indeed to be fated themselves. The walls inside the Jubilee Town Hall look "cracked and stained" (210); in the fairgrounds at the end of the Diagonal Road the bleachers are rickety and the fences disfigured. In the even more remote country around Jericho Valley, a sad region of decaying farms fading into bush, half the buildings seem to be burned-out or shored-up; and when we hear Garnet's sisters singing "This old barn is falling down" (224), we sense that both another barn and another bridge are in trouble. We learn, too, that the walls inside the Frenches' house carry watermarks from a former flood: for like pioneers in reverse, the Frenches live near the chaos from which the world once rose and to which it is now returning.

Against such a background Del is facing a death of her own, reaching the end of her schooldays at a time when no further career has opened up for her. She must equally leave behind her the world of childhood and adolescence — the world of *Lives of Girls and Women* in general — and with it the "old confidence" (187) that she remembers from the days of Art Chamberlain. At the same time various connections that have given her an identity until now are fast dissolving. As Mr. Jordan's fox-farming collapses, and Mrs. Jordan's more general enterprise in life, the two retreat from each other and from Del herself; her brother Owen seems a complete stranger now;

even her friendship with Naomi is petering out, in spite of one funny and pathetic reunion. Other Passion heroines see their worlds breaking up in much the same way: we find an old woman like Dorothy in "Marrakesh" nearing her death, a middle-aged woman like Rose losing her attractiveness along with what she gained from it, and a younger Violet giving up her hopes for marriage and a career.[71]

If the Passion stories show us disintegration in this way, they show more violent ways to come apart as well — ways that we first saw at the coming apart of a greater world in the initiatory stories, and must now see at the collapse of a lesser one. In the Exodus world we met Billy Pope the butcher; when Del goes to the Baptist Young People in "Baptizing" we hear about another butcher, Dutch Monk, in a sense the Young People's father. Later in the same story comes the loss of Del's virginity, metaphorically another piece of butchery since she turns the incident into a story about a tomcat tearing up a bird; and the climactic scuffle in the river is violent in the most direct way — Del is fighting for her life here. Presiding over the carnage, as it were, is Mrs. French the nurses' aid, who not only threatens to "scald the hide" off her children but has shocking tales to tell:

> She told me about accidents, a poisoned child who had been brought into the hospital recently turned as black as shoe polish, a man with a crushed hand, a boy who got a fishhook in his eye. (223)

Garnet, Mrs. French's dutiful son, works for a lumberyard — he is concerned, that is, with wood in a sawn-up condition:[72] and here the imagery of dismemberment acquires a biblical resonance, for in a story like "Baptizing" we naturally feel that the wood might be used to make a cross.

To sense a further biblical context, we can once again recall the Passover, the crisis in which death separated Israelite from Egyptian. The Passion, an antitype of this crisis, is similarly what "crisis" means, a judgment; and just as "Black Horse" anticipates the apocalyptic famine, so the Passion anticipates and already is the judgment of the world. We should not be surprised to hear echoes of the Apocalypse when, for instance, something gets separated to begin Del's departmental exams: "the Principal broke the seal before our eyes, and we signed an oath that it had never been broken before" (228).[73] The university party in "Simon's Luck," with its accusations and advocations, is among other things the same trial-scene again. According to a notably apocalyptic English professor, young disciples "trail around worshipping you and bothering you" (156), then cut you off; elders, on the other hand, should bow down before the lamb-like young. The professor himself takes great relish in cutting his students off, and we will be coming to more spectacular kinds of judgment: the great ordeals of fire and water in the central Passion stories.

In the face of such ordeals, the Passion group shows us what we have already seen in the Exodus group: where there is to be judgment — the great slicing — there will also be people waiting for its arrival, consciously or not. To mention only one type of arrival, we hear of a bus coming at the end of "Baptizing";[74] in "Simon's Luck" we find that, of the kinds of sociability Rose could feel at home with, the last would take place in "a little stucco house by the bus stop" (152). In other forms, waiting is more continuous with what it waits for: Mrs. Cross and Mrs. Kidd are waiting for death, and doing so in the "Home" that is itself a kind of death.[75] We also find, at whatever distribution from the centre of a story, people in graveyards — May in "A Trip to the Coast," Del in "Baptizing," the sad friends at the end of "Hard-Luck Stories." Del is virtually choosing the same location when, at the end of "Baptizing," she resolves to be "grave and simple" (242); in a sense this is where she has been throughout her affair with the "grave" (211) Garnet French, and where the whole world of this episode seems to be. For despite all the vital red and gold here, " 'A common greyness silvers everything' " (217): the greyness of the cold spring rain, the greyness of the preacher and of the ballplayers' uniforms — the greyness even of the smell when chicken is stewing.

*

When we concentrate this dying world into a human form, what we see resembles such Exodus figures as "Pop." In the last section of "Baptizing" we find a whole repertory of superannuated men — the tired-looking preacher, the listless old-timers at Garnet's baseball games, and, in a more Pop-like style, Mr. Buchanan the sardonic history-teacher and Presbyterian elder. Watching over it all is an equally sardonic figure, and one of the enthroned invalids of the terminal phase: Garnet's ancient father, with his Cheshire Cat's fading grin. Other such authorities are more wrathful than sardonic — for an extreme case we can think of Naomi's white-haired father, reappearing here to beat his daughter for drinking; and yet this "risen corpse" (193) is one of the patriarchs in Munro whose strength betrays infirmity, like the feisty but helpless little "King Billy" in "A Queer Streak." Among younger men, Blair King in "Marrakesh" is another king of sorrows: taking his name, evidently, from his job as a radio announcer, he may also take it from Blair's *Grave*, since he has his wife's fatal illness if not his own to contend with. In any case, "Blair" shows how we are once again in the doomed world of things Scottish or French; we are equally in that of victimized animals, including various shot groundhogs and racoons[76] (at one time the episode of the "old king rat" in "Images" belonged with material now in "Baptizing"[77]). As in the Exodus world medical care will plainly be needed, not to say ministerial, and in particular we should note the reappearance of "Murray Heal" the intending dentist: here again is Munro's death-and-life, which at this point we can simply call life dying.

To move from subsidiary figures to principal ones, the leading men of these stories present Munro's greatest constellation of suffering Undergods. Garnet French is the "grave," if sometimes infuriated, underling we have seen. Howard Troy is another, "still there, underneath, looking out, through all the things, the stupidity and ugliness, that had been put onto him and accepted by him" (141). Simon, while a good deal less accepting, is no less fatalistic — as is understandable in an ailing Jew who once barely escaped a death camp; Dane in "A Queer Streak" may be a compliant man, but there is the same fatalism in his air of mournful observance. The arrogant Douglas in "Hard-Luck Stories" seems at first quite different from these others, but like Duncan in "Dulse" he is a paradoxical limiting case:[78] the narrator comes to sense a mystery in this former "serviceman" (185), and we notice both his Scottish name and, at the end, the cross of St. Andrew beside the cross of St. George. "Miles" in "Differently" is in effect another soldier, helmeted and invading; he is also a pallid and intense man searching for "wrecks, and lost airplanes, and dead bodies" (231). Jack McNeil in "Mrs. Cross and Mrs. Kidd" is a simpler phenomenon — once a successful media-man like Blair King, now a helpless and weeping paralytic.

If not all these men are old, there is no reason why they need be to mean what they mean: in the Passion world as in that of the Exodus, the coming of death is also the taking away of life. Just as there is a young Eugene in "Dulse" afraid of drowning and given to "holler[ing] in his sleep" (49), so the leading male figures of the Passion stories include youngsters like Howard Troy and Garnet French —

there is in fact something still "boyish" (85) about Douglas, or even the aging Simon. And as elsewhere in Munro, sacrificial youths have mothers: most obviously in the case of Garnet, Mrs. French's chief support,[79] but discernibly in that of others as well. In "Mrs. Cross and Mrs. Kidd," for instance, the main figures may all be inmates of an old people's home, but Jack is much younger than Mrs. Cross, and quickly develops a mother-and-son intimacy with her. If a son dies in such a story, the mother becomes a figure like the mourning Isis or the bereft Jerusalem — who, we can note, reappears significantly in the gospel narrative of the Passion.[80] For our present phase, even more than the initiatory, is that of the figure we noted in *The Dry Salvages* — Mary as the *mater dolorosa*, grieving for her son and god. Mary may indeed have been doing this for some time: bleak old Dorothy in "Marrakesh" lost a son many years before the main story, the elegiac Aunt Ivie in "A Queer Streak" managed to lose three of them before having her daughters. The whole of time, in one perspective, is a Passion or the mourning that succeeds it.

*

The mortal god of these stories, then, can be old or young, a king or a sufferer — indeed he will always have something of both about him. We also find, and again as in the Exodus stories, that he can be one or many: Del Jordan, as seen by the philosophical Jerry Storey, demonstrates this state of affairs in a female version. On the one hand Del is a "handsome figger" (204) — some counterpart of the "fine figure" (208) that Mr. Buchanan sees in doomed saviours like Parnell; and remembering what Munro has to say elsewhere about figures and finishing,[81] we can see Parnell here as one uniting many before a catastrophe. But Del is a figure with a difference, since she proceeds to display three breasts as if turning into an omnibus mother goddess. Once again, it seems, we have a situation like that at the beginning of things, when time showed itself to be both the solitary Tyde and his three assailants; and while the manyness of this situation will be a tricky matter to deal with, we will need some idea of it if we are to appreciate Munro's vision of a disintegrating world.

In a way the particular number we are concerned with here does not matter: since any plurality is explicitly or implicitly set over against a contrasting unity — perhaps its own — we can increase its number as often as we like by combining this extraneous unity with the plurality itself. When Del turns triple-breasted, she accomplishes this feat by adding one to two. In the same way the pair constituted by Mrs. Cross and Mrs. Kidd turns into a trio when we add Charlotte, a woman unlike either yet a mirroring and combining image of both; and if we see Jack McNeil, the male contrary of all these, as an essential part of their situation, we are up to four. Conversely, numbers can be reduced in the same way as they are generated — in the present case we would soon have only Jack and a single female principle.[82] At the same time, particular numbers have an emblematic significance, traditional and even absolute if we think of the binary relation of before and after, or the ternary of past, present, and future. A weekend with Simon, Rose finds, is a weekend with a whole cast of characters, of whom we are told about three in particular. There is the Humble Workman, a furnace-repairer (that is, healer of something visceral) who sounds rather like Garnet French the lumberyard-worker and loyal agent of the "Heavenly Father" (216). There is also the Old Philosopher with his "memento mori" (161) — someone like Garnet's father himself, at least in his manifestation as a sardonic Buddha, or like Mr. Buchanan, or like the very similar English professor in "Simon's Luck." Lastly there is the Mad Satyr, a more lubricious counterpart of Garnet on his sensual side: in other words Simon is at once a son, a father, and a spirit of life. The hint of the Trinity here is matched by similar hints elsewhere: at the revival meeting in "Baptizing," for instance, Del encounters not only Garnet but a set of gospel singers — a quartet, to be sure, but once more we can do some reducing. The bass in the group is a fearsome man — thin, withered, and dark — who, unlike the others, does not draw the audience upward: in this way he is like the Old Philosopher, a reminder of the "base" of mortal experience. The others by themselves make a tidy threesome, which in turn is very much two plus one. Two, that is, are an ample and splendidly arrayed pair of women, each the other's image,[83] while the third is the tenor, "fat and yellow-skinned, smiling, munificent" (210) — as much a giver of life as Garnet with his "bounty" (241) and his "golden lover's skin" (238).

There is also a hint in "Mrs. Cross and Mrs. Kidd" worth investigating here. Just before the great reversal in that story we discover Mrs. Kidd playing scrabble with Charlotte, the servant who is about to take over as lady. Mrs. Kidd's word in the game is "elbow"; Charlotte works down from it to make "wind"; Mrs. Kidd, with a frown, makes "demon" across, and then proclaims a "triple word." Something triple is in the air, certainly: Jack is eagerly saying his characteristic "anh-anh-*anh*" (176) and is delighted when Charlotte asks what kind of word this may be. My own guess about the triple word is that, in the first place, Mrs. Kidd is playing for both herself and Mrs. Cross — the two are being thrown back into their old alliance as Charlotte's incipient defiance of them comes to the surface. Mrs. Kidd's two words, then, will do for herself and her friend, if only in making a high-and-low pair. And they seem to do this in any case. "Elbow" suggests an arm — vaguely an arm aloft, since Charlotte's word descends from it, and thus perhaps an authority such as a father, or Mrs. Kidd herself. "Wind," coming down, is spirit; "demon" is an under-figure, a son if we are to take "elbow" as a father. In any case it is a triple word — elbow, wind, and demon — that precipitates the crisis of the story; and I shall have more to say about "anh."[84]

What we have in these various threesomes is nothing as fixed as allegory. The inflection of their individual members varies — the Father as an imperious Mrs. Kidd is not the Father as a bowing Japanese philosopher, and a humble workman as such is not a demon. For that matter, we can make different alignments with Father, Son, and Holy Ghost — after all, a principle of multiplicity can also be one of metamorphosis. The fact remains that, at this point in our cycle of phases, we are confronted repeatedly by something like the Trinity, with something its make-up. We will find the same thing again if we consider how the Passion stories have a formal peculiarity: that of coming in groups like the tales told in the Exodus stories, and especially of coming in threes.

"Hard-Luck Stories" is just that: not a single story, except in its framing situation, but a collection.[85] The narrator's friend Julie has had a series of lovers (and here the number three seems to be significant[86]), Douglas has had a series of women, and the narrator herself refers to both a discarded husband and a lover previous to Douglas. It is interesting to find that the most important of the tales here was originally intended for Simon: before deciding on the "Simon's Luck" that we have in *Who Do You Think You Are?*, Munro advanced almost to publication with a set of three stories in which Simon went through a succession of mistresses.[87] In other words she conceived something formally close to "Baptizing"; and while the result (to have been called "Three Parties") could not have fitted into the novel we have, Munro's plans again suggest something trinitarian about her Passion world. In "Baptizing" itself there is no mistaking the effect of the three boyfriends, to use that term loosely. The first of these, Bert Matthews, is an aging man by Del's standards, pushing thirty; by occupation he is an inspector of poultry, which seems to include the girls at the creamery. He is also a man who, even in waiving his rules, asserts his authority, as when he grandly licenses Del to go to the bathroom; and when we hear of his making a bet with Naomi for "ten dollars" (185) we recognize one of Munro's lawgivers. Jerry Storey is more of a glorified son, a whiz-kid among doctors; Garnet French is a mysterious inspirer, associated both with pentecostal religion and its sexual counterpart. Or if we preferred we could emphasize how Jerry's abstracted intelligence allies him with the Spirit, and how Garnet is a different kind of Son, the Humble Workman I have mentioned. We would then have a negative rather than positive arc, and one ending in a figure of death rather than life: but this is only to say, once again, that trinities have something metamorphic about them.

There is one further male trinity needing to make its entrance here: for while the binary presentation of "A Queer Streak" somewhat obscures the fact, Violet has three important male consorts in her career. Trevor Auston, the first, is older and more official than herself, a man who believes in law and is headed for power. Wyck Tebbutt is somewhat harder to interpret: formerly a professional ballplayer, now an insurance agent, he is a quietly self-possessed man with whom Violet takes the same nervously bright tone that we will find Del taking with Jerry Storey. With Violet's nephew Dane we are on firmer ground, for Dane's role of melancholy sonship is very much that of Garnet French. All three of these men, we should note, have names associating them in some way with God: we can hear "Augustine" in Trevor Auston, busily erecting a United Church version of the city of God (even if "Trevor" means only a village); "Tebbutt" is a form of "Theobald," not really derived from *theós* but long associated with it; Dane's friend and *alter ego* is simply "Theo." For good measure this story has a female trinity to go with the male. When Aunt Ivie lost her three sons she replaced them with three daughters; and these last, while sometimes at odds, make an effective team — as we see in "Possession," where, in effect, the team is reconstituted. To feel its larger implication, we can as often in Munro look at the picture on the wall behind it: the three queens into whose hand the dying Arthur commits himself.[88]

*

Having distributed our mortal god into a company, we can go back now to treating him as an individual — evidently of a multifarious sort, as befits the strange self that possesses life and must die. Such a god is the one thing that is "the whole thing," as Del calls Garnet; conversely he is all things in one, for Del senses in him "all possibilities of fierceness and sweetness, pride and submissiveness, violence, self-containment" (214). Christianity imagines its composite deity as an upper rather than a lower principle: mystery and indeterminacy, on the other hand, are very much the qualities that we have been associating with an under-figure. Thus the composite lover met by Del in "Baptizing" may include the bright and integral Jerry Storey, but his multiplicity is better represented by the elusive Garnet French. Or we can think of the mysterious Simon, whom Rose affectionately calls an "idiot" (164) — a person who does things singly in some way — but who is not in the least single-minded. For one thing Simon is the opposite of a specialist: a polyglot, uncountried man with a miscellaneous stock of know-how about everything from insulation to fertilizer. By the same token he has a knack of taking on different roles — to use another key word of this story, he is a one-man party or "company" (162), with all the variousness of matter itself.[89] Rose imagines him as a harlequin, as does a mistress in one of the unpublished stories;[90] another mistress, unable to put him together, thinks of him as getting through all nets.[91] With Simon, in other words, we have returned to a figure like the motley Pied Piper or the slippery Old Man of the Sea — what the transcendent god of "Age of Faith" proves to be when really in the world.

Julie's lovers in "Hard-Luck Stories" have much the same Protean quality. The first is found on the ocean-beach; the second is a man of many facets — "how can you put it together?" (191) she wonders — and the third is Douglas Reider, at once a first-phase Poppy Cullender, a second-phase Art Chamberlain, and a third-phase Duncan. Jack McNeil, in spite of his undying devotion to one wife, is made similarly plural by his moodiness, which goes beyond any that Mrs. Cross supposed herself to be taking on. Garnet French may actually seem less variable than these others — it is precisely his simplicity and sincerity that Del contrasts with her own "complexity and play-acting" (238) — and yet she was not wrong in sensing his many possibilities. As the devout Baptist or the tender lover Garnet is very different from the violent self we ultimately see: Del has known — and been drawn to — all these Garnets from the beginning.

At this point we should acquaint ourselves with the hero around whom the main block of Munro's early drafting centres. This is a young man called Franklin, the ancestor not only of Garnet French (as his name suggests), but of numerous other characters or types in Munro. In different manuscripts we find a bold young trickster, a solitary trapper, a returned serviceman who will develop into Art Chamberlain (and thus Douglas Reider), a lover with a list of girlfriends much like Garnet's, and a kind of dying Christ. As for this last, there is one fragment in which the twelve-year-old Franklin, having got a nail in his foot, is carried through the barnyard by his father. "His long light body had collapsed, folded into a Z, his fair head drooped": and yet he manages to show the nail to Del Jordan (of whom there is a version here), and she thinks of him as "gallant and unlucky," sure to be killed in the war. In another form of his story, and the one that seems to be emerging most strongly in this material, Franklin is a soldier who survives for a homecoming. There is a great chicken dinner in his honour, much like that at the Frenches' in "Baptizing," and in the course of this we have what Munro later puts in "Monsieur les Deux Chapeaux": a confrontation of upper and lower in which the hero is seemingly shot by his brother. Franklin then reappears "risen from the dead" like Ross — for he too contains the mystery of transformation.[92]

*

Given the associations of names like "French" in Munro, "Franklin" would do for any representative of the Many rather than the One. But even "Franklin" suggests chiefly the darker side of manyness: can we find something less exclusively grave to call "the whole thing"? If names like "Del Jordan," or even their separate components, regularly prove to be oxymoronic, might there be a single one for humanity in general seen as a tissue of contradiction? In our exploration of Munro's naming we have not yet thought about "John" — in one form or another perhaps the commonest name in her writing. In an undergraduate story called "The Widower" we already find "John McManus": John the son of man, whose tragedy is that of all humanity bound to Nature in the guise of an enveloping wife. As we go on we run into a large troupe of Johnsons and Jacks and Janes and Joans and Janets. Every "jack, joke" seems to be here — from Jack Curtis the bold airman, for instance, to the same Jack as grounded in his later life, or from the capable to the impotent Jack McNeil, who for that matter has an intriguing surname in that it makes him either a champion or black or both.

When we begin to sort out the champions from the losers, we find that Duncan's list of girl-friends contains "serene socialite Jane" (52); we also find airy Jeanette in "Marrakesh," not to mention St. John's Church in "The Ottawa Valley," with its elevated ritual. On the other hand the lowly Ruby Carruthers, whose present name is close to Rose's, was once called Netta and contrasted with a Rose of a more upwardly mobile kind. Ruby, furthermore, is by no means a serene socialite; we may also remember that among Janet's Fleming aunts Jennet was the one who died, or that Jenkin's Bend takes its name from another death; in the same way, there is more to Jeanette than the flighty woman we first see. If we go back to "Day of the Butterfly" we may now notice how the butterfly brooch given to Myra by Helen comes out of a box of sticky and down-to-earth "Cracker Jacks" (404). In "Marrakesh," more pointedly, we learn from Jeanette about one's need to go to the "john" (168) — this being all she can think of when trying to appreciate Europe — and in "The Beggar Maid" we find Rose thinking the same thought as she contemplates other scholarship students. A further look at St. John's Church will reveal both saint and john — there is both a church and an outhouse here, each with its role in the story.[93] It should not be surprising, then, that in "The Found Boat" the list of names scrawled in the derelict station ends with Joanne:[94] John, so to speak, is what it all comes down to.

John is of course a biblical name, that of John the Baptist, John the Evangelist, and John the Divine; and as with Marys and Josephs, these various Johns readily coalesce into one. "Baptizing" turns out to be full of this composite figure. To stay with the last section of the story, where he appears in his third-phase form, we of course find him in Garnet French, the regenerate Baptist from Jordan Valley.[95] Garnet comes to Del during the great revival meeting, with its demand for religious conversion; he baptizes her sexually as no-one has quite done before; and he administers a very different baptism in the river when she refuses to join the Baptist Church. Garnet's appearance suggests the same identification again, for as first noticed by Del he has much the look of John the Baptist in his Nineteenth-Century version: "not very tall, dark-skinned; a bony face with deep eye-sockets, long slightly hollowed cheeks, a grave, unconsciously arrogant expression" (211).[96] To come at the same figure from a slightly different angle, we can compare Garnet with Don in "The Moons of Jupiter," "a tall ascetic-looking boy, with a St. Francis cap of black hair, a precise fringe of beard" (222).[97] And John himself appears in the Franklin material, where in one of his versions the hero turns into a lone riverside trapper, reminding Del's mother of a hermit:

No, thought Del, she means a pedlar, a hermit is dressed in furs. (She was thinking of John the Baptist in her grandmother's Bible, his fingers dripping locusts and wild honey). Nevertheless when she ran across the word again, she would think of Franklin, his sack and rubber boots and knitted cap, his self-sufficiency in those days when he had quit school and spent his time trapping.[98]

We can use all the hints Munro gives us here: Franklin, whom we saw first with the nail in his foot and then shot, more or less, by a jealous brother, is not only one of the lone recluses, pedlars, and trappers from Munro's first world but these as gathered into the last of the prophets and greatest of "idiots."

To these we can add the other biblical figures whom John gathers in. In one of the early fragments, Franklin pushing through a thicket is compared to Moses crossing the Red Sea — the Jordan used by John being metaphorically the same body of water. A different Franklin develops into Art Chamberlain: he leads, in other words, to a kind of David, and we can note that in some of Munro's versions of him David virtually merges with the hapless kind of John. David in "Simon's Luck," for instance, is betrayed by a woman, and we may recall as well how he appears "more or less symbolically" (156) between the lively host and the fateful Simon:[99] like the lone John sundered by Salome, the more sociable David is a one divided into, or between, a plurality. Then there is Simon himself: the Simeon (or Simon Peter, if we like) at the boundary between the old covenant and the new, seeing salvation but not, as unregenerate, having faith enough to grasp it.[100] And at the end of Old Testament history, with its Moses and David, we finally come to Jesus himself.

Here we are confronted by an ambiguity that will prove of major significance as we go on. Jesus is not John, of course — John is no more than a rough figure of the wilderness, representing an older dispensation and baptizing with a lesser element; and yet the *symboliste* John with whom Del falls in love in "Baptizing" is remarkably like the Pre-Raphaelite Jesus who so impressed her in "Age of Faith." In both cases she is confronted by a mysterious figure at a threshold: Garnet appears to her not only at the verge of her maturity but literally at the door of a house, dark against the sun. We have seen that "Chris" Watters in "How I Met My Husband" appears in the same way; when, on the other hand, we remember the dark bird against the sun at the "Simmonses' Gate" in "A Trip to the Coast," we may well wonder whether we are in the old dispensation or the new.

A minor character in "Dulse" can perhaps clarify the situation here. The "downcast" (37) John, the proprietor of the guest-house, has been a minister and carpenter in his time, and is now a different kind of minister — one who appears glumly waiting on table. If we go back to the *New Yorker* version of the story, we find that this John was once called "Josh" (32): Joshua, that is, a distinctly ambiguous biblical figure. Joshua lives under the Law, and under Moses; yet his name at least is the same as "Jesus," and even within the history of the Old Covenant he is able to cross the Jordan into the Promised Land while Moses must die in the wilderness. On the other hand, a Jesus who must die before his risen self can inherit the promised new Kingdom is still in the wilderness himself — still a forerunner;[101] and even the Jesus glorified in the Apocalypse may prove no more than this. The same thing can be said of the Trinity itself: while in its developed form it is not biblical, the idea of a plurality of persons having one mind is certainly so (notably, as it happens, in John's gospel); and in anything like the form we have seen, such a one-and-many can only be yet another shadowing. By the same token, a gospel on the terms of this shadowing can only be another Law: or as Del Jordan finds, the Garnet French who at last seems to offer true baptism may be baptizing only to repentance.

III. A Last Chance

A new gospel that turns out to be old law sounds like a tragic form of typology, in my sense of the word. Evidently, then, we will have to do as we did with the Exodus, and ask how the Passion story appears at different narrative levels. We found Munro's Exodus heroines managing to go for rides before returning disconsolately to Egypt, or perhaps arriving in a Promised Land that proved to be another Egypt itself; and while I have been imagining her Passion as a simpler linear descent to death, we have already had some glimpses of its more complex forms. In cyclical terms, people leaving Black Horse are bound for holidays, from which they will have to come back sooner or later: a common type of Passion story, similarly, is one in which the heroine herself tries escape before her final surrender. What is equally common is the freedom that is itself captivity — perhaps, as we will first be seeing, because it is a superficial kind of freedom, or more tragically because a deeper freedom only proves more deeply bound to its jailor.

Various characters in the Passion stories believe in the possibility of new life: as the Spanish Lady puts it,

> People believe in fresh starts, nowadays. Right up to the end of their lives. It has to be allowed. To start with a new person, your old selves known only to yourself: nobody can stop anyone fr' doing that. (188)

When Julie appears at the beginning of "Hard-Luck Stor'   oking unwontedly "gallant and absurd" (181) — the germ   .e whole story, according to Munro[102] — a fresh start of this '   just what she is attempting. Hitherto she has missed out on '   spite of her two possibilities, but now a third, Douglas Reid   as appeared as if by miracle. And there are a number of such '   les in Munro's Passion world, not all of them sexual: the sale   i encountered by the Spanish Lady has made a fresh start thr   h Rosicrucianism, while for others she has met — and she has a way of meeting them — it has been astrology or numerology or astral bodies. In the Garnet French episode sexual baptism is paralleled by the religious kind for Garnet and the academic for Del.

The youthful vitality in these stories, which we have already seen as the life death takes away, can readily be seen in this new perspective as well. Sometimes we have a sense of the young wanting their own lives in the midst of a hardening older world, like May in "A Trip to the Coast"; at other times it is older people themselves who, like the Spanish Lady, want to believe they still have a chance. The host at the party in "Simon's Luck" may be no youngster, but he looks wonderfully rejuvenated in his green "jumpsuit" (156); some of the Baptist Young People in the Garnet French story are not very young either, but then they are born again. Even the ancient grandmother in "A Trip to the Coast" has the impulse to get away from Black Horse and go on her great trip; Rose and the Spanish Lady do go on trips;[103] Dorothy in "Marrakesh" and Violet in "A Queer Streak," more home-bound in a geographical sense, have bizarre flings of their own before the end comes. The undoubted champion here is Simon: the man who, belonging to a scapegoat race, spends his whole life making lucky getaways. As a boy Simon just misses arrest and a death camp; he then survives a grave illness, and in later life this man who says "Move it along" (155) has his own felicity in moving along — moving away, most notably, from his entanglement with Rose.

Once more, then, we are seeing the gleam of fortune, now as the hope of the failing: and in its light we can reconsider the bridges in these stories — bridges that at first we saw only as leading to death. In "Executioners," a story full of passages, Helena not only walks a log bridge to the happier world of Robina's farm, but then triumphantly walks a plank over an open well. In the Garnet French story the revivalist pictures a bridge over a river of fire, "tied up at the banks of Paradise on the other side" (212); and we come even closer to the crossing of the Red Sea and the Jordan when Garnet and Del, late on a rainy evening, sit by the river in Garnet's truck. They are "still in the approaches to sex, circling, back-tracking" (218)[104] — unprepared to go the whole way; but even as things are they "cross over,[105] going into a country where there [is] perfect security" (214). The Third Bridge, it seems, need not lead directly to death.

There are various kinds of pleasure on the far side of this bridge: a specially conspicuous one is the communal eating and playing that we have already met in the Exodus stories. "Simon's Luck" — of which the prototype I have mentioned was to have been called "Three Parties" — has one festivity after another to show us: a catalogue of hospitalities to start with, then the party in Kingston, Rose's weekend with Simon, and, on the other side of the continent, the jolly television series with its automatic happy ending. More economically, "Hard-Luck Stories" uses a single chicken dinner as a framing situation; in the last section of "Baptizing" we find another chicken dinner at the centre of the action itself. The biblical resonance of such dinners is easy to feel. That at the Frenches' is — among other interesting things — a meal served to twelve, and the dinners attended by Violet and Trevor in "Anonymous Letters" carry the same kind of suggestion: for if these latter are short on wine (though long on cuts of meat), we are pointedly reminded that the United Church communion service is tea-total as well. It is not surprising, then, if the last of Mrs. Cross's three gifts in "Mrs. Cross and Mrs. Kidd" is "a picture of the Lord's Supper" (164). Mrs. Cross cannot, of course, enjoy the same sort of communion as Del and Garnet in the truck — after all, she is a resident of an old people's home. Yet being in such a place the old people have crossed a river of their own: and as they sit together at dinner or play cards in the Recreation Room, they are finding a security and companionship that might have seemed no longer possible.

*

Is this agreeable existence really life? — or, in terms we have been using, is it unity and freedom? It certainly seems to be. On the one hand, Violet is not the only person in these stories connected with the United Church: the Frenches for all their tatters were and are United, as Mrs. French stubbornly asserts. On the other hand, it seems that where there is no separating there is no confounding: the great academic party in "Simon's Luck" may be a triumph of sociability,[106] yet establishment and anti-establishment remain very much their preferred selves. And in this way they are like the components of the décor, which include (in the living-room alone) "a jukebox, barber-shop mirrors, turn-of-the-century advertisements . . . old silk lamp-shades, farmhouse bowls and jugs, primitive masks and sculptures" (154). Elsewhere the same easy syncretism meets us again and again. We might expect Rose's up-country village to be a simpler phenom-enon than the Kingston of the party, but in fact it is rather similar: some of the inhabitants are employed by a provincial mental institu-tion, others work or do not work in various ways except the obvious one of farming; and to match the swinging party in town, the local church "no longer served the discreet and respectable Protestant sect that had built it, but proclaimed itself a Temple of Nazareth, also a Holiness Centre, whatever that might be" (166). Violet is equally untrammelled when she finally settles with Wyck Tebbutt, since their house features items from assorted times and places, thrown together in a "temporary and haphazard" style (241) quite unlike that of her apartment over the bank. And so it seems that our question has answered itself: having recovered a kind of innocence, the born-again of the latter days happily and convivially do their thing — or their many things.

And yet there is something sham about all this: certainly — as Rose senses — there is something sham about the innocence. At the party in Kingston she notices the mirror trained on the bed; she finds other things no less self-conscious, especially the childlike hostess Shelley; for that matter she worries that her own dress may be "wrongly youthful or theatrical" (153). Perhaps she is unusually perceptive as well as unusually critical, being something of an outsider: but then the guests at this party are all really outsiders. For their world is one curiously unable to take itself for granted — it is like that of Jeanette's successive incarnations in "Marrakesh," or the charades in "Differ-ently," or the conversation in "Hard-Luck Stories," where it is very important to know that macramé is out. At its other extreme, to be sure, a motley world may seem to lack self-consciousness altogether, especially where it is an old world seen from the perspective of a new. The Frenches' farm, cluttered with everything from old bedsprings to Kotex ads, looks bizarre enough to a girl from town, and yet the Frenches themselves are at home with it. Even here, though, we will later find more awareness than we might suspect: we have arrived where we arrived with the Exodus stories, at a failure of Egyptian serenity in which brashness and misgiving, consciousness and unconsciousness, fall into a sensibility scramble of which neither member is its proper self.

To see order and freedom scrambled in the same way, we can first take the new world at its most simply and confidently up-to-date — which may in fact be its most naïve. Jerry Storey and his mother are the most modern of the modern, yet when Del feels something "affected" (205) about their manner, we could apply the same adjective to their unconventionality itself. The latter is real enough, to be sure, especially their talk about sex — on the subject of which Jerry's mother has all the breathtaking directness of a Mrs. Jordan.[107] Their bedtime snack, on the other hand, suggests a life of sanitized routine; Jerry's career is, by his lights, no less correctly plotted; and the fact is that those who defy convention are always very strict about following trends and setting themselves rules. This becomes even more apparent when simple modernity — what sets in in various Munro stories after the Second War — gives way to an even more modern cult of restoration. When Joan comes home in "Rose Matilda" she finds the once rejected old Logan reappearing, but in a deliberate form that makes it "strained, meticulous" (208): Dane in "A Queer Streak" is in fact a professional restorer, painstakingly changing the town back to "something like its original style" (241). If we look again at the party in "Simon's Luck" we may now be struck the familiar nature of the proceedings even at their most wayward — the party, like any party, is a ritual, as fixed in its way as a communion liturgy. Quite in keeping, then, are the "careful" (154) decoration and the hostess's authentic old gown: seeing her efforts in the kitchen, Rose wishes "that she could take such pains, that she could make ceremonies" (158).

Here we can take an important hint from "Walking on Water" — an initiatory story in ways we have seen, but also like terminal ones in its picture of a dying world clutching at life. Old Mr. Lougheed, having his difficulties with hippy Victoria, is particularly incensed by the more-holistic-than-thou young people at the health food store: "bread had been baked before" (71), he tells himself, reminding us of Rose's wish that she could do the same thing. Eugene finds the young people merely "boring" (a word used in more than one Passion story for the converted[108]): what they are really like, he suggests, is early Christians. If we consider the youngsters' "lilting, pious discussions" and the way "they took too much praise on themselves," we may think of still another group appearing in the Jewish world at roughly the same time as John and Jesus: the Pharisees. And there are numerous Pharisees, with or without capitalization, to be found in the Passion stories themselves.

In "Baptizing" Naomi joins a very strict group, that of working girls concerned with marriage and "showers" (181). If the Pharisees were upholders of legal purity, Naomi's friends are no less exercised by all kinds of "subtle formalities, courtesies, proprieties" (181–82), not to say "diets, skin-care routines, hair-shampooing methods, clothes, diaphragms" (179). And just as the Pharisees' rectitude was a preparation — for their own version of the Kingdom, as well as the afterlife in which they also believed — so Naomi's group lay up their own treasures in the form of household items, to be paid for by instalment and enjoyed when they achieve matrimony.[109] It is true that these girls breach accepted standards — they seem as offensive to the older women of Jubilee as the Pharisees to the more highly placed Sadducees. And yet it was the non-conformist Pharisees who preserved Judaism, and the practices of Naomi's circle are essential to the preservation of Jubilee: the town can take them in stride, since their real function is to bring a new generation into its order. The same thing can be said of the early Christians' liberty — offensive to the Pharisees themselves, of course — to the extent that this was only permitted license, affirming the Law rather than going beyond it. And it can be said of the liveliness, even mischief, of Munro's terminal phase in general as we have just been seeing it. Once again, this new life is not really new life at all: it only leads back to the letter that is death. Naomi puts herself through various escapades, including sex with a series of boys, but in the process manages to get pregnant, keep her baby, and force wedlock on the father (himself a telephone "lineman" [232]). Matrimony and legitimacy, in fact, were what she wanted all along.

We find the same process in Del's story as well: but in saying this we are venturing on larger issues, and if we want to see correspondence here we will first need to explore an apparent — indeed a very real — lack of it. Where "Simon's Luck" or "A Queer Streak" has only a single heroine, "Baptizing" is like "Lives of Girls and Women" in having two of them: the girls from River Street and Mason Street, more obviously contrasted than paralleled. The contemplative Del takes the general course in high school where the practical Naomi takes the vocational. Del, moreover, keeps apart from the laws and indulgences of Naomi's world; she associates with boys Naomi despises; she even falls in love. In a word — that of Naomi's last warning — she tries withdrawal, and withdrawal of a kind that is neither the one Naomi directly means nor the one she prudently allows herself. If Del, then, circles back like her friend, her circle is going to be far wider; if, more typologically, her liberty is the same thing as law, the paradox of their identification will be a far more intense one.

IV: Three Tries

Of the young men with whom Del keeps company in "Baptizing," the most important is obviously Garnet French — the third of three. We can best approach Garnet, however, through his two predecessors; and after the analogy I have suggested between Naomi and the Pharisees, it is interesting to see how the members of Del's trinity are themselves like forces in the turbulent New Testament world. First comes Bert Matthews: the poultry inspector[110] who by the same token is one of Munro's undertakers, inviting young girls out for the first time without ever going farther. In the same initiatory way we have found Bert to be a dealer of law: he is like the John or Jesus, then, who takes on a similar role — the Jesus, primarily, of Matthew's gospel, which sees salvation as based on legal righteousness. No doubt this Jesus is a convivial man as well, one who does not fast and is happy to eat with publicans and sinners. On the other hand he calls on his flock to set itself apart, refusing to eat and drink with the drunken:[111] for it is soon to inherit a kingdom. And in this way he eats and drinks with Matthew's opponents the Pharisees, who equally expect a historical kingdom for the virtuous.

Like "An Ounce of Cure," the Bert Matthews episode tells of a revel — one that, as in the earlier story again, takes place when a presiding figure, without giving up his authority, temporarily stops enforcing it. The Gay-la Dance Hall to which Bert lures Del and Naomi is, appropriately, a strange combination of the shut up and the wide open. We hear of a "black and rumoured place" (186), with dark pines, blind windows, and French safes for accessories; yet the raised dancing-platform inside looks "like a lighted ship floating above the earth and sawdust floor" (187). Once Del has had some whisky things float even more freely: the world comes to seem "temporary, and playful, and joyously improbable" (190), with no obligations attached. And soon we come to one of the convivial meals we are now used to: hot dogs and ginger ale in Bert's "happy home" (190) at the Brunswick Hotel.

Along with Bert the lively licenser goes a companion named Clive, who manages to look "dead-serious" (187) while proving himself a peppy dancer; and here John the Baptist enters our picture again. Whisky affects Del much as it does the babysitter in "An Ounce of Cure": when she looks at the dancers, "the heads seemed large, out of proportion to the bodies; I imagined them — though I did not really see them — detached from bodies, floating smoothly on invisible trays" (189). These heads are of course much like the floating dance-floor itself, but in the context they suggest something more that we have already glanced at: Del is seeing the head of John on its platter,[112] while herself falling into the role of Salome. Again, we find Bert at one point addressing Clive as "corporal" (188).[113] Perhaps this is because Clive is so physical — a dancer where Bert is more of an overseer — but there is another strand of association here as well: for presently Bert says "officer" (189), which fits the more military connotation of "corporal" just as it does Clive's sparring, his "machine-gun laugh," and his general hostility of manner. It is the same Clive who submits Del to a wily interrogation concerning capital punishment and women being "hung like men" (190); and while the distribution of roles is extremely ambiguous throughout this episode, we can sense a Herod here to match the Salome. There is perhaps a similar hint when Clive, for all the masterful style of his dancing, begs Del to "dance me loose" (188), and even "called me 'baby' in a cold languishing voice." To conflate two Herods, the ferocious military ruler who carries on with Salome seems to be unconsciously appealing to the innocents he has slaughtered.

Herod also slaughters prophets, of course, and indeed Clive may seem as odd a companion for a Bert "Matthews" as Matthew's John or Jesus for the Pharisees and their charges. But there is more than one sphere in which license and law can go together, and more than one source from which they can derive. Apart from being related to "cleave," "Clive" historically names a military and administrative hero of the British Empire: if Bert Matthews is a religious form of law, his associate suggests a more secular and imperial one. Again, we can note Clive's pretence to being a foreigner — a Dutchman:[114] for the Herods too were aliens in the eyes of their disgruntled Jewish subjects, and in fact their origin should be of special interest to readers of Munro. The Clive who calls to mind a red-coated British soldier is also a "foxy" (187) man, in colour as in manner: like the Idumaean or Edomite Herods, he points to red Esau, the angry brother.

It would take much longer to consider all the suggestions in this episode, and make all the necessary qualifications. What is plain, however, is that Bert and Clive make curious sparring-partners, shadow-boxing until ready to embrace. Their effect on Del is equally plain, for even at the height of her euphoria she experiences Clive's tongue as a cold rag: another of Munro's stoppers. By the time she is in Bert's hotel-room — Lair or Refuge depending on one's taste — she is starting to sober up, and on getting Bert's official permission to go to the bathroom goes farther than that. Beyond the "bubble-shaped container of red liquid" (190) that at first entranced her, she effects a kind of self-deposition by climbing down the fire-escape; then she simply goes home. Even now she easily gets confused, taking the wrong direction before taking the right. She also, before remembering her own house, knocks on the door of Naomi's: and what appears at this point is the thing she has really been flirting with all along. Naomi's father is the resurrected version of an old-fashioned bully; he obsesses himself with prophecies that he can understand only in the most fleshly way, while beating his daughter for looseness at the same time. As for the jovial Bert, his hair is receding: the inspector's temple is looking more and more like a bare dome.[115]

*

Among the more sublimated heroes of terminal stories — Chris Watters in his aeroplane, the Rosicrucian in the observation-car, the flying rug salesman in "A Trip to the Coast" — the most ethereal of all is no doubt Jerry Storey, Del's consort in the second stage of her baptism. I have suggested that, depending on where we put our emphasis, Jerry can be seen either as a glorified Son or as Spirit descending in the form of a brain. In any case he is "the scion of the fabulous fertilizer family" (197), offering the bread of heaven by abstracting himself from the earth: Jerry's world is one of pure consciousness, with anything more subversive admitted only as a joke. At his house Del is fed tricoloured jello pudding — the Egyptian jelly once again, here shaped like a "mosque" (201). His mother, similarly, attends winter meetings of the Eastern Star, and the great revelation of the episode comes as an epiphany for the wise on a snowy night. A whole tradition of oriental transcendence looms behind Jerry, while the western science that is his own religion rises high in the foreground.

Jerry is also what the wise men came to see. He "had long frail legs, a small head, curly hair, round bright eyes. He wore a plaid cap with fleece-lined earflaps . . ." (199). In other words he is a lamb, which means in the present context that he is the lamb of God — the mild Christ of the gospel of John. He "offer[s] himself up" (200), knowing himself to be unlike other boys (Jerry knows all things) but accepting the humiliating role he has to play among them. At the same time he never conceals his identity: "he was what he seemed" (200), says Del, who also remarks twice on his "conforming to type" (199, 201). Jerry, that is, is a pure manifestation — or at least that is his upper storey, since the Jerry beneath is very different. This latter talks about atrocities and apocalyptic weaponry with "a curious insistent relish" (198) — he is a lamb who unrolls a scroll of terrors; and however he may veil the fact by his joking and self-deprecation, he has ambitions. If the end of the world is coming in a few years, Jerry may still preside over it, since he "blasphemously" (199) thinks of winning the Nobel Prize by the age of thirty-five. Certainly he means to be vindicated: when the principal breaks the seal for the great examinations, Jerry is going to inherit "glory, glory, the top of the pinnacled A's" (207) — his destined place above the temple.

If Jerry has a special affinity with the gospel of John — the gospel in which Jesus washes his disciples' feet and urges them to be *katharoí* — he brings us back again to John the Baptist, not now as preacher of repentance or enemy of the Pharisees but as worker of purification. We will arrive at the same John if we follow yet another strand of allusion. Jerry sits with Del in the restaurant, "creasing a paper napkin into geometrical designs, wrapping it around a spoon, tearing it into fluttering strips" (198). Among other suggestions here we can notice that of a scroll of paper; if we want more napkins, Del finds that at the Storeys' house "the dishtowels were folded and ironed like the finest linen handkerchiefs and kept in a lemon-scented drawer" (201). The same care is taken with Jerry's I.Q.: to his mother it is like "an archaeological find . . . which she kept wrapped up in a drawer" (201). In recent times the leading discovery of concealed scrolls has been that at Qumran; and while, once again, I do not want to suggest anything like substitution allegory, it is worth noting that the Essenes

— close in various ways to John the Baptist and John the Evangelist — make an appropriate analogue for Jerry.

Of the various Israelite persuasions at the time of Christ, it is the Essenes who show most plainly the tendency of Judaism to withdraw from any world, even its own. They insist on perfect purity during the final conflict of light and darkness; they study the stars and systems of astrological determination for signs of the times; they take on themselves the role of suffering servants. Above all they consider themselves chosen, set apart by the same grace that bestows Jerry's brainpower; and in preparation they discipline themselves no less ruthlessly than Jerry getting ready for the departmentals. The name "Jerry" — to ignore lower associations here — belongs to a comparable figure: the great prophet of downfall, who reappears in the literature favoured at Qumran. If the same prophet sees downfall as the wages of whoredom,[116] this suits the Essene attitude to the establishment in Jerusalem and to much more: when Jerry examines Del with his "manual" (204) and then throws her into the basement, he is putting her down as the transcendent mind puts down the body of things in general.

All this is in honour of Jerry's mother Greta (or Margaret), the thoroughly up-to-date woman who shocks Del by recommending a "diaphragm" (202).[117] Del herself takes on various roles here. In a way she is utterly different from either the humble or the aspiring Jerry — another of Munro's "eggplants" (197), as he sees her, with "almost no capacity for abstract thought" (196) as opposed to mere metaphor. On the other hand, she lets herself be caught up for a time by Jerry as she had earlier been caught up by Bert Matthews: Del too wants A's, and cares enough about another kind of glory to present herself undressed for Jerry's inspection. In the main, however, she slips into a relation with him similar to the one he maintains with his mother — the high-strung, bantering sort of comradeship that we have seen in various central-phase couples. Jerry's relation to the world itself is the same, one that accommodates but does not risk any serious contamination or loss of power. And when Del, studying for the exams, turns facts into something "lovely, chaste, and obedient" (208), her own design on the world is like Jerry's.

What happens on the midwinter night follows the familiar pattern. Ascending the stairs to Jerry's room Del reveals herself, feeling no less "absurd and dazzling" (204) than when transformed by Bert's whisky. Then comes reversal — Mrs. Storey suddenly arrives home — and Del now finds herself stuffed naked into the basement, while

Jerry, in the kitchen above, enjoys one of Munro's vigils with biscuits in the form of cocoa and raisin buns with his mother. Disenchanted as at the Brunswick, Del has once more to escape, and from both a cross and a tomb — the wood of the steps against which she feels her nakedness, the tub across which she makes her way to get out a window. For Del has seen the Storeys manifested in a new way, as a priggish mother and frightened, dutiful son, while her own "offerings" (206) are left neglected. The best way to patch things up is to do as John's gospel does: going down the John Street Hill next day, the conspirators turn the whole affair into a "Great Comic Scene" (206), with Del naturally casting herself as "the woman taken in adultery" (207).

As usual, we can ask whether the heroine here has not been more implicated than she supposes — for Del's reserve is as controlling as Mrs. Storey's proprietorship, and remains so when she crawls out the window in disgust instead of pounding on the basement door. She does briefly show herself: as part of this story about napkins and towels — not to say "some old ragged curtain or piece of shelf-oil-cloth" (205) — she sheds her clothes, and notably her garter belt. But we have seen what kind of revelation this amounts to, and after a certain amount of yanking upwards and downwards,[118] Del is happy to get her coverings back. During a different sort of scene Jerry has dismissed all those who pretend to understand "without knowing any of the groundwork" (200). A remark like this sounds like another of Munro's archaeological digs; it also fits Jesus's attitude to questioners; and with greater irony it fits the kind of saviour that he himself is in John's gospel — an omniscient and imperturbable figure who in spite of everything never fully enters into human experience. Del is as capable as Jerry himself of playing such a role; at the same time her instinctual needs have "gone underground" (208), to reappear when she meets Garnet French.

*

The Del acceptable to Jerry Storey is a bright, hard-working girl — as much an Elizabeth in her own way as the practical Naomi in hers: indeed the "married" (200) relation between Del and Jerry matches Naomi's longed-for domesticity, whatever the latter's opinion of Jerry may be. Yet even at this time Del and Naomi are drifting apart, and when they meet again in the third section of the chapter, the brief revival of earlier closeness only shows how different they have now become. Naomi, even when losing her virginity, keeps her head:

throughout her story she remains no less strong-willed and controlled than Mrs. Jordan, and no less bent on worldly success as she conceives it. Del eventually takes another path. In dealing with the Exodus stories we saw a contrast between a communal Passover or Eucharistic meal and a lone communion more suggestive of Gethsemane. The two things, we found, could be simultaneous — even aspects of a single situation — yet they were often temporally disjunct, as when a character withdrew after a supper to meditate alone. Something like this movement now appears in the relation between Naomi and Del, since Del grows distant from her old friend, and the marital process generally, just as Naomi is consolidating her prospects. Del is proving to be not Elizabeth — or Martha — but Mary.

We can see the same movement within Del's own life. After her alliance with Jerry Storey — a bit eccentric like all her adventures in this chapter, but certainly convivial enough, and appropriate enough for a girl aiming at scholarships — Del turns to someone much deeper and more distant, both in himself and in his isolation from her normal circle. In doing so she also turns to love, offering herself in sheer "surrender," "an act of pure faith, freedom in humility" (218), like that of a convert at a revival meeting; and in this way she enters Munro's essential Passion story, where a heroine finds love after all in the presence of some form of death. This love, moreover, is of a very different kind from that of the Kingdom, at least if we emphasize the contrast between the two.[119] A Passion heroine is a deeply needing person; she seeks to give herself wholly and to trust another's self-giving; and inasmuch as she is able to do so she finds herself wonderfully favoured, gaining a freedom unlike any license possible in a merely legal arrangement. All through the earlier episodes of "Baptizing" there has been a Del who held back, unconvinced by a world of Berts and Jerrys and Naomis that was really the central one reinstated: now this Del — the authentic one, it would seem — comes into her own, responding to a call like none she has ever heard. It is as if the story of new life were just beginning.

*

The contrast between Del and Naomi here has no full counterpart in "Simon's Luck" (though the reappearing, cautioning Naomi corresponds structurally to Rose's fortune-telling neighbour); but Del herself has an evident counterpart in Rose — the woman who, inviting a man from a party to a private country weekend, offers herself to him passionately and heedlessly. And if Rose, then as at other times, is more a wandering *rosa mundi* than the quiet and secluded Mary of biblical tradition, we can discern the latter in some related heroines. Helena in "Executioners," for instance, is the diffident child in blue and white whom we found wanting to live alone in a tower, though at the same time someone who makes an offering — a very imprudent one, as the sequel shows — to a boy at school. As often, the same figure appears even more plainly in an early story: "Grace," the strange, shy girl who comes to Harry Brooke in the last part of "The Edge of Town," is also the girl who, at least in his dream, goes with him to St. Augustine, the city of Madonna lilies. Certain Exodus heroines, we can recall, have much the same air about them: the humble servant-girl Edie who worships her sky-borne lover; the Lois who works in the glove factory and, to Dick's surprise, gives herself in love like a mystic.

We thus find Mary and Elizabeth strongly polarized in such stories, and whenever that happens there are bound to be complications: the firmly installed, no-nonsense grandmother in "A Trip to the Coast," for example, suddenly yearns to go to California and even puts herself in the hands of a faith-healer. Apart from such changes in a single person, we can expect Mary and Elizabeth to trade characteristics here as elsewhere. Viola in "Marrakesh" is evidently one of Munro's Marys — a sweetly mannered woman with silver, wave-like hair, who picks blue-and-purple flowers for her husband's grave; Dorothy by contrast is a blunt and sexless Elizabeth. Yet it is Dorothy who suddenly turns impulsive and irrational, revealing a susceptible Mary hidden since childhood and making the self-possessed Viola seem an Elizabeth in comparison. Even more curious, from our present viewpoint, is the interchange of roles between Mrs. Cross and Mrs. Kidd. As little Marian Botherton the latter once wore a pinafore with angelic wings and lived above the Post Office, much like Helena in her imagined bank tower; later she skates in sky-blue and white; as an old woman she would like to live alone overlooking the sea. But unlike Helena Mrs. Kidd is not tragic in the least — she is the comic Mrs. "kid" here — and it is the coarser-grained, more practical Mrs. "cross" who in the event coddles Jack McNeil and cries on losing him.[120]

Thus prepared, we can turn to the extraordinary Violet in "A Queer Streak" — a woman who, as her nephew realizes, is not going to submit easily to "classification" (236). Violet's name, to begin there, connects her with Munro's Marys — Viola in "Marrakesh," of course, but some more abject figures as well, as we can see from her maiden name of "Thoms." This last, apart from making her a Tom, brings her close to "Violet Toombs" in "Changes and Ceremonies," the girl who is sexually had in the bicycle shed by the minister's son: and so Violet is related to such pitiful objects as Franny McGill and Ruby Carruthers. What makes this hard to accept is that in so many ways she is pure Elizabeth: bursting with energy and management, unwilling to have her life called tragic, contemptuous of the despondent, befuddled mother she once relegated to the barnyard. Yet the names we hear applied to the two — "Aunt Ivie" and "Aunt Violet" — are not dissimilar, and in fact there is a passionate Mary inside Violet just as there is inside the Dorothy of "Marrakesh."

In the course of her story, as we have seen, Violet forms intimacies with three men. As an eager young Elizabeth she becomes engaged to the divinity student Trevor Auston, a Bert Matthews in the sense that he wields a paternal sort of authority. Then she finds herself repudiated, on the suspicion of a "hereditary taint" (230), and desperation — or the family craziness, if we prefer — brings her close to suicide. When it is cast out by an imperative of service to others, her very acceptance exalts her: if still an Elizabeth, Violet will now be the kind we have also called a high Mary. In a way suggestive of Helena or young Marian Botherton she ensconces herself above the Royal Bank, making her apartment there into a neatly fitted *hortus conclusus* — we even hear of a small hedged-in yard, "as tidily enclosed, as susceptible to arrangement and decoration, as any living room" (236). This queenly woman, attired in the royal purple we have seen, gives the lie to any notion of taint (even if we find her "mortified" (238) by a scorch mark on the table-cloth); it is the same queen who is prepared for a Platonic dalliance with the self-possessed Wyck Tebbutt — an unconsummated central relationship of the kind we have found most recently in Del and Jerry. Violet softens somewhat when Wyck becomes available for marriage; then, after his death and with the approach of her own, a wildly different self is suddenly revealed. The craziness has been there all along, buried like the manure Violet imagines in the trunk; and while the question of love here will have to wait, we should at least remember the final incident in which her nephew finds her standing in flames. Violet has started the fire herself in an attempt to burn her papers: she is the terminal Mary here, trying recklessly to undo the past and give herself to some saving consummation.

*

Who is to be the consort of such a woman — in the terms we have been using, which sort of John? Not the John who is Bert or Clive, or Jerry Storey, all of whom belong in their different ways to the old world of Law. Instead, the Mary who is Del is drawn to Garnet French: for if her other boyfriends in the chapter are variously censors, revellers, and Platonic companions, Garnet is the purest example in Munro of John the lover. In the initiatory context of "Age of Faith" we saw that the "Mediterranean" Christ finds a way into people's hearts; and he does so as the bringer, not of purity or abstracted wisdom, but of experience. John in the biblical Salome story — or what has been made of it — is actually closer to this Undergod than to any of the actors in the Bert Matthews episode: he is the John who baptizes, and is baptized, into love and death. We can equally say that his baptism is into the body, if by that we mean, not the Egyptian corporation, but the self that refrains from controlling or articulating or otherwise raising itself above its creaturely need. Garnet is not only an intensely physical presence, but someone who hates "people trying to tie things together" (220). To be in his company is to see, as we have noted, not Jerry Storey's structured and ideated world, but "something not far from what I thought animals must see, the world without names" (221) — a world of pure reality to which, at this stage, Del reaches out as her truth.

Garnet's counterparts are the other Undergods of the Passion stories — figures we will now need to see for their sexual character. Simon, different as he is from Garnet in many ways, is like him as the same dark lover, sensual, mysterious, and rejected by the world. Douglas Reider is a wandering ladies' man, as indeed Munro first conceived Simon to be (and as Rose conceives him to be); and with men like these we can connect others who are not lovers in any strict sense. It may, for instance, seem far-fetched to say that Dane in "A Queer Streak" is Violet's third lover, since the love here is not directly expressed or even fully conscious. Dane is in fact kept remote from Violet through the central part of the action in which he figures, communicating with her mainly by telephone until just before the end; meanwhile two feminist girls not only carry her off to her past but, to Dane's considerable disquiet, enlist her against the male sex. Yet at the end Dane comes to Violet in the fire, and in due course we will be considering all that this means. Again, the Jack McNeil who companions Mrs. Cross is hardly an ordinary lover, being an aging, crippled man who shares Garnet French's inarticulateness to the point of physical inability to speak. On the other hand, Jack can point to a picture of pine trees and a red deer (hanging above "the church with the cross" [170]): and while he means only to say that he once worked in Red Deer, Alberta, he is clearly saying far more than that. By now we have met enough pine trees and enough of the Edomite red to recognize Munro's symbolism of fleshly suffering; and the pun on "deer" — not only a hunted animal but someone loved — is one of the oldest in English literature.

This lover who is reality is by the same token a "serviceman": but especially in the case of Garnet French we find service both taking a more sincere form and receiving a greater blessing than any we have seen before. Here, as it were, the low and the high, Gentile and Jew, are brought together: the despised boy from Jericho Valley is the equal of the town girl who gets A's. The Frenches, whom we can see now for their plain friendliness, offer Del a better hospitality than Bert Matthews or Jerry Storey; and in their presence she feels simple happiness — as if she were sharing, not a social ritual, but the genuine communion meal with its message of love. As for more private communion, we have seen how Del and Garnet cross into a Promised Land; or if we want to be more pentecostal, we can imagine them as receiving the traditional comfort of the Spirit — "Gifts. Various kisses, tongue touchings, suppliant and grateful noises. Audacity and revelation" (218). The Lord, it seems, has come to Mary at last, and is magnifying his handmaiden. After the consummation in the garden Del "marvels" (228) at herself, knowing the "glory" (227) of what has happened, while Garnet the hewer of wood appears in "triumph" (228).

*

And yet this glory fails. In the gospel, to see certain motifs in a certain way, we find Mary rebuffed by her Lord, and later standing at a distance when he is crucified. In Munro Del is confronted in the river by an enraged Garnet, Rose waits in vain for Simon to return — somehow the love of these stories always proves to have hatred and rejection for its other face. By the same token humility here is always shadowed by pride. "You think you're too good for it" (238), cries Garnet when Del refuses his baptism, and of course he is right: Del has no real intention of giving herself — nor has Rose, nor any of the other women who fall in love in these stories, as we see from their various gestures of defiance. As for Garnet, Del senses from the beginning the pride that goes with his submissiveness. The dark part of him, the part she thinks she wants, turns out when she gets it to be just this pride, now wounded and infuriated. And this means that Law — a hierarchy of aloof superior and resentful inferior — has not been put away at all. If in Elizabeth's world Law has license as a palliative, perhaps Mary's world is only one of greater license and greater calling to account. Garnet, we can note, is both a fornicating sexual baptizer and a cleaned-up member of the Baptist Church; his Baptist religion itself is a strange combination of pentecostal enthusiasm and legal strictness.

If this is so, then the simple love found in revival religion or revival sexuality can hardly be so simple after all. Del, like Rose and Julie, has to acknowledge her own deviousness, and Garnet, while obviously less calculating, is once again not merely different. When Del contrasts her own "play-acting" with his "true intent" (238), we should notice where the latter phrase comes from: the prologue to the Pyramus and Thisbe play in *A Midsummer Night's Dream*. The mechanicals' intent is not simple at all — it seems to be delight and repentance at once — nor is there anything simple about love in the world reflected by their play within a play. It is the same in Munro's story: in terms of hierarchy once again, Garnet is quite alive to the social status of his earlier girlfriends, and even in choosing Del at sight must have some instinct as to what she is, the clever and honoured girl from town. He is seeking to possess a superior being — or more exactly, one both superior and inferior, since on another side of his mind Garnet is not impressed by brainy townspeople, and assumes that it would be a privilege for Del to join his family.

For Garnet the "gypsy boy" (211) belongs at least emblematically to an ancient line.[121] While his people, like the inhabitants of Mission Creek, seem acquiescent enough, they know the value of what they are, and Garnet for one is roused to violence when this is affronted. If we cast about more widely in the Passion stories, we will find not merely alienation of one kind and another — as when lofty Egyptians are set apart from the barbarians who serve and invade them — but a festering resentment that is much less typical of the central world.[122] Biblically, the world that dreamed of a coming Messiah was at once an imperial and a revolutionary one (with the usual paradox that the rebels sought to impose a greater repression of their own kind than any imposed by their masters). *Mutatis mutandis*, the academic party in "Simon's Luck" — the party where Rose meets Simon — is not very different. We have noted the violent intrusion of David the student, the main incident of the episode in all its successive versions;

and we should remember as well the young faculty members with their jealousy of the older ones — as Simon later remarks, they too want "a chunk of the power" (161). Meanwhile the elders themselves make a "fucked-up jealous establishment" (158); and Rose, who can hardly tell whether she is establishment or outsider, is bitterly aware of being disadvantaged by her age and sex and precarious occupation.

The party here is presided over by Shelley,[123] the hostess who manages to combine an old-fashioned lady's dress with a "waif style" (153). If we follow Shelley into the cluster of "Caroline" stories that I have mentioned, we will find the tensions and paradoxes of the Kingston party in an even more volatile form. Most schematically, there is the situation in "Mrs. Cross and Mrs. Kidd," where the Charlotte who steals Jack McNeil from the two older women is first a handmaid offering "red felt" (174) purses and then a china-haired doll with a lady's smile. In "Hard-Luck Stories" the leading lady is Caroline herself, the rich woman with a taste for artists and ambiguities of rank. Martin the playwright has the role of servant, bringing her blankets; yet not only does he stand to profit from his service, but he is being tacitly applauded for another role in which he acts with his namesake's loftiness if not charity. Caroline in turn plays beggar, asking in her "submissive" (193) voice for a blanket, even seeming to beg for reassurance — while the hostile narrator sees a predator toying with its prey. Maya in "Differently" is the same predator, playing ruthless games with a husband, a lover, and a friend while surrounding herself with hippies and, again, artists; and like Caroline Maya greatly enjoys the role of underling. She appears in burlap — sackcloth, in effect[124] — to pose as "an acolyte, meekly and gracefully assisting" (225) the husband she despises; she puts up with another bullying lover; towards the end she even fancies a sacrificial queen in a temple[125] "getting her heart torn out or some gruesome thing" (221).[126] At the same time Maya really is this sacrifice, for she is the prey of her prey, a woman exploited by her protégés. And confronted by the fury of Georgia, the friend she has betrayed, Maya pleads with all the anguish of a doomed victim.

The imbroglio of the exalted and abased here can introduce us to a story about which I have so far said little: this is "Executioners," in which the sense of tyranny and revolt and their complexities is stronger than anywhere else in the Passion group. There can be no mistaking the importance of class here: Helena's patrician parents, the despised bootlegging Troys, Robina's family living in its unpainted house on the edge of the bush. Nor can we miss the bitter grudges — Jimmy and Duval in particular have, it seems, been cheated by various higher-ups, and turned into outlaws in the process. In a more adequate view, it is no easier here than elsewhere to tell the up from the down. Robina's family are as proud as their counterparts the Frenches; Robina, for that matter, considers herself the ally of her genteel employers (or does so until fired), reserving her hatred for the Troys, outcasts themselves. Or outcasts in one respect — for the Troys "flourish" (140) in the bootlegging trade while Jimmy and Duval, seemingly their rivals or former confederates, appear unable to do so. Stump Troy's secret, in the local view, is his power over a superior: because of the accident that cost him his legs, he can command a mill-owner's protection. Helena's father is another superior at the mercy of those below, having been — his daughter feels sure — "personally, tauntingly, shamefully rejected" (139) by the voters in an election. She herself may be dressed as a little lady, yet as mocked by her schoolmates is the most downcast of creatures. And so we come to the relation between Helena and her enemy Howard Troy, opposites and yet fellows in their misery and hidden rancour. Howard first accepts a favour from Helena; he then punishes her brutally — "for presumption[,] for condescension" (142), or perhaps, as she imagines, just for showing vulnerability. Helena dreams of punishment in return: all the pride and anger and need in the world is here, ready to explode at the story's crisis.

V: Story and Crisis

If the climax of a story like "Executioners" forces together all the passions in human experience — let us just say all the love and hate — then it is showing us a great dilemma: the human problem at its most intense. To give some account of this dilemma, it will first be necessary to establish certain parallels, both in content and structure, among the stories with which the rest of this chapter will mainly be dealing. These are the stories in which initial and final incidents give us a specially strong feeling of reciprocation: for while their opening sections may not be strongly "Passion" in character (the containing situation is likely to be much more so, as in the two novels), later and answering sections give us the Passion experience in its most unmistakable form.

At least this is so if we see what we have been seeing in recent pages: that a third-phase heroine reaching out for love is also, unwittingly, reaching for hate, to which we can add that the hate expressing itself by attack may also do so by rejection. If we bear these things in mind, seemingly different issues will become versions of a single one, and seemingly different structures the same structure. In the Garnet French episode — the story that most typifies the Passion group as we defined it earlier — love leads to hate; in "Simon's Luck," or more precisely in what I will take as its central phase, love leads to abandonment. In "A Queer Streak" a first love ending in abandon- ment leads to a final one — not so plainly love, and with a very different-seeming lover — in which abandonment is no longer possi- ble. In the closely related "Executioners" the first encounter is already its own little story of love turning to hate: Howard and Helena first "love" each other — in the sense that she passes him some paper and a pencil, which he takes — and then become deadly enemies. Their second meeting is a fiery climax of love-and-hate, as I will try to show, in which we sense revenge even more keenly than in "A Queer Streak" — revenge on Howard himself in this case, and revenge not for abandonment but for aggression.

To think in terms of narrative levels, any of these stories can be seen in a form as elementary as our linear figure. In "Executioners" the first meeting of the two principals — in which we can include both Helena's generosity to Howard Troy and his subsequent accosting of her on the road — leads to a distinct second meeting: and this simple kind of "crossing" is one we will need to keep in mind, since in "Executioners" as in the Garnet French story it has a strongly emblematic effect. When Howard tries to stop Helena on the road, she continues straight ahead; at the climax Howard himself runs straight through the door of his father's house; Robina, an especially emblematic figure in this story, marches straight through life gener- ally. But there is something more complex here as well: when Helena watches Howard run through the burning door, this situation reverses the earlier one in which it was Howard who watched and Helena who forced herself past as if "through a wall of flame" (142). What we are seeing now is cyclical return, in a dynamic version for which we can borrow Munro's word "reciprocity" (139). It was over the reciprocity issue, similarly, that Helena's father lost his seat in Parlia- ment, the loss itself being reciprocity as found in a two-party political system. In a less public way Jimmy and Duval are going to inflict reciprocity on the likes of Stump Troy; and we may as well apply the word to all the oscillating swings, doors, brooms, and arms in the story, not to say reciprocating games like "Red Rover" or "Aunty

Aunty over the Shanty" (146). Once again Robina seems at the heart of it all: as she strides through the bush, her body "seemed to . . . swing like a door on its hinges, controlled, but dangerous if you got in the way" (143). And when Helena, at the fire, does get in the way, Robina answers with "the hardest blow I had ever felt" (151) — the door has swung. It swings in "Simon's Luck" when David the student, whom Rose has absent-mindedly indulged and then forgotten, reappears at the party in Kingston to affront her: and the whole story will present the same rhythm of unthinking commitment leading to neglect or, in a larger reciprocity, to a disturbing reminder. In the Garnet French story, again, Del's commitment to Garnet, fervid yet not quite genuine, is answered in the end by his outraged demand for its fulfilment — after which he abandons her permanently.

*

Action that comes back on itself has a turning-point, of course, and the more this gathers neighbouring events around itself, the more we feel a central baptism as well as flanking ones. We have seen something of the central complex in the Garnet French story — the kissing and feasting at the Frenches, followed by sex in a more private situation. Helena's triumphant visit to Robina's family makes an obvious counterpart, and in "Simon's Luck" Rose's blissful weekend with Simon. In each of these episodes welcome leads to the same reversal, though there is some variation as to just how dire this is within the central complex itself. In "Simon's Luck" it is dire indeed: the happy weekend leads to a very different successor, when the figure appearing out of the night is not Simon — the "company" (164) Rose hoped for — but the lonely village woman who foresees similar loneliness for Rose. As we have seen, this woman is one of Munro's Counter-Strangers — a bringer of bad fortune; and soon afterwards Rose is keeping her midnight watch, alone and in despair. In more "hollow" stories the central reversal is a matter of signs and portents rather than actual disaster, but its presence is evident enough. The sexual consummation between Garnet and Del, already a turning away from the lively socializing before it, ends with both a collapse to the ground and an issue of blood. Reversal here may remain within the magic circle of the happy Sunday — indeed bring it to its final happiness — and yet the tone is shifting: presently we hear about a tomcat tearing a bird apart, and when Del proceeds to her ill-fated exams, the empty school is very much the janitors' building — one of Munro's Lairs.[127]

In "Executioners," as I have indicated, the central event is Helena's visit to Robina's family, an occasion on which she is no less happy than Del as the guest of the Frenches: but here again the scene proceeds to darken. Jimmy and Duval — the "play-fighters" (147) who hug Helena into something like Del's orgasmic pleasure in the garden — represent the more hostile side of play-fighting as well; and at the end of the episode Robina is grimly prophesying what the pair will do to their enemies. In particular, it seems, they are out to get Stump Troy, to whom Helena in her ensuing fantasy adds his son Howard: if we forgot the business of the Troys during their rivals' good-humoured celebration, it has stubbornly come back to be settled. In the latter part of "Possession" (the second half of "A Queer Streak") it is rather the past of a single family that needs settling. Violet at this stage is a much older woman than either Helena or Del: glory for her, after her husband's death, means simply getting out a bit and having her nephew Dane to count on. But now comes invasion, led by "King Billy" (243) — the family horse, that is, of whom Violet has a hallucination, but inevitably her much-bridled father as well. Another invader is the distraction suggestive of her mother Aunt Ivie; her sisters follow in the guise of the two feminist girls who inquire into family history and claim Violet for their own. Soon things have reached the point where she is seeing manure in place of the family papers.

By now Violet has retreated into the house, alarmed by her apparition; at the same time a tooth problem is keeping Dane away — once again a passion hero is virtually unable to speak.[128] The problem here, for which he is going to need a "root-canal job" (245), is another common one in these stories: after Jerry Storey, as we have noted, Del similarly imagines her need for love going "underground" like a "canny tooth-ache" (208). With Helena it is the unbearable word "fuck" that goes "underground" (143); with Violet it is the "infection" (252) — physical and emotional — that she speaks of as "running its course" through her veins. Now, as the story nears its crisis, the infection starts to come out: we find Helena, for instance, both wanting to burst Howard Troy's eye (whereupon "all kinds of pus, venomous substances, would spurt and flow" [149]) and preparing for an outburst of her own. And at last, in all of the stories we have just been considering, we come to a terminal baptism — seen in a cyclical reading as the third.[129] This baptism may have its own little story: in "Baptizing," for instance, we pass through a core of stillness and poise just as Garnet is starting to remind Del what she has contracted for, while Del herself indolently assumes the Crucifixion position in the water.

> The river was still as a pond; you couldn't tell to look at it which way the current was going. It held the reflection of the opposite banks. . . . (233)

Then death slices the day: soon Del and Garnet are trying to kill each other. Love has been answered by hate in spite of any cyclical diversion — in fact the diversion has only made the answer more terrible. Even more terribly, this answer is itself a form of love-making: love and death have become the same dark flash.

*

In such a flash the whole of the lovers' story is summed up — or the story of fallen humanity itself, as we can see by attending to some of Munro's allusions. These are best followed in "Executioners," at the climax of which we feel ourselves present not only at the burning of Troy but at every major theophany of the Bible. A previous scene of the same kind has been compared by Helena's mother to the Crucifixion; when we come to the fire itself, correspondingly, we notice a bystander's comment on the doomed man: " 'Jesus,' a man said reverently[;] 'Jesus, he'll be fried' " (151).[130] But the Crucifixion is all the crossings in history: other events are drawn to it as the Troys' neighbours are drawn to the fire or, in the Bible, kings are drawn from the east by a similar "proclamatory light." To step further back in time, we can note how the burning house in Munro's story is linked with the bursting eye in the previous paragraph — with a boil, then, and a flow of blood;[131] we find cars lined up as well, not to say Howard running through the door at an hour close to midnight.[132] And this Exodus is equally the encounter at Sinai: while others stand watching, Howard like Moses hears a call and passes through a fire-cloud to the Father. Within the life of Jesus the same event recurs as the Transfiguration, where we once more find onlookers, brightness, a voice from a cloud, and the disappearance of a chosen leader.

Nor does the Crucifixion only sum up the past: it points to the apocalyptic events that bring the world to its end. In this perspective, the place outside town in "Executioners" becomes that of the witnesses' martyrdom; it is also the place of the winepress where the grapes of wrath are trodden like the boil imagined by Helena, and blood flows to the horses' bridles; and if the fire here makes a noise like a lawnmower, what is taking place is the apocalyptic harvest as well. In the "hydrant" (150) gushing water we can make out a Dragon: the water that fails such a fire recalls, not only the river from the Dragon's mouth swallowed by the Earth, but the river dried up by one of the bowls of wrath — overturned like the "overturned basins" (149) in Helena's fantasy. We can remember, too, what this drying up prepares for, the coming of the kings of the east to the great battle; and we can remember how this is followed in turn by the most spectacular of all judgments, the fall of Babylon. Babylon is different things: at once a city, condemned like the carnal Temple elsewhere, and a whore filled like a tumour with impurities and blood. Babylon traffics sinfully, supplying the nations with her liquor; and in the end she is consumed by fire as the kings stand apart grieving. At the same time we hear the Song of Moses — the paean sung at the Exodus by the exultant Miriam, and paralleled at the Troys' fire by the manic yelling of Robina.

One further set of biblical connections will be necessary as we approach Munro's climax: these have to do with "stumps." Stump Troy, the man who cannot get out of the fire, is certainly stumped in the sense of baffled — a sense Munro draws attention to when applying the word to Mr. Lougheed in "Walking on Water" (74). He is stumped more obviously in the sense that he has lost his legs: he is one of the mutilated figures of the Passion stories. In "Something I've Been Meaning to Tell You," similarly, Jimmy Saunders goes "stumping" (19) about as a maimed war veteran,[133] and Jimmy has a further link with Stump Troy in being curtained out by Et Desmond — for Stump loses his eyes, metaphorically, when his son smashes the windows of his house, just as another man loses an eye literally in a fight with young Garnet French.[134] In "A Queer Streak," again, Aunt Ivie predicts that young Violet's bad temper will leave her with "stumps" (211) for teeth; at the end we appropriately find her "rooted" in a fire "like a big dark stump" (250). There are two biblical passages echoed here, I think. One that will prove important later deals with King Nebuchadnezzar, reduced to a "stump" in mind and body and compelled to eat grass like a beast.[135] And if we add one further image from Munro — the field of "stumps" in Jericho Valley near the "skeletons of a burned-out house and barn" (221) — we will arrive at an even more suggestive connection for the fire in "Executioners": John the Baptist's prophecy of judgment.

And now also the axe is laid unto the root of the trees; therefore every tree which bringeth not forth good fruit is hewn down, and cast into the fire.

I indeed baptize you with water unto repentance; but he that cometh after me is mightier than I, whose shoes I am not worthy to bear: he shall baptize you with the Holy Ghost, and with fire.

Whose fan is in this hand, and he will thoroughly purge his floor, and gather his wheat into the garner; but he will burn up the chaff with unquenchable fire.[136]

*

With the convergence of biblical motifs at the climax of "Execution- ers" we find metaphorically what we have also been seeing narra- tively, an ultimate confrontation in human experience that no earlier distinction and harmony has been able to avert. All the imagery of the Passion stories converges in the same way: if we follow it, we will be led to a single emblem for human suffering, and challenged to interpret that emblem. What may impress us first here is the elements themselves, and especially those most immediately associated by John with baptism — fire and water. Since fire is what "focus" means, Munro is playing with fire when the Fortune-Teller in "Simon's Luck" cannot get Simon "in focus" (165) or Dane's lapse into illness makes everything "out of focus to him" (245). Dane is later drawn into Violet's focus, of course, while "Executioners" is an even more focal kind of story. It is water, on the other hand, that dominates "Baptiz- ing" and plays an important part elsewhere — in the rain, for instance, that comes when Rose expected Simon. We can readily add the other elements to these two. The "concrete" (151) over which the fire moves like a lawnmower in "Executioners" is a form of earth; and the mortal red earth of Edom or Adam — present, I have suggested, in foxy Clive — is the dominant symbol in "Marra- kesh."[137] As for air, we can notice the "hot, creeping wind" (180) that springs up in the grass near the crisis of "A Trip to the Coast" — this on a day when darkness begins at mid-day, and we soon find ourselves with a saviour and a corpse. In "The Spanish Lady," again, there is a hot wind blowing as the heroine walks with the Rosicrucian at the Great Divide.[138]

If we find these elements individually, we also find them crossing — working both together and against each other like the elements of metaphor in general. "Executioners" contains a good deal of firewa- ter: that is what Helena's father drinks and the bootleggers bootleg, not to say what Helena herself is drinking (mixed with water) at the end. We find other inflammatory liquids here as well, inside the body and outside it. There is the pus in the boil imagined by Helena, and of course there is gasoline — another source of Jimmy and Duval's troubles with the police, also the means apparently used to start the fire at the Troys'. The grandmother in "A Trip to the Coast" sells gasoline; she also smokes and fries bacon on a fire, adding two other of the incendiary images that recur in these stories.[139] If, on the other hand, she "dampers" (176) the fire and later spits on it, we sense opposition of the elements: in which case either may be the winner. Fighting the fire at Stump Troy's with a hose would be, once again, like "spitting" (150),[140] and not of much effect; when Helena, on the other hand, passed through her own wall of flame, the season was the dead of winter, and "dog urine ran down the shoveled paths" (142). The hot element — here fluid — only freezes into the snow beneath, in a grim parody of the descent of spirit.

Along with alternatives of this kind, there is the reciprocation that we have found to be a structural principle in these stories as stories. The Garnet French episode begins with a revival sermon in which salvation is equated with the passing of a river of fire.[141] Del's acceptance of salvation here — religious or sexual — inevitably leads her, as it once led the Israelites, to the passing of a second river, this time one of water in which she is all but drowned. On the other hand, her first baptism is itself presented as leading to, or taking place in, a watery setting — the lovers' first sexual intimacy takes place in the rain beside the river — and compared to this gentle experience of water, it is the second baptism in the now shrunken river that is like one of fire. With such ambiguity, we can readily see how fire and water, like love and hate, might be the same baptism: the hot-blooded craziness, for instance, that courses in the veins of Violet Thoms, and once drove her sister to deal with "bad blood" (215) by sitting in the creek.

But elements are only that, and we can go on to the more organized vegetable world, exchanging the mown concrete of "Executioners" for grass to be cut or burned. When the Spanish Lady walks with the Rosicrucian in the hot wind, she does so at "Field," and we know from the Exodus stories what is endured by a counterpart of grass — the lichen bleached by the sun (not to say the dulse tried by the other ordeal of water). We should also remember that, when Uncle Craig is displayed to the world, the room is "like a haymow on a blazing afternoon" (58) — and that Allen Durrand in "The Ottawa Valley" is martyred in a real mow, itself burning hot.[142] Allen's high situation may also remind us that there are more vertical forms of vegetation than grass. When Helena's father in "Executioners" goes through an ordeal much like Stump Troy's, it is burning "brooms" (139) that he sees in front of him; when Violet runs from Wyck Tebbutt, in an earlier counterpart of the later fire scene, it is thornbushes that she runs into — not actually burning, but certainly prickling and trapping. And bushes can lead us to the most concentrated of vegetable images. We have recently been noticing stumps, with which we can put the log that Helena's imagination makes of Robina's hidden arm, or the three logs across the creek, or more generally Munro's lumberyards, hardwood floors, and blackboards.[143] In the crisis this world of wood becomes a single upright axis, ignited by the contrary principle of spirit. The "burning beam" (150) to which Robina is compared at the fire may be a beam of light, and in its context is equally the beam of a house: but it is also, I would suggest, a beam in the old sense of a tree — or of course a cross. We are coming, in other words, to discern the same tree and sun that we found in their worldly glory in the previous chapter, but now making an image of extremity.

As the image — a very cosmic one — of a tree becomes clearer, we begin to notice the animals, or their human counterparts, that archetypally gather to it. In "A Trip to the Coast" the grandmother dreams of a black bird against the sun; and we have seen other such images[144] — in one case that of Chris Watters, the airman who also terrifies Mrs. Peebles by flying in low. With a further concentration the bird may become the sun itself, as when Duval in "Executioners," sunstruck from working on a roof, cries "Get them feathers outa my face" (145); in the same way, the pieces of paper flying through the room at the climax of "A Queer Streak" appear to Dane as "flaming birds" (250). Such birds of course suggest doves, the images of fiery spirit; at the same time they recall birds of prey or carrion — the crows and buzzards elsewhere in Munro,[145] as well as in the Book of Revelation itself.[146]

Together with a bird at its top, the world-tree has a lower animal form — deer, lion, serpent — occupying its base; and the two are often to be found locked in combat. In another of the several references in "Executioners" to animals and birds (not to say an airport), we are told that Howard Troy has eyes like a cat — one of the many we have seen in Munro's stories. In the immediate context this cat is very much a victim, like her shot coons and groundhogs; on the other hand, the sight of Howard makes Helena afraid, and we can remember Del Jordan's notion of a tomcat tearing a bird apart.[147] It may be the bird, then, that is the cat's victim: for certainly there are dangerous beasts running loose in the Passion stories — "A Queer Streak" ends with a wild pig, and "Marrakesh" gives us a hint of the Cretan minotaur.[148] In the same story, as also in "Differently," Munro's world of Iberian sacrifice makes its appearance: the heroine's travels take her to Spain and the red Alhambra. Elsewhere in the Passion group, to go no farther, we find that the house shared by Violet with Wyck Tebbutt has a bullfighter on the living-room wall, and that Del fancies herself Carmen at the bullring, trying to get by an attacker who might as well be the bull itself.

With the help of "The Spanish Lady," still another "Iberian" story, we can take the final step necessary here. Combining its various suggestions, we see that "Field" (183) (to which we could add "God's Little Acre" [180–81]) is at once the arena of a bullfight, a field of honour or conquest, and the scene of an *auto da fe*. What is burning here, then, is also something human: a youthful Adam or Eve, to follow out other allusions in this story, or a "Rosicrucian" (184) in middle age, or an Old Man who flings his arms out in dying. "Executioners," with its concentration on a single spectacle, can focus our vision still more sharply. Even for the happy visit to Robina's family the creek has to be crossed on the three logs we have seen; and when Robina swings her arm out to do so, resembling in Helena's mind an injured bird, she also resembles a crucified human body. If we turn from this premonition to the story's climax, the burning house of wood there will appear as a human body again, set afire by its passion. When, moreover, Helena tells us that "the fire filled the house the way blood fills a boil" (149), we will think of what she has wanted to see punctured or exploded like a boil — Howard Troy's eyes; and if we keep looking at the house we will start to see both smashed eyes[149] and a flaming mouth. In the end, then, we have come to the place of the skull: the burning church at "Hedley's" Corners[150] or one of Munro's dying "temples." The head here is a locked one — Stump Troy cannot escape; and what is burning inside it is the source of all these images, the trapped and desperate human mind.

VI: The Baptism of Fire

What, then, happens in this happening that consumes humanity and its world? To begin with we can recall the setting: not only the burning house itself but the Troys' yard in its entirety. The house is on one side of it, watched by Howard. On the other side we find a similar configuration: Helena too is watching, and like Howard has someone to restrain her, in this case Robina. On this side of things, again, there is a parent behind the scene: Helena's mother is present inside a car but does not show herself to the others. As we might expect from such a correspondence, the climactic event comes on both sides of the yard at once: the burning house collapses, with Howard rushing through the door as it does; at the same moment Helena receives her stunning blow from Robina.

Helena is of course forced back where Howard goes forward — in relation to the fire — and there are other important differences here; but for the present we can treat the two events simply as parallel versions of a single one. Again, we could if we wanted distribute this event into something more serial, a sequence of action and reaction. First a situation of inert watching is disturbed by a call: when it occurs to Helena to ask the whereabouts of Jimmy and Duval, she yells the question to one of their sisters, while at about the same time Stump's cries reach Howard, or so some of the bystanders imagine. Then comes reciprocation: as another cry is heard, the roof falls in and Howard dashes through the door; across the yard Helena runs as it were into the arm of Robina — herself a door, as we have seen. But we can best stay for now with the idea of a single event (single in time in this case): simply a yell and a convulsive movement. At the Crucifixion, we remember, there is a corresponding event: Jesus asks his great question of the Father, utters a cry — whether of despair or desperate faith — and gives up his spirit.

Now we have gathered some of the manifest facts about Munro's climax; but what happened in a deeper sense as Howard ran through the door (to keep for the moment to his side of the yard)? Helena as narrator is at some pains to report the onlookers' explanations, which in general are not unlike the various explaining that has been applied to the Crucifixion.[151] First comes a theory that can serve as a model for all that follow: Howard, some say, lost his head and ran into the fire instead of running the other way. Other theories can best be reduced to two: Howard was either a hero or something more murky. Perhaps he was being loyal to his father, trying to get him out of a tight situation;[152] or perhaps the two had quarrelled — perhaps, then, Howard had set the fire, or if Stump had set it (for the insurance), Howard failed to rescue him, so that in either case his last act was prompted by "remorse . . . or fear of facing the authorities" (152).

Any of these theories is plausible enough to reassure the sensible part of one's mind; yet the fact remains that Howard ran into a burning, collapsing building when it was "far too late to save anybody, if that was his intention, too late to be saved himself" (152). In the same great event the reasonable joining and separating by which we relate things failed for once to do its work — boards flew, beams burned, concrete was mown, and flames tore at the sky. When Jesus dies, having likewise been called unable to save, a veil is rent, the earth opens, and the dead walk with the living. After such an event, something in us can only go on wondering — which in fact is what Helena is doing when we last see her as an old woman.

The fire, we can note, is described as making a "racket" (151), one that drowns out any cries on the part of Stump Troy. A racket is also what the various bootleggers of the story carry on, in alliance or out of it, not to say a weapon for reciprocal hitting. Perhaps, as in the Exodus stories, all the explanations of the fire amount to another racket: while play-fighting against each other, they band together to drown out or beat back something different altogether. Helena, suggestively, thinks that Robina hit her to keep something else from hitting her; in an earlier scene Helena's father, defeated in the play-fighting of Grits and Tories, tried to make an address and was jeered down by the mob with the burning brooms. If we are to get beyond the similar racket of explanation, we will have to do two opposite things, as generally in Munro: on the one hand, take what is given simply on its own terms, and, on the other, see it emblematically. For the facts — and indeed the recorded explanations, which are themselves facts — do give us an image of something.

Before proceeding with the fire in "Executioners," we can equip ourselves with an important analogue: in "A Queer Streak," as we have seen, we have another Passion story ending with a man and woman and a fire. We also have another story that plagues itself with explanation, for in each of its two halves there is an outbreak of strangeness to be accounted for. Violet and Dane, respectively, do their best with the job: the anonymous letters, it seems, are only Violet's sisters perpetrating a hoax; the strange goings-on in "Possession," which include not only another pair of girls but further papers (or manure), are feminism in the one case and senility in the other. But in both parts of the story the investigators sense something more that they cannot grasp. What have the sisters got against poor King Billy, as he himself wonders? The answer to the mystery is hidden in Dawn Rose's "innocent and evil" (226) grin. In "Possession" Dane senses another — or the same — mystery all around him, "a tiresome, silly, malicious sort of secret" (247). When, moreover, he questions his aunt about the past, her answer is only "a balky sort of grunt, *annhh*" (243) — the same teasing word that we found in "Mrs. Cross and Mrs. Kidd."

*

Another way of encountering the same mystery is to consider the title "A Queer Streak." This justifies itself in more than one way: not only is there the streak of craziness that runs in Violet's family, but at the climax, when Dane has streaked into the burning kitchen, Violet inexplicably streaks out of it. Afterwards, having said "annhh" (253) for a second time, she crazily imagines a wild pig running through corn — Munro's imagery of grass again, green in this case as Nature's bonfire can also be. And if we take streaking of this kind a bit farther, we arrive at still another kind. Running out of the kitchen and tumbling into some rose bushes, Violet is left with blood-smears on her arms. There is no need for Dettol, she says: every sort of infection has already "run its course" (252) through her veins. I have already connected this image with that of the poison in the "root-canal," and there is a link here as well with Dawn Rose, who once put off menstruation by driving the "bad blood" (215) back into her system. In any case the queer streak can be a streak of red, and red is something we find throughout this story. Dawn Rose, for instance, is not only red-haired[153] but red-faced and, when Violet catches her, literally red-handed, since strawberry juice is oozing from her fingers. The same colour appears in the "streak of red hair caught by the low sun, behind a juniper bush" (225) — the streak that reveals the two conspirators to Violet. Later Dane's only definite memory of Dawn Rose is one in which she is putting on a hat with a bright red ribbon.

By now we are on familiar ground: we have met red streaks, red sunsets, and red ribbons before, all of them forms of the line that crosses or seals a threshold. Now, of course, it is a final threshold we are concerned with; biblically, we need to see the blood at the Passover or the red thread of Rahab as final in the same way, which also means identifying them with their New Testament antitypes in the Passion and Apocalypse. In itself, though, what happens at the terminal threshold is like what happened at the initiatory: in linear terms, someone crosses; in cyclical, someone is turned back; in typological, someone both crosses and is turned back. In "Executioners" Howard goes through the door; Helena is struck back at the same time; and if events on the two sides of the yard parallel each other, the going through and the falling back are somehow one thing. We can see the Crucifixion itself in the same various ways. Jesus goes to the Father as the veil of the Temple is rent; Jesus also dies on the cross, crying that he has been forsaken; and in the view we must take here these two consummations are somehow the same.

Passage into a locked head, rejection, both at once: what all these amount to, certainly, is arrival at a barrier. We can call it a door; or, as the sun caught in the juniper bush indicates, we can say that it is our burning tree — for the transverse red streak is similarly a facing object confronting and blocking someone's way; and we can further imagine the barrier in what for "Executioners" is its most important form, that of a sexual threshold. In this case, inconveniently if significantly, the story itself makes a barrier, for its terminal baptism is one in which the hero and heroine, unlike Garnet and Del, seemingly have nothing to do with each other. At some earlier points in the story Munro has been concerned with inability to respond; now we find Helena standing back on one side of the yard — restrained by the Robina in herself, we might say — while Howard, who can hardly be aware of her presence, runs away from her. And yet I have already suggested that this climax, like that of "Baptizing," is the fatal coming together of two lovers.

*

To see how this might be so, we can first go back to the business of explaining. Nobody suggests, nor does it quite occur to Helena, that the right explanation for the fire might be Jimmy and Duval: yet the circumstances are suspicious to say the least. The two brothers are absent from an event at which everybody else is present, though as enemies of the Troys they would presumably want to be there; Helena, moreover, is swatted for asking where they are. Perhaps, then, they started the fire themselves — it would be like them to use gasoline from the can later found empty. Why do people not think of that? It could be simply that the rivalry between the two families is not well known, though such things are usually known and Robina for one is outspoken enough. In any case this explanation, as such, has the failing of other explanations: even if right it only takes us to more facts, or a reasonable account of the facts.[154] But now let us do the two things I have suggested as an antidote for explanation: let us

433

stay with Jimmy and Duval, and let us see them as emblems. For Jimmy and Duval mean something, and this something must be so disturbing that others do not want to know about it. As we have seen, the two brothers are specialists in play-fighting, and if as bootleggers they are the "rivals, or fallen-out accomplices" (148) of the Troys, then play-fighting is more than their rough-and-tumble at home. Perhaps play-fighting is behind the fire of the whole world—perhaps, then, it too is unthinkable.

If so, the same thing must be true of the love-hate that we have already seen as the matter of the terminal crisis: for that is what play-fighting amounts to. With Helena in the picture, moreover, we must see this love-hate, not just as the squabble over political office or the bootlegging market, but as that of sex. When Helena visits Robina's house, she herself becomes the object of the brothers' play-fighting — they put her between them, then tickle or hug her while calling "*Mine. Mine*" (147). In the rivalry of the two bootlegging families it is Helena again who stands in the middle — not necessarily as a factual cause (she would not have told Robina's family about her encounter with Howard) but simply as Helen, the woman who comes between Greece and Troy. And of course the same Helen comes between Helena and Howard Troy themselves: Helena, after all, is a pretty girl, not to say one who confers favours that Howard considers advances. It should not be too surprising to find her as a *casus belli* here: for in Munro the fire or blood in which the world is consummated can always be seen in sexual terms. When Del Jordan imagines the tomcat tearing up the bird, the blood she is trying to explain away is that of her sex with Garnet. "What do I have that's fur?" (154), wonders Rose innocently when a tomcat is himself killed in her dryer — another of Munro's images of "focus."

As certain things thus become clearer about fur[155] and feathers, they may also become so about vegetable types of our focal image. The burning tree that is, or is on, a height becomes in this context the sexual bush on the *mons Veneris*; there is the same sexuality in the door of the burning house and the red cord at the threshold — the threshold now of Babylon, with her blood and her fiery downfall. The ground of the burning bush, which we have seen as the "field" of an *auto da fe*, is equally the "plateau" (218) to which Del and Garnet come at the end of sexual "pleasure." So, we should add, are Munro's other sacrificial plates and trays,[156] which we can readily connect with the inner "tray" of the human body. Nor is the encounter simply a visceral matter: as we can see from the importance of the eye in "Executioners," the same fatal meeting is present in all fallen vision — that is, fallen knowledge. To match the burning house in "Executioners," "Marrakesh" offers various hot spaces that are ultimately a single enclosure — a glassed porch on which a man and woman make love while an old schoolteacher looks on. In a way, of course, Dorothy is the contrary of the lovers, with their pleasure and suffering; yet they reappear in the blackboarded schoolroom of her eye, and we have seen Munro's play on the word "stroke" (173). The sexual encounter and that of the critical eye with its object are really the same encounter: the carnal knowledge with which fallen consciousness meets flesh.

It is just this knowledge that is unbearable: for it is the coming together of things that cannot come together, or that come together only to destroy each other. Helena shrinks from it — when, like Rose crossing the bridge, she hears voices of "deadly innocence" (138) mocking her fur collar, she cannot wear it any longer; "we are shamefully made" (143), she thinks again when Howard Troy throws the forbidden sexual word at her. And then the shrinking back of shame becomes its opposite, the explosion of the burning head at the climax of the story. What is called sex is the most intimate and arousing and troubling of earthly knowledges: no wonder people take refuge in explanations.

VII: Real Life

If what happens at the great fire is something between Howard and Helena, we will need to understand how an encounter can at the same time be just the opposite: and for this we will have to think again about the metaphor of coming together and moving apart. We have seen how a protagonist goes through, or is turned back, or at once goes through and is turned back, depending on our level of interpretation. We have seen the same event in terms of a pair of opposites that do or do not come together, or both do and do not in a way that defies reason. If we think of these opposites as a pair of lovers we will again have various possibilities. At the baptism in the river Garnet and Del come together in a desperate scuffle, having come together as lovers just before. Simon comes to Rose and then, on the rainy night, does not come, whereupon Rose drives off to the west coast. After being separate for most of the final episode, Dane and Violet finally come together in the burning kitchen, though what happens there is especially complex: Dane rushes in to extinguish the fire, while Violet first stands like a stump and then rushes away — like Rose.

"Executioners" has something of all these stories: mutual hatred as in the Garnet French story, emphasis on the non-meeting of the protagonists as in "Simon's Luck," and of course various similarities to the climax of "A Queer Streak." It is also especially schematic, with its twin actions on mirroring sides of a yard; and now we will need to make it even more so. Each of the protagonists, in moving away from the other, goes to someone else: Howard runs to his father, and when Helena is struck by Robina and shrinks back into herself, she is becoming like her mother — the self-contained woman who has been waiting in the car behind her. "Deadeye Dick," the story with a burning red window in a half-blind door, has a very similar climax. Ignoring differences for the moment, we can note that when Morris crosses the street to date (or fail to date) Matilda, Joan is watching like Helena; at the same time, "far back in the house, Joan's mother is singing" (193). It was this mother who put Morris up to his enterprise; she is behind it as well in the sense of having drawn back from it.

Here it will be useful to make a distinction between love, or more adequately love-and-hate, and what in a broad sense we can call friendship. According to the narrator in "Hard-Luck Stories," there is the reasonable kind of love and there is the passionate kind,[157] the former always being neglected for the latter. The word "love" is applied to both sorts of feeling by this narrator, and in both cases means something between the sexes; but of course passionate love, not reasonable, is the truly sexual kind, and reasonable love may well be directed to a relative or friend — when Rose falls in love with Simon, for instance, her decent friendship with the woman next door becomes a less interesting alternative. Conversely, it often happens in Munro that someone (usually a man) abandons a sexual partner for a non-sexual concern that he finds more important: but in either case it seems that a choice has to be made. In "Executioners" the friendship that rivals sexual love — or rivals the hate that is the other side of such love — appears as loyalty to a parent, the person concealed on the periphery of the young people's circle.

In seeing a Counter-Stranger like Rose's neighbour as representing friendship, we will have to make a further distinction, this time between two kinds of Counter-Stranger. One is like the dark Arab who accosts Jeanette in "Marrakesh." The other is a member of the heroine's own sex, offering the companionship of that sex. In the Garnet French story Naomi is such a figure, as is Del's mother; Mary Fortune in "Red Dress — 1946" is a specially pure example, being a girl who wants female company and nothing else. In fact such a friend may herself take the form of a company: for if what is at the centre of our scheme is imagined as "one" — a coming together of two people — then what we find at the periphery may well be many. In "Possession," when Violet is approached by the two feminist girls, we hear about a whole "Isle of Women" (246) where men are kept in subjection; and Violet's lively interest reminds us that she presided over such a régime at home before having anything to do with boys. (Hooligan and Hayes, the far-off "outfit" who once bossed King Billy, advance into the foreground when we remember his complaint of having "a mule for a wife and a hooligan daughter running his house" [212].) "Marrakesh" has a muted version of the same situation: Blair King's wife, we hear, is "the sorority-girl type" (168), and the household of the three unattached women — the household from which Dorothy ultimately goes out to see Jeanette making love with a man — is implicitly another sorority. Compared to these female alliances, the relevant male figures seem weak and ephemeral: Blair King is as sad a ruler as King Billy; Dorothy's dead husband does not rate a mention. And in the background of "A Queer Streak" is the picture that Violet finds strangely moving: the three queens bound for their island with a stricken King Arthur in their power. If we substitute a biblical background for an Arthurian, we have the three Marys[158] who watch the Crucifixion from a distance — as for that matter do the three principal women in "Executioners."

But as the female sodality begins to form, a male counterpart is doing the same thing, and in a way that of course excludes rather than absorbs the heroine. Throughout the Garnet French story the hero has been praying to his "Heavenly Father" (216); he has also been doing the Father's work of looking after the Young People, not to say playing on an all-male baseball team — whose claims have to be met before he can get around to loving Del. After coming to her, in fact, he has always withdrawn in one way and another: for as Del learns at the revival meeting, he has a pledge to renew. Garnet is true to form, then, when he chooses in the end to be the father-worshipping kind of baptist rather than a lover of the opposite sex. Earlier in the story — at the time of some female Counter-Strangers, in fact — Del encounters unsettling male versions as well: the high-school principal and, in a more plural form, the bachelor trinity holding forth on the Flats Road. Revisiting her father there, she finds herself demoted to the role of drudge, kept physically away from her brother, and — in words she heard earlier from Garnet himself — refused the men's beer.[159] "Anonymous Letters" has much the same story to tell: when female craziness threatens embarrassment, Trevor Auston opts for his United god; in fact that is what Jesus himself can be seen as doing, and especially in the gospel of John. To see the matter from our current perspective (not the only one possible, of course), this not quite incarnate saviour would rather be one with the Father than share with humanity, and seals his choice by returning home in the end.

*

A centre and a periphery always behave like a pair of mirrors: if, then, we are seeing love set against friendship (in my present senses of those words), we can expect to see something more complex as well. We will remember how the Exodus stories feature Oedipal attachment, mainly between girls and fathers. The same attachment, mainly between sons and mothers now, returns in the Passion group, where it is obviously present in the case of Jerry Storey, and more covertly so if Bert and Clive are nothing but "cowboys" (191). To have something more passionate, we can remember how the suffering Undergod is at once the son of a *mater dolorosa* and a lover. So far we have not really identified these two roles, yet even with Del Garnet plays both — we can feel the child in his instinctive, freely infantile devotion, "the mouth closed frankly around the nipple" (218).[160] Martin in "Hard-Luck Stories" is a young man "in his early twenties" (193) — decidedly younger than his mistress Caroline; Jack McNeil, the lover from Red Deer, remains a little boy to the motherly Mrs. Cross. And for greater explicitness we can turn to "The Ferguson Girls Must Never Marry," where the "wild" (28) Maureen, the black-and-purple third in the trio of sisters, is attended by a frail, dreamy young man called Dave — young enough, as Maureen's sisters gleefully note, to be possibly her son. Behind all such lover-sons there looms Franklin, or one of the Franklins: the young man who, having smitten all the local girls, marries an aging woman whom strangers take for his mother.[161] At the same time this Franklin is the favourite of his real mother, a woman like Mrs. French as well as a Baptist convert — which of course brings us back to Garnet. We come back at the same time to the other object of Garnet's devotion: the

Father to whom as a Baptist he makes his pledge. It may seem far-fetched to say that there is sexuality here, yet there is certainly a strange intensity about male relations in these stories.

School belongs to the girls, we are told in one of the Franklin drafts:[162] being excluded from it, the boys have to assert themselves in whatever way they can. Miss Farris in "Changes and Ceremonies" is sure they play non-stop hockey, and without limiting ourselves to hockey we can see why she might think so. Garnet French goes in for baseball; Wyck Tebbutt used to do the same thing professionally, and is watching a football game with Dane at the time of his death. Jimmy and Duval have no such opportunities, but do well enough with their gymnastics and scuffling — their play-fighting, in other words. "I liked to think of this male ritual as the prelude to ours" (219), says Del; and yet her very wording suggests that the prelude is also an analogue. For there are two kinds of ballgame played in the Garnet French story — both perhaps ways of fighting, both perhaps ways of loving. When Howard Troy, then, runs through the burning door to Stump Troy, we may be seeing a queer streak of yet another kind: a going to the Father in hate and love (as the explanations in "Executioners" variously suggest) that might as well be sexual passion.

In this light we can look again at the fraternities and sororities of these stories. "A Queer Streak" itself has Dane living with another man; it equally has the girls from the Isle of Women who "make up their own plays" (246). Dorothy in "Marrakesh" wonders whether Jeanette was not living on her own Isle of Women during her African trip; and to bring Africa back to Ontario as the story invites us to do, we may wonder about the sorority in Dorothy's own house. Whether we could use the word "homosexual" for, say, Dorothy staring at Jeanette in a bikini is of little importance in itself: what matters is the way characters draw back from heterosexual relations to a friendship within their own sex that can take on its own sexual colouring. If it does so, it becomes less simply friendly: Dane's homelife may be peaceful enough, but sex is also present when various kinds of play — sports or politics or bootlegging — turn into fighting. It is present, for that matter, when men fight at dances — when their fighting has an association with women, in other words.[163] Art Chamberlain has been known to get angry on only one occasion, when another man tried to steal Fern Dogherty at the Tupperton Pavilion. "He yanked him off" (173), says Fern.

*

What we have now arrived at is a familiar triangle: in terms of parents and children we have, say, a father and a son with a mother between them, each bound to each of the other two in hate and love. "A Queer Streak" is especially important here, since the story of Dane and Violet not only offers itself in considerable detail but, through its allusions, projects itself onto the largest possible screen. Dane, as I have said, is a bit hard to imagine as a lover: apart from being celibate, the heavy-set middle-aged man of "Possession" — almost a staid Egyptian — seems utterly different from the slight, even haggard, John whom we find in the role elsewhere. But it appears that a lover can be fleshy as well: Dane himself seems to have spent his life alternating, physically and emotionally, between thick and thin.[164] At first a fat child, he is then left an orphan and spindly; when he finds a second mother in his virgin aunt, he gets stuffed with rich desserts. In a less direct way he gets starved as well, for Violet now starts to keep company with another man, Wyck Tebbutt the athlete. And what Dane feels is nothing less than shock: Wyck is a married man, for one thing, but Dane sees something here more heinous than mere social impropriety — something that, like others we have met, he can hardly bear to know. Violet has committed an unforgivable "treachery" (240), and his later tendency both to protect her and keep her at a distance makes us wonder how deep his supposed forgiveness has ever gone. When we last see him, he has lost weight again — from the infection in his root-canal.

Dane's name, which obviously belongs to Munro's Nordic complex, suggests that he may be a Great Dane — Violet's watchdog just as Garnet French is his mother's stalwart; and in any case there is a greater Dane in the background here, Hamlet the Prince of Denmark. Dane's quasi-mother, the lonely woman he would like to see closer to his father, involves herself with another man in what he experiences as a sickening adultery; he himself then fades into the role of disenchanted adviser, allying himself with a Horatio-like confidant in the process. In the end he is drawn back, literally and figuratively, into Violet's fire, where we find him sweating in a final struggle; and what has come at last, for him as for Hamlet, is as much a confrontation with a mother as with any other enemy. Yet Dane's name can suggest a different relation to a mother as well: another of Munro's Danes or Dans — a somewhat elusive group in her work, to be sure — may provide a suggestion here. In "The Shining Houses" the disaffected Mary walks off with her little son and companion Danny, a boy whose zipper she managed to do up while not signing the petition against Mrs. Fullerton. While this is as much as we are told about Danny, the impression he makes is of a potential vindicator — the son who might one day do what must be done for the helpless Mary. Dane, whom we first see as another child clinging shyly to his mother, has his own vindicator's role to play at the end. Whatever his old outrage and present detachment, his loyalty to Violet is by no means dead: he is dismayed by the evil that he senses threatening her, and when he rushes into the fire he is not only her antagonist in a way, but her rescuer.[165]

What we have in general, then, is on the one hand a Dane who defends a mother-figure, and on the other a Dane who, like his Shakespearean predecessor, nurses a resentment. Now we can make, or return to, a still more important connection. When the Spanish Lady first sees the chivalrous Spanish lord, the Rosicrucian — and before she receives her commission from a dying counterpart — the thought of "Dana" (182) Andrews comes into her mind. In other words, a Dane is associated here with Jesus: the great son who traditionally honours his consort-mother though also, as we have noted, a son who rejects her.[166] It is Jesus, correspondingly, whom we sense at various points in "A Queer Streak" — above all during Dane's agony in the fire, when "tears and sweat ran together down his face" (251). It is Mary — a very queenly Mary — whom we sense in the Violet installed over the Royal Bank; and it is a Mary of a more compromised and mortified kind who watches while Dane battles the fire. One odd couple, it seems, is playing another.

If we finally go back to the biblical origin of Dane's name, we will meet the paternal figure who makes this couple into a triangle. In the Book of Daniel we are introduced to the Ancient of Days, a father enthroned in fire;[167] the same passage shows us a loyal Son who does battle for him and is to be glorified in the end — the Son, we can also note, with whom Jesus identifies himself just before the Crucifixion.[168] The recapitulation of this prophecy in the Apocalypse adds a figure much like Mary: a heavenly Woman Crowned with Stars. The male child of this woman is destined to rule the nations with a rod of iron;[169] and since the same thing is later said of the victorious man on the white horse,[170] we can readily identify the child with this latter — and thus with the Christ, the Son who executes the Father's wrath on his enemies. This, at any rate, is one version of the situation: evil fails against a simple and harmonious alliance of almighty father, protected mother, and vindicating son. As echoed in Munro, the matter is not simply different, but it is more complex.

In the first place, the power of the male figures is more uncertain. I have already mentioned that the various stumps in Munro's stories point to another figure in the Book of Daniel — Nebuchadnezzar, the king who turns into a stumped tree as well as a beast of the field eating grass; we have connected the same images with the burned trees and chaff of John the Baptist. And so we come back to Stump Troy: another ancient seated in fire, but a singularly helpless one. If instead we choose to follow the apocalyptic white horse or its rider, we arrive again at a scrappy but ultimately helpless father, the wretched King Billy Thoms. Nor does the Son cut a much more consistent figure. In the Bible Daniel is an altogether worthy young man who braves a lion's den just as a trio of his companions brave a fiery furnace. In Munro the son-figure who enters a fire does so with much less aplomb; and by analogy Dane is, at least on his downcast and subservient side, King Billy all over again. As for the relation between father and son, we have seen its ambiguity in the case of Howard and Stump, not to say the various fighters they can be connected with. It is true that we hardly think of Dane as a fighter: as we have noted, he settles down quietly with "Theo," and even watches the football game with Wyck "Tebbutt" — amicably enough, it would seem. But perhaps the game on the screen is secretly their own: Wyck, after all, was once a ballplayer himself, and somewhere in Dane's root-canal an old animosity has gone on festering.

There remains Violet, whom Dane once revered as his virgin mother. In the Apocalypse the Woman Crowned with Stars, together with her unborn son, is kept safe from the jealous dragon; traditionally this woman is also Jerusalem, the bride of the Son though not of course the betrayer of the Father. As for Violet herself, she once worshipped Trevor Auston, and never permitted herself to rebel against the deity he represented; yet she had domineered over her own father, and when the two girls appear later from the Isle of Women she becomes wildly excited.[171] Earlier she dallied with Wyck Tebbutt, having already cosseted Dane himself in his adolescence; for the latter, in fact, this woman in royal purple who turned to a strange man became a Mary Magdalen, not to say a Babylon. And at the end she may be something else again: the betrothed who enforces from Dane the Undergod what she was denied by Trevor the Upper God. For we never know quite what to make of Violet and her infinite variety — is she the bossy mother-sister, the virgin in the tower, the distressed woman fleeing into the thorns of the wilderness, the bride claiming her bridegroom, or the incendiary who finally streaks away through the door? Or is she something beyond all of these, the crone who stands rooted in fire? If this last, she is herself a form of the stumped ancient in the story: and we will have to deal with her as such when we have finished with our more immediate business, the tragedy of the lover and the loved.

*

With "A Queer Streak" the transformative principle in Munro has made its masterpiece. Other of the ambiguities here will have to speak for themselves, but their general character seems plain: we have the sense, more almost than anywhere else in her work, that every human being plays all roles and takes all attitudes towards the roles played by others. Now let us try to see this confusing situation in terms of the general model we derived from "Executioners." At the centre of experience we have the union of male and female — a union that does not quite take place, or does so only in a rending way, since something is drawing the parties off to a periphery. This something, we have found, is often represented in parental terms, suggesting as it does a condition that the lovers have not been able to escape in their coming together; as a relation it is "friendship" that is not "love." But this friendship itself takes on the character of love, or love and hate, stealing these from the centre, and the figures at the periphery turn into another company with the same loves and squabbles. And so on: what I called a periphery might better be thought of as an expansion in which persons and relations multiply to infinity. To complicate matters further, we can turn our model inside out: we can put the natural lovers on the outside and think of some unnatural block coming between them. In "Deadeye Dick," for instance, Mrs. Fordyce may retreat to the interior of her house, but Loony Buttler does not: she stands right at the door, ordering Morris away while Matilda cowers somewhere in the background. But whichever picture we choose, we can now make the observation that must always be made with infinite regressions. The ever-expanding sphere can only reproduce the condition that generated it in the first place: the value of watching the expansion is precisely that it can show us this condition in an enlarged form. Like myths of origin — or consummation — "parents" can in one way only show us what is there in their "children."

This means that the children can stand for all couplings whatever. Throughout the Passion stories — and throughout Munro — we are challenged by emblematic pairs of one kind or another. As with Jimmy and Duval, these may consist of play-fighting males: the boys of the French family who do their own scuffling, Bert and Clive with their "shadow-boxing" (191), the acrobatic Walpole brothers among the Baptist Young People — to take acrobatics as a kind of play-fighting.[172] Or the pairs may be female, like Garnet's tricky sisters Lila and Phyllis; they may be serious, like the feminists in "Possession"; they may be lovers, like those (heterosexual in this case) that Del sees in passing through the cemetery. They may also — as pairs start expanding — be members of the Trinity, or the whole ruling class of the Isle of Women. But these pluralities are all really the same; and in their very multiplicity they point back to the single pair that we put in the centre of our picture. Indeed, we can say that they point to a single individual. The play-fighting Jimmy and Duval, and the lovers with whom we can link them, become Stump Troy, the man who sits alone in his fire.[173]

When we reduce the many in this way, variations in Munro that may have been bothering us need do so no longer — it does not matter, for instance, whether the person to whom the protagonist runs is a father, like Stump Troy, or a quasi-mother, like Violet, or whether in fact a parent rather than a child does the running, like Violet again. At the same time, we are bringing together things separated in our figure of expansion, and if these fully met, the collision would be just what we earlier saw as unbearable. For we live in a world where two people — or any other contraries we choose — cannot both unite and keep their own identities; to use again the term that Munro so often suggests, we are prisoners of Nature, including our natural selves. And so the explosive situation has to be neutralized: essentially, we do this by accepting one of its incompatible principles and refusing the other. We have been seeing some of the practical results. Love or friendship, with partners or parents, heterosexual or homosexual — with any sort of human bond (perhaps as found in a given situation) one of two forms is felt to be acceptable where the other is not. The rejected one is also liable to be called "unnatural": yet when we think our way down to principles we find that what is being rejected is one component of Nature itself. As that thoughtful woman Fern Dougherty remarks, "Natural or *un*natural, doesn't that depend" (186)?

The same thing is true with the more complex forms of our solution. To take the categories we are most concerned with here — similarity and difference, unity and independence — the easiest way of coping would be merely to call one of each pair right and the other wrong.

Applied strictly, though, this simple discrimination could only produce extreme doctrines of corporateness or individualism that could never really be put into practice. What is more common is to allow both of the opposites, but only one kind of relation between them: the sense compromise that we usually think of as natural. This gives us the acceptable "arrangements," such as ordinary wedlock, that we found to be the norm in the central-phase world. Conversely, societies tend to be uneasy when the partners in a sexual relation seem either too similar (hence taboos on incest and homosexuality) or too different (hence taboos on miscegenation of various kinds): one or other of the principles is seen as asserting itself in a way that endangers their compromise. And the compromise is an attractive one: if we could be satisfied with it, we would have a world that was at any rate stable. The problem is that our humanity needs something more — both authentic union and authentic individuality, and these as fulfilling one another, not just striking a bargain. The major Passion stories have shown us a last spasmodic attempt to satisfy this need; they have also shown us the outcome — a convulsion of love and rage, ending in total failure. Yet this was really inevitable from the start, for what we have been seeing here is only sensibility. Sensibility does not overcome the conditions of Nature: if sense is natural in the ordinary way, sensibility is its "unnatural" other face, equally part of Nature in a larger understanding. And here we have as good a way as any to epitomize the tragedy of the terminal phase, the tragedy of passion. The lovers in these stories cannot escape Nature: they can only try — finally and desperately — to do on Nature's terms what Nature will never permit.

*

Then, in Douglas Reider's phrase, the Sexual Revolution is over; and by the same token the world's regular arrangements are not. Del, unlike Naomi, may refuse domesticity in its usual form, but if so she must accept it in a further one — the drudgery of a job if not of marriage. The baptism of love or death, it seems, was by no means as final as it looked: the water from which Del expected drowning was not in fact high enough to reach her head.[174]

In more typological terms we must say, not just that the quest for baptism leads back to normality, but that ultimately the two are one. By turning to Garnet from the likes of Bert Matthews and Jerry Storey, Del is seeking real life; in the end "real life" (242) is just what she gets, but in the form she thought herself leaving behind.[175] And in a sense that is her baptism, for just as there are Del and Naomi, so there is a baptism of passion and a baptism of law or convention — indeed this is so even when both are administered by the same Garnet French. Receiving the one means receiving the other, and this in the sense not only that affairs lead to job-hunting, or passion to marriage,[176] but that passion itself — as the lovers find — is a compulsion, even a routine. Del does not, of course, accept marriage: in seeing that it would be intolerable, though, she is seeing the same thing about the baptism of passion itself — that she never really meant to share herself with Garnet, never wanted the water to reach her head. Both baptisms, in their opposite ways, require of her a surrender in which the autonomy of her private self would be forfeited. *'cause of parents example*

More ironically still, Del's autonomy would not be forfeited at all, nor would such a surrender be a surrender — for neither of these baptisms is as complete as it may seem. And here we can ask what Del in fact asks herself repeatedly in later years: what if she had let herself be baptized? To sense the full force of the question, we can take baptism here not just as a contracting for church membership, or the wedlock that goes with it in this story, but as the more extreme baptism of passion itself — the baptism of love or death. It will help if we recall the scene played by Rose in the epilogue to "Simon's Luck": one in which a young woman tries to throw herself into the ocean. Rose has the Comforter's role of preventing her, just as Robina prevents Helena from going into the ditch after the fire; Del plays her own Comforter when she saves herself from death in the river. But in our present view it would not matter if the passionate girls of these stories did go into the ocean or the ditch — as Violet does not once but twice; nor does it matter that Garnet does in fact push Del under the water, baptizing her in a real sense. For Del then walks away, shaken but self-possessed, and if she later passes through the cemetery she nevertheless ends at home.

What makes this strange is that baptism is supposed to be liberation, an exodus from an old life: and in rejecting the baptism she has received from Garnet Del is attempting yet another such exodus. If this too leads to bondage — the real life that is only a form of death — then we are seeing all the more fully what the Passion stories show us with their special intensity, the ability of the world's continuities to hold even in not holding. Rose in "Simon's Luck" tries for her own kind of new life, severing all ties at home to play in a new series in the west. But in a larger sense Rose has made no break at all: she has been in a series — which means "chain" — for a long time, and her successive efforts to escape involvement, as much as her impulsive courting of it, are the series' way of prolonging itself.[177] And to emblematize the terminal vision in the way we did the central, we can note why the girl in Rose's series is trying to drown herself. The trouble is pregnancy — the burden that threatened in "Lives of Girls and Women" and, more immediately and crucially, threatens throughout the Garnet French story. Naomi gets pregnant, and uses the situation to legalize her relation with Scott Geoghegan; Del does not get pregnant, though she hears herself saying she wants to; one of the Baptist Young People,[178] a frail girl from the "Chainway" (216) Store, seems actually to have had a baby out of wedlock. But a baby, as much as no baby, can show us how a binding remains unbroken: a baby is a new life, something that escapes from the dying of its parents, yet also the natural way in which the future is bound to the past. In this sense any baby is born within the chain of the Law, which means that there is no birth at all, merely "the old, old story" (213) declared by the born-again Baptists. In the same sense there is no loss of virginity — Del's own virginity being a notable example of continuity that stays intact even when disrupted.

The Del who comes home at the end is not entirely unhappy: like others who normalize, she feels an Elizabeth's "mild, sensible gratitude" (242); Rose even feels that she is having some luck of her own at last. And yet there is a tragedy here, and in its perspective the bad luck that Rose makes into worldly good luck is doubly bad, for it means forgetting something that, if remembered, might open a door leading beyond luck altogether. This is not to say that a passionate Simon or John or Dan could have opened such a door. The third-phase lover is the One who is not One, and whose love is the other side of hate; his gift of life is a gift of death, and his death only traps the heroine in natural life. Only through death of another kind might he become a different kind of lover, and baptize the heroine in a greater fire:[179] that is what we will see in Munro's fourth-phase stories.

NOTES

[1] This formula will do for present purposes, though I am consciously neglecting various complexities here. My claim is simply that the kinds of terminal situation and story presented in this chapter are in fact variations on a single theme: there is a movement away from a central worldly establishment, taking

447

the forms in Munro that I actually deal with.

2 As always there are variations: the brutality Flo experiences as a girl comes not from her parents themselves but from her later employer and his wife, the "bishop's sister" (43); it is these who agree to send her to school but do not; the lovely Miss Rush of the story is the bishop's sister herself, otherwise a snob and a bully; and it is this woman, not Flo's mother, who dies of cancer.

3 Rasporich, *Dance*, uses Isis at various points, though at none of these does she mention Isis's mourning and searching for Osiris.

4 See Wisd. 10–11, Prov. 8.

5 York, "The Rival Bards" (213), notes some of the Egyptian allusions here (as well as some in Tennyson's *The Princess*).

6 See Exod. 1:19.

7 Different perspectives are possible here, in a way that will become clearer as we proceed. Addie's travels began before the sojourn in Grandma Seeley's Egypt — though her escape from the farm was already an Exodus from the failed Egypt of a larger story. The travels also initiate the main story of the chapter.

8 Auntie Lou in "The Peace of Utrecht," explicitly called "Egyptian," is also said to have hair like "the dead end of hair on a ripe ear of corn" (203).

9 Gen. 44:1–2. The snake sounds Egyptian enough, though in the Genesis story what is hidden in the bag of meal is a silver cup.

10 See above, 48.

11 A limiting case here is Lydia in "Dulse," who gives up "all pride and sense" (50) in her surrender to Duncan: yet Lydia deeply resents this servility — which like Lois's is that of a proud woman. If we add the abject and sullen "Maria" in "Five Points," we will see how all such figures are special versions of the lowly and exalted Mary.

12 In drafts of "Something I've Been Meaning to Tell You" Et Desmond's name appears as Loretta (Tener 37.8.23–24).

13 The "Balm of Gilead Home" — for the aged — is a more ironic version of the same sort of house, perched "on the bluffs above Lake Huron" (52).

14 Anyone reminded of Milton's Eve here will be interested to know that "Edie" was at one stage "Eva" (Tener 37.17.12).

15 Note especially the dispenser that will not "disgorge" Kotex (39). In effect this dispenser is guarded by the janitor.

16 In this case we have lung cancer — virtually the "foundry disease" (3) contracted in the initiatory world of "Royal Beatings" and now completing its work.

17 See above, 440 for a counterpart in "A Queer Streak." See above, 290–91, for the portly central god, matched at times by a slim one like Clifford. What seems to me characteristic of the Exodus world is that fatness and thinness here are not only extreme but ominous, as in Pharaoh's dream (Gen. 41:1–4).

18 See Gen. 41. In Egyptian mythology Osiris is "the Listless One." Milkweed here can be compared to the cucumbers and milk taken by Addie Morrison (who

believes the combination to be poisonous) as a way of getting to Heaven. In Num. 11:5, similarly, the Israelites long for Egyptian "cucumbers" (as well as "onions" — what Flo gets from the clairvoyant along with the supposedly poisoned cake); on the other side of the Wilderness the Promised Land is "flowing with milk and honey" (Exod. 3:8, etc.).

19 See Num. 28, 29 for the Mosaic lambs without spot, also Heb. 9:14.

20 In Pop's Café in "Thanks for the Ride" note the "fly-speckled and slightly yellowed cutouts" of things to eat (44).

21 Her hair, we can also note, is "pulled tight from the middle parting" (75). Lois's hysterical mother has "skin straining over her temples" (52), and the same play on temples, with or without the word itself, is a recurrent one. With the failing Mrs. Jordan of "Baptizing" "the exposed white skin of the temple had an unhealthy suffering look" (183); Marion Sherriff's hair in "The Photographer" is "pinned unbecomingly back from the temples" (244).

22 Cf. Maria in "Five Points": a glum, stocky girl who in desperation gets "wild and sullen and mean" (39). Her sister, the suave Lisa, is a more competent version of Nile.

23 Even Edie in "How I Met My Husband" who seems both simpler and milder than these other women, not only has moods of her own, but feels the full pain of abandonment when her airman fails to write. In her concluding remark — "I like for people to think what pleases them and makes them happy" (66) — there is a touch of malice along with the blandness.

24 Dr. Peebles and Chris Watters's tent can perhaps be taken into a wider network of association. Mr. "Peebles" (180), the clergyman in "A Trip to the Coast," is of interest to the unmated Hazel, who is intrigued to think of him looking at her legs. In "The Dangerous One" it is Dr. "Coutes" of the Mountain Sanatorium who once gave the young heroine an autographed snapshot. "Coutes" or "Coutts" is the same word as "cotes" (cottages or sheep-cotes), so that once again we seem to be in the pastoral or nomadic world with its rough shelters — even if the Coutts family in *Lives of Girls and Women* are as lofty in Del's eyes as the Peebles in Edie's.

25 See "Privilege" 35.

26 See Budge 56.

27 If we transpose Egypt into the desert we find another god with four letters — Jehovah the tetragrammaton — who may indeed be relevant here.

28 The "downflash of a wing" can also suggest, among other things, the falcon-god Horus — the son who avenges Isis against Seth himself.

29 It may be pertinent that in Num. 12 Miriam and Aaron are fellow-rebels against their brother Moses.

30 Ruby Carruthers in Flo's anecdote is undertaken by each of the Three Jokers in turn: she understandably gets to the point of wanting to know "who I'm doing it with" (42).

31 Lydia is a "cooper" or barrel-maker ("Kuiper" in "Fits" is the Dutch

cognate) whom we find taking an interest in "Japanese boxwood" (37). Osiris is trapped in a chest.

32 David is younger than the other men I am concerned with here, and shows no signs of serious illness. But not only is he paralleled with Stella's dying father in the background: he has his own share of ailments, psychosomatic or other, and plays the same structural role as Bill Morrison or Rose's father.

33 In the background of "Five Points," the disabled Cornelius has to find work that he can do mainly sitting down; he is also dependent on Brenda, who among other things often does the driving when they go to look at Walley harbour.

34 In his apartment Duncan is of course Lydia's host — to the extent that we can say "host" of such a man — and there can be no doubt that in the end Lydia is his victim: once again, my present account brings out only one version of a highly ambiguous story. But to see Duncan himself as victim, we can note Lydia's therapeutic confession that she was "out to defeat" (55) him — which seems as much of the truth as other things she tells her psychiatrist.

35 Cf. Lydia's own paralysis on being abandoned: she sits in a chair for an hour outside the bathroom of an apartment.

36 Another variant takes place on the visit to Stella's father: David offers his annual tribute of whisky, yet this can only be drunk by breaking a rule, and a nurse later brings the father his allowed fruit juice.

37 "Love suffereth long, and is kind. . . . Love is not puffed up . . ." (154): see 1 Cor. 13:4.

38 For darkening of the sky at approximately noon cf. "A Trip to the Coast" 185; see above, 114–15.

39 See John 13:30.

40 The English verb "pass over" and noun "Passover" (translating different roots in Hebrew) produce a single idea with various associations: the Passover meal itself (Exod. 12:11), the passing of the Lord at midnight (Exod. 12:12), and the consequent passing of the Israelites over the Red Sea (Exod. 15:16) and later the Jordan.

41 It was at midnight, or five minutes before it, that the mining accident underlying "Five Points" took place, reducing Cornelius to his own lifelong agony. In "Memorial" the news of the father's death comes "at ten or eleven o'clock at night" (220): leaving Eileen's mother enough time to make tea-biscuits, we can put the vigil at close to midnight. But precision is not what matters here (we can think of Del's parents in "The Flats Road" playing their card-game and waiting for the war-news at ten — a late hour for such a family).

42 Much the same flash occurs in the last scene of "Princess Ida": when Mrs. Jordan has just vented her anger at Bill's bequest, Del has her momentary sense of the "downflash of a wing or knife" (91). The description of the Passover in the Wisdom of Solomon seems worth quoting here: "All things were lying in peace and silence, and night in her swift course was half-spent, when thy almighty Word leapt from thy royal throne in heaven into the midst of that doomed land

like a relentless warrior, bearing the sharp sword of thy inflexible decree, and stood and filled it all with death" (18:14-16). (Angels do not have wings in the Bible, but have acquired them long since.)

43 It is twenty after twelve when they get back to town.

44 Cf. Alice "Kelling," another aging and uncertain woman; she is also, as we can tell from her behaviour, one who senses the impending loss of her boyfriend.

45 The grandmother in "A Trip to the Coast" is very similar (see below, 473): this story could easily have been put with the Exodus group.

46 Duncan in "Dulse" writes on history, travelling like Mrs. Jordan to collect material. Rose's father is a reader and thinker (as well as someone who knows Rose's thoughts); and in "Lichen" we find David trying to reach Dina by phoning Michael "Read" (47).

47 Apart from Shylock and the pound of flesh, a reason for *The Merchant of Venice* among Rose's schoolbooks may be Portia, the wise woman who appears as a learned clerk.

48 The distinction between guilt and shame — not always worth making — becomes very marked here. The principal vows "to discover, expose, flog and expel" (40) the culprit: that is, he wants to find the real culprit and punish guilt according to a code of justice, no matter how absurd. As far as the senior girls are concerned, however, the Muriel Mason who has somehow got associated with the Kotex ought to die of shame, though they can hardly suppose that she put her own Kotex in the trophy case.

49 The country children in "Princess Ida" are equally knowing, with their "subtle, complicated embarrassment" (67), though they are not using their knowledge as a weapon.

50 Cf. the voices pursuing Helena in "Executioners" — "sweet voices . . . just on the edge of sincerity, deadly innocence" (138).

51 Cf. Flo losing the satin gloves given her by the bishop's sister (43). Another woman in this story bursts out "I saw your picture in a magazine, what was the name of that magazine, I have it at home" (53).

52 E.g., the "dark green blinds" (2) of Uncle Benny's house, or the "green blinds" (n.pag.) by which the contents of the Egyptian store are "shrouded" on Sundays in "The Widower."

53 The idea of broken chunks may also help us with the cooper and boxwood in "Dulse" (see above, 449-50 n31). In Duncan's anecdote it is boxes — separate containers — that he is arranging when approached by a bear (the anecdote in the *New Yorker* version of the story has bears themselves being chunked up [33]). Earlier we are told how Lydia copes with life after Duncan abandons her — "she set little blocks on top of one another and she had a day" (36); cf. Mr. Stanley and his meal (38).

54 See Matt. 5:3.

55 In Mrs. Jordan's painting "the mountains and the sheep looked alike, lumpy, woolly" (71-72). The "dead grass floating from the wires" (75) that she

once saw when approaching the barren farm is again close to the "moss" (41) or "pelt" (42) suggested to Stella by the lichen. When her mother parades at school, Del's only recourse is to concentrate on "indifferent straws of fact" (81) like the sweater ahead of her, with its "little nubby bits of wool sticking out" (80–81).

56 Muriel Mason in "Half a Grapefruit" is or has another (" 'You got the rag on to-day, Muriel?' " [40]), whoever the owner of the Kotex may be, and as a result gets exposed no less ruthlessly than lichen. In "Princess Ida" the oilcloth on the Morrison's table is nothing but a "rag" (76); cf. the rag on the clothesline after the family shooting in "Spelling" (177).

57 Stella's thought on discovering the lichen is "This is David's doing" (55). Cf. Matt. 21:42 (quoting Ps. 118:22–23): "The stone which the builders rejected, the same is become the head of the corner: this is the Lord's doing, and it is marvellous in our eyes."

58 As a Pied Piper Raymond Bolting is no match for Frank Wales: but he does take the narrator home, as Frank at least thinks of doing, and he makes the same comment as Frank — "I didn't realize you lived such a long ways out" (159).

59 See above, 340 n47.

60 Del has a similar falling-asleep vision of Frank Wales himself, and at the same structural point.

61 Along with being an accosted maid in a wealthy household, Alva is like Jessie in that she impresses the man of the house by her reading. She too has a taste for nineteenth-century novels of passion (she might actually read *The Red and the Black*), though like Jessie again she tends to avoid something — *King Lear* in her case, like the Grand Inquisitor in Jessie's.

62 See above, 245. We also find in "Baptizing" that Jerry Storey calls Del "eggplant" (197) when she has donned a "purply-wine coloured" dress.

63 It is "bright as glass" (157), though also "the black mirror of the north Atlantic" (169).

64 In an unpublished early piece, "The Green April" (Tener 37.15.4), a predecessor of "Averill" just manages to escape the fascination of her Aunts Meg and "Julie," whose aim is to trap her in their gothic household.

65 See above, 228.

66 See "Differently" 240. The central Passion stories naturally emphasize the termination of this terminal quest. Within the general story of "Baptizing," for instance — the story of Del's search for a lover as she comes to the end of adolescence — it is Garnet French who provides the terminal episode; and since Garnet gives us, so to speak, the Passion within the Passion, it is he who both makes the strongest impression on Del and gets much the most extensive treatment from Munro. Again, the third-phase episode inside the Garnet French story itself — the quarrel in the river — looms so large that one is inclined to call it central (what a terminal phase can always become in one perspective), with the earlier events of the affair as mere preludes to it.

67 See above, 395.

68 Cf. "Char" in "Something I've Been Meaning to Tell You." The name "Georgia" in "Differently" might be seen as a displacement of these Carolines and Charlottes; see also above, 252 n59. Of the historical Carolines the most important here is no doubt Lady Caroline Lamb — and we can, if we like, see figures like Martin the playwright in "Hard-Luck Stories" as Byronic.

69 Rev. 6:5.

70 In "June" in the *Album* the jokers drop a cat off the Third Bridge (Tener 37.13.10–13).

71 This comes at the end, not beginning, of "Anonymous Letters," but "Possession" thus becomes the story, most memorably, of an old woman — like Dorothy in "Marrakesh" — who gets a later chance after an early one came to a "tragic" (234) end.

72 For wood as the image of the material world, see above, 252 n63, 425–26, 428.

73 Cf. Rev. 5:1 ff.

74 It is also coming in "The Photographer" — in one perspective a pendant of "Baptizing." The last of the graffiti on the station wall in "The Found Boat" (apart from a set of names) reads "Waiting for a train" (133).

75 In "Winter Wind," again, the narrator will remark that the life of her grandmother and great-aunt is all "waiting time" (203).

76 See "Simon's Luck" 62; "Baptizing" 226. For "coons" see above, 56.

77 Tener 37.16.19.2.f3.

78 Conversely, John Brolier in "Oh, What Avails" is serious and intense like a typical Passion hero: we can see him as such a figure concentrated back into a central-phase worker of mischief. One result is that "Rose Matilda," the third part of "Oh, What Avails," is free to be as much an Apocalypse story as a terminal one.

79 This is also true of Garnet's counterpart Stu Sherriff in "The Idyllic Summer."

80 See Luke 23:28.

81 See above, 65.

82 With an experienced ladies' man like Garnet French we can go higher again: having already had four girlfriends, Garnet proceeds to a fifth, Del herself; and a true philanderer like Douglas in "Hard-Luck Stories" must have as many women in his collection as Duncan in "Dulse." In "Sheila," one of the earlier forms of "Simon's Luck," it is Simon who has a *catalogue raisonné* of mistresses (Tener 37.11.23–25).

83 We can also note that these women, while "coffee-coloured," are dressed in "emerald green, electric blue" — the colours of glory in Munro, very different from the appearance of the bass.

84 The "X" carved by Garnet French is like the "X" for Alex Walther in "Bardon Bus": it suggests four and it suggests Christ. So does the "crossword" in both "Princess Ida" (91) and "Baptizing" (242). "Anh" itself is a crossword

if, as seems natural enough in Munro, it can be associated with "ankh" — the Egyptian cross.

85 This is also true, if less explicitly, of its counterpart "Differently."

86 Julie tells of the two "possibilities" (187) that have come her way: she is now on her third.

87 See Tener 38.4.1.5. "Emily," close to "Simon's Luck" itself, was actually published.

88 Note the "three queens" (30) and the funeral game in "Privilege."

89 We can note especially Simon's "muddled European accent, mostly French" (155), which to Rose suggests "a richer and more complicated masculinity than the masculinity to be found in North America" (155–56) — one that is also "tinged with suffering, tenderness, and guile" (156).

90 See Tener 37.11.23.f11.

91 See "Angela": "she had never got the pieces of Simon to fall together to compose a revelation, the sort of thing she was after in her poems, something definitive as a buzzard or a rose. She had an idea he slipped through most nets" (Tener 38.4.3.f61).

92 For Franklin nailed see Tener 37.16.244.ff.; for Franklin shot see 37.13.12.f.20. In one version (Tener 37.16.29.2.f5) Franklin's severely pious sister Robina blesses the planks and sawhorses — crossing pieces of wood, that is — on which his homecoming meal will be set. The meal turns out to be an appropriately sacrificial one.

93 Eugene in "Dulse," the French ladies' man who also fears drowning, once got lost in Saint John. The John Street Hill in *Lives of Girls and Women* is associated both with learning and the woman taken in adultery (see above, 412).

94 An unpublished "Joanne," which seems to belong to the Simon group of stories in Tener 37.11.23–25, may have been intended to come last there, though the fragment we have is too short and unconnected with the others to enlighten us much. Munro does not mention it in her discussion of the group with Struthers ("The Real Material" 31).

95 In an early version of the Garnet French story (Tener 37.8.4) the revivalist's name is "Milton Johns." Garnet's surname was once "Fearjon" (Tener 37.8.6). (He later went through a phase of being "Fear.")

96 Cf. the "medieval face" of John Brolier in "Oh, What Avails," "long and pale and bony, with the smile she dismissed as tactical, the sober, glowing, not dismissible dark eyes" (205). Note that Joan thinks of Brolier's face by itself, as Del thinks of Garnet's (211) — as if these were severed heads. See also below, 408.

97 We can add that Don's girlfriend "Judith" points to a beheading like that of John at the behest of Salome, even if the solid Judith of this story leaves *femme fatale* qualities to her sister Nichola. In "Circle of Prayer" Trudy first attracts Dan's attention by dancing in front of him; he then introduces her to his fiancée as "Judy" (261), which she finds extremely funny. So Trudy as the dancing Salome may also be a decapitating Judith.

98 Tener 37.16.29.4.f4.

99 In the case of David in "Labor Day Dinner" the flanking opposites are girls — the bright Kimberley and dark Angela; we have also seen David in "Lichen" caught among his various women.

100 See above, 57.

101 Munro's melancholy Garnet Frenches and John Broliers seem to have behind them Cranly in Joyce's *Portrait of the Artist as a Young Man* (mentioned in a different connection by Struthers, "Reality and Ordering" 41). Cranly is at once a decollated John the Baptist and Christ himself as a figure of mere passion; in particular he ministers to women.

102 See above, 40 n14.

103 Some qualification is necessary here. Rose's trip is not the main exodus of "Simon's Luck" but a further one when that with Simon has failed. The Spanish Lady has already suffered the failure of her marriage; she is returning from a futile tour of relatives when she meets the Rosicrucian and, as it were, goes on an unscheduled trip to Spain.

104 See Num. 14.

105 In "Accident" the word "crossover" (83) is again used in a context of love-making; we also find the same quasi-mystical language as with Garnet and Del (see above, 417).

106 For the same party as a judgement, see above, 390–91.

107 See above, 72.

108 This is the word that Del, for instance, uses for Naomi's new self (182), and the Spanish Lady for the Rosicrucian (184).

109 The girls of the boarding-house in "Jesse and Meribeth" have much the same obsessions, rules, and ceremonies — including endless washing. They also have names like Beatrice and Evangeline: the grace they hope to win by strict observance can be put in a Christian as well as Pharisaic context.

110 Cf. Matt. 23:37, Luke 13:34.

111 See Matt. 24:49.

112 See above, 454 n96; also below, 459 n156.

113 Or the word "corporal" may be addressed to Del: but it suits what we are told about Clive in any case.

114 If the Dutch language sounds "warm and innocent" (188), Clive is a parody Dutchman — unless we take the further view that he is really a solid insurance adjustor all the time.

115 See above, 361 and 449 n21.

116 See especially Jer. 13:22–27.

117 Apart from its obvious sense here and its association with breathing (and thus spirit), a diaphragm is more generally a partition. This seems worth noting in an episode where we have "Storeys" living in "half of a double house" (201).

118 See John 12:32.

119 In a limiting case the difference would merely be one of perspective, but

it is very clear in the two novels and can be discerned more generally. Basically, a heroine loses something that has come too easily and not been fully appreciated; then, perhaps after a time of desolation in which she learns her true need, she gets a miraculous second chance. We may find something of this even during a central affair, as when Frances in "Accident" fears the "crossover" (83) will not succeed again; conversely, the third-phase experience can be an affair (if a passionate and even trusting one) like Georgia's in "Differently." But the pattern holds if we make necessary qualifications (see also above, 347–48 n141). In "Differently" Munro wants to contrast the relatively self-possessed Georgia with the abandoned Maya. In "A Queer Streak" Munro wants to contrast the enterprising love of Violet and Trevor Auston with its final counterpart, the very terminal relation of Violet and Dane. The Exile stories, with their already bereft and longing heroines, are much closer to the Passion group than are the Mischief stories.

120 By the same token the Mrs. "Kidd" who says "Joy to the World" (167) is associating herself with the infancy of Jesus, where Mrs. "Cross" belongs with the other end of his life. A kid is also, of course, like a lamb: destined for rejection or sacrifice.

121 See above, 81 for the suggestion that Garnet is Esau — the deprived older brother — as well as the motif of Esau's revenge.

122 It is interesting to note various hints that give these stories their flavour: Parnell in the Garnet French story, the "Sexual Revolution" (186) in "Hard-Luck Stories," the era of "revolutionary costumes" (222–23) in "Differently" — not to say communes and secretly radical hired companions. And the dream of levelling pervades everything from revival meetings to TV series about kindly flophouses.

123 Along with shells — thin or thick — Shelley reminds one of another Shelley, the ethereal revolutionary. Shelley was in fact a radical gentleman.

124 Caroline wears "a gray cotton dress with a hood. No makeup" (193). Cf. Nancy in "Monsieur les Deux Chapeaux" 68.

125 As well as being a queen immured in a temple, Maya wears her hair "parted high at one temple" (224); Caroline in "Hard-Luck Stories" similarly has a "high white forehead" (193). For temples, with their indication both of legal restriction and of the sacrifice it decrees, see above, 361 and 449 n21.

126 The name "Maya," apart from suggesting the "Mary" family, takes us back to Munro's Latin American allusions, including Indian ones. We can note in particular that in "Fits" Nora Weeble comes back from Yucatan with a story about sacrificed virgins (106). Caroline in "The Photographer" is very much a sacrifice, ritually laid on tombstones (246).

127 After the exam Del is invited for "coke" (228) at a former blacksmith shop. The invitation comes from another Counter-Stranger: an ungifted, unromantic drudge of a country girl whom Del has not been taking seriously, but who now wants an answer to exam questions about "social stability" (229). As the summer goes on other people raise more or less the same issue: the mother who waits for

Del to come home at night, the Naomi who reappears from the past with her warning against attempted withdrawal.

¹²⁸ See above, 416, for the silent Passion lover. Dane's speechlessness recapitulates that of Trevor Auston, plagued by a sore throat in his last interview with Violet.

¹²⁹ In "Simon's Luck" the "third baptism" is, within the central episode, Simon's failure to return on the second weekend. In a larger story, and more specially answering the party at Kingston (with its "suicide woman" [159]), there is a further baptism: Simon in effect returns from the dead at the end, both rebuking Rose and doing something more that will concern us in the next chapter.

¹³⁰ Dane's words on finding Violet in a corresponding fire are "Jesus, Jesus, what are you doing" (250), and the same not quite casual use of "Jesus" or "Christ" occurs in various places in Munro.

¹³¹ For the plague of boils, see Exod. 9:9 ff.; for the turning of waters into blood, see Exod. 7:17 ff. There is also, of course, the plague of darkness itself (Exod. 10:21 ff.).

¹³² Helena has gone to bed, since she sees the light of the fire from her bedroom window. Older people are not yet in bed, or are willing to get up again, since "it was not yet midnight" (151). Since it takes time for them to get to the fire, and for the house itself to collapse, the fatal running of Howard Troy through the burning door occurs roughly at midnight. For the Passover at midnight, see above, 372–73.

¹³³ The old horse Mack in "Boys and Girls" tries to find the "stump" (120) of a molar.

¹³⁴ For half-blinded men elsewhere in Munro see above, 257 n113. Here we can add figures like Jack McNeil with his paralyzed left side, and Mr. Buchanan in "Baptizing" with "half his stomach cut away for ulcers" (208).

¹³⁵ See Dan. 4.

¹³⁶ Matt. 3:10–12.

¹³⁷ See above, 81.

¹³⁸ On the other hand Munro sometimes has pointed references to the absence of wind: there is none, someone remarks, at the fire in "Executioners," none in the cold weather of "Fits" ("If there was any wind it'd be murder," says Karen [115]), and none when the narrator's pants slip in "The Ottawa Valley." It seems to me that in each of these cases there is a wind — or spirit — that the speaker is unaware of. The OT word "ruach" means any or all of wind, breath, and spirit.

¹³⁹ When Violet goes to the A. & P., her interest in "smoked meats and back bacon" (243), not to say strong coffee, may remind us both of the "greasy bit of bacon" (147) at Robina's and of Jimmy and Duval's smell of "Buckingham's Fine Cut" (148). Later, of course, Stump Troy gets "fried" (151), and we can also remember the "greasy shame, . . . indigestible bad secrets" (143) lodged in Helena by the word "fuck." Grease, while hard to digest, is easy to ignite: at the fire in "A Queer Streak" Dane is concerned about grease on the walls. Presently we

hear about a wild pig — the animal that turns into bacon.

[140] Cf. the spitting during the Passion (Matt. 26:67), also Jesus healing by spittle (Mark 7:33, 8:23).

[141] "Brantford," mentioned three times in Munro's stories and once in the Garnet French episode itself (225), seems to be — metaphorically, not etymologically — another "burning ford." (Cf. "Brandon" in "The Time of Death," with his incendiary effect on Patricia.)

[142] "Brent Duprey," the name of the hot-gospelling husband in "Pictures of the Ice," sounds like "burned" and "field" (*pré*). (See previous note.) We should also note Munro's image of the "yard" here — burning when Mary Agnes in "Heirs of the Living Body" looks through a pane of red glass and says "Yard's on fire" (41). In "Executioners" we have the "yard" (152) before the burning house. Earlier we saw a Christ-like wounded Franklin carried through a barnyard (above, 399) — which is also where Jack McNeil's stroke occurs. See also below, 460 n172.

[143] For the imagery of wood see above, 252 n63. Violet's burning paper in "A Queer Streak" is a related image.

[144] See above, 148, 159 n60.

[145] See above, 187, for a few examples of crows. The Arthur Comber who flaps his black gown like crow's wings also looks like "the priest from Holy Cross" (16). It seems appropriate, then, that Nola in "The Ferguson Girls," reflecting on a sickly Undergod like Maureen's young man Dave, would exclaim "Holy crow" (33). The grandmother in "Winter Wind," herself a martyr, once had to wear "something with floppy sleeves . . . and a sort of vest with crisscrossed velvet trim" (194). For the Photographer in Del's secret novel, see below, 495.

[146] See Rev. 19:17–21.

[147] We also have Garnet sinking into Del "like a shot gull" (236), and one of the portents in "Walking on Water" is a blue jay brought in, as Mr. Lougheed speculates, by a cat (78). Kamboureli (38) points out the importance of the tomcat and bird in "Baptizing," although her interpretation differs from mine.

[148] See above, 63.

[149] For blinded or half-blinded men see above, 256 n113; 457 n134. The house in "The Peace of Utrecht" has a "little blind window of coloured glass beside the front door" (197). We are not told that anyone sees the yard on fire through it (see above, 457 n138), but the surrounding imagery is fiery enough — a red brick house in a heatwave, with a note in "flamboyant" handwriting on the door and a bouquet of "phlox" inside (see above, 147). See also "Deadeye Dick" 184, 192, and above, 235.

[150] "Heirs of the Living Body" 61.

[151] This is the "covering" that I discussed earlier (see above, 31). Another much-explained event is the shooting in "Fits": "Robert listened to all these explanations but did not believe any of them. . . . Equally plausible, these seemed

to him, equally hollow and useless" (119–20). "Fits" is — more literally than "Executioners" — a story about an exploding head, and once again something crucial is omitted: here from Peg's account of finding the bodies.

152 Carrington (51) suggests the analogy of Aeneas rescuing Anchises from the burning city of Troy.

153 King Billy transmits his red hair to both Bonnie Hope and Dawn Rose, and through the latter to Dane, a red-headed boy and later a "ruddy" (240) man. For "ruddy" see above, 285.

154 Even if they were perceived as setting the fire, Jimmy and Duval would hardly provide a sensible explanation for Howard's final act in itself. What matters here is simply that in all the explaining they are left out: thus their play-fighting can stand for something more that is left out.

155 We have also seen fur in Munro as associated with sacrificial animals — skinned foxes and the like. But the two associations readily go together: Mrs. French, who superintends the world of sensuality in "Baptizing," threatens to skin her children alive. The squirrel fur collar that Helena comes to find embarrassing has "something too soft about it, private, humiliating" (139).

156 See above, 408 for heads on trays. This is really the same image, in a more tragic version, as that of the sun in the tree or crown of petals (see above, 297).

157 She compares this second kind to "possession" (195): the word used for the title of the second part of "A Queer Streak."

158 See John 19:25. While the Greek is ambiguous, John seems to intend four women of whom three are Marys.

159 Various people are denied drink in Munro: see above, 185, 370–71, 472–73, 537 n28. Within the Passion world we can note Violet taking King Billy's whisky away; in "The Idyllic Summer" Mr. Sherriff laughingly offers Clara beer, but his wife says no.

160 Garnet must in fact be several years older than Del if he is twenty-three (215) and she is in Grade XIII. But we are hardly made to feel this difference in age, and Garnet seems to Del a "young man, boy" (211).

161 See Tener 37.13.10–12.

162 See Tener 37.16.28.12.

163 Jimmy and Duval were once beaten up — on the orders of Stump Troy, Robina is sure — outside a dance hall (148). King Billy Thoms was beaten up at a dance before he learned to turn the tables at the next dance (210). Garnet French left a man one-eyed outside a beer parlour (215) — a festive if not directly sexual place.

164 For Exodus counterparts, see above, 360, 361. For fatness and thinness in central and terminal contexts see above, 342 n75.

165 There is a Franklin whom I have not yet introduced: an observant outsider who waits on the fringe of things, "calmly puzzled, not giving trouble," as poems like "The Destruction of Sennacherib" — Byron on the delivery of Israel from Assyria — ferment inside him. See Tener 37.16.28.12.f2–3.

[166] See above, 417. In the gospels see John 2:4, also Matt. 12:46 ff.

[167] See Dan. 7:9–10: "his throne was like the fiery flame, and his wheels as burning fire. A fiery stream issued and came forth from before him."

[168] See Matt. 26:64.

[169] Rev. 12. The rod of iron in verse 5 is specifically from Psalm 2:9: "Thou shalt break them with a rod of iron."

[170] Rev. 19:15.

[171] For allusion to Joan of Arc see Carrington 182.

[172] Note the word "yard" again in some of these cases: Jimmy and Duval do their acrobatics in "the dust of the yard" (147); the younger French boys in "Baptizing" scuffle in the "yard" (220). Another pair of gymnasts are Sam and Edgar Grazier in "The Moon in the Orange Street Skating Rink," who work out in a "vacant lot" (135). See above, 458, n142.

[173] The French family similarly includes not only the tricky Lila and Phyllis (grace and nature in a very natural context) but the sulky and self-absorbed "Thelma" ("will"). Cf. the jealous Aunt Thelma of "At The Other Place," — "hungry, watchful, distempered" (132) — not to say "Willa" Cather.

[174] Cf. other escapes: Helena in "Executioners," struck by Robina, gets away with a cut inside her lip, Violet gets away from the fire with scratches. In all such cases, as with Dorothy's "stroke" (173) in "Marrakesh," we have to say in the immediate perspective that nothing has really happened.

[175] The relation between "Garnet French" and "real life" (242) at the end of "Baptizing" can be understood in different ways, as can its two members. Here I am saying that baptism and the unregenerate real life opposed to it can be seen as the same thing.

[176] Thus Macdonald (209) asks whether Garnet, "despite initial appearances, has not simply offered Del another route to the garrison" ("garrison" being his term for the world as containment).

[177] The Garnet French story has a remarkable collection of chains, including not only the kind that gets a car out of mud but others as tenuous as a thread-bridge or strip of skin. In the end these all hold firmly, as do others that seem to break.

[178] I will venture the suggestion that the various Young People hint at the tradition of Christian reform — which is a tradition as surely as what it reforms against. For "Dutch Monk" see above, 202.

[179] I agree with Struthers, "Reality and Ordering," 43, that in the climactic scene of "Baptizing,' Del rejects the wrong kind of baptism before accepting the right, though I myself would not quite identify the two acts. Struthers sees the end of "Baptizing" as corresponding to that of Joyce's *Portrait*: I prefer the end of "The Photographer," and would emphasize the difference as much as the (unquestionable) similarity between Del's "Yes" and Molly Bloom's.

A Link Beyond the Usual

A. THE APOCALYPSE

I: Introduction

After the stories that I have put in a Passion group there remain others at the ends of Munro's collections making a distinct, if again somewhat heterogeneous, group of their own. I have suggested that certain "late" Passion stories — "Marrakesh" and "The Spanish Lady" are the clearest cases — touch this later group by their character as well as position. "Rose Matilda," the third part of "Oh, What Avails," is as much fourth-phase as third-phase (there being no separate fourth part of this story). And we can add, where convenient, any other story that sufficiently emphasizes some kind of "extra" experience, either in its whole course or near its end. "Eskimo," for example, which I have put in an Annunciation sub-group, leads to a long dream-epilogue in which something beyond mere Passion is being announced; we can detect the same greater annunciation in stories like "Hold Me Fast, Don't Let Me Pass" and "Pictures of the Ice."[1] An uncollected story that I have used elsewhere, "The Ferguson Girls Must Never Marry," will prove still another good resource here — especially, once again, in its final incident. For reasons already sketched,[2] I associate stories like these with the biblical Apocalypse: in fact we will be seeing an even greater apocalypse, to the extent that the biblical one remains confined in the world of our earlier phases.

When we come from Munro's Passion group to the groups of stories at the ends of her collections, the first thing we may notice is a settled finality about them — a life of one kind or another is not just nearing its end but decidedly ending or ended. A title like "Memorial" speaks for itself: Douglas is dead. So is Tracy Lee in "Circle of Prayer"; so is the mother in "The Peace of Utrecht" who fought so hard against death; indeed Jubilee, if we are to believe Mrs. Jordan in "The Photographer," is a veritable town of suicides. And death in the strict sense is not the only way to be finished: as Joan remarks in "Rose Matilda," "people . . . disappear, and they don't all die to do it" (209). The aging Rose, desperately trying for love in "Simon's Luck," is not doing so in "Spelling" or "Who Do You Think You Are?" — or at any rate that is not what these stories are primarily about.[3] In "Winter Wind" a once "baffled and struggling" (206) girl must now see herself as a fixture: a neglected old woman, shut away for good in her unchanging house. It is true that some characters see themselves as happier kinds of fixture: the mother in "The Ottawa Valley," for instance, returns to her childhood home prepared for triumph. But she too feels that something is settled; and characters may feel this even when what is settled belongs to the future. The Jerry Storey of "The Photographer" looks forward to a scientifically programmed "Brave New World" (245), as Del calls it, while Del herself is going to produce a not so brave new world by fixing Jubilee in her gothic novel. Nor are all expected settlements as imaginary as these. At the end of "White Dump" Sophie turns to the Prose Edda: "it is too late to talk of this now," she reads, "it has been decided" (309). Sophie might have read the same thing in herself, for she knows that choices have been made, that events will now lead where they must. Del in "The Photographer," waiting for her exam results, takes delay only as "reprieve" (249), knowing she will not get the scholarship she hoped for.

Limiting ourselves to the tragic kind of fatality, we can say that the acceptance of failure, perhaps after initial reluctance, is a second major feature of these stories — more major, certainly, than in either the Exodus or Passion groups. In "Spelling" Rose accepts Flo's senility, as Flo must do in her own way; the father in "The Moons of Jupiter" accepts the operation he is not likely to survive; the triumphant mother in "The Ottawa Valley," as her daughter somehow knows, has consented to her own approaching death. As is specially clear in this instance, last tries such as we found in the third phase now aim more at producing a different version of the inevitable than at challenging its inevitability. The mother here is seeking to put the best face on her death — or on the living death of Parkinson's disease; and whatever face it may present, we often find people contemplating or displaying what their lives have amounted to.[4] The "The Ottawa Valley" mother has brought her daughters to see the world of her earlier life; the father in "The Moons of Jupiter" has recollections about his own. A specially suggestive image here is that of Flo on the sun-porch looking at her souvenirs — emblems that sum up the whole of our series of temporal phases, here at the point of completion. In more spatial terms we have Jerry and Del, soon to leave Jubilee, looking down from the railroad bridge: below them lies the town in which they have done their growing up, its pattern exposed both by winter and by their own kind of coldness.

The gloomy prospect here finds a notable counterpart in, once more, "The Ottawa Valley": when, at the end of a long train ride, the narrator's mother gestures into the darkness and announces the place of the story's title, it is a valley of shadow that she is pointing to. In "Visitors," similarly, we come to the little house with its coffin-sized coffee table where Wilfred and Mildred do "fine" (199); if we go with them for a drive we come to a sign reading "Dead end. No winter maintenance beyond this point" (210). And we can make a more specific connection between the imageries of these last two stories, at least if we take into account a variant form of the latter. In its collected version, Wilfred produces an anecdote about sailing on the Kamloops to Sault Ste. Marie — following a loop, perhaps, to end in the falling waters of Mary. In the *New Yorker* version there was a comparable but rather more pointed suggestion here: it was the "Lethbridge" — Lethe bridge, from the sound of it — that Wilfred was taking, and the place he was bound for was Port Arthur. As for this last name, we may notice that, in both versions, Mildred at one point calls herself "Her Majesty the Queen" (200); in "The Ottawa Valley" we similarly hear of "Her Majesty" (228), as Aunt Dodie calls her — the narrator's aunt, a legal secretary in black and red.[5] And when we see Dodie herself wearing "a man's hat without a crown" (229) and hear the mother quoting Tennyson's King Arthur, we realize what we have come to.[6]

For this is the place Violet tried so hard to avoid in "A Queer Streak": the sombre realm of the presiding queens and the dead king. In "Memorial" the stricken mother believes herself connected with Arthur Meighen, "former Prime Minister of Canada" (213); and to see what happens to this kind of Arthur, we can recall how Mrs. Kidd once regained her self-possession — by retorting "Who cares?" (179) when asked the name of a prime minister. In "The Ottawa Valley" we hear of another king — Mackenzie King — who, as Aunt Dodie assures her visitors, is too small a man to get elected locally. Mackenzie King did get elected, of course, and became a very royal prime minister in the larger Ottawa Valley of which the smaller is an epitome. But election seems a dubious thing in such a place, and a king may be chosen only for a minister's suffering. "The Ottawa Valley" shows us a valley of kings as a graveyard: if, indeed, we think of the "large cube of dark blue granite, flecked white" (239) that makes its most impressive monument, we can see how the whole night sky might be the same graveyard or gravestone — the world fixed forever by the judgment of death.

*

Before going farther, we can stop to consider the status of this dark vision within our scheme of phases. The fourth phase is evidently a strange one, coming after what is already a termination: and in fact "after" does not have its usual sense here, for there is a curious disjunctness about the Apocalypse stories. In the two novels, both of which have a clear temporal sequence, the final chapters stand outside this in each case. Del Jordan's meeting with Bobby Sherriff takes place not after her affair with Garnet French but in the course of it, and there is no ordinary causal connection between the two episodes. The main incidents in "Spelling" and "Who Do You Think You Are?" seem actually to happen before Rose's affair with Simon in the previous chapter — if we can establish any clear temporal relation at all. And whereas "Simon's Luck" represents a definite stage in Rose's love life after "Mischief" and "Providence," the concluding chapters do not show us stages in the same way: the meeting with Ralph Gillespie, for instance, is a casual and unsexual encounter at a time when Rose is making plans to sleep with someone else.

This is not to say that the fourth phase has nothing to do with the third: in one view it is just what the third was in relation to the central second, a distribution of its predecessor's falling movement — this is why it is often easy to read a story in either a terminal or an Apocalypse way. Yet not only can this movement complicate itself, as we have seen with other phases, but we also sense something radically new here, different in kind from the cycle of phases that has come before. If we think again of the fourth-phase characteristics we have just been noting — finality, disjunctness, reflectiveness — it may occur to us that these are typical of the late recognition in an individual story: the "extra" that is not an event in the same way as others but a vision of what events mean. Such a vision will for one thing act as a reinforcement, showing us the way of the world with an ultimate clarity; and since we have been considering this way as a tragic one, our first job here will be to see the world's tragedy in a definitive form. But tragedy is only one of the possibilities that Munro offers us. It is not just that the world can show comic luck as well as tragic necessity — dependence on either is ultimately the same bondage, and in this way the world remains tragic as a whole; but in recognizing this we have a key to escape from it, and access to what can most easily be called a larger comedy. At last we are seeing the world for what it is; and if this can be the most paralyzing and gorgon-like of visions, we can also choose to make it the opposite — a vision of freedom. This is the vision that constitutes the fourth phase proper: a phase contrasting with our tragically conceived third phase instead of merely extending it.

One way to imagine this new phase is as a new kind of narrative, and for the purpose we will have to add another figure — if we want to call it that — to the ones we have used for narrative so far. (At the same time, we can reduce this figure to typological or even cyclical terms, and for simplicity's sake I will often be doing so without special notice.) Here we must take up where we left off in considering the forms of stories earlier. We saw narrative figures growing more complex as they expressed increasing degrees of differentiation and identification — at least as these were possible on the natural terms we were confined to. On its own principle this development could go on to infinity, but typology can well represent the endless end of it — the joining of contraries in all their contrariety that I have called coinherence. Coinherence is still not genuine identity; while we can see it as sealing the world, it equally displays the world's inability to be, on its own terms, more than an integration without integrity. But this very display can suggest a better counterpart: there can be a recognition, beyond typology or any complicating of it, in which the world's terms are themselves changed and an infinite regression reverses itself. In a way this new recognition returns us to the simple figure with which our exploration of narrative began — the point, that is, as a miraculous "happening" defying the conditions of time. Because it had no extension and in that sense could not be a story at all, the point was a limiting case at one end of our sequence,

functioning as the germ of the properly narrative figures. The transformed vision in Munro's fourth-phase stories tends to come as
another special, brief experience — an epiphany once again: but what
it shows us now is a wholeness of life going beyond multiplicity rather
than stopping short of it.

As usual an example or two from outside Munro may be useful,
though at present we must limit ourselves to a very few of the
fourth-phase characteristics. For a fairly simple case, we can think of
the epilogue to Shaw's *St. Joan*. The play is finished, yet it is not —
its characters meet again in a timeless nowhere; and as they reflect
on their story, it takes on a new appearance quite different from the
one it had presented within its temporal shell. Or, to take a more
realistic ending, we can think of *The Prelude*: with the complete
turning of the revolutionary wheel, Wordsworth is able to imagine
things differently, envisaging a new kind of brotherhood in an
immediate present that as such had no place on the wheel. In Eliot's
Quartets, where we have seen *The Dry Salvages* as the poem of the
dying god and the sorrowing mother, *Little Gidding* deals not so
much with dying as with the condition of being dead; and through
death or "detachment," by the greatest of paradoxes, a new communion and expression becomes possible — one located in the "never
and always" that is also now and here.[7]

II: The Restored Temple

With Eliot's never and always we have glimpsed the fourth-phase
vision in a way that we will now have to abandon for a while: for
what we started with was death, and we must deal with the different
versions of this — a story in itself, as we will see later — before going
on to a life comprehending it. But there is certainly a kind of life to
be dealt with here as well: one that is contained by, or is a form of,
death itself. The third-phase story, we found, need not move straight
to its conclusion: like other tragedies it may pass through prosperity
on the way. We could even, if we wanted, say that it ends in prosperity
— the domesticity, for instance, that a Naomi finds satisfying enough
— though such prosperity is adversity from Del's point of view. Taken
as a distribution of the third phase, the fourth has the same possibilities, if on its own terms; and since we have already seen it as a tragedy
of the simplest kind, we can now consider its more triumphant
elements.

Having arrived at her destination in the pitch dark, the narrator of "The Ottawa Valley" wakes up next morning to see that it is not really a valley at all. Certainly it is no valley of death: and some of the things to be found here are positively exalted. If we look not at the graveyard but inside the Church of St. John, we see an impressive ceremony taking place, with a picturesque company assembled for it. Allen Durrand, once a martyr, is now a "big Holstein man" (233);[8] his consort is a West in blue with a hat like a wheel. The narrator's mother makes her own proud appearance, her grey enlivened by a discreet form of scarlet. And the choir, as we expect at an apocalyptic celebration, sings "All Things Bright and Beautiful":

Thou art worthy, O Lord, to receive glory and honour and power: for thou hast created all things, and for thy pleasure they are and were created.[9]

An apocalyptic flavouring, as we saw, has already come into third-phase gatherings: the Eucharistic meal, after all, is not only a feast within the world but the proleptic celebration of a future kingdom, even the kingdom itself already come. In "Simon's Luck," for instance, we have sensed the Apocalypse at the opening party in Kingston, with its bowing elders and turn-of-the-century décor; perhaps we can sense the same thing again when Rose has followed the "Hope-Princeton highway" (171) to the western ocean. Here she flourishes playing "utter tripe" (172) on television — Munro's far or final vision again; in the epilogue that is the story's own fourth phase we find her starring in a "scene" (the New Testament word for "tabernacle") set near "Salt Spring" (171) Island, famous for its lamb. In the Apocalypse group itself "Memorial" has a comparable scene: at the great reception June performs with all the professionalism of a Rose, and the house where she does so, overlooking the same western ocean, sits on "Hollyburn" (218) Mountain — the mountain of a holy burn or stream. Perhaps there is also a burning tree here, as at the fire in "Executioners" — where, for that matter, we found apocalyptic imagery in a Passion context. But here the context is one of final glory.

We might not expect such glory to prove as worldly as in — most recently — the corresponding aspect of the third phase. Yet June's reception, memorial or not, is very much of the world; so, in an unsympathetic view, is the city of the biblical apocalypse itself: for once again, it would seem, Egypt has expanded to absorb anything beyond its borders. This greater Egypt may have the same giddy, syncretistic quality we found in the swinging new world of the third-phase stories — the eclecticism of Ewart and June in "Memorial" being a prime example; what is more impressive here is a return of the old stability, now more stable than ever. Along with the apocalyptic kingdom itself, the final stories display our various worldly empires again — there is a Japanese garden, a Chinese tomb, King George and Queen Elizabeth on a china mug[10] — and more generally we find an atmosphere of economic recovery. The setting of "The Photographer" may be the one we saw in decay in the Garnet French story, but now we are shown a different aspect of it: since the end of the War, as Bobby Sherriff explains, people are all buying. And evidently they have good reason, for the prosperity, financial and other, looks as if it is going to last.

This means that something else has not lasted. There may have been a danger that June would not get over her early misgivings, but "I *really* did it in Gestalt. I worked it all out and finished with it" (221). June also has a system for finishing with the garbage, and, in concert with her husband, a larger system for finishing with experiences generally — "all of them accepted, chewed and altered, assimilated, destroyed" (216). If a memorial service is called for, her arrangements are so accomplished that "everything was thought of, everything was done" (218).[11] Laurence and Magda in "White Dump" have fixed their world up in much the same way; so, severally, have Morris and Joan in "Rose Matilda," and various less affluent people like the tidy grandmother in "Winter Wind" or the ever-lucky Wilfred in "Visitors." So, we might add, have another group we have met before — the inmates of homes for the elderly,[12] not to say hospitals. At the Home in "Spelling," with its order and amenities, former things have passed away. The old folk are now free to enjoy their ageless afterlives, some of them happier than ever before; the regulars at the Legion in "Who Do You Think You Are?" enjoy an agelessness of their own kind. Even the children of Uncle James and Aunt Lena in "The Ottawa Valley" can be put with these happily adjusted people: once physically and morally beaten, they have turned into "decent friendly wage-earners, not a criminal or as far as I know even a neurotic among them" (246) — adults so normal that neither law nor psychology can find anything wrong.[13]

And so the world has reached Gestalt, so to speak; at the same time its stability, like that of Egypt again, can incorporate any amount of change. One thing Rose notices at the Home is a mobile, in which "cutout birds of blue and yellow paper were bobbing and dancing, on undetectable currents of air" (181). Other constructions use currents of a more definite and circular kind: the purpose of the garbage-system in "Memorial" is "recycling" (209), and the Japanese garden in the same story seems to maintain itself on a system of circulating water. In fact Ewart and June are a recycling system themselves — the digestion that can dispose of anything can restore itself through anything, making even the death of a son into an "occasion" (214), to quote a word that sticks in Eileen's mind. And this changelessness-in-change has the same apocalyptic ring as simpler forms of permanence. In "Who Do You Think You Are" we are told at length about Hanratty's Orange Walk, in which is proclaimed the putting down of Antichrist by the man on the white horse — a triumphant version of King Billy. Nothing could be more definitive, and yet the parade is both a succession and, Munro implies, a cycle: it runs from King Billy on his white horse to the Black Knights on darker ones at the rear, and these Black Knights wear not only "the ancient father-to-son top hats" but ouroboric "swallow-tail coats" (192). Hanratty itself, as the story makes us see it, is a larger-scale version of the same cycle and even something more. Since Rose was a girl everything has changed and nothing has changed — Milton Homer, for instance, no longer has the Orange Walk to attend to, but watches the cars on the highway instead.[14]

*

If the apocalyptic fixture, with or without movable parts, is what everything arrives at, what it arrives at is everything. What Ewart and June have thought of and done is everything; what they have experienced in the Growth Group is everything; their collection of adopted children takes in all races and cultures, as does their décor — the latter extending to pottery by a former convict now absorbed into the Unitarian Church. The church in "The Ottawa Valley" could hardly be Unitarian, but from what we are told it may well be United; and in any case it is the church of St. John — John the Divine, it would seem, who shows us the creator of everything receiving his praise. When the narrator's mother upstages the minister it seems to be her church too, and appropriately enough: for as we have seen, this institutional woman reminds her daughter of a department store, with its well-classified "plenitude" (227). As a girl she once co-operated in sewing up the fly of Allen Durrand's "overalls" (235), causing such plenitude that he had to reveal "the full view" (236) to get relief. Later she saves her daughter from a similar fate by donating a safety-pin to keep up her pants (for what it is worth, St. John's word for "all things" is *pánta*).[15] The mother thus belongs with the various characters, in the Apocalypse stories and elsewhere, who exert themselves to keep the world in one piece; Allen himself, for that matter, was soon able to "put it all together" (236) as his name suggests he might.[16]

The place to celebrate this all is of course a temple — the establishment we imagined for the god of the central phase and can now imagine as more finally established. St. John's Church is a sacred form of it; a department store is a secular one; more official, and reminding the narrator no less of her mother, is the Union Station in Toronto — "like a church with its high curved roof and great windows" (228). Transcending all of these in its way — and again compared explicitly with a temple — is the Planetarium in "The Moons of Jupiter": here the same curved roof contains the whole sky, the sanctuary where a father-planet sits enthroned among his turning satellites. In "White Dump," similarly, the honoured Laurence is ensconced in an aeroplane and taken for a panoramic ride, a parallel to the moon-flight in the same story. We have seen the sky in a very different way — as the grave of a dead king, mourned by attendant queens; but in our present vision death is swallowed up in victory.

At the same time there remains something elusive about these places — an auditory and visual ambiguity, for one thing. Sometimes they seem very quiet, as is natural enough when they are in fact funeral homes. In one such, as we are told in "The Widower," "the thick carpet hushed every footstep": the "heavy, creamy, soft" (218) carpet and curtains in June's living-room must have a similar effect. On the other hand there may be sonorous noises — what we also find in the Apocalypse itself, of course, with its heavenly voice like the sound of waters or thunder.[17] Munro's funeral homes have wall-to-wall music to match the carpets; the "thunder of trains" (228) resounds through the Union Station; and there as in the Planetarium an "amplified voice" makes solemn proclamations. What is more remarkable about these noises is that we cannot make out their origin: for they seem to come "out of the walls" (230), like the announcer's voice in the Planetarium, or perhaps from behind them, like the noise of the trains.[18] In the same way the announcements in the station "could not quite be understood" (228) — a recurrent problem in these stories.[19] There is something curiously artificial about sound that for all its definitiveness is so indefinite, and indeed much of it is magnified, recorded, electric, or simply unauthentic.[20] The announcer in the Planetarium turns on an "eloquent professional voice" (230) — like the minister in St. John's Church, no doubt, and certainly the preacher in "The Widower"; the music in the funeral homes sounds religious but is not. Above all, there is "a faint echo-chamber effect":[21] we cannot be sure whether we are hearing voices from the beyond or the inside.

It is much the same if we think in visual terms. On the one hand, the temple has its walls and perhaps curtains, closed in the case of a funeral parlour. On the other, it may well be a room with a view: June's house on its mountain has a splendid panorama, and a Planetarium is in a sense all view — a room that turns into the heavens themselves. The same thing is true of more modest settings: to mention only one, the County Home in "Spelling" has its own advertised view.[22] Once again, however, it is difficult to locate what our senses offer us, for light here is as confusing as sound. In a funeral parlour it may be concealed by "little wall-bracket lights behind heavy pink glass";[23] it may even seem, like the sound, "to come right out of the pink walls."[24] In any case what we see by this light may be another wall, and where the view recedes picturesquely into the distance it may be only a picture hanging on the same sort of blank surface. It may for that matter, as at the Planetarium, be a projection: if, then, we peek behind the wall, as Nola in "The Ferguson Girls" does while at the Art Gallery, we will not find anything to enlighten us much.

All in all, it would seem, the temple is like Ewart's Japanese garden, which looks like a real landscape only when you are not looking at anything else; and the landscape of the universe itself may be no less deceptive. We can remember here what Janet sees projected onto a screen in the hospital: the heart of her dying father. Perhaps the proud Jupiter not only of the Planetarium but of the real heavens is no more than this father; perhaps people's experiences of floating to the ceiling at death are no more than this projection. We have seen how Munro's stories of going out and coming in have the same reflecting quality: if, in showing us an Exodus and a Promised Land, they keep us imprisoned all the while, they too are only sounds and images rebounding inside a closed chamber. The Apocalypse itself, with its stunning sound-effects and massed choirs and opening *skené*, may do no more than complete the illusion — in which case eternity, as we are seeing it, is only one of the Counter-Stranger's recesses that manage to counterfeit larger and freer worlds. The temple, as Janet feels, may be "slightly phony" (232).

*

The confinement here will be more evident if we focus the prison into a jailor. For the temple is also a body — the cosmetic pink of the different funeral-parlours is that of Egyptian skin — and with its "high curved roof"[25] it is one of our places of the skull as well. Its deity is thus, in the first place, the god of the locked head, whether we see him as a central-phase sun-god or as an ultimate Jupiter with his moons. But we have also seen this god as involved with a goddess; and if we are concerned with the temple as a mysterious and inviolable container, we may prefer at this stage to imagine the goddess as containing the god (never forgetting that both represent aspects of us all, men and women alike).

No doubt the mother in "The Ottawa Valley" has to commandeer the church from the minister if she wants it, but to her daughter's way of thinking it is already her kind of place. We have seen others like her: "Memorial" has shown us June — that is, Juno — very much in charge; earlier we met Isis, not just a bereft wanderer but the all-comprehending veiled mother who, in a more swaddling way than the apocalyptic god, is all that is and was and will be.[26] In fact each chapter in the second part of this book has ended with the same goddess. First we came to Mother Nature — the great egg, breakable yet unbreakable, that holds the entirety of things in its shell. In a more attractive way, we found, this mother is Venus, in a crazier way Loony Buttler; as time itself, she is ancient Mrs. "Cronin." With the central stories we arrived at indifferent old Mrs. Wright and the Jenkin's Bend aunts, from whom Del, like Uncle Craig, finds it impossible to escape. In the terminal groups we found how Stella and Robina, not to say Rose, exert themselves to keep people from going into the ditch or ocean or otherwise "passing out."[27]

Beside the woman who keeps people out of the water we can set the one who keeps them from drinking it. We have seen various Flos and Stellas who take drink away or deny it in the first place;[28] and there is one incident in which Munro's whole world of arousal and denial seems epitomized. In a story of Robina's, Duval takes sun-stroke while working on a hot roof without a hat; and what he says in his delirium is "Please Grandma, get me a drink of water" (145) — the fair-skinned boy who climbed in the sun has become a helpless victim crying "I thirst" to a pitiless old woman. For a more corporeal example of the Old Woman, as I am going to call her generally, we can turn to the grandmother in "A Trip to the Coast," who forbids May to swim, controls the supply of various liquids, and defeats a would-be saviour's efforts to charm her with a bottle-opener. We can recall her temple here: the Egyptian store purveying onions and oranges and cookies. She herself can be found sitting in state beside the ice-cream freezer with the silvery foil behind her[29] — evidently she is not just a fertility goddess but a queen of heaven, with certain touches linking her especially to the moon. She is the clock-face as well, almost hidden by a ripening tomato and some powder for her false teeth; and when she talks about having a "headstone" (177) she becomes the grave itself — what she most resembles, in fact, is a walking skeleton, topped by a huge skull.

She sits alone and autonomous: for she has long outlived her husband, and, to quote her guiding principle, "I look after my ownself" (179). It is true that the store is decaying; the grandmother has come to disbelieve even her own reasons; and she dies when the faith-healer coaxes her out of the doubt that is her only existence. Yet as May finds, she does not die in dying any more than she sleeps in sleeping; life and death, it appears, are both subject to her:[30]

> It seemed to [May] that any place she went her grandmother would be there beforehand; anything she found out her grandmother would know already, or else could prove to be of no account. (175)[31]

The mother in "The Ottawa Valley" may be a believer rather than a doubter — she is like June with her values and Mrs. Jordan with her notions — and yet this pantocratic woman is not really so different from May's grandmother: alone, self-sufficient, restricting, and completely obtuse to a daughter's sensitivities. She too survives her own death, as the daughter learns in trying to exorcise her; she too has her own temple — one of glacial rock and ice whose limits cannot be passed because, as with other temples we have seen, they cannot be defined:

> She is heavy as always, she weighs everything down, and yet she is indistinct, her edges melt and flow. Which means she has stuck to me as close as ever and refused to fall away. (246)

473

III: The Thief in the Night

The Old Woman's power seems absolute and final; what is strange is that, for all her ability to keep things on track, various people in the Apocalypse stories manage to go off it — to escape into the ditch or the swamp or the river. "The Photographer" in particular is full of such escapes. When the strange hero in Del's novel disappears his car is found empty, "overturned beside a bridge, overturned in a ditch beside a dry creek" (247). Caroline, Del's heroine, manages a similar end, and so in real life do Marion Sherriff and the Miss Farris recalled here from "Changes and Ceremonies" — to mention only those who go into the ditch in a more or less literal way. And in one perspective at least, all these people are acting to free themselves: perhaps the Old Woman's reign is not so absolute after all.

"Take your life," says Helen in "The Peace of Utrecht" to her sister Maddy, intending to "finish this" (210). Like many things said at the end of Munro stories — and, as we have seen, things said about finishing in the present group of stories — this advice needs some pondering. Maddy has sacrificed her mother's life to her own: one thing we hear in Helen's words is the Old Woman enforcing her law in return, telling Maddy to kill herself. Or, like the aunt who has just handed down the dead mother's clothes, Helen is saying that Maddy must take up a life of remorse — which would only be death in another form. But what Helen more plainly means is something else: she is inviting Maddy to get away from Jubilee, to take the life that her mother's ghost is denying her; and while we will need to return to the other meanings, there is no reason not to take the obvious one seriously. We will, at the same time, have to see what the taking of one's life in this last sense entails. Since the Old Woman has got the whole world in her power, any escape to life will in a way have to be an escape from it, an escape to death; and death must not, in our present view, be merely something the Old Woman sponsors and incorporates — another member for her Trinity or province for her Egypt. If Maddy's taking of her life means dying after all, she must die on her own terms, and finish like a true finish-woman.

Dying in this sense — and we can see any death as at least an emblem of it — is just what the Old Woman works to prevent; and yet there are people she does not seem to notice or take seriously, stones that she rejected in building her temple.[32] In Rose's TV series, we are told, nice people are not allowed to die; others, however — "peripheral and unappealing characters" (172) — do get away with it. There is an evident hint here at Simon, who in fact is peripheral not only to others surviving him but to the Trinity of his own "characters" (161). And we have met other supernumeraries: the aging victims of the Exodus stories, the unappealing bass of the Gospel Quartet in "Baptizing," Munro's whole array of janitors and hermits — of whom there is something in the abject Caroline and the washed-up Maddy. We have also seen the treatment such people generally get at the hands of the less excluded. The dying old man in "The Spanish Lady," to add an important example, is ignored by half the people around him and merely gawked at by the rest; Marion Sherriff may be a tale and a picture on the wall, but that itself disposes of her. What we must now see is the privilege of such people: it is the despised and afflicted who get free of the Old Woman's demonic life — or life-and-death — and acquire the authority of independence.

*

If the Old Woman is unable to keep her prisoners in, her troubles do not stop there: she has others of her own. We could, again, see these as part of her stability — her smooth rotation on her axis — and yet there is a deeper uncertainty in her that we sense from her very need to assert herself. Robina, very much the Old Woman in some ways, is unable to control the great fire and so has to pretend a victory; the grandmother in "A Trip to the Coast," for all her proclaimed self-satisfaction, feels her sudden compulsion to sell the store and go west. Such figures often give themselves away, as we have seen: the triumphant June, for instance, makes the mistake of wearing silver-green eye-shadow, a "hint of something hectic, unsure" (218), and the mother in "The Ottawa Valley" is making a similar mistake when she enters church with her slip showing. In this last case, moreover, our minds go back to the mother's earlier slip, the revealing of her voyeur's joke on Allen Durrand:

My mother looked from me to Aunt Dodie and back with an unusual expression on her face: helplessness. . . . She just looked as if there was a point at which she might give up. (236)

Giving up here would for one thing mean showing pleasure: what the Old Woman cannot help wanting and thus one threat to her self-sufficiency. Flo, as Rose finds in "Spelling," can be baited by things like "trifle" (181); Robina's arousal at the burning of her enemies' house is positively orgasmic. At the same time we may sense something very different disturbing the Old Woman's equanimity: the fear that we earlier saw besetting the central world. Behind the ambitious plans of the grandmother in "A Trip to the Coast" is the unacknowledged fact that she will soon die; and in "The Ottawa Valley," with its cemetery and gloomy poetry, death seems a looming presence in the minds of all the older women. Aunt Lena is afraid that her children will be killed in accidents; the mother is haunted by her own approaching death; even Aunt Dodie, who has the jittery brightness of other secretly frightened women in Munro,[33] tells the narrator about death when ostensibly telling her about life. This death will acquire a more definite face if we notice its connection with Munro's absent male figures.

Although they never say so directly, the female Old Women of these stories are often haunted by someone, usually though not necessarily male,[34] who may be lamented but has also been disposed of in some way, and is dreaded for that reason. "He is not Dead but Sleepeth" (239), reads a stone in St. John's churchyard, quoting the biblical account of Lazarus: and the idea of a sleeper who might wake has a special thrust here, since the same story includes not only the sleeping King Arthur but the martyred Allen Durrand and, all but unmentioned, the dead husband whom the mother would not allow to drink. In the case of other women, an uneasiness like this mother's is related to something passing in the night — our dark flash again, or light itself coming into a dark camera through a tiny aperture. We have seen old Dorothy in "Marrakesh" with her fear of a midnight stroke; among the bedeviled old women in "Spelling," who seem generally to feel they have been robbed, one is sure that a man has been watching her undress through a crack in the blind. It seems to be fear of a similar invader that has Flo behaving like a thief in the night herself or marching off to hide the cutting board. Even in the Home she does not feel quite safe, for if she wore the wig that looks like a dead animal, "somebody'd be sure to take a shot at me" (187). The last of her souvenirs is in fact the picture of a family shot by its father in the middle of the night: it must take a good deal of bravado for Flo to insist, as she does at the end, that her gallstones be shown to her husband.

Here we have one way to understand the tremors that afflict so many of these women, particularly in their arms or hands. The shaking hand of the mother in "The Ottawa Valley" is technically the result of Parkinson's disease, but if the hands of Maddy in "The Peace of Utrecht" shake as well, making her drop her valuable fruit-bowl, there must be something more here: something to which the biblical palsy gives a suggestive echo. In the same way Robina "trembles" (150) even when showing her arm in victory, and the arm she does not show is incapacitated — amputated in this case. On the night of the great rearrangement in "Spelling" it is "as if someone had wielded a big shaky spoon" (175): the invader himself, Flo might say, but Flo as well in her defiance of him. For light on such strange behaviour we can go back to the church scene in "The Ottawa Valley," during which the mother is confronted by a sweaty old man "whose hand . . . she did not want to shake" (242). The same man remembers her as "the best-lookin'" (241) of his teachers:[35] since what she once looked at was the trapped Allen Durrand trying to get his fly open — his hand "fairly clawin' and yankin' every which way" (235) — one can see why the thought of shaking hands with the old Adam would be enough to make her own hand shake.

What Allen Durrand does to the mother at the church service may not seem very drastic — he simply fails to speak to her — but in his implicit repudiation we can see something that leads to her doom, structurally if not mechanically. Uncle James, while as much a failure as Allen is now a success, snubs the ferocious Aunt Lena in much the same way — "you would think Aunt Lena had nothing to do with him" (233). And as we can tell from the echo here, it is once again Jesus who is looming in the background, the Jesus who refuses his mother's authority.[36] The same Jesus rises from the dead, and will return in the end as the Old Woman's judge: for if the official Last Judgment is merely a show — her own, in fact — she will eventually have to appear at a more authentic counterpart.

To invoke a further range of biblical imagery, a stone is rolled away at the Resurrection. Later some heavier things will move from their places — mountains and stars and enormous hail; and when that happens Babylon herself will fall, having been split open at last. There are various forms, and readings, of the comparable imagery in Munro: for the present we can take it all as pointing simply to the collapse of the Old Woman herself.[37] It is she, we can say, who is starting to fail when cracks appear in walls, heavy weights topple, and the world appears as "rubble."[38] If we go back here to the emblematic gravestone in "The Ottawa Valley," we will note how it is "balanced on one corner" (239), sharing that ominous position with other things in the same story; and we can note that this stone, which we have connected with the universe, is equally "like a cooking

pot" (239) — one of Flo's, we might say, and we can recall here
Maddy's shattering bowl in "The Peace of Utrecht." Indeed a number
of things in the latter story suggest the same falling stone or slipping
bowl: the old red-brick house with its cracks and sagging verandah,
the pavements "broken up" by the "bombardment" (194) of winter,
the townsfolk borne down by the Atlas's weight of the summer heat,
"as if you have to carry the whole burning sky on your head" (197).
In the closely related "Memorial," again, guilt was once "piled onto"
(213) Eileen, and later something else was piled onto the unfortunate
Douglas: his car poised, tipped, and fell on him — as June
demonstrates at the end with a "slightly trembling" (226) hand.
Earlier in the story, of course, June does not tremble, nor does Ewart,
for they would rather display their values than have "the fact of a
death set up whole and unavoidable, in front of everybody's eyes"
(215). But in the process they set up their own abomination of
desolation,[39] and finally we see how shaky it is.

IV: The Tragic Cycle

My account of the Old Woman and the dreaded revenant has been a
very simplified one, leaving questions that will themselves return in
the end. First, though, there are other matters that need attention. So
far we have thought about the Apocalypse stories in relation to other
groups — as part, that is, of a larger structure; but we have not
considered structure as we find it inside the Apocalypse group itself.
And this means that we have not considered either the phases of
individual stories or the corresponding phases of the group as a whole
— sub-groupings like those that helped us to sort out the Central and
Passion stories. In principle, the sequence of such phases will be less
temporal now than before: if the fourth phase represents the condition at which the world finally arrives, its sub-phases will represent
the different versions of this condition, as we have already started to
see. But any sequence in Munro corresponds to the phases of a story,
and we have not yet seen what kind of story her Apocalypse makes.
We have, though, begun to see two apocalypses, a tragic and a comic,
and I have suggested that the relation between these might make a
larger story: a tragedy, to go no farther for the present, in the middle
of which we will find an unstable comedy.
    First we can glance at two stories that will remind us of our
initiatory phase, now recurring to begin a tragic story of conclusion.

"Winter Wind" puts us where fallen experience first discovered itself: in a blizzard from which travellers take shelter as best they can. Like others we have seen, the narrator's family have migrated to the new world and managed to settle, though to judge from the rigid and lonely grandmother of this story, settlement is only a trap within chaos itself — confinement "on the edge of the wilderness" (192). In "Visitors" the general tone is more humorous, and Wilfred and Mildred seem happy enough crammed inside their tiny house; yet the situations in the two stories are not dissimilar. An orphan thrown out at the age of twelve by his foster-father, Wilfred has spent most of his life as one of Munro's wanderers — a sailor, a gambler, a worker at various jobs in various places, a man who once followed a gleaming light through a blizzard to win a game of darts.

Late in life Wilfred has met the generous Mildred and settled down, even if his old restlessness has not quite left him (he still checks the tomatoes every half hour). But now he is visited by kinsfolk from a much less enclosed and sustaining world: his brother Albert arrives with his wife and sister-in-law from dry Saskatchewan. In "Winter Wind" a grand-daughter, the narrator of the story, similarly arrives in town from a chaotic farm and an equally chaotic mother, not to say a chaotic snowstorm (wet being much like dry, as elsewhere in Munro). Once again there are obvious differences — the grand-mother does not want her lively grand-daughter to go, Wilfred does not want his taciturn relatives to stay — yet in each case the visit is linked with something more disturbing: a visitation, as we can call it. The piece of news that sums this up brings the initiatory character of these stories sharply into focus. In "Winter Wind" an old friend of the grandmother has been lost in the storm on her way to the barn, having failed to attach herself with a clothesline; in "Visitors" we learn of a man who disappeared into a swamp. By the end both the grandmother and Wilfred are crying, loudly or silently: and what they are crying for is not only the others they have lost but themselves — the drowning or marooned castaways that they once were and will always be.

"Winter Wind" makes an appropriate opening for the Apocalypse group in *Something I've Been Meaning to Tell You*; at the end in the various collections come stories like "The Photographer" and "Dance of the Happy Shades," a distinct sub-group of their own. Do the stories in the middle make a sub-group in the same way? Not a clear-cut one, it must be said. A story like "Circle of Prayer" becomes at its close much like Munro's final group, while stories actually final in their collections, such as "The Ottawa Valley" and "Wigtime," may have much in common with those I am going to classify as medial (hence my use of these two stories in the following account). On the hither side of the middle, "Winter Wind" and (especially) "Visitors" come close to a story like "The Peace of Utrecht"; and as always, what we see depends partly on the way we do our seeing. Yet there remains a distinction here that is worth taking note of, and that can at times be very marked. *Who Do You Think You Are?* concludes with two chapters — "Spelling" and "Who Do You Think You Are?" itself — which are clearly contrasted and give us no sense of redundancy;[40] the contrast between "The Peace of Utrecht" and "Dance of the Happy Shades" is equally clear. And if we set some of our medial stories beside each other, we will find striking resemblances.

*

If we put together three typical cases — "Memorial," "The Peace of Utrecht," and "Visitors," seen now in their medial aspect — what may impress us at once is that all of them deal with siblings: Helen and Maddy, June and Eileen, Wilfred and Albert. We also find this last pair shadowed by the sisters Grace and Vera in a way that leaves Mildred, an only child, puzzled at the strange phenomenon of brothers and sisters. Other medial stories (for which "Sibling stories" can now perhaps serve as a more concrete name[41]) have siblings in a more extended sense — old friends like Anita and Margot in "Wigtime," cousins like the mother and Dodie in "The Ottawa Valley," a mother and daughter in "Circle of Prayer," a mother and step-daughter (in addition to a brother and sister) in "Spelling." But in every case there is emphasis on a certain kind of bond: what I have called friendship as opposed to sexual love.

Some years before the visit that makes the main action of "The Peace of Utrecht," Helen and Maddy entered into a pact for the care of their ailing mother — a pact renewed in a more general sense by the visit itself. There are various similar pacts in "Circle of Prayer": the high-school secret societies once belonged to by Janet, the confederacy of girls who drop their jewellery into Tracy Lee's coffin, the fellowship symbolized by the mugs in the home for the retarded, not to say the Circle of Prayer itself. We could say the same thing about the various Growth Groups and the like surrounding Ewart and June in "Memorial," including the one that assembles for the memorial service. And a more cosmogonic sort of pact is that linking Trudy to

Robin or June to Eileen: the bond of nature itself. For if a story like "Winter Wind" recalls the blustery origin of things, a Sibling story recalls the arrangement that made the world a world. In the beginning, as we have imagined, a primal identity fell from itself — an eternal bond was broken, giving rise to chaos; then the quarrelsome opposites remaining contracted for a lesser bond, the bond that is natural kinship of one sort or another. Emblematically, Rose and Flo made their "truce" (5); Et and Char made their own curious arrangement. Yet the world thus created has never ceased to be a troubled one, and the parties to its arrangement seem destined to a final re-encounter. Like Maddy and Helen they must try to "finish this" (210) — to normalize relations yet again, but in some more permanent way.

The self lost before the arrangement is suggested, in the Sibling stories as in initiatory ones, by lost victims young and old. As for the former, just as we find a drowned Sandy in "Something I've Been Meaning to Tell You," so we find Douglas in "Memorial" and Tracy Lee in "Circle of Prayer," both teenagers killed in car accidents. Equally important are lost elders such as — most conspicuously — the dead or soon-to-be-dead mothers in the background or foreground of "Royal Beatings," "Memorial," "The Peace of Utrecht," "The Ottawa Valley," and "Wigtime." Less conspicuous are husbands and fathers: indeed inconspicuousness has its own significance here. The father's war-death in "Memorial" can barely be told; dead fathers are recalled only briefly in "Spelling" and "The Ottawa Valley"; a father in "The Peace of Utrecht" is never mentioned at all, though his presence or absence would seem crucial in the family's difficulties. And this may remind us of the Douglas who is scarcely mentioned in conversation — or mentioned only in a brisk way that effectively denies his death. Douglas is properly memorialized, of course, and Tracy Lee displayed in true Egyptian style at the funeral home: but as with Uncle Craig, display itself is a kind of hiding here. One thing we may notice is that Douglas and Tracy Lee have the air of substitutes, as parents in their stories anxiously reflect: Douglas might have been Eileen's daughter Margot, Tracy Lee might have been Trudy's daughter Robin. The dead, that is, might have been those lucky enough to go on living, and we sense that their death has in some way made possible the others' life.[42]

Were they, then, sacrificed? As usual in Munro we can make no simple assignment of guilt, or of roles. But one version of what happened is of special importance at this point, even if we will later need others as well: we often detect a figure we have already noted, a guilty Old Woman haunted by the consort she has put away. For a hero is certainly missing in this world — an Arthur, so to speak, has been buried in the Ottawa Valley, and all that is left is the ineffectual shadow we first met in "Something I've Been Meaning to Tell You." Fred Powell in "The Peace of Utrecht," the very similar Ewart in "Memorial," even Dan in "Circle of Prayer" are all somewhat easy-going, passive men compared to their striding partners. Reuel Gault in "Wigtime," while much less accommodating, is even farther from heroism; and we can note that, while his given name suggests "rule" or "royal," his surname would seem to connect him with Munro's Golleys and Gauleys — gods fallen into holes.[43] What, then, of the women in such stories? One possibility is the yearning Teresa, Reuel's abandoned and crazed war-bride, for whom he is still an unfallen hero; and we can see that Margot and Anita, the "siblings" of the story, have secret longings like Teresa's. But they are also women who learn to handle their men,[44] and are quite capable of betraying. The story of such siblings' relation to one another will mean betrayal again. Helen senses her "secret, guilty estrangement" (201) from Maddy; Anita and Margot in "Wigtime" part ways after the latter's appropriation of Reuel; in "Circle of Prayer" there is not only the overt rivalry for Dan between Trudy and other women, but a more covert rivalry for him between Trudy and Robin themselves.

*

Now we can briefly follow the siblings' immediate story, which recapitulates the larger one of their falling out and in. With whatever lost self in the background, the two first come together for a renewal of their alliance. In each of our stories they have become different persons with different lives — lives, indeed, that may be the opposite of what we would expect. June, the shy and dependent younger sister, is now a true Juno, where Eileen has grown inert, pensive, and sensual, a drifter in the world. Margot is no less formidable in her way than June, and no less a chatelaine;[45] the adventuring Anita — who became a nurse and travelled as Margot wanted to do — is the Eileen here. In "The Peace of Utrecht" it is Maddy, formerly a satirical outsider to Jubilee, who has become a stay-at-home and even conformist, while the younger Helen has flown off to a new life elsewhere. And to say this is to show how the peace of this latter story has been broken. Each sister, by the terms of their agreement, was to have four years away from their mother (it is a sick mother who is being disposed of here[46]); yet Helen has married and not come back, while Maddy for her part has broken the treaty — or kept it in a provocative way — by remaining home and turning into the kind of person both sisters had resolved not to be. And as we later find, Maddy has broken the treaty in a deeper way: by abandoning her patient.

At the high point of such a story, the sibling who has chosen to claim success — always a wilful "Wilfred" in some way — celebrates this in a temple dedicated to it. That is what we have seen the "Ottawa Valley" mother doing literally when she appears in St. John's Church; it is equally what Margot in the "Wigtime" frame-story does when she appears in her gaudy new house by the lake, or June when she appears in her mansion by the sea, ready to make an occasion out of her son's death.[47] "The Peace of Utrecht" has nothing quite like this,[48] but Maddy is clearly flaunting herself to Helen as to others, since like June she has the trick of turning misery into conspicuous optimism. The high point of her display, moreover, comes at an affair oddly similar to June's reception: a lakeside party at which she joins some resolutely with-it friends, themselves dressed up much like June for the occasion. When Wilfred in "Visitors" tells his success stories, there is the same bravado producing the same rebelliousness in other people; both are particularly intense on the central trip to the Conservation Area, during which Wilfred carries on almost belligerently while the others notice the ominous signs out the window. These last, such as "Dead End" (210), are ominous indeed: for all these occasions are really funereal, displays of a life that is only a braving of death.

Having been navigated through the official preserve that is also a swamp, Wilfred is brought to the almost obliterated family homestead — conservation people "don't leave you much" (212), he reflects; and this means for one thing that he has been drawn to the Lair of a Counter-Stranger, played at this point by the brooding Albert.[49] Helen, making a final visit to her aged aunts, is drawn to the "darker parts of the house" (204), where Aunt Annie gives her the clothes of her dead mother to wear. And we have already seen what happens in the wake of June's memorial festivities: Eileen, to whom the proceedings merely look like "fraud" (221), counters with some fraud of her own. Like Helen at the lakeside party, she drinks too much and then falls asleep — her reawakening, I have suggested, can be seen as a kind of sleep-walking — and like Helen again she retires to a car. It is in this Lair that she accepts sexual possession by her sister's husband and so gathers him into her own possession: that of misfortune or, in its meaning for Ewart, death itself. Within Margot's "wigtime" anecdote the same role is played by "Lana," a girl whose name comes close to both "Eileen" and "Helen" and who impresses Margot as "slightly lonesome, or unlucky" (267). Albert in "Visitors," while far less wayward than Eileen, tells stories containing "neither luck nor money" (215), and is emblematically another bringer of misfortune.[50]

In the end the rivals meet again to settle their differences, providing the heart-to-heart talk with which several of these stories conclude. And here, in an optimistic view, there is reconciliation: the Peace of Utrecht — first made years before, and again for Helen's return visit to Jubilee — is at last definitively concluded. What makes such a treaty possible appears plainly in "Memorial": for Eileen, who has not "helped you the way I meant to" (225), has helped in the opposite way, by her very subversion of June's unreal triumph. The disloyal Helen now urges Maddy to live her life (to understand Helen's ambiguous phrase in that sense here);[51] in the case of Flo and Rose there is not only a final laugh but agreement on the "comedy" (187) that the elder is passing on to the younger. We may even sense a greater comedy as Eileen reaches out to her troubled sister, or Margot and Anita in the frame-story of "Wigtime" look out to a world "bright and distinct and harmless" (273).

But to the extent that it remains within a tragic cycle, comedy at this stage can achieve only an "unconsummated relationship":[52] still a pact between conspirators, even a contracting for further "haunts." The Peace of Utrecht, as we learn from Helen's old school notes, "brought an end to the War of the Spanish Succession" (201); it also brought renewed war, the deadly struggle between England and France that filled the ensuing century.[53] And in whatever treaties may follow, the world will remain a balance of power endlessly breaking down and restoring itself — endlessly making itself from its own unmaking. Nor are all treaties successfully concluded. Maddy cannot bring herself to leave Jubilee, restrained in part by the very existence of Helen, with her incriminating knowledge; "Visitors," to read as we are now reading, arrives at a general misunderstanding in a café, and ends with an Albert gone forever and a Wilfred crying in his sleep. When the ambiguous comedy of the Sibling stories fails in this way, what confronts us is the tragic aspect, or tragic terminal phase, of the Apocalypse cycle. There is no need to elaborate such a phase, since it can only repeat, on more conclusive terms, the one of which it is a distribution: but we can note here the primary sense of "The Ottawa Valley" and "White Dump," final stories in their collections. In both cases an old woman is repudiated, and in both cases she reasserts her dark power at the end of everything.

These two stories, however, are not the only final ones; nor have we exhausted the ways of reading those we have just examined. I have already proposed that in the very sealing of the world we might find its unsealing; and this can mean a taking of life for which the siblings' treaty is no more than an image. For a hint of such an opportunity we can turn to the last scene in "Spelling." Flo, who has made a peace of sorts with her step-daughter, must also be seen here as the implacable Old Woman, a power that will ultimately make peace with no-one; set against this power, Rose becomes the self that rightly desires independence. Successfully humoured, Flo drops off to sleep at the end. Until she wakes again, Rose is free to have a new kind of adventure, perhaps discover a new kind of peace — in "Wigtime" the mad Teresa even imagines that her lost lover is waiting for her. For at last, and in a greater context than the central one, we have arrived at the point where we found Egypt to be vulnerable: that of death or birth before any further cycling of time.

V: The Messenger

Among the final stories in Munro's books we find several — her Epilogue stories, as I am going to call them — that make perhaps the most distinct group in all of her work, even if its motifs can often be discerned at corresponding points elsewhere.[54] As I have noted, *Who Do You Think You Are?* has for its Apocalypse both "Spelling" — predominantly a Sibling story — and the final title-chapter: the very fact of two chapters here invites us to see them as different, and they are in fact very different. Chatting with Ralph Gillespie is not like grappling with Flo:[55] it is more like visiting the obsolete, silly, and magical Miss Marsalles in "Dance of the Happy Shades," the final story of its collection, or passing an hour with the amiably demented Bobby Sherriff. We must of course make our usual provisos: Sibling stories may, for instance, merge with Epilogues rather than stand out against them. In such a case the difference may be between parts of a story, as when "Circle of Prayer" leads to the final communing of Trudy and Kelvin, or "Memorial" to that of Eileen and June. For that matter stories as wholes may have a double aspect: and yet the

difference between a Sibling story and an Epilogue is clear in principle, and remains so even when we compare Epilogues as comic
resolution with the same resolution in the Sibling stories. Epilogue
stories as such are not about the restoration of the world on the
world's terms: they look forward, or outward, to something other
than the world. This is specially true, again, of their own epilogues
— for the present I am going to treat these as if they were simply
Epilogue stories in their own right.

What are the conditions for an epilogue experience, as we can call
it? In the first place, it seems essential that something worldly not be
there. In "Spelling," as we have just seen, a crotchety stepmother falls
asleep; in "Who Do You Think You Are?" she is as it were sleeping
throughout, safely installed in the County Home. In "The Photographer" Bobby Sherriff's daunting mother is no less absent, having gone
off to Toronto for the time being. Alternatively, supervisory characters who might have put in an appearance fail significantly to do so.
At Miss Marsalles's recital, for instance, a point is made of the fact
that some of the mother's friends have not come — particularly
"Marg French," a woman with twins and a comprehensive name,
both Elizabeth and Mary.[56] A male absentee is Tom Shepherd, Janet's
former lover in "The Moons of Jupiter," who turns out to be
unavailable in the crisis "as if we had planned to meet in a public
place and then he hadn't shown up" (224). Interestingly, Munro
chooses the same name for a lover who fails to show up in "Who Do
You Think You Are?" This latter is not expected, to be sure, but the
thought of him and his whereabouts occurs to Rose just before her
interview with Ralph Gillespie: once again, a shepherding Tom is
somewhere else.[57]

When we try to connect this situation temporally with the Apocalypse cycle we have been following, we find the same curious
disjunctness as with our fourth phase generally in relation to the third.
Rose, when she visits the Legion, is in town to deal with the family
house after dealing with Flo; but her visit — and certainly her meeting
with Ralph — is not otherwise connected with the events in "Spelling." In more spatial terms, the Epilogue stories take us back to
Munro's region of out-places and out-buildings. All these stories are,
in some sense or other, located in the Ottawa Valley, a place central
enough from a provincial point of view but otherwise the remote
"backwoods" (493) that it seems to the narrator. We can of course
read "The Ottawa Valley" in a different way, with St. John's Church
appearing as a grand temple; yet as grandeur fades, we are more likely

to notice how puny a temple this is — after the Toronto Union Station only a little country church with an outhouse. Other temples in these stories are no grander: neither the Hanratty Legion nor Miss Marsalles's modest brick house by the tracks impresses the visitor through whose eyes we see it, and the Sherriffs in "The Photographer" live in what is itself a kind of outhouse — a little stucco bungalow behind the *Herald-Advance* building.

There is something peripheral again about the epilogue experience itself. On the slack morning of "The Photographer" or the slack evening of "Who Do You Think You Are?" a meeting takes place that seems quite by the way — tea and lemonade with a madman, a casual encounter with an old school-acquaintance. Such an incident, Rose feels, is hardly worth passing on, and in their narratorial capacities the first-person tellers of these stories plainly agree: some of the events we will be most concerned with appear only because a narrator has slipped them in as an afterthought. Janet, we have seen, doubles back to tell about her vision in the Chinese garden, as if it were merely trivial, not to say embarrassing; the narrator of "The Ottawa Valley" feels that, to have a "proper story" (246), she should not have added the poetry-reciting.

If we look now at the human embodiment of epilogue, what we will find is a counterpart of all these dubious extras: the "Messenger," as I am going to call this figure for reasons that will become clearer, is the distillation of all Munro's misfits and barbarians. As someone who appears (or perhaps reappears) in a neglected place, he sounds like a Counter-Stranger or even the revenant feared by the Old Woman; and while we are going to see ways in which he is neither unfortunate nor terrible, we should see first how he does answer such a description. To begin with, he is strange, not to say crazy. Bobby Sherriff, most obviously, is a lunatic from an asylum; Ralph Gillespie, who spends his time "being idiotic" (202), is at least a fool, while his shadow Milton Homer is "not all there" (193) — and another "idiot" as Phoebe sees him. Kelvin in "Circle of Prayer," who plays Messenger at the end, has a corresponding "gentle head fog" (257), in his case mainly an inability to judge people's motives. Miss Marsalles is an oddment of her own kind, flanked once again by "idiots" (222) — the mongoloid children she takes under her wing.[58] In fact Miss Marsalles is a child herself, or someone both old and young — much like Ralph with his "aging jauntiness" and "petrified adolescence" (204), or the middle-aged Milton Homer who still licks ice-cream cones.[59]

These people are very much the world's losers, doomed to death, an institution, or some less official form of confinement. Ralph is no doubt the most accident-prone of all — blown up in the navy, then pieced together "from scratch" (201), then killed falling downstairs not long after the main incident of the story. At the time when Rose sees him, moreover, he is already what accident has made him: a discarded, shrivelling man who hangs around the Legion, resented for what little he gets in the way of a pension. Bobby, an academic failure named like other doomed sons in Munro,[60] is now a prisoner of both the asylum and his mother; the Misses Marsalles have gone steadily downhill from their Rosedale gentility. The father in "The Moons of Jupiter," while no idiot in the usual sense,[61] is nevertheless what his daughter sees at the hospital: "an old man trapped here by his leaky heart" (220).

Such figures, like counterparts in the Sibling stories, have the air of scapegoat substitutes — perhaps outright victims like Milton Homer, perhaps simply people whom others feel compelled to abandon: for "you have to survive" (230) as Janet explains in "The Moons of Jupiter," having detached herself both from her endangered daughter and later from her dying father.[62] Like these, the Messenger is a marked person — at times, indeed, in a physically precise way. Ralph Gillespie has his limping foot; Miss Marsalles is marked quite literally by her feverish rouge, echoed in the purple blotches on her dress. Ted Braddock, whose role as Messenger we will be touching on later, not only comes of a despised family but was once a slight young man with a "black smudge" (43) on his forehead for Ash Wednesday. Putting motifs together, we can perhaps see how Ewart in "Memorial," much like the Ted of later years, is at once an establishment figure and another Messenger, disadvantaged by the very wealth that "marks" him like "a mulberry splotch on the face, a club foot" (212).

Ewart, moreover, can provide us with an analogy we may now be expecting: when Eileen wakes in the night and finds her way into the tomb-like garage, it is this burdened minister who comes to her in the role of a gardener, even calling her by name.[63] The hint of Christ here (with the usual waywardness in the distribution of roles) may remind us of various touches in the presentation of Milton Homer, the "hangdog-looking" (195) idiot who is also known to stand at the door "with his big head on one side and his fist raised to knock" (190). We find a figure of the same sort in the afflicted Dolores Boyle of "Dance of the Happy Shades" — sitting "ungracefully at the piano with her head hanging down" (222) — or in the humiliated Kelvin of "Circle of Prayer," with his sagging face and look of being "old, sunk into himself, wrapped in a thick bewilderment" (273). Kelvin has in fact been treacherously asked to choose between a Marie and a Josephine: it is no wonder he looks like the Undergod we have met so often in this book, or even a lock-headed upper counterpart fallen into the same misery.[64]

*

But if Munro's Messengers, in one view, are continuous with her Undergods, we have begun to see that they are very different as well. It may help here to remember that undergods often take on the role of Counter-Stranger, and that a Counter-Stranger can turn into a much more amiable figure: the Messenger as Messenger is the furthest distribution of this transformed loser, one who indeed transforms distribution itself. Kelvin in the epilogue scene of "Circle of Prayer" is at first locked in his misery, then reappears from it to share a mysterious comfort with Trudy. Bobby Sherriff has been a prisoner of the asylum and his grim mother, even no doubt the henchman that his name suggests, but on the morning of the story he is his own man: a Robin Hood, not a Sherriff, inviting Del to join his robber band. His counterpart in Del's secret novel is based on Frankie Hall, and Frankie is not the tragic kind of French but the lordly — the "grown idiot" (245–46) who, once in the cycle of each year, rides free on the merry-go-round at the fair, smiling and waving.

It seems that madness, for which the world confines the Messenger, also liberates him from worldly constraint — that, more than brains, is what is not there in Milton Homer:

What was missing was a sense of precaution, Rose thought now. Social inhibition, though there was no such name for it at that time. Whatever it is that ordinary people lose when they are drunk, Milton Homer never had. (193–94)

Some of the same precaution is lacking in the Ralph Gillespie who "don't know when to stop" (202), and a generous amount is lacking in Miss Marsalles, with her absurd costumes and entertainments and illusions about her pupils. The Misses Marsalles are allowed such things because they are what Maddy in "The Peace of Utrecht" tries in vain to be, "sexless, wild and gentle creatures, bizarre yet domestic, living in their house in Rosedale outside the complications of time"

(214). Nor is the Messenger in his released form merely tolerated: just as Frankie Hall waves with "a royal negligence" (246), so Bobby Sherriff himself is king for a day, enthroned on the old wicker chair with the lumpy cushion. The father in "The Moons of Jupiter" is a similar figure when Janet last sees him: doomed and bound to the hospital, no doubt, but out of bed and presiding benignly in his chair. Even Ralph Gillespie, while less regal, presides in his own way at the Legion, as Miss Marsalles certainly does at her party. And from this presidential position the Messenger acts as an "affable host":[65] he invites the heroine to share in his pleasure and his bounty, the "gift" that Del somehow knows to be in his bestowing.

The result is the maddest of parties, but also the most gracious. A gentlemanly Bobby offers insipid cake and lemonade; a ladylike Miss Marsalles offers stale sandwiches and flat punch, sure that her house is Elysium and her guests a troop of dancing shades. And if the Messenger's world features this happy make-believe, by the same token it features play and art. What joins Rose and Ralph, both in high school and again years later, is a shared love of jokes and mimicry; when Janet pays her last visit to her father in the hospital, they play the quasi-game of naming the moons of Jupiter; in "The Ottawa Valley" a group of elders forget their troubles and differences to recite poetry remembered from school.[66] The content of such poetry may be sad enough — dying heroes and a dying year. Yet the very fact of poetry or a charade seems to do what Orpheus's music does for Eurydice, or the favour of Jupiter for Ganymede: it lifts the mortal from a lower realm — the Ottawa Valley with its dark queens — to a world of new life. And when at the end Bobby poises on his toes like a dancer, he shows how there is life out of death for a god himself: Bobby here is a risen and ascending Christ,[67] and in blessing Del he is inviting her to come where he is. The vigil with biscuits — an indulging in natural life or waiting for natural death, as we first saw it — has been changed into a heavenly banquet.[68]

*

If each of our phases is also a relation, what kind of relation have we now come to? When we looked at the phases of the worldly cycle, what we found was — in the appropriate senses — friendship and love, the bonds of those who are naturally parallel and naturally opposite. According to this distinction our "siblings" were primarily related by friendship; correspondingly, the central phase of our larger cycle showed us the friendship of Egypt, a domesticity that is also a celibacy of one kind or another. The third phase, on the other hand, turned out to be primarily that of love: passion like Del's for Garnet or Rose's for Simon. But now we have arrived at what is most distinctive in the fourth phase, the odd communing of people like Del and Bobby, Rose and Ralph Gillespie. When we ask whether Bobby is a friend or a lover, we see how we have entered a new world: for if he is both in a way, there is also an important sense in which he is neither.

In the first place, Bobby is not a relative of Del's, nor have they known each other before the morning of the story as more than faces on the street; indeed Bobby is the inmate of an asylum, divided from Del by the gulf that separates the certified from the uncertified. The "impossible" (214) Miss Marsalles is no friend of the family, just an eccentric and shabby-genteel object of its patronage. Ralph Gillespie may have been a high-school friend of Rose's, even a quasi-brother or the partner in a "spurious domesticity" (200): but the spuriousness here is as significant as the domesticity. Because of the alphabetical arrangement of the class the two happened to sit next to each other, and because of a common lack of survival skills became secret allies. They had no relation outside school, nor do they have any after Ralph leaves it: like Bobby and Del, they are merely people who recognize each other on the street. Even when he is a relative, for that matter, the Messenger as Messenger has something of the same alienness about him. Janet's father sitting in state is a gracious host, even Jupiter or his minion, but he is not simply the down-to-earth father we met earlier; and when Denise in "White Dump" plays Messenger to her father, she appears to him not as herself but as a fairy godmother.

Yet the Messenger who is not a friend does not seem to be a lover either. During her meeting with Ralph at the Legion Rose feels obliged to do a little flirting, but — as she herself knows — the sexual relation between the two is as insubstantial as their friendship.[69] Ralph in school was much like Frank Wales: a passer of secret messages, an attracting artist, but more a child on the border of sexuality than someone who had crossed it.[70] Bobby Sherriff is sexless altogether — his sexlessness is in fact the thought in Del's mind as it wanders from what he is saying. What unites such poor conversationalists is no more than what Kelvin and Trudy share at the end — a "halfway joke" carrying with it "some oblique feeling of conspiracy" (274): and this itself is the communion we must try to understand here. Ralph, "one slot over" from Rose (206), may not be bound to her by either of the connections that maintain the world, yet at the end, when they have shared a brief joke and conspiracy of their own, she feels him closer than any of the men she has loved with the world's kind of love. Karin in "Pictures of the Ice" — to see this story now for its epilogue quality — is taken on as some kind of housekeeper by old Austin Cobbett. In vanishing he contrives an odd understanding between them, and she is left feeling a "link beyond the usual" (155) — even, to take her words beyond her conscious intention, a sense that "she could be the one for him."

We are going to want a term for this strange link beyond other links, and one as suggestive as any is "courtesy." Miss Marsalles and Bobby Sherriff will of course come to mind, with their quaint, obliging good manners; or we may find equal considerateness being expressed in a less formal way. In Janet's last visit to her father, for example, all we have is two people engaged in ordinary chat and banter, sensitive to anything hurtful in their words, and in the end saying good-bye as simply as if they were not separating forever. We can think of other scenes we have touched on: that in "The Ottawa Valley" where the family good-heartedly encourage one another to recite poetry, that in "Rose Matilda" where Joan and Morris do the same thing. Discordant notes may come into such scenes, and for that matter their courtesy itself may not be entirely genuine — that is something we will have to return to; yet there is a precious spirit here, a beautiful giving and receiving for which some kind of formal ceremony makes an apt if not indispensable garment.

*

The Bobby who gives so courteously is also the Bobby who says shyly "I know you" (251): there is an act of recognition here as well. And if we consider the wave of "kindness, of sympathy and forgiveness" (205) that flows from Ralph to Rose, we will see that this recognition is itself courtesy — a greeting or blessing (Munro is fond of the word "offering"). It presupposes, of course, the seeing and respecting of another's difference from oneself; above all it does not take advantage of another's creaturely weakness. In the world of "The Ottawa Valley," for instance, it does not do what is done to Allen Durrand in the mow, or to Dodie when she is jilted, or to the mother when the narrator points to her shaking arm. More positively, courtesy is the "circle of prayer" made possible by just this forbearance.

As a Sibling story "Circle of Prayer" works to restore a natural kind of bond: most obviously, that of Trudy and her daughter Robin. But from the vantage-point of the little epilogue scene between Trudy and the mad Kelvin, any such bond may seem as foolish as Janet's secret clique of women praying for each other's natural hankerings. Kelvin takes a different view: if he knew what to pray for, he says, he would not have to. This is a hard enough saying — and all the harder for suggesting the preamble to the Lord's Prayer[71] — but it clearly points beyond any sort of prayer that only tightens the bond of natural connection. The gifts of the Messengers in the Epilogue stories all have a rarefied quality: party sweets from Bobby Sherriff, a delicate old piano piece from the mongoloid girl in "Dance of the Happy Shades." In the same way, Kelvin's gift to Trudy does not bring her any solid comfort — like Ralph Gillespie, he simply shares for a moment his wry sense of a situation. And yet it is this sharing, not the bond of natural demand answered by natural giving or forgiving, that is the true circle of prayer. It is like the water-lily that Trudy imagines at the end — an Egyptian flower as we saw it earlier, but here expressing an utterly different kind of infolding.[72]

The Messenger's real gift is thus as much the gift of yourself as of himself: he invites you to be the someone whom you did not know to be there. Austin Cobbett makes Karin feel strangely "approved of" (155); Bobby knows Del is going to win scholarships; Miss Marsalles not only knows that there is music in her pupils' hearts, but effortlessly calls it out from one of them. We have found Miss Farris trying a more direct method: bullying her pupils into dancing, "as if she could pull out of us what nobody else, and not we ourselves, could guess was there" (130). This has only a zapping effect, and Miss Farris herself is only a forerunner — one of the suicides of "The Photographer," in fact. The dark hero of Del's secret novel is equally a forerunner, and yet after his mysterious disappearance, followed by the suicide of the importuning Caroline, her simpleton brother notices something strange, the black-to-white reversal of Caroline's eyes in the class photograph.[73] In the same way, the real-life Bobby Sherriff notices the aptness in Del that she has lost sight of: he is a Pied Piper who can call her out of herself to be her more genuine self.[74] This is why the epilogue recognition, when contrasted with the typological, produces not amazement, much less shock, but a strange sort of wonder: a feeling of ease and familiarity that is at the same time utterly unfamiliar.

In conferring this gift Bobby asks for trust: something that we found to be a concern of Munro's initiatory stories, and will need to consider again later, but that is also important at the stage we have reached. Trust of course is hard for Del to give here: she knows that her aspirations have ended in failure, and in any case Bobby is not an easy person to put one's trust in. For the gift he offers is never "given" — if typological identification is there only for the understanding, the identity announced by the Messenger is not "there" at all. Bobby is not telling the objective truth when he says that Del will get a scholarship: what we can say provisionally is that he is asking for belief in make-believe — in a fairy-tale world like Munro's Avalon or Elysium or Olympus. "Belief" here means taking one's life in the sense of accepting an offered gift without concern for what may be behind it: Del must share in the insubstantial banquet Bobby sets before her and say "yes" (254) to the blessing and calling with which he takes it away. If there is more to the episode than that, this simpler account of it is not wrong.[75]

B. UNREFINED FLOUR

I The Bonds of Death

As we have imagined the matter so far, Bobby simply invites Del for cakes and lemonade. This makes a finely ethereal image: and yet if Bobby's offering contained or meant no more it would remain, paradoxically, only an offering of the world, and we would have yet another story of Egypt triumphing in someone's seeming escape from it. In fact there are some distinctly sinister touches about the Bobby who uses his "ironic" (249) good manners to play spider and fly — as he himself puts it — with the apprehensive Del: perhaps he is no Robin Hood but a bobby after all, even Robert the Devil. If we go back to other Messengers we will notice some diabolic motifs there too. Ralph has both a lame leg and a history of explosions, like Milton Homer when full of "bad intentions" (197); Miss Marsalles is made up like a harlot and displays Mary Queen of Scots on the wall; and if we remember the blotches and smudges marking the Messengers generally, we may now suspect the sinister presence of Cain.[76] Matching these questionable hosts are guests who, to a sceptical eye, do not look any more appealing. The listeners at Miss Marsalles's recital experience only boredom and irritation, turning to dismay at the Dance of the Happy Shades. The narrator is equally dismayed;

so is Del listening to Bobby, to the extent that she again is not just bored.[77] If such people are aware of an invitation, some say no to it, like Jeanette in "Marrakesh" when proposed to by the blue-eyed arab, while others say the yes-and-no that is no better divinity — when Del, for instance, says yes, she does so "naturally, a bit distractedly" (254), and without bothering to say thank you.[78] The old human situation, it appears, is still there: at best these people seem like Helena in her state of shock after the fire, intending to respond, or thinking she has responded, yet unable to do what could only be done if she were more fully awake.[79]

An Epilogue can always be taken as such a story of temptation or of failure to meet a test: tragedy, like comedy, is present in all events in time. And we must recognize this fact to deal with the tragedy of "The Ottawa Valley," in which the narrator ends possessed by a ghost, or in a more sexual version the epilogue to "White Dump." In the latter we find an airman whose blue eyes at first seem "most innocent, genial, and kind" (305), not inviting to any grossness — for the beginning of love is the "pure part" (308); we equally find a responsive woman, not to say one who breathes magical happiness into her family, expressed in a typical epilogue game of charades. Yet all this is the onset of an affair leading in the end to bitterness and a wrecked marriage;[80] and "The Photographer," from our present perspective, is not very different. A less blue-eyed counterpart of the pilot here is the diabolic hero of Del's novel, coupled with his no less diabolic leman: on the one hand an evil-eyed camera man, with black hair "combed back in two wings" (246), on the other the dark and wayward Caroline, the woman who seduces men but survives them like a black widow. The Photographer himself seems to have been one of Caroline's victims, while for his own part he has impregnated her only to leave her in despair, a suicide with a still-born child. In the main story, which we must see as in one way parallel to the novel, it is Del who in effect plays harlot, giving Bobby no alternative but to pass away in one sense or another — it would be literally by his death if he were Ralph Gillespie. Nor does Bobby do any better by Del: he practises his arts on her, implants in her a longing for something she can never attain, then abandons her to wretchedness.

For what awaits Del now is a "heart-breaking" (253) fate of labouring and never giving birth, of accumulating graceless facts without ever bringing them to wholeness or life. In saying "Yes" she has been like Maddy in a tragic reading of "The Peace of Utrecht" — the Maddy who says "Yes I will" (210) without really meaning it:

and the only choice for such a person is between equally grim ways of taking her life. One of these, Caroline's and perhaps Marion's, is suicide; the other, which is not really other at all, is a new enslavement to the cycle of time, and this is Del's way. She has entered into a covenant — without full sincerity, of course, just as Bobby has made his offer without sincerity, but that only makes the natural covenant the more binding. As a result she will soon find herself in Egypt: a labourer like her Uncle Craig, as she herself realizes. She seems equally bound to something like Israelite Law, for the vocation of art passed on to her by Bobby may be only the curse of the "Halloways" (244), the judge's family based on the Sherriffs in Del's novel. When we think along these lines, we begin to see the Photographer's camera — an all-seeing eye in a box behind which he hides veiled in "black cloth" (246) — as an ark or tabernacle. No doubt he is more of a rising Christ when he disappears from his overturned car — a similar box with a similar cloth; but then he does so only to evaporate like a ghost. Caroline, the "sacrifice" (246) spread against tombstones, trees, and mud, is this same frustrating Christ playing the trick of passivity. And Bobby is the same demon yet again: at once the god of a phony temple and the equally phony rebel who calls Del out of the temple as a way of luring her back into it.

*

Once again, it seems, someone has reached for what seemed "well" and got a painful surprise. To speak in the terms we began with, someone has reached for truth and got reality: and that is just the problem. The meeting with the Messenger, as I first presented it, is only a truth, a flying away from something, and as such it hardly seems an adequate form for what we found courtesy to be — a self-offering grounded on respect for the human condition. But even in "Dance of the Happy Shades" — the earliest of the Epilogue stories, also the simplest in the way it makes Elysian truth supervene on shabby reality — something more than truth is being offered; and in "The Photographer," as we will see presently, the airy Bobby Sherriff recommends as a means to life something that is not airy at all. In effect Bobby is presenting reality itself as a way of presenting more; and since it would be denying reality not to share in it, we must add that his own role as Messenger cannot just be one of magical exemption. Rather, we should now think of a Messenger as someone who has fully entered into his reality — implicitly his death — and so reached a greater life in which reality and truth are one. Having done so, he can offer the same life to others: that is where his courtesy lies.[81]

There is a story to be followed here, for what I have been treating in the last pages as a sequence of readings is also the internal course of the Epilogue as a narrative. Simple forms of this have in fact appeared as we went along, but for the integration we are now concerned with we will need the fuller one of typology — beyond which we will be able to see what transcends typology itself. Within the larger Apocalypse story, the Epilogue comes when something has already fallen: in narrative terms there has been a central reversal, and we find the sort of situation this always leads to. We can start, then, by putting ourselves in one of the typically out-of-the-way, Lair-like Epilogue settings — the little stucco house behind the newspaper office or the little brick house by the tracks. The Epilogue heroines themselves are not unlike such places, for compared to the brisk and believing Junes of the Sibling stories they are sad to behold — rather like the Eileens of whom they make a distributed form, though now it is what they receive rather than what they do that we are to hear about. Several of them take a dim view of their native towns; the narrator of "Dance of the Happy Shades" takes the same view of her decaying old piano teacher. And when they view themselves they are no more impressed, for what they see is failure and meanness — even the narrator-heroine of "Dance of the Happy Shades" knows herself an inferior performer, older than the others, trying not to let sullenness get the better of her. And yet these heroines are proud in their very dejection: not in the pharisaical way of a June, but with Eileen's obscure pride in disillusionment itself — to use more traditional language, the pride of despair. The demoralized narrator of "Dance of the Happy Shades" is a snob at least partly for this reason; Del takes Bobby's admiration for granted; and Rose especially can show us all the contradictory things felt by such a heroine. She is ashamed — ashamed of her age, her profession, and something more elusive, "a failure she couldn't seize upon or explain" (203); yet she too feels superior to her surroundings — much like a shadow self she meets, the woman who finds Hanratty a great comedown after Sarnia.

What first happens to this collapsed yet still inflated heroine is something that teases her pride: typically she is invited to be a guest of honour, even if the occasion is one of which she has no great opinion. Del is offered congratulations and a seat on the Sherriffs' porch; in the Planetarium episode of "The Moons of Jupiter" — a comparable scene though structurally a subordinate meditation within a larger story — Janet finds herself installed in a luxurious chair and taken on a tour of the sky. Other formalities at this stage may be less splendid, but at least appear reasonably successful: in "Dance of the Happy Shades," for instance, Miss Marsalles's musical party seems to be going without a major hitch, the narrator's mother has achieved a "dreamy, distant look" (220), and the narrator herself is called on to perform. Now comes the upset, simplest perhaps in this same story. As the narrator is rendering the minuet from *Berenice*,[82] the "idiot" children invade from the "Greenhill School." They too have been invited to the party: their inclusion is the substance of its hospitality, the reality of its truth. We find the same upset in a more exhibited form when Janet, having seen the wonders of Jupiter, is brought back to the "red soil" (231) of Mars. In "The Photographer" Del has made her own bid to fly to the heavens — by winning scholarships that will take her away from Jubilee. She has also been planning the novel that will contain and transform the town, and in particular she has been transforming the stolid Marion Sherriff into the romantic Caroline. So far these flights have not quite crashed: yet now, noticing the plainness of her surroundings, Del notices something more — Caroline was only Marion, her death an end without glamour. That does for the novel: "it is a shock, when you have dealt so cunningly, powerfully, with reality, to come back and find it still there" (251). And Del herself is trapped — the temple has proved to be a prison and Bobby a jailor.[83]

If the story showed us nothing beyond this, or more complex later equivalents, it would be only the tragedy we have recently seen in it. Yet the Del who finds herself a prisoner also finds neither jail nor jailor as bad as she might have expected: what is remarkable here, more than any evil, is ordinariness — a not unpleasant ordinariness. The mad Bobby Sherriff, when she takes a good look at him, seems an innocent young man, well-groomed and well-mannered; the Sherriffs' yard is a tidy little area with flowers. The Lair, in other words, is a Refuge, and reality has its own value. And there is something more here: in watching Bobby, Del senses the mysterious gift in his madness. In "Dance of the Happy Shades" the narrator finds, not only that the mongoloid children are gentle enough — their faces "marked only by an infantile openness and calm" (221) — but that one of them brings a gift of her own: it is her playing that turns Miss Marsalles's poor living-room into Elysium.

If we use this pattern for our Epilogues, we can treat further distributions from the centre as simply reinforcing it. We may, for instance, find that the promised gift arrives only in a spiritual form some time after the Messenger's departure in the flesh — as with the message from Ralph Gillespie that Rose senses when she has left Ralph's uncommunicative presence.[84] But in any case the gist of the story, seen in our new way, is the same. To single out "The Photographer" again, Bobby serves Del the insubstantial cake and lemonade of truth; he then tells her about the need for reality, the unrefined flour that is "nourishment for the brain" (252); and in the end, offering her his blessing, he rises a spiritual body.[85]

*

With Bobby's whole-wheat flour to sustain us, we can now consider the transformations in some specially suggestive stories. To begin with, we can go back to the strange events of "Eskimo," in which Mary Jo the nurse meets a Métis man and Eskimo woman on her flight to Tahiti. I have already associated this story with an Annunciation group within the larger terminal one: a heroine bound on a journey senses a new life when shown a passion she has never recognized in herself. But while a terminal story as such can go no farther, "Eskimo" has hints at the end of a love beyond love, greater than the earthly if also its source. I have also connected this story with others like "Marrakesh" and "The Spanish Lady" — stories about the vision of life at the threshold of death; and in its riddling way "Eskimo" tells us even more than these last about such a vision.

The heroines in these three stories all reach a point of radical doubt — about themselves, about others, about the world. The Spanish Lady broods on her lost marriage; Dorothy in "Marrakesh" sits disconsolately on the bed, looking at her witch's face in the mirror. Mary Jo, after her unsettling failure to get the Eskimo girl away from the bullying Métis, looks into another glass — the reflecting window of the plane, now darkened — and arrives at much the same view of things as Dorothy's. In particular she feels the danger and uselessness of interfering with others: we are lost in the dim mirror of our own minds, and there is no communion beyond it. This is, of course, the self-absorbed scepticism that we have found before at the collapse of pride, but here we need to see it in its greatest implication, as a vision containing the whole of fallen human experience. Mary Jo then returns to her seat and is ignored by her neighbours — they too seem self-absorbed.

While this makes a story in itself, Mary Jo's reflections do not stop here. She is never consciously aware (in spite of an emblematic movie screen[86]) that in the overbearing Métis and submissive Eskimo she is seeing a projection of her employer-lover and herself; she does, though, think of Dr. Streeter again at just this point. The worthy heart specialist is one of Munro's self-contained, impervious figures, sure to point out the futility of overmuch concern.[87] And yet, thinks Mary Jo, he does feel concern. For all his pomposity he is a burdened and obedient man, dedicated to his work of saving hearts — even if, at this stage of her meditation, the hearts in question are only physical ones. Mary Jo's own calling, "baffled, cautious, permanent" (203), is to love such a man: for like the god-gifted "Dorothy," another sensible Elizabeth on the outside, she is secretly the passionate Mary indicated by her name.[88] And now, even more than Dorothy, she will be shown where her austere devotion leads.

First we find the sudden vision of intimacy that is a feature of both "Eskimo" and "Marrakesh" — a vision that takes in the whole Passion experience of love and death. Mary Jo sees the Eskimo girl absorbed in sexual worship of the Métis and, like Dorothy having her "stroke" (173) on seeing the lovers, is wildly aroused. With arousal goes disgust, and as her thoughts turn again to Dr. Streeter, he becomes the Dr. Streeter of her doubt, not faith, the man who takes a "sly and natural satisfaction" (205) in being professionally exempted from caring. Now, however, she is to receive the intimation of a lover beyond either of the figures that she has imposed on herself — the chosen officiant and the sly fraud; and beyond the woman tormented by them she is to sense another Mary Jo. For she has seen in the Eskimo girl's devotion — a devotion "that takes every bit of her concentration and her self but in which her self is lost" (204) — something that points beyond passion itself.

In the mysterious fantasy-turning-dream that follows,[89] Mary Jo as an Elizabeth is trying to make things "work out better" (205); and so they do, but in ways that Elizabeth alone cannot comprehend. First comes a recapitulation of the larger story — most immediately of the later events on the plane, but also of what those themselves recapitulate, Mary Jo's relation with her employer. As the dream begins she is inviting the Eskimo girl, successfully this time, into the sanctuary of a ladies' washroom, safe from any battering Métis. But she finds her washbasin something less than immaculate, and the Eskimo girl a rubber doll with an all-but-severed head. As for Mary Jo, she is to "choose [her] own" (206), according to a mysterious white-haired woman beside her — though Elizabeth is not one to accept the condemnation the woman seems to imply. Then, instead of returning to the plane as she intends, Mary Jo finds herself where she began: in Dr. Streeter's office. A large figure in bandages, some unknown victim of fire, is carried past on the way to an inner garden where, as she hears from the same woman, there is to be a "court" or perhaps "count" (207) — and Mary Jo senses a further meaning here that she cannot quite make out, something to do with Dr. Streeter. Briefly, we can note the biblical echoes in this part of her dream: the suffering servant, agony in a garden, trial. And to these we can add mockery, for Mary Jo suspects that the woman is calling Dr. Streeter "count" to make fun of him — as the white-haired Mrs. Streeter might do, or his rebellious daughter. Once more, then, Dr. Streeter — to see that "bulky" (189) man as the figure in bandages — has appeared as a figure of passion. Now, however, we are seeing this passion not just as the ministry of a glorified son or the secret pleasure of a hypocrite, but as obedience unto death. Dr. Streeter is a patient as well as a doctor: and we are coming to see that Mary Jo, for all her nurse's competence and fuss, is another patient.

If we see this, perhaps we can grasp the rest of this mysterious episode, or read the whole of it in a new way. The figure in bandages is like Christ, or the bound Lazarus who "is not dead but sleepeth," to recall again the words on the gravestone in "The Ottawa Valley." The white-haired woman shows Mary Jo flowers "like snowdrops, but blue" (207) — Mary's flowers;[90] the word "court" itself, she explains, means flowers as well. Once again, of course, Mary Jo's sceptical self interposes, and yet I will suggest that the dream was sent by a deeper self: a Mary Jo who knows that flowers go with "court" when they go with courting, and that there is a courtly variety of count as well. Beyond the sufferings of an Undergod a noble lord is waiting to court his lady, though this can happen only in an enclosed garden at the heart of a dream. And after a story that has repeatedly asked "What do you want?" the lady in the garden will answer "I will as you will."[91] The waking Mary Jo will now go on to a tourist's island, but she has already received her Christmas present.

We will see the same transformation in a more summary form if we turn to the final scene of "Simon's Luck" — one that completes a terminal story (and sets it within a Sibling story[92]), but that hints at yet a further story. In general, we have found, "Simon's Luck" is concerned with the lucky and the unlucky, the established and the disestablished, who are not always easy to tell apart. Rose herself feels anything but established: she is intensely aware both of her mortal body, now well on the way to corruption, and of the difference between herself and men — who even in middle age, it seems, can take or reject at their pleasure. But in the final scene Rose has to think again, for as the Suicide Woman from Kingston is negotiating her Sibling's truce, she delivers news of which Rose has been ignorant: Simon is dead, after suffering for some time from cancer of the pancreas. Simon, that is, shared the condition of *pân kréas*, all flesh: like Dr. Streeter he was not only a man of some privilege but one subject to death like the rest of humanity, including Rose. And with this revelation Rose finds herself seeing in a strange new way — it may even be that the dead Simon is appearing at this "late date" (173) to join her again.[93]

In the apocalyptic language of this episode, the news of Simon's death suggests "new judgments and solutions" (173) — even a courtship beyond a judging court. More schematically, we can think of the new narrative "figure" that I have said our present phase would require — a new identification, in other words, resolving the limitations and contradictions of earlier ones. This identification, I noted, is not "there" as even the typological is there: to see where it is, we can first follow the sequence of identifications as they present themselves in a single story. At the centre of "The Spanish Lady" the heroine encounters a stranger in the dome-car of a train: a man in mustard yellow and burgundy red who looks dashing enough to remind her of Dana Andrews.[94] The counterpart on Mary Jo's plane-ride is a strange-looking man in similar colours who, as she cannot resist thinking, just might be a glamorous Khan from Afghanistan. Unfortunately the conquistadors in these stories all turn out to be wretched natives: the Khan and his wife are only Canadians — a Métis and an Eskimo — and the seeming Dana Andrewes is, so to speak, only a con-man of a different sort, a real-estate salesman. Primary Strangers, in other words, have to be connected to their counter-selves: but then there is further connecting to be done.

The Rosicrucian in "The Spanish Lady" — he is a con-man in that sense as well, a man with a faith — is someone whose eagerness masks uncertainty and whose theory of reincarnation masks the fact of death. The Spanish Lady has just parted from a comparable man, but a Neighbour in my sense: her husband Hugh, a self-satisfied professional who beneath his assurance remains the nervous young fiancé she once met in the Vancouver train station. She is thinking of the same meeting in the same station when a great deal comes together at once — for the reader and, to a considerable extent, for her own conscious self. The old man utters his cry, and "by that cry Hugh, and Margaret, and the Rosicrucian, and I, everyone alive, is pushed back. What we say and feel no longer rings true, it is slightly beside the point" (190). The Rosicrucian is like Hugh; both are like the Spanish Lady; and all, as merely living, are rebuked by this dying man, the ultimate alien whose cry comes "from outside myself" (189). Yet, once again, something like a courtship is taking place,

> as if we were all wound up a long time ago and were spinning out or control, whirring, making noises, but at a touch could stop, and see each other for the first time, harmless and still. (190–91)[95]

If death can so touch life, this means a greater uniting than any we accommodated in our earlier scheme: the coming together not only of what is, but of what is and what is not — death or nothingness. And, as we will need to see, it means their coming together as more than two objective states.

*

We can note here the simple fact that the Spanish Lady is seeing something. The present chapter has taken us into a theatrical world of screens and processions and views and scenes, not to say the television that Munro is so fond of putting in her conclusions. One reason for this, I have suggested, is that an Apocalypse story as a whole, and *a fortiori* an Epilogue story, corresponds to the late recognition within any story. And in particular it corresponds to the final showings we have just examined — a man dying in public, for instance, or another's death opening windows to show a new world. But now we should notice something more about such spectacles: they are not only something seen but something in the seeing. The person who goes through a reversal here is the experiencer herself, and the union to which her reversal leads is of a kind that is only possible as experience, fully conscious or not. When Rose sees that Simon is dead, she apprehends not only a fact but one that, as it were, calls her into itself. And that is a very different matter, though a book like the present one can offer only a few tentative thoughts about it.

What the things of an object world have in common, if nothing else, is that they are things; yet as things they can never be one. To be a thing is precisely to exclude other things; and this remains true even if we unite them typologically or metaphorically, since we are still concerned only with what is — an objective situation.[96] Perhaps the union of subject and object themselves can be imagined in the same way, yet their relation is more distant and more intimate than any we have found so far, and can represent something different in kind. Two things related as subject and object lose their common ground altogether, since in this relation they cannot both be things in the same way: each, so to speak, is nothing to the other's something. Their relation is thus like that between the Spanish Lady and the dying old man, Rose and the dead Simon — the meeting of the something of life with the nothing of death; and if death is the fate of *pân kréas*, we could even say that this meeting is of nothing with nothing, and is itself nothing. But perhaps it is just such a nothing that can become everything.

Rose and Simon are both people who "seriously lack power" (173): in that way they are nothing. But this nothing is itself what they have in common and what, if accepted, can bring them together — enable them to touch each other as the carnal lovers of the inner phases can never quite do. To pick up a persistent hint in the late-phase stories, we can say that one self gives its life for the other, and in that way invites a mutual giving of the same kind. It is not that the death of Ralph Gillespie, say, is in any mechanical sense the cause of Rose's continued life — we are beyond that kind of causation here. Rather, two people give up their natural life as separate entities; and by this means they open themselves to a life that is more than natural, so that the distant Ralph becomes "close, closer" (206) to Rose than any of her lovers. In more cognitive terms, Rose and Ralph are like viewer and reflection — as we can say if we now give the idea of a mirror a deeper meaning than any we have used before. The reflection here is fully other than the viewer, yet each gives itself and the two become one.

Of course not all mirroring, or all knowledge, has this unitive character. The all-incorporating Egyptian knowledge is only a carnal analogue of it, and the dejection of exiles only an opposite kind of analogue. In this latter condition we think Mary Jo's desolate thought that the world cannot be known, or perhaps that it can be known only the way doubt knows it — as utterly alien to oneself or a mere projection of oneself. Mary Jo at this point is of course looking at a reflection, and seeing it in a certain way: she is like Del Jordan after her loss of Garnet French, watching a strange sufferer in the mirror who is herself yet not herself at all. And no doubt this really is one end represented by the Apocalypse phase, as we have found: a dead world seen with dead vision. But knowledge of this kind is itself a phase in a story, and not necessarily the final one. Beyond it there may be, most immediately, a crisis — that of the Spanish Lady as simply "pushed back" (190) by the dying man in the station, or Rose dismayed by the news about Simon. Rose finds that the man she loved is now lost to her forever; she also realizes that in his very mortality he shared something with her. And through this terrible double awareness comes the intimation of something new — of "inappropriate unforgettable scenery" (173). There remains, of course, the "scene" (171) to which Rose's natural self has to go back: the *skené*, once again, of theatre, mystery, and law. But here Rose is glimpsing a country in which Simon might return to her, and not just as one of Munro's accusing revenants.[97]

II. Mrs. Carbuncle

Before entering this country, however, we have some important unfinished business. In the last few pages we have been imagining a heroine's relation to a Messenger — one who must be acknowledged in both his high and low roles, as both truth and reality. At the same time, of course, we have seen that a shadow must be cast out, the negation I have often called "the world." But there is still a danger here: it is all too easy to isolate a heroine and hero (if that is what they happen to be), see the negativity in their surroundings, and reject along with that a recalcitrance, even perverseness, that is essential to reality itself and its paradoxical work of saving. We should think again of the person who appeared when we looked hard at the world: an ageless, self-willed, denying Old Woman (or Old Man, but I suggested that the Old Woman is a more useful figure in Munro). In the Epilogue stories we have found this Old Woman as the Mrs. Sherriff got around by Bobby and Del, or the Misses Milton got around by Milton Homer and his avatars; in a less outsmartable form she is Sophie in "White Dump" or the mother in "The Ottawa Valley" — in any case a great block. But what if the Old Woman, like the Messenger, proved to be not one thing but different things? And what if one of these were like the vitamins that must not be refined out of the flour? Perhaps there is an Old Woman who helps us to affirmation, even though she has to use denial as her means: if so, then she too needs to be included in our circle of prayer.

One characteristic of the Old Woman that we have already noticed is her rashness — her way of overextending herself or reaching for a bait: in fact the guardian who tries to keep others on the track has a mystifying tendency to go off it herself.[98] There is something of this, for instance, when Et Desmond tells her inexplicable fib, or Dorothy in "Marrakesh" turns into a Peeping Tom; in "Spelling" we find it with women who are actually senile, and Violet in "Possession" is another clear case of senility in the sense of Alzheimer's disease. But we do not have to limit ourselves to the clinical here. Et and Dorothy are not senile, and for that matter strange doings are by no means limited to the old — in "A Queer Streak," for instance, various ages contribute to the general "Female Craziness" (248). The Old Woman is something in all women, as in all men; and this makes it the more remarkable that her craziness, wherever we find it, should have a consistent feature — that, to quote "Spelling," it is always "meant to tell" (174). When the grandmother in "A Trip to the Coast" cannot resist starting off for California, or the Misses Milton get up the petition that brings their own downfall, we have the feeling that they are courting disaster, perhaps turning victory itself into disaster by displaying it. It is as if they positively wanted their slips to show, and this in order to show something more.[99]

What might this something be? The feminist girls in "A Queer Streak" have a ready label for the female craziness in Violet's family — "anti-patriarchal rage" (248): but while they may be right in a sense beyond the one they intend, and to some extent even in an immediate sense, there is a great deal that they leave unaccounted for. Dawn Rose's "innocent and evil" (226) smile, as I have argued,[100] goes beyond any ordinary grudge against her feeble-witted and hen-pecked father; Violet in her bouts of strangeness even seems to be asking a man to take her over — though again there is more to the matter than that.[101] In any case, one thing that looms out of all the craziness is a need for sympathy. We have already seen the Old Woman as both hostile and frightened, dreading the return of the consort she has put out of the way; now it is time to see her as the loving wife or mother who has been deprived of him.

*

"A Queer Streak" gives us a direct glimpse of something that remains only implicit in a story like "The Ottawa Valley." We have found the enterprising Violet to be secretly the same person as her "helpless and distracted, dull and stubborn" (244) mother; we have also seen these two as "Hooligan and Hayes" (213) putting a bridle on King Billy. At the same time we must remember the picture in the parlour: the three queens standing at the side of the dying Arthur. To Violet this scene conveys "unbearable sweetness and sorrow" (209); and whether or not she supposes the three queens to be mourning, there can be little doubt that her own mother is doing so — for at some time in the shadowy past Aunt Ivie lost her three sons.[102] Already an untameable initiatory figure, she now turned into a plainly crazy one: in later life she prowls dejectedly about the barnyard, looking for out-of-sight chicken's eggs.

It appears, then, that the queens of the world — of whom Aunt Ivie herself produced three on losing her sons — are figures of bereavement; and the universal mother is an Isis not only in her completeness but her incompleteness, what drives her to search endlessly for her lost offspring or consort. By the same token she is the Mary who has lost her son and lord: she is even a Mary whose lord has abandoned her or driven her away. Trevor Auston rejects Violet, to her shock; in "The Ottawa Valley," again, this is one way we must see, not only the jilting of Aunt Dodie, but Allen Durrand's snubbing of the mother; and if we turn to "Rose Matilda" we find Morris cheating a whole trio of women. We even find the Old Woman taking on the role of martyr, for in reciting the last words of Tennyson's Arthur, the mother in "The Ottawa Valley" is preparing for her own death. When she silently darkens and withdraws from the daughter who has exposed her mortality, this martyr's role becomes that of a crucified Christ — as we can see from counterparts like Marion Sherriff, hanging on the wall with lowered face and darkened eyes.[103] Aunt Ivie in her "man's felt hat" (213) can be taken as the same Undergod; so can the Aunt Dodie whom we have seen to wear "a man's hat without a crown" (229); and when we are told of the mother in "The Peace of Utrecht" with her "dead and burning" (200) eyes, we recognize the same universal sufferer as at the climax of "Executioners."

But as someone bereaved or dying, the old woman is like those who despise and resist her: she too is subject to the fate of *pân kréas*, and in showing her bereavement she is reaching out to her fellows. We may be reminded here of the women who try for reconciliation at the end of Sibling stories, or the Suicide Woman who tells Rose of Simon's death: for in her very display of triumph this woman is also making an appeal,[104] as is Robina in "Executioners" offering to show Helena her hidden arm. In this last case, to be sure, the arm is an Old Woman's "sign of perversity and power" (144) — a companion to the more visible one that stuns Helena at the fire; yet we must also see it as being just what it is, a crippled arm. And in being that, it may also be a mysterious treasure: the narrator of "The Ottawa Valley" may be forfeiting the same treasure when she puts demands on another crippled arm, that of her dying mother.

This brings us to the heart of the matter: if the Old Woman can be a figure of reconciliation in a Sibling story, perhaps she might also be the Messenger in an Epilogue, an offerer of grace.[105] Once again we can use Mary Jo's dream in "Eskimo" as a paradigm. Apart from Mary Jo herself, the only figure present throughout this dream is the strange white-haired woman in the red sari, a person of some authority. At first this woman appears a tidy nurse like Mary Jo, covering the rusty sink with her hands; she seemingly turns accuser to say "You'll get a chance to choose your own" (206) — her own punishment, Mary Jo assumes, dismissing the woman as "crazy." Yet Mary Jo, with her programme of withdrawal, has come to a rusty patch of her own and is in some danger of going down the drain. If an accuser, the woman in the sari is also a Rescuer, and may even be helping Mary Jo to choose her own in another sense: for in the last part of the dream she speaks as a friend, shows Mary Jo the blue snowdrops, and explains that "court" refers to these flowers.

*

Now let us go back now to the two Old Women most important in Munro's concluding stories: the mother in "The Ottawa Valley" and Sophie in "White Dump." Earlier we saw these as fates — inexorable old guardians of a dark wisdom. If we wanted to see "The Ottawa Valley" as the simplest form of Epilogue, the mother could of course only be a more composed version of the imprisoning Mrs. Sherriff — one who may give her last pin to keep her daughter's pants up, but has containment for her only motive. Hence this mother is to be outwitted and exposed: it is Dodie the trickster who, more than anyone else, knows how to bring down both the mother and the priggish daughter with the right words. Yet not only is the mother more formidable than such a reading lets us see: the question of good and bad will is also more complex. The words that are enough to bring the daughter's pants down are "Some people don't deserve Christian" (239) — a ruthless assertion of Law on Dodie's part, since nobody deserves Christian. On the other hand, the mother who descends into the outhouse to save her daughter from shame, and even takes shame on herself by appearing in church with her slip showing, is performing a kindness. And we should add that Dodie herself once performed a like kindness: she looked after a dying woman whose own children were kept at bay for fear of infection. Both the mother and Dodie, in their opposite ways, are figures of grace: both offer the narrator something for which, if she were less self-absorbed, she might say thank you.

With "White Dump" we have no single experiencer, and hence an even greater complexity of readings, but here too the unappreciated old woman is an essential presence. The humourless and obtuse and directorial Sophie, with her habits and her opinions, is once again just the person to be covertly laughed at, and indeed rebuked to her face when she makes her sensational appearance at breakfast; and yet there is more to her than her son and daughter-in-law will ever admit. This "Old Norse" (280), I have suggested, is a kind of earth-mother: she remains unimpressed by her son's accomplishments and disinclined to the official sort of television, preferring to brood on prophecies in her dank Log House with its ancient stove. When taken to the upper element in a plane she shrivels with dread, aware that something ominous has happened to herself and her children. And in fact two ominous events have taken place on this same day, both of them like the plane ride itself: the first moon-shot and the appearance of three young hippies by the lake where Sophie goes for her daily swim.

In each case we can say that a goddess is exposed and violated. The hippies steal and rip Sophie's bathrobe in the course of some posturing and play-fighting — in the latter, we can note, a boy apparently rips off a girl's pants. As a result of this incident a triumphant birthday is badly disrupted: the man who likes to see his pretty wife in a bikini finds himself looking at his aged mother in nothing. "Christ, Mother!" (300) cries Laurence, scrambling to get the tablecloth over this woman whose garment has been taken and rent.[106] Isabel for her part thinks of Sophie's hypocrisy — her sham innocence, her concealed desire to humiliate her son. Nor, as we have found, does Isabel like the hippies any better: they are only "arrogant brats" (301) who preach peace and enlightenment while secretly craving violence — like Sophie herself, as she observes elsewhere of this woman who reads sagas. Presently Isabel is having an affair with the pilot from the skyride, deeply humiliating her husband in the process; yet it would not occur to her that the three of them are behaving like the three hippies in the role of brats, or that she is doing what she has attributed to Sophie. Nor would it occur to her that Sophie might be, among other things, a messenger of genuine peace and freedom: a mother offering her squabbling children what they prefer to take by force.

*

If we return to other stories with these two in mind, certain questions will now need further answers. In "The Peace of Utrecht" what are we to make of Aunt Annie's gift of the dead woman's clothing? Is it a gesture of simple innocence, is it a trick to keep Helen under control, or — what we will now be wondering — does it also have the innocence of a greater wisdom and a greater charity? What about Helen's own invitation to Maddy, the invitation to take her life? What about Flo's passing on of the wig and gallstones at the end of "Spelling?" To go back to the beginning of things, what about the carryings-on of Loony Buttler, also known as Mrs. Carbuncle? One reason for this latter name is given us explicitly — Loony Buttler is altogether "knobby, deadened, awkward, intractable" (185); but perhaps she is mysteriously a carbuncle of a different kind, one found in the garden of God.[107] After all, the daughter who goes on to looniness of her own appears in the end as "Rose Matilda," possessed of every virtue and grace.

One more example of an ambiguous old woman, or women, can help us see what is at issue here. Miss Marsalles, or we can say the two Misses Marsalles,[108] are obviously Messenger figures, close cousins of Bobby Sherriff or Ralph Gillespie. The Misses Milton in "Who Do You Think You Are?" are just as obviously the contrary, law-enforcers whom anyone would want to trick and avoid. Yet the more we consider these two pairs of old ladies, the more alike they seem: for in their own way the Misses Mattie and Hattie are giving the same mad party as the Misses Marsalles. In each case we have two aging spinsters, stranded members of an order whose collapse they will not acknowledge; in each case there is the absurd gathering with its insipid refreshments and entertainment. Each of these gatherings, moreover, is inspired by a sense of mission: missionary work in the one case, the mission of bringing music to children in the other, accompanied by books with titles like *Little Mission Friends*. As for the guests, it is simply taken for granted that they are innocents eager to receive the gospel in question — the revelation from a far country.

In the one story, to be sure, the revelation is of dancing spirits, while in the other it is of hard work in darkest China; but that raises just the question that needs raising here. Can the legal Misses Milton be workers in the same mission as the all-indulgent Misses Marsalles? This is like asking whether the Sophie who represents fate can also be an offerer of grace, or whether Aunt Dodie's eyes can flash both malice and a saving kindness; and there is an important sense in which the answer seems to be yes.[109]

*

We have seen the cosmogonic tragedy of Aunt Ivie: the loss of the three sons in a swamp, followed by the generation of the three daughters. To go back a step farther, Aunt Ivie herself was once an unwanted daughter, and so ineligible as a wife that only a King Billy would have her. To see why she was unwanted, we will have to go back farther still — to the very beginning of things as we have found Munro imagining it. Before the world, even before chaos, an eternal identity fell from itself, giving rise to the separated principles of our present experience. One of these can most readily be thought of as male: an active creator who from doubt and fear withdraws into the security of himself, deeply weakened though gaining a kind of strength, not to say aggressiveness, from his isolation. A complementary figure can be thought of as female: not an aggressor but a resister, spitefully refusing to be known or loved.[110] Simply as matter this figure is what we might call Earth; as the enveloping principle I have called Nature she takes on a form of her own; and yet all the while she remains like the recalcitrant Mrs. Fullerton, the unfathomable Old Woman with pits for eyes. The only way for the story to find a resolution is that of Munro's Epilogues, or of what they enable us to glimpse beyond themselves: the parties must come to acknowledge their oneness in difference, and thus reach back through the fallen condition they share to the unfallen identity they have lost.

This primal story begets two mirroring lesser forms of itself; and while, like any mirror-images, these readily dissolve into one another, the distinction between them remains important. In one of these it is the God, as I am going to call him, who is the injured party: he still represents the unfallen identity and calls a fallen Nature to return to it. He may call directly, but this by itself does not seem to work: the only language Nature understands is her own. And so the God has to become a principle of negation himself — in the first place, a principle of Law. Within this role he may play a further one: turning into the contrary of what he was as an upper authority, he becomes the figure of incarnation — of passion and death — whom we have called the Undergod. In this way he regains the love of Nature: or in the typological version of the story indicated by this duality of gods, he arouses Nature, leaves her to feel his loss, and receives her again when she learns to recognize him in loss itself. Thus we have in a positive form Munro's story of the withdrawing or inscrutable lover — Simon, Dr. Streeter, in "Bardon Bus" simply "X": a lover who might later say in all integrity "I loved you; I love you now."[111] We correspondingly have the heroines who overcome their bitterness, if they do, when they see that they were loved — that what they have been going through has been a process of purgation and learning. When Rose's father writes "Scald strawberries to remove acid" (3) his words ultimately point, like much else in Munro, to this sweetening of Nature.[112] And so we find one way to make sense of what happens in the world and solve the problem of evil: except that the story in this single version readily identifies the unfallen with the fallen — with a god who cannot act with such sincerity. To go back to the theodicy of "Age of Faith," we are to believe that the god of that story acted for the best in what he did to his son, or in what father and son as a pair do to the rest of Creation; and after a good look at the Crucifixion Del finds such a creed hard to accept.

A form of the story with Nature as the aggrieved party is no less one-sided, but its inadequacy complements that of the other version in a way that can lead us beyond either. In this second version, to quote the narrator of "Tell Me Yes or No," "You told me that you loved me years ago. Years ago. And I said that I too, I was in love with you in those days" (106). In the beginning the active "male" principle loved the "female" and was loved in return: then, in a great betrayal, the male withdrew. Within the fallen state, and on its terms, the God has offered love again, and Nature has said "Yes"; but again he has abandoned her, breaching his contract, and Nature accordingly must hold him to it. To describe her way of doing so will be to review much of what we have already seen in this book, though now we must look at it in a new way, as a means of recalling a lost life to itself. For one thing, we will find simple Law again — Nature behaving like the "categorical" (227) mother in "The Ottawa Valley" or the formidable Aunt Lena, the kind of woman who lays down the law as law.[113] And Nature may also use a more devious kind of law, or anti-law: where the "Ottawa Valley" mother — or, from what we are told, Auntie Lou in "The Peace of Utrecht" — is noted for her directness, Aunt Annie is a spirit of mischief. When Eileen in "Memorial" receives Ewart into herself, it is mischief again that she represents in the deeper form of elusiveness and drift. No doubt these things seem less formidable than June's proclaimed values, yet Ewart finds them no easier to resist — fortune, not to say mortality itself, is exerting its own compulsion, here in a sexual guise.

*

If we combine Nature's two methods — to be imagined here as ways of reclaiming a lover — we arrive at a female counterpart of the male double play we have often seen in this book.[114] And while directness and indirectness — law and mischief — are weapons of God and Nature alike in the myths I am sketching, the less assertive principle of indirectness seems the more female by comparison.[115] Nature here is not simply the God facing in the other direction, but rather a principle of contrariety as such: where the God is truth she is reality, with all its stubbornness, waywardness, and mystery. And so, in the first place, Nature is a trickster — the same essentially that we have met before, but in a different context. When Munro contrasts the straightforwardness of Garnet French or Ewart with the indirections of Del Jordan or the deviousness of Eileen, we have the difference between the archetypally male and female in a simple form. When, on the other hand, we find a male figure adopting a role of "tricks and . . . trap doors" (124), like the lover in "Tell Me Yes or No," or turning protean like the heroes of the Passion stories, we can think of him as taking on the female role of fraud rather than force — a role played in fact by a number of Munro's men.

And if we are dealing with Nature as a trickster, we should note the tricky form that she herself assumes for the purpose. In positing first an opposition of male and female, then a combination of opposite methods on the part of either, we have once again invoked the business of pairing — of this and that — that has been with us throughout this book. When we associate pairing with female contrariety, even the double play of Upper God and Undergod takes on a female character; Nature's own double play does so, of course; and Nature herself readily becomes double. It will be important here to reconsider the female pairs that are such a typical feature of Munro's stories: not only the Misses Marsalles and the Misses Milton but, as we have just seen, Auntie Lou and Aunt Annie, June and Eileen — and the countless others that will immediately suggest themselves. What matters at present is that all these pairs can be thought of as teams of tricksters. One member will tend to play straight-woman, even to be the victim of the other's jokes — in "The Ottawa Valley," for instance, the mother is a stately Egyptian, while Aunt Dodie is the laughing "gypsy" (243) who repeatedly upsets her cousin's dignity. But in our present perspective this is all part of the act, as are the partners' routines more generally: all the high and low, tragic and comic, Mary and Elizabeth that make up the world as a baffling duality.

In particular, we can recall, one of the two partners is an escape artist, someone who takes life in the sense of bursting out of its more contained form — or making others do so; the other's specialty is keeping herself and her charges safely inside. And to concentrate, we can see the same doubleness in any single duplicity. It is true that Dodie and the mother in "The Ottawa Valley" are most readily contrasted — Dodie in effect pulls the narrator's pants down, the mother pins them up again. Yet we can easily see the whole pair in either one of them: the Victorian mother looking as if she might secretly be amused, Aunt Dodie secretly crying in the night or even flashing her malice and kindness at the same time.[116] And almost the first thing the narrator sees her aunt do is to hold a slopping milk-pail for a calf while at the same time "laughing and scolding and hitting it, trying to make it slow down" (229).

Flow and restriction are nicely combined again in the star performance of the pair as a pair, the trick played on Allen Durrand. Allen is sewn up, filled with lemonade and vinegar, and then left for the result: in the hot mow "he just finally went past caring and gave up and ripped down his overalls altogether and let 'er fly" (236). Dodie's experience in this line began earlier: when her own dying mother had been swollen with "fluid," "they came one time and took it out of her by the pailful" (243), while Dodie played her part by rolling the mother onto "her heart side," causing death. No doubt this weighs on Dodie — as the narrator's own dead mother will weigh on the narrator — but it is the turn itself that concerns us at present. For the dropsical mother is one of the capsizing bodies we have noted in this story and "Memorial" — the car that rolls over onto Douglas, the gravestone in the cemetery, or even in a sense the dead Dave McColl, who would get rolled out of his grave if Dodie had her way. In all such cases, it seems, the same double pressure tactic is being applied:

something is swollen with fullness or heaviness, then tumbled by an opposite force. If we now translate physical pressure into different terms, we will arrive at a form of the same tactic specially important here: important for the Apocalypse stories, important more generally as showing us both the full cruelty of an Old Woman's tricks and a benevolence in cruelty itself.

*

A number of characters in Munro have tricks like the one played on Allen Durrand — Helena virtually ignites the house in which Howard Troy meets his death, the Jenkin's Bend aunts draw the world into the burning "haymow" (58) of the parlour, Dorothy contrives the fiery scene at the end of "Marrakesh." Dorothy, we can add, is showing the value of upgrading, having once had to spent hot summers in Toronto for the purpose. At that time the Department of Education tried to teach her new "methods and perspectives" (105); now she manoeuvres the lovers into a hot glassed porch and watches them have sex. She watches with a well-trained eye, of course: the sexual encounter here, as we have found, is being combined with a critical one. What we must do now is to see all natural knowledge whatever as the same Old Woman's trick: the holding of victims in a cognitive as well as physical kind of "focus."

Nature's camera — for of course that is what we are dealing with — can equally be seen in terms of another image I have used repeatedly: a chamber of mirrors, duplicity working as reflection. Once again we have something that both opens out and closes in, since a mirror, as we noted earlier, draws the viewer to itself while also reflecting him back. The walls that serve as viewing screens in Munro's carnal temples are much the same: and here, if we like, we can again imagine two Old Women at work. One, like Miss Hattie with her slides, is the spirit of projection; the other is like the wall, a spirit of reflection or resistance. Both spirits, and their subtle co-oper-ation, can be felt in a story like "The Moons of Jupiter," where a great deal of display is combined with a pervasive sense that you should not put on an act or otherwise "make a fuss" (220). More emblem-atically, we find the workings of the father's heart projected outwards from him and reappearing as an image on a screen.

A different kind of screen, or wall, is Janet's alarm at such a procedure:

It seemed to me that paying such close attention — in fact, dramatizing what ought to be a most secret activity — was asking for trouble. Anything exposed that way was apt to flare up and go crazy. (217–18)

In "Heirs of the Living Body," to draw the obvious parallel, Del is no less disturbed to see her Uncle Craig on view in his coffin; his own heart attack was his way of flaring up, an explosive rebellion against Egyptian idolization and confinement. Yet we have seen how, through all such misgivings and explosions, the mirror trick continues to work. Indeed it is at work in all natural perception — within the confinement of nature things are kept apart while being at the same time exposed to each other, made to be alien images on distant screens. And the result goes beyond any physical suffering: it is also the torment of shame that we have met so often in this book. Allen Durrand is ashamed to have been seen naked; Laurence is ashamed to see his mother in the same state. It is no less shaming to be covered up, like Mary Agnes Oliphant, or shut out by another's coverings, like Jimmy Saunders. Looming behind all such situations, as I have argued, is that of Jesus on the cross, bound and exposed, seeing and being seen — and ultimately crying out in desperation.

But that is not the whole of the picture we need here. If we live by projecting and screening, no doubt that is something forced upon us by the malicious Old Woman who is Nature: and yet it is something more as well. For one thing, as we have just found in Janet and Del and Uncle Craig, it can also be seen as expressing the victims' opposition, even overt challenge, to the Old Woman. And what if we do as we have begun to do, and take the Old Woman herself as a victim — someone unjustly regarded or disregarded by an abandoning God? Certainly the distress we have seen is also hers: that of the dying mother in "The Peace of Utrecht," for instance, at once boarded in and subjected to the eyes of her tormentors. Perhaps the Old Woman's camera show is not just a mean-spirited trick, but another challenge, even an act of good will. And it may be from good will that the Old Woman includes a special attraction in the show: her own martyrdom.

*

At the end of "Spelling" we find Flo asking Rose "Did you show your father" (188)? All Flo means to refer to is the egg-sized gallstones

which, supposedly, were once removed from her insides, and which
Rose pretends to have taken home. But the imaginings of Flo's senility
are very suggestive: eggs and gall are what we expect from the
stubborn Old Woman that she is, and Rose is accepting the Old
Woman's role in taking them to herself. Gall, like the vinegar supplied
to Allen Durrand, also makes us think of the Crucifixion — with
Jesus in mind, we may even hear a Johannine ring in Flo's wording.[117]
In such a resonant context, the meaning of her question seems
multiple. Did Rose show the gallstones to her father? Did she show
more than that — perhaps himself? Did she "show him" in the sense
of showing herself to him as well, forcing him to know the gall of her
spite or her suffering? And beyond all this did she show him in the
sense of revealing him — revealing, that is, not his betraying shadow
but his genuine self?

In the first place, it would be typical for the Old Woman to be
showing something to somebody. "Look here, look there" (297), says
the professorial Sophie; "This is the Ottawa Valley" (229), says
another pedagogical mother. The Old Woman in us, it seems, forever
wants to be indicating things; nor does she have any hesitation about
indicating them to themselves. Here the champion is Flo herself,
whose byword is "You have to let them know" (57) and who, for
example, lets Rose know what she thinks of her appearance in a
semi-topless *Trojan Women*. When it comes to showing the father
himself in this indicating sense, Flo's method in "Half a Grapefruit"
is simple but effective — she holds up his stained underwear; we have
equally seen her disposing of George the prize-winner with a forthright "Look at the Nigger!" (187).[118]

On the other hand there is the showing of oneself that, in one form,
is "showing off." I have remarked on the high incidence of this in
"The Moons of Jupiter," whatever the family's code of self-effacement
may be. Janet wants fame as a writer, going against her father's implied
disapproval; the father himself, whenever his mood lifts, shows off
his knowledge of poetry or the hospital slang or the moons of Jupiter,
keeping the tone light for self-protection. He is almost overtly
delighted at the accomplishments of his other daughter's family, their
"innocent energetic showing-off" (227); he is more guardedly
approving of Janet's own. And in "Who Do You Think You Are?"
showing off becomes unmistakably the central theme of a story. Ralph
does it, Rose does it, their archetype Milton Homer does it more freely
than anyone else, storming boisterously through town, strutting in
the parades, exposing himself (as well as getting exposed) in line-ups.

Hanratty, for that matter, does it too, most notably in the great Orange Walk; and even the unparading Misses Milton manage to display themselves quite plainly. Everything about them — their slide-shows, of course, but also their house, their clothing, their general demeanour — declares who they think they are.

Miss Hattie also, of course, wants to know who Rose thinks she is: declaring herself goes with challenging another.[119] In fact, as an older Rose learns from her interviewing experiences, everybody secretly wants to challenge in this way — "to show somebody, to show everybody"; and if Miss Hattie herself is sedate about it, others of no less dignity want to "make a face" (97). Here we can note another feature of the showing that is challenging: it always seems to be mimicry as well. Flo, who endlessly makes faces, may warn Rose against Milton Homer's "monkey[ing] around" (194), but she has a monkey face of her own as well as a talent for aping people: her faces presumably include the mimetic kind. For Rose and Ralph, of course, showing off is always mimicry, as Rose demonstrates by turning into an actress. We have the opposite form of the same thing when, as it were, someone forces another to become a mimic — the Spanish Lady, for example, wanting to make her husband suffer like herself no less than to make a face of her own:

I could say, *Now you know, don't you, now you see.* Yes. In his extremest pain I would show him my little, satisfied, withdrawing smile. I would show it. (188)

Here we have the trick of showing in all its cruelty, irresistible for this proud woman who has herself been so cruelly shown. Flo is no less ruthless when she brandishes the underwear: indeed her general effect on the other members of the family is that "there was not a thing in their lives they were protected from" (47). But — as we must now ask — might there also be kindness in such ruthlessness, and honesty in its trickery?[120] Eileen in "Memorial" believes, with whatever belief her Old Woman's unbelief is capable of, that "acts done without faith may restore faith" (226); and perhaps she is right in a way that goes beyond the mere diplomacy of a Sibling story.

We should think again about the bad faith to which such acts are a mirroring — that is, mimicking — response.[121] In the world of "Memorial" bad faith is easy enough to see, since it has all the self-conscious posing and syncretism about it that we first noted in the terminal stories. Old-time Hanratty is a simpler and soberer place:

it will not do there to be parading. But this, of course, simply means that one should conceal the fact of parading — not seem too aware of one's parade as a parade. Even better, one should not consciously *be* too aware of it: at the Legion Rose is made to feel objectionable, not only for "parading" (203) around the room, but for asking questions — "who was this, when was that" — about pictures on the wall that are not meant to be looked at or thought about. If one wants to go successfully about the business of life, in this case playing cards and drinking beer, sense dictates that one not let oneself be aware of too much, that one take the world for granted. And in the apocalyptic context, it is just this numbness that is the worst faith of all. The stuffy Legion — or Hanratty, or the settled world in general — is like the quarantine room where Rose and Brian wait out the measles, protected by a quilt over the window to keep the light from blinding them.[122] That is precisely why the Old Woman, as represented by the story's mimics, poses such a threat. No doubt Milton Homer and Ralph Gillespie are mere "idiots" (193) — people who are only themselves. But they are also legion: like the idiot Simon, they have the protean knack of playing all roles. Ralph, indeed, might take the covering off the more official Legion to reveal a tomb full of demoniacs.[123]

Ralph is of course grudgingly accepted as a local fixture; so was his predecessor. If worldly perceiving or representing can only deal with an alien object and thus inevitably produce a caricature, then "it wouldn't be a parade without Milton Homer" (193) — Hanratty must let him carry on while keeping him as tamed as possible. The mimics, however, are not content to keep the parade going: they want to disrupt it. It is true that they confound themselves in the process, for the bringing in of light can have harmful effects on all concerned — Milton and Homer went blind,[124] while Ralph apparently meets his end stumbling in a blindness of his own. And the mimics go on too long for their own good: comedians, whether Ralph or — as we can now say — the Misses Milton themselves, never know when to stop, so that things "just blow up in their faces" (197). But they are willing to let this happen; indeed it seems that people who make faces positively want "to sabotage themselves."[125] Seeing Ralph do Milton Homer, Rose wants "to fill up in that magical, releasing way" (200) — to bring on her own explosion, in effect. And the mother in "The Ottawa Valley," who arranges similar performances, finally appears in one of her own: for this contained and inflated woman chooses to die.

With this we can return to the question of the Old Woman's underlying motive. I have suggested that she is not just malicious but desperate, and perhaps we can now say the same thing in a more adequate way. Why, the daughter wonders in "The Ottawa Valley," did her mother choose as she did? It seems she wanted to show somebody — to have "display, of a sort." She wanted "revenge of a sort as well," a wild remedy against an injustice; and beyond this there was "more, that nobody could ever understand" (244), the endless mystery of the Old Woman's recalcitrance. Yet there remains something else about the mother that is clear enough, something that takes us past worldly understanding altogether: this woman once gave herself for her child.[126] Perhaps she is doing so in her death; and perhaps the Old Woman who shows the father is offering a similar gift. She sets him up as a foolish King Billy in an Orange Parade; she even turns him into a martyr like Munro's other King Billy; and by exposing him in his torment, she forces him to explode — to go past caring, to reveal his anger and need and mortal weakness. But something more is ultimately needed: if, like the dying Simon, she can show him that his mortality is also hers, that will achieve what mischief alone can not. In saying "Now you know, don't you, now you see" (188), she will be not mocking him but asking for his love.

And so, in one way or another, the Old Woman keeps her man to his bond. "Hold me fast, don't let me pass," pleads the Tam Lin who has been spirited away by the fairies. Hazel, in the story named after the ballad, rejects the same unspoken plea from her husband, leaving him "gray and insubstantial" (104) — an abstracted ghost. But the Jennet of the ballad does hold fast, whatever the cost may be, and after an explosion of shape-changing Tam Lin himself lies free in her arms. In the end the God held by the Old Woman is freed in the same way: and now at last he can be revealed, not just as a fool or a martyr, but as someone who always loved her and counted on her to save him. Now, too, she herself is free to reassume her genuine form. The froward Eileen once glimpsed a loving woman in a mirror: in the end she will simply be that woman, and as for the Old Woman of disaffection or presumption, it is time to "let 'er fly." The demon within the natural self can finally be cast out, the crotchety step-mother can fall asleep, the chilly schoolteacher can melt away.

C. TAKING YOUR LIFE

I: Believe Me

At the end of "A Queer Streak" we find Violet explaining how she was once extricated by Wyck Tebbutt from some bushes — like others in Munro, she had gone off the road. "We" were laughing, she says, meaning most obviously herself and Wyck. After all the female craziness in this story one readily thinks of a different meaning as well: "we" are the sorority that has already appeared in various forms, and Violet's helplessness was one of its customary tricks on the opposite sex. Now, however, we are ready for a meaning that transcends this second one: "we" are the woman and the man again, done at last with their old scrap and ready to share the fun of it. Nor is this sharing merely a defiance of reality (of Wyck Tebbutt's dismal wife, for instance) since we have now reached a more comprehending way of seeing the Messenger's courtesy. Properly understood, the place to which he is inviting — the shining Jubilee, for instance, that Bobby Sherriff inspires Del to want — is a visionary world that also gathers the real one wholly to itself: "every last thing, every layer of speech and thought, stroke of light on bark or walls, every smell, pothole, pain, crack, delusion" (253).[127] So whatever there is of good will inside the cracked and deluded Old Woman is welcome here too: outside this city she may have to play a mocking and accusing shadow, but inside it she can be revealed as a bride, the other who is also oneself. And this revelation is neither a showing nor a showing off, since there is no alienation of self and other here; by the same token there is neither covering nor exposure, and no place for shame.[128]

In giving Del his blessing and commission Bobby asks, as we have seen, for belief. The city for which she is setting out certainly takes some believing: in fact we have noted how the new world of the Epilogue stories — the new relation, in other words — is not "there" at all apart from one's experience of it. To appreciate this world, then, we will have to return again to the question of knowing and, what this amounts to in the world of courtesy, the question of communicating. We have already considered this last in an earlier chapter, as a problem for narrators caught between worldly opposites;[129] now, however, we can put the same problem in its ultimate context, that of a Messenger and his message.

More perhaps than any other group in Munro, the Apocalypse stories show us the extraordinary difficulty of communication.[130] We may think especially of "Memorial" and "The Moons of Jupiter," in which Eileen and Janet make so many futile attempts to say the right thing. We may also think of the "unsatisfactory conversation" (205) when Rose and Ralph come together: the two can no more speak to each other directly than they can love each other directly, nor would they be able to do so at any later time. And if Rose means not only to talk to Ralph but to talk about him to others, she runs into the same difficulty. She senses, to her shame, that the ability to "report antics" is not enough: there is "a tone, a depth, a light" (205) — the same thing in effect as a "lack of material" (206) — that baffles her Old Woman's craft of acting and tale-telling. Some feelings, it seems, require "translation" (205), and translation is never successful. Indeed the whole of "Who Do You Think You Are?" is presented as an explanation of Rose's failure.

To the extent that all this is so, the Apocalypse epilogue remains within a tragic world. Intimations here are only that: obscure messages of a kind that cannot be understood or delivered, like the fallen words that can never be congruent with reality or the reality that can never be put adequately into words.[131] Eileen, horrified by the memorial service, wishes that the reality of suffering and death could be left alone: "Words are all shameful. They ought to crumble in shame. . . . Silence the only possible thing" (221). Silence, however, has its own peril — as we see in "Executioners," the story in which Helena fails to respond to Robina's offer on the road. When, later, Helena does want to speak, it is the offended Robina who turns away; and at the heart of the story we have the great blow by which Robina — and everything she represents — strikes Helena dumb. We may even, as situations like these indicate, have the shamefulness of speech and that of silence side by side, perhaps as represented by the two sexes. We sometimes find haranguing or garrulous women opposed to men who clam up, as in the interview between Rose and Ralph; or it may be the Rosicrucian or Bobby Sherriff or the breezy neighbour at June's reception who does the talking, and the defensive heroine who retreats into discretion — or tries to, for the battle between a need to talk and a need to be quiet is fought inside as well as out.

*

To have an appropriate image for this world of expression gone wrong, we can return once again to the palsied mother: the old woman who, literally or figuratively, has lost her power to speak if not her desire to do so. We have met such women in stories like "The

Ottawa Valley," "The Peace of Utrecht," and "Memorial" — in every case mothers who need to express themselves but cannot; and "Winter Wind," where we find still another, is perhaps Munro's richest treatment of maimed communication. I have suggested that this story harks back to the chaotic initiatory phase: one way in which it does so is just in its pervasive concern with speech and silence. In the background loom the settlers who chose reclusiveness and secrecy — the great-grandfather who strangely left his convivial life in Ireland, the grandfather who withdrew into his books. In the present there is Mr. Harmer, the teacher from the old country who spends the evenings reading in his lonely room; there is the narrator's mother, half speechless from Parkinson's disease; and at the heart of the story there is the grandmother, the woman who has disciplined herself to duty and concealment.

The mother cannot speak, the grandmother will not; and both are like another solitary in this story, a Mrs. Gershom Bell known to the older generation as Susie Heferman. When this woman dies in a blizzard trying to reach the cows in her barn, the reason, as we have seen, is that she did not tie a line to the door: a line of communication, we can now say, like the line roads and telephone lines in the story's background.[132] Beyond such material lines, often useless in the story, there is a more occult kind that is not: independently of information, or even of the normal ability to size up another person, the narrator senses her grandmother's desperation. Tragically, this intuition is only a hunch, something she cannot understand and has no idea what to do with — for even at the time of the story she too is becoming palsied, stiffening with shame at her arts.[133] Yet the narrator trusts her strange message against all evidence or lack of it; and the names in the story provide some vindication of her trust. Some of these are straightforward enough — "Heferman" suits the woman who tries to get to her cows, "Bell" goes with telephones; the name of Gershom, Moses's first son, means or was thought by the biblical writers to mean "sojourner,"[134] appropriately enough for one of the isolated settlers of this story. More curiously, "Susie" and, for that matter, "Bell" suggest that we may be close to the Book of Daniel again: and as it happens "Winter Wind" is a story about not only exile but occult connections, divination, even perhaps a wind of prophecy in a desolate time. As much as any Munro story, it forces us to reconsider the question of evidence and the belief we accord it.

*

The belief proper to the world of sense is that of "luminously sane" (108) people like Mr. Jordan in "Age of Faith": people who neither believe nor disbelieve in any very committed way, but maintain a reasonable deference toward the unknowable while going about their own affairs. As we pass into the world of sensibility we begin to meet believers of the more intense kind — the assorted enthusiasts, for example, who gravitate to the Spanish Lady. We are equally in this world when Mrs. Jordan asserts her opinions, or June upholds her values, or Ted Braddock in "The Ferguson Girls" clings to religious beliefs that Bonnie finds preposterous. Again, this is the world of Munro's nuns and ministers: it includes both Dr. Streeter and Mary Jo, for instance, as given to secret, unreasonable devotion. On the other hand it includes the burglars, sceptics like Bonnie herself or the Spanish Lady or Eileen — for these no more resemble the sensible Mr. Jordan than do the Teds and Junes. In fact it includes Mr. Jordan himself in other than sensible versions: we can recall the conscientious butcher of Del's nightmare, or the man who, like his counterparts in "Winter Wind," withdraws into isolation and silence. Even when masked by good sense, the nonsense of belief and doubt seems always to be there.

In an extreme form, sensibility gives us the paranoia of a Joe Phippen, so afraid of his shadow that he takes it for the hostile Silases. And Joe, we notice, has two sides to him. He is one of Munro's Counter-Strangers, the witness to a reality others would like to forget; yet here reality goes with wild delusion, since the Silases he guards against are, as Ben Jordan puts it, "just nobody" (43). To have the same thing in an opposite form, we can set the feeble-minded Joe, holed up in his terror, beside the Jerry Storey of "The Photographer," a world-class intellect whom we see at one point walking confidently along a bridge. Jerry is anything but benighted: he goes by scientific evidence. He can prove that everyone is about to be blown up; he can equally prove that there is going to be a brave new world of programmed behaviour, safe from any accident. In other words, Jerry is not unlike Joe: he looks at the world with the same combination of mistrust and conviction, seeing a threat against which only total security will prevail. Once again, then, we are seeing the paranoia that is reality and truth in an insane conspiracy.

To get the better of this conspiracy, we can first reconsider a story that I have already grouped with "Winter Wind." "Visitors" is very much about communication, with its lines to be held to, its misunderstandings between members of a family, and its pentecostals from a dry region who believe in "tongues" that are "the voice of God" (202). The swamp to which the main characters of the story are drawn is said to resound with voices of its own — "squawks, calls, screeches, and cries" (213); and the mention of these leads to Albert's tale of Lloyd Sallows, a man who, if he did not spend time in a fiery furnace, did survive an Ontario winter naked in the same swamp. Wilfred, as his wife reflects, would not have told such a story, or told it the same way. He would have given it more reason and point, with a happy ending to tie matters together — in his own fashion, Wilfred is a purveyor of truth. But the dour Albert speaks for reality: his version of the story has no seeming shape and contains "neither luck nor money" (215). For that matter, as he himself claims, "It's not a story. It's something that happened." Once again Munro is raising the question of belief.

Of the two brothers, it is Wilfred who knows answers and believes things — including those he makes up. Albert is much the more sceptical, both of other people's knowledge and of his own: he shows himself highly circumspect, for instance, when trying to recall the family homestead. This makes it doubly strange that he would cling to his Lloyd Sallows story, for he did not see Lloyd Sallows, and the story itself is far more unlikely than any of Wilfred's. What Albert demonstrates again is the way obsession with reality turns into a fanatic's belief in truth: as we watch him telling his dark tale, looking "fierce, concentrating" (212) and slicing up a hamburger, we might be seeing Joe Phippen himself. And so neither brother, taken simply on his own terms, makes a very satisfactory Daniel: Wilfred remains in his phony temple of facile belief, Albert in his lair of doubt — the doubt that only becomes a crazier kind of certitude.

But perhaps this story of two brothers could be taken a step farther. Lloyd Sallows goes as wild as Albert, eating "flesh" (214) the way Albert eats hamburger; but at the end of the same anecdote, though not any end acceptable to sense, a remarkable thing happens: the vanished man, both of whose names mean "pale"[135] and thus suggest the wan Albert himself, reappears out of his swamp as a kind of white innocent. What if the story of one's belief in such stories led to something similar? What if, properly interpreted, the tongues that echo through temple or station or swamp were not just the voice of a lost man but the genuine voice of God? That at any rate is what "Grace" and "Vera" might claim, speaking as "one" (202).[136]

*

The contrast between Wilfred and Albert may remind us of a similar contrast in "The Progress of Love," where the sisters Marietta and Beryl have conflicting versions of an incident in their mother's early life. In promoting these they of course assume that one rather than the other has to be chosen; but Phemie, the heir of both these older women, treats a corresponding story in a different way. When she recalls her mother burning some inheritance money, watched by her father, she knows that this incident could not have taken place as she remembers it: yet it somehow has a greater authority than that of mere fact. "How hard it is for me to believe I made that up. It seems so much the truth it is the truth; it's what I believe about them" (30). Phemie here is feeling as Mary in "The Shining Houses" feels about Mrs. Fullerton's stories, which, as we have noted, have "a pure reality that usually attaches to things which are at least part legend" (19).[137] In the same way, Albert's tale in "Visitors" is most adequately described neither as a story, in the sense of an empty fiction, nor as something that happened in a merely factual sense. Rather, it is in a narrative form what I have called courtesy in another context: fiction and fact offer themselves to one another, and so gain an authority that neither can have in separation.

Belief in such an authority is paranoia turned inside out; and it is just this belief that Munro's Messengers are asking for. With their merely natural selves, of course, these strange people are as deluded as any Joe Phippen: the Rosicrucian believes in reincarnation, Ted Braddock believes in saving the soul by relocating the body, Bobby Sherriff believes that lack of vitamins is the sufficient cause of mental breakdowns. Yet we should compare Bobby with Jerry Storey, as Munro herself invites us to do — the Bobby who says "Believe me" (253) when he rises absurdly into the air, the Jerry who sings "Be-*lieff* me" (245) as he goose-steps along the rails. Both can be considered crazy, but where Jerry's craziness is only oppressive, Bobby's has his mysterious gift to offer. What Jerry envisages is, in the terms we have been using, a reality wholly conformed to truth: matter, that is, compelled by the abstract idea of a programmer with total and arbitrary control over it. (At the same time Jerry sees this world as coming by physical necessity, which delivers it to a counter-truth in reality itself). Bobby too calls up a shining world beyond the vicissitudes of this one, and his world is equally a bonding of reality to truth; yet in Bobby's world human experience is recalled to humanity by the love that invites and that says "yes" — reality and truth here are not a prisoner and a jailor but indivisible partners in the life so achieved. Jerry's world is a monstrous coupling of fact and science fiction; Bobby's is neither fact nor fiction but, as I have said, make-believe, to which we can now give the stronger name of creation. By the same token, Jerry's authority is only that of a projection onto a blank wall, whereas Bobby's that of his authentic self — he is a "Tom Shepherd"[138] worth trusting.

*

To know the good shepherd here we cannot simply accept Bobby's conscious beliefs; rather, we must see these as the parables by which a deeper authority in him is teaching us. And if we can hear such a teacher when Bobby insists on the all-importance of vitamins, we will be able to hear and accept him when other people make equally improbable claims. We will believe the God of "Age of Faith" when he claims to have tried and abandoned humanity for its own good; in more secular terms, we will believe Eric Cryderman when he claims to be giving Jessie a lesson, or Dan in "Circle of Prayer" when he claims to be leaving Trudy only as "a test of love" (264), a way of creating new opportunities in her life; we will even believe that whisky does Joe Phippen's cat no harm, or that the Department of Education has betterment in mind when it stuffs Dorothy into the hot room in Toronto. Along the same lines, we will believe that Robina is jostling Helena only to keep her out of the ditch, and that Aunt Lena beats her children to give them a good start in life.

An especially illuminating story in this connection is "Walking on Water," where still another unpleasant pedagogical device is used to "give people a jolt" (77), and ultimately to give something more. In this "serious kind of joke" (74) gravity and levity again work together — in fact they do so literally, since the way in which young Eugene makes fun of old Mr. Lougheed is to try, unsuccessfully, to walk off a pier onto the Pacific Ocean. This remarkable "demonstration" (68) is the focus for a world of similar ones: having retired to Victoria in the hippie era, Mr. Lougheed finds himself surrounded by occult signs, sexual exhibitions, hints at the biblical miracles, and endless pharisaical "showing off" (71) on the part of the young people around him. He watches these things sceptically but obsessively, like Dorothy or the Spanish Lady — while a rational man and a very sober one, he somehow apprehends the coming of a "message" (80). And in some sense this will be the message of foolishness itself: Eugene, certainly, is prepared to make a fool of himself, or more precisely show a fool who is already there.[139]

"Show the fool, yes, expose the fool, but isn't the fool just yourself, isn't it there all the time? Show yourself. What else can you do?" (78)

This is something Mr. Lougheed has never done. In his life as a druggist he has had the sense to "skate along affably" (67) while keeping his own counsel. Now he finds himself walking on water: he has joined the precarious world of the young and the old, a world of despair and desperate belief. Read in one way, "Walking on Water" is the tragedy of such belief: Eugene is simply a deluded young man whose ungrounded faith lets him down. At the central reversal of the story he sinks into the ocean and, having discovered that being under water is better than trying to stay on top of it, goes on to drown himself — that, at any rate, is one plausible explanation of his later disappearance. Mr. Lougheed goes through a similar process himself, but the role he plays with Eugene is a complementary one: that of the father-god who might save his son and does not. Though solicitous throughout, he gives Eugene no support in his venture; and solicitude and unreliability, as usual, make a perilous combination here — Mr. Lougheed arrives at the pier just in time to call Eugene out of the water, whereupon Eugene "bowed his head and went under" (86).[140] And as he is settling his nerves with coffee afterwards, Mr. Lougheed remembers or imagines something he has long been unable to bring back, the ending of a recurrent dream. This last arose from an early incident of his own life, a crisis in which his father had not trusted a son's ability to follow him; as a boy in the dream Mr. Lougheed does follow, but only to find himself alone on a rickety bridge, looking down at another boy lying on the river-bottom. Waking to the present, he is seized with anxiety, for Eugene and less overtly for himself — at the end of the story he is about to move to higher lodgings.

The most positive interpretation we can put on the story, taken in this way, is that the Old Woman has done her work: Eugene and Mr. Lougheed in their different ways have gone past caring and exposed their fallenness, both severally and in their mutual attachment and betrayal. And Mr. Lougheed for one has learned a lesson, if a bitter one. But this account leaves out what takes us beyond the Old Woman's tricks: in particular it leaves out an element of the dream that the lock-headed Mr. Lougheed himself is quick to dismiss with his waking mind. To his dreaming self the boy seen from the bridge had not appeared a cause of anxiety at all: he had been lying quietly among stones in the shallow water, appearing "just as natural a sight as the stones, and as clean and white" (90). What is foolishness to the rational world here is an innocent's vision of innocence, like the simpleton's vision of Caroline's eyes as white, or the children's vision of Lloyd Sallows as a "white fellow" (215) in the swamp. Such a vision is "pure reality" again,[141] something more than either fact or fiction. It is sent by the self in which Mr. Lougheed and Eugene are one, here using the agency of Eugene — the Eugene who found he liked being under water — to unlock a memory beyond memory in Mr. Lougheed.

*

If the over-anxious Mr. Lougheed could believe with his waking self what he believes in his dream, he would know the right way to walk on water and could help Eugene to do so. The ending of the story is suggestive here: Mr. Lougheed appeals to Calla, the moon-like female member of the downstairs trio, and finds her response to Eugene's possible suicide one of complete equanimity — "if that's what he was going to do, then nobody ought to stop him, should they? Or feel sad about him" (92). Perhaps Calla's callousness is as unsatisfactory as Mr. Lougheed's anxiety, but it too gives us one image of a greater wisdom — of love that is also forbearance, thoughtfulness that is not taking thought. The faith that sees, and is, the boy lying quietly in the river is not a desperate attempt to get or give rescue, or even a confidence that rescue will come, but the assurance that rescue is not needed — the assurance of a "well" in which there is no danger.[142] With faith of this kind a higher self — Eugene's or Mr. Lougheed's — looks down at the lower one that has entered the natural element of experience, while both selves pass over in safety.

We have another image of this faith, if again only an image, in what I take to be a sister-story, "Miles City, Montana." Here, as we have found,[143] parents' ability to rescue a daughter from drowning is something that cannot be relied on. Better, the narrator feels, the simple indifference to his son shown by Steve Gauley's father, even if that meant letting Steve drown. Better still, one might add, the family scene that we found Phemie imagining at the end of "The Progress of Love" — her mother burning the inheritance money, her father present not to interfere but to give her his support:

> People doing something that seems to them natural and neces-
> sary. At least, one of them is doing what seems natural and

necessary, and the other believes that the important thing is for that person to be free, to go ahead. (30)

The mother here is the self that goes down into the water; the father is the self that watches; and both in this moment make up the greater self that is faith, unity in freedom. Children, as the narrator of "Miles City, Montana" understands, know that "by rights they should have sprung up free, to live a new, superior kind of life, not to be caught in the snares of vanquished grownups, with their sex and funerals" (104).[144] The faith that makes this claim is not a belief that sex and funerals can be avoided — it does not deny the fact of nature. Rather, it is the power of a Lloyd Sallows who can live in the ice or fire of the world, feeding on the flesh of carnality itself; and by the same token it is "God real, and really in the world" (115) — the genuine form of such a God, that is, for which the elusive and indifferent God in "Age of Faith" provides only a spectre.

In "Who Do You Think You Are?" we can find this faith in Milton Homer, who along with his mimicking makes a practice of baptizing the local babies.[145] In doing so he predicts that the child will live or die as the case may be, but that in either event it will not sin. He does not say that it will make no mistakes: the "major explosion of *lives*" (191), as he intones the word, can well stand for the various blow-ups into which he and others always manage to stumble. But Milton frees the children in advance from the guilt he has had loaded onto himself (it is Milton who comes across the bridge yelling "I did not and I did not and I did not!" [189] as if the ten commandments were being thrown at him one by one). He is thus like the Miss Marsalles who knows that children have music in their hearts, or the Bobby Sherriff who knows that Del is a scholar. And in the end Rose receives Milton's baptism in a further way: as the wave of forgiveness flowing to her from another doomed fool, Ralph Gillespie. Elsewhere in Munro forgiveness is a trick played to ensnare victims;[146] here it is an invitation to a bond of faith. And through this bond the divided can also be "the same, the same" (204) — two people can be one, the past can be the present[147] beyond the mere natural continuance or coinherence that is Hanratty.[148] Ralph warrants Rose to be in her way what he has been in his, calling her to himself while giving her her liberty; and so they will keep their mysterious closeness as she goes on with her own life and he goes to his own death.[149]

II: A Whole Word

When Bobby Sherriff offers Del his parting gesture, this seems to her "a letter, or a whole word, in an alphabet I did not know" (254). A word (or "letter," no doubt with a secondary meaning to it) would certainly be the most concentrated form of the stories and discourses we have just been looking at; and much earlier we found Rose sensing wholeness — a resolving of all contrariety — in the word "drum-lin."[150] At that point I had been speaking in terms of presentation, a story as delivered by one person to another. Afterwards we turned to the world of the presented by itself, but in the end we found there what we had found before: that wholeness in its genuine form is a one made by the mutual self-offering of two. Such a wholeness is not "there" but has its life in the offering itself — which indicates for one thing that we no longer need our distinction between presentation and presented. But it seems that this acceptable offering is also acceptable speech (or expression more generally, since Bobby's gesture is hardly a "word" of the usual kind). If this is so we can ask again, and now in a more adequate context, what magic there can be in a word like "drumlin": the word that for Rose means the opening of a door no common power can open.

Asking this question will also take us back to the strange business of mediation. On the one hand, something that only mediates -- a mere sign such as a word -- seems nothing in itself. On the other hand, this nothing can be very much a something: a trickster-servant, as we imagined earlier, who increasingly plays the master. And whatever its supposed function, mediation can be the thickest of obstacles if those it connects would like to unite beyond mere connection — or any more complex form of the same thing. In Del Jordan's gothic novel the heroine's general habit of slipping sideways comes from efforts to "get through a crack in an invisible wall" (246).[151]

Del herself, as she sits on the Sherriffs' front porch, is looking at another wall, that of the building across the street. In fact she observes this wall in precise detail:

> That back wall had no windows in it; it had certain stains, chipped bricks, a long crack running down diagonally, starting a bit before the middle and ending up at the bottom corner next to the Chainway store. (252)

Perhaps the echoes here of Diagonal Roads, menials enslaved to the Chainway, and so on, can speak for themselves, as can the resemblance between what Del is faced with and Munro's other blank partitions, photographer's screens, and planetarium ceilings — some of which have cracks like the wall that Del sees here.[152] Any of these may have the effect of drawing one on — the particular wall Del is facing is that of the *Herald-Advance* building — but that does not make them less opaque. And as Del sits staring, other things are equally so. She notices the burning of refuse; she thinks of the banks opening, the bus leaving at the meridian hour:[153] and like what Bobby is saying to her, these things all remain a blank wall, observed with the curiosity of boredom.[154] It is true that, like her heroine, Del notices the crack in the wall — Munro's streak again, now suggesting an opening; she even perceives that Caroline is Marion. But at the point she has reached, this identity remains only a disturbing paradox.[155]

There are two complementary ways to imagine the overcoming of this paradox, and both of them can be of help to us here. When Del sees that Caroline and Marion are the same, she is on the point of discovering that there is no wall, only a trickster's illusion of one: and this means an end to the same wall in the form of images and signs — words in our extended sense. But in another view words are the opposite of something to be got through and got rid of. We saw how characters in Munro's Exodus stories covet what we can loosely call things: mental or physical entities to be accumulated. We also saw how words themselves, as accumulated in the various Great Books, may only be more things — pieces of natural wisdom like the melting candy in country stores.[156] But this carnal bread might turn into Bobby Sherriff's more nourishing kind if were gathered into a "whole word" — the word of which it is the broken fragments.[157]

Such a word is neither nothing nor an obstructive something, but in the truest sense everything: what we have seen as only connecting, and by the same token separating, we can now see as comprehending. In the same way metaphor, transcending itself, has become not a yoking together of contraries but a oneness in which contrariety is transformed. As they near a final threshold Munro's characters often find something troubling about words as such: in effect, their meta-phorical nature. Rose, we have seen, will not put her faith in "translation" (205), which means the same thing as "metaphor"; Mrs. Jordan frets over the lost "crossword" (91).[158] Her daughter is of course equally puzzled by Bobby's parting message — but then this is the Del who also sits staring at a wall. If Del understood Bobby's word, she would find it to be not one that crosses in the sense of either blocking or penetrating, but one in which all things cross. What it expresses is itself, and that is why Bobby is speaking with authority. So are Albert and Phemie when the stories they produce, however unsatisfactory as fact or fiction, are in the deepest sense their own stories.

The question of communicating leads to the same resolution. We have found Munro's characters holding back — on grounds of "honorable restraint" (206), Rose would like to think — and we have found them chattering and lecturing. But beyond this natural discretion or indiscretion there is the baptismal sentence conveyed by Ralph to Rose — "though certainly no words of that kind had been spoken" (205) — or Janet's bond with the father and daughter who, in different ways, choose to remain "incommunicado" (230). There is more, as well as less, than "honorable restraint" in Rose's decision not to tell about Ralph Gillespie, or Phemie's decision not to tell about her mother's burning of the money. There is more, similarly, in speech itself when it reaches beyond communication to communion. This is the language, not of Del's stillborn gothic thriller or her equally stillborn collection of facts, but of the novel that she — or her author — does give to the world, where the something she has been meaning to tell is told in the only way possible. It is the presence of this better language that redeems the merely natural, in which truth and reality can do no more than point to each other. Having its benediction, Rose can go safely on in her Old Woman's career of mimicry and tattling — entertainer's tricks that, with their best will, serve something beyond trickery.

*

With the assent to Bobby's word, and Ralph's, opposites thus return to their origin: a simplicity like that of the point which, as I have suggested, both begins and ends the series of narrative figures.[159] If this were so in merely a cyclical sense, we might feel that the problem of opposition with which this study began was never there, or there as a meaningless illusion that could as well have been ignored. But as we also saw, this is what we are tempted to feel whenever a polarity confounds itself: when, for instance, we find Mary and Elizabeth turning into each another. And what must be said to the temptation is always the same thing. The opposites are not ultimately separate things, yet we do experience them as separate, even as opposed, and this experience is not meaningless or worthless. The only oneness our humanity can ultimately accept is that in which two, while affirming their individual selves, also freely and knowingly offer these selves to one another; and for a vision of such oneness we must imagine a story — to take the temporal route we have followed in the last chapters — in which the two first move apart and then unite again. Nor is their reunion merely cyclical or even typological: they are now "held still and held together"[160] in a story that has become a single word — one that can enfold the full human story, the word that is life itself.

It is this word that we may be hearing, in an odd way, when Rose investigates the County Home in "Spelling." She finds there a senile old woman who can do nothing but spell words, using all her remaining power to keep the thread of letters unbroken to the end.[161] We have seen this retentive old creature as an Elizabeth, and we might have seen her as our more comprehensive Old Woman, with the Old Woman's limitations; yet there could be more to her than that. Perhaps, as Rose imagines, she finds in words only their ordinary meanings, or no meaning at all; perhaps, though, each word for her is "marvelous and distinct and alive as a new animal" (184). We could say the same thing about the words, or word, of Almeda Roth's poetry, and especially the poem that was to have been the Meneseteung River itself. Almeda, like the woman in "Spelling," has her natural shortcomings: she looks askance at the hapless Queen Aggie, and turns to her poem when unable to love her neighbour Jarvis Poulter. The poem itself is conceived in a state of delusion; if it were actually written out it would not — judging from the rest of Almeda's output — be any masterpiece. Yet she has at least imagined a word of life, and for our present concern that is what matters: image here is substance, and the willingness to say a word is itself the word. That is why this withdrawn spinster can also be a Messenger speaking to the narrator from beyond the grave.[162]

Almeda identifies herself with a river: Del Jordan's name, we can recall, makes the same kind of identification.[163] So, if we like, does the name "Alice Munro" — "Munro" being derived from the river Roe in Ireland;[164] and in any case there is a more local river with which Munro can be associated. In 1974 she published a short article[165] about her home, "Loretown" — a "straggling, unincorporated, sometimes legendary non-part" of Wingham, Ontario; the same article introduces the local river, the Maitland which is also the Meneseteung. In this river are fish like those caught to begin the world in "The Flats Road," a Flood that comes with "Biblical inevitability," and a great deal more: for "I am still partly convinced that this river

— not even the whole river, but this little stretch of it — will provide whatever myths you want, whatever adventures." The same thing, as I have tried to indicate, is true of Munro's writing itself as it follows its not very extensive course. And while its adventures may often come to tragic ends — the river itself supposedly has "deep holes, ominous beckoning places," eerie enough to satisfy Uncle Benny — there is something here that transforms even the depths.

We saw how an unincorporated region like the Ottawa Valley can equally be the Church of St. John, where the Creator is celebrated for the bright and beautiful things he has made. Munro speaks with the same wonder of the living creatures along the river, or the names which they also are: "I name the plants, I name the fish, and every name seems to me triumphant, every leaf and quick fish remarkably valuable." And so, she concludes, "this ordinary place is sufficient, everything here touchable and mysterious." The touchability of things is their reality, the mystery of them is their truth — or, if we prefer, their truth is what can be grasped and their reality what remains mysterious, as in a way reality always does; but in either case it is by the grace of naming, and its counterpart story-telling, that these contraries are gathered into one. Through names and stories, then, Munro offers us true reality: the ordinary made marvellous in its distinctness and the abundance of its life.

NOTES

[1] See also 33–37, and the incidents referred to there.

[2] See above, 166, 174.

[3] In "Rose Matilda" Joan has a lover, but as for her old life of passion, "it's as if she had once gone in for skydiving" (207). In "Wigtime" the two friends have given up on earlier sexual hopes, and now sit recalling their adventures.

[4] "We never behave as if we believed we were going to die," says Georgia at the end of "Differently" (242). With their retrospective character, the Caroline stories — including in a way "The Photographer" — are haunted by the same sense of a mistaken and now unchangeable past. The sense of useless memory appears at the very end of certain other Passion stories as well, such as "Baptizing" and "Executioners"; it is very much on Joan's mind as she returns to Logan in "Rose Matilda."

[5] The aunt's name is Bernice; the minuet from *Berenice* is also what the narrator plays in "Dance of the Happy Shades." The Bernice of Acts 25–26 was a queen, later the mistress of an emperor.

[6] This means that both Dodie and the mother are playing the role of tragic king as well as of queen: but it is the role itself that matters here. See above, 504

ff., for further considerations.

7 See above, 157 n32. In relation to *The Dry Salvages* as cyclical, *Little Gidding* can be seen typologically, but here I am seeing it as expressing a greater identity than any in the merely given world. See above, 503–05

8 In other words, Allen is one of Munro's cowboys (see above, 240–41). Perhaps we can also hear words like "whole," "hole," and "stein" in "Holstein": that would at any rate be in keeping with the rest of the story.

9 Rev. 4:11.

10 In "The Moons of Jupiter" the voice in the Planetarium reminds Janet of the way radio announcers used to describe "the progress of the Royal Family to Westminster Abbey on one of their royal occasions" (230).

11 Cf. John 19:30; also of course the many references to ending in Revelation.

12 See above, 391, 403.

13 Cf. the baby produced by the Crydermans in "Jesse and Meribeth": "quite normal, as far as anyone knew" (186).

14 Billy Pope's splendid car in "Half a Grapefruit" was of the same type that, in "The Photographer," people are buying on postwar money — a new Oldsmobile.

15 It may be significant that in "Labor Day Dinner" Valerie's daughters beg her, "Don't put on your *panty* hose" (138). Apart from the word "pants" itself, the missing garter belt in the Jerry Storey episode can be seen the same way — without it Del cannot put on her stockings and more generally pull herself together.

16 I have noted the derivation of "Allen" from "Alan," a barbarian Germanic tribe (see above, 249 n19); but the word itself means "all men."

17 Rev. 14:2.

18 In the hospital in "The Moons of Jupiter" announcements are similarly made on a loudspeaker (233). "The Funeral Goer" features a hidden singer.

19 At the Art Gallery in "The Ferguson Girls," Nola hears from behind the walls "constant, muffled sounds" (35) (actually of quarrelling in this case) which she cannot make out.

20 In "The Ferguson Girls," for instance, there is "the canned music of an electric organ" (31).

21 "The Moons of Jupiter" 230.

22 Here Munro's "temples" shade into a large number of rooms that we first met as Refuges (see above, 142–44).

23 See "Circle of Prayer" 262.

24 "The Widower" n.pag.

25 Cf. the "bowl of the ceiling" (which turns into the night sky) at the Planetarium in "The Moons of Jupiter" 230.

26 When Stella in "Lichen" is referred to by Catherine as "older," David starts to wonder: "Older than the house? Older than Lake Huron? Older than the cat?" (that is, Hercules the tomcat) (33).

27 See "Lichen" 46.

28 I have noted various maternal figures who refuse drink (see references in 459 n159 above). For Apocalypse examples see "The Ottawa Valley" 237, also "Winter Wind" — in which the family patriarch was a "a drinker, a great celebrator" who changed his ways to become a hard-working settler with a "mollified wife" (194).

29 See above, 242–43.

30 Although a skeleton, the grandmother has a look of pregnancy: she contains the whole cycle of things, like the ribs or shell that seem to contain the dawn of the story's opening. But as May discovers, there can be no birth from her.

31 Cf. the wise women of the Exodus stories, to which "A Trip to the Coast" is clearly related. See above, 373–74

32 There are also those whom the Old Woman notices but in some way cannot grasp, for all her wisdom. The fortune-telling neighbour in "Simon's Luck" cannot get Simon into her "focus" (165); Bugs in "Goodness and Mercy" cannot get her satirical claws into the captain; Callie at the end of "The Moon in the Orange Street Skating Rink" cannot understand what Sam wants. The captain and Sam are not of course simple outcasts, any more than Rose's neighbour in "Simon's Luck" is simply the malevolent Old Woman: but precisely in not being "needy" (167) — as Averill imagines — the captain has a curious independence. Sam is, if not an outcast, certainly an outsider to the circle in which Callie keeps Edgar contentedly imprisoned.

33 The cousins in "Connection," for instance, and especially Iris, "brash and greedy and scared" (16).

34 At the end of "The Ottawa Valley" the narrator herself has become an Old Woman haunted by her mother. In "Home" it is again a mother who plays revenant — haunting Irlma or more precisely the narrator's acceptance of Irlma.

35 I have noted the same wordplay in "Oranges and Apples," 106 (see above, 349 n159).

36 See above, 417, 460 n166.

37 For the "tiplady" see above, 224, 233, 256 n104.

38 See "Rose Matilda" 208.

39 See Matt. 25:15.

40 *Lives of Girls and Women*, with no distinct chapter to correspond to "Spelling," has the estrangement and temporary reunion of Del and Naomi within "Baptizing."

41 The thematic use of siblings, as Martin notes (*Paradox* 23), is widespread in Munro: what I mean here by "Sibling stories," however, is somewhat more special.

42 See above, 228.

43 See above, 204. At the end of the story Anita reflects that, after years of having one's life "undermined" by a man, "one day there's nothing, just a hollow where he was" (273) — and she seems to be thinking of Reuel as well as, no

doubt, the man for whom she left her husband.

44 We can think, for instance, of the two fathers. Anita's is decidedly upstaged by her increasingly assertive mother; Margot's seems to go in for royal beatings, an alternative to the more passive kind of weakness. Anita may well be right in thinking that Margot is more frightened than she pretends; but when Margot chooses a similarly bullying man for herself, she gets control of him in the end. And while Anita's style is different, her men eventually make a collection in her mind, a "tidy buildup" (272).

45 There is also a striking resemblance between Margot and Trudy in "Circle of Prayer." Margot too is staggeringly blunt; she plays up to the man she wants, is callous to the older woman she supplants, and in later life finds herself in the older woman's situation.

46 In "Visitors" we hear of a mother who died giving birth to Wilfred, bringing about the separation of the family. This mother was not disposed of, nor are Wilfred and Albert conspirators in any ordinary sense: once again, I am emphasizing a particular version of the story.

47 "Wigtime" resembles other stories in the group partly in its main action and partly in its frame-story. In the latter we have Margot's new house triumphantly on display; we then have Margot blurting out "Do you want to know really how I got this house?" (263), and telling the "wigtime" anecdote. In the presentation, what has come just before Margot's outburst is the central fact in the two women's relation: Margot once took Reuel for herself while keeping the business a secret from Anita. Anita says nothing of this, yet it is evidently on her mind; and no doubt her very presence would be enough to force Margot's confession after a while — the confession that Margot herself has been betrayed, and that the house is only a compensation.

48 Structurally "The Peace of Utrecht" is two stories, typographically distinguished. It is in the first of these that Helen undermines Maddy's triumph at the party; in the second Aunt Annie undermines the bond between the sisters much more deeply by her revelation and her offer of the dead mother's clothes.

49 The homestead, on higher ground than the swamp, is potentially an upper Refuge, again with a message if the visitors could make it out.

50 As always, we can see the same agency as that of fate or law rather than chance: the Flo of "Spelling" is the most relentless of legalists and scorners. Rose here, wanting victory in her "old, old competition" (179) with Brian, first means to be Flo's triumphantly dutiful nurse, then at least to get her smoothly into the County Home. Flo thinks otherwise.

51 Lana within the "wigtime" story unwittingly helps Margot to get a new house, though what matters at the end is the comradeship of Margot and Anita — who has in effect played confessor to her friend.

52 See above, 297–300 for the same kind of relation in the context of the main central phase.

53 Cf. the war between Rose and Brian ("who is the better person, who has

chosen the better work?" [179]), which they are somehow unable to stop. Secretly they want each other's approval, "which perhaps they meant to grant, in full, but not yet."

54 A few other non-final stories with an Epilogue flavour at their endings or throughout are "Home" (closely related to "The Moons of Jupiter"), "The Spanish Lady," "Simon's Luck," "Dulse," "Hold Me Fast, Don't Let Me Pass," "Pictures of the Ice," and "The Ferguson Girls Must Never Marry." And there is an Epilogue tinge to any Judges story — any story, that is, about a Pied Piper.

55 Note also that after the war between the siblings — Brian and Rose — in "Spelling," "Who Do You Think You Are?" immediately shows their almost magical solidarity when recalling Milton Homer.

56 For the final scene of "Circle of Prayer" the inmates of the Home are all safely asleep, including the two who had given Kelvin trouble earlier, "Marie and Josephine" (270). In "The Ottawa Valley" Bernice the legal secretary fails to meet the train in Toronto: the story is going to be an Epilogue among other things.

57 This particular Tom is made to sound like Tom in "Providence" — a fatherly but sceptical and undependable bearer of the name. For "Tom" see above, 56–57.

58 For other "idiots" — numerous in Munro — see above, 266, 397.

59 Kelvin in "Circle of Prayer" is fifty-two but still "boyish" (257). Another boyish man, and certainly a Messenger among other things, is the middle-aged Dudley Brown in "Hold Me Fast, Don't Let Me Pass."

60 See above, 58.

61 The dying fathers in "Home" and "The Moons of Jupiter" are exceptions that prove a rule: they have intimations they consider idiotic while doing their best to be sane.

62 Note that she applies the same word to her father's younger self: "the survivor" (220).

63 See John 20:16.

64 Among the "lock-headed fathers" (see above, 33) the one in "Home" especially has the same exhausted and uncomprehending look as Kelvin.

65 "The Moons of Jupiter" 232. Formally, the Messenger can be either host or visitor in a given situation: when Denise plays Fairy Godmother at one point in "White Dump," she is acting as visitor.

66 Cf. Rose and Brian laughing together in "Who Do You Think You Are?" when Rose does her imitation; Trudy and Kelvin playing Crazy Eights in "Circle of Prayer"; Hazel and Dudley Brown in "Hold Me Fast, Don't Let Me Pass" sharing "Tam Lin" as well as a silly naming contest; Joan and Morris in "Rose Matilda" remembering Landor's "Rose Aylmer."

67 Several specific times are mentioned during Del's visit, and for what it is worth, I will suggest that Del is going through a kind of crucifixion — as Bobby has done already. (This means condensing a day into a morning, and in any case the biblical "hours" do not mean the same thing as our own.) At six o'clock the

priestly Mrs. Sherriff makes her departure: in the story of the Crucifixion, correspondingly, it is at the sixth hour that the natural order fails and darkness covers the earth. As she sits on the Sherriffs' porch Del herself has reached the ninth hour ("between nine and ten o'clock" [248]), when Jesus dies. After Jesus's death comes the opening of temple, earth, and graves: in Jubilee the banks will open at ten. Just after noon a bus will go through town, stopping if flagged at Haines's Restaurant, where Del and Jerry have been meeting to plan their great escape. Noon here may seem to break the correspondence, but we have seen how Munro associates mid-day and midnight; and the latter is the time of the original Passover, prefiguring both death and liberation in the Passion. See above, 114–15, 372–73.

68 See also Bailey 117, for suggestive thoughts on Bobby as Jungian Wise Man, or as Wise Fool.

69 See Martin, *Paradox* 126. Martin also comments on the motif of art in the final stories.

70 In the epilogue at the end of "Hold Me Fast, Don't Let Me Pass" — a conversation in a neglected lounge between a lonely tourist and a boyish, elusive local bachelor — sexual feeling does well up, but has to pass before the Epilogue experience can continue. What happens in the central incident of "The Spanish Lady" is fairly similar: the heroine converses briefly, and not quite sexually, with a lonely and unsuccessful real-estate man met on a train.

71 See Matt. 6:8. (Also Rom. 8:26).

72 See Blodgett's discussion of this passage (150). Having argued that Munro's characters must learn to accept contradiction and uncertainty — "to be 'at the mercy' without asking for much more" (126) — he sees "possibilities of archetypal coherence" (151) here, and suggests that these may put other stories in a new light. Cf. also Sam's musing in "The Moon in the Orange Street Skating Rink" as he thinks back to the moment of happiness on the train many years before: "do such moments really mean, as they seem to, that we have a life of happiness with which we only occasionally, knowingly, intersect?" (160). Trudy in "Circle of Prayer" thinks of these moments as "breathing spaces" (273) in which we stand outside our own unhappiness — though they also occur as a sadness outside happiness, and are thus a transcendence of what we usually mean by these terms altogether.

73 York (*Other Side* 39–40) sees this passage somewhat differently.

74 In "The Beggar Maid" Rose has an intimation of a "radiantly kind and innocent Rose and Patrick, hardly ever visible, in the shadow of their usual selves" (95).

75 My argument at this stage is different from Carrington's in her thoughtful study. I fully agree that "shame, humiliation, and the abdication of power" (5) are prominent features of Munro's stories, that the afflicted split themselves apart to become watchers of their own experience, and that they may achieve a working if precarious *modus vivendi* — which, as Munro herself has said, we all need if

we are to survive in the world as it is. But what Munro's Epilogue experiences ask for is something other than control, or even controlled indulgence. The mundane outcome of such experiences is another matter — they may help one to keep going, they may get one into trouble — but the vision they offer is life itself. This is why I would understand the true "walking on water," for instance, as the opposite of control (see below, 529), and see Eileen's appearance in the mirror as something more than a self-serving delusion. Dahlie's argument in "Unconsummated Relationships: Isolation and Rejection in Alice Munro" is similar to Carrington's.

[76] See above, 488; also 253 n71.

[77] For boredom as a response to an unshared belief, see above, 406, and 455 n108.

[78] In Godard's view (Miller 69) Del, having used and disposed of Garnet French, is now using and disposing of Bobby, quite properly in both cases; she is thus becoming "assertive, independent, her own being" (70). But what the narrating Del says here is that at the time she was too self-absorbed to be grateful for a kindness.

[79] Laurence in "White Dump," receiving his daughter's fairy blessing, is or pretends to be more appreciative, but like Del he clearly assumes that he is only getting his just deserts. Even someone like the narrator of "Tell Me Yes or No," who at one point says "Yes" (113) with tears of gratitude, does not fully understand what she is saying, as we can see from her bewilderment at the sequel.

[80] See above, 36, where I emphasize what is genuine in this same experience.

[81] When Austin Cobbett, similarly, sends Karin the pictures of the glittering ice, he himself is not present in them — or is present precisely in being absent. For as Karin now knows, he has given himself to the different ice of reality: "Shaft Lake" near "Thunder Bay" (152) (which, incidentally, is the same place as Port Arthur).

[82] See above, 535 n5.

[83] We must never expect strict correspondence between stories. In a way Del remains proud to the end, and hardly conscious of any rapport with Bobby; Rose, who is less proud, already feels a flash of camaraderie with Ralph Gillespie at what is structurally the mid-point of the action — though she will falter when she tries to communicate with him directly, and experience her sense of mysterious closeness only later.

[84] Similarly the full significance of the Dance of the Happy Shades comes as a communiqué from Miss Marsalles as the narrator is driving home.

[85] See Eldredge 113–15, for a similar analysis of "The Photographer."

[86] The screen has been taken up by the time she returns to her seat. What this means, I think, is that outer vision is going to become inner.

[87] In other words he is like any central-phase high god. A more immediate analogue is Hugh in "The Spanish Lady"; another important one is the captain in "Goodness and Mercy," since this story develops, on its ambiguous terms, all

the way to the epilogue experience we are concerned with here.

88 Cf. the spoken and unspoken taunting of Mary Jo by "Rhea" (see above, 251 n52): "you think he's God . . . the Great Healer" (191).

89 For different readings of this dream, see Carrington 161–62; Rasporich, *Dance* 117.

90 These are like certain of the flowers of late summer noticed by Mildred in "Visitors": "Goldenrod she knew, and wild carrot, but what were these little white flowers on a low bush, and this blue one with coarse petals, and this feathery purple?" (211).

91 Cf. Luke 1:38.

92 The Suicide Woman, with her hair blowing across her face, is one of the story's several figures of fortune — the Occasion whom you must take by the forelock; but in spite of her own good fortune in the form of a well-heeled new husband, she plays the same role as Eileen here, undermining Rose's success by bringing the news of Simon's death. She toys with this news in a way that suggests — to Rose herself as well as the reader — that there is rivalry between the two women. Yet "that slyness could ask for help, as well as measure victories and surprises" (172): we sense that the Suicide Woman herself had responded to Simon, and is asking for reconciliation on that basis.

93 Martin sees Rose, like Del, as reaching "increasing stability, self-knowledge, and sense of purpose" (*Paradox*, 106); thus she is able to cope with "disarrangements" like the news of Simon's death. I see less stability in either heroine, and feel that, such as it is, it serves partly as a barrier against the greater illumination offered in the "disarrangement." Thus I am also less inclined to see the all-arranging Valerie, for instance, simply as a model. At the same time, Martin brings out Valerie's openness and considerateness: these qualities can be seen as continuous with the greater "courtesy" in my sense, even if — as I feel — we also need to see a discontinuity here. Howells's reading of "Simon's Luck" is essentially similar to Martin's: to gain "self-possession" (81) Rose must "readjust" to reality (86), of which the news of Simon's death is a part.

94 For the associations of "Dan" see above, 440–42. Austin Cobbett in "Pictures of the Ice," another sacrificial figure as well as a man of faith, wears similar colours. "Burgundy" suggests not only a world of chivalry but wine — or blood. "Mustard" seems to mean different things in Munro (something hot, for example), but both faith and the Kingdom of Heaven are like mustard seed (Matt. 13:31, 17:20), and mustard would seem to have this association in, for instance, "Walking on Water" (79), very much a story about faith.

95 Note a similar phrase giving an epilogue tone to the end of "Wigtime": "everything seems bright and distinct and harmless. Spellbound" (273).

96 If we see one of the things as the indefinite, as in some contemporary criticism, we have still not overcome the stubbornness of their opposition: we have only defined indefiniteness as another kind of thing, and taken infinite regression a step further. See Kamboureli 31 ff.

[97] In "The Ferguson Girls Must Never Marry" Bonnie reaches complete isolation and indifference as she walks across town. At the Braddocks' house she hears Ted's words about the saving of Nola's soul, and suddenly sees her vision of souls as pilgrims. Then comes her sense of rending birth-pains: and in the end Ted says simply "You're welcome to stay" (64).

[98] See "Spelling" 174.

[99] For similar behaviour in a different context, see above, 32–33.

[100] See above, 431–32.

[101] "Did she really want to be rescued?" (196) wonders the narrator. The rest of this section will suggest an answer.

[102] "Ivie" is not only "ivy" but fairly close to "Eve." (As mentioned above, 448 n14, "Edie" in "How I Met My Husband" was once "Eva.") Among other grieving mothers there is the very mythical Mrs. Brooke in "The Edge of Town" with her two lost sons.

[103] June in "Memorial" belongs here as a secretly grieving mother: having made her "offering" at the end, she sits with "downward profile" (226).

[104] See above, 542 n92. In "Memorial" it is the death of her husband that makes the mother show herself to Eileen as someone "frail and still; almost, almost . . . an ordinary woman" (221).

[105] To see the Old Woman suggesting one of the paradoxically royal Messengers, we can think of the dream-Flo in "Spelling" (184), enthroned and speaking with authority, an oracular bird in a marvellous cage. The terms used for the dream-mother in "Friend of My Youth" (26) are notably similar.

[106] I think we can sense here both the rent veil of the Temple and the garment of Christ. See above, 238.

[107] See Ezek. 28:13, also above, 250 n41.

[108] The other Miss Marsalles is older and grimmer (and not directly present, suggesting figures like the absent Mrs. Sherriff), but we are told that both sisters are kindly, and they can readily be seen as allies like the confident Miss Hattie and the withdrawing Miss Mattie.

[109] Dodie looks like a "gypsy" (243) here, suggesting that we might reconsider our view of gipsies. Flora in "Friend of My Youth," whom the narrator suspects of trickery, seemed to the narrator's mother to have something splendid about her: "A gypsy queen, my mother thought she looked like, with her . . . lithe and bold serenity" (8).

[110] Once again, this is not to say that the "woman" must be represented by a female character in Munro. We have "male" and "female" archetypes here if we see assertion as a masculine principle and reception as a feminine; but even within the world of archetypal myths these principles quickly trade roles to produce their own contraries — dominating female figures and withdrawn or elusive male ones. These are archetypes, moreover, and not concrete human beings (real or fictitious): the closer we come to these latter, the harder it is to make generalizations. I cannot agree with critics who argue that enforcing or arranging or

theorizing is largely found in Munro's male characters, and resistance to it largely in her female: the evidence seems to me much too varied for that. Rather, I have been trying to show in this book how roles and players shift their alignments in her work, and also how, in an adequate analysis, these roles are played reciprocally — what is done to us is what we do to others. When Rose sees what she sees at the end of "Simon's Luck" — that opposite people share the same human condition — she is approaching the heart of Munro's vision.

111 "Tell Me Yes or No" 111. The narrator's lover declares himself when the two meet years after their initial encounter: this makes a story in itself, though here part of a larger tragedy in which the heroine is abandoned.

112 One important example comes at the end of "Material," when Gabriel leaves the vindictive narrator alone to "get over it" (44) — acting for her own good, in our present reading.

113 In any case it is the business of such old women to hand out their "five dollar bills," "making sure the haunts we have contracted for are with us, not one gone without" ("The Peace of Utrecht" 209). See above, 208–09

114 See above, 215–16, 393–94, 437–38.

115 Note that the relation between "male" and "female" here is like that between Upper God and Undergod.

116 There can be any number of variations. The triumphant mother turns out to be dying; the luckless and subversive Dodie, who tells the narrator about death, is a laughing Comforter. The "coquettish" (203) Aunt Annie plays the subversive role again, but without any note of comfort. Eileen proves "hospitable" (223) as well as subversive, though through most of the story she is the brooding sister and June the seemingly cheerful one.

117 See John 14:8–11.

118 Auntie Grace in "Heirs of the Living Body" masquerades as a "darky" herself to jump out at the Austrian (the counterpart of "Mr. Black" in "The Stone in the Field"): "I made up my mind I'd show him" (33), she says.

119 Cf. "Spelling" 186: "Of course it was possible that [Rose] did, secretly, want Flo to come [to the prize-giving], wanted to show Flo, intimidate her, finally remove herself from Flo's shade. That would be a natural thing to want to do."

120 For the same question in a different context, see above, 154.

121 Note especially that Eileen "would try when desperate to turn June's own language against her, using it flippantly and high-handedly" (210).

122 We can also think here of all Munro's blinds, some with "lightning cracks" ("Images" 31, and see above, 114–16, 238). The Old Woman may be hiding inside the blind ("Spelling," 174) or tricking others who are doing so: this depends on which form of the "God and Nature" story we are seeing.

123 See Mark 5:9.

124 These may seem odd archetypes for Munro's Milton Homer: evidently the relation is partly an ironic one. But they too practised the art of mimesis — we can even say that in asserting eternal providence as an objective fact they made

a mockery of it; conversely, Milton Homer's foolery includes baptism that we have to take seriously.

125 "The Beggar Maid" 97.

126 Cf. Flora in "Friend of My Youth," an initiatory story related to others like "The Progress of Love," yet sharing more with "The Ottawa Valley" than its setting. The mysterious Flora is like the mother and Dodie together, a strict (if not priggish) woman who also has the air of a gipsy. (If met later in life she would smile with both kindness and "a degree of mockery, a faint, self-assured malice" [26]). Flora may be a saint or a witch or neither: what matters at present is that she does sacrifice herself.

127 Cf. the "St. Augustine" for which Harry Brooke sets out in the end: a city of God, though dark as well as bright and offering Peach "Melba" (see above, 62).

128 Another motif important here appears at the end of "Wigtime," where the mad Teresa believes that her lover is coming to herself alone — "lucky her" (273). The theme of the man who cannot satisfy a plurality of women goes back to Munro's very early "Story for Sunday" and recurs in, for instance, "Circle of Prayer" and "Hold Me Fast, Don't Let Me Pass." To reverse the sexes we can think of Duval and Jimmy crying *Mine. Mine* over Helena. But the visionary city here is at once Del's own and a place for everybody and everything.

129 See above, 25–27.

130 See New, "Pronouns and Prepositions."

131 Del cannot understand Bobby Sherriff's strange parting gesture; the Spanish Lady cannot deliver the message received from the dying old man. When Rose hears Flo's "clear authoritative" (184) words in her dream in "Spelling," she cannot remember them on waking up.

132 Cf. the undersea telephone cable in "Dulse," the Telephone Road in "Labor Day Dinner."

133 See above, 27.

134 Exod. 2:22, 18:3.

135 "Lloyd" means "grey, hoary"; "sallow," of course, also means "willow," a symbol of mourning.

136 If we see a polarity in the names "Grace" and "Vera," Vera must be veracity in the sense of reality, not "truth" as elsewhere in the present book. See John 1:14 for "grace and truth."

137 Cf. "Miles City, Montana," in which the narrator remembers the bringing back of the dead Steve Gauley, though "I don't think I really saw all this" (84).

138 See above, 486.

139 Along with the echo of 1 Cor. 15:52 (Mr. Lougheed expects "a message that could flash out almost too quick for the eye to catch it" [80]) we can hear Paul in Eugene's cheerful acceptance of his own foolishness (see for instance 1 Cor. 1).

140 See John 19:30.

141 See above, 9.

142 Cf. the dream-mother's assurance in "Friend of My Youth" that her daughter's "bitter lump of love" (26) — the "bugbear" memory (4) of a woman dying from Parkinson's Disease — was not necessary. Once again, as with previous slicings and flashes, we learn that nothing really happened; but now the situation has been turned inside out — the comfort is not that the world is safe but that it does not need to be. The daughter, we can note, feels a bit cheated: like Mr. Lougheed she does not entirely want to give up her distress.

143 See above, 221.

144 Austin Cobbett in "Pictures of the Ice" says more or less the same thing, though from an opposite perspective: "Oh, what a tangled web we weave, when first we — have children. They always want us to be the same, they want us to be parents" (146). In "Walking on Water," read as we are now reading, Frank McArter's climactic piece of insanity, the killing of his father and mother, only demonstrates the killing of a relation as such: the interdependence of parent and child which must be outgrown if one is to reach freedom.

145 Note that Milton baptizes on his own authority — which means that he does not "call on the Father or the Son or do any business with water" (190).

146 See above, 328, for the aunts' forgiveness in "Heirs of the Living Body." In "Eskimo," one indication that the Eskimo girl's devotion is an "Epilogue" matter is the fact that it has "nothing so presumptuous as forgiveness or consolation" (204) about it. Ralph's "forgiveness" (205) is evidently like this non-forgiveness.

147 "I loved you for linking me with my past," says the narrator in "Tell Me Yes or No": "my life did not altogether fall away, in separate pieces, lost" (113). Lydia in "Dulse" is attracted to Vincent for the same reason, though in both stories, as we would expect, the bond we are now concerned with is involved with more imprisoning kinds.

148 See above, 268, 275. As a kind of Gideon, Frank Wales has an authority independent of worldly succession. Martin's idea of "the transmission and the inheritance of human tradition and spirit" (52) seems close to what I am trying to characterize here.

149 The main characters in "The Moons of Jupiter" are natural kin as Rose and Ralph are not, but inasmuch as they give one another the same warrant, nature itself becomes more than natural: "my father had chosen and Nichola had chosen. Someday, probably soon, I would hear from her, but it came to the same thing" (233). What the father has chosen is to chance a heart operation — to "go ahead" (30) as Phemie would put it.

150 See above, 38–39.

151 In Part II, Ch. 3 I treat Munro's Carolines as Passion figures: Caroline in "The Photographer," whose eyes turn from black to white after her death, takes us farther.

152 Cf. the walls of the family house in "The Peace of Utrecht" (197), of the

Jubilee town hall in "Baptizing" (210), and of the Chinese temples in "Who Do You Think You Are?" (197).

153 See above, 539 n67.

154 In other Epilogue stories we find variants. Janet in "The Moons of Jupiter" has always meant to look at the "relief carvings" (233) going round the tomb at the museum, but never quite does so; Rose looks at the pictures "all around the walls" (202) at the Legion, but without much interest — and is afterwards mainly concerned about the propriety of what she has done.

155 Del here is like Rose in "Simon's Luck" discovering that Simon was mortal like herself: see above, 501–02. In both cases this experience of shock is followed by an intimation of calling.

156 See above, 378–79.

157 See John 6:48, 63.

158 For the "crossword," see above, 377: Mrs. Jordan cannot remember the missing word "to save my soul" (91). At the end of "Baptizing" the same Mrs. Jordan has "torn the crossword out and taken it up to bed" (242): and so her daughter as well is denied the word that would save her. In the *New Yorker* version of "White Dump" the Log House contains a Scrabble set "with the X and one of the U's missing" (26): in the final version (279) Munro has changed the "X" to "Y" — as if a missing "X" in a word-game had come to seem too obvious a motif.

159 See above, 465–66.

160 *Lives of Girls and Women* 253.

161 Cf. the ancient Miss Dobie reciting her ballad in "Hold Me Fast, Don't Let Me Pass," "getting it out in the right order — word after word, line after line, verse after verse" (95).

162 "Meneseteung" is not in the main an Epilogue story, but Almeda herself — a lonely misfit, also a quaintly ceremonious one and, of course, a dabbler in the arts — comes into her own as a Messenger in her relation to the narrator (in a framing story, that is).

163 See above, 47–48.

164 Since "Del" and "Alice" are both "Ad-" names, we can if we like see "Del Jordan" as the counterpart of "Alice Munro."

165 "Everything Here Is Touchable and Mysterious" (33).

CONTENTS OF MUNRO'S BOOKS

Dance of the Happy Shades

"Walker Brothers Cowboy"
"The Shining Houses"
"Images"
"Thanks for the Ride"
"The Office"
"An Ounce of Cure"
"The Time of Death"
"Day of the Butterfly"
"Boys and Girls"
"Postcard"
"Red Dress — 1946"
"Sunday Afternoon"
"A Trip to the Coast"
"The Peace of Utrecht"
"Dance of the Happy Shades"

Lives of Girls and Women

"The Flats Road"
"Heirs of the Living Body"
"Princess Ida"
"Age of Faith"
"Changes and Ceremonies"
"Lives of Girls and Women"
"Baptizing"
    [1. Bert Matthews]
    [2. Jerry Storey]
    [3. Garnet French]
"Epilogue: The Photographer"

Something I've Been Meaning to Tell You

"Something I've Been Meaning to Tell You"
"Material"
"How I Met My Husband"
"Walking on Water"
"Forgiveness in Families"
"Tell Me Yes or No"
"The Found Boat"
"Executioners"
"Marrakesh"
"The Spanish Lady"
"Winter Wind"
"Memorial"
"The Ottawa Valley"

Who Do You Think You Are?

"Royal Beatings"
"Privilege"
"Half a Grapefruit"
"Wild Swans"
"The Beggar Maid"
"Mischief"
"Providence"
"Simon's Luck"
"Spelling"
"Who Do You Think You Are?"

The Moons of Jupiter

"Chaddeleys and Flemings"
   1. Connection
   2. The Stone in the Field
"Dulse"
"The Turkey Season"
"Accident"
"Bardon Bus"
"Prue"

"Labor Day Dinner"
"Mrs. Cross and Mrs. Kidd"
"Hard-Luck Stories"
"Visitors"
"The Moons of Jupiter"

The Progress of Love

"The Progress of Love"
"Lichen"
"Monsieur les Deux Chapeaux"
"Miles City, Montana"
"Fits"
"The Moon in the Orange Street Skating Rink"
"Jesse and Meribeth"
"Eskimo"
"A Queer Streak"
    1. Anonymous Letters
    2. Possession
"Circle of Prayer"
"White Dump"

Friend of My Youth

"Friend of My Youth"
"Five Points"
"Meneseteung"
"Hold Me Fast, Don't Let Me Pass
"Oranges and Apples"
"Pictures of the Ice"
"Goodness and Mercy"
"Oh, What Avails"
    1. Deadeye Dick
    2. Frazil Ice
    3. Rose Matilda
"Differently"
"Wigtime"

WRITINGS REFERRED TO

Bibliographies

Moore, Jean M., and Jean F. Tener. *The Alice Munro Papers, First Accession: An Inventory of the Archives at the University of Calgary Libraries.* Calgary: U of Calgary P, 1986.

Moore, Jean M. *The Alice Munro Papers, Second Accession: An Inventory of the Archives at the University of Calgary Libraries.* Calgary: U of Calgary P, 1987.

Writings by Alice Munro

(a) Books

Dance of the Happy Shades. Toronto: Ryerson, 1968.
Friend of My Youth. Toronto: McClelland, 1990.
Lives of Girls and Women. Toronto: McGraw-Hill, 1971.
The Moons of Jupiter. Toronto: Macmillan, 1982.
The Progress of Love. Toronto: Macmillan, 1986.
Something I've Been Meaning to Tell You. Toronto: McGraw-Hill, 1974.
Who Do You Think You Are? Toronto: Macmillan, 1978. Published as *The Beggar Maid* in the United States (New York: Knopf, 1979) and Great Britain (London: Allen Lane, 1980).

(b) Uncollected Published Stories

"At the Other Place." *Canadian Forum* Sept. 1955: 131–33.
"A Basket of Strawberries." *Mayfair* Nov. 1953: 32+.
"Characters." *Ploughshares* 4.3 (1978): 72–82.
"The Dangerous One." *Chatelaine* July 1957: 49–51.
"The Edge of Town." *Queen's Quarterly* 62 (1955): 368–80.
"The Ferguson Girls Must Never Marry." *Grand Street* 1.3 (1982): 27–64.
"Home." *New Canadian Stories: 74.* Ed. David Helwig and Joan Harcourt. Ottawa: Oberon, 1974. 133–53.
"How Could I Do That?" *Chatelaine* Mar. 1956: 16+.

"The Idyllic Summer." *Canadian Forum* Aug. 1954: 106+.
"The Widower." *Folio* 5 Apr. 1951: n. pag.
"Wood." *New Yorker* 24 Nov. 1980: 46–54.
"Working for a Living." *A Grand Street Reader*. Ed. Ben Sonnenberg. New York: Summit, 1986. 17–45.

(c) Earlier Published Versions of Collected Stories

"Dulse." *The New Yorker* 21 July 1980: 30–39.
"Emily." *Viva* Aug. 1978: 99–105 ("Simon's Luck").
"Royal Beatings." *The New Yorker* 14 Mar. 1977: 36–44.
"White Dump." *The New Yorker* 28 July 1986: 25–43.

(d) Articles

"Everything Here Is Touchable and Mysterious." *Weekend Magazine (Toronto Star)* 11 May 1974: 33.
"Remember Roger Mortimer: Dickens' *Child's History of England* remembered." *The Montrealer* Feb. 1962: 34–37.
"The Colonel's Hash Resettled." *The Native Voice: Short Stories and Reflections by Canadian Writers*, ed. John Metcalf (Toronto: McGraw-Hill Ryerson, 1972): 181–83.

Interviews and Secondary Sources

Bailey, Nancy L. "The Masculine Image in *Lives of Girls and Women*." *Canadian Literature* 80 (1979): 113–20
Blodgett, E.D. *Alice Munro*. Boston: Twayne, 1988.
Budge, E.A. Wallis, ed. *The Book of the Dead*. New York: Bell, 1960.
Carrington, Ildikó de Papp. *Controlling the Uncontrollable: The Fiction of Alice Munro*. DeKalb, IL.: Northern Illinois UP, 1989.
Carscallen, James. "The Shining House: A Group of Stories." Miller, 85–101.
Conron, Brandon. "Munro's Wonderland." *Canadian Literature* 78 (1978): 109–23.
Dahlie, Hallvard. *Alice Munro and Her Works*. Toronto: ECW, 1985.
——— . "Unconsummated Relationships: Isolation and Rejection in Alice Munro's Stories." *World Literature Written in English* 11.1 (1972): 43–48.
Desroches-Noblecourt, Christiane. *Tutankhamen*. Boston: New York Graphic Society, 1976.
Djwa, Sandra. "Deep Caves and Kitchen Linoleum: Psychological Violence in the Fiction of Alice Munro." *Violence in the Canadian Novel*

since 1960. Ed. Virginia Harger-Grinling and Terry Goldie. St. John's: Memorial UP, 1981. 177–90.

Eldredge, L.M. "A Sense of Ending in *Lives of Girls and Women.*" *Studies in Canadian Literature* 9 (1984): 110–15.

Godard, Barbara. " 'Heirs of the Living Body': Alice Munro and the Question of Female Aesthetics." Miller, 43–71.

Hancock, Geoff. "An Interview with Alice Munro." *Canadian Fiction Magazine* 43 (1982): 75–114.

Howells, Coral. *Private and Fictional Words: Canadian Women Novelists of the 1970s and 1980s.* London: Methuen, 1987.

Hoy, Helen. " 'Dull, Simple, Amazing, and Unfathomable': Paradox and Double Vision in Alice Munro's Fiction." *Studies in Canadian Literature* 5 (1980): 100–15.

Kamboureli, Smaro. "The Body as Audience and Performance in the Writings of Alice Munro." *A Mazing Space: Writing Canadian Women Writing.* Ed. Shirley Neuman and Smaro Kamboureli. Edmonton: Longspoon/Newest, 1986. 31–38.

Keith, W.J. *A Sense of Style: Studies in the Art of Fiction in English-speaking Canada.* Toronto: ECW, 1989.

Macdonald, Rae McCarthy. "Structure and Detail in *Lives of Girls and Women.*" *Studies in Canadian Literature* 3 (1978): 199–210.

MacKendrick, Louis K., ed. *Probable Fictions: Alice Munro's Narrative Acts.* Downsview, ON: ECW, 1983.

Martin, W.R. "Alice Munro and James Joyce." *Journal of Canadian Fiction* 24 (1979): 120–26.

——. *Alice Munro: Paradox and Parallel.* Edmonton: U of Alberta P, 1987.

——. "The Strange and the Familiar in Alice Munro." *Studies in Canadian Literature* 7 (1982): 214–26.

Mathews, Lawrence. "*Who Do You Think You Are?*: Alice Munro's Art of Disarrangement." MacKendrick, 181–93.

McMullen, Lorraine. " 'Shameless, Marvellous, Shattering Absurdity': The Humour of Paradox in Alice Munro." MacKendrick, 144–62.

Miller, Judith, ed. *The Art of Alice Munro: Saying the Unsayable.* Waterloo, ON: U of Waterloo P, 1984.

Monaghan, David. "Confinement and Escape in Alice Munro's 'The Flats Road.' " *Studies in Short Fiction* 14 (1977): 165–68.

New, W.H. "Pronouns and Prepositions: Alice Munro's *Something I've Been Meaning to Tell You,*" in New, *Dreams of Speech and Violence.* Toronto: U of Toronto P, 1987. 201–10.

Noonan, Gerald. "The Structure of Style in Alice Munro's Fiction." MacKendrick, 163–80.

Orange, John. "Alice Munro and a Maze of Time." MacKendrick, 83–98.

Osachoff, Margaret Gail. " 'Treacheries of the Heart': Memoir, Confession, and Meditation in the Stories of Alice Munro." MacKendrick, 61–82.

Rasporich, Beverley J. "Child-Women and Primitives in the Fiction of Alice Munro." *Atlantis* 1.2 (1976): 4–14.

_____ . *Dance of the Sexes: Art and Gender in the Fiction of Alice Munro.* Edmonton: U of Alberta P, 1990.

Ross, Catherine Sheldrick. " 'At Least Part Legend': The Fiction of Alice Munro." MacKendrick, 112–26.

Slopen, Beverley. "PW Interviews Alice Munro." *Publisher's Weekly* 22 Aug. 1986: 76–77.

Struthers, J.R. (Tim). "Reality and Ordering: The Growth of a Young Artist in *Lives of Girls and Women*." *Essays on Canadian Writing* 3 (1975): 32–46.

_____ . "The Real Material: An Interview with Alice Munro." MacKendrick, 5–36.

Taylor, Michael. "The Unimaginable Vancouvers: Alice Munro's Words." MacKendrick, 127–43.

Thacker, Robert. " 'Clear Jelly': Alice Munro's Narrative Dialectics." MacKendrick, 37–60.

Wallace, Bronwen. "Women's Lives: Alice Munro." *The Human Elements: Critical Essays.* Ed. David Helwig. Ottawa: Oberon, 1978. 52–67.

York, Lorraine. " 'Distant Parts of Myself': The Topography of Alice Munro's Fiction." *American Review of Canadian Studies* 18.1 (1988): 33–38.

_____ . *The Other side of Dailiness: Photography in the Works of Alice Munro, Timothy Findley, Michael Ondaatje, and Margaret Laurence.* Toronto: ECW, 1988.

_____ . "The Rival Bards: Alice Munro's *Lives of Girls and Women* and Victorian Poetry." *Canadian Literature* 112 (1987): 211–16.

INDEX OF TITLES AND CHARACTERS

The following index lists only references by name: to Munro's writings — mainly her stories — and to individual characters with names mentioned by her or, as in the case of Del Jordan's parents, readily inferred. (Writers on Munro are listed in a separate index.) Since a reader can hardly be expected to remember Uncle Benny's surname or Mr. Chaddeley's given name, double-named characters have been entered — somewhat arbitrarily, no doubt — under whichever name seemed more likely to be familiar (generally the given one); the other appears with a cross-reference. The same practice is followed in the case of characters having both maiden and married names. The characters in Del Jordan's secret novel have been promoted to full membership in *Lives of Girls and Women*. References to the heroine of "The Spanish Lady" (whom I have regularly called after her story) will be found in the story's own entry; a very few other characters with regular "epithets" in Munro — such as the Rosicrucian in the same story — have entries of their own. Many important characters, lacking stated names, have remained absent, though they are of course identified whenever they come up in the text. The protagonists in the two novels, Del Jordan and Rose, are absent for a different reason: their omnipresence in this book. One might as well read it as look them up.

Heal, Murray: see Murray
Healey, Gladys: see Gladys
Heather Sue Murray: see Murray
Heferman, Susie: see Susie
"Heirs of the Living Body" (*Lives of Girls and Women*) 49, 50, 58, 68, 72, 78, 84, 102, 115, 141, 142–43, 152, 158, 165, 199, 228, 240, 255, 256–57, 261, 277–78, 279, 280, 282, 288, 289, 292, 306, 308, 309, 310, 318, 319, 321, 322, 327, 328, 343, 345, 346–47, 349, 360, 458, 516, 544, 546
Helen
("Day of the Butterfly") 51, 67, 68, 70, 72, 85, 90, 91, 92, 209, 336, 399
(Aunt) ("Heirs of the Living Body") 84, 85, 306
("Pastime of a Saturday Night") 100
("The Peace of Utrecht") 74, 84, 99, 147, 299, 345, 474, 480, 481, 482, 483, 484, 510, 538
("Postcard") 80, 85, 96, 142, 175, 281, 282, 289, 291, 299, 302, 304, 306, 311, 324, 327, 330, 331, 332, 334, 335, 342
Helena ("Executioners") 10, 18, 62–63, 64, 71, 85, 92, 108, 130, 131, 142, 403, 414, 415, 419, 420, 421–22, 423, 424–25, 426–27, 428, 429–31, 433–34, 435, 436, 446, 451, 457, 459, 460, 507–08, 515, 522, 527, 545
Helena Rose Armour ("Connection") 251
Henry Bailey ("Boys and Girls") 213–14, 215, 246, 254
Henry Streets ("The Turkey Season") 213, 254

Henshawe, Dr. ("The Beggar Maid") 265, 270, 271, 273, 345
Herb Abbott ("The Turkey Season") 93, 212, 214, 215, 225, 228, 254–55, 285, 291, 301, 340, 342
Hobden, Miss ("The Funeral-Goer") 308
"Hold Me Fast, Don't Let Me Pass" (*Friend of My Youth*) 73, 75, 99, 100, 159, 205, 248, 250, 253, 254, 255, 261, 337, 345, 461, 520, 539, 540, 545, 547
Holy Betty: see Betty
"Home" (uncollected) 24–25, 26, 29, 33, 57, 66, 69, 74, 75, 87, 99, 122, 213, 537, 539
Homer, Milton: see Milton
Horse Nicholson ("Half a Grapefruit") 300
"How Could I Do That?" (uncollected) 100, 156
"How I Met My Husband" (*Something I've Been Meaning to Tell You*) 17, 121, 124, 148, 186, 255, 346, 351, 352, 355, 356, 357, 358, 374, 400, 449, 543
Howard Troy ("Executioners") 85, 108, 130, 131, 392, 392, 420, 421, 423, 424, 428, 429, 430–31, 432–33, 435, 436, 439, 442, 457, 459, 515
Howey — Madeleine, Mason: see under given names
Howie ("Memorial") 251
Hugh ("The Spanish Lady") 502–03, 541
Hugo Johnson ("Material") 18, 60, 98, 201, 251, 257, 280, 293, 298, 304, 307, 308, 315, 330, 338, 343, 344, 347, 348

INDEX OF WRITERS ON
MUNRO REFERRED TO